Frommer's 96

New England

**by Lisa M. Legarde
and Dale Northrup**

Macmillan • USA

ABOUT THE AUTHORS

Lisa M. Legarde (Chapters 1–10) was born in New Orleans and graduated from Wellesley College with a B.A. in English. She worked as an assistant editor at Macmillan Travel before embarking on her career as a travel writer. Lisa has traveled extensively in Europe and North America and is the author of several Frommer's guides. **Dale Northrup** (Chapters 11–13) lives in Portland, Maine, and has reported on travel from over 60 countries and has visited more than 7,000 hotels. His radio commentary is regularly heard on "Weekend Travel," and he is author of *Frommer's The Carolinas & Georgia* as well as regional editor of *America on Wheels Florida*.

MACMILLAN TRAVEL

A Simon & Schuster Macmillan Company
1633 Broadway
New York, NY 10019

Find us online at **http://www.mcp.com/mgr/travel** or on America Online at Keyword: **SuperLibrary.**

ISBN 0-02-860877-1
ISSN 1044-2286

Editor: Michael Feist
Production Editor: Amy DeAngelis
Design by Michele Laseau
Digital Cartography by Geografix Inc. and Ortelius Design

SPECIAL SALES

Bulk purchases (10+ copies) of Frommer's Travel Guides are available to corporations at special discounts. The Special Sales Department can produce custom editions to be used as premiums and/or for sales promotion to suit individual needs. Existing editions can be produced with custom cover imprints such as corporate logos. For more information write to: Special Sales, Macmillan Publishing, 1633 Broadway, New York, NY 10019.

Manufactured in the United States of America

Contents

7 Martha's Vineyard & Nantucket 255

8 Central & Western Massachusetts 289

9 Rhode Island 334

10 Connecticut 376

List of Maps

AN INVITATION TO THE READERS

In researching this book, we discovered many wonderful places—hotels, restaurants, shops, and more. We're sure you'll find others. Please tell us about them, so we can share the information with your fellow travelers in upcoming editions. If you were disappointed with a recommendation, we'd love to know that, too. Please write to:

Lisa M. Legarde and Dale Northrup
Frommer's New England '96
c/o Macmillan Travel
1633 Broadway
New York, NY 10019

AN ADDITIONAL NOTE

Please be advised that travel information is subject to change at any time—and this is especially true of prices. We therefore suggest that you write or call ahead for confirmation when making your travel plans. The authors, editors, and publisher cannot be held responsible for the experiences of readers while traveling. Your safety is important to us, however, so we encourage you to stay alert and be aware of your surroundings. Keep a close eye on cameras, purses, and wallets, all favorite targets of thieves and pickpockets.

WHAT THE SYMBOLS MEAN

✪ Frommer's Favorites

Hotels, restaurants, attractions, and entertainment you should not miss.

Ⓢ Super-Special Values

Hotels and restaurants that offer great value for your money.

The following abbreviations are used for credit cards:

AE	American Express	EU	Eurocard
CB	Carte Blanche	JCB	Japan Credit Bank
DC	Diners Club	MC	MasterCard
DISC	Discover	V	Visa
ER	enRoute		

Getting to Know New England

When it comes to American history and culture, New England is where it all began. Certainly history is not the only thing to attract you to the six states that make up this region: Connecticut, Rhode Island, Massachusetts, Maine, New Hampshire, and Vermont. Each state has natural beauties worth bragging about—like the beaches of Rhode Island, the windswept dunes of Cape Cod, the rugged coasts of Maine, or the Green Mountains of Vermont. And there's the local cuisine, particularly the seafood: lobster, the freshest you can get; clam chowder, easily the best in the world; Vermont Cheddar cheese; and hotcakes with New Hampshire's maple syrup.

New England is not all cities and civilization, either—despite all the talk about the eastern megalopolises. The Appalachian Trail has its beginning here; the sandy shores of Cape Cod are more than 100 miles long; Vermont alone has more than two dozen challenging ski areas; and if these places are too busy for you, head for the untracked wilderness forests of northern Maine. In fact, it's not really the big cities such as Hartford, Providence, and Boston that set the tone of New England community life, but rather the small villages—Litchfield, Conn.; Newfane, Vt.; Kennebunkport, Me.—each with its village green surrounded by the church, school, library, and town hall, each separated from its neighbor by rolling pastures, lush woodland, and glacial lakes.

Although there's more to New England than just history, one soon discovers that New Englanders love their region because of its history and its traditions. Only here can you see Plymouth Rock, climb Bunker Hill, and visit the site of the very first Thanksgiving feast. At Connecticut's Mystic Seaport, you can see a re-created New England maritime town of the past in full operation; and at Sturbridge Village and Plimoth Plantation, the crafts of the colonial period are performed as they were centuries ago.

Even in modern Boston the history of New England is everywhere. From the observation deck atop a sleek skyscraper, you can look down on the charming colonial buildings ranged along gas-lit cobblestone streets on Beacon Hill. Wander through Faneuil Hall, where American colonists debated the abuses of British rule, then plow through the crowds thronging the renovated Quincy Market, Boston's favorite gathering place. Make an excursion out to the suburban towns of Lexington and Concord, where the first battles of the American Revolution were fought more than 200 years ago,

New England

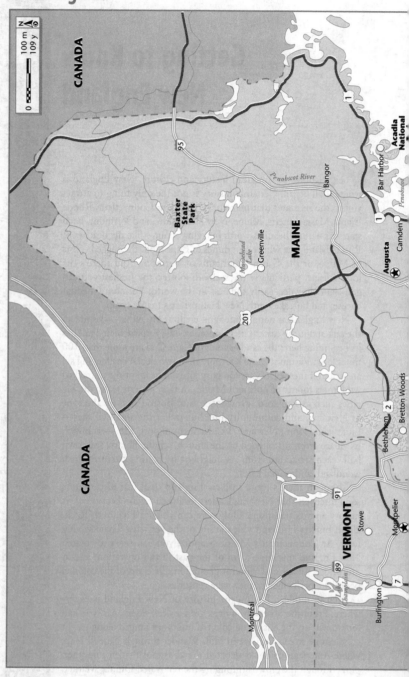

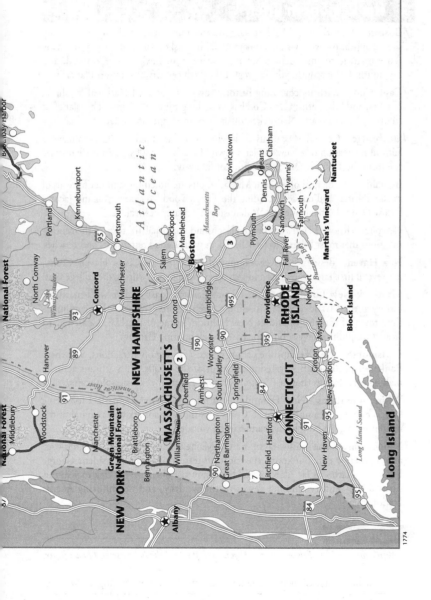

1774

and you'll cross Route 128, the nexus of high-technology research and development for the eastern United States.

New England's paradoxical loves of both tradition and innovation have coexisted peacefully from the very beginning, when men and women came to this area to escape the strictures of Reformation Europe and experiment with new religious and societal frameworks. They built a new way of life on this continent, but they included in it the things they loved best about the old countries they had left behind.

1 The Regions in Brief

Boston New England's oldest, largest, and most historically significant city should appear on every visitor's itinerary. Within a short drive of the city are many more historic towns, such as Salem, Marblehead, Lexington, Concord, and Plymouth. In Plymouth, you can revisit the 17th century at Plimoth Plantation.

Cape Cod With its charming historic towns, Cape Cod National Seashore, beaches, and bike paths, Cape Cod has something for every visitor. The islands of Martha's Vineyard and Nantucket, offshore of the Cape, are equally fascinating.

Sturbridge Central Massachusetts is where you'll find old Sturbridge Village, a faithful re-creation of a New England town of the early 1800s. A similarly historic site from the 1700s is **Old Deerfield,** not far away.

Berkshires The hills of western Massachusetts are noted for summer festivals of music, theater, and dance, including the Tanglewood Music Festival and Jacob's Pillow Dance Festival, and the Williamstown Theater Festival.

Newport Rhode Island's oceanside playground boasts palatial turn-of-the-century mansions that must be seen to be believed, as well as good restaurants and beaches.

New Haven Besides the lovely campus of Yale University, New Haven, Conn., has several first-rank museums and a lively cultural season during the college year.

Mystic & New London Connecticut's eastern coast is alive with maritime history at the Mystic Seaport Museum, a carefully preserved New England maritime town of the 1800s; and at New London, home of the U.S. Coast Guard Academy, and the navy submarine base at neighboring Groton.

Portsmouth New Hampshire's short seacoast is long on attractions. Strawbery Banke, in Portsmouth, is a living museum of the 1700s, with artisans actually making their livings (not just "demonstrating") at their centuries-old crafts.

White Mountains New Hampshire's White Mountains are perfect for scenic drives, hiking, or camping. North Conway is the outdoor activities capital of the region; Franconia Notch has many natural wonders.

Maine Coast The southwestern coast of Maine is lined with pretty beach towns, among them Kennebunkport, the vacation retreat of former President George Bush. Bar Harbor is far "down east," but many visitors make the trek to visit this turn-of-the-century summer resort of the wealthy, and neighboring Acadia National Park.

Impressions

I think you [in New England] have beyond all question the happiest and best country going.
    —Arthur Hugh Clough, in a letter to Charles Eliot Norton, August 29, 1853

❷ Did You Know?

- Basketball was invented in 1891 by Dr. James Naismith in Springfield, Mass. You can visit the Basketball Hall of Fame there.
- In 1895 William Morgan invented volleyball in Holyoke, Mass.
- The dollar bills in your wallet were probably printed on paper produced by the Crane Paper Co. of Dalton, Mass., main supplier to the U.S. Mint.
- Great Barrington, Mass., was the first town in the world to have electric streetlights, in 1886.
- Sylvester Graham (1794–1851) of Northampton, Mass., advocating a diet of vegetables and coarse-milled grains, invented the Graham cracker.
- Boston is at a latitude similar to that of Barcelona, Rome, and Istanbul.
- Harvard University, founded in 1636, is America's oldest institution of higher learning.
- Of the hundreds of people accused of witchcraft in Salem in 1692, only one confessed—and she claimed that others had forced her into evil.
- Mount Washington (6,288 feet), the highest summit east of the Rockies, holds the record for the strongest winds ever recorded: 231 miles per hour. The summit qualifies as an arctic climate zone.
- Boston's subway system was the first built in the western hemisphere.

Green Mountains   From gracious Bennington in the south to alpine Stowe in the north, Vermont's Green Mountains are dotted with cozy inns, charming New England villages clustered around their commons, and excellent possibilities for outdoor activities. Drive Vt. 100 for a good introduction to the Green Mountain state. Just south of Burlington, the Shelburne Museum has perhaps the best and fullest collection of Americana ever assembled.

2   A Look at the Past

HISTORY

To understand New England and its people, you must take at least a quick look at the region's history. To a surprising extent, today's New Englanders think and act as they do because of how their ancestors thought and acted.

EUROPEAN EXPLORERS   Historians think the Vikings were the first Europeans to explore North America's shores, but there is evidence—none of it conclusive—that the discoverers may have been Irish, Spanish, or Portuguese. We do know that the Norse came to this area about 1000 B.C. and may have founded settlements in the land they called Vinland. Though the land was fruitful, the settlers found it hard going, mostly because the indigenous peoples fought the settlers ferociously. The great Nordic leaders did not judge the land to be worth the deaths of many of their people, so they withdrew to their more easily ruled settlements in Greenland and Iceland.

Dateline

- 9000 B.C. Immigrants from Asia reach what is now New England.
- 1000 B.C. Norse mariners explore parts of the New England coast.
- 1497 Giovanni Caboto (John Cabot) lands on the New England mainland and claims it for the king of England.

continues

■ 1524 Giovanni da Verrazano sails along the New England coast, naming Rhode Island.

■ 1602 Bartholomew Gosnold and colonists arrive in New England, name Cape Cod and Martha's Vineyard, and set up a colony that lasts only 22 days.

■ 1614 Capt. John Smith returns to England with a rich cargo of fish and furs from what he calls "New England," the first use of the region's name.

■ 1620 Pilgrims aboard the *Mayflower* reach the tip of Cape Cod in November and Plymouth in December.

■ 1636 Harvard College is founded to educate young men for the ministry.

■ 1638–39 Portsmouth, R.I., is founded; Hartford, Windsor, and Wethersfield, Conn., join to form the Connecticut Colony.

■ 1692 Witch trials are held in Salem, Mass.

■ 1765–67 Passage of the Stamp Act and Townshend

continues

By the time the intrepid Columbus set out on his epoch-making voyage 500 years later (1492), Europe had become ready to profit from discoveries of new lands. Columbus was followed by other explorers, including Giovanni Caboto (known as John Cabot), who sailed under the English flag in 1497 and claimed all of what would become New England for his master, Henry VII.

It took a century before the English monarch was ready to exploit his claims. During the early 1600s, expeditions were sent out under Sir Humphrey Gilbert, Bartholomew Gosnold, Martin Pring, and George Weymouth. These brought back useful intelligence on the new land (and Weymouth brought back a Native American named Squanto, who learned English before returning to his homeland), but it was Capt. John Smith who studied the land seriously with an eye to colonization and who gave it the name "New England."

COLONIAL NEW ENGLAND   Before Gilbert, Gosnold, and Smith set out for the New World, several hundred Puritans had already left England for Holland in search of religious freedom. Their stay in Leyden was not a happy one, since they found the morals of the local people to be less than strict; so a number of these Puritan "pilgrims" returned to England and, in late summer of 1620, set sail in the *Mayflower* for the New World. In November they arrived at what is now Provincetown, on the tip of Cape Cod, and paused there long enough to draft and sign the Mayflower Compact, which would be their governing law. But Cape Cod's sandy terrain and scrubby vegetation, which delight present-day vacationers, were too poor for the Pilgrims' purposes, and the search for more fertile land finally brought them to Plymouth Rock, south of Massachusetts Bay, in the middle of the frigid month of December in 1620.

Half the Pilgrims died that winter of disease and privation. But luck was with the rest: Squanto, George Weymouth's prisoner, found them and persuaded Massasoit, *sachem* (chief) of the Wampanoags, to agree to 50 years of peace between his people and the colonists. In 1621 more colonists arrived, and in a few years Plymouth was a sturdy colony. At first, land was held and worked in common, but this system was abandoned when it was realized that family plots would be worked more diligently.

Land north and south of Plymouth proved to be more fertile, and soon there were several thriving communities nearby ready to welcome new settlers.

The Founders, as they are called, were followed in 1628 by another group of Pilgrims who established the colony of Massachusetts Bay. By 1637 the colony had several thousand inhabitants, and new towns were being founded up and down the coast, and even inland at Concord, Dedham, and Watertown. The Puritan settlers must have seen a bright future, for in 1636 they set up Harvard College to educate young men for the ministry.

By 1640 there were sturdy communities of settlers in Connecticut and Rhode Island as well as in Massachusetts. By 1680 the indigenous peoples who had lived here before the coming of the settlers were reduced to only a few thousand souls as a result of fierce warfare, European-introduced disease, and alcohol addiction.

SPIRIT OF INDEPENDENCE   The settlers of New England governed themselves while paying lip service to the sovereignty of the British Crown. They built their own prosperity despite laws promulgated in London that placed burdens and restraints on their economic activities. Governors sent out by the king were universally disliked and were often forced to return home by the cantankerous colonists.

It was George III (reigned 1760–1820) who forced the issue, refusing to bear the irritation of the Americans' independent spirit any longer. Taxes were imposed on the colonies, even though the colonists had no elected representatives and no voice in Parliament. Resentment grew as the colonists chafed under the burden of taxation without representation. In March 1770 a crowd of Bostonians began taunting royal army sentries, and soon the mob got out of hand. Greatly outnumbered, the soldiers fired into the crowd, killing five citizens in what would be known as the Boston Massacre.

Life in Boston was outwardly peaceful for a few years, but king and Parliament were still determined to rule the unruly colonists, and the colonists were determined not to permit interference with their privileges of self-government, now a century and a half old. As a symbol of London's supremacy, a tax was placed on tea shipped to the colonies. The tax was widely reviled, not so much for its economic impact, which was minimal, but because of its symbolic importance: Virtually everyone drank tea, and thus everyone was forced to pay the tax. The political temperature rose as American patriots formed secret societies, such as the Sons of Liberty and the Committees of Correspondence, and worked out plans of resistance to London's control.

In the autumn of 1773 matters came to a head as the patriotic activists insisted that the king's governor order HMS *Dartmouth,* arriving in Boston with a cargo of taxable tea, to go back where it came from. Governor Hutchinson would not give the order, so on the night of

Acts infuriate American colonists.

■ March 1770 Boston Massacre heralds the beginning of the American Revolution.

■ December 16, 1773 Boston Tea Party goads Parliament to pass strict laws strangling New England's economy.

■ April 19, 1775 Minutemen of Lexington and Concord battle British regulars, beginning the American Revolution.

■ June 17, 1775 Revolutionary forces inflict heavy casualties on the British at the Battle of Bunker Hill.

■ 1777 Vermont declares independence from Great Britain as a republic.

■ 1783 In the Treaty of Versailles, Great Britain recognizes the independence of the United States.

■ 1790s Salem shipowner and merchant Elias Hasket Derby becomes America's first millionaire; Eli Whitney's cotton

continues

gin provides cheap thread for New England's burgeoning textile industry.

- 1820 Maine, once part of colonial Massachusetts, becomes 23rd state.

- 1845 Thoreau builds his cabin on Walden Pond in Concord, Mass.

- 1852 Harriet Beecher Stowe's book *Uncle Tom's Cabin* inspires Abolitionists.

- 1857 Discovery of petroleum in Pennsylvania sounds the death knell for New England's whalers and rich whale-oil trade.

- 1929 Stock market crash signals the end of New England's commercial and industrial greatness.

- 1944 World monetary conference held at Bretton Woods, N.H.

- 1954 USS *Nautilus,* the world's first nuclear-powered submarine, is launched at Groton, Conn.

- 1960–63 John F. Kennedy, of Brookline, Mass., serves as President of the United States.

continues

December 16, bands of patriots disguised as Native Americans and African Americans emptied the *Dartmouth* and two other ships of their cargoes. The tea was dumped into Boston Harbor, and the night's action became known as the Boston Tea Party. When London learned of this rebellious act, laws were passed that were meant to strangle the colonial economy and to teach the nasty colonists a lesson. The political temperature in New England neared the boiling point.

REVOLUTIONARY WAR   Seeing war as inevitable, farmers and tradesmen began to stockpile arms, ammunition, and material. Boston and other large towns were under the direct control of sizable royal garrisons, but the countryside and its villages belonged to the revolutionists, so this "arms race" went on uninhibited.

In an effort to stop the colonists' arms collecting, a British expeditionary force marched secretly to Concord on the night of April 18, 1775, to make surprise searches of suspected illegal arms caches at dawn the next day. But American spies learned of the plan and set up a system to warn their countrymen. If the redcoats departed Boston along the isthmus that linked it to the mainland, one lantern would be hung in the steeple of Boston's Old North Church. If the troops instead boarded boats to row across the water and march on a different route, two lanterns would be hung.

As the British filled the boats, two lanterns appeared in the steeple, easily visible from the far shore where Paul Revere, William Dawes, and Samuel Prescott waited on horseback. These messengers rode into the dark hinterland, sounding the alarm in each village. The American intelligence network was so good that the citizens of Lexington and Concord leapt from their beds long before Major Pitcairn and his royal infantry were anywhere near. As dawn broke, 70 Lexington Minutemen faced Pitcairn's regiments on Lexington's town green.

The Minutemen were ordered by Major Pitcairn to disperse. They stood their ground. Taunts were exchanged. A shot was fired, and that triggered a battle. When the smoke cleared, eight Minutemen were dead, and the British troops went on a rampage that was stopped only with difficulty by their commanders, who immediately marched them in the direction of Concord.

On June 17, 1775, full war broke out when the Americans fortified Breed's Hill, next to Bunker Hill, in Charlestown, just across the harbor from Boston. General Gage, the British commander, was forced to attack this threat, but from their entrenched positions the Americans shot more than a thousand of his soldiers. As the battle raged, the Americans' ammunition ran low and their commander, Col. William Prescott, said to his troops, "Don't fire until you see the whites of their eyes," in order to make every shot count. Their ammunition exhausted, the Revolutionary forces abandoned their positions, having won another important victory.

■ 1970s Computer boom brings renewed prosperity to New England.

A year later on July 4, 1776, in Philadelphia, American leaders signed a Declaration of Independence from Great Britain.

Though many of the most important battles of the Revolutionary War were later to be fought in New York and Pennsylvania, New England prides itself on having been the place where it all began. Patriots Day (April 19) is a holiday in Massachusetts, and hundreds of citizens and visitors turn out at dawn to witness reenactments of the Battles of Lexington and Concord staged by groups in period uniforms.

By 1781 the Revolutionary War was over and the American colonies were free and independent states. But the forging of a strong and effective central government for the former British territories would not be accomplished until 1789. In the meantime, the removal of British legal restrictions on trade meant that New England merchants were at last free to trade with the world as they liked. New Englanders put to sea in ships built in Maine, Massachusetts, Rhode Island, and Connecticut and were soon returning with the riches of Europe, Africa, China, and India in trade. Whaling ships out of Salem and New Bedford brought back whale-oil wealth of similar greatness. Though the renewal of war with Great Britain (the War of 1812) disrupted New England's progress for a time, the seas were soon open again.

THE INDUSTRIAL REVOLUTION   Across the open sea from Great Britain, a young man named Samuel Slater had arrived in 1789. Slater had worked in England's new cotton-spinning factories. Though it was against British law to "export" knowledge of the machines, which were making Great Britain the world's wealthiest textile producer, Slater slipped out of the country and established a cotton-spinning mill at Pawtucket, R.I., based on his knowledge of English

---

The Battle of Concord: Echoing Still

Word of the Lexington engagement was rushed to Concord, where the local Minutemen retreated across the North Bridge over the Concord River in the face of the powerful British force. The Battle of Concord was fought for command of the bridge. The British forces were unable to take it, which was a victory for the much smaller colonial force. But the redcoats pursued their mission in town, discovering and burning some wooden gun carriages. The smoke rising from the town convinced the Minutemen, holding their position at North Bridge, that their homes were in flames, and they fought all the more fiercely.

The "shot heard 'round the world" was fired from a Minuteman's musket at Concord North Bridge, where this band of farmers held off professional soldiers. However, this first battle of the American Revolution was actually won by the colonists as the British retreated. Sniping from behind trees and stonewalls along the road back to Boston, Minutemen brought the British casualty count up to 200, a grievous and embarrassing loss for the powerful forces of the Crown.

machine design. The mill revolutionized the weaving of textiles in the New World and set the stage for New England's great weaving industry.

Throughout the 19th century, as New England's clipper ships and whalers swept through the world's oceans, land-bound New Englanders exploited the region's waterpower resources to run their new mills, and industrial towns sprang to life along New England's rivers. The textile factories grew and grew, and some, like the gigantic Amoskeag Mills in Manchester, N.H., had many-windowed facades that marched along the riverbank for more than a quarter of a mile. Next to the factories were new houses for the armies of workers, many of whom were women. Company stores and company-financed civic buildings filled the streets of the new towns, which were founded on the wealth from weaving.

From some of the factories it was not textiles but machinery, firearms, shoes, watches, and instruments that marched out the doors on their way to the markets of the world. New England inventors and New England engineers gained a repu-tation for ingenuity that survives today, and samples of "Yankee ingenuity" are still proudly displayed.

New England's commercial success brought New Englanders wealth and sophis-tication. Boston, the chief city of the region, was proud to call itself the "Athens of America." But changing times brought changed circumstances to the region in the next century.

CONTEMPORARY NEW ENGLAND   After the prosperity of the 1800s, the steamship replaced the New England clipper; natural gas, petroleum, and electricity replaced whale-oil lamps; and textile manufacturers moved their operations to southern states, where wages were lower. Millions of immigrants who had come from abroad to share in New England's commercial boom were left with minimal skills in a diminishing job market. New England's farms, set on rocky soil in a northern climate, were outproduced and outsold by the vast farms in other areas of the country.

The 1929 stock market crash and its aftermath spelled the bitter end of New England's golden age. What had once been America's richest, proudest, and most cultured region was now economically depressed, politically corrupt, and spiritu-ally defeated.

However, New England was still beautiful, historic, and proud. In the years after World War II, New Englanders realized that their land had other kinds of wealth. New England's hundreds of colleges and universities were leaders in education. The New England landscape was sprinkled with graceful towns and villages. New Englanders were as ingenious as ever, and the chilly waters of the Atlantic still held a wealth of seafood, so New England survived and even prospered again.

In recent decades, graduates of New England's universities, no matter where they came from, settled here and founded small companies—including Wang Laboratories and Digital Equipment—that became large companies employing tens of thousands. The sturdy 19th-century textile mills of brick and granite were recycled as computer-company offices and factories. The name of Route 128 became synonymous with the computer industry. New England's picturesque towns and villages found a new vocation as the great old houses were transformed into historic inns, and the more modest houses began to provide bed-and-breakfast accommodations to travelers and vacationers.

Today New England is known for its beautiful landscapes and settlements, its rich history, its technical expertise, its medical research, and, well, its "livability" and charm. More than one New Englander will proudly claim that this is America's first and best—and after your visit here, we think you'll agree.

3 Art & Architecture

ART   Early New England art was folk art. Colonial women produced wonderful patchwork quilts that were both practical bed coverings and delightful works of art. Sailors, particularly those on the whaling ships that might be at sea for months at a time, carved household utensils, buttons, letter openers, and corset stays from whale bone and tooth. Often these objects were decorated with etched designs known as scrimshaw. The delicacy of scrimshaw scenes, many of which feature ships and other nautical subjects, is impressive, not merely because the artists were self-taught but because their tools were sometimes no more refined than pocket knives.

The Shaker religious communities in Maine, New Hampshire, and western Massachusetts looked on honest work as a prayer and each object crafted by hand as an offering to God of one's labor and creativity. Pieces of Shaker furniture, especially the famous Shaker chairs, are valued heirlooms and antiques today.

Metalworking was highly advanced as well. Besides being an active patriot and partisan of the American cause, Paul Revere (1735–1818) was a renowned silversmith. His simple, harmonious design for a silver or pewter bowl ("Revere bowl") is still a favorite among connoisseurs in New England.

Painting was a craft, then an art, in New England. The primitive works of untrained daubers decorated many a colonial household. Fine portraits of the great and powerful graced the mansions of the upper class. During and after the Revolutionary War, painters turned their efforts to the American cause, producing patriotic works that are still revered. Archibald Willard (1836–1918), whose famous painting *The Spirit of '76* hangs in Abbot Hall in Marblehead, Mass., was trained to decorate carriages but soon showed his skill with oil on canvas.

During the mid- and late 19th century, New England's world-class painters had to move to more sophisticated regions in order to prosper and be recognized. James Abbott McNeill Whistler (1834–1903) was born in Lowell, Mass., and though he lived abroad for much of his life, New England still claims him as one of its own. After living in St. Petersburg and Paris, he established himself in London, where his belief in "art for art's sake" was very unconventional. While others were making paintings of almost photographic quality, Whistler held to his credo that a painting was essentially an "arrangement of light, form and color." His most famous painting, of his mother sitting in a chair, is entitled *Arrangement in Grey and Black;* we know it better as *Whistler's Mother.* Whistler's *Girl in a White Dress* hangs in the National Gallery in Washington, D.C.

John Singer Sargent (1856–1925) was born in Florence, Italy, and worked mostly in Paris and London, but he also gained a reputation as a painter of portraits of many famous and socially prominent Bostonians and other New

Englanders. In the 1890s Sargent did a series of murals depicting *The History of Religion* for the Boston Public Library.

An earlier painter of the same last name, Henry Sargent (1770–1845), was born in Gloucester, Mass., and studied in London with Benjamin West. Two of his most famous works, *The Tea Party* and *The Dinner Party,* are in the Museum of Fine Arts in Boston; his famous portrait of Peter Faneuil hangs in Boston's Faneuil Hall.

By the turn of the century, New England had painters content to use local scenes as subject matter. Childe Hassam (1859–1935) was born in Boston, and though he studied in Paris, he returned to his native city to create enchanting impressionist-influenced paintings of the Boston Common, the Isles of Shoals, and a church in Gloucester.

Winslow Homer (1836–1910), also a Boston native, began his career as a magazine illustrator of Civil War scenes, but took up painting full-time at the age of 40. His direct, realistic, and colorful style was just right for the nautical and coastal scenes he favored, taken mostly from life in Maine.

Though Grandma Moses (Anna Mary Robertson Moses, 1860–1961) did most of her painting in Washington County in New York state, her themes and subjects are familiar to New Englanders. The Bennington Museum in Bennington, Vt., just across the state line from the painter's hometown of Hoosick Falls, N.Y., now holds an outstanding collection of her charming primitives. Most were painted after the artist's 70th birthday, some when she was more than 100.

ARCHITECTURE   Colonial Style   The early colonists who came to New England brought no visions of grand mansions or stately churches. Their homes were simple, as befitted a people of strict religious beliefs. Their public building was usually a simple meetinghouse (what others might call a church). For a look at buildings remaining from the 1600s, visit the Hoxie House (1637) in Sandwich, on Cape Cod, or the Whipple House (1640) in Ipswich, on Boston's north shore. Plimoth Plantation, near Plymouth, Mass., gives perhaps the best glimpse of 17th-century life and architecture. The simple, homespun design and decoration used in early New England has become what we think of as colonial style.

Georgian Style   America is a rich land of great potential, and it wasn't long before the colonists were prosperous. Along with prosperity came a waning of religious strictures; along with trade came glimpses of how life was lived in other countries, particularly in England. After the Great Fire of 1666, London had been rebuilt in Palladian style by Inigo Jones and Sir Christopher Wren. This updated classicism, which we call the Georgian style, appealed to colonial New England's builders, who happily used Wren's designs in building some of the region's most famous and stately churches. Harvard University is a riot of Georgian red brick and white cornice. Throughout New England you'll run across the Palladian window,

Impressions

New England is a finished place. Its destiny is that of Florence or Venice. . . . It is the first American section to be finished, to achieve stability in its conditions of life. It is the first old civilization, the first permanent civilization in America.
—Bernard Devoto, *New England: There She Stands—Forays and Rebuttals,* 1936

Impressions

You can always tell the Irish,
You can always tell the Dutch;
You can always tell a Yankee,
But you cannot tell him much.

—Eric Knight, All Yankees Are Liars, before 1943

the epitome of the style, in building after building. Georgian houses were built up to the time of the Revolution—and in beautiful Litchfield, Conn., until the end of the 1700s.

Federal Style   With political independence came even more prosperity. The ship-owners and merchants of New England's great maritime ports—Salem, Mass.; Portsmouth, N.H.; and Providence, R.I., for example—wanted large, comfortable, imposing houses, and local architects gave them just what they wanted in the years following the Revolution. Domestic Federal architecture was straightforward and commodious: large rectangular two-story wooden buildings with rows of windows, chimneys at both ends, and a grand portal centered in the facade. The famous Charles Bulfinch, who designed the State House (Massachusetts's state capitol), on Beacon Hill in Boston, is New England's most famous Federalist architect; lesser-known Samuel McIntire of Salem left his indelible imprint on the older streets of his hometown. In Providence, College Hill boasts many handsome Federal-style houses.

Greek Revival   Spacious domes, soaring columns topped by Ionic capitals, and noble echoes of the Doric order—this is Greek Revival. There are fewer Greek Revival houses and public buildings in New England than in other parts of the United States, but the ones that remain here are particularly fine. Boston's Quincy Market building (1825), now the centerpiece of Faneuil Hall Marketplace, is perhaps the best-known example. The Arcade (1828) in Providence is another. For good specimens of domestic Greek Revival architecture, visit Grafton, Vt., a veritable museum of the style carefully preserved by its sensitive residents.

Late 19th- & 20th-Century Styles   The great textile mills that were built along the rivers of New England were Federal style, but the mill owners wanted something fancier. As the 1800s wore on, they employed Henry Hobson Richardson, the firm of McKim, Mead and White, and other designers to build worldly fantasies: Egyptian temples, Renaissance palaces, Romanesque temples, and Gothic churches. Trinity Church, at Copley Square in Boston, is a fine example of the period. Newport, R.I.'s elegant mansions—many of them actually small palaces—demonstrate how this late-century exuberance would end. Among the "common people," exuberance led to Victorian gingerbread, some of the best of which survives in the town of Oak Bluffs on Martha's Vineyard island in Massachusetts.

During the 20th century skyscrapers began to soar above the quaint old neighborhoods of Boston, Providence, and Hartford. Many were undistinguished, and few had echoes of New England's past. But among the great commercial towers were some of imposing form and striking originality, such as Boston's slender, mirror-covered John Hancock Tower and Hartford's glass ellipse.

4 New England Literary Tradition

From the Puritan sermons and devotional writings of Increase Mather (1639–1723) and his son, Cotton Mather (1663–1728), New England literature has come all the way to the punchy Spenser thrillers of Robert Parker. Along the way, New England has fostered some of America's greatest writers.

The runaway bestseller of the early 1800s was not a book of sermons or a novel or even a history of the late war with England: It was the *American Dictionary of the English Language,* by Yale graduate Noah Webster (1758–1843). First published in 1828, Webster's 70,000-word dictionary was bought by hundreds of thousands of Americans every year—and still is.

Among the writers most closely associated with New England is Ralph Waldo Emerson (1803–82). Emerson's beliefs in the mystical unity of nature, and Thoreau's championing of the simple life in tune with nature's laws, were radical in 19th-century Concord, Mass. Along with other writers, Emerson was a founder of the Transcendental movement and had more effect on American literature than any other New Englander.

Henry David Thoreau (1817–62), a friend of Emerson's, is best remembered for *Walden, or Life in the Woods* (1854). This journal of observations and opinions written during his solitary sojourn (1845–47) on Walden Pond in Concord, Mass., may be the best-known book on New England. Thoreau was also known for *Civil Disobedience* and for his accounts of walking trips, entitled *The Maine Woods* and *Cape Cod.*

Nathaniel Hawthorne (1804–64) was born in Salem, Mass.; attended Bowdoin College in Maine; then pursued a career that produced *The Scarlet Letter, Twice-Told Tales,* and *The House of the Seven Gables,* among other titles. Hawthorne is thought by many to be the writer who established the American short story. His contemporary, Edgar Allan Poe (1809–49), was born in Boston but pursued his career in Virginia.

Among New England poets, the 1800s belonged to Henry Wadsworth Longfellow (1807–82). Born in Portland, Me., he attended Bowdoin, taught at Harvard, and lived in a big yellow house on Brattle Street in Cambridge that is now a historic landmark. Several of Longfellow's poems are a part of Americana: *Paul Revere's Ride, The Song of Hiawatha,* "The Village Blacksmith," "Excelsior," and "The Wreck of the Hesperus" are among the better-known ones.

Impressions

Those New England States, I do believe, will be the noblest country in the world in a little while. They will be the salvation of that very great body with a very little soul, the rest of the United States; they are the pith and marrow, heart and core, head and spirit of that country.
—Fanny Kemble (Mrs. Butler), *A Year of Consolation,* 1847

No author, without a trial, can conceive of the difficulty of writing a romance about a country [New England] where there is no shadow, no antiquity, no mystery, no pictur-esque and gloomy wrong, nor anything but a commonplace prosperity, in broad and simple daylight, as is happily the case with my dear native land.
—Nathaniel Hawthorne, *Transformations, The Marble Faun,* 1860

Preceding and during the Civil War, New England writers such as abolitionist William Lloyd Garrison (1805–79) and John Greenleaf Whittier (1807–92) contributed their literary and poetic talents to the struggle to end slavery.

Few Americans realize that Samuel Clemens (1835–1910), better known as Mark Twain, settled in Hartford, Conn., at the age of 35. Though Missouri-born, Twain wrote his masterpieces *Tom Sawyer* and *Huckleberry Finn* in Hartford, as well as *The Prince and the Pauper* and *A Connecticut Yankee in King Arthur's Court.* Touring his grand Victorian mansion at Nook Farm is the high point of a visit to Hartford.

In the 1800s, many excellent New England women's colleges produced graduates instilled with a spirit of independence and self-reliance. Harriet Beecher Stowe (1811–96) exposed the injustice of slavery in her novel *Uncle Tom's Cabin* (1852), which sold an amazing 300,000 copies in one year.

Opposite in temperament to the energetic Ms. Stowe was poet Emily Dickinson (1830–86), a native of Amherst, Mass., who lived there in near seclusion most of her life. Only seven of her poems were published during her lifetime, but the posthumous editing and publishing of nearly 1,000 poems established her reputation. Her influence on American poetry is matched only by that of Robert Frost.

Among New England's other famous female poets is Katharine Lee Bates (1859–1929), a native of Falmouth, Mass., and a graduate of Wellesley College. Though much of her work is unfamiliar today, every American knows her patriotic hymn *America the Beautiful.*

Robert Frost (1874–1963) was born in San Francisco to a New England family. He moved to New England early in his life, attended Dartmouth and Harvard without taking a degree, and later returned to teach poetry at both Amherst and Harvard. His many books capture the quintessence of New England living and the Yankee soul.

5 A Taste of New England

Seafood is New England's strong suit, of course. Many kinds of fish are taken in New England's waters.

In colonial times the codfish was so important to the region's economy that a codfish carved in pine had a place of honor in the Massachusetts State House (you can still see it there today). Filets of choice little codfish (or any other whitefish) are called scrod, sautéed in lemon butter or topped with cheese sauce; it's pretty bland, as is halibut. Bluefish, smoked and served as an appetizer or broiled for a main course, has a fuller flavor. Monkfish sautéed in butter tastes mildly like lobster. Swordfish and fresh tuna steaks are best if grilled over charcoal. Fish chowder, as made in New England, uses bland whitefish, potatoes, corn, and milk.

Shellfish are also important. Everyone knows about Maine lobster, but Massachusetts has a large lobstering fleet as well, and the state supports hatcheries where baby lobsters are raised before being released to sea.

Clams come in several varieties. Soft-shell clams have shells that chip and crack easily. The clams are usually steamed in the shells, which gave rise to their other name: steamers. Hard-shell clams have very hard porcelainlike shells; among the most popular varieties are littlenecks and cherrystones. These can be steamed, baked, or served raw on the half shell with lemon, tomato sauce, or a dab of horseradish. Quahogs (*ko*-hogs) are clams larger than your fist; they're often cut into strips, fried in batter, and served as fried clams at roadside or beachfront snack stands, or they can be minced for use in clam chowder.

New England clam chowder contains clams and potatoes in a base of milk or cream. It's quite different from Manhattan clam chowder, which uses tomato instead of milk. Oysters from Chatham, Wellfleet, and Cotuit on Cape Cod are usually eaten raw on the half shell or served whole in milk-based oyster stew.

Whether you're on the beach around a driftwood fire, at a backyard cookout, or in a restaurant, chances are you'll encounter the traditional clambake during your stay in New England. The true clambake takes place on the beach, starting with the digging of the clams, but the backyard and restaurant versions are good substitutes—provided you observe the rituals properly.

The three essential courses are steamed soft-shell clams, corn on the cob, and lobsters. Here's a recipe: Take one very large pot, fill it with clean seawater, and place it on the fire to boil. Put live lobsters in the bottom, then a layer of seaweed, then ears of corn, more seaweed, and finally a layer of "steamers" (soft-shell clams for steaming). When the clams open, they're ready.

Take a clam, open it completely, and lift out the meat. The "neck" is black and covered with a wrinkled black membrane. Shuck the membrane off (you pick up the knack for this by about the fifth clam), hold the clam by the neck, and dip it in "clam broth" (seawater that has had clams steamed in it—even in a restaurant you'll be provided with it). The "broth" is strictly for dipping, not for drinking; the dip washes any sand off the clam. Next, dip in the melted butter provided, then enjoy.

When you've had your fill of clams, it's on to the buttered ears of corn and finally to the lobsters. Eating a lobster is an art in itself.

Restaurants will prepare lobsters in any number of elaborate ways, but to a true New Englander there are but three ways to cook a lobster: boil (steam) it, broil it, or grill it. To broil or grill, take a live lobster, make a straight cut underneath from head to tail, and place cut-upward under the broiler or cut-downward on the grill.

Boiling or steaming is even easier. Put the live lobsters into a pot that has a few inches of boiling seawater in it, cover, bring to a boil again, and let them cook until they turn bright red (10 to 12 minutes, longer for lobsters of several pounds or more). When you take them out, they'll be very hot and full of hot water, too. Give the lobster a few minutes to cool.

Many traditional New England foods are not often served anymore. Boston may be famous for baked beans (navy beans, molasses, salt pork, and onions cooked slowly in a crock), but very few restaurants serve them, and then mostly for sentimental or touristic reasons. New England boiled dinner, a chunk of beef boiled with cabbage, carrots, and potatoes, is also rarely served—and perhaps that's just as well.

Vermont is dairy country, known for Cheddar cheese and delicious Ben & Jerry's ice cream. All the New England states produce delicious pure maple syrup in the late winter and early spring. Many inns and some restaurants serve it with breakfast pancakes and waffles.

As for dessert, fresh fruit and fruit pies are the best. Strawberry season is early to mid-June; rhubarb is also ripe then, and if you come across a strawberry-rhubarb pie, don't let it get away whole. Late June to mid-July is blueberry season, when pies of fresh blueberries appear. Autumn brings peaches, plums, and apples, plus gallons of fresh apple cider. Look for it at roadside stands throughout the region.

New Englanders are as famous for what they don't (or didn't) drink as for what they do drink. Oak Bluffs on Martha's Vineyard and Rockport on Cape Ann (both in Massachusetts) are "dry" towns where alcoholic beverages may not be bought or sold.

Though New Englanders' taste in drinks is largely the same as that of most Americans, there are some specialties. Maine's Poland Spring water is now bottled and shipped throughout the country. In the autumn, fresh apple cider is the beverage of choice throughout the region. Cranberry juice, from berries raised in the bogs of southeastern Massachusetts, is usually mixed with other liquids to ease its tartness.

The urge for better, more distinctive beers led to the rise of Boston's own Samuel Adams lager and also Schooner, both premium brews.

Despite the area's rocky soil and uncooperative weather, enterprising New England vintners have identified hospitable microclimates for the culture of hybrid and vinifera wine grapes. You should definitely sample the vintages offered by Rhode Island's Sakonnet Vineyards; Chicama Vineyards on Martha's Vineyard; Haight Vineyards near Litchfield, Conn.; and Hopkins Vineyard on Connecticut's Lake Waramaug. Nashoba Valley Winery, near Concord, Mass., harvests fruit from its own orchards and produces delicious colonial-style fruit wines.

By the way, many New Englanders still call a carbonated soft drink a "tonic" and the neighborhood food shop where you buy a tonic a "spa."

2 Planning a Trip to New England

The smoothest trips are those that are properly prepared in advance. Here's the information you'll need to get ready for your New England sojourn.

1 Visitor Information

There are both public and private sources of information. Each state has a tourism office that issues brochures, maps, lists of festivals and special events, and other useful materials. Municipal governments often have their own tourism offices as well, but the job of providing information in a town or city is done mostly by the local chamber of commerce or convention and visitors bureau. We've written the names, addresses, and telephone numbers of these chambers and bureaus in the relevant chapters. See also **Travelers Aid Society** under "Emergencies" under "Fast Facts: New England," later in this chapter.

Here are the addresses and telephone numbers of the state tourism offices: **Connecticut Department of Economic Development, Tourist Division** 865 Brook St., Rocky Hill, Conn. 06067-3405 (☎ **203/258-4355** or **800/282-6863**); **Maine Publicity Bureau,** P.O. Box 2300, Hallowell, Me. 04347 (☎ **207/623-0363** or **800/533-9595** outside Maine); **Massachusetts Office of Travel & Tourism,** 100 Cambridge St., 13th Floor, Boston, Mass. 02202 (☎ **617/727-3201** or **800/447-6277** for a free Massachusetts Getaway Guide and map); **New Hampshire Office of Travel and Tourism,** 172 Pembroke Rd. (P.O. Box 1856), Concord, N.H. 03302 (☎ **603/271-2666**); **Rhode Island Department of Economic Development,** 7 Jackson Walkway, Providence, R.I. 02903 (☎ **401/277-2601** or **800/556-2484**); **Vermont Travel and Tourism,** 134 State St., Montpelier, Vt. 05602 (☎ **802/828-3237** for general information; ☎ **802/828-3236** for a vacation packet; ☎ **800/833-9756** to access visitor information by fax).

2 When to Go

CLIMATE Without doubt, the best times to tour New England are summer (June through August) and autumn (September and October), unless you're coming for skiing. You can enjoy a visit here

What Things Cost in Boston	U.S. $
Taxi from airport to downtown Boston	16.00–22.00
Bus from airport to downtown Boston	8.00
MBTA subway token	.85
Double at the Four Seasons Hotel (very expensive)	300.00–460.00
Double at Boston Park Plaza Hotel & Towers (expensive)	155.00–245.00
Double at Copley Square Hotel (moderate)	135.00–175.00
Lunch for one at Zuma's Tex-Mex Café (moderate)	6.95–17.95
Lunch for one at Samuel Adams Brewhouse (budget)	5.95–9.50
Dinner for one, without wine, at Aujourd'hui (deluxe)	26.00–35.50
Dinner for one, without wine, at Rocco's (moderate)	9.00–24.00
Dinner for one, without wine, at Jimbo's Fish Shanty (budget)	6.00–16.00
Glass of beer	2.75–4.00
Coca-Cola	1.00
Cup of coffee	1.00
Roll of ASA 100 Kodacolor film, 36 exposures	6.75–7.75
Admission to the Museum of Fine Arts, Boston	8.00
Movie ticket	7.00–7.50
Theater ticket	30.00–90.00

any time of year if you prepare for the weather and are wary of the busy times when hotels, restaurants, and transportation are filled to capacity.

THE SEASONS   Weather in New England is a much-discussed topic because it's so unpredictable. However, there are some generalizations that seem to hold true from year to year, and these may affect your plans on when to visit New England.

Coming very late and staying very briefly, **spring** tends to be a disappointment. The week or two of spring days in the normal year are a delight, with cool temperatures in the evening and just the perfect degree of warmth during the day. In the countryside the thaw brings "mud time," the period between frost and spring planting. Mud time is the slowest season for tourist facilities, coming after ski season and before summer warmth. Thus many country inns, resorts, and amusements close for a few weeks in April or thereabouts.

By mid-June, **summer** is well established and, despite the region's northerly and coastal location, it can be pretty hot and sometimes quite humid. When it's 85°F (or even up to 95°F) and humid, as it often is through mid-September, head for the beaches, the islands, mountains, lakes, and riverbanks. Sailing, along the coast or on the rivers, is a choice activity, as is a hike to the top of Mount Washington or a week at a beach on Narragansett Bay. A drive through the Berkshires or along the Connecticut coast can also be very satisfying.

Autumn is undoubtedly New England's glory and its finest season, and if you have a choice of vacation times, this is the one to pick. Although you may have to forsake swimming, the famous fall foliage is a worthy substitute; it's at its peak

What Things Cost in Portland	U.S. $
Taxi from airport to a downtown hotel	7.00
Local telephone call	.25
Double room at the Danforth Inn (very expensive)	95.00–155.00
Double room at the Portland Regency (expensive)	115.00–195.00
Double room at one of Exit 8 hotels (moderate)	45.00–70.00
Lunch at The Seaman's Club	8.00–10.00
Lunch at Gilbert's Chowder House	6.00–8.00
Dinner for two (lobster) at the Lobster Shack	32.00
Dinner for two (with dessert) at the Pepper Club	28.00
Pint of beer at Taps	2.75
Pepsi-Cola and hot pretzel from Freeport	2.50
Specialty coffee at Coffee by Design	1.00–2.25
Roll of ASA 100 film, 24 exposures	2.99
Movie ticket at Clark's Pond Cinemas	7.00
Movie ticket at Nickelodeon Cinemas Downtown	2.25

usually in late September and early October, starting in northern Maine, New Hampshire, and Vermont and moving southward and eastward as the weeks pass. Days are still warm and very pleasant, nights a bit chilly but not uncomfortably so. City people load their bikes into the car and head for the country, picking up fresh apple cider, pumpkins, and squash from farm stands on the way home. Fresh cranberries are on sale in the markets all autumn, and although the blueberry-picking season is past, many apple orchards open so that you can "pick-your-own" and get the freshest fruit possible at a very low price.

If you're heading to New England specifically to enjoy the fall foliage, you should make sure you'll be there during "peak color." You can call the following number in each state to find out about fall-foliage: Connecticut (☎ 800/CT-BOUND), Maine (☎ 207/623-0363 or 800/533-9595), Massachusetts (☎ 617/727-3201), New Hampshire (☎ 800/258-3608), Rhode Island (☎ 800/556-2484), and Vermont (☎ 802/828-3239).

Most tourist resorts and inns stay open through September and often to Columbus Day. Those that stay open all year sometimes close for two weeks or so from mid-October to early December to give the staff a break before the advent of the ski season. By Thanksgiving, everyone's getting in shape for the ski season.

After a period of chilly weather in October, New England usually gets a respite, with a short period of warm weather known as "Indian summer," which can occur in late October or November. It's not dependable and may be brief, but it's glorious all the same.

Impressions

I believe no one attempts to praise the climate of New England.
—Harriet Martineau, *Retrospect of Western Travel*, 1838

Impressions

The most serious charge which can be brought against New England is not Puritanism but February.

—Joseph Wood Krutch, "February," *The Twelve Seasons,* 1949

Winter, as they say, depends: Snow might begin in November, which is very early, for the first flurries usually come in mid-December. Sometimes snow wishes are too well answered, as in the Great Blizzard of 1978, which piled six feet of snow on Boston, closing the city for a week. Ski reports appear in newspapers and the broadcast media, and the special skiing-condition phone lines go into operation. January through March is cold and snowy, and the skiing may be quite good through April; gray snowy days alternate with brilliant, crisp, sunny days when the air is very cold but the sun's warmth makes it pleasant. Those who aren't skiing take advantage of the cities' cultural seasons or perhaps escape to an inn somewhere in the snow-clad mountains for a weekend.

Mount Washington Weather: None of this applies to Mount Washington in New Hampshire, of course. This "highest peak in New England" is said to have the worst weather in all 50 states, and New Englanders delight in exchanging horror stories of the latest report: winds of 150 miles per hour (the record is 231 mph!), temperatures of –40°F, and windchill factors that don't seem earthly.

HOLIDAYS & TRAVEL SEASONS   The same major holidays that are celebrated throughout the rest of the United States are observed in New England. That would include: **New Year's Day, Martin Luther King Day, Presidents' Day** (particularly busy in ski country), **Easter, Memorial Day, Independence Day, Labor Day, Columbus Day, Election Day, Veterans Day, Thanksgiving,** and **Christmas.** In addition, **Patriot's Day** is widely celebrated in Massachusetts.

Beginning around January 15, ski season begins in earnest, and many ski lodges and inns offer money-saving packages during this time, especially if you plan to stay on weekdays rather than weekends. Ski season continues sometimes well into March and even April, depending on when the last snowstorm occurs.

The end of March and early April are "mud time" in much of New England. Farmers take advantage of the warming weather and rising sap for "sugaring off": tapping their maple trees for sap and boiling it down to make pure maple syrup. Also in April, many country inns close for all or part of the month.

May is the time when seasonal travel areas (like Cape Cod) begin opening their doors to tourists. The weekend closest to Memorial Day signals the official start of the summer tourism season. Rooms are in great demand at this time.

You won't have much trouble getting a room in early June before school lets out for the summer, but the end of the month is particularly busy. July and August are also popular travel months. You'll also need to make travel plans early if you're going to be traveling on Labor Day weekend, in September.

October is high season in many areas in New England because it is the month during which New England's famed fall foliage is in full color. October is also a popular conventioneers month in Boston.

November is a slower month, and December is the beginning (albeit a slow one) to the ski season.

NEW ENGLAND CALENDAR OF EVENTS

For up-to-date information on events throughout New England, buy the Thursday edition of the *Boston Globe,* which carries a separate calendar section with detailed listings on all sorts of happenings.

January
- **First Night.** The arrival of the new year is celebrated with festivities in Boston, Mass.; Providence, R.I.; Stamford, Conn.; Burlington, Vt.; and other cities and towns. New Year's Eve.
- **Stowe Winter Carnival,** Stowe, Vt. Ski races, parties, and other festivities, many of them outdoors. Third week.

February
- **Dartmouth Winter Carnival,** Hanover, N.H. Dartmouth College's annual snow celebration. Second week.

March
- **Maine Maple Sunday.** Maple sugarhouses throughout the state open their doors to visitors. Third Sunday.

April
- **Boothbay Harbor Fishermen's Festival,** Boothbay Harbor, Me. Seafood feasts, exhibits, and games. Second weekend.
- ✪ **Patriots Day.** Reenactment of the battles between Minutemen and redcoats at Lexington Green and Concord North Bridge, with real musket fire (but no bullets). To do it right, be at Lexington Green by dawn for the Lexington battle, then walk along Battle Road to Concord North Bridge (eight miles) for the Concord one.

     Where: Lexington and Concord, Mass. **When:** Patriots Day, April 19 (celebrated on the third Monday), a holiday in Massachusetts. **How:** For information, contact Minuteman National Historical Park (☎ **508/369-6944**), the Lexington Visitors Center (☎ **617/862-1450**), or the Concord Chamber of Commerce (☎ **508/369-3120**).
- **Boston Marathon.** Patriots Day, April 19.

May
- **Brimfield Antiques Fair,** Brimfield, Mass. Up to 2,000 dealers fill several fields near this central Massachusetts town, with similar fairs in early or mid-July and mid-September. Mid-May.
- **Lobster Weekend,** Mystic Seaport in Mystic, Conn. Lobster feasts and live entertainment. Late May.

June
- **Yale-Harvard Regatta,** on the Thames River in New London, Conn. Early June.
- **Taste of Block Island Seafood Festival,** Block Island, R.I. Chowder cookoff, games, crafts, and live entertainment. Mid-June.
- **Blessing of the Fleet,** Gloucester, Mass. Festivities, seafood fests, dancing, and exhibits. Late June.
- **Jacob's Pillow Dance Festival,** Becket, Mass. The region's premier summer dance festival. Contact Jacob's Pillow Dance Festival, P.O. Box 287, Lee, Mass. 01238 (☎ **413/243-0745**). June to August.

July

- **New Haven Jazz Festival,** concerts on the green in New Haven, Conn. Early to late July.

❂ **Independence Week.** A week of concerts, exhibits, and special events culminates in the famous Boston Pops Fourth of July concert at the Hatch Memorial Shell on the Esplanade; after Tchaikovsky's *1812 Overture* (with real cannons), a mammoth fireworks display goes off over the Charles River. **Where:** Various locations in Boston.

  When: Week of July 4. **How:** For information and schedules, contact the Greater Boston Convention & Visitors Bureau, Prudential Plaza (P.O. Box 490), Boston, MA 02199 (☎ **617/536-4100** or **800/888-5515**; fax 617/424-7664), or phone the Special Events Group (☎ **617/267-2400**).

- **Great Schooner Race,** Rockland, Me. First or second Friday.
- **Newport Music Festival,** Newport, R.I. Chamber music concerts are held in the great mansions. Second and third weeks.
- **Historic Homes Tour,** Litchfield, Conn. One day is your only opportunity to tour this beautiful town's historic houses. Call ☎ **203/567-4506** for details. Mid-July.
- **Barnstable County Fair,** Hatchville, Mass., on Cape Cod. An old-time county fair complete with rides, food, and livestock contests. Late July.
- **Friendship Sloop Boothbay Harbor Regatta,** Boothbay Harbor, Me. A three-day event, this series of boat races culminates in a parade of sloops. Last week.
- **Bar Harbor Music Festival,** Bar Harbor, Me. Classical and popular concerts. July to August.
- **Marlboro Music Festival,** Marlboro, Vt. Among New England's oldest and most renowned. July to August.

❂ **Tanglewood.** The summer season of the Boston Symphony Orchestra brings symphony and chamber concerts and solo recitals to the Berkshire hills. **Where:** Tanglewood, near Lenox, Mass. **When:** July to August. **How:** Write for a program: Symphony Hall, 301 Massachusetts Ave., Boston, MA 02115 (☎ **617/266-1492**), or call the Tanglewood Concert Line (☎ **413/637-1666** in July and August only).

August

- **Maine Lobster Festival,** Rockland, Me. Celebration of the lobster and the region's maritime history. Arts and crafts, entertainment, a parade, and lots of lobster. Call ☎ **207/596-0376** for more information. First weekend.

❂ **Newport Folk Festival & Jvc Jazz Festival.** Thousands of music lovers congregate at Fort Adams State Park on alternate weekends in July and August. Performers include such big names as Suzanne Vega, Randy Newman, B.B. King, Ray Charles, and Tony Bennett.

  Where: Newport, R.I. **When:** Second week in August. **How:** For information on schedules and tickets, call the Newport Festival Office (☎ **401/847-3700**) or Ticketmaster (☎ **401/331-2211**). For tickets and information by mail, write the Newport Festival Office at P.O. Box 605, Newport, RI 02840. Tickets can also be purchased at the Festival Office, located at 670 Fame Street.

- **League of New Hampshire Craftsmen Fair,** Mount Sunapee State Park, near Newbury, N.H. Crafts displays and demonstrations amid other festivities. Admission is charged. Call ☎ **603/224-1471** for more information. Second week.

- **Bennington Battle Days,** Bennington, Vt. Commemorates the Battle of Bennington (August 11, 1777) with exhibits, speeches, and celebrations. Second week.

September

- **Blue Hill Fair,** Blue Hill, Me. A country fair with rides, games, and lots to eat. Labor Day and the four days preceding it.
- **Vermont State Fair,** Rutland, Vt. Agricultural exhibits, games, rides, and entertainment. Labor Day weekend.
- **Providence Waterfront Festival,** Providence, R.I. Performances, art exhibits, boat races, and multiethnic feasts. Early September.
- **New Haven Fall Antiques Show.** Among the region's largest shows. Mid-September.
- ✪ **Eastern States Exposition.** "The Big E" is New England's largest agricultural fair, with a midway, games, rides, agricultural judgings, lots of eats, and general fun. **Where:** West Springfield, Mass. **When:** Mid-September. **How:** Contact the Eastern States Exposition (☎ **413/737-2443**) or the Greater Springfield Convention and Visitors Bureau, 34 Boland Way, Springfield, Mass. 01103(☎ **413/787-1548**).
- **National Traditional Old-Time Fiddler's Context,** Barre, Vt. Lots of good music. Late September.
- **Northeast Kingdom Fall Foliage Festival.** Hometown church breakfasts, crafts sales, and open-house tours in the towns of Barnet, Cabot, Groton, Peacham, Plainfield, and Walden, Vt. Late September to early October.

October

- **Festival of Vermont Crafts,** Montpelier, Vt. Crafts both traditional and modern. Late October.

November

- **Thanksgiving Celebration,** Plymouth, Mass. Authentic colonial food, dress, and festivities in town and at nearby Plimouth Plantation. Third Thursday.

December

- **Boston Tea Party Reenactment,** Boston, Mass. At the Tea Party Ship and Museum on Boston's Museum Wharf. Mid-December.
- **Christmas Eve and Christmas Day.** Special festivities throughout New England. In Newport, R.I., several of the great mansions have special tours; Mystic Seaport in Mystic, Conn., has a special program of Christmas festivities; Nantucket, Mass., features carolers in Victorian garb, art exhibits, and tours of historic houses. December 24–25.

3   The Active Vacation Planner

The mountains, forests, seacoasts, and rivers of New England are all venues for exciting, memorable outdoor adventures, from biking the back roads of Vermont to braving the bracing waters of the Maine coast in a sea kayak.

WALKING/HIKING   Country Walkers, Inc., P.O. Box 180, Waterbury, Vt. 05676-0180 (☎ **802/244-1387**), organizes 5- to 11-day walking trips in New England and other parts of the world. Walking tours typically cover 4 to 12 miles per day, in three to five hours. You walk at your own pace with similarly paced participants, who range in age from 30 to 70; luggage is transported in a van.

Lodging is in rooms with private baths at nice country inns; all three meals are included. There's a five-day trip on the coast of Maine that costs $825, and a five-day trip in central Vermont for $789 per person.

New England Hiking Holidays, P.O. Box 1648, North Conway, N.H. 03860 (☎ **800/869-0949**), runs two- to five-day hiking trips in New England and other areas, providing accommodation at country inns at night. Call or write for a detailed brochure of their offerings.

BICYCLE TOURING   Vermont Bicycle Touring, Box 711-AN, Bristol, Vt. 05443 (☎ **802/453-4811**), offers tours for all ages and abilities. Call for information on their upcoming tours and prices.

You can arrange your own bicycle tours on Cape Cod with the aid of **The Cape Cod Bike Book,** which has maps and details on bike paths, rest stops, places to take a break, and where to rent or repair a bicycle. You can buy the book ($2.99) in many stores on the Cape, or order it ($3.75) from Cape Cod Bike Book, P.O. Box 627, South Dennis, Ma. 02660.

MOUNTAIN BIKING   Touring the backwoods by bike can be exhilarating, especially during New England's autumn foliage season. If you plan to do your biking from mid-September to mid-October, make your reservations well ahead of time.

The **Craftsbury Center,** P.O. Box 31, Craftsbury Common, Vt. 05827 (☎ **802/586-7767**), has a program of mountain-bike tours that includes accommodations and meals at lower prices than most other organized tours. If you bring your own bike and use a room with shared bath as your base, you may pay less than $70 per person per day; for more comfortable accommodations with private bath and all meals, the rate is about $100 per person per day. Tours range in length from two-day weekend jaunts to five-day excursions.

SEA KAYAKING & SCHOONER CRUISES   Maine Island Kayak Co., 70 Luther St., Peaks Island, Me. 04108 (☎ **207/766-2373**), 20 minutes by ferry from Portland, offers half-day and full-day trips by sea kayak among the Diamond Islands, long weekend excursions featuring camping on the islands, and 5- to 10-day expeditions along the most beautiful stretches of the Maine coast. Most trips require no previous knowledge or experience of sea kayaking, so beginners are welcome. "If you can walk a few miles," they say, "you can paddle between camps."

SKIING   You'll also find good skiing in the Berkshires in Massachusetts. Downhill skiing is available at Catamount, Butternut, Jiminy Peak, Brodie, and Bosquet ski areas. All of these areas offer children's ski programs, and some areas offer special rates for senior citizens. Rentals are available at all ski areas. Snowboarding is also popular at most areas.

The grounds of Tanglewood (known for its summer concert series) are open in winter for cross-country skiing, and there are state parks and wildlife sanctuaries in the area that maintain groomed trails. Many of the downhill areas listed above also maintain challenging cross-country ski trails.

Call the ski areas or the Berkshire Visitors Bureau for details (☎ 413/443-9186 or 800/237-5747).

While northern New England ski areas don't enjoy the reputation of resorts in the West such as Aspen, Deer Valley, or Whistler Mountain, the tri-state area of Maine, New Hampshire, and Vermont does welcome hundreds of thousands of downhill skiers each season. The rugged terrain and annual snowfall usually guarantee excellent skiing.

Skiing in New England

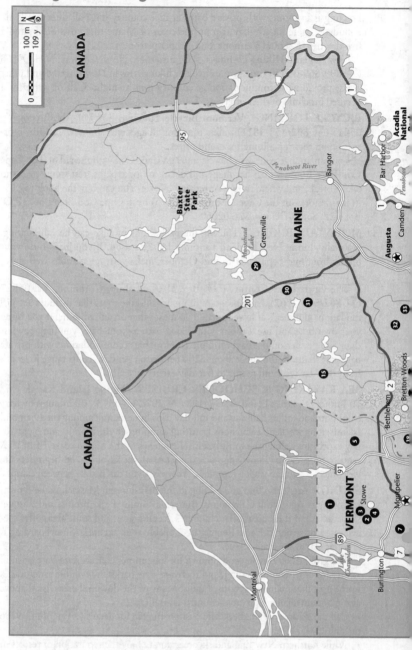

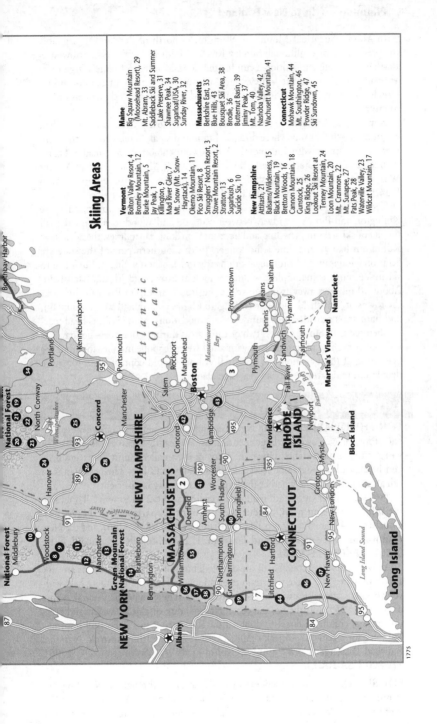

Skiing Areas

Vermont
Bolton Valley Resort, 4
Bromley Mountain, 12
Burke Mountain, 5
Jay Peak, 1
Killington, 9
Mad River Glen, 7
Mt. Snow (Mt. Snow-Haystack), 14
Okemo Mountain, 11
Pico Ski Resort, 8
Smugglers' Notch Resort, 3
Stowe Mountain Resort, 2
Stratton, 13
Sugarbush, 6
Suicide Six, 10

New Hampshire
Attitash, 21
Balsams/Wilderness, 15
Black Mountain, 19
Bretton Woods, 16
Cannon Mountain, 18
Gunstock, 25
King Ridge, 26
Lookout Ski Resort at Tenney Mountain, 24
Loon Mountain, 20
Mt. Cranmore, 22
Mt. Sunapee, 27
Pats Peak, 28
Waterville Valley, 23
Wildcat Mountain, 17

Maine
Big Squaw Mountain (Moosehead Resort), 29
Mt. Abram, 33
Saddleback Ski and Summer Lake Preserve, 31
Shawnee Peak, 34
Sugarloaf/USA, 30
Sunday River, 32

Massachusetts
Berkshire East, 35
Blue Hills, 43
Bousquet Ski Area, 38
Brodie, 36
Butternut Basin, 39
Jiminy Peak, 37
Mt. Tom, 40
Nashoba Valley, 42
Wachusett Mountain, 41

Connecticut
Mohawk Mountain, 44
Mt. Southington, 46
Powder Ridge, 47
Ski Sundown, 45

1775

In Maine, Sugarloaf Mountain, 90 minutes north of Portland, is arguably the premiere choice, although Sunday River, in Bethel, 75 minutes northwest of Portland gives all competition a run for the slopes. Closer to Maine's largest city are Saddleback and Lost Valley. Each area offers an array of condominium rentals and nearby hotels. Sugarloaf and Sunday River have lodge hotels on the mountain.

New Hampshire tends to have its ski facilities in close proximity to each other. Begin in North Conway where dozens of inns and small hotels cater to the summer and winter crowds with aplomb. Among your choices are the small but commendable Mount Cranmore and the larger Wildcat Mountain. Also in Mount Washington Valley are Attitash and Black mountains. Continue north toward Franconia Notch, and there you'll find Cannon and Loon mountains.

Central Vermont offers a core of downhill areas, too. The most popular are Killington and Pico, set midway between Rutland and Woodstock. Now that all the major ski areas in New England have snow-making capabilities, the advantage Killington had at one time is no longer. In the southern part of the state are Stratton Mountain and Bromley, both handy to Manchester village. But a trip to ski in Vermont is incomplete without a look at Stowe and Mount Mansfield. About 30 minutes away from Stowe are Sugarbush and Mad River Glenn, near the towns of Waitsfield and Warren. Sugarbush has a north and south mountain, and both areas provide a spectrum of accommodations. Many visitors headquarter themselves in Stowe and ski two or three areas during a one-week holiday. Almost every ski area promotes itself with a toll-free telephone number found in the beginning of those sections, so potential visitors should contact them for more details and reservations. All have package plans.

4 Tips for Special Travelers

FOR THE DISABLED   All of New England's major hotels and most museums, and stores, as well as other large institutions, are readily accessible to visitors in wheelchairs or on crutches. However, many of the smaller country inns and bed-and-breakfast houses are not accessible or not fully accessible. The best plan is to call ahead to determine whether the level of accessibility is sufficient.

Two states offer information about accessible facilities and events. To receive the information you need, contact the **Vermont Department of Travel and Tourism**, 134 State St., Montpelier, VT 05602 (☎ **802/828-3236**), and the **New Hampshire Office of Travel and Tourism**, 172 Pembroke Rd., Concord, N.H. 03301 (☎ **603/271-2666**).

Amtrak trains are accessible to the disabled, but not all Amtrak stations are; ask about this when you make your train reservations, and also inquire about help with your baggage, special seating, and other assistance. There's a bonus: Amtrak grants discounts of 25% (off the normal coach fare) to adult disabled travelers and 50% (off normal children's fares) to disabled travelers aged 2 to 12. For full information, ask for a copy of Amtrak's annual *Travel Planner* from **Amtrak**, National Railroad Passenger Corp., 400 N. Capitol St. NW, Washington, DC 20001 (☎ **800/USA-RAIL**).

FOR SENIORS   Senior discounts are readily available throughout New England at museums, parks, attractions, and some hotels and on Amtrak trains, so make sure to carry some convincing form of photo identification. It's best to request discounts on hotel rates, train and plane fares, and rental-car fees *when you make your reservation,* not when you're paying for the services. For more information about senior discounts in general and for a good-as-gold discount card, contact the **American Association of Retired Persons (AARP),** 601 E St., NW, Washington, D.C. 20049 (☎ **202/434-2277** Monday through Friday from 9am to 5pm).

By the way, Boston is the home of **Elderhostel,** 75 Federal St., Boston, Mass. 02110-1941 (☎ **617/426-7788**), with innovative educational programs throughout the world for those 55 years and older.

FOR FAMILIES   New England is a favorite destination for families on vacation, and many price breaks are available. Museums, amusement attractions, whale-watch expeditions, and most other sights offer reduced admission rates for children. Many offer even better deals in the form of family plans, whereby one admission price covers an entire family; the price is lower than the sum of two adult and two children's tickets.

Some attractions (outdoor concerts, state parks, beaches, and so forth) charge admission "per car," so families on a driving vacation pay as little as solo travelers.

Often a family of four or even five can stay in the same hotel room. Most modern hotels and motels allow children to stay for free with their parents if the parents pay the normal two-person rate (not a special discount rate) and the children use the room's existing beds. In a room with two double beds, a family of four can stay as cheaply as two. If there are three children and a rollaway bed is necessary, there'll be a small charge ($10 to $20) for it. The age permissible for children under the "family plan" varies; for some plans, there is no age limit. Some inns follow the same policy, but at many others children are not accepted.

A good source of information for family travel is *Frommer's New England with Kids.*

5   Getting There

Three major gateways to New England are New York City, Montréal, and Boston. Most train and bus routes to New England pass through either New York or Montréal, and a large number of transcontinental and transatlantic flights arrive at the airports in these cities. Many travelers choose to fly directly to Boston, of course. All these routes are covered below, along with information on how to travel around New England by bus, rail, air, and car.

BY PLANE

FLIGHTS FROM NEW YORK CITY   You can easily catch a connecting flight from New York to Boston. There are several flights daily from each of the three major airports: John F. Kennedy, LaGuardia, and Newark, N.J. Airlines flying between New York and Boston include American (☎ 800/433-7300), Continental (☎ 800/525-0280), Delta (☎ 800/221-1212), Northwest (☎ 800/225-2525), and USAir (☎ 800/247-8786).

If you find no convenient connecting flight, consider taking the airport transfer bus to LaGuardia to catch an air shuttle. Some shuttle flights depart every hour on the hour, others on the half hour, between 6am and 9pm. No advance reservations are needed—you're guaranteed a seat.

Flights from New York City go daily to these other airports in the region as well: Albany, N.Y.; Bangor, Me.; Bridgeport, Conn.; Burlington, Vt.; Hartford, Conn.; Hyannis, Mass.; Lebanon, N.H.; Manchester, N.H.; Martha's Vineyard, Mass.; Nantucket, Mass.; New Haven, Conn.; New London, Conn.; Portland, Me.; Presque Isle, Me.; Providence, R.I.; and Worcester, Mass.

FLIGHTS FROM CHICAGO   Flights take off from the city's four airports— O'Hare International, Midway, Pal-Waukee, and Merrill C. Meigs—daily for New England and nearby destinations, including Albany, N.Y.; Bangor, Me.; Boston, Mass.; Burlington, Vt.; Hartford, Conn.; Manchester, N.H.; Portland, Me.; Providence, R.I.; and Worcester, Mass. The most active airlines are American, Northwest, United, and USAir.

FLIGHTS FROM CANADA   Delta Airlines operates routes from Montréal's Dorval Airport to Boston and Hartford; and Air Canada's commuter line, Air Alliance, flies from Dorval to Boston as well. Either flight takes just over an hour.

DISCOUNT TICKETS   Discount airfares normally have three constraints attached to them. First, you must make your reservations and purchase your tickets in advance. Usually you must close the deal at least a week before you fly, but some airfares require even more time, perhaps two or three weeks.

Second, you cannot change your plans without paying some sort of penalty. This penalty ranges from 25% to 100% of the price you've paid.

The third constraint is that airlines may offer very few seats on each flight at the lowest fare.

Are there ways around these rules? Yes! Nothing can substitute for good advance planning, so make your plans and talk to your travel agent well in advance of your trip.

An agent willing to "dig" into the plethora of airfares and discover a special fare or a special routing that will save you money is **1-800/FLY ASAP** (the company name and toll-free phone number are the same). Make your reservations, but don't buy your ticket until you're required to do so. When the time comes to buy your ticket, ask the agent to take another look to see whether the situation has changed. The reservations and airfare business is so complex that seats on particular flights may be "reserved"and "released" many times before the plane even leaves the ground, and fares go up and down almost daily.

As for penalties, airlines rarely levy a penalty if you advance your return date— that is, if you come back to your starting point early.

Foreign visitors can sometimes take advantage of special air-travel passes that offer unlimited flying for a period of time (three weeks, a month, several months, etc.) on a particular airline's routes. You must buy the pass before you leave home (Europe, Japan, etc.), you cannot fly during holiday blackout periods, you cannot backtrack, and there may be a minimum or maximum number of takeoffs. There's also the constraint of the airline's route system: Does it operate flights to the places you want to visit? But these passes provide indisputable bargains when they are offered.

BY CAR

FROM NEW YORK CITY   Starting from New York City, choose your route according to your destination:

For **northwestern Connecticut, the Massachusetts Berkshires, and southern and western Vermont,** follow the Henry Hudson Parkway or I-87 north to the

Saw Mill River Parkway, which connects with the Taconic State Parkway north. The Taconic is a beautiful road, and trucks are not allowed.

To **southwestern Connecticut, Hartford, central Massachusetts, Boston, eastern Vermont, New Hampshire, and Maine,** take the Henry Hudson Parkway or I-87 north to the Saw Mill River Parkway, and that north to I-684. At the junction with I-84, go east via Danbury and Waterbury to Hartford and beyond.

If you're heading for points along the **Connecticut and Rhode Island coasts** (New Haven, New London, Mystic, Providence, Newport), Cape Cod and the islands, New Bedford, and Plymouth, follow the Henry Hudson Parkway or I-87 north to I-287. Head east on I-287 to the Hutchinson River Parkway north; after a few miles this road enters Connecticut and becomes the Merritt Parkway. Unlike the alternative route, I-95, this scenic road is not open to trucks, making it even more pleasant. Beyond Bridgeport, the Merritt Parkway is named the Wilbur Cross Parkway; it continues past New Haven and north to Meriden, where it's best to take I-91 north. To head east along the coast from New Haven, take I-95, unless you want to slow down and take the older U.S. 1, an interesting route that goes through many coastal towns—and red lights.

FROM CHICAGO   Interstate 80 is very heavily traveled to Cleveland and not particularly pleasant to drive, but it's the most direct route. For scenery and a more relaxed time, take I-94 to Detroit, then cross the border into Canada to follow Highway 401 to Hamilton before heading down via Niagara Falls to Buffalo to pick up I-90, the New York State Thruway, to Albany and Boston.

FROM TORONTO   From Toronto, the Hamilton–Niagara–Buffalo–Albany route is the logical choice unless you're headed for northern New England, in which case you might want to drive via Montréal (see below).

FROM MONTREAL   The most direct route from Montréal to Vermont, southern New Hampshire, and the southern New England states is to cross the Pont Victoria and follow Canada 10, the Autoroute des Cantons de l'Est, eastward 22km (13 miles) to Canada 35 south; this is all expressway. Beyond Iberville, the route is marked as Québec Highway 133 and is a fairly fast two-lane highway through flat farming country. At the U.S. border, the road becomes I-89 south and continues via Burlington and Montpelier to White River Junction, Vt., where it intersects with I-91. Continue on I-89 to Concord and Manchester, N.H., and to Boston; take I-91 south to southern Vermont and New Hampshire, central Massachusetts, and central Connecticut around Hartford.

For the western parts of Vermont, Massachusetts, and Connecticut, take the Pont Victoria or Pont Jacques-Cartier east out of Montréal and follow Canada 15 due south to the U.S. border, where the highway becomes I-87. You can leave this road at Exit 39 north of Plattsburgh, N.Y., to catch a ferry from Gordon Landing over to Grand Isle and thence via U.S. 2 to I-89 and Burlington; or you can take an exit farther south to get to Port Kent and the ferry across Lake Champlain directly to Burlington (for details on this service, see "Burlington," in Chapter 13). Near Albany, roads go east to Bennington in southern Vermont, Williamstown, Mass., and the Berkshires; just south of Albany, I-87 intersects with I-90, the Massachusetts Turnpike to Boston. If you're headed farther south, follow I-90 east from I-87 to the Taconic State Parkway, a pleasant, fast road open only to cars, not to trucks.

From Montréal to northern New Hampshire and Maine, take the Pont Victoria, follow Canada 10, the Autoroute des Cantons de l'Est, eastward as far as Magog.

Turn south here on Canada 55 to the U.S. border. South of the border the highway is I-93, which leads straight to New Hampshire's White Mountains. To get to Maine, you can take U.S. 2 or U.S. 302 eastward from I-93.

Another route to Maine, slower and less scenic, with fewer tourist services, is to continue on Canada 10 east from Magog and through Sherbrooke. Beyond Sherbrooke, the road becomes two lanes and is numbered Québec 112. Follow 112 to the small town of St-Gérard, then follow Québec 161 through Lac-Mégantic to the U.S. border. In Maine, the road is Me. 27, a lonely route through forests and mountains, finally bringing you to Augusta, the state capital.

BY TRAIN

Amtrak's schedules are carried in all the major airline systems, and any travel agency with one of the airlines' computerized reservation systems can give you information on Amtrak schedules and fares, and can sell you tickets.

Amtrak's rail passenger service travels coast to coast. From the south, trains speed north along the eastern seaboard to Washington, D.C., the southern end of **the "Northeast Corridor"** (Washington-Boston route). Most passengers who come to New England by train take this line via New York City.

Amtrak's *Lake Shore Limited* travels nightly **from Chicago** to New England, departing Chicago's Union Station and arriving in Springfield, Mass., the next day. Several through cars from the *Lake Shore Limited* continue to Boston. From Springfield, you can also continue north by bus, east or south by train.

One train daily, the *Maple Leaf,* departs **Toronto** and arrives at Albany-Rensselaer. From Albany, it's a short hop by bus to the Berkshires or southern Vermont. There's only one train a day, the *Lake Shore Limited* (see above), connecting Albany-Rensselaer with Boston. If you've come this far on the *Maple Leaf,* you must continue by bus or stay overnight and catch the *Lake Shore Limited* the next day.

Two Amtrak trains run daily **from Montréal**'s Central Station (beneath the Queen Elizabeth Hotel) to New York City, a distance of 450 miles. The *Adirondack* is a day train (10 hours) departing Montréal. If you get off the train at Albany, you can take a bus to southern Vermont or to the Berkshires.

The *Montrealer* is a night train (12 hours) that arrives in New York around 7am.

Schedules may change, so call **Amtrak** (☎ **800/USA-RAIL**) for a current schedule.

Note: Besides Amtrak service from Penn Station, there is **Metro North** train service on the Connecticut Department of Transportation's New Haven Line from New York's Grand Central Terminal to New Haven, Conn., every hour on the hour from 7am until after midnight on weekdays, with extra trains during the peak morning and evening hours. Service on Saturday, Sunday, and holidays is almost as frequent, with a train at least every two hours. The trip from Grand Central to New Haven takes $1^3/_4$ hours. For exact schedule information, call ☎ **212/ 532-4900.**

TRAINS TO CAPE COD   During the peak summer vacation season of July and August (through Labor Day weekend), Amtrak operates special weekend trains from New York City to Hyannis on Cape Cod.

The *Cape Codder* departs Washington, D.C., in mid-afternoon on Friday, stops at New York's Pennsylvania Station in late afternoon, departs New Haven at suppertime, and arrives in Hyannis at bedtime. On Saturday, trains from Washington and New York connect with the *Clamdigger* at Providence, R.I., for the final run to Hyannis. Return trips from Hyannis to Providence, New York, and Washington depart Saturday morning and Sunday afternoon.

For the latest information on ever-changing fares and schedules, call ☎ **800/USA-RAIL**, which is **800/872-7245**.

Remember that unless you travel first class in a club or sleeping car, meals are not included in Amtrak's prices; you must either pay for meals on the train when you receive them or carry your own food.

BY BUS

In **New York,** the main bus station is the **Port Authority Bus Terminal,** Eighth Avenue and 42nd Street (☎ **212/564-8484**). From Newark International Airport, shuttle buses go directly to the Port Authority terminal. From LaGuardia Airport or John F. Kennedy International Airport, take a Carey airport bus to Grand Central Terminal (Park Avenue and 42nd Street) and walk (or take a taxi) five blocks west along 42nd Street to the bus terminal.

BUS LINES   From the Port Authority Bus Terminal, various lines run to different parts of New England.

Bonanza Bus Lines   Bonanza's (☎ **800/556-3815**) routes go to Albany, N.Y., via the Berkshires (Great Barrington, Stockbridge, Lee, Lenox, and Pittsfield, Mass.) from New York City; and from New York City to Cape Cod (Falmouth, Woods Hole, and Hyannis, Mass.) via Providence, R.I. During the winter months, service to Falmouth and Woods Hole (for the ferries to Martha's Vineyard and Nantucket) is via a connection at Bourne, Mass. Bonanza also operates between New York City and Providence and Newport, R.I., and New Bedford, Mass. Buy your tickets in New York's Port Authority Bus Terminal at the Adirondack Trailways Ticket Plaza.

Greyhound Lines   Greyhound (☎ **800/231-2222**) operates buses from New York City to Hartford, Springfield, Worcester, New Haven, New London, and Providence. Service to Cape Cod is provided in conjunction with Bonanza. The Boston service has a few buses daily. The direct trip to Boston takes about $4^{3}/_{4}$ hours. From Boston, connections are made to points in Maine, New Hampshire, and Vermont.

Vermont Transit Lines   Vermont Transit (☎ **800/451-3292, 800/642-3133** in Vermont) operates in conjunction with Greyhound to serve Vermont's ski and vacation regions as well as Montréal and several points in New Hampshire.

The major bus routes to New England **from Chicago and Toronto** enter the region at Albany and Montréal, and you may find yourself changing buses at one of these points to reach your final destination. The distance by road to Boston from Chicago is almost 1,000 miles; from Toronto, 550 miles.

Vermont Transit buses depart at least three times daily **from Montréal's** central bus station, the Terminus Voyageur, 505 bd. de Maisonneuve est (☎ **514/842-2281**), en route to Boston (nine hours). In summer, Greyhound operates daily service from Montréal to Burlington, Vt.; North Conway, N.H.; Old Orchard Beach, Me.; and Boston. Other Greyhound buses head due south along Canada 15 and I-87 to New York City, stopping in Albany along the way.

6 Getting Around

Whether you use your own car or a rental (hired) car, driving is perhaps the best way to see New England. The forested hills, winding river valleys, and historic New England towns and villages are most accessible and best appreciated when seen from a car traveling at moderate speed on secondary roads. But other means of transportation are available as well.

BY CAR

Within New England you'll normally drive only an hour or two to your next destination. From Boston, it's only about an hour's drive to Providence, Plymouth, Manchester, or Portsmouth; about two hours to Hartford, Portland, Mystic, or Cape Cod; about three hours to New Haven, the Berkshires, southern Vermont, Boothbay Harbor, or New Hampshire's White Mountains; and only about four hours to New York City or central Vermont. Five hours takes you from Boston to the resort and national park at Bar Harbor, Me., and not much more than six hours' driving deposits you in beautiful Montréal.

CAR RENTAL   To rent a car in New York or New England, you must be 21 years of age and have a valid driver's license. A credit or charge card is almost always a necessity. Without one, you must leave a sizable cash deposit, perhaps $100 per day for the estimated length of the rental, or perhaps a flat $2,000 or more.

Major International Companies   Rental rates vary among companies. Most expensive are the well-known international companies with car-rental desks right in the major airports; cheapest are small local agencies in major cities. In between are the moderate-size agencies with airport shuttle buses to take you to their "off-airport" locations.

Lowest rates are for the smallest cars, rented on "weekends" (Thursday noon through Monday noon) or for an entire week or more with unlimited mileage, and returned to the place of rental or at least to the city of rental. Always return a rental car to the agency with as much gas in it as when the rental began (usually a full tank). Agencies will charge you if they must refuel the car, and some charge high prices at their pumps.

Among the high charges for car rental are those for insurance. The so-called Collision Damage Waiver (CDW) or Loss Damage Waiver (LDW) can cost $8 to $14 or more per day. These charges are currently the subject of legal debate and may be abolished or regulated by state governments in the future. For now, you can avoid them several ways. If your own auto insurance covers damage to a rental car, you needn't waste money on CDW or LDW; check with your auto insurance broker to be sure. Otherwise, your American Express card or gold Visa or MasterCard may provide coverage for any car rented with the card; check your card agreement to see what coverage is provided. In case of damage, rental-car companies may require not only that you pay for repairs but also that you pay normal rental fees for all the time that the rental car is out of commission for repairs.

If you're under 25, you might also get charged an extra $8 a day, depending on the company you choose, so be sure to ask. Rental cars from the national companies may be reserved through any travel agent or by calling a car-rental company directly on its toll-free line. Here are the toll-free numbers of the national companies: **Alamo** (☎ **800/327-9633**), **Avis** (☎ **800/331-1212**), **Budget**

(☎ 800/527-0700), **Dollar** (☎ 800/421-6868), **Hertz** (☎ 800/654-3131), **National** (☎ 800/227-7368), **Rent-A-Wreck** (☎ 800/535-1391), and **Thrifty** (☎ 800/367-2277).

Local Car-Rental Companies   Besides the large national companies, there are many small, local car-rental companies in each New England city. Look in the yellow pages telephone directory under "Automobile Renting & Leasing." Though they don't have the national companies' far-flung systems of agents, many of these local companies provide good local service at excellent rates. Most offer free delivery and pickup at the airport or at a hotel, unlimited mileage, and good late-model cars. Since New England is not a large region, you may not be too far from the rental agency if a problem arises.

DRIVING RULES   Highway and street speed limits, licensing of drivers, and all other rules governing automobile use are set by each state's legislature. In general, you must be 18 years old to get a driver's license. Maximum speed on most expressways in New England is 55 m.p.h., though many drivers regularly exceed that. A few expressways (mostly in New Hampshire) have speed limits of 65 m.p.h. Fines for speeding are $75 to $100 or more per offense, and after several offenses, your driver's license is revoked for a period of time.

Police use radar to detect speeding drivers, but some drivers use radar detectors to warn them about police speed traps. In Connecticut, it's illegal to mount or to use a radar detector. If you are caught speeding in Connecticut and you have a radar detector in your car (whether or not it's connected or in use), fines may total upward of $300. If you must go very fast, take an airplane; it will cost less than getting caught speeding!

Laws requiring use of car safety belts are common, and every intelligent driver knows that the chances of surviving an accident and avoiding injury are increased greatly if safety belts are worn. Throughout the United States, infants and small children (under 4) are required by law to be placed in child safety seats secured by seat belts. Child safety seats are available from car-rental firms at a small extra charge.

ROAD MAPS   New England maps are sold in the region's bookstores and gas stations for $1 or $2.50. Maps of each state drawn with greater detail are available, usually for free or for less than $2, from official state tourism departments by mail, or from state roadside information centers located on major highways near state borders. For addresses of the state tourism offices, see "Visitor Information," at the beginning of this chapter.

BREAKDOWNS/ASSISTANCE   Several Interstate highways have Motorist Aid Call Boxes posted at regular intervals along the side of the roadway. State police officers patrol all major highways to assist travelers with car problems. If your car stops and you can't get it going, wait in your car until a patrol car stops. The officer can call a repair or tow truck to help you. If you're driving a rental car, remember to call the rental company before authorizing a mechanic to do more than the most minor repairs.

If you're a member of the **American Automobile Association** (☎ 800/ 222-4357), the AAA will provide simple towing and breakdown assistance at no charge, although long-distance tows and more expensive repairs are your responsibility. To become a member of the AAA, you join a local AAA-affiliated automobile club near your home, paying that club's normal membership dues.

Members of some foreign auto clubs can use the AAA. AAA-affiliated clubs offer trip-related financial services and issue road maps and guidebooks at no charge to members. The AAA can also provide foreign visitors to the United States with "Touring Permits" validating your home driver's license for use in the United States.

BY RECREATIONAL VEHICLE

Among the most pleasant ways to tour the country is in a recreational vehicle (RV, motor home, or camper). RVs come in all sizes and shapes and in dozens of models. They usually sleep four to six people comfortably, include a full kitchen (with cooking range, refrigerator, and running water), and are air-conditioned; some even come equipped with a shower! Hundreds of campgrounds in New England can provide electrical, water, and sewer hookups for $15 to $20 per night. Some RVs are so self-sufficient that they can operate for several days without hookups. In an RV, you're completely independent, and you can save money by cooking your own meals and not paying for expensive hotel rooms. The advantages to families with young children are obvious. Family travel in a rental RV can be a very cost-effective way to tour New England.

Renting an RV has its disadvantages as well. Rentals are fairly expensive, and you should work out estimated budgets for a trip in an RV versus a trip using a rental car and hotels before making your final decision. When figuring costs, keep in mind that RVs are heavy vehicles, and they use a lot more fuel than do passenger cars. During the busy summer months, you may not be able to find the campsite you want in the location you want, since many of New England's choicest campgrounds fill up early in the day. You may have to reserve in advance, which takes some of the fun out of footloose vagabond travel. Finally, New England is a region with many delightful country inns. If you've rented an RV at considerable expense, you may not feel that you can pay to stay in country inns very often.

RV RESOURCES   For more information on RVs, contact the **Recreation Vehicle Industry Association,** 1896 Preston White Dr., Reston, Va. 22090 (☎ **703/620-6003** or **800/336-0355;** fax 703/591-0734); for $5 they'll send you a 40-page catalog listing locations, services, and rates of the various RV rental agencies. The **Recreation Vehicle Dealers Association,** 3930 University Dr., Fairfax, Va. 22030 (☎ **703/591-7130**) is another good source. Call **Go Camping America** (☎ **800/47-SUNNY**) for a free 16-page camping vacation planner to help you plan fun and successful camping and RV vacations.

RV RENTAL COMPANIES   Companies renting recreational vehicles are listed in yellow pages telephone directories under "Recreational Vehicles—Renting & Leasing," "Motor Homes—Renting & Leasing," and "Trailers—Camping & Travel." (Don't let the word "Trailers" mislead you; this section has lots of listings for RVs, since many businesses rent both trailers and RVs.) One of the largest national franchisers is **Cruise America and RV Depot** (☎ **800/327-7778**).

Several companies in the Boston area rent RVs. The listings below are for your convenience, since RV rentals should be arranged in advance, and you might otherwise find it impossible to learn who rents RVs in Boston. For information on a company's reputation, you can contact Boston's **Better Business Bureau, Inc.,** 20 Park Plaza, Suite 820, Boston, Mass. 02116-4344 (☎ **617/426-9000**). Try **Trip Makers, Inc.,** P.O. Box 9132, Foxboro, Mass. 02035 (☎ **508/660-5000**).

BY PLANE

The larger cities, such as Boston, Providence, Hartford, Portland, and Burlington, all have good air service provided by the larger domestic airlines. Numerous regional "feeder" airlines fly between the larger cities and smaller ones. There are also many connections by regional carrier to New York City.

Almost all the small regional airlines operate in conjunction with larger national and international airlines. The regional airlines' flights are included in the flight schedules of the larger airlines, including American, Continental, Delta, and USAir. Call these airlines for information on flights, fares, and cities served.

BY TRAIN

Amtrak operates trains connecting Boston with Springfield and Pittsfield, Mass., and Albany, N.Y.; Hartford, New Haven, New London, and Mystic, Conn.; Providence, R.I.; and (via Springfield) Brattleboro, White River Junction, and Montpelier, Vt.; and Montréal, Québec. There is no interstate train service northeast of Boston (that is, to Maine or central and eastern New Hampshire), but there are buses that run from Amtrak's terminus at Boston's South Station to Portsmouth, N.H., and to major cities and towns in eastern Maine. Trains on routes between Boston and points south and west are fast and frequent, but to get to points in Vermont from Boston, connections are not good and service is infrequent.

BY BUS

Bus service is quite good in New England. Here are some of the major companies, their phone numbers, and the areas they serve:

American Eagle (☎ **508/993-5040**), New Bedford Terminal, operates frequent buses daily between Boston and New Bedford.

Bonanza Bus Lines (☎ **617/720-4110** or **800/556-3815**), Back Bay Terminal, 145 Dartmouth St., runs from Boston to Cape Cod (Falmouth and Woods Hole) and Fall River, Mass., and Newport and Providence, R.I. Other routes run from Providence to central and western Connecticut and the Berkshires of Massachusetts, and from Providence to Cape Cod.

Concord Trailways (☎ **617/426-8080**) is the line to take to New Hampshire. Buses start at Logan Airport and the Peter Pan Trailways Terminal in Boston, then head north to Concord, Laconia and North Conway, Plymouth, Waterville Valley, and Franconia. Another route goes to Alton and Wolfboro.

Greyhound (☎ **800/231-2222**), with its terminal at South Station in Boston (any Red Line subway to South Station), operates many of the long-distance routes in New England, and connects the region with the rest of the country. Greyhound buses operate from Boston via Hartford and New Haven to New York City; from New York City via New Haven and Hartford to Springfield, Mass., connecting with Vermont Transit buses for points in Vermont, and Montréal, Québec.

Another Greyhound route is from Boston via Portsmouth, N.H., to the Maine coast, stopping at Portland, Freeport, Brunswick, and Bangor (with connecting service to Ellsworth for Bar Harbor); this route connects with Canadian SMT buses headed for New Brunswick and Nova Scotia.

Greyhound also connects New York City via New Haven and New London, Conn., with Providence, R.I., and also to Plymouth and Brockton Bus Lines, which service the Cape Cod area of Massachusetts.

Another route is between Islip, N.Y. (on Long Island), via New Haven and Hartford, Conn., and Boston.

Greyhound also operates buses heading due west from Boston, stopping at Worcester and Springfield, Mass., and Albany, N.Y., with connecting service to points west in both the United States and Canada.

Peter Pan Trailways (☎ **617/426-7838** or **800/237-8747**), at the Peter Pan Trailways Terminal in Dewey Square, opposite Amtrak's South Station, runs between Boston and Albany, Amherst, Bridgeport, Danbury, Hartford, Holyoke, Lee, Middletown, New Britain, New Haven, New York City, Northampton, Norwalk, Pittsfield, Springfield, Sturbridge, Waterbury, and Worcester. Other routes connect Springfield, Mass., with Bradley International Airport and Hartford, Conn.

Plymouth & Brockton Street Railway Co. (☎ **508/746-0378**), Peter Pan Trailways Terminal in Dewey Square, is the one to take from Boston to Plymouth, Sagamore, Barnstable, Hyannis, and Provincetown on Cape Cod. Many P&B runs start at Logan Airport, then head into Boston for stops at Park Square, the Peter Pan Trailways Terminal, and South Station. You can take any P&B bus from Logan Airport and transfer to another one downtown.

Vermont Transit Lines (☎ **800/451-3292, 800/642-3133** in Vermont), Greyhound Terminal, in collaboration with Greyhound Lines, operates from New York City via Albany to Bennington, Manchester, East Dorset, Rutland (with connecting service to Killington, Woodstock, and White River Junction), Middlebury, and Burlington. Connecting service from Burlington goes on to Montréal.

Another service is from Boston via Manchester, Concord, Mount Sunapee, and Hanover, N.H., to White River Junction (with connecting service to Woodstock, Killington, and Rutland), then to Barre, Montpelier, Burlington, and Montréal.

Vermont Transit also runs buses between Portland, Me.; Burlington, Vt.; and Montréal, stopping at North Conway and Bretton Woods, N.H.; and St. Johnsbury, White River Junction, and Montpelier, Vt.

Another route takes travelers from New York City or Boston to White River Junction for connections to St. Johnsbury and Newport, Vt., and Sherbrooke and Québec City.

To get to Stowe, Vt., you must first go to Burlington or Newport, Vt.

HITCHHIKING

Hitchhiking is not a good way to get around New England, either within cities or between cities and towns. It's illegal to hitchhike on expressways. Incidents of robbery and violence by driver or hitcher, though few in number, have left most motorists unwilling to stop for hitchhikers.

SUGGESTED ITINERARIES

Many visitors to New England have specific destinations and activities in mind when they plan their visits: rambling along the Maine coast looking for antiques, visiting the sites where the American Revolution began in and around Boston, or inn-hopping in Vermont. If you have no such itinerary already in mind, refer to the features entitled "What's Special About . . ." at the beginning of each chapter. These features may help you decide what you want to see and do in the time available to you.

PLANNING YOUR ITINERARY

For first-time visitors, here are sample itineraries covering many of the high points:

BOSTON & VICINITY
If You Have 3 to 4 Days

Here's one suggestion for a way to see the Boston area:

Day 1   Follow the Freedom Trail around Boston's most historic sights, have lunch in or near Faneuil Hall Marketplace, spend some time shopping at Downtown Crossing or along Newbury Street, and have dinner in one of the city's better restaurants.

Day 2   Visit one or two of the city's better museums (Museum of Fine Arts, Gardner Museum, Museum of Science, Museum Wharf), then take the subway to Harvard Square for some cafe-sitting, shopping, and a tour of Harvard University.

Day 3   Drive, or take the suburban train, to Concord for a walk around that historic town and out to Old North Bridge, where the second battle of the Revolutionary War was fought. If you're driving, follow the course of Battle Road from Cambridge through Lexington and Concord in the Minuteman National Historic Park. Or instead of heading west to Concord, drive or take a train north to Salem to explore New England's maritime history at the Essex Institute, Peabody Museum, and Salem Maritime National Historic Site. You can get a look at some of Salem's witch lore as well.

Day 4   With an extra day, you can do both of the excursions outlined in Day 3. Or if Pilgrim lore is fascinating to you, drive or take a Plymouth & Brockton bus south to Plymouth for a look at Plymouth Rock, the *Mayflower II,* and other sites in Plymouth, then spend the afternoon at Plimoth Plantation, south of town.

SOUTHERN NEW ENGLAND
If You Have 7 to 10 Days

Here's a loop tour by car that starts at Boston but can actually be started anywhere along the loop:

Day 1   Drive west for 90 minutes on the Massachusetts Turnpike (I-90) to Sturbridge for a visit to Old Sturbridge Village. Stay in the area or continue westward to Amherst or Northampton. Visit Old Deerfield if you have extra time.

Day 2   Head for the Berkshires. Enjoy a picnic; visit the Norman Rockwell Museum in Stockbridge, Chesterwood, or perhaps the Hancock Shaker Village; and take in an evening performance at Tanglewood, Jacob's Pillow, the Berkshire Theater Festival, or some other cultural venue.

Day 3   Drive south to Lake Waramaug and Litchfield for a look at this pristine 18th-century town. Continue south down the Naugatuck River Valley along Conn. 8 to Derby, then east on Conn. 34 to New Haven for dinner.

Day 4   Explore Yale University and its museums in the morning and drive east along the Connecticut Turnpike (I-95) to Essex, Ivoryton, and Old Lyme. Choose a place for lunch, and tour these towns at the mouth of the Connecticut River. Continue to New London or Mystic for the night. (If you're starting your tour from New York City, this would be Day 1).

Day 5   Visit the Mystic Seaport Museum or, if you prefer, the U.S. Coast Guard Academy and Navy Submarine Base. Spend the night in Mystic, Stonington, or Watch Hill.

Day 6   Drive to Newport to tour the fabulous mansions along Bellevue Avenue, ride bicycles along Ocean Drive, amble along Cliff Walk, and enjoy an excellent seafood dinner.

Day 7   If time is short, head for Plymouth to view Plymouth Rock and visit Plimoth Plantation before heading back to Boston. If you have a few more days, head for Cape Cod. It's best not to attempt the drive all the way to Provincetown today; choose a town on the "lower cape" or "mid-cape" for the night.

Day 8   Enjoy Cape Cod: Tour the national seashore, lunch on fried clams and french fries, and take a swim. If you're in the mood for a circus atmosphere, drive out to the tip for a look at Provincetown. Or, from Woods Hole or Hyannis, take a day-trip or an overnight excursion to Martha's Vineyard or Nantucket (going by plane will save time).

Day 9   Continue your explorations of Cape Cod, Martha's Vineyard, or Nantucket.

Day 10   Head back to Boston, stopping at Plymouth for a look at "The Rock" and a few hours at Plimoth Plantation.

NORTHERN NEW ENGLAND
If You Have 6 to 10 Days

Northern New England has its cultural side, but most people who tour here are looking for outdoor adventure. The following itinerary can also be followed as two shorter trips. Look on Days 1 through 4 as a short tour of the Maine coast, returning to Boston on Day 4. To make a six-day tour of New Hampshire and Vermont, drive north from Boston to North Conway, N.H., and pick up the itinerary at that point on Day 5.

Day 1   Head north from Boston on I-93, then I-95, stopping at Portsmouth, N.H., for lunch and a tour of Strawbery Banke. Continue to the Maine coast, staying the night in Ogunquit or Kennebunkport, or if you prefer, in Portland.

Day 2   Continue northward along I-95, stopping for some shopping in Freeport, home of L. L. Bean and many factory outlets. Just before Brunswick, follow U.S. 1, continuing through Bath. Spend part of the day around Boothbay Harbor, Camden, or Blue Hill, but plan to stay the night in one of Bar Harbor's sumptuous inns.

Day 3   Explore Acadia National Park and Bar Harbor, with another overnight here.

Day 4   Return to Portland and drive north on the Maine Turnpike and Me. 26, via Sabbathday Lake and Poland Spring, to Bethel for the night.

Day 5   Follow U.S. 2 west to Gorham, then N.H. 16 south through Pinkham Notch to Glen and North Conway. Have lunch in North Conway or buy supplies for a picnic, then drive westward along the Kancamagus Highway, the heart of the White Mountains. Stop for a picnic and a short hike at one of the national forest areas along the highway. Spend the night at Lincoln, at the western end of the highway.

Day 6   Drive north from Lincoln through Franconia Notch, stopping to see the Old Man of the Mountain and "The Flume." Stop for lunch in Littleton, then head southwest on U.S. 302. You may want to take a look at the Rock of Ages quarry and Hope Cemetery in Barre. Spend the night in Stowe, Burlington, or Sugarbush Valley.

Day 7   Visit the Shelburne Museum south of Burlington, then follow U.S. 7 south through Middlebury and the Middlebury Gap to Hancock, on Vt. 100. Drive south on Vt. 100, perhaps with a detour to Woodstock or Plymouth. Stay the night in Woodstock, Weston, or Grafton.

Day 8   Spend today exploring the beautiful villages of southern Vermont: Manchester, Dorset, Grafton, Newfane, and Weston. Spend the night in any one of these.

Day 9   From Manchester, go south along U.S. 7 via Arlington to Bennington for a visit to Old Bennington, the Bennington Battle Monument, and Bennington Museum. If you have the time, you can slip across the state line to see Williamstown, Mass., and the wonderful Clark Art Institute. Stay the night in Bennington.

Day 10   Go east along Vt. 9, the Molly Stark Trail, via Marlboro to Brattleboro, perhaps with a detour to Newfane for lunch. Continue via Keene, N.H., and Mount Monadnock back to Boston.

FAST FACTS: New England

Banks and ATM Networks   Most banks are open Monday through Friday from 9am to 3pm, and many have extended hours until 5pm (or even 8 or 9pm on Thursday) and on Saturday from 9am to 2pm or later. All banks are closed Sunday except currency-exchange booths at Boston's Logan Airport. Most banks and supermarkets and shopping malls have automatic-teller machines (ATMs) for after-hours transactions. If you have a bank card, you can obtain cash from an ATM that's on the same network (PLUS, Cirrus, and so on). If you have a major credit or charge card (American Express, MasterCard/Access/EuroCard, or Visa), you may be able to obtain cash from an ATM. Ask anyone for the location of the nearest ATM or call one of the major ATM networks: **Cirrus** (☎ 800/424-7787) or **PLUS** (☎ 800/843-7587).

Business Hours   Business hours in **public and private offices** are usually Monday through Friday from 8 or 9am to 5pm. Most **stores** are open Monday through Saturday from 9:30 or 10am to 5:30 or 6pm; many are also open on Sunday from 11am or noon to 5pm. All cities and large towns have at least a few "convenience stores" for food, beverages, newspapers, and some household items; many are open 24 hours. In cities, most **supermarkets** stay open from 8 or 9am to 9 or 10pm, with shorter hours on Sunday; some are open almost 24 hours a day. For bank hours, see "Banks," above.

Car Rentals   See "Getting Around" earlier in this chapter.

Climate   See "When to Go," earlier in this chapter.

Driving Rules   See "Getting Around," earlier in this chapter.

Embassies and Consulates   See Chapter 3, "For Foreign Visitors."

Emergencies   In major cities, dial **911** from any telephone (no coin needed at pay telephones/call boxes) to contact the local police, fire department, or ambulance. In areas without 911 service, dial "**0**" (zero) to reach an operator who will direct your call to the proper emergency service. Local numbers for emergency services are also listed on the inside front cover of most telephone directories.

The **Travelers Aid Society,** 17 East St., Boston, MA 02111 (☎ 617/542-7286), is a nonprofit social service agency dedicated to helping travelers solve problems large and small. Professional staff members provide crisis intervention counseling, referrals to community resources, and emergency financial assistance to travelers in crisis. Travelers Aid volunteers at Logan Airport (☎ 617/567-5385) and the Greyhound Bus Terminal at South Station (☎ 617/737-2880) will help you find an address, a hospital, lost luggage, a way to get money from home, or the solution to any other travel dilemma.

Health Services   All New England cities have hospitals; blue signs bearing a white H mark the way. Boston is one of the country's most renowned medical centers, with dozens of hospitals and medical facilities. To use most of these facilities, however, you'll need health insurance, since prices for services are astronomical. A three-day stay in a hospital can cost more than $1,000 just for the room and basic services; medical procedures and doctors' fees might cost several thousand more.

Information   See "Visitor Information," at the beginning of this chapter and specific chapters for local information offices.

Liquor Laws   In Maine, New Hampshire, and Vermont, liquor is sold in government-operated stores only; in Connecticut, Massachusetts, and Rhode Island, liquor is sold privately. Liquor is not sold on Sunday, though most restaurants and bars with liquor licenses may serve liquor by the drink on Sunday. The minimum age for drinking varies by state, but in most it's 21 years. A few towns in New England, such as Rockport, Mass., are "dry," which means that no shop, restaurant, or hotel may sell liquor, but it's not illegal to bring in your own liquor and drink it. You serve yourself in restaurants.

Restaurants have either a full liquor license (for liquor, wine, and beer), a wine and beer license, or no license. At some restaurants that have no license, you can bring your own liquor; others don't allow this.

It's illegal to drink alcohol in public areas, such as streets and parks or on benches. If you're discreet, you can usually have wine or beer with your picnic.

Maps   See "Getting Around," earlier in this chapter.

Newspapers/Magazines   Each of the larger cities in New England has its own daily newspaper. The *Boston Globe* and the *Boston Herald* are distributed throughout New England, as is the *New York Times,* and, in most cities, the *Washington Post.* The national newspapers *USA Today* and the *Christian Science Monitor* are also available. You can also buy the *International Herald Tribune* at Boston's Logan Airport and at some newsstands in large cities.

Police   In an emergency, dial **911**.

Post Offices   Most post offices are open Monday through Friday from 8am to 5pm and Saturday from 8am to noon or 2pm. A few major post offices stay open until 5:30 or 6pm, and the post office at Boston's Logan Airport stays open until midnight. To receive mail at a post office, have it sent to you c/o General Delivery (Poste Restante) in the town where you'd like to pick up your mail. Specify the name of the post office where you'd like to pick up your mail; if in doubt, write "Main Post Office." You'll need to show identification, such as a passport or driver's license, to pick up your mail.

Safety   Whenever you're traveling in an unfamiliar city or country, stay alert and keep a close eye on your possessions.

Taxes   Taxes on hotel rooms, restaurant meals, some transportation services, and purchases in general are levied by each state and by some cities. Taxes on rooms, meals, and other purchases (which can be as high as 11% or 12%) are not included in the price. Here are the current tax rates by state: Connecticut, 8%; Maine, 6% (7% on lodging); Massachusetts, 5% (9.7% on lodging); New Hampshire, 8%; Rhode Island, 7% (12% on lodging); and Vermont, 6% (8% on rooms and meals).

3 For Foreign Visitors

Although American fads and fashions have spread across Europe and other parts of the world so that America may seem like familiar territory before your arrival, there are still many peculiarities and uniquely American situations that any foreign visitor will encounter.

1 Preparing for Your Trip

ENTRY REQUIREMENTS

DOCUMENT REGULATIONS   Canadian citizens may enter the United States without visas; they need only proof of Canadian residence.

Citizens of the U.K., New Zealand, Japan, and most western European countries traveling with valid passports may not need a visa for fewer than 90 days of holiday or business travel to the United States, providing that they hold a round-trip or return ticket and enter the United States on an airline or cruise line participating in the visa-waiver program. (Note that citizens of these visa-exempt countries who first enter the United States may then visit Mexico, Canada, Bermuda, and/or the Caribbean islands and then reenter the United States, by any mode of transportation, without needing a visa. Further information is available from any U.S embassy or consulate.)

Citizens of countries other than those stipulated above, including citizens of Australia, must have two documents: a valid passport, with an expiration date at least six months later than the scheduled end of the visit to the United States; and a tourist visa, available without charge from the nearest U.S. consulate. To obtain a visa, the traveler must submit a completed application form (either in person or by mail) with a $1^1/2$-inch-square photo and demonstrate binding ties to the residence abroad.

Usually you can obtain a visa at once or within 24 hours, but it may take longer during the summer rush from June to August. If you cannot go in person, contact the nearest U.S. embassy or consulate for directions on applying by mail. Your travel agent or airline office may also be able to provide you with visa applications and instructions. The U.S. consulate or embassy that issues your visa will determine whether you will be issued a multiple- or single-entry visa and any restrictions regarding the length of your stay.

MEDICAL REQUIREMENTS   No inoculations are needed to enter the United States unless you are coming from, or have stopped over in, areas known to be suffering from epidemics, particularly cholera or yellow fever.

If you have a disease requiring treatment with medications containing narcotics or drugs requiring a syringe, carry a valid signed prescription from your physician to allay any suspicions that you are smuggling drugs.

CUSTOMS REQUIREMENTS   Every adult visitor may bring in, free of duty: 1 liter of wine or hard liquor; 200 cigarettes or 100 cigars (but no cigars from Cuba) or 3 pounds of smoking tobacco; and $100 worth of gifts. These exemptions are offered to travelers who spend at least 72 hours in the United States and who have not claimed them within the preceding six months. It is altogether forbidden to bring into the country foodstuffs (particularly cheese, fruit, cooked meats, and canned goods) and plants (vegetables, seeds, tropical plants, and so on). Foreign tourists may bring in or take out up to $10,000 in U.S. or foreign currency with no formalities; larger sums must be declared to Customs on entering or leaving.

INSURANCE

There is no national health system in the United States. Because the cost of medical care is extremely high, we strongly advise every traveler to secure health coverage before setting out.

You may want to take out a comprehensive travel policy that covers (for a relatively low premium) sickness or injury costs (medical, surgical, and hospital); loss or theft of your baggage; trip-cancellation costs; guarantee of bail in case you are arrested; costs of accident, repatriation, or death. Such packages (for example, "Europe Assistance" in Europe) are sold by automobile clubs at attractive rates, as well as by insurance companies and travel agencies.

MONEY

CURRENCY & EXCHANGE   The U.S. monetary system has a decimal base: one American **dollar** ($1) = 100 **cents** (100¢).

Dollar bills commonly come in $1 (a "buck"), $5, $10, $20, $50, and $100 denominations (the last two are not welcome when paying for small purchases and are not accepted in taxis or at subway ticket booths). There are also $2 bills (seldom encountered).

There are six denominations of coins: 1¢ (one cent or "penny"), 5¢ (five cents, or a "nickel"), 10¢ (ten cents, or a "dime"), 25¢ (twenty-five cents, or a "quarter"), 50¢ (fifty cents, or a "half dollar"), and the rare $1 piece.

TRAVELER'S CHECKS   Traveler's checks denominated in U.S. dollars are readily accepted at most hotels, motels, restaurants, and large stores. But the best place to change traveler's checks is at a bank. Do not bring traveler's checks denominated in other currencies.

CREDIT CARDS   The method of payment most widely used is the credit card: Visa (BarclayCard in Britain), MasterCard (EuroCard in Europe, Access in Britain, Chargex in Canada), American Express, Diners Club, Discover, and Carte Blanche. You can save yourself trouble by using "plastic money" rather than cash or traveler's checks in most hotels, motels, restaurants, and retail stores (a growing number of food and liquor stores now accept credit cards). You must have a credit card to rent a car. It can also be used as proof of identity (often carrying more weight than a passport), or as a "cash card," enabling you to draw money from banks that accept them.

Note: The "foreign-exchange bureaus" so common in Europe are rare even at airports in the United States, and nonexistent outside major cities. Try to avoid having to change foreign money, or traveler's checks denominated other than in U.S. dollars, at a small-town bank, or even a branch in a big city; in fact, leave any currency other than U.S. dollars at home—it may prove a greater nuisance to you than it's worth.

SAFETY

GENERAL While tourist areas are generally safe, crime is on the increase everywhere, and U.S. urban areas tend to be less safe than those in Europe or Japan. Visitors should always stay alert. This is particularly true of large U.S. cities. It is wise to ask the city's or area's tourist office if you're in doubt about which neighborhoods are safe. Don't go into any city part at night unless there is an event that attracts crowds—for example, Boston's concerts in the parks. Generally speaking, you can feel safe in areas where there are many people and many open establishments.

Avoid carrying valuables with you on the street, and don't display expensive cameras or electronic equipment.

Remember also that hotels are open to the public, and in a large hotel, security may not be able to screen everyone entering. Don't assume that once inside your hotel you are automatically safe and no longer need be aware of your surroundings.

DRIVING Question your rental agency about personal safety, or ask for a brochure of traveler safety tips when you pick up your car. Obtain written directions, or a map with the route clearly marked, from the agency, showing how to get to your destination. And, if possible, arrive and depart during daylight hours.

Recently, more and more crime in all U.S. cities has involved cars and drivers, most notably, what is called "car jacking." If you drive off a highway into a doubtful neighborhood, leave the area as quickly as possible. If you have an accident, even on the highway, stay in your car with the doors locked until you assess the situation or until the police arrive. If you are bumped from behind on the street or are involved in a minor accident with no injuries and the situation appears to be suspicious, motion to the other driver to follow you to the nearest police precinct, well-lighted service station, or all-night store. *Never* get out of your car in such situations.

If you see someone on the road who indicates a need for help, do *not* stop. Take note of the location, drive on to a well-lighted area, and telephone the police by dialing 911.

Park in well-lighted, well-traveled areas if possible. Always keep your car doors locked, whether attended or unattended. Look around you before you get out of your car, and never leave any packages or valuables in sight. If someone attempts to rob you or steal your car, do *not* try to resist the thief/carjacker—report the incident to the police department immediately.

You may wish to contact the Greater Boston Convention and Visitors Bureau and other information centers listed in Chapter 4 before you arrive. They can provide you with safety brochures.

2 Getting to the U.S.

Travelers from overseas can take advantage of the **APEX (Advance Purchase Excursion) fares** offered by all the major U.S. and European carriers. Aside from these, attractive values are offered by **Icelandair** on flights from Luxembourg to New York and by **Virgin Atlantic Airways** from London to New York/Newark.

British travelers should check out **British Airways** (☎ **081/897-4000** in the U.K., or **800/247-9297** in the U.S.), which offers direct flights from London to New York, as does **Virgin Atlantic Airways** (☎ **01/293-74-77-47** in the U.K., or **800/862-8621** in the U.S.). Other helpful numbers to call for U.S. airline reservations are **American** (☎ **0181/572-5555**) and **United** (☎ **0181/990-9900**). Canadian travelers might book flights on **Air Canada** (☎ **800/776-3000**), which offers service from Toronto and Montréal to New York and Boston. In addition, many other international carriers serve the New York airports, and several service Boston as well.

The visitor arriving by air, no matter what the port of entry, should cultivate patience and resignation before setting foot on U.S. soil. Getting through Immigration control may take as long as two hours on some days, especially summer weekends. Add the time it takes to clear Customs and you'll see that you should make very generous allowance for delay in planning connections between international and domestic flights—an average of two to three hours at least.

In contrast, travelers arriving by car or by rail from Canada will find border-crossing formalities streamlined to the vanishing point. And air travelers from Canada, Bermuda, and some places in the Caribbean can sometimes go through Customs and Immigration at the point of departure, which is much quicker and less painful.

3 Getting Around the U.S.

Some large American airlines (for example, TWA, American Airlines, Northwest, United, and Delta) offer travelers on their transatlantic or transpacific flights special discount tickets under the name **Visit USA,** allowing travel between any U.S. destinations at minimum rates. They are not on sale in the United States and must, therefore, be purchased before you leave your foreign point of departure. This system is the best, easiest, and fastest way to see the United States at low cost. You should obtain information well in advance from your travel agent or the office of the airline concerned, since the conditions attached to these discount tickets can be changed without advance notice.

Travel by car gives visitors the freedom to make—and alter—their itineraries to suit their own needs and interests. And it offers the possibility of visiting some of the off-the-beaten-path locations, places that cannot be reached easily by public transportation. For information on renting cars in the United States, see "Getting Around," in Chapter 2, and "Automobile Organizations" under "Fast Facts: For the Foreign Traveler," below.

International visitors can also buy a **USA Railpass,** good for 15 or 30 days of unlimited travel on Amtrak. The pass is available through many foreign travel agents. Prices in 1995 for a 15-day pass were $229 off-peak, $344 peak; a 30-day pass costs $339 off-peak, $425 peak. (With a foreign passport, you can also buy passes at some Amtrak offices in the United States, including locations in San Francisco, Los Angeles, Chicago, New York, Miami, Boston, and Washington, D.C.) Reservations are generally required and should be made for each part of your trip as early as possible.

Visitors should also be aware of the limitations of long-distance rail travel in the United States. With a few notable exceptions (for instance, the Northeast Corridor line between Boston and Washington, D.C.), service is rarely up to European standards: Delays are common, routes are limited and often infrequently served, and fares are rarely significantly lower than discount airfares. Thus, cross-country train travel should be approached with caution.

The cheapest way to travel in the United States is by bus. **Greyhound,** the nationwide bus line, offers an Ameripass for unlimited travel for 7 days (for $259), 15 days (for $459), and 30 days (for $559). Bus travel in the United States can be both slow and uncomfortable, so this option is not for everyone.

FAST FACTS: For the Foreign Traveler

Automobile Organizations   Auto clubs will supply maps, suggested routes, guidebooks, accident and bail-bond insurance, and emergency road service. The major auto club in the United States, with 955 offices nationwide, is the **American Automobile Association (AAA).** Members of some foreign auto clubs have reciprocal arrangements with the AAA and enjoy its services at no charge. If you belong to an auto club, inquire about AAA reciprocity before you leave. The AAA can provide you with an **International Driving Permit** validating your foreign license. You may be able to join the AAA even if you are not a member of a reciprocal club. To inquire, call ☎ **800/222-4357.** In addition, some automobile-rental agencies now provide these services, so you should inquire about their availability when you rent your car.

Business Hours   See "Fast Facts: New England" in Chapter 2.

Climate   See Chapter 2, "When to Go."

Currency Exchange   You will find currency-exchange services in major airports with international service. Elsewhere, they may be quite difficult to come by. In Boston, a reliable choice is **Thomas Cook Currency Services, Inc.,** 160 Franklin St., Boston, MA (☎ 617/426-0016) which has been in business since 1841 and offers a wide range of services. There is also an office in Cambridge at 39 JFK St. (☎ 617/868-6605). They sell commission-free foreign and U.S. traveler's checks, drafts, and wire transfers; they also do check collections (including Eurochecks). Their rates are competitive and service excellent. Other places in Boston at which to change money are the Boston Bank of Commerce, 133 Federal Street (☎ 617/457-4400); Ruesch International, 45 Milk St. (☎ 617/482-8600); BayBank, 1414 Massachusetts Ave. (☎ 617/556-6050); and Shawmut Bank, One Federal St. (☎ 617/292-3964). Check the yellow pages of the telephone directory in other major cities and small towns.

Drinking Laws   The legal drinking age is 21.

Electric Current   The U.S. uses 110–120 volts, 60 cycles, compared to 220–240 volts, 50 cycles, as in most of Europe. Besides a 100-volt converter, small appliances of non-American manufacture, such as hairdryers or shavers, will require a plug adapter, with two flat, parallel pins.

Embassies/Consulates All embassies are located in the national capital, Washington, D.C.; some consulates are located in major cities, and most nations have a mission to the United Nations in New York City.

Listed here are the embassies and New York or Boston consulates of the major English-speaking countries—Australia, Britain, Canada, Ireland, and New Zealand. If you are from another country, you can get the telephone number of your embassy by calling "Information" in Washington, D.C. (☎ 202/ 555-1212).

The **Australian embassy** is at 1601 Massachusetts Ave. NW, Washington, D.C. 20036 (☎ 202/797-3000). The **consulate** is located at the International Building, 630 Fifth Ave., Suite 420, New York, N.Y. 10111 (☎ 212/408-8400). The consulate in Los Angeles is located at 611 N. Larchmont, Los Angeles, Cal. 90004 (☎ 213/469-4300).

The **British embassy** is at 3100 Massachusetts Ave. NW, Washington, D.C. 20008 (☎ 202/462-1340). The **consulate** is located at 600 Atlantic Ave., Federal Reserve Plaza, 25th floor, Boston, Mass. 02210 (☎ 617/248-9555). The consulate in New York is located at 845 Third Ave., New York, N.Y. 10022 (☎ 212/745-0200). The consulate in Los Angeles is located at 11766 Wilshire Blvd., Suite 400, Los Angeles, Cal. 90025 (☎ 310/477-3322).

The **Canadian embassy** is at 501 Pennsylvania Ave. NW, Washington, D.C. 20001 (☎ 202/682-1740). The **consulate** is located at 1251 Ave. of the Americas, New York, N.Y. 10020 (☎ 212/596-1600), and 3 Copley Place, Suite 400, Boston, Mass. 02116 (☎ 617/262-3760). The consulate in Los Angeles is located at 300 Santa Grand Ave., Suite 1000, Los Angeles, Cal. 90071 (☎ 213/ 346-2700).

The **Irish embassy** is at 2234 Massachusetts Ave. NW, Washington, D.C. 20008 (☎ 202/462-3939). The **consulate** is located at 345 Park Ave., 17th floor, New York, N.Y. 10022 (☎ 212/319-2555). The consulate in San Francisco is located at 655 Montgomery St., Suite 930, San Francisco, Cal. 94111 (☎ 415/ 392-4214).

The **New Zealand embassy** is at 37 Observatory Circle NW, Washington, D.C. 20008 (☎ 202/328-4800). The **consulate** is located at 780 3rd Ave., Suite 1904, New York, N.Y. 10017-2024 (☎ 212/832-4038). The consulate in Los Angeles is located at 12400 Wilshire Blvd., Suite 1150, Los Angeles, Cal. 90025 (☎ 310/207-1605).

Emergencies Call **911** for fire, police, and ambulance. If you encounter such travelers' problems as sickness, accident, or lost or stolen baggage, call the **Travelers Aid Society,** an organization that specializes in helping distressed travelers, whether American or foreign. In Boston the number is ☎ 617/ 542-7286 (they are open Monday through Friday from 8:30am to 4:30pm).

Gasoline [Petrol] One U.S. gallon equals 3.75 liters, while 1.2 U.S. gallons equal one Imperial gallon. You'll notice there are several grades (and price levels) of gasoline available at most gas stations. And you'll also notice that their names change from company to company. Unleaded gas with the highest octane is the most expensive. Each gas company has a different name for the various levels of octane, but most fall into the "regular," "super," and "plus" categories (most rental cars take the least expensive "regular" unleaded).

Holidays On the following legal national holidays, banks, government offices, post offices, and many stores, restaurants, and museums are closed: January 1

(New Year's Day), third Monday in January (Martin Luther King Jr. Day), third Monday in February (Presidents' Day), February 21 (Easter), April 15 (Patriots' Day), last Monday in May (Memorial Day), July 4 (Independence Day), first Monday in September (Labor Day), second Monday in October (Columbus Day), November 11 (Veterans Day/Armistice Day), fourth Thursday in November (Thanksgiving Day), and December 25 (Christmas Day).

Finally, the Tuesday following the first Monday in November is Election Day, and is a legal holiday in presidential-election years.

Legal Aid   The well-meaning foreign tourist will probably never become involved with the American legal system. However, there are a few things you should know just in case. If you are pulled over for a minor infraction (for example, of the highway code, such as speeding), never attempt to pay the fine directly to a police officer; you may wind up arrested on the much more serious charge of attempted bribery. Pay fines by mail, or directly into the hands of the clerk of the court. If accused of a more serious offense, it's wise to say and do nothing before consulting a lawyer. Under U.S. law, an arrested person is allowed one telephone call to a party of his or her choice. Call your embassy or consulate.

Mail   If you want your mail to follow you on your vacation and you aren't sure of your address, your mail can be sent to you, in your name, **c/o General Delivery** at the main post office of the city or region where you expect to be. The addressee must pick it up in person and produce proof of identity (driver's license, credit card, passport, etc.).

Generally to be found at intersections, mailboxes are blue with a red-and-white stripe and carry the inscription U.S. MAIL. If your mail is addressed to a U.S. destination, don't forget to add the five- or nine-digit postal code, or ZIP (Zone Improvement Plan) code, after the two-letter abbreviation of the state to which the mail is addressed (CT for Connecticut, MA for Massachusetts, ME for Maine, NH for New Hampshire, NY for New York, RI for Rhode Island, and VT for Vermont).

Newspapers/Magazines   The *New York Times, USA Today,* and the *Wall Street Journal*—widely available in large cities—and the magazines *Newsweek* and *Time* cover world news. Most magazine racks at drugstores, airports, and hotels stock a selection of foreign periodicals, such as *Stern, Der Spiegel, The Economist,* and *Le Monde.* For more details, see "Newspapers/Magazines" under "Fast Facts: New England," in Chapter 2.

Radio/Television   Audiovisual media, with four coast-to-coast networks—ABC, CBS, NBC, and Fox—joined in recent years by the Public Broadcasting System (PBS) and the cable network CNN, play a major part in American life. In big cities, televiewers have a choice of a few dozen channels (including basic cable), most of them transmitting 24 hours a day, without counting the pay-TV channels showing recent movies or sports events. All options are usually indicated on your hotel TV set. You'll also find a wide choice of local radio stations, each broadcasting particular kinds of talk shows and/or music—classical, country, jazz, pop, gospel—punctuated by news broadcasts and frequent commercials.

Safety   Whenever you're traveling in an unfamiliar city or country, stay alert. Be aware of your immediate surroundings. Wear a moneybelt and don't flash expensive jewelry and cameras in public. This will minimize the possibility of your becoming a crime victim. Be alert even in heavily touristed areas. For more details, see "Safety" under "Preparing for Your Trip," earlier in this chapter.

Taxes   In the United States there is no VAT (value-added tax) or other indirect tax at a national level. Every state, and each city in it, is allowed to levy its own local tax on all purchases (including hotel and restaurant checks, airline tickets, and so on) and services. Taxes are already included in the price of certain services, such as public transportation, cab fares, telephone calls, and gasoline. The amount of sales tax varies from about 4% to 10%, depending on the state and city, so when you're making major purchases, such as photographic equipment, clothing, or stereo components, it can be a significant part of the cost.

For the state taxes levied in the New England region, see "Taxes" under "Fast Facts: New England," in Chapter 2.

Telephone/Telegraph/Telex   The telephone system in the United States is run by private corporations, so rates, especially for long-distance service, can vary widely—even on calls made from public telephones. Local calls in the United States usually cost 25¢.

Generally, hotel surcharges on long-distance and local calls are astronomical. You are usually better off using a **public pay telephone,** which you will find clearly marked in most public buildings and private establishments as well as on the street. Outside metropolitan areas, public telephones are more difficult to find. Stores and gas stations are your best bet.

Most long-distance and international calls can be dialed directly from any phone. For calls to Canada and other parts of the United States, dial 1 followed by the area code and the seven-digit number. For international calls, dial 011 followed by the country code, city code, and the telephone number of the person you wish to call.

Note that all calls to area code 800 are toll free. However, calls to numbers in area codes 700 and 900 (chat lines, bulletin boards, "dating" services, etc.) can be very expensive—usually a charge of 95¢ to $3 or more per minute, and they sometimes have minimum charges that can run as high as $15 or more.

For **reversed-charge** or **collect calls,** and for **person-to-person calls,** dial 0 (zero, not the letter "O") followed by the area code and number you want; an operator will then come on the line, and you should specify that you are calling collect, or person-to-person, or both. If your operator-assisted call is international, ask for the overseas operator.

For local directory assistance ("Information"), dial 411; for long-distance information, dial 1, then the appropriate area code and 555-1212.

Like the telephone system, **telegraph** and **telex** services are provided by private corporations like ITT, MCI, and above all, Western Union. You can bring your telegram in to the nearest Western Union office (there are hundreds across the country) or dictate it over the phone (☎ **800/325-6000**). You can also telegraph money (using a major credit or charge card), or have it telegraphed to you, very quickly over the Western Union system. (Note, however, that this service can be very expensive—the service charge can run as high as 15% to 25% of the amount sent.)

Telephone Directory   There are two kinds of telephone directories available to you. The general directory is the so-called **white pages,** in which private and business subscribers are listed in alphabetical order. The inside front cover lists the emergency number for police, fire, and ambulance, and other vital numbers (like the Coast Guard, poison-control center, crime-victims hotline, and so on). The first few pages are devoted to community-service numbers, including a guide to long-distance and international calling, complete with country codes and area codes.

The second directory, printed on yellow paper (hence its name, **yellow pages**), lists all local services, businesses, and industries by type of activity, with an index at the back. The listings cover not only such obvious items as automobile repairs by make of car, or drugstores (pharmacies), often by geographical location, but also restaurants by type of cuisine and geographical location, bookstores by special subject and/or language, places of worship by religious denomination, and other information that the tourist might otherwise not readily find. The yellow pages also include city plans or detailed area maps, often showing postal ZIP codes and public transportation routes.

Time   The United States is divided into four time zones (six, if Alaska and Hawaii are included). From east to west, these are: Eastern Standard Time (EST), Central Standard Time (CST), Mountain Standard Time (MST), Pacific Standard Time (PST), Alaska Standard Time (AST), and Hawaii Standard Time (HST). Always keep changing time zones in mind if you are traveling (or even telephoning) long distances in the United States. For example, noon in New York City (EST) is 11am in Chicago (CST), 10am in Denver (MST), 9am in Los Angeles (PST), 8am in Anchorage (AST), and 7am in Honolulu (HST).

Daylight Saving Time   is in effect from the first Sunday in April through the last Saturday in October (actually, the change is made at 2am on Sunday) except in Arizona, Hawaii, part of Indiana, and Puerto Rico. Daylight Saving Time moves the clock one hour ahead of standard time.

Tipping   This is part of the American way of life, based on the principle that you should pay for any special service you receive. Here are some rules of thumb: bartenders: 10% to 15%; bellhops: at least 50¢ per piece, $2 to $3 for a lot of baggage; cab drivers: 15% of the fare; cafeterias, fast-food restaurants: no tip; chambermaids: $1 a day; checkroom attendants (restaurants, theaters): $1 per garment; cinemas, movies, theaters: no tip; doormen (hotels or restaurants): not obligatory; gas-station attendants: no tip; hairdressers: 15% to 20%; redcaps (airport and railroad station): at least 50¢ per piece, $2 to $3 for a lot of baggage; restaurants, nightclubs: 15% to 20% of the check; sleeping-car porters: $2 to $3 per night to your attendant; valet parking attendants: $1.

Toilets   Foreign visitors often complain that public toilets are hard to find in most U.S. cities. True, there are none on the streets, but the visitor can usually find one in a bar, restaurant, hotel, museum, department store, or service station—and it will probably be clean (although the last-mentioned sometimes leaves much to be desired). Note, however, a growing practice in some restaurants and bars of displaying a sign TOILETS ARE FOR THE USE OF PATRONS ONLY. You can ignore this sign, or better yet, avoid arguments by paying for a cup of coffee or soft drink, which will qualify you as a patron. The cleanliness of toilets at railroad stations and bus depots may be open to question. Some public places are equipped with pay toilets, which require you to insert one or more coins into a slot on the door before it will open.

THE AMERICAN SYSTEM OF MEASUREMENTS

Length

1 inch (in.)			=	2.54cm				
1 foot (ft.)	=	2 in.	=	30.48cm	=	.305m		
1 yard (yd.)	=	3 ft.			=	.915m		
1 mile	=	5,280 ft.					=	1.609km

To convert miles to kilometers, multiply the number of miles by 1.61 (for example, 50 mi. × 1.61 = 80.5km). Note that this conversion can be used to convert speeds from miles per hour (m.p.h.) to kilometers per hour (kmph).

To convert kilometers to miles, multiply the number of kilometers by .62 (example, 25 km × .62 = 15.5 mi.). Note that this same conversion can be used to convert speeds from kilometers per hour to miles per hour.

Capacity

1 fluid ounce (fl. oz.)			=	.03 liters		
1 pint (pt.)	=	16 fl. oz.	=	.47 liters		
1 quart (qt.)	=	2 pints	=	.94 liters		
1 gallon (gal.)	=	4 quarts	=	3.79 liters	=	83 Imperial gal.

To convert U.S. gallons to liters, multiply the number of gallons by 3.79 (example, 12 gal. × 3.79 = 45.48 liters).

To convert U.S. gallons to Imperial gallons, multiply the number of U.S. gallons by .83 (example, 12 U.S. gal. × .83 = 9.95 Imperial gal.).

To convert liters to U.S. gallons, multiply the number of liters by .26 (example, 50 liters × .26 = 13 U.S. gal.).

To convert Imperial gallons to U.S. gallons, multiply the number of Imperial gallons by 1.2 (example, 8 Imperial gal. × 1.2 = 9.6 U.S. gal.).

Weight

1 ounce (oz.)			=	28.35g				
1 pound (lb.)	=	16 oz.	=	453.6g	=	.45 kg		
1 ton	=	2,000 lb.	=		907kg	=	.91 metric tons	

To convert pounds to kilograms, multiply the number of pounds by .45 (example, 90 lb. × .45 = 40.5kg).

To convert kilograms to pounds, multiply the number of kilos by 2.2 (example, 75kg × 2.2 = 165 lb.).

Area

1 acre			=	.41 ha		
1 square mile	=	640 acres	=	2.59 ha	=	2.6 km

To convert square miles to square kilometers, multiply the number of square miles by 2.6 (example, 80 sq. mi × 2.6 = 208km).

To convert hectares to acres, multiply the number of hectares by 2.47 (example, 20ha × 2.47 = 49.4 acres).

To convert square kilometers to square miles, multiply the number of square kilometers by .39 (example, 150km × .39 = 58.5 sq. mi.).

Temperature

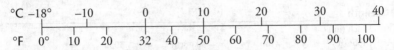

To convert degrees Fahrenheit to degrees Celsius, subtract 32 from °F, multiply by 5, then divide by 9 (example, 85°F–32 × ⁵/₉ = 29.4°C).

To convert degrees Celsius to degrees Fahrenheit, multiply °C by 9, divide by 5, and add 32 (example, 20°C × ⁹/₅ + 32 = 68°F).

Boston 4

"Boston is the Hub of the Universe"—or at least that's what many people remember Dr. Oliver Wendell Holmes as saying. Actually, his statement about his beloved city was less ambitious: "Boston Statehouse is the hub of the solar system." No matter, because to Bostonians their city is still "The Hub," the center of the world. And though outsiders may quibble about its being the Hub of the Universe, they must accept the fact that Boston is and always has been the capital of New England. The Pilgrims settled on the shores of Massachusetts Bay in the 1620s, and the other great cities of this six-state region were offshoots from this colony: Thomas Hooker, the man who founded Hartford, went there from Cambridge in 1636, and about the same time Roger Williams fled the area to found Providence. The pattern of arriving in Boston and then pushing on into the hills beyond was to be a permanent feature of New England life, and consequently today the city is a rich mixture of ethnic neighborhoods. Immigrants from all over the world arrived at Boston's docks and established communities of their own within the city. Second-generation immigrants then moved out across the state and across the nation.

What gives Bostonians the idea they're special? Well, theirs was the first large town in the region, first in resistance to British measures that brought on the Revolution, and first in science and culture during the 19th and early 20th centuries. Their city is the home of the Boston Celtics (basketball), the Boston Bruins (ice hockey), and the Boston Red Sox (baseball), as well as the Boston Pops Orchestra.

The city of Boston itself is a fairly small area with a population of something over 600,000. But if one adds in the populations of the neighboring cities Cambridge, Somerville, Charlestown, Chelsea, Brookline, and so on, the total population in Greater Boston comes to about three million. And yet Boston is one of the most livable and manageable cities in the world, with big-city economic and cultural resources yet small-city spirit and pace of life.

1 Orientation

ARRIVING

As major American cities go, Boston is eminently approachable. The airport is less than a 15-minute taxi or subway ride from the center of the city. The train station is right downtown, as are the two bus terminals. Once you arrive, however, Boston's famous twisty colonial streets take over and its notoriously careless drivers threaten, so read the sections below carefully.

BY PLANE

Boston's **Logan International Airport** (☎ **617/561-1919** or **800/235-6426**) is one of the busiest in the country, but it's well organized and has the advantage of being very near the center of the city, as airports go. After you get your bags, look for the signs to buses, taxis, and "limo," and after a few steps you'll see the stops.

GETTING DOWNTOWN   By Subway   The **Massport Shuttle Bus** (run by the Massachusetts Port Authority) runs the airport loop and is free. The bus goes to all the terminals and to the MBTA "Airport" subway stop, where you can take a Blue Line train downtown. The subway into town costs 85¢, and a person in a booth will make change for you except during late-night hours. Trains run every 8 to 12 minutes from 5:30am to 1am; the ride takes only 10 minutes. Some of the hotels recommended in this book are within a few blocks of the Government Center stop, but for most places you'll have to change at Government Center from the Blue Line to Green Line trains bound for Boston College, Cleveland Circle, Riverside, or Arborway (all of which pass near the hotels recommended). For Cambridge, take the Blue Line to Government Center, then the Green Line to Park Street (one stop), and change to the Red Line for Harvard or Alewife. It's a fairly long haul to Cambridge, with these two subway transfers.

By Water Shuttle   Vehicular traffic through the tunnels connecting the airport to Boston has become very heavy in recent years. One innovative solution to the problem is the **Airport Water Shuttle** (☎ **617/330-8680**) service between the airport's own dock and Rowes Wharf, on Atlantic Avenue in downtown Boston. A one-way ticket for the seven-minute shuttle boat costs $8 for adults, $4 for seniors, free for children under 12. Trips run every 15 minutes between 6am and 8pm on weekdays, every half hour from noon to 8pm on Sunday and holidays. There's no service on Saturday, July 4, Thanksgiving, Christmas, or New Year's Day. From Rowes Wharf, it's only a few blocks to South Station's train, subway, and bus stations.

By Limo   If you'd rather arrange for private transportation from the airport, call **Carey Limousine Boston** (☎ **617/623-8700**) or **Stagecoach Executive Sedan Service, Inc.** (☎ **617/723-9393** or **800/922-9500**). You should make arrangements prior to your arrival.

By Taxi   A taxi from Logan airport to downtown Boston will cost between $6 and $22 for the ride (including toll, excess baggage charge, and tip).

GETTING BEYOND BOSTON   Chances are good that you won't be roaring straight through Boston on your way north, west, or south, but in case you are, you should know about these services to areas outside Boston. If you have questions, you can call the **Logan Airport information office** (☎ **800/235-LOGAN**).

What's Special About Boston

Museums
- Museum of Fine Arts, one of America's best, noted especially for its collection of impressionist paintings.
- Isabella Stewart Gardner Museum, a Renaissance palace imported from Italy and stuffed with precious art by its eccentric owner.
- Computer Museum, with its amazing machines, old and new.

Parks & Gardens
- Boston Common, one of the country's oldest public parks.
- Public Garden, the flowery formal counterpart to the Common.
- The "Green Necklace," Frederick Law Olmsted's system of parks and verdant thoroughfares.
- Arnold Arboretum, Boston's "living collection" of plants.

Architectural Highlights
- Beacon Hill, its quaint streets lined with 19th-century Federal and Greek Revival town houses.
- Massachusetts State House (1798), Charles Bulfinch's masterpiece.
- Faneuil Hall Marketplace, Boston's "stomach" in 1825, now restored (1970s) to be its "palate."
- Old North Church (1723), Boston's oldest and most graceful and historic place of worship.
- Trinity Church (1877), Henry Hobson Richardson's harmonious Romanesque Revival masterpiece.
- John Hancock Tower (1974), the towering mirror-glass rhomboid designed by I. M. Pei and Partners.
- Christian Science Center, with its dignified Mother Church, reflecting pool, and clean-lined tower.

Shopping
- Filene's Basement, the nation's first and best bargain-basement store.
- Downtown Crossing, Boston's commercial heart, for pedestrians only.
- Newbury Street, with its elegant and fashionable boutiques.

Events & Festivals
- Boston Pops concerts on the riverside Esplanade, especially the July 4 concert with cannons and fireworks.
- First Night, a New Year's Eve festival with ice sculpture, performances, and parades.
- Boston Marathon, the famous footrace run on Patriots Day (April 19).

Especially for Kids
- Swan Boat rides on the lake in the Public Garden, setting for the children's classic *Make Way for Ducklings.*
- Boston Children's Museum, designed especially for kids of all ages.
- Museum of Science, with lots of hands-on scientific and technical exhibits.
- New England Aquarium, a spellbinding undersea world on view.
- USS *Constitution,* the mighty ship that battled the British in 1812.
- Boston Tea Party Ship and Museum, where kids can wander around a recreation of a Revolutionary War–era ship.

Boston At A Glance

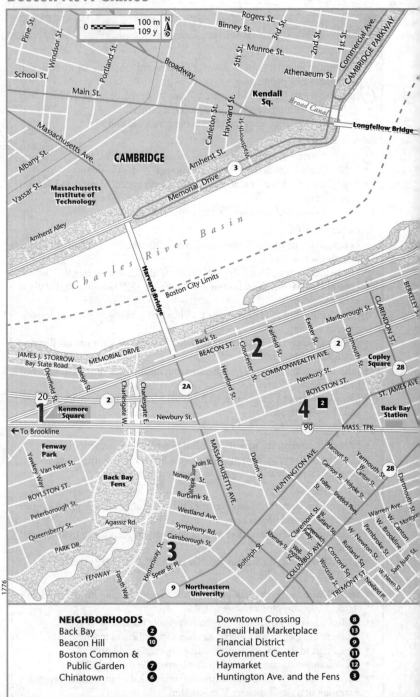

NEIGHBORHOODS

Back Bay	**2**	Downtown Crossing	**8**
Beacon Hill	**10**	Faneuil Hall Marketplace	**13**
Boston Common &		Financial District	**9**
Public Garden	**7**	Government Center	**11**
Chinatown	**6**	Haymarket	**12**
		Huntington Ave. and the Fens	**3**

Kenmore Square ①
The North End ⑮
Prudential Center ④
South End ⑤
Waterfront ⑭

VISITOR CENTERS
Boston Common Visitor
 Information Center ▮1
Prudential Visitor Center ▮2
Visitor Center ▮3

Share-a-Cab   In principle it works like this: Call the **Massport Dispatcher**, which can be reached by calling (☎ **800/235-LOGAN**), or simply pick up one of the special Share-a-Cab phones near the baggage-claim areas. Give your name and destination (any suburban community, but not Boston itself), and within 15 minutes you'll be on your way, sharing the expense of the cab with several other passengers going to or near the same destination. In practice, this excellent idea has been languishing of late because of competition from suburban limo companies. You may or may not find that Share-a-Cab works for you. Best time to try is at rush hour, of course.

Buses to Eastern Massachusetts   To Plymouth or Hyannis, call the **Plymouth & Brockton Street Railway Co.** (☎ **508/746-0378**).

Buses to Rhode Island   Bonanza Bus Lines (☎ **800/556-3815**) goes from Logan Airport right to Providence, a 1¹/₂-hour trip, daily every hour on the half hour between 8:30am and 10:30pm, with a final trip at 11:45pm.

Buses to New Hampshire   Concord Trailways (☎ **603/228-3300**) will take you to Manchester, Concord, Lake Winnipesaukee, North Conway, Jackson, Glen, and Hanover, right from the airport.

Buses to Vermont   Vermont Transit (☎ **800/451-3292**) operates from the airport to New Hampshire, Vermont, and Montréal.

By Car

One of the country's most ambitious construction projects is currently underway right in the heart of Boston. The city's "Central Artery," the John F. Fitzgerald Expressway, is being put underground, and a third tunnel is being dug across the harbor to connect Boston with East Boston and Logan International Airport. Construction detours are confusing, and delays may be long. The guidance given below is subject to change as construction progresses.

The easiest and fastest way to enter Boston by car from the west is via the **Massachusetts Turnpike** ("Mass. Pike"), which goes right through Back Bay to the center of the city; then it connects with the John F. Fitzgerald Expressway, also called the **Central Artery.** There are exits at Prudential Center and Chinatown (Kneeland Street).

You may approach Boston from the south on Mass. 3, the Southeast Expressway, as it comes up from the South Shore (Cape Cod and Plymouth). It's the main commuter route from everywhere south of Boston and is traveled very heavily; at rush hours there are frequent tie-ups.

From the north, the approach to Boston is by I-93, which crosses the Tobin Bridge to join the Central Artery; or by U.S. 1, which comes through East Boston.

Two divided highways skirt the Charles River toward Cambridge, the faster and busier one being **Storrow Drive** on the southern bank, the more scenic being **Memorial Drive** in Cambridge on the northern bank of the Charles. Take either one to go between Boston and Harvard Square. Go all the way to the Larz Andersen Bridge and Cambridge's John F. Kennedy Street, then turn right (north) for Harvard Square.

Once you are downtown, the Central Artery construction project and Boston's warren of winding, confusing streets, most of them one-way, will try your patience, but once you make your way to a hotel, you should park the car and try to forget it for the rest of your visit. Driving downtown makes little sense, and driving to Harvard Square even less sense (the parking problem there is even worse). Take the car out to go to Lexington, Concord, or the North Shore, but otherwise leave it parked.

BY TRAIN

Amtrak trains operate into and out of Boston's **South Station** and/or **Back Bay Station** (☎ **617/482-3660** or **800/USA-RAIL**). If you plan to stay downtown or in Cambridge, take the Red Line subway from South Station inbound toward "Alewife." In two stops, you'll be at Park Street for downtown hotels; if you stay on the Red Line, you'll get to Harvard Square. The Back Bay Station is on the Orange Line subway. To reach the Red Line, travel three stops to the Downtown Crossing stop.

BY BUS

Boston has three bus stations. Many local, commuter, and regional bus lines operate from a bus area next to Amtrak's South Station. **Peter Pan Trailways,** 555 Atlantic Ave. (☎ **617/426-7838, 413/781-3320,** or **800/237-8747**), is located in its own terminal in Dewey Square, just across from South Station. It offers service to and from Maine, New Hampshire, Connecticut, Rhode Island, and Massachusetts. To find your way downtown, look for the towering silver Federal Reserve Bank building, which resembles an enormous truck radiator. It's right in Dewey Square.

   Greyhound Lines is located in South Station (☎ **800/231-2222**) at the corner of Atlantic Avenue and Sumner Street. The South Station subway stop is on the Red Line. If you call the toll-free number above, you can get information about service to Portland, ME, New York City, and Hartford.

ESSENTIALS

Before coming to Boston, contact the **Greater Boston Convention & Visitors Bureau,** Prudential Tower (P.O. Box 490), Boston, MA 02199 (☎ **617/ 536-4100** or **800/888-5515 outside MA;** fax 617/424-7664), and request its information packet. You can also get a comprehensive guidebook ($4.95) and a "Kids Love Boston" guidebook. If you're looking for up-to-date information on attractions, performing arts, nightlife, gallery openings, and travel services, call **Boston By Phone** at ☎ **800/374-7400.**

   If you have access to the Internet and want information before you leave home, go to http://www.city.net/countries/united states/massachusetts/boston.

   If you call the **Massachusetts Tourism Office,** 100 Cambridge St., 13th floor, Boston, MA 02202 (☎ **617/727-3201** or **800/447-6277**) and leave your name and address, they'll send you a Massachusetts Vacation Kit.

   Much of Boston's historic downtown area is now part of the Boston National Historical Park, and so the National Park Service maintains a **Visitor Center** at 15 State St. (☎ **617/242-5642**). Free guided Freedom Trail tours are available in the spring, summer, and fall. The information center is open daily from 9am to 5pm. You'll see park rangers here and there at historic spots, ready to help with directions or information.

   On Boston Common (Green Line or Red Line to the Park Street station), at the intersection of Tremont and Winter Streets just a few steps from Park Street Station, there's the **Boston Common Visitor Information Center,** 410 Tremont St., (☎ **617/536-4100**), open year-round Monday through Saturday from 8:30am to 5pm and Sunday from 9am to 5pm. There you can get maps and booklets describing the Freedom Trail and other visitor information, as well as visitor "T" passes here. Ask for a free travel planner with seasonal events and accommodations listings.

The best calendar of current happenings for free is *Where* magazine, available at visitor information desks and in hotel lobbies. It's a complete listing of the best plays, sports events, concerts, special exhibits, and programs. The *Boston Globe* has a special "Calendar" supplement each Thursday, listing theater, concert, cinema, and lecture events as well as many other activities, with locations, prices, and telephone numbers. If you miss the *Globe* on Thursday, look for a similar supplement in the Boston Herald called "Scene." The *Boston Phoenix* is also a good source, and the *Tab* is a neighborhood specific publication that can be picked up at street corners. *Boston Magazine* is a monthly publication that also features a section detailing theater, lecture, and concert events.

CITY LAYOUT

In its earliest days Boston was called "Trimountain," for the three hills around which the settlement was built. At that time Trimountain was almost an island, connected to the mainland only by the narrow natural causeway called Boston Neck.

In the 19th century, an ambitious development plan resulted in the leveling of two of the hills and the moving of the dirt to fill in around Boston Neck; the marsh and bogs that were filled in to make the Back Bay quarter soon became a prime residential district with a Manhattan-style grid of streets and a wide, shady central boulevard called Commonwealth Avenue.

From the time when Trimountain had only a few winding pathways, the city has grown to be a maze of twisty streets difficult to get through in a car and easy to get lost in on foot.

Main Arteries   Boston is mostly a city of districts and neighborhoods, with few grand boulevards. The exception is the Back Bay area, which was a planned development built on filled land. **Commonwealth Avenue,** a wide tree-lined divided boulevard, is the main thoroughfare of Back Bay. **Beacon Street** to the north and **Boylston Street** to the south are the other major east-west streets. The shorter north-south streets of Back Bay have been named in alphabetical order. Thus, if you go west along Commonwealth Avenue from the Public Garden, you'll cross Arlington, Berkeley, Clarendon, Dartmouth, Exeter, and so on.

Finding an Address   This can be difficult in Boston, as there are many short streets downtown, and even having the name of a nearby cross street may be of little help. Bostonians are used to giving directions by means of landmarks and neighborhoods: "On Federal Street near South Station in the financial district" or "On Hanover Street in the North End near the post office." Remember to get more information than just the address. If you have the telephone number, call and ask for directions by means of neighborhood, landmarks, and subway stops.

NEIGHBORHOOD IN BRIEF

The North End   Starting at the very northeastern tip of Boston's peninsula, this is one of the city's oldest quarters. Old North Church is its best-known landmark; Paul Revere's House, the city's oldest house still standing, is another. The narrow streets and four-story brick buildings are now home to Italian-American families who preserve much of the old country's daily life in their Italian groceries, butcher shops, cafes, vegetable stands, and restaurants.

Impression

Boston State-house is the hub of the solar system.
—Oliver Wendell Holmes, *The Autocrat of the Breakfast Table*

Haymarket　Squeezed in the midst of Government Center, the North End, and Faneuil Hall Marketplace, this is where Boston's big open-air food market is held every Friday and Saturday. Most of the costermongers are old-timers from the North End.

Faneuil Hall Marketplace　This phenomenally successful restoration of Boston's historic Quincy Market, North Market, and South Market buildings is not only beautiful and historically important but also just plain fun. The marketplace, just east of Government Center, deserves its own restaurant guide for the dozens of places to buy the snacks, lunches, or elegant dinners that are provided here.

Waterfront　East of Faneuil Hall Marketplace and south of the North End is Boston's Waterfront, another area in which restoration has brought new life and vitality. The solid old brick and granite buildings that once served as warehouses for India and China traders have been modernized and converted to offices, shops, restaurants, and apartments. The New England Aquarium, Marriott Long Wharf Hotel, and Boston Harbor Hotel are at the southern end of the "new" Waterfront.

Government Center　All the districts mentioned above touch on Government Center, a bureaucrats' corral surrounded by striking modern buildings housing city, state, and federal offices, and dominated by the City Hall, placed in the midst of a brick-paved plaza that covers several acres. The plaza, with its sunken fountain, is a focus of outdoor activities in summer—free concerts, plays, and exhibits.

Financial District　South of Government Center is the city's financial district, centered on State Street, Milk Street, Devonshire Street, and the surrounding ways. The skyscrapers tower above such old Boston landmarks as the Old State House, Old South Meetinghouse, and the Old Corner Bookstore.

Beacon Hill　Due west of Government Center is Beacon Hill, last of the three hills of Trimountain and now an exclusive residential section with a surprisingly old-world ambience. The crown on the hill is Bulfinch's great State House, topped by its gold dome; the building is the home of the "Great and General Court of Massachusetts Bay" (the state legislature). Beautiful Louisburg Square is famous as the hill's most picturesque collection of houses. The Charles River Esplanade is the river's edge of Beacon Hill, on the north side. With a marina, the Hatch Memorial Shell for summer concerts, a bikepath, and lots of benches, it's the loveliest part of the Charles's banks.

Boston Common & Public Garden　South of Beacon Hill is the Boston Common, the city's "central park," with its Frog Pond—filled with splashing children in summer and skaters in winter—statues and monuments, walkways, and benches. Park Street Station, at the Common's southeastern corner (intersection of Park and Tremont Streets), is the heart of the "T," Boston's subway system, and also a gathering place for soapbox orators, one-person bands, religious zealots, panhandlers, mimes, and hawkers. The Public Garden, just west of the Common, has flower beds and lawns kept meticulously. The famous Swan Boats (run by pedalpower) slowly cruise sightseers around the pond. The Bull & Finch Pub in the Hampshire House, facing the Public Garden on the north, is famous as the inspiration for the television show "Cheers."

Downtown Crossing   Southeast of the Common on Washington Street, between West and Winter Streets, is the city's downtown shopping district, a pedestrian zone called Downtown Crossing. Take the subway to Washington Station and you can enter either of the two big department stores, Jordan Marsh or Filene's, directly from the subway station.

Chinatown   A few blocks south of Downtown Crossing, packed into the area around Beach Street, Tyler Street, and Harrison Avenue, are dozens of good Chinese restaurants, groceries, businesses, and churches. Like the North End, Chinatown is a place where the language of the old country may greet your ears more frequently than English.

Back Bay   West of the Public Garden is the large section called Back Bay, with Commonwealth Avenue its residential axis and Boylston Street its axis of business and pleasure, with office buildings, restaurants, clubs, and shops. Walking west on Boylston Street in Back Bay will bring you to Copley Square, one of Boston's most genteel areas, bounded by the classic Boston Public Library, the elegant Copley Plaza Hotel, and Henry Hobson Richardson's famous Trinity Church, built in the late 1800s. Modern intruders on this gentility are the striking mirror-glass shaft of the John Hancock Tower and the sprawling complex called Copley Place.

Prudential Center   Even farther west along Boylston Street, this was Back Bay's first large-scale redevelopment scheme, with the Prudential Tower ("the Pru") as its centerpiece, flanked by the mammoth Sheraton Boston Hotel, several blocks of luxury apartments, and stores such as Lord & Taylor. Also in the Pru complex is the Hynes Convention Center, the scene of everything from rock concerts to the boat show.

Huntington Avenue & the Fens   After the Pru Center, Huntington Avenue (which runs along the Pru's southern side) passes the Christian Science Center, Symphony Hall, Northeastern University, and the Museum of Fine Arts on what might be called Boston's "Cultural Highway." The Back Bay Fens sound uninviting, but actually this unappetizing name designates the first links in Frederick Law Olmsted's "Green Necklace," a chain of green parks, copses, and waterways for the residential districts of Back Bay, Roxbury, Jamaica Plain, and Brookline, stretching for miles from the green banks of the Charles River to the Arnold Arboretum to the south.

Kenmore Square   This is the westernmost part of the city of Boston, at the intersection of Commonwealth Avenue, Beacon Street, and Brookline Avenue. Boston University is just a few blocks west of the square, and Kenmore's life is dominated by its student denizens, who flock to its cafeterias, book and record stores, movies, and clubs. On the Boston skyline at night, you can always locate Kenmore Square by the huge red Citgo delta sign.

Impressions

The Bostonians take their learning too sadly: culture with them is an accomplishment rather than an atmosphere; their "Hub" as they call it, is the paradise of prigs.
—Oscar Wilde, "The American Invasion," *Court and Society Review,* March 1887

OUTLYING DISTRICTS   Although the city of Boston is fairly large, it's dwarfed by Greater Boston, officially termed the Metropolitan District, which consists of a dozen other cities as well as some outlying sections of Boston proper. Charlestown, north of the tip of Boston peninsula, is dominated by the Bunker Hill Monument obelisk; the USS *Constitution* (Old Ironsides) is berthed nearby in the old Boston Navy Yard.

East Boston, northeast of Charlestown, is reached by two tunnels: Callahan Tunnel runs north (outbound; no toll); Sumner Tunnel runs south (inbound; toll). And the big industry here is Logan International Airport.

South Boston, southeast of the financial district, is separated from the city proper by the Fort Point Channel. "Southie" is the city's Irish bastion, and here St. Patrick's Day is the national holiday. (*Note:* If someone mentions the **South End,** he or she is referring to the residential district just south of Back Bay. The South End and South Boston are, confusingly, completely separate places.)

NEIGHBORING CITIES   West of Boston is **Brookline,** a large, mostly residential city and the former hometown of the Kennedy family. On the northern banks of the Charles River, Cambridge got most of the riverfront land, while **Somerville** had to be content with a mere foothold. The banks of the Charles from the Charles River Dam (topped by the Museum of Science) all the way to Harvard University are covered by grass and trees, and in summer the grass is covered with sunbathers and picnickers.

2 Getting Around

BY SUBWAY & BUS   The best way to get around downtown and Back Bay is on the "T" (short for Massachusetts Bay Transportation Authority, or MBTA, which runs Boston's subway and bus network).

Transportation Information   The **MBTA Information Booth** is in Park Street Station. For information by telephone, call these numbers: for route information, ☎ **617/722-3200;** for MBTA commuter railroad schedules, ☎ **617/722-3200.** If you're going to be riding the subway a great deal during your stay in Boston, you might consider purchasing the book, *Car-Free*™ *in Boston: The Guide to Public Transit in Greater Boston and New England* (published by the Association for Public Transportation, Inc.). It was most recently published in 1995 and is an invaluable source for information pertaining to any and all aspects of public transportation in Boston.

Fares   Fares are 85¢ on the subway and 60¢ on local buses. Buses that go to outlying communities (Salem, Marblehead, Lexington, etc.) charge up to $2.25 one-way for the ride. All fares are payable in exact change. On buses and trolleys, you must have the exact fare; at subway stations, there are change booths open during service hours.

Children 5 to 11 are charged half fare on subways and buses; children under 5 ride free. Seniors pay 20¢ on the subway, 15¢ on the bus if they have an MBTA identity card.

The MBTA sells the **Boston Visitor Passport** that allows unlimited travel on the subway and on local buses in Greater Boston. Passes good for three consecutive days cost $9, seven-day passes are $18, and one-day passes cost $5. You can buy your Passport at the Airport Station, North Station, South Station, Government

Center, Harvard, and Riverside subway stops, as well as at the information centers at Boston Common and Quincy Market. Many hotels also sell the Passports. If you'd like to get it in advance of your trip, call ☎ **617/722-5218.**

Hours   Times on subway and bus lines vary, but you're pretty sure of being able to take the "T" any day from 5am to 12:30am (and up to 1am on some lines). After that, be prepared to take a cab. Hours may vary on Sunday.

Subway Lines   Subway lines are color-coded: The **Red Line** goes from Alewife in Cambridge via Harvard Square through Boston's main subway station at Park Street, then on to the suburbs of Quincy, Braintree, Dorchester, and Mattapan. The **Green Line** goes from Lechmere Square near the Museum of Science in East Cambridge through Park Street and downtown, then out to the western suburbs. The **Blue Line** connects downtown Boston with the Airport stop at Logan International Airport; you can also use the Blue Line to reach the New England Aquarium. There is an **Orange Line** as well.

   On several subway lines (most notably the Green Line) the cars surface and serve as trolleys after they leave the central part of the city. After an outbound car emerges from underground, passengers boarding aboveground ride for free. If you catch an inbound Green Line trolley aboveground, however, you pay the entire fare to your destination (which may cost up to $2) when you get on. Make sure you have exact change when traveling from a station that doesn't have a token booth. You can purchase subway tokens at downtown stations (many of the aboveground stops don't have token booths, so you must have exact change or a previously purchased token), and now you can also get tokens from the MBTA's token-vending machines. You'll find the machines at the "Airport" station (Blue Line), Back Bay (Red Line), Prudential (Green Line), and South Station (Red Line).

   A note for disabled travelers: The Americans with Disabilities Act (ADA), effective in 1992, requires all forms of public transportation to provide special services to persons with disabilities. All MBTA buses have lifts or kneelers (call ☎ **800/LIFT-BUS** for more information). While some bus routes are wheelchair accessible at all times you might have to make a reservation as much as a day in advance for others. For reduced fares in public transportation, persons with disablities can obtain an **MBTA Transportation Access Pass (TAP)** from the Downtown Crossing Station during the week from 8:30am to 4:15pm. For more information, call ☎ **617/722-5438** in advance of your trip. A TAP will cost you $3, and it's valid for five years.

BY CAR   It's not wise for a visitor to drive much in Boston. Its colonial layout of narrow streets (said to follow cattle paths) is confusing enough on foot, let alone in a car. Boston drivers are famous throughout the country for their careless maneuvers; they act as though no one else is on the road. Parking (see below) is difficult to find and expensive when you find it.

   If you make an excursion to Cambridge, take the Red Line of the subway, not your car. For places around Boston such as Concord, Salem, and Plymouth, a car is the best way to go.

   See also "Getting Around," in Chapter 2.

Rentals   There are car-rental desks at Logan International Airport and at various locations downtown. For more information on renting cars, see "Car Rental" under "Getting Around," in Chapter 2.

Parking   Parking meters in downtown Boston charge 25¢ per 15 minutes, and parking lots charge much more, up to $8 for the first half hour. Fines for parking illegally are routinely $50 or higher. If you stay for some time in Boston, don't accumulate a backlog of unpaid parking tickets: Cars are towed or fitted with a "Denver boot" and held hostage until the tickets are paid.

For the visitor unfamiliar with the city, try the large **Boston Common Underground Garage,** entered from Charles Street between the Common and the Public Garden. Here the rates are moderate, and there's a free shuttle bus to take you to nearby points.

BY TAXI   Fares in Boston and Cambridge are computed by the mile. In Boston, the first quarter mile costs $1.50, and each additional eighth of a mile costs 27¢. In Cambridge the fare is $1 for the first seventh of a mile and 27¢ per additional one-seventh mile thereafter. There's no charge for normal luggage, but trunks cost extra.

Boston companies include **Town Taxi** (☎ 617/536-5000) and **Checker Taxi** (☎ 617/536-7000). In Cambridge, call **Yellow Cab** (☎ 617/547-3000) or **Ambassador Cab** (☎ 617/492-1100).

If you have a complaint against a driver, get the hackney carriage medallion number and the driver's name and number (from his permit, posted in the cab), record the date and time of the occurrence, and call the **Boston Police Department's Hackney Carriage office** (☎ 343-4475).

BY BICYCLE   Boston is a good town for bicycling: The hills are gentle, the views are fine, and there are marked bike paths, one running from near the center of town along the beautiful Esplanade and the south bank of the Charles River all the way to Harvard Square. Bring a strong lock or heavy chain to prevent theft. Perhaps the greatest advantage of biking in Boston and Cambridge is the ease and cheapness of parking: Any lamppost will do, and it's free. You can rent bikes in Boston or Cambridge. Rental shops are listed in the yellow pages under "Bicycles—Renting." See also "Outdoor Activities," later in this chapter.

ON FOOT   Walking is the best way to see the sights in Boston. Indeed, if you want to follow the famous Freedom Trail, you've got to do some walking. For suggestions on where to walk, see the two "Walking Tours," later in this chapter.

FAST FACTS: Boston

American Express   The company has several travel agencies in the Boston area. The main office is at 1 Court St. (☎ 617/723-8400; subway: Government Center). There's also an office near Harvard Square, Cambridge, at 44 Brattle St. (☎ 617/661-0005; subway: Harvard). To report a lost or stolen American Express charge card, call ☎ 800/528-4800; to report lost or stolen American Express traveler's checks, call ☎ 800/221-7282. American Express also offers a currency exchange and money-wiring services.

Area Code   Boston's telephone area code is **617;** a number of outlying cities and towns, including Cambridge, Lexington, and Marblehead, are also in the **617** area. Other towns just slightly farther away (Concord, Salem, Cape Ann, Plymouth) have an area code of **508.** All telephones on Cape Cod, Martha's Vineyard, and Nantucket are in the **508** area.

Airport   See "Arriving," earlier in this chapter.

Boston MBTA Rapid Transit Lines

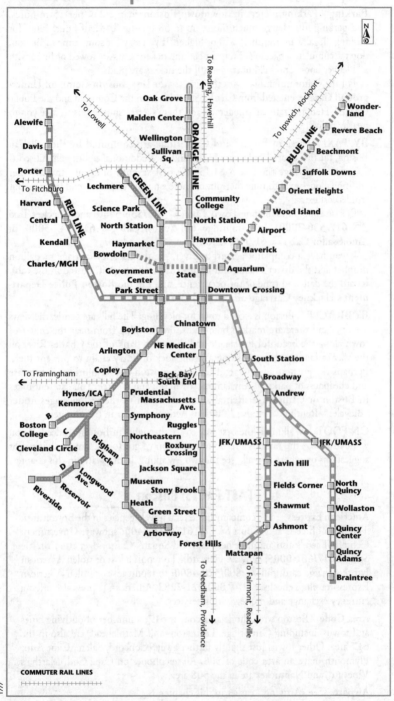

Babysitters Many of the larger hotels can arrange for babysitters; ask about this when you make reservations. Otherwise, nanny and babysitting services are listed in the yellow pages telephone directory under "Sitting Services," which includes house-sitting, pet-sitting, and elder-care services as well.

Business Hours See "Fast Facts: New England," in Chapter 2.

Car Rentals See "Getting Around," earlier in this chapter and in Chapter 2.

Climate See "When to Go," in Chapter 2.

Dentist Boston has lots of dentists. If you can't wait to go to your own dentist at home, refer to the yellow pages telephone directory under "Dentists" for listings by name, by practice specialty, and by location. You might also ask at your hotel for the name of a dentist who has given satisfactory care to someone on the hotel staff.

Doctor Boston doctors are listed by name and by specialty in the yellow pages. Most of Boston's hospitals operate physician referral services; if you call the service, they will put you in touch with a doctor who can treat your ailment. Here are several referral services: **Beth Israel Hospital Physician Referral** (☎ **617/735-5356**), **Massachusetts General Hospital Physician Referral Service** (☎ **617/726-5800**), and **New England Deaconess Hospital Physician Referral Service** (☎ **617/732-8006,** 24 hours a day).

Drugstores See "Pharmacies," below.

Embassies/Consulates See Chapter 3, "For Foreign Visitors."

Emergencies Dial **911** from any telephone (no coin needed at pay phones) for police, fire, ambulance, or any other emergency.

Eyeglass Repair There are many professional opticians able to repair glasses or fit you with eyeglasses or contact lenses quickly, whether or not you have a copy of your eyeglass prescription (if you can, you should take your glasses, even if they're broken). Look in the yellow pages telephone directory, under "Opticians." Many opticians, like LensCrafters, promise new glasses "in about an hour." Eye World, located at 481 Washington (☎ 617/357-9747) and at 699 Boylston (☎ 617/437-1070) offers same-day service.

Some pharmacies (drugstores/chemists) have racks of inexpensive eyeglasses, which might solve your problem (at least until you return home), and the cost is a fraction of that for custom-fitted glasses.

Hospitals Boston has some of the best hospitals in the country. Let's hope you don't need one during your stay, but here are some names for your reference: **Beth Israel Hospital,** 330 Brookline Ave. (☎ **617/735-2000,** or **617/735-3337** in an emergency); **Brigham and Women's Hospital,** 75 Francis St. (☎ **617/732-5500**); **Cambridge Hospital,** 1493 Cambridge St. (☎ **617/498-1000,** or **617/498-1429** in an emergency); **Children's Hospital,** 300 Longwood Ave. (☎ **617/735-6000,** or **617/735-6611** in an emergency); and **Massachusetts General Hospital,** 55 Fruit St. (☎ **617/726-2000,** or **617/726-3375** for children).

Hotlines AIDS hotline, ☎ 617/424-5916; Rape Crisis, ☎ 617/492-7273; Massachusetts Poison Control System, ☎ 617/232-2120; and Suicide Samaritans, ☎ 617/247-0220.

Information See "Essentials" earlier in this chapter.

Liquor Laws   See "Fast Facts: New England," in Chapter 2.

Lost Property   If you have lost or found something on an MBTA bus or subway, call ☎ **617/722-5000.**

Maps   See "City Layout" earlier in this chapter.

Newspapers/Magazines   Boston has two daily newspapers: the *Boston Globe* and the *Boston Herald.* They both have information about what's going on in town. A very good guide is the Globe's "Calendar" section, an added supplement every Thursday. The *Boston Phoenix,* a weekly, reports everything that's happening in town on the art, theater, music, and dance fronts. *Boston Magazine* is published monthly.

Pharmacies   There's sure to be a pharmacy (drugstore/chemist) nearby. Look in shopping centers and downtown commercial districts, or ask at your hotel. Most pharmacies have business hours from about 8am to 8pm, but times vary. To buy medicines 24 hours a day, seven days a week, go to Phillips Drug Co., 155 Charles St., Boston (☎ **617/523-1028** or **617/523-4372;** fax 523-1094; subway: Charles); or CVS Pharmacy, Porter Square Shopping Center, Massachusetts Avenue, Cambridge (☎ **617/876-5519;** subway: Porter); or to the emergency room of the nearest hospital.

Police   For police emergency, call **911;** for other business, call ☎ **617/ 247-4200.**

Post Office   For general postal information, call ☎ **617/451-9922.** Boston's postal center is the General Mail Facility, 25 Dorchester Ave. (☎ **617/ 654-5327**), next to South Station at Fort Point Channel (subway: South Station). Another convenient post office is the McCormack State Post Office Building at Post Office Square (☎ **617/654-5684;** subway: State). For more information on post offices, see "Fast Facts: New England," in Chapter 2.

Restrooms   See "Toilets" under "Fast Facts: For the Foreign Traveler," in Chapter 3.

Safety   Boston is as safe as any large American city, and safer than many. Follow the general rules: Watch out for pickpockets on subway trains and buses; don't go into parks after dark; don't venture into rundown neighborhoods, especially at night.

Taxes   See "Fast Facts: New England," in Chapter 2.

Taxis   See "Getting Around," earlier in this chapter.

Transit Information   See "Getting Around," earlier in this chapter.

Weather   Call ☎ **617/936-1234.**

3 Accommodations

Boston has a very fine selection of downtown hotels, each with something special to recommend it. The best way to get to know this wonderful city is to stay right downtown, where the action is. This can be expensive, however; a double room in one of Boston's fine hotels often costs nearly $200 or more per night, and the city's 9.7% room tax can hike that lofty price to almost $220.

My price categories below are as follows: Double rooms that are $200 and up are "Very Expensive," $175 and up are "Expensive," $100 and up are "Moderate," and $80 and up are "Budget." Note that, unless otherwise specified, each room comes with a private bath.

MONEY-SAVING TIPS   Visit on a Weekend   If you want to stay right downtown, by all means plan your visit for a weekend! A double room at any luxury hotel right in downtown Boston may cost $200 during the week. But if you sign up for a two-night stay on Friday and Saturday, you may get that same room for something like $135, plus a bottle of champagne, breakfast in bed, the morning's newspaper, and free parking. These "weekend specials" are offered by all the city's luxury hotels, and many are even lower in price. It even makes sense to detour out of town—to Salem and the North Shore, to Cape Cod, or to Old Sturbridge Village—in order to arrive in Boston on Friday afternoon or evening. (By the way, country inns and resorts are most crowded, and highest in price, on weekends, so it makes sense to visit the country places during the week.)

Reserve from a Tourist Information Center   A number of moderate-to-expensive downtown Boston hotels routinely offer special prices to travelers calling from tourist information centers for same-day reservations. For instance, if you arrive at the airport or train station, or are driving up from Cape Cod or Plymouth and stop at the **Regional Information Complex for Visitors** on Mass. 3 at Exit 5 and pick up the hotel's brochure, inside you may find a leaflet offering a special low price. The price may be extremely good, such as $65 to $75 for a room that normally rents for $110 to $125, single or double. What's the catch? You can usually reserve that same day only, you may be limited to a stay of two or three days, and you must call from the information center and tell the reservations agent the name of the center you're calling from. The offers are based on availability of rooms, and if the hotel is pretty full, they might not grant you the discount price. Why do hotels do this? They want to fill rooms that may otherwise go empty that night.

Try a Bed-&-Breakfast or a Guesthouse   Another way to save money is to try a bed-and-breakfast room. Several agencies will make reservations and arrangements for you, and they are listed below. By staying in a bed-and-breakfast you can pay half or even a third of the downtown hotel price and make new friends in the bargain.

Try calling on of the following agencies for a reservation:

A B & B Agency of Boston (and Boston Harbor Bed and Breakfast) at 47 Commercial Wharf, Boston, MA 02110 (☎ **617/720-3540** or **800/248-9262 in the United States, 0800895128 in the U.K.**), will find you anything from a guest room in a historic Boston home to a fully furnished studio or one-, two-, or three-bedroom apartment, with a completely outfitted kitchen, television, and telephone, depending on your needs. The 120 privately owned properties are located all around Boston, and you may rent for two nights or more. Some of the agency's clients are business travelers, but many of the units are equally well equipped and welcoming of families with children, which is a plus because most bed-and-breakfasts don't allow children.

Boston Accommodations

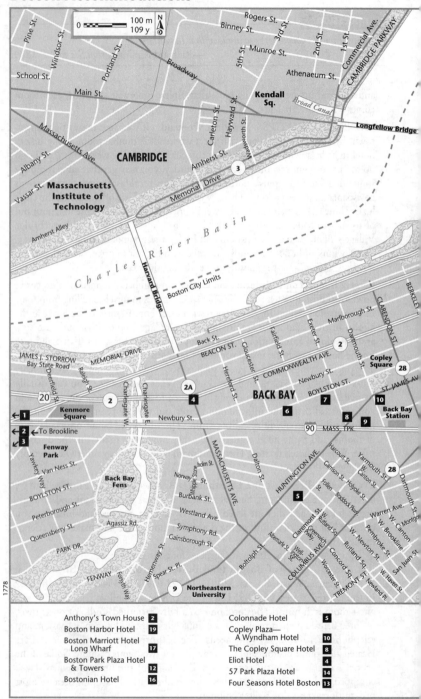

Anthony's Town House	2	Colonnade Hotel	5
Boston Harbor Hotel	19	Copley Plaza— A Wyndham Hotel	10
Boston Marriott Hotel Long Wharf	17	The Copley Square Hotel	8
Boston Park Plaza Hotel & Towers	12	Eliot Hotel	4
Bostonian Hotel	16	57 Park Plaza Hotel	14
		Four Seasons Hotel Boston	13

1778

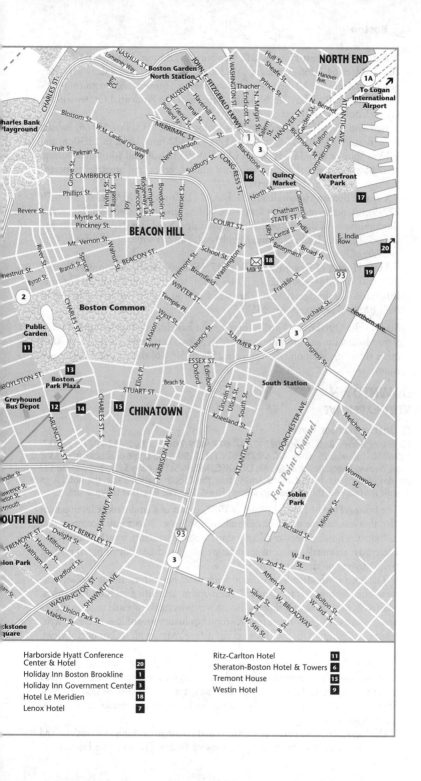

Harborside Hyatt Conference Center & Hotel	**20**	Ritz-Carlton Hotel	**11**
Holiday Inn Boston Brookline	**1**	Sheraton-Boston Hotel & Towers	**6**
Holiday Inn Government Center	**3**	Tremont House	**15**
Hotel Le Meridien	**18**	Westin Hotel	**9**
Lenox Hotel	**7**		

Beacon Inn Guest Houses, 248 Newbury St., Boston, MA 02116 (☎ 617/ 262-1771 or 617/266-7142; fax 617/266-7276), will arrange a daily or weekly room rental for you. All their rooms are in renovated brownstone apartment buildings located in Back Bay, on Newbury Street near the Prudential Center and the Hynes Convention Center.

Bed and Breakfast Associates Bay Colony Ltd., P.O. Box 57166, Babson Park, Boston, MA 02157-0166 (☎ 617/449-5302 from 10am to 12:30pm and 1:30 to 5pm, or 800/347-5088; fax 617/449-5958), will send you sample listings describing hundreds of home stays, inns, studios, suites, and apartments located throughout eastern Massachusetts.

Greater Boston Hospitality, P.O. Box 1142, Brookline, MA 02146 (☎ 617/ 277-5430), makes reservations for private homes, private city clubs, small inns, and condominiums in Boston, Brookline, Cambridge, Needham, Newton, Wellesley, Quincy, Scituate, Gloucester, and Marblehead. You can write, or call from 8:30am to 5:30pm.

Host Homes of Boston, P.O. Box 117, Waban Branch, Boston, MA 02168-0001 (☎ 617/244-1308; fax 617/244-5156), will find you a room in Newton, Brookline, Cambridge, Boston. They will send you a free descriptive directory of their B&Bs. They accept AE, MC, V.

Stay on the Outskirts   Finally, there are the hostelries on the outskirts of town. If you have a car and are willing to stay in Salem, Lexington, Concord, or some other suburban location, you can save 25% to 50% of the cost of a downtown room.

DOWNTOWN
VERY EXPENSIVE

✪ Boston Harbor Hotel

70 Rowes Wharf, Boston, MA 02110. ☎ **617/439-7000** or 800/752-7077. Fax 617/ 330-9450. 230 rms, 26 suites. A/C MINIBAR TV TEL. $200–$385 single or double; from $350 suite. Weekend packages available. AE, DC, DISC, MC, V. Self-parking $21; valet parking $23 per day. Directions: From Central Artery, take the "South Station" exit; the hotel is on Atlantic Avenue near the intersection of High Street. Subway: Blue Line to Aquarium.

The Boston Harbor Hotel, opened in 1987, is part of a landmark redevelopment plan that restored the dramatic old buildings at Rowes Wharf into a complex that includes the hotel, offices, condominiums, shops, restaurants, a yacht marina, and a ferryboat terminal—you can spot the striking flat-domed main portal easily if you're driving on the Central Artery.

The hotel is wonderfully luxurious: Each room has its own sitting area separate from the sleeping area. Standard guest-room amenities include bathrobes, hairdryers, umbrellas, and slippers. Room windows can be opened to let in the sea breezes, and each guest room features top-class luxury furnishings in classic style. Besides the standard rooms, the hotel has deluxe rooms with harbor or city views, plus luxury suites.

The public spaces are classic, conservative, and beautiful, and suggest wealth and richness—from the lavish use of colored marble to the crystal chandeliers, the thick patterned carpets, and the displays of antique maps and charts of Boston and New England. Classical music murmurs in the background, or a piano tinkles in the spacious sea-view lounge.

Dining/Entertainment: The Rowes Wharf restaurant features fresh seafood and American cuisine and has a sweeping view of Boston Harbor. The Harborview

Lounge serves afternoon tea and evening cocktails. The Rowes Wharf Bar, serving cocktails and light fare, is open from 11:30am to midnight. Seasonal dining is also available outdoors in the Rowes Walk Café (open late May to early September).

Services: 24-hour room service, free shoeshine service, chamber service twice daily.

Facilities: 60-foot lap pool, whirlpool, sauna, steambaths, massage rooms, exercise equipment, spa-treatment facilities, aerobics classes, weight-training instruction.

Boston Marriott Hotel Long Wharf

296 State St., Boston, MA 02109. ☎ **617/227-0800** or 800/228-9290. Fax 617/227-2867. 400 rms. A/C TV TEL. $139–$279 double. Weekend packages available. AE, DC, DISC, MC, V. Valet parking $22. Subway: Blue Line to Aquarium.

This seven-story luxury hotel has a modern design done along traditional lines to help it fit into the waterfront cityscape. Located right on the waterfront, off Atlantic Avenue near the New England Aquarium and Faneuil Hall Marketplace, the hotel has a decor that's up-to-date and quietly dramatic, with lofty public spaces and a second-floor lobby reached by escalator. Many guest rooms have views of the wharves and the water. .

Dining/Entertainment: The spacious Oceana Restaurant offers a grand harbor view, and Wave's Bar and Grill is a popular watering hole.

Facilities: Indoor pool with outdoor terrace deck, exercise room and sauna, games room, business center.

Bostonian Hotel

Faneuil Hall Marketplace, Boston, MA 02109. ☎ **617/523-3600** or 800/343-0922. 152 rms, 11 suites. A/C MINIBAR TV TEL. $235–$275 double; $375–$650 suite. Weekend packages start at $149 per night. Children under 12 stay free in parents' room. AE, CB, DC, MC, V. Valet parking $20 per night. Subway: Green or Blue Line to Government Center or Haymarket.

"What a perfect place for a hotel!" That's how the Bostonian introduces itself. It's true: Next to Faneuil Hall, Government Center, the weekend fruit-and-vegetable market, the North End's Italian shops and restaurants, the Bostonian is in the midst of the action. Modern with colonial accents, the hotel boasts tiny balconies overlooking Faneuil Hall on most of its individually decorated rooms. Some rooms even have working fireplaces. It's a small low-rise (seven-floor) luxury hotel. Honeymoon suites have Jacuzzis and fireplaces.

Dining/Entertainment: On the fourth-floor rooftop is the glass-enclosed Seasons Restaurant, featuring Creative American cuisine. The restaurant is reached by its own glass elevator.

Services: Evening turndown, shoeshine, limousine service to the airport and parts of Boston.

Harborside Hyatt Conference Center & Hotel

101 Harborside Dr., Boston, MA 02128. ☎ **617/568-1234** or 800/233-1284. Fax 617/568-6080. 270 rms. A/C TV TEL. $195 single or double. AE, CB, DC, DISC, MC, V. Parking $7 maximum for overnight guests. Directions: Follow the signs to the grounds of Boston's Logan International Airport and take Harborside Drive.

With a nautical theme and waterfront location, the Harborside Hyatt is one of Boston's newest hotels, and it offers unobstructed views of Boston Harbor and the city's skyline. The architecture is striking; fiber-optic stars change color in the sky dome ceiling in the reception area. Anchoring one end of the building is a lighthouse whose light is turned on and off by the Logan Airport control tower so that it doesn't interfere with the runway traffic. The decor in the public rooms resembles that of old cruise ships, with lots of nautical memorabilia. The first-class guest rooms have all the amenities you'd expect from a deluxe hotel, plus such extras as irons and ironing boards in each room, luxury baths, desks, dataport access on all guest-room phones, fine woods, and views of the harbor or airport.

Dining/Entertainment: The hotel's restaurant serves breakfast, lunch, and dinner. Floor-to-ceiling windows allow for spectacular views.

Services: Water taxi to Rowes Wharf that leaves from the hotel dock, 24-hour airport shuttle service.

Facilities: Full health club complete with indoor lap pool.

Hotel Le Meridien Boston

250 Franklin St., at Post Office Sq., Boston, MA 02110. ☎ **617/451-1900** or 800/543-4300. Fax 617/423-2844. 326 rms, 22 suites. A/C MINIBAR TV TEL. $235–$260 double; $450 suite. Extra bed $20. AE, DC, DISC, MC, V. Valet parking $17. Subway: Orange or Blue Line to State Street.

Located in the Old Federal Reserve Bank (1922) building, which was designed by R. Clipston Sturgis to resemble a 16th-century Roman palazzo, Hotel le Meridien is a historic landmark. Incorporated into its design are some of the bank's elegant architectural details, like the original grand marble staircase that leads to the dining area. Two murals by N.C. Wyeth grace the walls of the bar, and ornately carved marble fireplaces and floor-to-ceiling arched windows take you back in time.

While the Meridien is especially convenient for business travelers, it is also a good location for vacationers because it is within walking distance of major sightseeing attractions. First and foremost, though, it's a great place for anyone who wants to be pampered. One guest room is not identical to another here. In fact, there are 153 different room configurations, including dramatic loft suites with a first-floor living room, a bedroom in the loft area, and bathrooms on both levels. A glass mansard roof was later added to the structure and as a result, several rooms have glass walls and extraordinary views. *Note:* At press time, the Hotel le Meridien was undergoing a $5.5 million renovation to its guest rooms. It should be completed before the beginning of 1996.

Dining/Entertainment: A historic coffered gold-leafed ceiling tops the elegant Julien restaurant and bar. A six-story glass atrium creates a perennial garden court for the Cafe Fleuri, which serves breakfast, lunch, dinner, a seasonal Saturday "Chocolate Bar Buffet," and Sunday jazz brunch. La Terrasse is the hotel's seasonal outdoor cafe.

Services: 24-hour room service, concierge, laundry and dry cleaning service, daily weather report.

Facilities: Indoor pool and health club, full-service business center. Two floors for nonsmokers, 15 rooms for the disabled.

EXPENSIVE

Holiday Inn Government Center

5 Blossom St., Boston, MA 02114. ☎ **617/742-7630** or 800/HOLIDAY. Fax 617/742-4192. 303 rms, 2 suites. A/C MINIBAR TV TEL. $199 single or double. $15 for rollaway. Additional person $20 extra. Children under 18 stay free in parents' room. AE, DC, DISC, JCB, MC, V. Parking $16 per day in covered parking adjacent to the hotel. Subway: Blue or Green Line to Government Center.

Just off Cambridge Street, between Government Center and the Longfellow Bridge over the Charles River, is a high-rise haven slightly out of the center of things. It's several blocks from Government Center, then several blocks again from Government Center to the Boston Common. But prices are not too bad in this modern building, and the facilities are good. There are two restaurants (one on the rooftop), as well as a cocktail lounge. A seasonal outdoor pool and a nearby health club are available for guest use.

BACK BAY

VERY EXPENSIVE

✪ Four Seasons Hotel Boston

200 Boylston St., Boston, MA 02116. ☎ **617/338-4400** or 800/332-3442. Fax 617/ 426-7199. 288 rms, 80 suites. A/C MINIBAR TV TEL. $300–$460 double; from $650 one-bedroom suite; from $1,100 two-bedroom suite; $1,550 three-bedroom suite. Weekend packages available. AE, CB, DC, MC, V. Valet parking $22. Subway: Green Line to Arlington.

The elegant Four Seasons, a small brick-and-glass structure overlooking the Public Garden and Beacon Hill, has earned an impressive reputation since its 1985 opening. The newly refurbished guest rooms and suites are in harmony with the old-world charm of Boston and the simplicity that marks today's architectural styles. Each room is elegantly appointed and has a unique view of the city. The beds are large and comfortable, and a breakfront conceals the 19-inch remote-control TV and minibar. The suites range from Four Seasons Executive Suites, which have enlarged alcove areas for entertaining or business meetings, to luxurious one-, two-, and three-bedroom deluxe suites that are the utmost in elegance, privacy, and comfort. All rooms have bay windows that open, plus individual climate control, digital alarm clock radios, three two-line telephones with computer and fax capability, hairdryers, and terry-cloth bathrobes. Children receive bedtime snacks and toys. Small pets are accepted and get the royal treatment with a special pet menu and amenities.

Dining/Entertainment: Aujourd'hui is one of Boston's finest French restaurants. The Bristol Lounge is open for lunch, afternoon tea, dinner, and breakfast on Sunday. The Bristol features live entertainment nightly.

Services: Twice-daily maid service, complimentary overnight shoeshine, complimentary limousine service to downtown Boston addresses, 24-hour valet and room services, concierge. For those who lose luggage en route, the staff of the Four Seasons will purchase new items and will provide you with a full set of toiletries and other necessary items.

Facilities: Indoor pool, health spa with weight machines, StairMasters, and treadmills, private masseuse, and sauna (the pool and spa are shared with residents of the condominiums that occupy upper floors of the hotel). Five nonsmoking floors; rooms for the disabled.

✪ Ritz-Carlton Hotel

15 Arlington St., Boston, MA 02117. ☎ **617/536-5700** or 800/241-3333. Fax 617/ 536-9340. 278 rms, 48 suites. A/C MINIBAR TV TEL. $265–$385 double; $500–$2,150 suite. AE, DC, DISC, MC, V. Valet parking $20 per night. Subway: Green Line to Arlington.

This is Boston's grande dame in the luxury class, with careful service and a prime location facing the Public Garden. Guest rooms are very comfortable and classically styled. The location puts you near the upscale boutiques and trendy nightlife of Newbury Street and Back Bay. Many rooms have classic French provincial furnishings accented with imported floral fabrics and crystal chandeliers; each has a refrigerator, a well-stocked honor bar, a clock radio, and phones with voice mail. The baths are surfaced with Vermont marble. There are two sections: the older, original building with the lobby and Ritz Dining Room, and the newer, more modern addition. Many guests prefer the charm of the older rooms.

Dining/Entertainment: The dining room overlooking the Public Garden serves excellent continental cuisine with impeccable service, while The Café, on Newbury Street, serves equally good fare in simpler surroundings and at lower prices. Sipping tea in the lounge or martinis in the dignified bar are well-practiced Boston customs. The dress code in all three establishments states that men must wear a jacket and tie after 5pm. The roof is the hotel's seasonal outdoor grill, offering dining and dancing weekends from May to September.

Services: 24-hour room service, concierge, babysitting, multilingual staff, complimentary limousine, twice-daily chamber service, guest privileges at a nearby spa. The Junior Presidential Suite is available for children.

Facilities: Fitness center, flower and gift shop, hair salon, jewelry shop.

Sheraton Boston Hotel and Towers

39 Dalton St., Boston, MA 02199. ☎ **617/236-2000** or 800/325-3535. Fax 617/236-6061. 1,187 rms, 85 suites. A/C MINIBAR TV TEL. $220 double; from $255 suite. Children under 17 stay free in parent's room. AE, CB, DC, DISC, ER, JCB, MC, V. Parking $16. Subway: Green Line to Prudential or Hynes Convention Center/ICA.

With its three top-rated restaurants and its attractive rooms, this hotel is one of the most popular in the city. It's actually two hotels in one—the original Sheraton and the luxurious Sheraton Towers with private elevators to the top floors. The complex is connected to the Hynes Convention Center.

The rooms are decorated with traditional mahogany and cherrywood furnishings and accented with floral drapes and bedspreads. Many of the suites have an extra phone in the bathroom, a wet bar, and a refrigerator. Guests who stay on the club level will enjoy free local calls and no access charges on long-distance calls, as well as complimentary breakfasts and evening hors d'oeuvres (both are served in the club level lounge). In-room amenities on the club level include a desk, phone with a dataport, morning newspaper, coffeemaker, and iron.

The Sheraton Towers, located on the 26th floor of the hotel, features private check-in, an elegant atmosphere accented by antiques, and a wonderful view from the lounge, where Tower guests can enjoy complimentary breakfast, afternoon tea, and late-day hors d'oeuvres and beverages. Luxury touches in the Tower rooms include Egyptian cotton sheets, goose down comforters, plush bathrobes, electric blankets, a "valet-hanger" for suites, shoe trees, and phones in the bathroom (some even have a wall-mounted TV). Guests staying on this floor have their own personal butler.

Dining/Entertainment: Open for breakfast, lunch, and dinner, the Mass. Bay Company features an eclectic, seasonal menu. A Steak in the Neighborhood offers dining in a casual atmosphere. Serving breakfast, lunch, and dinner, the menu suits all tastes and offers over 70 different beers.

Services: 24-hour room service.

Facilities: Tropical domed pool pavilion with Jacuzzi, Universal, and other fitness equipment; special accommodations for the disabled; nonsmoking rooms. Indoor/outdoor pool, fitness equipment.

Westin Hotel

10 Huntington Ave., Boston, MA 02116. ☎ **617/262-9600** or 800/228-3000. Fax 617/424-7483. 800 rms, 46 suites. A/C MINIBAR TV TEL. $169–$250 double; $285–$1,500 suite. Additional person $20 extra, $30 on Executive Club Level. Weekend packages available. AE, CB, DC, DISC, ER, JCB, MC, V. Valet parking $21. Subway: Green Line to Copley or Prudential, or the Orange Line to Back Bay.

Dominating the busy corner at Dartmouth Street and Huntington Avenue, this 36-story hotel is a concrete-and-glass marvel at the gateway to Copley Place, Boston's shopping mecca. You're greeted by two-story-high, twin waterfalls cascading into flower-banked pools at the glass pedestrian entrance opposite the Boston Public Library. Escalators carry guests between the falls to the Grand Lobby. The guest rooms are spacious and airy with excellent views from the large bay windows—you might request a view of downtown Boston, the airport and harbor, or the Charles River and Cambridge when making reservations. Furnishings are oak and mahogany, and each room has an in-room safe. This is a chain hotel, so guest rooms are standard throughout.

Dining/Entertainment: Three restaurants and three bars offer a variety of dining experiences. Ten Huntington is a casual bar serving light meals. Seafood is the specialty of Turner Fisheries, which has an oyster bar and greenhouse-style lounge and features live jazz nightly. The Brasserie, an informal dining room by the waterfall is open for breakfast and lunch. The lobby lounge is a relaxing spot for drinks and conversation.

Services: Valet service, 24-hour room service, multilingual staff.

Facilities: Health club, indoor pool, nonsmoking rooms. Forty rooms for the disabled, which adjoin standard rooms to accommodate guests traveling with disabled persons.

EXPENSIVE

Boston Park Plaza Hotel & Towers

64 Arlington St. at Park Plaza, Boston, MA 02116-3912. ☎ **617/426-2000** or 800/225-2008, 800/462-2022 in Massachusetts. Fax 617/426-1708. 960 rms, 24 suites. A/C TV TEL. Main hotel, $155–$215 single or double. Towers, $195–$245 single or double; $375–$1,500 suite. Children stay free in parents' room. AE, DC, MC, V. Parking $18. Subway: Green Line to Arlington.

Built as the great Statler Hilton in 1927, the hotel is proud of its history though equally proud of its renovations. The nice old features—such as the spacious lobby with a crystal chandelier, lots of gilt trim, and red-carpeted corridors—have been kept, but the rooms have been updated with many modern comforts. The clientele includes many groups as well as thrifty families, both domestic and foreign. The location is very central, a scant block from the Boston Common and Public Gardens and only a block or so from the theater district.

Dining/Entertainment: Guests can enjoy themselves at the Café Rouge Bistro (serving breakfast and lunch) with continental cuisine; a branch of Boston's famous Legal Sea Food restaurant; and Captains Bar, Café Eurosia, and Swans Court in the Grand Lobby. There are many other restaurants in the neighborhood as well.

Services: 24-hour room service; concierge; shoeshine.

Facilities: Health club, travel agency, hairdresser, airport shuttle stop, foreign-currency exchange, Amtrak and many airline ticket offices, gift shop, pharmacy, beauty salon, game room for kids, nonsmoking floors.

⊕ Family-Friendly Hotels

Boston Park Plaza Hotel & Towers *(see p. 79)*   The Cub Club provides children with a coupon book for Boston attractions, a special children's menu, Red Sox ice-cream sundaes, a free Swan Boat ride, Story Hour, and Benny's Den (a fully outfitted games room for children). Saturday is Pizza & Movie night.

Charles Hotel *(see p. 142)*   Adjoining the hotel is the Le Pli Day Spa, which features family swim time. Room-service menus offer specialties that kids enjoy, including pizza, and all snack bars are adequately stocked with juice, milk, and cookies.

The Four Seasons *(see p. 77)*   Kids love the pool and spa and the executive suite where they can get children's videos, milk and cookies delivered by room service, child-size bathrobes, and many other children's accessories.

Ritz-Carlton Hotel *(see p. 77)*   If you can afford the splurge, your kids will love the video library, games, toys, and snacks served in the Junior Presidential Suite. The Ritz also hosts special weekends for children.

Royal Sonesta Hotel *(see p. 144)*   During Summerfest, the Royal Sonesta features supervised children's programs for kids 5 to 12, including complimentary use of bicycles, health club, indoor/outdoor pool, boat rides on the Charles, and unlimited amounts of ice cream.

57 Park Plaza Hotel

200 Stuart St., Boston, MA 02116. ☎ **617/482-1800** or 800/HOTEL-57. Fax 617/451-2750. 350 rms, 10 suites. A/C TV TEL. $140–$155 double; $140–$165 single or double suite; $120–$165 minisuite. Additional person $15 extra. Children under 18 stay free in parents' room. AARP discounts available to those with ID. Weekend and family packages available. AE, DC, MC, V. Free parking. Subway: Green Line to Boylston or Arlington.

This well-located upper-range hotel is only two blocks from the Boston Common and the Public Garden, and is right near the Greyhound bus terminal, in a multipurpose complex of buildings that includes a parking garage, two cinemas, two lounges, and two restaurants. Business meetings provide a big part of its clientele, both because of the facilities and because of its central location. Each guest room has a private balcony with a commanding city view and a king-size bed or two double beds, and is decorated in soft, pleasant tones. A pool and a sauna are available for year-round guest use.

⑨ Tremont House

275 Tremont St., Boston, MA 02116-5694. ☎ **617/426-1400** or 800/331-9998. Fax 617/482-6730. 281 rms, 34 suites. A/C TV TEL. $130–$145 double; $170–$270 suite. Additional person $15 extra. Children under 12 stay free in parents' room. AE, CB, DC, MC, V. Valet parking $15. Directions: Take the Chinatown/Kneeland Street exit from the Mass. Pike or I-93, follow Kneeland to Tremont, and turn left. Subway: Green Line to Boylston or Orange Line to New England Medical Center.

Built in 1925 as the headquarters of the Benevolent Protective Order of Elks, this well-located downtown hotel three blocks south of the Boston Common was later called the Bradford, and as such it hosted live radio broadcast from its rooftop nightclub. Later a favorite stopping place for actors and artists, it has been extensively (and expensively) redone recently from top to bottom. The elegance of the original neoclassical architecture shines through and is delightful. The guest rooms, tastefully done in Early American style with prints of works in Boston's Museum of Fine Arts, are small but comfortable, with twin, double, queen-size, and king-size beds. There are several units that feature kitchenettes with a range, sink, and refrigerator—a great choice for a family.

Dining/Entertainment: Broadway's Restaurant & Bar serves a pub-style menu at breakfast, lunch, and dinner. The Roxy nightclub features Top 40s hits and international music, and the NYC Juke Box Club offers the greatest hits of the 90s on Thursday, Friday, and Saturday evenings.

Services: Room service, concierge, dry cleaning.

Facilities: Nonsmoking floors, handicapped-accessible rooms.

COPLEY SQUARE/CONVENTION CENTER/ MASSACHUSETTS AVENUE
VERY EXPENSIVE

The Colonnade Hotel

120 Huntington Ave., Boston, MA 02116. ☎ **617/424-7000** or 800/962-3030. Fax 617/ 424-1717. 288 rms, 15 suites. A/C MINIBAR TV TEL. Standard, $240 double; superior, $245 double; deluxe, $270 double, $450–$1,400 suite. AE, CB, DC, MC, V. Parking $20 per day. Subway: Green Line to Prudential or Symphony.

Located in the historic Back Bay, across from the Prudential Shopping Center, the Colonnade is one of Boston's finest. The hotel's contemporary European atmosphere is enhanced by a friendly, professional staff whose members give every guest personalized VIP service. The rooms in this independent family-owned hotel boast many extra touches in addition to the amenities you'd expect in a luxury hotel. Guest rooms either feature contemporary oak furnishings and are decorated in a coppery autumn color with dark accents or contain mahogany furnishings against a rose-colored backdrop. The newly designed suites have dining rooms and sitting areas decorated in a "residential" motif. Marbled baths have pedestal sinks, bathrobes, and hairdryers.

Dining/Entertainment: The Café Promenade, open daily from 7am to 11pm, features seasonal menus, as well as gourmet pizzas, in a bistro setting. Every Friday and Saturday night you'll find dinner and dancing with the Winiker Swing Orchestra in Zachary's Bar.

Services: 24-hour room service, concierge, nightly turndown, multilingual staff, Hertz car rental in the lobby.

Facilities: Seasonal rooftop pool and resort area; fitness room.

The Copley Plaza—A Wyndham Hotel

138 St. James Ave., Boston, MA 02116. ☎ **617/267-5300** or 800/822-4200. Fax 617/ 247-6681. 373 rms, 53 suites. A/C MINIBAR TV TEL. $245–$295 double; $395–$1,400 suite. Additional person $20 extra. AE, CB, DC, MC, V. Valet parking $20 per night. Subway: Green Line to Copley.

The Copley Plaza, facing Copley Square, is a wonderful grand old Boston hotel. The attractions are the hotel's grand style and original touches: a quiet cocktail lounge that is, in fact, a comfortable club library, complete with oil portraits and brass-nailed leather chairs; the striking, ornate, elegant Plaza Dining Room, in which the ceilings are heavily gilded, the mantelpieces are marble, and the maître d' is a soft-spoken and very suave man in a tuxedo; and Copley's, a mirror-laden brass-rail bar serving drinks and sandwiches, with trompe l'oeil paintings on the mirrors and doors.

Dining/Entertainment: The Plaza Dining Room serves French cuisine with 700 wine-cellar selections. Copley's Restaurant & Bar offers New England fare and serves breakfast, lunch, and dinner. For cocktails, The Plaza Bar and The Library Bar fit the bill.

Services: 24-hour room service, twice-daily chamber service.

Facilities: On-site fitness facility for hotel guests. Complimentary use of Le Pli Spa.

EXPENSIVE

✪ Eliot Hotel

370 Commonwealth Ave., Boston, MA 02215. ☎ **617/267-1607** or 800/44-ELIOT. Fax 617/536-9114. 16 rms, 78 suites. A/C MINIBAR TV TEL. $175–$195 double; $185–$205 suite for one, $195–$215 suite for two. AE, DC, MC, V. Valet parking $18. Subway: Green Line to Hynes Convention Center/ICA.

The Eliot, at Massachusetts and Commonwealth Avenues, one block from trendy Newbury Street, is one of Boston's undiscovered delights. Located in a parklike setting, the hotel is adjacent to the Harvard Club and just minutes from shopping, dining, and cultural sites. The stunning portico, sparkling five-foot-wide imported lobby crystal chandelier, and richly upholstered period furnishings are an elegant introduction to the nine-story European-suite hotel. Spacious suites are furnished with traditional English-style chintz, authentic botanical prints, and antique furnishings. French doors separate the living rooms and bedrooms, and modern conveniences—such as Italian marble baths, dual-line telephones, two TVs, and coffeemakers—are standard. Many suites also have an icemaker, a microwave, and a well-stocked refrigerator.

Dining/Entertainment: Breakfast is served in the Charles Eliot Room, where guests enjoy classical music and the *Wall Street Journal.*

Services: Room service, concierge.

Lenox Hotel

710 Boylston St., Boston, MA 02116. ☎ **617/536-5300** or 800/225-7676. Fax 617/267-1237. 214 rms. A/C TV TEL. $180–$235 double. Additional person $20 extra. Children under 18 stay free in parents' room. AE, DC, DISC, ER, MC, V. Valet parking $24, self-parking $22. Subway: Green Line to Copley.

Enjoy the pleasures of the Prudential Center and Copley Place by staying at the Lenox, where you're right on the same block as the Pru. The guest rooms have Chippendale-style furnishing, big closets, and high ceilings; some even have fireplaces and marble bathrooms. Besides being right in the Prudential Center, the Lenox is at Boylston and Exeter Streets, right next to the Boston Public Library and only a block from Copley Square.

Dining/Entertainment: The Upstairs Grille and the Samuel Adams Brewhouse both serve full meals.

Services: *USA Today* room delivery, babysitting, airport shuttle service (for a nominal fee).

Facilities: Exercise room.

MODERATE

⑤ Copley Square Hotel

47 Huntington Ave. (at Exeter St.), Boston, MA 02116. ☎ **617/536-9000** or 800/225-7062. Fax 617/267-3547. 143 rms. A/C TV TEL. $135–$175 double. Additional person (up to four) $10 extra. Children under 18 stay free in parents' room. Special winter rates and

package plans available. AE, DC, DISC, MC, V. Transportation: Airport shuttle service $7.50 per person. Parking: Available next door for $16. Subway: Green Line to Copley.

This is perhaps the best bargain in the area of the Prudential Center, Copley Place, Symphony Hall, and the Christian Science Center. As in most of the older hotels in Boston, its rooms have been carefully refurbished and maintained, and are very comfortable. Though much less fancy than the big places, this is a full-service hotel. The rooms are pleasantly decorated, with coffeemakers, hairdryers, alarm clock radios, and safes, as well as cable TVs with movie channels.

Dining/Entertainment: Café Budapest restaurant, a Boston tradition, serves continental cuisine. Pop's Place is the informal cafe/bistro. The Original Sports Saloon is a great place for a light meal.

KENMORE SQUARE & ENVIRONS

Holiday Inn Boston Brookline

1200 Beacon St., Brookline, MA 02146. ☎ **617/277-1200** or 800/HOLIDAY. 208 rms, 8 suites. A/C TV TEL. $100–$170 double; $150–$190 suite. AE, DC, DISC, JCB, MC, V. Free parking. Directions: Go west on Beacon Street; the hotel is just across the city line in Brookline. Subway: Green Line "Cleveland Circle" train.

Just 10 minutes from downtown by subway, this sparkling hotel is built around a colorful atrium with a garden lounge, putting green, sun deck, and 40-foot swimming pool plus whirlpool. Rooms are furnished in pecan-, walnut-, or oak-finished pieces. An entire floor is designated for nonsmokers, and 10 rooms are equipped for handicapped guests. There's the popular Cafe on the Green and two lounges.

A BED & BREAKFAST IN BROOKLINE

Anthony's Town House

1085 Beacon St., Brookline, MA 02146. ☎ **617/566-3972**. 10 rms (none with bath). TV. $35–$75 single or double. No credit cards. Free parking. Directions: From downtown Boston, follow Beacon Street west, cross the city line into Brookline, and look for the guesthouse on the left-hand side of the street. Subway: Green Line "C" train to the Hawes Street stop (the second surface stop after Kenmore).

This restored turn-of-the-century brownstone town house offers guest rooms at reasonable rates in a lovely Victorian atmosphere. Anthony's Town House has been owned and operated by the same family for over 50 years and is listed in the historic register.

MOTELS ON THE OUTSKIRTS

Although it's preferable to stay downtown and not get snarled in city traffic, you may want to know that Boston has several representatives of the budget-priced **Susse Chalet** motel chain. Prices generally run in the range of $49 to $65 for a single and $54 to $69 for a double. If you're not sure where exactly you'd like to stay in relation to the city, call one of the toll-free numbers (☎ **800/258-1980, 800/858-5008** in eastern Canada), because they handle all the Susse Chalets in the area. If you'd rather call directly to the location of your choice, there are two in Neponset: one at 800 Morrissey Blvd. (☎ **617/287-9100**), and the other at 900 Morrissey Blvd. (☎ **617/287-9200**). There's also one in Newton at 160 Boylston St. (☎ **617/527-9000**), which is accessible by subway. All the motels listed above have outdoor swimming pools (except for the one at 900 Morrissey in Neponset—its guests use the pool at the Susse Chalet at 800 Morrissey) and coin-op laundries, as well as color TVs.

4 Dining

Dining possibilities in Boston are virtually limitless. The city's array of restaurants includes at least one representative of every notable cuisine in the world, and usually more than one—in the Boston area there are more than 150 Chinese restaurants alone. Most of Boston's restaurants take advantage of the fresh seafood that comes to the docks daily, whether the specialty is seafood or not.

For my recommendations, I've chosen favorites, places that I've found satisfactory in every way. Remember that the many very fine hotel restaurants, lounges, and coffee shops are covered along with the hotels themselves in the preceding section. The good restaurants and coffeehouses in Cambridge are described in Chapter 5, "Around Boston"; keep in mind that most of them are within walking distance of the Red Line's Harvard subway station, and the trip can be made from central Boston in 10 or 15 minutes. The good restaurant in the Museum of Fine Arts, the best place for lunch if you're seeing the MFA or the Gardner Museum, is described along with the museum itself in the sightseeing section.

In the more expensive establishments, it's good to call ahead for reservations if they'll take them—many Boston places do not. This is true especially on weekends and holidays. If you're driving, be sure to ask what the parking arrangements are before you leave.

BEACON HILL/PUBLIC GARDEN

The Bay Tower

60 State St. ☎ **617/723-1666.** Reservations recommended. Main courses $15–$36. AE, DC, MC, V. Dinner only Mon–Thurs 5:30–10pm, Fri–Sat 5:30–11pm. Subway: Orange or Blue Line to State Street. CREATIVE AMERICAN.

Every table in this restaurant, which is right next to Boston's Faneuil Hall, has a marvelous view of the Custom House Tower, Boston Harbor, Logan Airport, and the hills beyond (because it's located on the 33rd floor). A cocktail lounge with a band for dancing (Friday and Saturday) is on the mezzanine level (open 4:30pm to 1am Monday through Thursday, to 2am on Friday and Saturday). There is a $9 cover charge in the lounge after 9:30pm on Fridays and Saturdays; dining room customers are exempt. A jacket is required in the dining room. The menu is long and inclusive, expensive but not outrageous. You can start with lobster ravioli with ginger and basil, or a simple soup. Fish and shellfish, fowl, and grilled meats are all featured; specialties are roast rack of lamb with rosemary, garlic, and cracked pepper in a zinfandel sauce, and a seafood mixed grill of lobster, swordfish, and sea scallops. The menu changes seasonally.

✪ Biba Food Hall

272 Boylston St. ☎ **617/426-7878.** Reservations required. Main courses $17–$34. CB, DC, DISC, MC, V. Mon–Fri 11:30am–2pm, Sun 11:30am–2:30pm; Sun–Thurs 5:30–9:30pm, Fri–Sat 5:30–10:30pm. Bar menu offered until 2am. Subway: Green Line to Arlington. AMERICAN.

Biba is disconcerting, expensive, and lots of fun. Enter past the valet parking attendant to the high-ceilinged bar where the flashy decoration is on the people, not the walls. Located in the building called Heritage on the Common, to the right of the Four Seasons, this is among Boston's trendiest places for the young and well-heeled to drink and dine. Upstairs past the wine racks is the large low-ceilinged dining room done in an eclectic, spare style with hints at art deco and the Southwest. Chef-owner Lydia Shire's menu is unlike anything you've ever seen, but the food is excellent. Categories are fish, offal, meat, starch, legumina, specials, and sweets. Order two or three appetizers if you like, or split a main course or two—anything goes. You might get a chance to try lobster pizza; crab accented with scallions and ginger, served on a bed of Asian noodles; Nero Indian-spiced sirlion of lamb in tandoor; or breast of chicken broiled simply with arugula and served with a warm lentil salad. Lunch is equally original. The latest favorite desserts are stacked crème brûlée with apricot glaze and little angel food cakes with mint ice cream and chocolate fudge sauce. The staff is friendly and well informed, the clientele is youngish and professional, and there's no dress code.

Ritz-Carlton Dining Room

15 Arlington St. ☎ **617/536-5700.** Reservations recommended. Main courses $28.50–$43; dinner $65–$80. AE, DC, DISC, MC, V. Dinner Sun–Thurs 5:30–10pm, Fri–Sat 5:30–11pm; Grand Sunday Brunch 10:45am–2:30pm; Saturday Fashion Lunch noon–2:30pm. Subway: Green Line to Arlington. CONTINENTAL.

The genteel atmosphere here makes a good place for a fine lunch or dinner, where diners look onto the Public Garden, its trees and flowers, or snow scenes as the case may be. Elegance is all around: gold tracery on the cream-colored ceiling, lofty many-paned windows surrounded by blue-and-white print drapes, crystal chandeliers, and sconces, potted plants, a tinkling piano, and impeccable service. The menu changes daily, but a typical luncheon might offer you beef tenderloin Diane, prepared tableside; a broiled veal chop demi-glace with mushrooms; or perhaps a selection from the cold buffet. At dinner, start with smoked North Atlantic salmon or the duck-liver-and-leek terrine, and then go on to a rack of spring lamb with thyme, or lobster prepared with whisky, or medallions of venison with cranberries and chestnuts. For dessert, have one of the several dessert soufflés, which are first a dream, then ambrosia, then a fond memory.

WATERFRONT

Anthony's Pier 4

140 Northern Ave. ☎ **617/423-6363.** Reservations are recommended. Main courses $9.95–$24.95 at lunch, $13.95–$29.95 at dinner. AE, CB, DC, MC, V. Mon–Sat 11:30am–11pm, Sun and holidays 12:30–10:30pm. Closed Christmas. Free parking on the wharf. Subway: Red Line to South Station. SEAFOOD.

This is one of the most outstanding restaurants in New England, and it has won the Business Executive's Dining Award first prize as America's most popular restaurant for many years. Dramatically situated at the end of a pier, the restaurant's waterfront walls are made of glass, allowing clear views of incoming sea vessels.

To start, you're served marinated mushrooms and relishes, then hot popovers. There are, of course, a number of other appetizers, including Oysters Rockefeller (some of the best I've tasted) and an excellent clam chowder. Among the featured dishes are fresh New England seafood, Dover sole from the English Channel (flown over especially for Anthony's), bouillabaisse, roast beef, and if you're in the mood to splurge, lobster Savannah with mushrooms, peppers, spices, wines, and Mornay sauce. This is also a good place to try a traditional clambake. Leave a little room for dessert. Some of my favorites are the Grand Marnier soufflé (served with a lovely zabaglione sauce) and the baked Alaska with a strawberry sauce. The pecan pie and Anthony's bread pudding are also good. If you haven't yet had a

Boston Dining

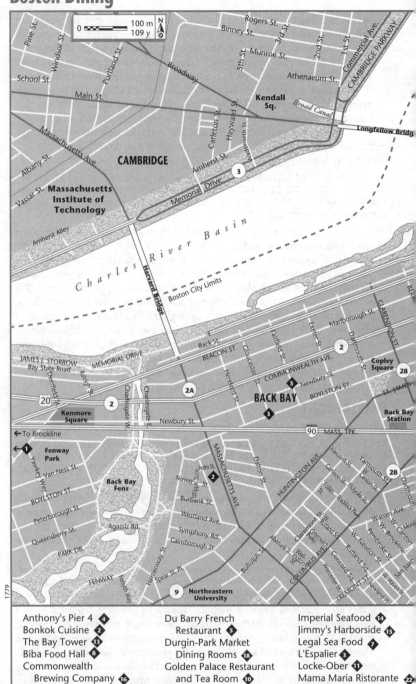

Anthony's Pier 4 **④**	Du Barry French	Imperial Seafood **⑭**
Bonkok Cuisine **②**	Restaurant **⑤**	Jimmy's Harborside **⑮**
The Bay Tower **⑬**	Durgin-Park Market	Legal Sea Food **⑦**
Biba Food Hall **⑧**	Dining Rooms **⑱**	L'Espalier **③**
Commonwealth	Golden Palace Restaurant	Locke-Ober **⑪**
Brewing Company **⑯**	and Tea Room **⑩**	Mama Maria Ristorante **㉒**
Cornucopia on the Wharf **⑳**	Hamersley's Bistro **⑥**	Maison Robert **⑫**

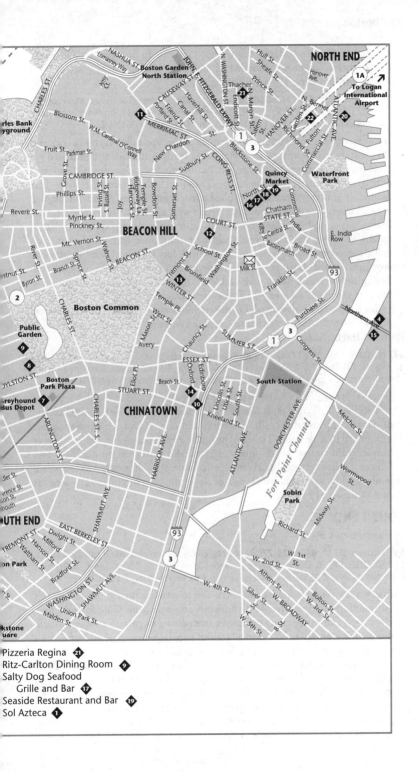

Pizzeria Regina 🔶21

Ritz-Carlton Dining Room 🔶9

Salty Dog Seafood
   Grille and Bar 🔶17

Seaside Restaurant and Bar 🔶19

Sol Azteca 🔶1

chance to try Indian pudding, this is a good place to do that. It's best to drive to this restaurant. Jackets are requested for men at dinner.

✪ Cornucopia on the Wharf

100 Atlantic Ave. ☎ **617/367-0300.** Reservations recommended at dinner. Main courses $13.50–$23.95. AE, MC, V. Daily 11:30am–2:30pm; 5:30–10:30pm. Patio open daily 11:30am–9:30pm. Subway: Blue Line to Aquarium. AMERICAN REGIONAL.

If you're spending the morning or afternoon at the Aquarium, Cornucopia on the Wharf is an excellent spot for lunch. The modern interior is dominated by hand-painted columns and a large bar. Picture windows allow diners clear views of neighboring wharves and the harbor. The menu is short, offering favorites like broiled scrod with roasted-garlic mashed potatoes and braised leeks with almond brown butter. The grilled swordfish niçoise with tomatoes, *haricots verts* (green beans), olives, grilled potato, and roasted red onion is also a good choice. Vegetarians will enjoy the *pan bagna,* flatbread pizza topped with eggplant spread, grilled vegetables, wilted greens, and topped with Ipswich goat cheese (my personal favorite). Another favorite of mine is the codfish cakes with baked beans and Boston brown bread. Along with each dish, the chef's wine recommendation is listed on the menu—a lovely touch for those who have a difficult time choosing a wine to accompany their meal. For dessert you've got to try the chocolate mousse in a chocolate meringue cage with a cinnamon anglaise.

Jimmy's Harborside

242 Northern Ave., ☎ **617/423-1000.** Reservations recommended. Main courses $10.95–$22.95. AE, CB, DC, MC, V. Mon–Sat noon–9:30pm, Sun 4–9pm. Subway: Red Line to South Station, then no. 7 bus, "City Point–South Station" (taxi is preferable). SEAFOOD.

Jimmy's, "Home of the Chowder King," located at the end of Northern Avenue on Fish Pier, due east of downtown Boston across the Fort Point Channel, has lots of nautical memorabilia, plush carpets and chairs, and a boat-shaped bar surrounded by little cocktail tables. The lunch special includes chowder or lobster bisque, main course, salad, potato, dessert, and coffee. At dinner, have two "chicken" lobsters (weighing about a pound apiece), with french fries and salad, jumbo shrimp, swordfish shish kebab, or one of the pasta specialties. The wine list runs to almost 115 items.

SOUTH END

✪ Hamersley's Bistro

553 Tremont St. ☎ **617/423-2700.** Reservations recommended. Main courses $17.50–$22.50. DISC, MC, V. Dinner only, Mon–Fri 6–10pm, Sat 5:30–10pm, Sun 5:30–9:30pm. Valet parking available. Subway: Orange Line to Back Bay/South End. ECLECTIC.

In just a few years Hamersley's has been able to establish itself as one of Boston's outstanding eateries. Created by husband-and-wife team Gordon and Fiona Hamersley, Hamersley's once occupied a small dining room with an open kitchen, but the space proved to be too small for this popular restaurant, and Hamersley's moved across the street into a historic 19th-century building.

A limited number of entrées are on the menu, but each is prepared with an emphasis on taste and texture. For example, the roast chicken that has become a standard is crispy outside, moist inside; flavored with a marinade of garlic, lemon, and parsley; and served with roast potato, roast onions, and whole cloves of baked garlic that become sweet when cooked. There are several seafood dishes, vegetarian plates, and an excellent Moroccan-inspired braised lamb with chick-peas, couscous, and preserved lemon; occasionally you'll find pheasant and sausage choucroûte with mustards and cornichons. The menu changes seasonally. Some excellent and expensive vintages are featured on the wine list, along with wine by the glass.

COPLEY SQUARE AREA

L'Espalier

30 Gloucester St. ☎ **617/262-3023**. Reservations required. Fixed-price four-course dinner $62. AE, CB, DC, MC, V. Mon–Sat 6–10pm. Subway: Green Line to Copley. CREATIVE AMERICAN.

Many Bostonians would agree that L'Espalier is one of the finest restaurants in town. For the city's ultimate dining experience, it may be equaled but can't be beat. This is an elegant restaurant in a turn-of-the-century Back Bay town house off Commonwealth Avenue. Reservations are sometimes difficult to get. You enter through a vestibule and walk up a flight of stairs to reach one of three formal dining rooms. Waiters in black and white attend to you immediately and are professional, polished, and friendly in their work. The menu changes daily and lists the chef's latest creations of contemporary American cuisine, which, though sometimes exotic, are really inspired and delicious. The wine list is extensive, offering more than 200 bottles. You won't soon forget a meal here.

NORTH END

⑤ Commonwealth Brewing Company

138 Portland St. ☎ **617/523-8383**. Reservations not required. Main courses $8–$15. AE, DC, DISC, MC, V. Mon–Thurs 11:30am–midnight, Fri–Sat 11:30am–1am, Sun noon–10:30pm. Subway: Green Line to Haymarket or North Station. AMERICAN.

Through the huge windows of this working brewery and restaurant near North Station and Boston Garden, the antique copper brewing equipment gleams and shines. In the high-ceilinged main dining room are long brass-clad tables and a long stand-up bar running the length of the back wall. There's a spirit of conviviality, inspired by the decor but forcefully encouraged by the Commonwealth's forte: golden ale, amber ale, bitter, and stout, brewed right here and served live. If you descend to the basement (where there are more tables and another long bar), you can witness the brewing. On weekends, the basement plays host to reggae and calypso bands. The menu is long and satisfying: Yankee rib fest grand-prize–winning ribs and a huge variety of fresh grilled offerings are a couple of examples.

Mama Maria Ristorante

3 North Sq. ☎ **617/523-0077**. Reservations are recommended. Main courses $7.50–$10.50 at lunch, $14.50–$25.75 at dinner. AE, DC, DISC, MC, V. Tues–Sat 11:30am–2:30pm; Mon–Sat 5–10pm, Sun 5–10pm. Valet parking available every evening (a wonderful bonus in the crowded North End). Subway: Haymarket (Green or Orange Line). NORTHERN ITALIAN.

🐤 Family-Friendly Restaurants

Pizzeria Regina *(see p. 90)*   One of Boston's best, and best-known, pizza parlors is always a best bet for children, and you can feed the whole family here for little more than $20, including beverages.

Serendipity 3   At Faneuil Hall Marketplace (☎ **617/523-2339**). Kids love to read the whimsical menu here and to eat such favorites as the foot-long chili hot dog, Tom Sawyer's potato skins, and the unforgettable frozen hot chocolate.

If you enjoy northern Italian cooking and Mediterranean cuisine, try this upscale North End restaurant. Favorites include grilled lamb chops served with roasted red peppers and veal tenderloins with shiitake mushrooms. Appetizers include scampi alla Nizza, shrimp served with warm tomato pulp, basil, and virgin olive oil; and fichi alla San Lorenzo, a combination of figs, goat cheese, prosciutto, and herbed vinaigrette. The pasta dishes are especially delicious prepared with seafood—lobster, shrimp, calamari, scallops, or mussels. And a full order can be split to serve two as a first course.

Pizzeria Regina

11¹/₂ Thacher St. ☎ **617/227-0765.** Reservations not required. Pizza $4.95–$14.25. No credit cards. Mon–Sat 10am–10pm. Subway: Orange Line to Haymarket. PIZZA.

If you have trouble finding Boston's most famous pizza place, located at the corner of Thacher and North Margin Streets, just ask anyone in the North End. Old dark-wood booths with Formica tables and a small bar for the solitary lunchers make up the interior. The decor is simple, but the pizzas are fancy, for the cooks know the secret of making a good one: the best imported cheese and tomato sauce, and a few dashes of real olive oil. A small, simple 10-inch cheese pizza feeds two moderately hungry people for lunch. You pay somewhat more with mushrooms, anchovies, sausage, or other toppings. The elaborate 16-inch Giambotta easily feeds a party of three or four. Beer and wine are served.

DOWNTOWN CROSSING

Locke-Ober

3 Winter Place. ☎ **617/542-1340.** Reservations recommended. Main courses $8–$22 at lunch, $17–$40 at dinner. AE, DC, MC, V. Mon–Fri 11:30am–3pm; Fri 6–10:30pm, Sat 5:30–10:30pm, Sun 5:30–10pm. Subway: Red or Orange Line to Downtown Crossing. AMERICAN.

This restaurant is a legend in town. Some Bostonians have lunch here every day at the same table and, even though there's a huge menu, choose the same classic favorites at each meal. The plates are stacked high, and so are the prices. Part of the attraction is the setting—the carved paneling, silver-plated service pieces, and mammoth German silver buffet covers on the long mirrored downstairs bar, which dates from 1880. The peach-complexioned nude in the painting over the bar is famous—many years ago one of Boston's morals-watching societies wanted her body covered. The upstairs dining room with a crystal chandelier, heraldic stained-glass windows, and leather chairs is the choice of those who prefer a clublike atmosphere.

But, of course, you've come for the food: rack of lamb, finnan haddie, wienerschnitzel à la Holstein, lobster stew, and the greatest dish on the menu, lobster Savannah, Locke-Ober's star for decades. It might be difficult to choose among them, but order one of the many desserts.

NEAR FANEUIL HALL/GOVERNMENT CENTER/ FINANCIAL DISTRICT

Durgin-Park Market Dining Rooms

North Market Bldg., 340 Faneuil Hall Marketplace. ☎ **617/227-2038.** Reservations not accepted. Main courses $4.95–$15.95. AE, MC, V. Mon–Sat 11:30am–10pm, Sun 11am–9pm. Subway: Green or Blue Line to Government Center. TRADITIONAL NEW ENGLAND.

Durgin-Park, a Boston institution for many years, boasts that it was "established before you were born," and adds that "Your grandfather and great-grandfather may have dined with us, too." As you mount the stairs to the dining room, it crosses your mind that you must have taken the wrong stairway, for there before you is all the dishwashing machinery and hard-working kitchen help, and right next to this, the kitchen itself, with cooks and waitresses scurrying here and there. To left and right are large, plain rooms with steam pipes running about on the ceiling, and several sets of long tables covered with checkered cloths. The menu, plainly printed with notices of daily specials stapled to it, bears pithy reminders and warnings such as "WASHROOM DOWNSTAIRS" and "WE ARE NOT RESPONSIBLE FOR ANY STEAK ORDERED WELL DONE." The food is of the highest quality, and portions are very large—after all, food is what you go to a restaurant for.

If you can, go for "dinner" (old Bostonese for the noontime meal) and order the Poor Man's roast beef or Yankee pot roast. At supper, try the huge prime rib (while it lasts, for this is the specialty). All steaks and chops are broiled on an open wood-burning fireplace. Seafood is received twice daily, and fish dinners are broiled to order. Be sure to try their clam chowder and Boston baked beans. (Buy some to take home at the Beanery in the Marketplace.) Homemade cornbread comes with every meal. For dessert, I strongly recommend that venerable New England specialty, baked Indian pudding (a molasses and cornmeal concoction, slow baked for hours and hours), luscious with ice cream; or the strawberry shortcake with fresh berries and whipped cream.

If you're going for "dinner," beat the crowd by getting there before 11:30am. Otherwise the long line may drive you to drink; happily, a stop at the Gaslight Pub downstairs permits you to wait in a shorter line before being seated upstairs. And, on Sunday when every other restaurant is serving a brunch of eggs and quiche, you can feast on full-course Durgin-Park dinners at their midday rates until 2:30pm. Perhaps the best time to go is at lunch, when the crowds are thinner, the portions are more manageable, and the prices are lower.

✪ Maison Robert

45 School St. ☎ **617/227-3370.** Reservations recommended. Main courses $16–$30; fixed-price meals $17 or $23 at dinner. AE, CB, DC, MC, V. Mon–Fri 11:30am–2pm; Mon–Sat 5:30–10pm. Paid valet parking available for both restaurants. Subway: Red or Green Line to Park Street. INNOVATIVE FRENCH.

Maison Robert is one of the finest French restaurants anywhere—to be exact, two of the finest French restaurants: the elegantly formal Bonhomme Richard on the main floor and the cozy Le Cafe on the ground floor. When the great chefs of France come to Boston, they dine with Lucien Robert, a restauranteur of uncompromising standards.

Decorated in French Second Empire style, the Bonhomme Richard is a gracious dining room with ornate moldings, crystal chandeliers, and stunning fresh flower arrangements. The new peach-and-rust color scheme is picked up in the modern Villeroy & Boch china. Lunch and dinner are served in the classical French tradition. Start with the wonderful *soufflé au crabe* (crab, corn, and mustard soufflé with a mango and lemon sauce) or *la tarte aux poireaux* (sautéed leek tart with saffron butter, sour cream, and caviar). As you proceed to the main course, you'll feast on the likes of *le carré d'agneau provençale à la française* (French-cut rack of lamb with garlic sauce), *le canard à l'Orientale* (roast Long Island duck breast with rice noodles, shiitake mushrooms, bok choy, and collard greens in a ginger garlic broth with deep-fried horseradish), and *la sole de la manche meunière* (Dover sole pan-fried with butter and lemon). Desserts are excellent. I love the *profiteroles exotiques* (profiteroles filled with toasted coconut ice cream in a warm dark rum sauce) and the *dessert aux cinq chocolates* (white and dark frozen chocolate torte in a chocolate almond cake with Godiva chocolate sauce). The service is as superb as the food, and there is a well-selected wine list that includes sauternes and ports and liqueurs.

Le Cafe has a less formal environment, and meals are less expensive, though they are thoroughly French in style and prepared with equal care.

If you're here in summer, get a table on the outdoor terrace next to the statue of Benjamin Franklin. This was the first outdoor statue in Puritan New England. There's jazz on the terrace in summer from 5:30 to 7:30pm.

Ⓢ Salty Dog Seafood Grille and Bar

Lower level of Quincy Market. ☎ **617742-2094.** Reservations not accepted. Main courses $4.95–$18.95; blackboard specials $8.95–$12.95. AE, DISC, MC, V. Daily 11:30am–11pm. Directions: Take the Green or Blue Line to Government Center; face the front of Quincy Market, with your back to Faneuil Hall, and walk to the right of the market facade; just under the southwest corner of the market is the stairway down to the Salty Dog. SEAFOOD.

Good fresh seafood and charcoal-grilled steak in congenial surroundings is the formula at this seafood grille and bar where you can have fish and chips, clams on the half shell, or any one of several fried or baked fish plates. In recent years, owner Roland Prevost has upgraded service and decor, and has added interesting specialties (Cajun, barbecue) to the menu. The oyster stew seems expensive, but you'll find at least half a dozen whole, succulent oysters in each bowlful. The double-tall Bloody Mary comes with a shrimp. There's a sidewalk cafe and open-air oyster bar for those who prefer eating outside.

Seaside Restaurant and Bar

188 South Market Bldg., Faneuil Hall Marketplace. ☎ **617/742-8728.** Reservations not required. Main courses $4.95–$8.95 at lunch, $9.95–$16.95 at dinner. AE, DC, MC, V. Daily 11:30am–10pm. Subway: Green or Blue Line to Government Center. SEAFOOD/AMERICAN.

Lunch is the time to dine here, although Seaside is busy all day. Elaborate sandwiches, complex salads, seafood, and quiches make up the midday bill of fare. Besides the natural-wood tables, Seaside has a bar at which you can sit to have a drink or a sandwich, or both. There's also an outdoor cafe on the main concourse of Faneuil Hall Marketplace, open for lunch, cocktails, and light dinner, weather permitting. At dinnertime Seaside features steaks, lots of seafood, and the chef's daily specialties; and on Wednesday, Friday, and Saturday there's live entertainment. Also, Sunday through Friday from 5 to 7pm you can take advantage of the $9.95 "Drive Time" three-course menu.

BACK BAY

Bangkok Cuisine

177a Massachusetts Ave. ☎ **617/262-5377.** Reservations not accepted. Main courses $8–$13.50. AE, DC, MC, V. Mon–Sat 11:30am–3pm; Mon–Thurs 5–10:30pm, Fri 5–11pm, Sat 3–11pm, Sun 4–10pm. Subway: Green Line to Hynes Convention Center/ICA. THAI.

This small, attractive place near Boylston Street is always busy serving Thai classics: clear soups made with scallions, shrimp, and hot peppers; savory dishes of duck with hot curry, tamarind sauce, snow peas, green peas, onions, and pimientos. Once you've tried the food here, you may indeed want to take off for Bangkok.

Have soup or an appetizer; a main course based on seafood, pork, beef, or chicken; a dessert; and a bottle of Thai beer. *A warning:* Soups are marked "moderately hot," but they're very spicy-hot (and very good).

Du Barry French Restaurant

159 Newbury St. ☎ **617/262-2445.** Reservations recommended. Main courses $4.25–$20 at lunch, $12–$20 at dinner. AE, CB, DC, DISC, MC, V. Mon–Fri noon–2:30pm, Sat 12:30–3pm; Mon–Sat 5:30–10pm, Sun 5:30–9:30pm Subway: Green Line to Copley. FRENCH.

Traditional French cuisine is Du Barry's specialty, and it can be enjoyed in the cozy dining room and, during the summer, in the private open garden and enclosed terrace. All the specialties from escargots to crepes Suzette are made to order. Consider coq au vin de bourgogne, chateaubriand sauce béarnaise, or brochette d'agneau grillé bordelaise, with an authentic French onion soup gratinée as an appetizer. At lunch you can have the onion soup with a salad at $5, or choose from a range of other entrées, including soft-shelled crabs, frogs' legs, and sea scallops.

This is also a great place to brush up on your French. Teachers have been bringing their students here to practice their language skills for many years.

Legal Sea Food

35 Columbus Ave. ☎ **617/426-4444.** Reservations recommended. Main courses $6–$22; meals $22–$36. AE, DC, DISC, MC, V. Mon–Thurs 11am–1:30pm and 4:30pm–10pm, Fri 11:30am–1:30pm and 4:30pm–11pm, Sat noon–11pm, Sun noon–10pm. Subway: Green Line to Arlington. SEAFOOD.

This Boston institution, located in the Boston Park Plaza Hotel, is a no-nonsense operation that prides itself on freshness and reasonable prices. The light and attractive restaurant is big, but nicely arranged into cozy sections. The menu is encyclopedic, listing close to 100 items, but this is for reference: When fresh stocks run out, that's it for any particular fish. Start with a shrimp cocktail or oysters on the half shell, and go on to scrod, bluefish, trout, lobster, salmon, or scallops. Note that there's often a wait for a table, and it's especially long on weekends.

CHINATOWN

Golden Palace Restaurant and Teahouse

20 Tyler St. ☎ **617/423-4565.** Reservations not required. Main courses $4–$7 at lunch; $5–$12 at dinner. AE, MC, V. Daily 8:30am–11:30pm. Subway: Orange Line to Chinatown or New England Medical Center. CHINESE.

The cuisine of Hong Kong is served at this enormous and ornate establishment. The food isn't the usual American-Chinese fare, a fact that hasn't escaped the local Chinese residents, who you'll see dining here every day. Good bets are the fried pork chop Peking style and the shrimp dinners. The dim sum, served daily from 8:30am to 3pm, is one of the best in Boston. As a result, the place is packed with diners and dim sum carts at lunchtime. The lunch menu also offers some good, inexpensive items, but the real reason to make a trip to the Golden Palace Restaurant and Teahouse is for the dim sum.

Imperial Seafood

70 Beach St. ☎ **617/426-8439.** Reservations recommended. Main courses $4.25–$5.50 at lunch; $9.95–$14.95 at dinner; dim sum $1.25–$2.75 per piece. AE, MC, V. Daily 9am–2am (dim sum served 9am–3pm). Subway: Orange Line to Essex. CANTONESE.

This restaurant in the heart of Boston's small Chinatown has been around for a long time, but has only recently been recognized for what it is: the best place in town for dim sum yum chai. The best time to go for the classic meal of Chinese

uvres is between 10 and 11am, or after 1:30pm on weekdays; other times,
l is dense.

Most of the patrons here are Chinese Bostonians who know a good thing, or
rather, things: spareribs, water chestnuts in gelatin, pork dumplings, tofu, green
sugarcane leaves stuffed with sweet rice, pork, and quail eggs, even fried duck
feet. Sit in the upstairs room for dim sum. The à la carte restaurant downstairs is
not as good. The system is this: You pick what you like from the carts, which
appear in a steady stream throughout the morning and afternoon. Each plate on
the cart has about three portions of the item (so it's good to do dim summing with
two friends). When you've had enough, the waiter counts up the plates and gives
you the bill, which will be very low considering the amount and quality of the
food.

BROOKLINE

Sol Azteca

914a Beacon St., Brookline. ☎ **617/262-0909.** Reservations recommended. Main courses
$9.85–$14.75. AE, MC, V. Dinner only, Mon–Thurs 5–10:30pm, Fri–Sat 5–11pm, Sun
5–10pm. Subway: Take a Green Line "Cleveland Circle" train and get off at the first stop
aboveground. MEXICAN.

The word got around quickly among devotees of Mexican food that the
guacamole, enchiladas (rojas, verdes, or Suizas), tacos, and tostadas at Sol Azteca
were authentic, delicious, and moderately priced. In fact, it's now considered by
many to be the best Mexican food in Boston. Dinner starts with chips, salsa, and
a bottle of Dos Equis or a glass of wine. Appetizers include the standard nachos
as well as other expected dishes, but also more exotic fare, such as cactus, which
is quite good. If you want a little of everything, try one of the combination
platters—they're a best buy. On Friday and Saturday, especially during college
term, it's very crowded, so get there early.

5 Attractions

THE TOP ATTRACTIONS
THE FREEDOM TRAIL

The sights of Revolutionary Boston are linked together by the Freedom Trail,
marked by a red line or double row of red bricks on the sidewalk. The trail leads
past almost all the important sights in 1¹/₂ miles; the outer loop of the trail goes
to the Bunker Hill Monument and the USS *Constitution* (Old Ironsides), across
Boston's Inner Harbor in Charlestown, 2¹/₂ miles from the Boston Common.

The Freedom Trail does, however, leave out many other important things to see.
The Freedom Trail has been divided into two walking tours here so that you can
see more without retracing your steps. If you follow "Beacon Hill and Downtown
Boston" and "North End and Charlestown," you'll have seen most of the sights
along the Freedom Trail, and many others besides.

If you'd rather not walk all of the Freedom Trail, you can ride the red
Beantown Trolley, 439 High St., Randolph (☎ **617/236-2148**), operated by
Brush Hill/Gray Line Tours. Schedules for the trolleylike bus vary with the
seasons, summer being the time when service is most frequent (about every 15
minutes from 9am to 4pm). Fare is $14 per adult ($10 for seniors), $7 per child
11 and under (kids under 5 ride free). Your ticket entitles you to hop on and off

Freedom Trail Attractions

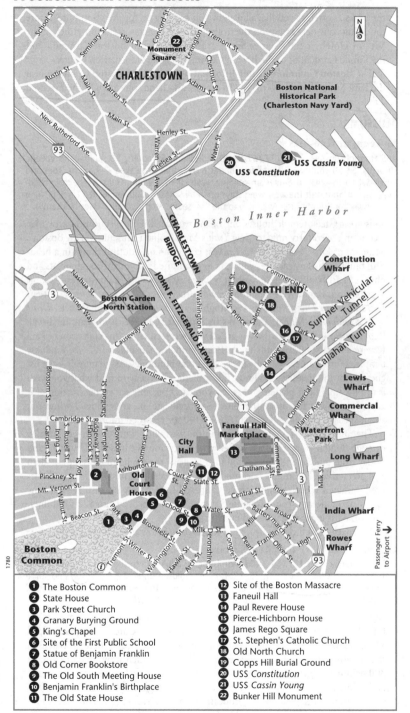

① The Boston Common
② State House
③ Park Street Church
④ Granary Burying Ground
⑤ King's Chapel
⑥ Site of the First Public School
⑦ Statue of Benjamin Franklin
⑧ Old Corner Bookstore
⑨ The Old South Meeting House
⑩ Benjamin Franklin's Birthplace
⑪ The Old State House
⑫ Site of the Boston Massacre
⑬ Faneuil Hall
⑭ Paul Revere House
⑮ Pierce-Hichborn House
⑯ James Rego Square
⑰ St. Stephen's Catholic Church
⑱ Old North Church
⑲ Copps Hill Burial Ground
⑳ USS Constitution
㉑ USS Cassin Young
㉒ Bunker Hill Monument

the buses as often as you like all day, or you can stay on for the 90-minute lecture tour. Buy your ticket right on the trolley, or at the Sheraton Boston Hotel, at the Westin Hotel, at the Charles Street crosswalk between Boston Common and the Public Garden, or at the Boston Common Visitor Information Center.

The **Boston Common Visitor Information Center,** on Boston Common near the Park Street Station (☎ **617/426-3115**), also hands out maps of the Freedom Trail.

MUSEUMS

Museum of Fine Arts

465 Huntington Ave. ☎ **617/267-9300.** Admission $8 adults, $6 seniors and college students, $3.50 youths 6–17, children under 6 free; free to all Wed 4–9:45pm. Tues and Thurs–Sat 10am–4:45pm, Sun 10am–5:45pm, Wed 10am–9:45pm. Thurs–Fri the main building closes at 5pm, but the west wing stays open till 9:45pm. Subway: Green Line "E" train ("Arborway" or "Huntington Avenue") to the "Museum" stop (just after "Northeastern").

This great Greek temple houses one of the world's finest collections of artworks, second in the country only to New York's Metropolitan Museum of Art. Boston's Museum of Fine Arts is a wonder, a vast collection of beautiful things in a beautiful building. Many pictures you may have admired for years through prints and photos in art books are here: Gilbert Stuart's *Athenaeum Head* portrait of George Washington; Renoir's *Le Bal à Bougival;* Burne-Jones's *The Love Song;* Whistler's *Girl in a White Dress;* works by van Gogh, Gauguin, Degas; lots of Monets; *Death of Maximilian* by Manet; and works by Japanese, Chinese, European, medieval, Renaissance, and baroque masters are all well represented. A fine collection of Paul Revere silver, several rooms taken from French châteaux, a full-size Japanese temple, a 9th-century Spanish chapel, Egyptian mummies, Assyrian seals—the list goes on for the treasures of almost 200 galleries. The way to find what you want is to pick up a floor plan as you enter; you can't possibly see even a fraction of it all, so pick out a few areas or rooms to concentrate on, and enjoy. To find out about special exhibits, call ☎ **617/267-9300** for recorded information.

The museum's restaurant is located in the west wing. Lunch is served Tuesday through Sunday from 11:30am to 2:30pm; dinner, on Wednesday, Thursday, and Friday from 5:30 to 8:30pm. Surrounded by glass, the dining room is ultramodern and attractive. The menu is often keyed to special exhibits—Chinese dishes predominated when the impressive Chinese bronzes were on display—and the prices are moderate. You can figure $10 to $12 for lunch, $18 to $22 for dinner. The wine list is short, good, and fairly priced.

For snacks and pick-me-ups, head for the cafe below the restaurant.

✪ Isabella Stewart Gardner Museum

280 The Fenway. ☎ **617/566-1401.** Admission $7 adults, $5 seniors and college students with ID ($3 on Wed), $3 youth 12–17, free for children under 12. Tues–Sun and some national holidays 11am–5pm. Directions: Walk west from the Museum of Fine Arts around its parking lot to the Fenway; turn right and walk two short blocks.

After visiting the Museum of Fine Arts, try to spend at least a few hours at the Isabella Stewart Gardner Museum nearby. "Mrs. Jack" Gardner early developed a love of art, and with her considerable wealth and the services of Bernard Berenson she set about to build an outstanding collection, which now includes almost 300 paintings, almost as many pieces of sculpture, close to 500 pieces of furniture, and hundreds of works in textiles, ceramics, and glass. Most of the holdings are from the great periods of European art, but classical and Asian civilizations are also represented. Not the least of the exhibits is the house itself, which was finished in 1901, and the museum opened in 1903. "Fenway Court" is not much to look at from the outside, but inside it's Mrs. Gardner's vision of a 15th-century Venetian palace, with many doors, columns, windows, and the like, which were brought from Europe and assembled around an open court topped by a glass canopy. The court is always planted with flowers, in bloom summer and winter, and several fountains bubble merrily at one end. Upstairs in one room is a dramatic portrait of "Mrs. Jack" herself, displayed with various masterpieces above a floor covered in tiles from Henry Mercer's Moravian tile and pottery works in Pennsylvania. Along a long gallery nearby, look for mementos of Mrs. Gardner's years, including letters from many of the great and famous of the turn of the century.

In March 1990 this lovely museum suffered a tragedy when art thieves dressed as police officers tricked the guards and made off with 12 masterpieces, including paintings by Degas and Rembrandt and a rare Chinese vase, worth hundreds of millions of dollars. The museum has bounced back, opening a special-exhibitions gallery on the first floor. Three to four changing exhibitions a year feature works from the museum's collections, as well as loans from private and public collections.

The Gardner Museum's popular concert series runs from September through May, with performances on Saturday and Sunday at 1:30pm in the elegant Tapestry Room. A concert fee of $4 (in addition to museum admission) is charged. The museum cafe offers a full bistro-style lunch menu and is open Tuesday through Friday from 11:30am to 3pm, until 4pm on Saturday and Sunday.

Museum of Science

Science Park. ☎ **617/723-2500.** Admission $7 adults, $5 children 3–14 and seniors, free for children under 3. Sun–Thurs 9am–5pm, Fri 9am–9pm. Closed Thanksgiving and Christmas. Subway: Green Line "Lechmere" train to Science Park.

Children are especially delighted here, for they can, for example, pat a reptile, confront a live owl or porcupine eyeball to eyeball, "stop" a drop of water in mid-air, weigh themselves in moon measurements, or climb into a space module. Exhibits run the gamut from a giant chicken egg incubator to a life-size replica of a *Tyrannosaurus* to a gargantuan magnifying glass.

The Big Dig takes museum-goers on a tour of Boston's Central Artery project. The exhibit—planned and executed in conjunction with state and federal transportation officials—includes cutaways of vehicles, a computer program that allows visitors the opportunity to "work as" a highway planner or crane operator, a simulated elevator ride into an excavation site, and several other interactive exhibits. There's also a brand-new preschool Discovery Center to help children become interested in science early in life.

In addition, there's the **Thomson Theater of Electricity,** where artificial lightning is produced twice daily, and an exhibit on the human brain, where you can test your brain's reactions to different stimuli. The museum also hosts national and international traveling exhibitions and special events. You should call to see what's featured while you're in town.

Don't miss the adjoining **Mugar Omni Theater,** where the movie screen actually wraps around the entire theater. You might be surrounded by penguins under Antarctic icebergs or go whizzing through outer space.

Across from the Omni Theater is the **Charles Hayden Planetarium** (there's an extra charge for the planetarium, and you should buy your ticket when you enter the museum, even if it's quite some time before the performances, since the shows sell out early), which puts on daily star shows. On weekends the planetarium hosts rock-'n'-roll laser programs.

Parking in the museum's own garage costs $2 an hour, with a maximum of $10 a day. Besides the rooftop Skyline Cafeteria, there's a Friendly's snack shop.

○ Boston Children's Museum

300 Congress St. ☎ **617/426-8855**. Admission $7 adults, $6 children 2–15, $2 1-year-olds, free for infants; $1 for everyone Fri 5–9pm. Sept–June, Tues–Sun 10am–5pm (until 9pm on Fri); June–Aug, daily 10am–5pm (until 9pm on Fri). Subway: Red Line to South Station; then follow the signs to Museum Wharf.

A short walk from Faneuil Hall and South Station, the Children's Museum is a great destination for families. Cultural exhibits allow families to explore the lifestyles of kids around the globe. Children can discover the world of science with exhibits featuring unusual physical science experiments; or they can set out on an adventure in the climbing exhibits that will take them up, up, and away. Some 30 current exhibits include *Teen Tokyo*, where kids can ride an authentic Japanese subway car, grapple with a sumo wrestler, and sing karaoke. *The Kids Bridge* is an interactive video tour that teaches children to value their own race and work against discrimination. The museum offers a series of rotating science exhibits, including *Under the Dock*, an environmental exhibit designed to teach kids about Boston's seaside eco-system, and kids can also play on the Science Playground.

Computer Museum

Museum Wharf. ☎ **617/423-6758**, or 617/426-2800 for the museum offices. Admission $7 adults, $5 students and seniors, free for children 4 and under; half price for everyone Sun 3–5pm. Labor Day–June 21, Tues–Sun 10am–5pm; June 22–Labor Day, daily 10am–6pm. Subway: Red Line to South Station.

"What?" you may say. "Computers aren't old enough to have a museum!" But they are. Some of the calculating and computing devices that are part of the collection at the Computer Museum on Museum Wharf go back centuries. It seems that we've always had a passion for number-crunching but have been unable fully to realize that passion until today. The abacus has been used in China for a millennium; Scottish mathematician John Napier (1550–1617), inventor of the logarithm, came up with a calculator called "Napier's Bones."

A $1-million interactive exhibit, *People and Computers: Milestones of a Revolution*, opened in 1991. A walk through the exhibit gives you an excellent briefing on how computers came to affect our lives so deeply. Another recently installed exhibit, *Tools & Toys*, allows visitors hands-on experience with 35 different exhibits, including a flight simulator.

In addition, the museum has 75 other hands-on, interactive exhibits. You can do everything from designing a bicycle on a graphics terminal to flying an airplane; creating your all-computer-generated music, animation, or even a commercial; or haggling over the price of strawberries with a computerized "vendor." There's an exhibition of vintage robots and computers, but perhaps most fascinating of all is the Walk-Through Computer™, a gigantic working personal computer you can use by trying out its 25-foot-long keyboard; results are displayed on a 108-square-foot monitor. Walk through the computer, past the giant chips, to find out how it all works. A major technical upgrade was planned for the fifth anniversary of the Walk-Through Computer™ in October 1995. Also, in November 1994 the museum opened a global computer networks exhibit called *The Networked Planet*.

The Computer Museum is right next door to the Children's Museum across Fort Point Channel from the Boston Tea Party Ship and Museum

SUGGESTED ITINERARIES

If You Have 1 Day

The best way to get the flavor of Boston both old and new is to walk the Freedom Trail. Besides leading you to many of the city's historical sites, the trail takes you past the financial and government districts to fun-filled Faneuil Hall Marketplace and the picturesque North End. Have lunch in Faneuil Hall Marketplace or the North End. To enjoy the trail fully will take a full day; if you cut it short, you may have time in the afternoon for a visit to one of the top museums—the Museum of Fine Arts or the Gardner Museum for the aesthetic-minded, the Museum of Science or the Computer Museum for those of a scientific bent. The kids are sure to like the New England Aquarium, the Children's Museum, and the Boston Tea Party Ship and Museum.

If You Have 2 Days

Start your second day with a walk through the Boston Common, the Public Garden, and Back Bay. Be sure to see some of the wonderful old houses along Commonwealth Avenue and the shops, cafes, and boutiques along Newbury Street. In the afternoon, pick another of the top museums or do some shopping and cafe-sitting. For nightlife, look into the current roster of musical events (there are dozens each night) or see what's doing in the Theater District.

If You Have 3 Days

On your third day it's time to cross the river for a look at Harvard Square and Harvard University in Cambridge. You can easily spend a full morning sightseeing, shopping, and cafe-sitting around the square. In the afternoon, head for Boston's Downtown Crossing. Take the Red Line subway from Harvard Square, get off at Downtown Crossing, and you can exit the station directly into Filene's Basement. For more shopping tips, see "Shopping," later in this chapter.

If You Have 5 Days

With five days to spend you can really get to know Boston. You'll have time to visit the Kennedy Library, the Boston Athenaeum, the Arnold Arboretum, and the Mapparium in the Christian Science Center. If you prefer, spend a day on an excursion to Salem, Gloucester, Rockport, Concord, or Plymouth (see Chapter 5, "Around Boston," for details).

MORE ATTRACTIONS

New England Aquarium

Central Wharf. ☎ **617/973-5200.** Admission $8.50 adults, $7.50 seniors, $4.50 children 3–11, free for children under 3; $1 off for everyone onThurs 4–7:30pm and Wed in summer. Mon–Tues and Fri 9am–6pm, Wed–Thurs 9am–8pm, Sat–Sun and holidays 9am–7pm. Winter hours vary. Subway: Blue Line to Aquarium.

It seems fitting that a sea-conscious city such as Boston should have a major aquarium, and it has exactly that in the New England Aquarium, on Central Wharf off Atlantic Avenue and two blocks from Faneuil Hall Market in the

❓ Did You Know?

- Boston area residents eat more ice cream per capita than do those of any other city in the country.
- Martin Luther King Jr. studied at Boston University and left it many of his important papers.
- "America" was first sung in the Park Street Church on July 4, 1831.
- The police commissioner of Boston ordered his officers to shave daily in 1901—the same year the Gillette Safety Razor Company was founded in Boston.
- The Boston subway system, which opened in 1897, was the first in the Western Hemisphere.
- Benjamin Franklin was born in Boston in 1706.
- Paul Revere, patriot, silversmith, dentist, and entrepreneur, was also the father of 16 children.
- Scollay Square, once the home of several storied strip joints, is now the site of Government Center and Boston City Hall.
- The Boston Red Sox sold Babe Ruth, who was their pitching star, to the New York Yankees in 1919 for $100,000.
- The Boston Stone, embedded in the side of a gift shop across from the Hancock House, at 10 Marshall St., was once the official center point of the city. All distances to and from Boston were measured from this point.
- Susan B. Anthony was arrested in Boston in 1872 for trying to vote in the presidential election.
- Kahlil Gibran, the Lebanese-American poet who wrote *The Prophet,* grew up in Boston's South End.
- A reproduction of the garret where Alexander Graham Bell invented the telephone and transmitted speech sounds over wire on June 3, 1875, is in the New England Telephone Building at 185 Federal St.
- The toothpick was first used in the United States at the Union Oyster House. The owner hired Harvard boys to dine there and ask for toothpicks as a way to promote his new business.
- Ether was first used to treat patients in the Bulfinch Pavilion at Massachusetts General Hospital.
- The first school in America, attended by John Hancock and Benjamin Franklin among others, was located in Boston. You'll find a plaque marking the spot on School Street.

redeveloped waterfront area (look for the twin Harbor Towers apartment buildings). The pride of the aquarium is one of the largest cylindrical, glass-enclosed saltwater tanks in the world, and this and other exhibit tanks are stocked with more than 600 species of marine life, from electric eels to sharks. In the ship *Discovery,* moored next door, sea lion presentations are put on daily for aquarium visitors (call for current show times). The variety of fishes is truly astounding, and the shapes, colors, and forms that evolution and adaptation have produced in these creatures really give one a sense of the richness of the marine environment.

The price of admission covers all exhibits, including the *Everglade* which features alligators, spiders, snakes, turtles, and fishes—plus daily multimedia presentations.

Boston Tea Party Ship and Museum

Congress Street Bridge. ☎ **617/338-1773.** Admission $6.50 adults, $5.20 students, $3.25 children 6–12, free for children under 6. Ship and museum, Mar 1–Nov 30, daily 9am–dusk (about 6pm in summer, 5pm in winter). Closed Dec 1–Feb 28 and Thanksgiving. Directions: Take the Red Line subway to South Station, walk north on Atlantic Avenue one block past the Federal Reserve Bank (which looks like a mammoth space-age radiator), turn right onto Congress Street and walk a block to the water, and there's the ship at Congress Street Bridge.

The events recalled here are very much a part of colonial Boston's struggle for independence. What you see here is the brig *Beaver II*, a full-size replica of one of the merchant ships emptied by the "Indians" on the night of the tea-party raid, and a museum with exhibits outlining the "tea party." Visitors can dump their very own bale of tea right into the waters of Boston Harbor. At the nearby Tea Party Store, you can buy some tea. Complimentary Salada tea is served—iced in summer, hot in winter.

Boston Athenaeum

10½ Beacon St. ☎ **617/227-0270.** Free admission. June–Sept, Mon–Fri 9am–5:30pm; Oct–May, Mon 9am–8pm, Tues–Fri 9am–5:30pm, Sat 9am–4pm. Subway: Red or Green Line to Park Street.

Tucked away atop Beacon Hill, facing the State House, is the Boston Athenaeum, near the Boston Common, an independent research library founded in 1807. The athenaeum's collections are strong in the history and literature of Boston and New England; its picture and sculpture collections were once, de facto, Boston's premier art museum. The neoclassical 19th-century reading rooms of this grand old Boston institution are used by members, their guests, and other approved researchers (you must have references). You can visit the athenaeum's second-floor gallery to view the current exhibition, or call and reserve a place on a guided tour of the building (Tuesday and Thursday at 3pm).

Institute of Contemporary Art

955 Boylston St. ☎ **617/266-5152,** or 617/266-5151 for recorded information. Admission $5.25 adults, $3.25 students, $2.25 seniors and children under 16; free for everyone Thurs 5–9pm. Wed–Thurs noon–9pm, Wed and Fri–Sun noon–5pm (call ahead for hours to be sure). Subway: Green Line "Boston College," "Riverside," or "Cleveland Circle" car to Hynes Convention Center/ICA Station.

Located across the street from the Prudential Center, the institute is a beautifully modern place inside a historic Richardsonian structure. Founded in 1936, the ICA is the oldest institution in the world dedicated to the presentation of contemporary art. The ICA has no permanent collection; rather, it presents an ever-changing series of exhibitions and programs. Shows may be anything from exhibits of sculpture and painting to photography, installations, and video. Special events include video programs, musical concerts, and evening lectures. All exhibitions change about every 6 to 10 weeks.

Boston Architectural Center

320 Newbury St. ☎ **617/536-3170.** Free admission. Mon–Thurs 9am–9pm, Fri–Sat 9am–5pm. Subway: Green Line to Hynes Convention Center/ICA.

There's often an interesting exhibit in the lobby of the Boston Architectural Center, at the corner of Hereford Street. The show will be connected in some way with architecture, whether it be the life and work of Henry Mercer, the

ner Boston Attractions

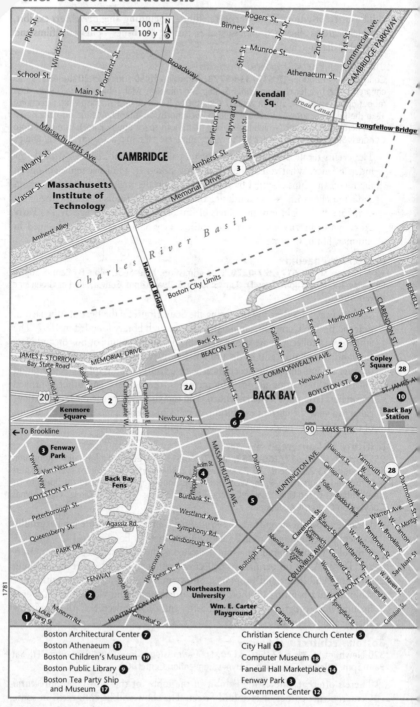

Boston Architectural Center **7**	Christian Science Church Center **5**
Boston Athenaeum **11**	City Hall **13**
Boston Children's Museum **19**	Computer Museum **18**
Boston Public Library **9**	Faneuil Hall Marketplace **14**
Boston Tea Party Ship and Museum **17**	Fenway Park **3**
	Government Center **12**

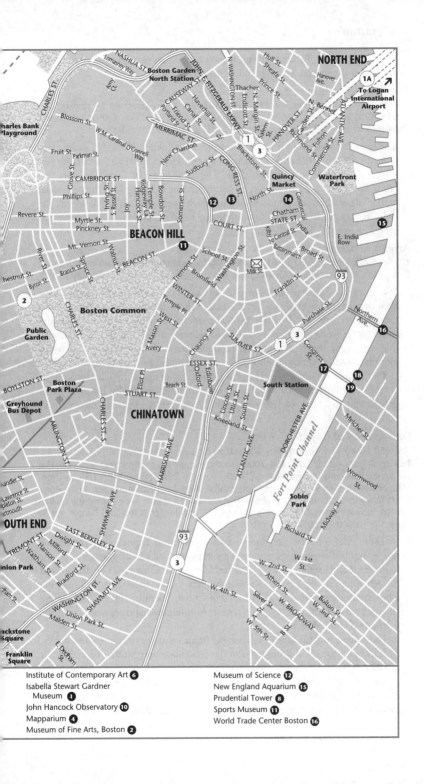

Institute of Contemporary Art ⑥

Isabella Stewart Gardner
Museum ①

John Hancock Observatory ⑩

Mapparium ④

Museum of Fine Arts, Boston ②

Museum of Science ⑫

New England Aquarium ⑮

Prudential Tower ⑧

Sports Museum ⑪

World Trade Center Boston ⑯

turn-of-the-century Pennsylvania tile maker; a collection of neon signs; or the thesis projects of the Boston Architectural School graduates.

The Kennedy Library

Columbia Point, Dorchester. ☎ **617/929-4523.** Admission $6 adults, $4 students and seniors, $2 children 6–15, free for children under 6. Daily 9am–5pm. Closed New Year's, Thanksgiving, and Christmas Days. Subway: Red Line to JFK/U. Mass. Station.

The nation's memorial to JFK is the museum at the John F. Kennedy Library. This dramatic chalk-white building, designed by the distinguished architect I. M. Pei, sits on a peninsula on Dorchester Bay. The landscaping of Cape Cod roses, sea grass, and weeping willows serves to harmonize the building with the peninsula, harbor islands, and sea. A new museum, which opened late in 1993, uses all the latest in audiovisual and museum technology to tell, chronologically, the story of John F. Kennedy's life and career.

Arnold Arboretum

125 Arborway, Jamacia Plain. ☎ **617/524-1718.** Free admission. Daily dawn–dusk. Subway: Orange Line to Forest Hills, or Green Line to Arborway (the Orange Line's probably faster).

Ever since this 265-acre park was given to the city by Harvard, Bostonians have been coming here to enjoy the peacefulness of the park and the more than 14,000 trees, plants, and shrubs from various parts of the world that make up the arboretum's "living collection." Spring is a fine time to catch the first blossoms like the lilacs, early summer brings the rhododendrons, and all through the warm months the scents here will bring back any nose dulled by the city air.

The Arnold Arboretum of Harvard University, designed by Charles Sprague Sargent and Frederick Law Olmsted, is maintained jointly by Boston's parks department and Harvard University, which uses it as an open-air classroom in botany.

First Church of Christ Scientist
(World Headquarters of the Christian Science Church)

175 Huntington Ave. ☎ **617/450-2000.** Hourly tours are arranged for free, or you can visit the various buildings on your own. Church, Tues–Fri 10am–4pm, Sun 11:30am–2pm; Mapparium, Tues–Fri 9:30am–4pm; Bible Exhibit, Wed–Sat 10am–4pm, Sun 11am–4pm. Hours may vary seasonally, so call ahead. Free parking is available while visiting the Church Center. Subway: Green Line "Boston College," "Riverside," or "Cleveland Center" car to Hynes Convention Center/ICA or Symphony.

In 1866 a devout New England woman experienced a quick recovery from a severe accident, attributing her cure to a glimpse of God's healing power as taught in the Bible and lived by Jesus. Thereafter, Mary Baker Eddy (1821–1910) devoted the remainder of her long life to better understanding, practicing, and teaching Christian healing; founding the Church of Christ, Scientist; and establishing the church's periodicals, including the renowned international daily newspaper, the *Christian Science Monitor.*

Today the Christian Science religion has branch churches in some 70 countries, with its headquarters in Boston, site of the denomination's Mother Church, built in 1894. Next to the church stands the Christian Science Publishing Society, home of the *Monitor* and other Christian Science publications. Two church office buildings and the Sunday school complete the church center. The whole complex, near Symphony Hall at the intersection of Huntington and Massachusetts Avenues, is a new Boston landmark, and it's right between two other landmarks, Symphony Hall and the Prudential Center.

Observing Boston from the Air

Take the Green Line to Copley Station or the Orange Line to the Back Bay stop for the **John Hancock Observatory,** 200 Clarendon St., at Copley Square (☎ **617/247-1977**). The ticket office entrance is on the corner of Trinity Place and St. James Avenue. This is the tallest building in New England. The observatory offers five multimedia exhibits, including *Boston 1775,* a sound-and-light show about the Revolution, as well as five new interactive computer exhibits that test your knowledge of Boston past and present. It's open Monday through Saturday from 9am to 11pm year-round; on Sunday, May to October hours are 10am to 11pm, and the rest of the year they're noon to 11pm. The last ticket is sold at 10pm. Adults pay $3.75; seniors and children 5 to 17, $2.75; children under 5 enter free.

The **Prudential Tower,** 800 Boylston St. (☎ **617/236-3318**), centerpiece of the Prudential Center, has a **skywalk** on the 50th floor with a full-circle panorama of the city. It's open from 10am to 10pm Monday through Saturday, and noon to 10pm on Sunday. Admission is $3.50 for adults, $2.75 for children 5 to 15 and seniors; children under 5 enter free. Two floors above is the Top of the Hub restaurant and cocktail lounge, and you can see the city for free when you buy a drink or a meal. To get to the Pru, take a Green Line "Arborway" car to Prudential Station, or a "Boston College," "Cleveland Circle," or "Riverside" car to Hynes Convention Center/ICA Station or Copley Station.

The main points of interest are the plaza and reflecting pool, the exterior of the Mother Church and its grand extension where services are held, and the Publishing Society's Mapparium and elegant sales room. You can take a 15- to 30-minute tour through the Mother Church or just take the elevator up to see the auditorium. This huge chamber is the main inner space of the church, which is built on the plan of a Byzantine church with its great dome and two semidomes.

The church's newest addition is a multimedia Bible exhibit, located across from the Sheraton Hotel & Towers, displaying rare Bibles and a giant Plexiglas map.

Sports Museum of New England

In the CambridgeSide Galleria, 100 CambridgeSide Place. ☎ **617/57-SPORT.** Admission $6 adults, $4.50 seniors and children 4–11, free for children under 4. Mon–Sat 10am–9:30pm, Sun noon–6pm. Subway: Green Line to Lechmere, then a short walk; or Red Line to Kendall Square, then a shuttle bus ride.

This museum is home to a collection of memorabilia from outstanding moments in New England sports history. There are bats, balls, skates, and sneakers (some size 15½) that belonged to the superstars of sports. Larger-than-life statues of Larry Bird, Bobby Orr, Eusebio, and Carl Yastremski stand by the cases displaying jerseys, baseball cards, programs, and print articles. Visitors can watch sports highlights in minitheaters modeled after Fenway Park, the Boston Garden, and Harvard Stadium. There are nine interactive exhibits, including *Catching Clemens, In the Net,* and *Stump Haggerty* (a sports-trivia contest). The museum's newest exhibits at press time include *Boston Bruins: Saluting 70 Years of Boston Bruins Hockey History,* and two more interactive exhibits (*Treadwall* helps you learn to climb rock walls, and *The Exploder* measures your vertical leap).

Frommer's Favorite Boston Experiences

Springtime in the Public Garden. Take time to smell the flowers—tulips, pansies, and flowering trees and shrubs. Ride the Swan Boats, feed the ducks, bring a sandwich and have lunch. Relax away from the bustle of the city.

Shopping at the Nostalgia Factory. You won't believe your eyes when you walk into the Nostalgia Factory, located on Newbury Street. Collectors of the odd and unique will lose themselves for hours here as they browse through things like old postcards, political pins, advertisements, and old posters. There's a gallery attached, in which you'll learn a thing or two about this country's recent history and social attitudes.

A Nighttime View from the Top. From a perch high up in the Hancock Tower of the Prudential Center, view the city in its nighttime glamour, a panorama of light all across town, from the Charles River to Boston Harbor.

Friday or Saturday Afternoon at the Haymarket. Whether you're in the market for fresh produce or not, the Haymarket is an experience you shouldn't miss. In addition to fruits and vegetables, there are some great shops for buying meats and cheeses here on Blackstone Street between North and Hanover streets. At the end of the day on Saturday, you might even walk away with a bargain or two.

An Evening at Boston Pops. The music at Symphony Hall is light and sparkling, like the champagne that is served. Pleasant music and great fun, especially on Old Timer's Night when everyone joins in the sing-along.

An Afternoon at the Sports Museum of New England. Sports enthusiasts will love visiting this museum with its incredible collection of sports memorabilia that includes bats, balls, jerseys, lifesize statues, and even shoes of New England sports greats.

A Visit to Faneuil Hall Marketplace and the Waterfront. Soak up the ocean breezes, walk along the waterfront, get some goodies at the food stalls, and watch the street performers at the marketplace—it's great fun at any time of day.

World Trade Center Boston

164 Northern Ave. ☎ **617/439-5000.** Admission varies with the event.

This 850,000-square-foot convention center, located on the waterfront, has a worldwide video-teleconference center, an exhibition hall, a conference center, and office space. The facility hosts more than 1,100 events throughout the year, including international, national, and regional trade shows; conferences; and special events. Call the center to find out what events will be going on during your visit.

TOURS

ORGANIZED TOURS **Bus Tours** A guided bus tour is the easiest way of all to get acquainted with the city and its landmarks, and the price for such an introduction is reasonable. **Boston Tours, Inc.,** 56 Williams St., Waltham (☎ **617/899-1454**), offers fully lectured tours of Boston's Freedom Trail and Cambridge daily from suburban hotels. **Harvard and MIT Tours** leave every day at various times and cost $20 for people 13 years and older; nothing, if you're 12 or under.

Sea Cliffs on the Atlantic. A trip to the rocky coastline north of the city in Marblehead and Rockport will be well worth your efforts. Climb the rocky cliffs along the shore and look out the sea, watch the sailboats, and admire the luxurious cabin cruisers.

A Few Hours at the Samuel Adams Brewery. Learn how this famous Boston beer is made, right at the brewery. You'll get a guided tour and will enjoy free tastings of the lager.

A Holiday Visit to the Isabella Stewart Gardner Museum. In December, the museum's garden courtyard is massed with brilliant poinsettias and the skylit atrium is ablaze with color. It's just delightful.

A Meal at No-Name. It doesn't look like much, you'll sit at communal tables with people you've never seen before, and it's filled to the bursting point with locals, businesspeople, and tourists, but don't let that stop you from heading on in (after you wait in line first). The fish served here is excellent. No-Name is located at 15¹/₂ Fish Pier.

Second-hand Book Shopping. In my opinion, the best place to shop for second-hand books is at Avenue Victor Hugo on Newbury Street. On a rainy day, you'll have no qualms about spending hours digging through the well-selected stock.

A Trip to the Boston Children's Museum. If you've got kids in tow, there's no better place to take them than the Boston Children's Museum. It's one of the best in the country, and it features multicultural interactive, educational exhibits.

A Walk Down Hanover Street. You'll feel like you've been transported right into the heart of Italy. Hanover Street is, in fact, the center of Boston's Little Italy, and it's a real treat to walk along enjoying the people and sights of this colorful neighborhood.

Shopping on Newbury Street. Don't miss a visit to this wonderful boutique-lined thoroughfare. It's a great place to pick up some unique clothing and accessories. It's also a pleasant place to do some window shopping.

They also offer a Boston Freedom Trail shuttle tour that uses open-air double-decker buses. Fares are $14 for adults, $5 for children. Contact them by phone (for Harvard tours: ☎ 617/495-1575; for MIT: ☎ 617/253-1000) or at the sightseeing desk of one of the larger hotels.

Cruises   A novel way to get acquainted with Boston is by taking a cruise in the harbor and Massachusetts Bay. **Bay State Cruise Company,** 67 Long Wharf, Boston, MA 02110 (☎ 617/723-7800; fax 617/457-1425), operates vessels that tour the waters of Boston from early spring to late fall. Ninety-minute cruises to Boston's Outer Harbor, with an optional visit at Geroge's Island State Park, depart several times a day; the price is $6.50 for adults, $5.50 for seniors, and $4.50 for children under 12. A 55-minute cruise of Boston's Inner Harbor is also available, with the option of going ashore at the Charlestown Navy Yard. Adult fare is $5, seniors $4, and children $3. These boats depart from the RED Ticket Office halfway down Long Wharf, opposite the Chart House Restaurant, near the Aquarium (Blue Line) subway station. In addition, cruises to Provincetown, Cape

Cod, and whale watches are also available. Call for exact dates and schedules. Bay State's administrative offices are located at 184 High Street, Suite 501, Boston, MA 02110.

Boston Harbor Cruises, One Long Wharf, White Ticket Center (☎ 617/ 227-4321), specializes in historic sightseeing tours. There are inner-harbor *Constitution* cruises, day and evening whale-watching safaris, and John F. Kennedy Library water shuttles. Call for details.

WALKING TOURS　For in-depth, self-guided walking tours, call **Cushing Tour Tapes,** 20 Park Plaza (☎ 800/998-TAPE). This company offers walking-tour audiocassettes that will guide you through Harvard/Cambridge and Beacon Hill and along the Freedom Trail. It provides you with the tape, the cassette player, and a color souvenir map. Call for information on where to go to rent the tapes.

The **Black Heritage Trail** is a walking tour of Beacon Hill and other Boston locales that figured prominently in the lives and careers of Bostonian African Americans. For information and trail pamphlets, contact the Boston African American National Service (☎ 617/742-5415) or the Museum of Afro-American History, 46 Joy St., on Beacon Hill (☎ 617/742-1854).

The **Boston Women's Heritage Trail** publishes a guidebook ($4) detailing walks that highlight the accomplishments of Boston women. The guidebook is sold at several stops on the Freedom Trail, including Old South Meeting House, the Paul Revere House, Old North Church, and the Globe Corner Bookstore. You can order it by mail ($5) from Boston Women's Heritage Trail Guidebook, 22 Holbrook St., Jamaica Plain, MA 02130 (☎ 617/522-2872).

If you prefer guided walking tours to hoofing it on your own, **Boston By Foot,** 77 N. Washington St., (☎ 617/367-2345 or 617/367-3766 for 24-hour recorded information) conducts architectural tours of Beacon Hill and other areas of interest from May through October. The guides, or docents, have completed a special instructional program and are quite knowledgeable about the architecture and history of the city. The 90-minute tours are given rain or shine. The "Heart of the Freedom Trail" tour starts at the statue of Samuel Adams in front of Faneuil Hall on Congress Street, Monday through Saturday at 10am and Sunday at 2pm. Tours of Beacon Hill begin at the foot of the State House steps on Beacon Street, Monday through Friday at 5:30pm, Saturday at 10am, and Sunday at 2pm. Other tours and meeting places are Copley Square tour, Trinity Church at noon on Friday and Saturday; the Waterfront tour, at the statue of Samuel Adams in front of Faneuil Hall on Congress Street, Sunday at 10am; and North End tour, at the statue of Samuel Adams at Faneuil Hall, Saturday at 2pm, Sunday at noon. Rates are $7 for adults and $5 for children; reservations are not required. Tickets may be purchased from the guide at any time of the tour.

Special-theme tours may be arranged if there are enough requests. Included in the request tours is the Boston Women's Heritage Trail, which covers areas in the North End, downtown, Chinatown, and Back Bay.

An especially noteworthy offering (also by Boston By Foot) is **Boston By Little Feet,** geared to children from 6 to 12 years old. The guide will present a child's-eye view of the architecture on the Freedom Trail and of Boston's role in the American Revolution. Children must be accompanied by an adult, and a free explorer's map is provided. Tours meet at the statue of Samuel Adams in front of Faneuil Hall on Congress Street, Saturday at 10am, Sunday at 2pm, rain or shine, and the cost is $5 per person.

Historic Neighborhoods Foundation, 2 Boylston St. (☎ 617/42
offers several walking tours that focus on neighborhood landmarks, i
Beacon Hill, North End, Chinatown, the waterfront, and financial dist...... The
"Make Way for Ducklings" tour, very popular with children and adults, includes
a ride on the Swan Boats in the Public Garden.

Schedules change with the season, and the programs are based on themes, such
as social history and topographical development. Write or call Historic Neighborhoods Foundation for current schedules and meeting places.

In addition, the **National Park Service** (☎ 617/242-5642) organizes daily free
walking tours of historic sights in downtown Boston.

You can't pick the flowers, but you can have a wonderful time on the Boston
Park Rangers' free guided **walking tours of Boston's "Emerald Necklace,"** a
network of green spaces tying the city to the suburbs designed by landscape
architect Frederick Law Olmstead. This tour covers outstanding parks and gardens,
including Boston Common, Public Garden, Back Bay, Commonwealth Avenue
Mall, Muddy River in the Fenway, Olmstead Park, Jamaica Pond, Arnold
Arboretum, and Franklin Park. The full six-hour walk includes a one-hour tour
of any of the sites. For hours and schedules, call ☎ 617/635-7383.

Of course, you can also follow the two walking tours below.

Sail Loft
80 Atlantic Ave.

WALKING TOUR 1
Beacon Hill & Downtown Boston

Start: Boston Common (subway: Red or Green Line to Park Street).
Finish: Faneuil Hall Marketplace.
Time: Two hours, more if you tour several buildings; the distance is about a mile.
Best Times: Sunday morning is most peaceful, but any morning will do. (Note
that the State House is closed on the weekend.)

From Park Street station, exit at the easternmost corner of the:

1. **Boston Common,** the colonial town's "common pasture land," to which any
citizen's cows could be brought. Though this is now the city's most popular
park, the pasture ordinance is still in effect. No one seems to take advantage of
it—as if with all the picnickers, sunbathers, soapbox orators, street buskers, and
pitch persons there'd be any room left for a cow to graze! The entrance to Park
Street Station is Boston's unofficial "speaker's corner," where ideologues hold
forth on their political, social, and religious beliefs.

Stroll through the Common as you like, making your way up the slope to the:

2. **Massachusetts State House** (☎ 617/727-3676), which dominates Beacon Hill
and the Boston Common, its gold dome shining and visible for miles. It was
designed by Charles Bulfinch, Boston's most famous and best-loved architect,
and built at the end of the 1700s. This is where the Massachusetts General
Court (legislature) sits today; in its archives (which you can visit) are curious and
famous documents relating to the history of the colony of Massachusetts Bay
and the early republic. The State House is open Monday through Friday from
10am to 4pm.

From the rear (north) side of the State House, turn left and walk along:

3. **Mount Vernon Street,** the prettiest street on Beacon Hill, Boston's prettiest
residential neighborhood. The brick Federal-style houses (see "Art and Architecture" in Chapter 1) are all superbly kept. In a few minutes you'll come to:

4. **Louisburg Square,** laid out in the 1840s with its tiny private park. The square is Beacon Hill's architectural gem and its most prestigious address. The park is owned in common by the residents of the houses facing the square.

   Continue down the hill on Mt. Vernon to West Cedar Street and turn left. The next street on the left is:

5. **Acorn Street,** a short street that's so picturesque it's almost synonymous with Beacon Hill. If you see a photograph of a Beacon Hill street, it's probably Acorn Street.

   Continue to the next corner and turn right onto Willow Street, following it to Chestnut Street, like Mt. Vernon Street lined with fine Federal brick row houses. Go left. At the top of Chestnut Street turn left, then right on Mt. Vernon, then left on Joy Street. Descend the hill on Joy to the corner with Myrtle, near which you'll see the:

6. **African Meeting House,** 46 Joy St., at Smith Court (☎ **617/742-1854**), built in 1806 and now the nation's oldest African-American church building. Though it's now set up as a museum, it was once the venue for speeches by abolitionists William Lloyd Garrison and Frederick Douglass. The meeting house is open for tours on Saturday and Sunday at 10am, noon, and 2pm. Admission is free. Equally interesting is the:

7. **Museum of Afro-American History,** also at 46 Joy St. (☎ **617/742-1854**), open Monday through Friday from 10am to 4pm.

   Walk back up Joy Street, around to the front of the State House and down Park Street, back to the intersection of Park and Tremont Streets. Directly across Park Street from the subway station entrance is the:

8. **Park Street Church** (☎ **617/523-3383**), the tall-steepled, graceful church designed by Peter Banner and built in 1809. William Lloyd Garrison thundered against slavery from the pulpit here in 1829 and thus began his long abolitionist campaign. Take a look inside so that you can compare this early 19th-century church with the earlier churches farther along the Freedom Trail. The church is open to visitors from late June to late August, Tuesday through Saturday from 9:30am to 4pm; closed, July 4. Congregational services are held all year on Sunday at 10:30am and 6:30pm.

   Exit the church, turn left, and walk along Tremont Street a few steps to the:

9. **Old Granary Burying Ground,** last resting place for some of the American Revolution's most famous figures, including Samuel Adams, Peter Faneuil, John Hancock, and Paul Revere. Crispus Attucks and the other victims of the Boston Massacre (March 1770) were laid to rest here, as were Benjamin Franklin's parents. The cemetery took its name from a nearby granary, now long gone. Take a walk through—you'll constantly be surprised and delighted by the names, dates, and mottoes on the finely carved headstones.

   Continue northeast on Tremont Street to the intersection with School Street, and you'll see:

10. **King's Chapel,** which dates from 1754. Once the Anglican church of the royal governors, then the Episcopalian church of Boston's great personages, this dark mass of granite is now a Unitarian meeting house. The bell was cast by Paul Revere and is the largest he ever made. In the burying ground next to the chapel are the graves of John Winthrop (1588–1649), first governor of the Massachusetts Bay colony, and many of his family, as well as other Boston notables.

Walking Tour—Beacon Hill & Downtown Boston

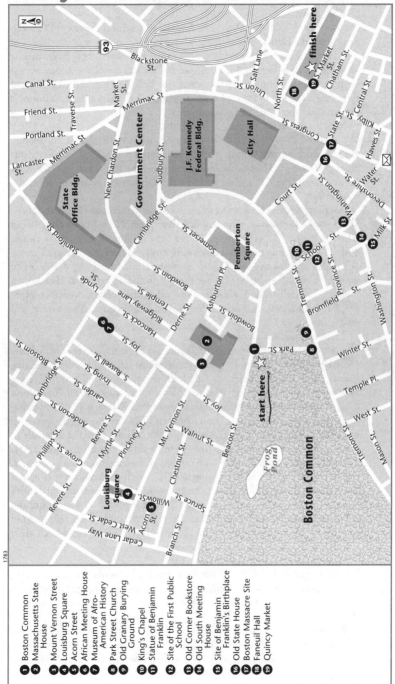

1783

① Boston Common
② Massachusetts State House
③ Mount Vernon Street
④ Louisburg Square
⑤ Acorn Street
⑥ African Meeting House
⑦ Museum of Afro-American History
⑧ Park Street Church
⑨ Old Granary Burying Ground
⑩ King's Chapel
⑪ Statue of Benjamin Franklin
⑫ Site of the First Public School
⑬ Old Corner Bookstore
⑭ Old South Meeting House
⑮ Site of Benjamin Franklin's Birthplace
⑯ Old State House
⑰ Boston Massacre Site
⑱ Faneuil Hall
⑲ Quincy Market

Walk down School Street to the:

11. Statue of Benjamin Franklin. Most Americans remember the story of Franklin getting off the boat in Philadelphia with very little money and two loaves of bread for sustenance to begin his famous career, but some people forget that he was coming from Boston, his birthplace (1706) and childhood home; he was born in a house on nearby Milk Street (see below). This statue by Richard Greenough (1856), in front of Boston's old city hall, pays tribute to Boston's famous son, who is buried in Philadelphia.

Near the statue (follow the red line) is the:

12. Site of the First Public School to be established in the American colonies (1635), which boasted Cotton Mather, Benjamin Franklin, and Samuel Adams among its alumni. Though the building is gone, the school survives as Boston Latin School, the city's most prestigious high school, now located in the western part of the city.

Continue down School Street to the corner of Washington Street and the:

13. Old Corner Bookstore. The building dates from 1718, but its fame began when it became a gathering place for famous American authors in the 19th century. At that time bookstores were also publishers, and Messrs. Ticknor & Fields, who ran the Old Corner Bookstore, published and drank coffee with the outstanding literary men of the age, including Emerson, Hawthorne, Holmes, Longfellow, and Whittier. Now called the Globe Corner Bookstore (☎ **617/523-6658**), at 3 School St., it specializes in books about travel and adventure.

Turn right and walk a block to the:

14. Old South Meeting House, at 310 Washington St., at the corner of Milk Street (☎ **617/482-6439**). New England congregations call their buildings meeting houses rather than churches, and it's from this that the Old South Meeting House gets its name, although it was used for town meetings as well. (Old North Church, from which the lanterns hung to signal Paul Revere, is a different building farther along the Freedom Trail.) Built in 1729, the meeting house saw its most famous meeting on December 16, 1773, when a group of colonials in Native American dress set out from here to throw the Boston Tea Party. Today the building is a museum with exhibits of historical documents, currency, furniture, and a scale model of Boston in 1775, which gives you a very clear idea of the size and layout of the town. An audiovisual show recounts Old South's history. Admission to Old South costs $2.50 for adults, $2 for seniors and college students, $1 for children 6 to 18; children under 6 free. Open April through October, daily from 9:30am to 5pm; November through March, daily from 10am to 4pm (to 5pm on weekends).

Around the corner on Milk Street is the:

15. Site of Benjamin Franklin's Birthplace, marked by an obscure plaque on the side of a skyscraper. Though Franklin (1706–90) made his fame and fortune in Philadelphia, he was a Boston native who learned his printing trade here in the shop of his half brother, James.

Backtrack on Washington Street, past the Old Corner Bookstore, to find the:

16. Old State House, at 206 Washington St. The charming brick building dates from 1713 and was built to house the colonial government. After the Revolution it was known as the State House, and after the present State House was built in 1795, this one became the Old State House. The Declaration of Independence was first read to Bostonians from its balcony in 1776. From that same balcony, Washington addressed the citizens of Boston in 1789. Now that the building is hemmed in by giant buildings on all sides, much of the dignity it must have held for colonial and Revolutionary Americans is lost. Inside, a museum has changing exhibits. Historical talks are given on the hour. There's an entry fee to the museum (☎ **617/720-3290**): $2 for adults, $1.50 for senior citizens and students, 75¢ for children 6 to 18, free for children under 6. Summer hours are 9:30am to 5pm every day.

Walk east down Court and State Streets two short blocks to the:

17. Boston Massacre Site, near the corner of State and Congress Streets, where on March 5, 1770, colonists protesting the excesses of the royal government confronted some British soldiers who then fired into the crowd, killing five men. The incident served to enflame anti-British feeling in the colonies, which led, five years later, to the outbreak of the Revolutionary War.

Turn left and go down Congress Street half a block to:

18. Faneuil Hall (*fan*-yool or *fan*-l), the "Cradle of Liberty," so called because of citizens' meetings that were held here before and during the Revolution. The handsome brick building was erected by the town of Boston in 1742 with money given by Peter Faneuil; designed by John Simbert, it was later enlarged by Charles Bulfinch (1805). The ground floor was originally a food market and is now filled with shops; the second floor was—and is—used for public meetings; and the third floor houses the headquarters of Boston's most famous chowder-and-marching society, the Ancient and Honorable Artillery Company. The entrance to the second-floor meeting hall is from the east side; National Park Service guides are on hand to tell you all about the building: The huge painting dominating the front of the hall, they will tell you, is of Daniel Webster speaking on the virtues of a close union of states (as opposed to states' rights). The speech was given in Washington in 1830, not in Faneuil Hall, but the painting must have inspired hundreds of less-talented, although perhaps equally long-winded, orators. Entrance to the hall is free.

Facing Faneuil Hall is the stout gray granite facade of:

19. Quincy Market, named for Boston Mayor Josiah Quincy, who had it erected in 1826, along with the large Greek Revival market buildings on either side. Quincy Market was Boston's larder for a century before the changing patterns of commerce and provisioning led to its decline. Its restoration in the 1970s, along with the North Market and South Market buildings, has created the booming Faneuil Hall Marketplace you see today. (For details on shopping in the marketplace, see "Shopping," later in this chapter.)

🔊 TAKE A BREAK   Faneuil Hall Marketplace is filled with snack shops, chowder houses, cafes, delis, bakeries, and restaurants. If you want only a snack or light lunch, wander through **Quincy Market** and pick up freshly baked bagels, bags of dried apricots, nuts or Turkish figs, fragrant French bread, Italian salads, Chinese finger food, or any of a hundred other treats. For restaurant suggestions, see "Dining," earlier in this chapter. If it's raw clams or oysters you crave, drop in for a dozen at the **Union Oyster House,** Boston's oldest restaurant (see "Walking Tour 2," below).

WALKING TOUR 2
North End & Charlestown

Start: Faneuil Hall Marketplace (subway: Green Line to Government Center).
Finish: USS *Constitution* (Old Ironsides) in Charlestown.
Time: Two hours, more if you tour several buildings; the distance is about two miles.
Best Times: Anytime; the open-air market is on Friday and Saturday; Old North Church has services Sunday morning.

From Faneuil Hall Marketplace, cross North Street and walk up Union Street past:

1. Ye Olde Union Oyster House, at 41 Union St. (☎ 617/227-2750), Boston's oldest restaurant still in operation; it's been here since 1826.

Continue walking north, then turn right, and if it's Friday or Saturday you'll be in the midst of:

2. Haymarket, the name by which Boston's open-air produce market is generally known. Every Friday and Saturday, this area is thronged with costermongers selling fresh fruits and vegetables in Boston's weekly outdoor market. To get to the North End, look for the pedestrian passage beneath the Central Artery (Fitzgerald Expressway). (*Note:* The massive Central Artery construction project may have changed the face of this area by the time you arrive. Watch for Freedom Trail signs or signs for Paul Revere's House.)

On the northeastern side of the Central Artery is the North End, Boston's "Little Italy." The first street you'll see is:

3. Salem Street, the narrow street lined with Italian groceries, butchers, fish stores, and other shops. Turn right and walk one block to:

4. Hanover Street, the "main street" of the North End, lined with Italian-style cafes and stores. Walk two blocks up Hanover to Prince Street and turn right to reach North Square and the:

5. Paul Revere House, at 19 North Sq. (☎ 617/523-2338), a small clapboard dwelling surrounded by crooked cobblestone streets. It's the only house left in downtown Boston that was built in the 1600s. Paul Revere moved in about a century after the house was built, and he lived here during the Revolutionary period. The house would be interesting even if the great patriot had never set foot in it, with its quaint weathered exterior, small windows, and wide floorboards. But furnished in colonial style, with explanatory materials, the house is better than an hour's history lecture. Admission is $2.50 for adults, $2 for seniors and college students, $1 for children 5 to 17, free for children under 5. No photography is allowed inside the house. Hours are 9:30am to 4:15pm in winter, to 5:15pm in summer; closed Monday January through March.

Walk back down Prince Street to Hanover Street, turn right, and walk a few very short blocks to the:

6. Paul Revere Mall, with its equestrian statue of the Revolutionary hero. The church at the southeastern end of the mall and across Hanover Street is St. Stephen's, built by Boston's favorite architect, Charles Bulfinch.

At the northwest end of the mall stands:

7. Old North Church, at 193 Salem St. (☎ 617/523-6676). You can see by the church's location why it was a good place from which to give a signal. The code, as every schoolchild knows, was "one if by land, two if by sea," and it was two lanterns hung in the tower that started Paul Revere on his fateful night ride to warn the colonials that British troops were heading out from Boston to search for hidden arms. It's the oldest church building in Boston (1723) and is today officially known as Christ Church in the city of Boston. A walk around inside turns up many curiosities that bear on the history of Boston and the United States, plus memorial plaques to famous men, nameplates on the very high pews. The tall graceful windows of Old North Church are exceptionally fine.

Although it's hemmed in by houses and shops on all sides, Old North Church does have a set of tiny terraces and gardens on its north side, open to the public. The small formal garden and the fountain are good to refresh your spirit on a hot day, and the memorial plaques set into the walls are, in some cases, delightful. Donations are appreciated. It's open daily from 9am to 5pm; visitors are also welcome for Sunday services at 9am, 11am, and 4pm. There's also a gift shop that's open daily from 9am to 5pm.

Go left on Salem Street until you reach Hull Street. Turn right and walk uphill on Hull Street past no. 44, the narrowest house in Boston, to find:

8. Copps Hill Burying Ground, the second-oldest cemetery (1660) in the city. Among the cemetery's permanent inhabitants is fiery Puritan preacher Cotton Mather. Some of the tombstones were marked by British musket balls during the Revolution. You can visit daily from 9am to 4pm. While you're up on Copps Hill, look across to Bunker Hill, with its obelisk monument, and the old Charlestown Navy Yard to see the tall masts and complicated rigging of the USS *Constitution.* To reach the ship you must walk over a mile, across the Charlestown Bridge and to the right; you might want to take a taxi instead.

9. Bunker Hill. The 200-foot granite obelisk that towers above Charlestown marks the spot where Col. William Prescott of the Continental Army stood with his small force and held off wave after wave of attack by British regulars on June 17, 1775. Their ammunition running low, Col. Prescott cried to his men, "Don't fire until you see the whites of their eyes" in order to make each shot count. When their ammunition was exhausted, the Americans were forced to retreat, but the battle had caused grievous casualties to Boston's British garrison. Most of Charlestown surrounding the hill was burnt by the British during the engagement.

Construction began on the monument in 1828, half a century after the battle. There's a fine view of Charlestown, the navy yard, and Boston from the top, 295 steps up (no elevator!).

Down the hill, docked in the decommissioned navy yard, is the:

10. USS *Constitution* (Old Ironsides) (☎ 617/242-1812). Launched in 1797, it's the oldest commissioned warship in the world still afloat. Today you can see more of Old Ironsides than ever before as it sits in Dry Dock No. 1 at the Charlestown Navy Yard for inspection and repairs. Free guided tours led by sailors in 1812 uniforms are available 365 days a year from 9:30am to 3:50pm, and self-guided tours are permitted from 3:50pm to sunset. The nearby USS *Constitution* Museum (☎ 617/426-1812; $3 for adults, $2 for students and seniors, $1.50 for kids 6 to 16, free for children under 6 and active military) houses many artifacts dealing with the *Constitution*'s history and its 40 battles at sea (all won). There is also a *Life at Sea* exhibit showing what shipboard life was like in 1812. The Boston National Historical Park at the Charlestown Navy Yard also offers programs on the yard and the history of American shipbuilding in the Visitor Information Center in Building 5.

Walking Tour—North End & Charlestown

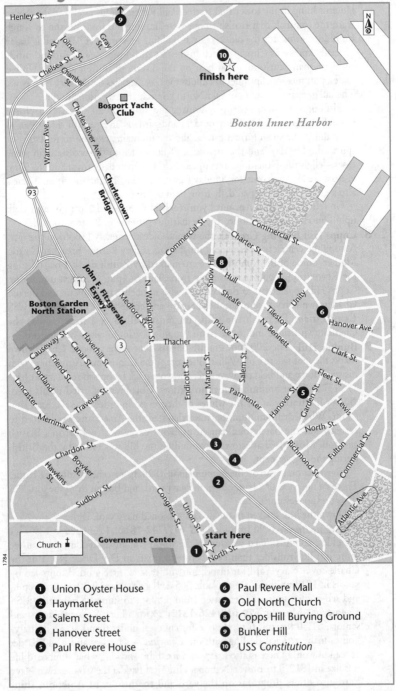

1. Union Oyster House
2. Haymarket
3. Salem Street
4. Hanover Street
5. Paul Revere House
6. Paul Revere Mall
7. Old North Church
8. Copps Hill Burying Ground
9. Bunker Hill
10. USS *Constitution*

Henley St.
Park St.
Joiner St.
Gray St.
Chelsea St.
Chamber St.
Charles River Ave.
Warren Ave.
Charlestown Bridge
93
Bosport Yacht Club
Boston Inner Harbor
finish here
John F. Fitzgerald Expwy.
1
Boston Garden North Station
Medford St.
N. Washington St.
Commercial St.
Charter St.
Commercial St.
Snow Hill
Hull
Sheafe
Unity
Tileston
N. Bennett
Hanover Ave.
Clark St.
Fleet St.
Lewis
Prince St.
Thacher
Endicott St.
N. Margin St.
Salem St.
Parmenter
Hanover St.
Garden St.
North St.
Richmond St.
Fulton
Commercial St.
Causeway St.
Haverhill St.
Canal St.
Friend St.
Portland
Lancaster
Traverse St.
Merrimac St.
Chardon St.
Bowker St.
Hawkins St.
Sudbury St.
Congress St.
Union St.
Government Center
start here
North St.
Atlantic Ave.
Church
1784

6 Special & Free Events

Lots of films are shown for free in Boston, or very nearly for free—the **college film series** at many Boston colleges often charge as little as $1 for admission. Newspaper listings may or may not have information about college film series, and indeed the movie to be shown, place of screening, and even date and time may change without notice except for a few mimeographed flyers stuck up here and there on the campus. Still, try calling one of the college switchboards and asking about "the film series." For Harvard, check the *Gazette,* a weekly (less often when classes are not in session) newspaper about the university available for free in the University Information Office, Holyoke Center, Harvard Square.

More dependable and predictable than the college film series are the films shown fairly regularly by these institutions, all for free. The **Boston Public Library** (☎ **617/536-5400**) shows various films in the lecture hall and at the library's branches throughout the city. Take the Green Line to Copley. The **Institute of Contemporary Art,** 955 Boylston St. (☎ **617/266-5151**), screens various films usually having to do with modern art or artists; see "Attractions," earlier in this chapter, for transportation details.

7 Outdoor Activities

BEACHES

Although Boston is situated right on the water, people don't come here for surf and sand. There are several beaches in South Boston (Castle Island Beach, M Street Beach, Pleasure Bay, Carson Beach, and City Point Beach, off Day Boulevard) and Dorchester (Malibu Beach, Tenean Beach, and Savin Hill Beach, off Morrissey Boulevard); however, they're not the nicest of spots, so I'd recommend that you look beyond the Greater Boston Area for a day at the beach. You might take an hour's drive south on Route 3 or take a boat to **Nantasket Beach,** a large, well-equipped public beach in Hull. Or you can go farther south to **Duxbury** near Plymouth for a clean, quiet, 9-mile beach with dunes. The beach is located off Routes 3A and 139. Public parking is at the north end. Going north from Boston, try **Revere Beach,** which has an expanse of sandy beach and a gentle surf. Parking along the beach is free. Or take the MBTA to Revere Beach or Wonderland stations, 20 minutes from downtown. If you have a car, drive up to the end of the beach, near Point of Pines and the General Edwards Bridge, for less crowded swimming. Even more spacious, with clear, cold water for swimming, is **Nahant Beach,** about 3 miles north. (I should warn you that the temperature of the water at the North Shore beaches is apt to be quite low; they're not as cold as the beaches of Maine, but not as warm as those on the South Shore and Cape Cod.) If you're going to Nahant, get there early in the morning, especially on the weekends, since parking is just $1 and spaces fill up fast.

You could also take a one-day trip to Salem, where you can explore old houses and some outstanding museums, swim at Salem Willows, or take a boat ride to historic Marblehead, home of the American navy and now host to the chic yachting set, a great place to walk around, with its quaint streets, vintage houses, and fun shops; continue on to Gloucester, home of the fishing fleet; and to the picturesque artists' colony at Rockport. But for the very best swimming on the

North Shore, you should drive rather (a little more than an hour from the city) to Ipswich's beautiful **Crane Beach,** with its picturesque dunes, miles of white sand, and crisp, cold water. Admission is $6.50 during the week, $10 on weekends, but it's worth it, since many of the other North Short beaches are for residents only. The drive, incidentally, will take you through what is called "John P. Marquand country"— those elegant little villages where the Boston Brahmins have long escaped the summer heat.

If the parking lot at Crane is full (get there by 10am), try some of the other North Shore beaches. There are two fine places in Gloucester. **Wingaersheek Beach,** just off Route 128 (Exit 13), has beautiful white sand, a fantastic view, and sand dunes for climbing or hiding behind to seek privacy. It's open through Labor Day, and there's also a charge for parking. **Stage Fort Park,** Route 128 (Exit 13), is at Gloucester Harbor and has 100 acres of oceanfront with sheltered beaches, playgrounds, picnic and cookout areas, and an old fort site for the kids to explore. If you'd like a stretch of several beach areas with magnificent dunes and a strong surf (surf fishing is allowed), take Route 1A to Newburyport and **Plum Island,** which is part of the Parker River Wildlife Refuge, with nature trails, observation towers, and wildlife. There is no admission or parking charge, but the small lots fill up early—sometimes cars are turned away at 9am.

Just a word of warning: Wingaersheek, Plum Island, and Crane beaches are host to greenhead flies as well as swimmers for a few weeks in late July and early August. Bring insect repellent with you. These beaches have lifeguard services and bathhouses.

Other fine area beaches include **Salisbury Beach,** Route 1A, south of the New Hampshire border, which has spectacular surf; and **Good Harbor Beach,** Gloucester, also with a fine surf, on Thatcher Road off Route 127A.

HARBOR ISLANDS EXPLORATION

Boston's Harbor Islands are treasures that the locals like to keep to themselves. There are 30 islands in the outer harbor, some of which are open for exploring, camping, or swimming—great spots for the day-tripper. George's Island is the most popular, with an old fort built in 1834; it's open for guided tours and is rumored to have a resident ghost! There is a visitor's center, refreshment area, fishing pier, place for picnics, and a wonderful view of Boston's skyline. From there, free water taxis run to Lovell, Gallops, Peddocks, Bumpkin, and Grape Islands, which have picnic areas and campsites (permits are required—call ☎ 617/740-1605). Lovell Island has a sandy beach and is the only one with supervised swimming. Boats leave from Long Wharf and Rowes Wharf. The islands are part of the Boston Harbor Islands State Park.

Impressions

When I got into the streets [of Boston] upon this Sunday morning, the air was so clear, the houses were so bright and gay; the signboards were painted in such gaudy colours; the gilded letters were so very golden; the bricks were so very red . . . that I almost believed the whole affair could be taken up piecemeal like a child's toy, and crammed into a little box.

—Charles Dickens, *American Notes,* 1842

BIKING

Boston is a great city for biking, whether on marked bike paths or not. The **Dr. Paul Dudley White Charles River Bike Path** is a 17.7-mile course that begins at Science Park (near the Museum of Science) and will take you through Boston, Cambridge, and to Watertown Square. You'll ride along both sides of the river if you take this path. There are multiple entrances along the way. It's managed and maintained by the Metropolitan District Commission (MDC, 20 Somerset St., ☎ 617/727-5114, ext. 555). Another good bike path is the **Southwest Corridor Linear Park Bikepath.** It runs alongside the MBTA's Orange Line and is four miles long. Pedestrian and bike paths are separate in this park. The 11-mile **Minuteman Bicycle Trail** follows the route of an old railroad track (it's actually in the railroad bed) and runs from the Alewife "T" station in Cambridge through Arlington, Lexington, and Bedford. The **Greenbelt Bikeway** runs along the 8-mile perimeter of the "Emerald Necklace," a famous Boston chain of parks that includes Boston Common and Franklin Park. In addition to the bike paths listed above, on Sundays from 11am to 7pm, Memorial Drive, along the Charles River, is closed to traffic—bicycles are allowed.

For additional information on Boston bike paths, call the **MDC** at ☎ 617/727-5114, ext. 555, or the **Boston Area Bicycle Coalition,** ☎ 617/491-7433).

Bicycles are allowed on the subway system (except the Green Line) during off-peak hours, and you can generally get away with riding on the sidewalk as long as you're careful of pedestrians.

For rentals, repairs, and general help, try **Earth Bikes** at 35 Huntington Ave. (☎ 617/267-GREEN). You can take an organized or self-guided tour with Earth Bikes, and they'll supply you with a bike lock and helmet with your rental. Other bike shops to try are **Back Bay Bicycles,** 333 Newbury St. (☎ 617/247-2336) and **Community Bike Shop** at 496 Tremont St. (☎ 617/542-8623).

BOATING

If you're looking for adventures in boating, you'll have several options. **Community Boating, Inc.,** 21 Embankment Road (☎ 617/523-1038) offers sailing lessons and boating programs for children and adults from April to November. **Courageous Sailing Center** (☎ 617/635-4505) in the Charlestown Navy Yard offers youth program lessons year-round. **Boston Sailing Center**, 54 Lewis Wharf (☎ 617/277-4198) offers lessons for sailors of all ability levels. The center is open all year.

For those who prefer kayaking or canoeing, **Charles River Canoe and Kayak Center,** located at 2401 Commonwealth Avenue in Newton (☎ 617/965-5110), rents canoes, kayaks, and sculls at their dock. Lessons are available.

If you've brought your own boat and are looking for a place to launch it, call the MDC at ☎ 617/727-0537.

Pleasure boating is allowed on the Charles River and Boston Harbor. The MDC will inform you of regulations.

FISHING

Freshwater fishing is permitted at **Turtle Pond** in the Stony Brook Reservation in Hyde Park, as well as **on the banks of the Charles River.** For off-shore salt-water fishing, the Harbor Islands are a good choice. You might also try heading out to South Boston to the pier at City Point, and the John J. McCorkle Fishing Pier. Both are located off Day Boulevard.

For information about fishing around the state, contact **Massachusetts State Parks,** 100 Cambridge St., Room 1905, Boston, MA 02202 (☎ 617/727-3180 or 800/831-0569).

GOLF

There's a large number of golf courses (both public and private) located around Boston. A few of the courses you might like to try are the **Fresh Pond Golf Course,** 691 Huron Ave., in Cambridge (☎ 617/349-6282); the **George Wright Golf Course,** 420 West St., Hyde Park (☎ 617/361-8313); and the **Newton Commonwealth Golf Course,** 91 Algonquin Rd., Brookline (☎ 617/630-1971).

The **Massachusetts Golf Association** (175 Highland Ave, Needham, ☎ 617/449-3000) represents over 270 golf courses around the state and will send you a list of courses. Call or write the above address. In addition, **Tee Times,** 199 Wells Ave., Suite 9, Newton, MA 02159 (☎ 617/969-0638) organizes golf outings.

HIKING

In addition to the Harbor Islands, listed above, the MDC (☎ 617/727-0460) maintains hiking trails at several reservation parks throughout the state, some of which are within short driving distance of the city. They include the **Blue Hills Reservation, Beaverbrook Reservation, Breakheart Reservation, Hemlock Gorge, Middlesex Fells Reservation, and Belle Isle Marsh Reservation.** Call the above number for information on how to get maps. You might also try **Stony Brook Reservation** in Hyde Park.

The **Boston Harbor Islands** also offer great hiking. Contact Boston Harbor Island State Park, 349 Lincoln St., Building 45, Hingham, MA 02043 (☎ 617/740-1605).

ICE-SKATING

If ice-skating is more your speed, there are several options. Try **Steriti Memorial Rink** in Boston (☎ 617/727-4708); **Simoni Memorial Rink** in Cambridge (☎ 617/727-4708); **Porazzo Memorial Rink** in East Boston (☎ 617/662-8370); **Veterans Memorial Rink** in Somerville (☎ 617/727-4708); and **Bajko Memorial Rink** in Hyde Park (☎ 617/727-6034).

IN-LINE SKATING

A favorite spot for in-line skaters is the **Esplanade.** In addition, on Sundays in summer, **Memorial Drive** in Cambridge is closed to traffic, and rollerbladers from all over the city take to the street. If you didn't bring your own skates to Boston, try the Beacon Hill Skate Shop, located at 135 Charles Street South (☎ 617/482-7400).

If you have access to the Internet and want to know what's hot on the in-line skating scene before you get to Boston, go to **Inline On-line:** http://www.sk8net.tiac.net/users/sk8man/icb.html.

JOGGING

City residents love to jog along the Charles River. Other sources of information on jogging include the **MDC** as well as the **Bill Rodgers Running Center,** located in Faneuil Hall (☎ 617/723-5612). In addition, virtually every hotel in Boston provides jogging maps for hotel guests.

Boston's Swan Boats

You should try to take at least one turn around the lagoon at the Boston Public Garden on the most famous ride of all—the **Swan Boats** (☎ 617/522-1966). Built in the shape of a swan, with graceful neck and outspread wings, these pedal-powered boats still look as they did when first created in 1877, except that now they're made out of fiberglass instead of wood. Oliver Wendell Holmes called them "as native to Boston as baked beans." Sailing along with the real swans and ducks in the lagoon, they operate from mid-April until the last Sunday in September (weather permitting). Hours are 10am to 6pm (and from noon until 4pm after Labor Day). The fare is $1.25 for adults, 75¢ for children, and $1 for seniors.

TENNIS

There are public courts available at no charge, throughout the city. They are maintained by the MDC. To find the one nearest you, call the **MDC** at ☎ 617/727-0460.

8 Spectator Sports

The love affair carried on by the people of Boston with the city's professional sports teams is unlike anything you'll find in other American cities. In addition, there are several colleges in the area that play a good game of football or hockey.

Whenever you go to Boston, you'll find an incredible array of scheduled sports events.

MAJOR SPORTS VENUES

The real sports meccas in Boston—not just for local fans, but for pilgrims from all over new England and beyond—are FleetCenter (the new Boston Garden), home of the NBA Celtics and the NHL Bruins, and Fenway Park, the ancient, stale-smelling, and much-beloved home of baseball's perennial second bananas, the Red Sox.

Fenway Park

24 Yawkey Way. ☎ **617/267-9440** for information, 617/267-1700 for tickets.

The oldest ballpark in the United States, Fenway Park opened in 1912 and has been the place to see the everyday face of Boston ever since—not to mention a baseball game. The dimensions and architecture of the park create a feeling not found in the uniform stadiums or domes of most other cities—in Fenway, the game is played on a field of real grass and dirt, bounded by walls that jut out at weird angles and, in the case of the famed Green Monster, climb to bizarre heights. The fans closely ring the field in a narrow cordon; the cramped seats aren't all that comfortable, but you'll love the feeling of sitting right on top of the game. Eat a hot dog, watch the numbers change on the old hand-operated scoreboard, listen to the cheesy organ and the deafening shouts of the vendors, and enjoy the game— Fenway Park hasn't changed all that much since the early 1900s, and baseball is a game that improves with history and tradition.

Fenway is a small park, and the Red Sox have a loyal following. Whether the home team is winning or losing as you plan your vacation, call as far in advance as possible if you'd like to see a game. Seating for the disabled and nonalcoholic sections are available.

Admission to lower boxes $18, upper boxes $14, grandstand $10, bleachers $7. Games often begin at 7:30pm on weeknights and at 1 or 2pm on weekend afternoons. MBTA: Kenmore Sq. (Green Line, B, C, or D train).

FleetCenter

150 Causeway St. ☎ **617/624-1000** (for recorded events) or 617/931-2000 (for Ticketmaster). MBTA: North Station (Green or Orange Line).

The Celtics and the Bruins, legends in their respective sports of basketball and hockey, have a new home in the brand-new, five-story FleetCenter, which houses considerably more spectators than their old hangout, the Boston Garden. The Bruins haven't won the Stanley Cup in recent years, but historically they're one of the NHL's most successful franchises; and the Celtics have won a great many NBA championships.

The FleetCenter is located right next to the Boston Garden.

BASEBALL

The **Boston Red Sox** play at Fenway Park (see above) from early April to early October (as long as nobody is on strike). This American League team hasn't won a World Series in 78 years. You can get tickets while you're in Boston or in advance by calling Ticketron or Bostix. For Red Sox information, call ☎ 617/267-1700.

BASKETBALL

The **Boston Celtics** is the city's famed professional basketball team. The Celtics, who play at FleetCenter, have won 16 NBA Championships since 1960. Following the baseball season, basketball season runs from early October to May. For information, call FleetCenter above.

DOG RACING

If you're a greyhound fan, there's racing at Wonderland Park in Revere (☎ 617/284-1300), reached via the "T" on the Blue Line.

FOOTBALL

The **New England Patriots** play football (not very well in recent years) during the fall and winter out at Sullivan Stadium (☎ 800/543-1776) in Foxboro, about a half-hour drive south of the city. You can drive or catch a bus from the entrance of South Station, the Riverside "T" station, or Shopper's World in Framingham (west of the city).

College football is played by Boston College (Alumni Stadium, Chestnut Hill, ☎ 617/552-3004), Boston University (Nickerson Field, Commonwealth Ave., ☎ 617/353-2872), Harvard University (Harvard Stadium, N. Harvard St., ☎ 617/495-2206), and Northeastern University (Parsons Field, Kent St., Brookline, ☎ 617/373-2672).

HOCKEY

Boston Bruins hockey games are always exciting, but if you're lucky enough to be in town when they're playing Montreal, you're in for a treat. Tickets for all their games (held at FleetCenter, see above) sell out early. For tickets and information, call FleetCenter above.

Colleges with hockey teams include Boston College (Conte Forum, Chestnut Hill, ☎ 617/552-3004), Boston University (Walter Brown Arena, 285 Babcock St., ☎ 617/353-2872), Harvard University (Bright Hockey Center, 60 JFK St., Cambridge, ☎ 617/495-2206), and Northeastern University (Matthews Arena, St. Botolph St., ☎ 617/373-2672).

MARATHON

Every year on Patriots Day (April 19), the Boston Marathon is run from Hopkington to Copley Square in Boston. Call the Greater Boston Convention & Visitors Bureau (☎ 617/536-4100) for more information.

ROWING

Another celebrated annual event is the Head of the Charles Regatta. It's held in October, and over 800 crews from all over the world participate. Shells leave the Boston University boathouse every 10 seconds or so. It's a major social event as well. Thousands of people gather along the banks of the Charles River to picnic and watch the shells glide by.

TENNIS TOURNAMENT

The U.S. Tennis Championship at Longwood is held every year in July at the Longwood Cricket Club (564 Hammond St., Brookline). Call ☎ 617/731-4500 for tickets and information about the week-long event.

9 Shopping

Like New York, Washington, and other great American cities, Boston has its special places to buy things, whether you're in the market for the mundane or the exotic. Here are some of the prime locales for getting rid of money.

DOWNTOWN CROSSING   The two Boston giants are **Jordan Marsh Company** and **Filene's,** located cheek-by-jowl in the downtown pedestrian shopping district on Washington Street (subway: Red or Orange Line to Washington) called Downtown Crossing. Jordan's is a large department store with a vast assortment of items for sale, everything from baubles to bar stools. Jordan's Great Basement Store is admittedly great in terms of size, but is outdone in popularity by neighboring Filene's Basement, which has become a New England legend. Tales circulate about women changing clothes right between the dress racks to try things on, of the crowds one must fight, of the "automatic reduction" policy—which dictates that if an item is not sold in a certain amount of time, it's simply given away just to get rid of it.

Well, the basement has become a bit more refined now that it's famous, and the prices in many cases are similar to those in any of the big new suburban discount stores. As for the automatic reductions, they're still in operation; but few items reach the date when they're given away, and if they do it's usually because they're too torn or ugly or useless to be bought—and even so they're given away to charity (Goodwill Industries, for example) as a tax write-off and not to you. But the basement is still busy, often crowded, and it's because people know that there's a good chance they'll run into something that suits them at a very good price. Don't go to Filene's Basement to buy a pair of shoes, but rather go to dig around in the shoe bins and see what there is in your size and at a good price—you may find something that makes good sense to buy. And look through the other clothes departments, accessory counters, and various sections—a $400 outfit with a marked-down $40 price tag could very well be waiting there for you.

Surplus merchandise from famous stores such as Lou Lattimer's in Houston and Saks in New York comes frequently to Filene's Basement, with such classy labels as I. Magnin and Yves Saint Laurent. Don't be disappointed if you don't find anything. Come back in a few days, for the stock moves incredibly fast and new shipments arrive daily.

Also at Downtown Crossing is **Lafayette Place,** a vast shopping mall with a central courtyard for sipping and dining, a 500-room hotel, and hundreds of shops.

Washington Street, the pedestrian thoroughfare of Downtown Crossing, has its own lineup of shops. Across from Filene's, at 333 and 387 Washington St., for instance, are entrances to the **Jeweler's Building,** a warren of little shops in a homely building. The building may not look like much, but the display cases in each shop are laden with fortunes in gold, diamonds, rubies, and emeralds. If you're at all interested in jewelry, take a stroll through here. Prices can be very good.

FANEUIL HALL MARKETPLACE   The Faneuil Hall Marketplace is a whole complex of buildings including **Faneuil Hall** and **Quincy Market,** flanked by the **North and South Markets** on either side.

Quincy Market is the centerpiece of this imaginative and fantastically successful redevelopment venture by the Rouse Company with the guidance of Cambridge architect Benjamin Thompson. For years the area was a rundown waterfront slum, with only the 19th-century-style butchers' shops and provisioners to provide life. The early plan was to have the buildings razed to the ground and replaced by a modern shopping center, but architect Thompson changed the thinking to conservation, and the result is a beauty. Behind Faneuil Hall, the market is busy with crowds of customers from sunrise to sundown every day of the week. A granite-block pavement is spread between Faneuil Hall and the market's pillared classic Greek facade, and inside, the long main hall stretches for a city block on two floors.

Downstairs are **food shops,** where you can buy everything from take-out snacks to a full picnic-style meal, to a pound of Camembert for the kitchen at home. On a recent stroll through Quincy Market I noted the following items for sale (partial list): a dozen kinds of bagels right out of the oven on the premises, an infinite array of deli sandwiches, southern fried chicken, shish kebab, subgum chow mein, Baby Watson cheesecake, German blutwurst, French Brie, Châteauneuf-du-Pape, live lobsters, mixed nuts, cold cuts (domestic and imported), rumpsteak, fresh doughnuts, and, at the clam bar, half a dozen cherrystone clams opened and ready to eat.

The wings of the market are of glass, and shelter **restaurants, drinking places, and singles' hangouts** patronized by the good-looking and well-to-do from the business, financial, and government offices nearby. In the basement are various shops selling fish, meat, health foods, and imported delicacies.

On the second floor the emphasis is on **crafts and exotic imports**—rugs from Persia, jewelry from India, baskets from China and Mexico. There's a fine **flower shop** in a very handsome all-glass building in front, on the granite pavement, and benches set out under the trees between the market and the adjoining buildings.

About the best purchase you can make here at Faneuil Hall Marketplace is tickets to the theater, concerts, ballet, shows, and so on. **Bostix** (☎ 617/ **723-5181**), in a kiosk right next to Faneuil Hall itself, sells half-price seats for

Impressions

On another occasion a guest at a White House reception eased up to the president and remarked: "Mr. President, I'm from Boston." His blue eyes rested only briefly on her as he said: "You'll never get over it."

—I. Ross, *Grace Coolidge and Her Era,* 1962

today's performances—and this is the only place in the city where you can buy them. Plan your nightlife while you're here, rather than coming all the way back. It's cash-only for same-day, half-price seats—that's the policy.

Street performers of all varieties are always on hand to entertain in the market promenades, and a genial mounted police officer draws scores of children, all wanting to pat his mount's nose. The whole complex is an all-year, day-and-night carnival you shouldn't miss, open for free. For restaurant details, see "Dining," earlier in this chapter. To get to Faneuil Hall Marketplace, take the Green or Blue Line to Government Center, or the Blue or Red Line to State Street.

NEWBURY STREET   Boston's famous street of boutiques, galleries, and cafes runs from fashion to funk. It starts at the intersection of Arlington and Newbury, right next to Burberry's and the Ritz-Carlton Hotel, and the shoppers' and strollers' delights continue for half a dozen blocks. Shops sell everything from the sublime (and expensive) to the ridiculous (and expensive); galleries can be chic or somewhat traditional. Cafes are good and bad, expensive and cheap, and all possible permutations of those four qualities.

Serious shoppers and gallerygoers should pick up two useful brochures, available at information booths (City Hall, Boston Common, Boston Public Library), entitled "The Newbury Street League Map," which gives a list of most of the shops and some of the cafes along the street, their specialties, addresses, and phone numbers; and "Map of the Newbury Street Art Galleries," which gives brief descriptions of the 30 galleries on the street, times of operation, special services, and so forth.

Newbury Street starts at the Ritz, and the shops in the first few blocks are, naturally, the most expensive. All the shops mentioned below are along the first six blocks or so of Newbury Street, starting at Arlington.

If you're shopping for classic and high-fashion clothing, look for big names such as **Burberry's, Brooks Brothers, Cartier, Giorgio Armani, Ann Taylor, Laura Ashley,** and **Guy Laroche,** as well as Boston-based designers **Charles Sumner, Louis-Boston,** and **Robert Todd.** For furs, there's **Kakas.** For more contemporary wear, seek out **Joseph Abboud, Martini Carl, In Wear Martinique, The Gap, Banana Republic, Reebok, Claire Williams,** and **Agnes B.** For outrageous fashions, try **Alan Bilzerian.** Jewelry crafters include **Body Sculpture,** at no. 127, and **Silver & Gold—The Finest Hour,** at no. 274. **F.A.O. Schwarz,** the famous New York toy store, has two branches in Boston, at 40 Newbury St. and in the Prudential Center.

Streets in the Back Bay were laid out in a grid, and the cross streets that run north-south were given names with initial letters running from A to H—Arlington, Berkeley, Clarendon, Dartmouth, and so on—so it's easy to know how far you are from the start of Newbury Street at Arlington Street. The second cross street, then, is Berkeley.

COPLEY PLACE   Just off Copley Square is Copley Place, a vast ultramodern shopping, dining, lodging, and entertainment complex. **Neiman Marcus** is the big store here, but there are dozens of shops as well. **Ralph Lauren, Williams-Sonoma, Saint Laurent Rive Gauche, Jaeger, Gucci,** and **Godiva,** among others, all have outlets. Hours are normally 10am to 9pm Monday through Friday, to 7pm on Saturday, and noon to 5pm on Sunday. The hotels in the complex are the Boston Marriott Copley Place and the Westin Hotel Copley Place.

10   Boston After Dark

Forget everything you've ever heard about things being "banned in Boston," for at night in this big city it seems as though anything goes. The opportunities for evening activities are bewildering in their variety, and because of all the students in town, nightlife is very active, available, and—in many cases—not all that expensive. This section will give you some idea of what's going on, with details on a selection of the better things to see and do.

Bostonians have been known to call their city "The Athens of America"—they did this even before the city had a sizable Greek population. The reason, of course, is Boston's lively cultural and artistic life. It could fairly be said that on any given day of the year one could take a pick of a dozen or more lectures, concerts, or dance and theater offerings, and at least a few of these would be free of charge.

The best way to find out what's on is to buy the *Boston Globe* on Thursday; that issue includes a free "Calendar" guide to happenings in Boston and vicinity, with locations and phone numbers.

Another useful publication is the tabloid "alternative" weekly newspaper, the *Boston Phoenix.*

Bostix (☎ **617/723-5181** for a recording) sells all kinds of tickets to all sorts of events in Boston and beyond. You can buy a ticket to almost anything in eastern Massachusetts here. You'll pay the regular price plus a small service charge. This is a useful service.

But the best deal at Bostix is the sale of tickets at half price on the day of performance. Theaters, concerts, shows, and so on are put on a "daily list" of half-price offerings, and you must stop by the Bostix kiosk next to Faneuil Hall in Faneuil Hall Marketplace (subway: Green or Blue Line to Government Center) to read the list—they won't give it to you over the telephone. For same-day, half-price seats, you must pay in cash, no refunds or exchanges; for advance bookings, you may pay with a check drawn on a Massachusetts bank. No credit cards are accepted. Bostix is open Tuesday through Saturday from 10am to 6pm (half-price tickets go on sale at 11am), on Sunday from 11am to 4pm.

THE PERFORMING ARTS
MAJOR PERFORMING ARTS COMPANIES
Boston Symphony Orchestra

301 Massachusetts Ave. ☎ **617/266-1492,** CON-CERT for program information, and 617/266-1200 to charge tickets in advance.

The Boston Symphony Orchestra (BSO) preserves a reputation for excellence and innovation that it has had for over a century. The formal symphony season runs from October through April, with performances in Symphony Hall. The hall was designed in 1900 by McKim, Mead, and White, who carried out one of the earliest-known scientific acoustical studies for such a structure, and their careful work has been an outstanding success for nearly a century.

To get to Symphony Hall by subway, take the Green Line "Brigham Circle" car (also called the "E" train) to Symphony (literally right outside the front door of the BSO) or any other Green Line train to Hynes Convention Center/ICA. Turn left as you leave the station, and walk down Massachusetts Avenue. Bus no. 1 runs from Dudley to Harvard Square and back, down Massachusetts Avenue and right by Symphony Hall.

Symphony tickets range in price from $20 to $60. You can purchase tickets in person at the Symphony Hall Box Office, open from 10am to 6pm Monday through Saturday and 1 to 6pm on Sunday, and also during concerts through the first intermission. You can also order tickets by phone at the above number; there's a handling fee of $2.25 per ticket ordered by phone.

There are ways to enjoy the Boston Symphony Orchestra without paying full price: **rush seats and open rehearsals.**

A limited number of tickets for each BSO concert (Tuesday and Thursday evening and Friday matinee) are held back, to be sold only on the day of the concert, one to a customer, in the Massachusetts Avenue lobby of Symphony Hall. These rush seats go on sale on Friday at 9am and on Tuesday, Thursday, and Saturday at 5pm, and cost a mere $11.50 each. You must buy them in person, not by phone or mail, and there's a limit of one ticket per customer.

During the symphony season, open rehearsals are held on six Wednesday evenings at 7:30pm (doors open at 6:15pm, with a lecture at 6:30pm), and four Thursday mornings at 10:30am (complimentary coffee and pastries are served between 9:15 and 9:30am). The rehearsals, preceded by a half-hour lecture on the musical program, are almost the same as a full-fledged concert, but tickets cost only $11.50.

Tanglewood   In July, the indefatigable members of the orchestra move out to the Berkshire hills in western Massachusetts for the Tanglewood Music Festival in Lenox. The Tanglewood season runs from July through Labor Day weekend. Chamber music concerts, recitals, and full-symphony concerts fill each week, and a jazz festival ends the season on Labor Day weekend. Again, these performances are very heavily attended, and it's best to go early to get a good seat (you can sit inside the "Music Shed" or on the lawn outside, depending on how much you want to spend for a ticket); even more important than going early to the concert is to get a room reservation nearby, unless you plan to drive out ($2^1/_2$ to 3 hours) and back the same day.

Special excursions to Tanglewood concerts are offered by Peter Pan Trailways (☎ **617/426-7838**).

For more information on Tanglewood, refer to "Lenox," in Chapter 8.

The Boston Pops
Symphony Hall, 301 Massachusetts Ave. ☎ **617/266-1492** for general information, ☎ 617/266-2378 (Apr–June) for the latest program information, ☎ 617/266-1200 for tickets.

The Boston Pops concerts of light classical works, music from the cinema and Broadway, and catchy orchestral arrangements of popular tunes run from early May through mid-July and are performed Tuesday through Sunday. The floor in Symphony Hall is cleared of seats; cafe tables and chairs are brought in; and light refreshments, beer, and wine are served to those on the floor (but not in the balconies).

The rules for Pops tickets are similar to those for buying symphony tickets (see above). Pops concert ticket prices range from $12 to $32, with a $2.50 service charge.

The Boston Pops performs free concerts during the first week in July in the Hatch Memorial Shell, on the Charles River Esplanade (subway: Red Line to Charles). The highlight of the series is the traditional Fourth of July performance, which always ends with Tchaikovsky's *1812 Overture,* accompanied by a battery of cannons and followed by a mammoth display of fireworks over the river.

OTHER CONCERTS

Two well-known music schools offer frequent concerts by students, faculty, and visiting groups of performers.

New England Conservatory of Music

30 Gainsborough St. ☎ **617/262-1120,** ext. 700.

The conservatory has frequent concerts, most of them free, in its performance halls, which include Jordan Hall. Thought to be one of the most acoustically perfect music halls in the world, Jordan Hall is at the center of the New England Conservatory's musical life. Not only is it a primary performance space, but it also serves as a classroom and rehearsal hall. It's located one block from Symphony Hall, on Gainsborough Street at Huntington Avenue, close to the Boston YMCA and Northeastern University (Green Line's "Arborway" or "Northeastern U" car to Symphony Station, or to the first stop aboveground; or take the Orange Line to Massachusetts Avenue; or take bus no. 39, "Forest Hills," from Copley Square and Back Bay). A monthly calendar of events is available on request.

Berklee College of Music

136 Massachusetts Ave. ☎ **617/266-7455** for a recorded schedule or 617/266-1400 for a human being.

The Berklee Performance Center, on Massachusetts Avenue (near the corner of Boylston Street) is for larger groups, while the Recital Hall, at 1140 Boylston St., is for small ensembles. There's also the Berklee Concert Pavilion, an urban amphitheater, for outdoors events. Take the Green Line "Boston College," "Cleveland Circle," or "Riverside" car to Hynes Convention Center/ICA Station for both places. Both halls are fairly near the Prudential Center. Call Ticketmaster at ☎ 617/931-2000 for reservations.

Handel and Haydn Society

300 Massachusetts Ave. ☎ **617/262-1815** for general information, 617/266-3605 for the box office.

Few Boston institutions predate the society, which has been giving concerts in Boston since 1815. The Handel and Haydn's season runs year-round, with a Symphony Hall Series and a Chamber Series at Jordan Hall at the New England Conservatory and at Sanders Theatre. The society, older even than the Boston

Impressions

We really are 15 countries, and it's really remarkable that each of us thinks we represent the real America. The Midwesterner in Kansas, the black American in Durham— both are certain they are the real America. And Boston just knows it is.
                                                    —Maya Angelou, *Time,* April 24, 1978

Symphony Orchestra, has a closely guarded reputation for high excellence in its performances. The artistic director of the Handel and Haydn Society is the internationally renowned conductor, Christopher Hogwood.

DANCE

Ballet Theater of Boston

186 Massachusetts Ave. ☎ **617/262-0961.**

If you're interested in contemporary ballet, you should definitely check the paper for performances by the Ballet Theater of Boston. They're a small, relatively new troupe, but their performances are excellent—both original and innovative. Call for ticket information.

Boston Ballet

19 Clarendon St. ☎ **617/695-6950,** or 617/931-ARTS for tickets.

Some may not know it, but the Boston Ballet is the fourth-largest dance company in America. For 32 years it has maintained a high standard of artistic excellence and vision. Under artistic director Bruce Marks, the Boston Ballet's repertory is an eclectic mix of classic story ballets, contemporary ballets, and avant-garde works. Watch for notices and times in the papers, then go to the Wang Center Box Office, 270 Tremont St., Monday through Saturday from 10am to 6pm to purchase tickets. Prices range from $14 to $65.

THEATERS

Boston's taste in theater runs the gamut from previews of Broadway musicals to the most experimental of experimental. The offering is so rich and varied it would be impossible in this small space even to give an idea of the range available. Groups will pop up here and there, struggle to survive, and in the meantime put on fine performances, and then fail financially and disperse, having left many theatergoers with a lasting impression. I would stress that people interested in the theater should not limit themselves to the possibilities outlined below, but should take the time to seek out the new groups performing in odd places, for they're often at the frontier.

Nevertheless, if you have only a little time to spend in Boston and you'd like to take in a play or a musical, start with the theaters that follow. Besides these, the universities have a great many drama offerings, usually at fairly low prices; and during the summer the city of Boston and other organizations sponsor outdoor performances in City Hall Plaza, in other public squares, and along the Charles River Esplanade. (See also "Cambridge," in Chapter 5.) Note that the old-line theaters with musicals and plays slated for Broadway are all downtown near the Green Line's Boylston Station.

Charles Playhouse

74–76 Warrenton St. ☎ **617/426-6912.**

Good drama is the rule at the Charles Playhouse, located right down behind the Shubert and Wilbur Theaters and the Tremont House Hotel (subway: Green Line to Boylston; Warrenton is parallel to Tremont one block west, but it's only a block long). At press time, the Charles Playhouse was featuring Blue Man Group (from New York City), and *Shear Madness* (see "More Entertainment," below).

Wang Center for the Performing Arts

270 Tremont St. ☎ **617/931-2000.**

With 3,700 seats, the Wang Center (formerly the Metropolitan Theater) was known as Boston's most important landmark of the Roaring '20s. The Wang presents a variety of performing arts to the Boston communities, as well as providing educational and outreach programs like "Young at Arts." The theater, declared a historical landmark, has been restored to its original glory and is home to the Boston Ballet and the Bank of Boston Celebrity Dance Series. Wang Center tours are now available. Call the **Snow Palace Hotline** at ☎ **617/ 482-9393,** ext. 271 (TTY ☎ 617/482-5257).

THE CLUB & MUSIC SCENE

The Boston area's more than 75 colleges and universities give downtown nightlife a particularly lively character; a lot of graduates get to like the town so much they settle down here, and so Boston's crew of "young professionals" is also very large and very conspicuous in the clubs.

Despite the fact that Boston is one of this country's most expensive cities, a night on the town won't kill your budget. Drinks are mostly $4 to $7, and beer or a glass of wine is $3 to $6.

COMEDY CLUBS

Boston attracts a wide range of comic talent. A couple of places to check when you're in town are the **Comedy Connection** in Faneuil Hall (☎ **617/248-9700**) and **Nick's Comedy Stop** at 100 Warrenton St. (☎ **617/482-0930**).

FOLK & COUNTRY

Nameless Coffeehouse
3 Church St. No cover.

The Nameless attracts an enthusiastic young crowd that enjoys the wide range of music presented, the storytelling, and the free refreshments—coffee, cider, tea, cocoa, and cookies. Open September to May, Friday and Saturday from 7:30pm to midnight.

Passim
47 Palmer St., Cambridge. ☎ **617/492-7679.** Cover $6–$15, depending on the performers.

The best-known spot for folk music is Passim, behind the Coop. It was the focus of the folk boom in the 1960s and early 1970s and still has a national reputation as an outstanding showcase for folk musicians. Concerts are presented five nights a week. At other times it's a charming coffeehouse that offers lunch and light meals. Alcoholic beverages aren't served here, but you can purchase artwork and jewelry. Open Monday through Saturday from 11:30am to 11pm.

ROCK CLUBS

Boston has innumerable rock clubs. The ones listed below are just a smattering of those that were most popular at the time this book was going to press.

Local 186
186 Harvard Ave. ☎ **617/351-2660.** Cover charge varies; call ahead.

This is a very popular spot for local talent and local residents. It's usually crowded, but if you're lucky you might be able to secure one of the two pool tables. Open daily from 9pm to 2am.

Man Ray
21 Brookline St. ☎ **617/864-0400.**

Man Ray advertizes itself as "a smoky haven for black-clad lovers of dissonance"—and they aren't lying. This is the place where Boston's "artsy" crowd likes to gather, and it's where you'll find anything from the Top 40 to "Industrial Alternative Noise." You should call ahead if you're interested in live music, because you won't always find it here. Thursday is reserved for gay men. Open Tuesday through Sunday from 8pm to 1 or to 2am.

The Rathskeller (The Rat)

528 Commonwealth Ave. ☎ **617/536-2750.**

The Rathskeller, locally known as "the Rat," remains loyal to its punk-rock heritage. Located in the Kenmore Square area, it is Boston's oldest rock-'n'-roll bar and grill, with live music Thursday through Sunday nights in the lower level of the club. The restaurant menu ranges from barbecued ribs of considerable renown to sandwiches and vegetarian meals. The restaurant is open from 11am to 10pm, the bar until 2am. Call for a schedule of events and cover charges

T.T. The Bear's Place

10 Brookline St., Cambridge. ☎ **617/492-0082.**

This is one of the few clubs that admits guests under 21. It's "18 plus" to get in, and "the Bear" is usually packed with young people. Entertainment is offered from 9pm on. Monday night is Stone Soup Poetry night, and on Sunday Ethiopian food is served from 3pm to 11pm. There are also two pool tables. Call for a schedule of events and cover charges.

The Tam

1648 Beacon St. ☎ **617/277-0982.** Cover charge varies, depending on the entertainment.

Currently, the Tam is extremely popular with the "just out of college" crowd. The music selections are fairly standard (but they also occasionally book alternative rock bands), and there's live entertainment—mainly featuring local bands. Dinner is available daily until 10pm. Open Sunday through Friday from 5:30pm to 2am and Saturday from 5pm to 2am.

JAZZ & BLUES

Boston and Cambridge are enjoying a jazz revival. Many top musicians perform regularly in lounges and clubs throughout the area. You can even listen to live jazz in the shopping malls and outdoor plazas such as the Prudential Center in Boston and Charles Square in Cambridge. There's also a weekend Cabaret Jazz Boat from Long Wharf. (Check the newspapers for listings.) To find out what's doing on the jazz scene, call **Jazzline** at ☎ **617/787-9700.**

House of Blues

96 Winthrop St. ☎ **617/491-BLUE.** Cover charge varies; call ahead.

One of Boston's most popular eateries, the House of Blues is also one of Boston's newest music hotspots. Blues bands play several nights a week, and often more than one show is scheduled for a night. Advance reservations are highly recommended. Call for tickets and show times.

Regattabar

In the Charles Hotel, 1 Bennett St., Cambridge. ☎ **617/937-4020.** Cover $6–$20.

Featuring local and national artists, this nightclub offers the best jazz in the metropolitan area. The large third-floor room has a 21-foot picture window from which you can see the flag plaza of Charles Square and the bustle of Harvard

Square while enjoying drinks. Buy tickets at the door or in advance from Concertix (☎ 617/876-7777). Open Wednesday through Saturday with performances at 8 and 10pm.

Ryles
212 Hampshire St., Inman Sq., Cambridge. ☎ **617/876-9330.**

Serious jazz fans head to Ryles for its choice of bands on two levels. Downstairs, where dinner is served, you can socialize with music as the background. (Between sets, spin a few tunes on the jukebox—it's one of the best around.) Upstairs has great acoustics and a wide variety of first-rate jazz performances. Both offer good music and a friendly atmosphere. Call for schedule and cover charges.

Scullers Jazz Club
In the Doubletree Guest Suites Hotel, 400 Soldiers Field Rd., in Cambridge. ☎ **617/ 562-4111.** Cover $7–$25 depending on performer.

The Scullers Jazz Club hosts top jazz singers and instrumentalists in a comfortable room with a view of the Charles River. Shows are usually Monday through Saturday. There's also an excellent monthly dinner-jazz show.

Sticky Mike's Blues Bar
Boylston Pl. ☎ **617/351-2450.**

Hear live blues every night, but don't expect to get a seat. Seating is at the bar only, and there's no dance floor, but that doesn't stop everyone from dancing anyway.

Willow Jazz Club
699 Broadway, Somerville. ☎ **617/623-9874.** Average cover $12.

Alternative jazz is featured here daily. The Willow's proximity to Tufts University campus makes it a popular student nightspot, but the top-notch musicians who play here lure jazz aficionados from miles around.

DANCE CLUBS

Avalon
15 Landsdowne St. ☎ **617/262-2424.** Average cover $10.

This is a multilevel club with a full concert stage, private booths and lounges, large dance floors, and a spectacular light show. The dress code calls for jackets, shirts with collars, and no jeans or athletic wear; thus, it attracts a slightly older crowd than Axis. Open Thursday to Sunday.

Axis
13 Landsdowne St. ☎ **617/262-2437.** Cover $6–$12.

Axis attracts a young crowd with its progressive rock music and "creative dress." Special nights for hard rock, heavy metal, and alternative rock. Open Tuesday to Sunday 10pm to 2am.

MORE ENTERTAINMENT

Shear Madness
Charles Playhouse Stage II, 74 Warrenton St. ☎ **617/426-5225.** Tickets $23 and $28.

Shear Madness is the longest-running nonmusical play in American theater history (as acknowledged by the *Guinness Book of World Records*), and it makes its home in Boston, as it has for the last 15 years. It's a zany whodunit that takes place in a hairstyling salon. A concert pianist (Isabel Czerny) who lived in the apartment

Impressions

Boston prides itself on virtue and ancient lineage—it doesn't impress me in either direction. It is musty, like the Faubourg St. Germain. I often want to ask them what constitutes the amazing virtue they are so conscious of.
          —Bertrand Russell, letter to Margaret Llewellyn Davies, April 12, 1914

above the salon was murdered, and the salon staff, as well as several of its customers, are suspects. Much of the show is improvised, and no matter how many times you see it, you'll never see the same show twice. The Charles Playhouse is a 199-seat cabaret-style theater with full bar service. Shows are Tuesday through Friday at 8pm, Saturday at 6:30 and 9:30pm, and Sunday at 3 and 7:30pm.

FILM

Films are a big part of Boston's nighttime entertainment picture, and the hot-topic big releases are always crowded during the first few weeks. But besides major releases, silent movies, golden oldies, and bestsellers of the recent past are always available. Prices range from free admission to $7.50 per seat.

The local listings will let you know what's on tonight. What you may find of help is directions on how to get to the principal movie theaters. Remember to check out Cambridge movies as well, listed separately in the Cambridge section (see Chapter 5). Here are the prime movie houses in Boston:

Cheri
50 Dalton St. ☎ **617/536-2870.**

Next to Hynes Convention Center in the Prudential Center complex. Take the Green Line "Boston College," "Cleveland Circle," or "Riverside" car to Hynes Convention Center/Auditorium, turn left out of the station, left again down Boylston, and look right.

Cinema 57
200 Stuart St. ☎ **617/482-1222.**

In the tall 57 Park Plaza Hotel—Howard Johnson, in Park Square. Take the Green Line to Boylston, then walk along the edge of the Common on Boylston Street to the intersection with Charles Street and turn left—it's right in front of you.

Coolidge Corner
290 Harvard St., in suburban Brookline. ☎ **617/734-2500.**

Take the Green Line "Cleveland Circle" car along Beacon Street to the junction with Harvard Street, called Coolidge Corner. This art deco cinema is the place to go for offbeat movies and foreign films.

Loews Nickelodeon Cinemas
606 Commonwealth Ave., near Kenmore Sq. ☎ **617/424-1500.**

This is actually slightly off Commonwealth, behind Boston University's College of Communication, but you'll see the cinema's big sign as you walk west along Commonwealth from Kenmore Square.

Museum of Fine Arts
465 Huntington Ave. ☎ **617/267-9300,** ext. 888.

The M.F.A. has many film programs, with screenings most Thursday and Friday evenings. Call for recorded information.

Wang Center for the Performing Arts

270 Tremont St. ☎ **617/931-2000.**

Near Stuart Street in the Theater District, this place is often booked with theater, dance, and concerts, but it does have several subscription film series, too. Take the Green Line to Boylston, then walk south (away from the Common) two blocks on Tremont Street. The Wang Center is on the left.

THE COMBAT ZONE

Police hate it, politicians want to get rid of it, some citizens revel in it—the several blocks of Washington Street between Avery and Stuart streets (subway: Green Line to Boylston or Orange Line to Essex) are perhaps the most "un-Bostonlike" part of Boston. No grand old traditions are here except that of "the oldest profession"; no lofty artistry unless one can call nude dancing art. The Combat Zone, as it's known to all, is Boston's tenderloin: several blocks of prime downtown real estate full of strip shows, porno films, and generally sleazy diversions.

Despite its sinister name and gamy appearance, the Combat Zone is not a wildly dangerous place to stroll through, and many of the bars and clubs and movie houses are safe enough to enter as long as you don't go late at night, and definitely don't go alone. In most places women are as welcome as men.

Around Boston 5

The towns around Boston can be neatly divided into three full-day excursions: Cambridge, Lexington, and Concord are to the west; Salem, Marblehead, Gloucester, and Rockport are to the north, known as the North Shore; and Plymouth, New Bedford, and Fall River are to the south.

WEST OF BOSTON As Paul Revere sped through the country-side along another road, William Dawes made a famous midnight ride that took him from the banks of the Charles through the communities of **Cambridge** (once called Newtown), **Lexington,** and **Concord.** Boston's expansion, like America's, was westward toward the mountains, and these important communities west of the city were large enough to play a significant role in the Revolution.

Today, Cambridge, Lexington, and Concord are linked by Battle Road, a designation given by the National Park Service, which harks back to that historic day when Revere and Dawes rode out, followed by troops of redcoats. The story of Battle Road and the events of that day in 1775 are clearly told in the exhibits at Minuteman National Historic Park in Lexington and Concord, but before heading off in search of Revolutionary history you should make a stop in Cambridge, home city of Harvard College, which was founded long before the Revolution. Cambridge is easily reached from Boston by bus or subway. Buses run to Lexington, and commuter trains go from Boston's North Station and the Red Line's Porter Square station in Cambridge directly to Concord.

THE NORTH SHORE North of Boston are many of the towns that brought great wealth to the North Shore of Massachusetts Bay in the 18th and 19th centuries. Ships from these Essex County towns would sail to Asia and Africa and return several years later with cargoes so rich that everyone involved in the voyage became wealthy overnight.

The gracious houses and public buildings constructed during this era are still here to be seen, and the museums in **Salem** hold a treasure of mementos and artifacts from the maritime boom. **Marblehead** and **Rockport** are still important as yacht harbors and excursion points, but all three towns now make their living primarily from the land: as "bedroom" communities for Boston and as vacation stops for Bostonians and those who come from farther away. Commuter trains run frequently from Boston's North Station

What's Special About Boston's Environs

Museums
- Harvard's University Museums of Cultural and Natural History, with everything from glass flowers to Mayan ruins.
- Harvard's art museums, with treasures of European, Middle Eastern, and Asian art.
- Concord Museum, where a colonial town comes alive.
- Peabody/Essex Museum in Salem, exhibiting the riches and exotica of the China trade.
- New Bedford Whaling Museum, showing how New England lit its lamps before electricity.
- Plimoth Plantation, a "living museum" re-creating the life of the Pilgrims in the 1600s.

Architectural Highlights
- Harvard University's campus, especially historic Harvard Yard.
- Pretty town greens in Lexington and Concord, surrounded by historic buildings.
- Handsome 19th-century ship captains' houses in Salem.
- New Bedford's restored historic district.
- The great granite mill buildings of Fall River.

Shopping
- Rockport's boutiques and artists' galleries, especially along Bearskin Neck.
- Fall River's huge factory outlets, selling everything from haberdashery to housewares.

Events & Festivals
- Patriots Day (April 19), when the first battles of the Revolution are reenacted at Lexington and Concord.
- St. Peter's Festival in Gloucester, with games, rides, and the blessing of the fleet.

Cool for Kids
- *Mayflower II* in Plymouth, an authentic replica of the original *Mayflower*.
- Canoeing down the Concord River to Old North Bridge, where the Minutemen fought the redcoats.
- Whale-watching expeditions out of Gloucester.

Literary Shrines
- Ralph Waldo Emerson's house in Concord, the birthplace of transcendentalism.
- Site of Thoreau's cabin on Walden Pond in Concord.
- Orchard House in Concord, home of Louisa May Alcott and her family.
- Longfellow's house in Cambridge.
- The Old Manse in Concord, where Nathaniel Hawthorne lived and worked.
- The House of the Seven Gables in Salem, setting for one of Hawthorne's most famous novels.

to Salem and **Gloucester**; Marblehead and Rockport can be reached by commuter train, then bus.

THE SOUTH SHORE   Of the many communities on the South Shore of Massachusetts Bay, **Plymouth** is easily the most famous. Crowds of visitors make the pilgrimage every summer to see one of the places where this country began.

   Though Plymouth makes a logical day trip, you would probably want to visit the 19th-century whaling port of **New Bedford** and the old textile center of **Fall River** (made famous by Lizzie Borden) on your way to Cape Cod, Providence, or Newport. By car is the best way to go, though buses travel from Boston to all three towns.

1 Cambridge

3 miles W of downtown Boston, 6 miles SE of Lexington, 15 miles SE of Concord

Cambridge means Harvard to most visitors who come to Boston, and although Harvard is not the only thing in the city of Cambridge (MIT's there too, after all), it is certainly the city's most important institution. Harvard Square, at the intersection of Massachusetts Avenue, Brattle Street, and John F. Kennedy Street, is a crossroad that teems with evidence of a hundred lifestyles, from the stuffily academic to the loosest of dropouts.

GETTING THERE   By Subway   The MBTA's Red Line connects Harvard Square to Park Street Station on Boston Common. The Red Line is the fastest, most frequent, and most comfortable in the system, and the journey normally takes about 15 minutes from turnstile to turnstile. Going from Harvard Square into Boston, take any "Inbound" train; all trains stop at Park Street Station. From Boston to Harvard Square, take an "Outbound" train marked "Alewife" or "Harvard."

By Bus   Those staying in Boston's Back Bay section might find it easier to walk to Massachusetts Avenue and catch bus no. 1 ("Harvard-Dudley"), which goes past MIT, through Central Square, directly to Harvard Square, the last stop. From areas nearer to Boston Common, the Red Line subway is faster the bus.

By Car   From Boston, take Storrow Drive westbound along the south bank of the Charles River, or Memorial Drive westbound along the north bank, and follow the signs to Harvard Square. You can also follow Massachusetts Avenue from Boston across the Charles River and all the way to Harvard Square.

ESSENTIALS   The **telephone area code** is **617.** There's an information kiosk right in the center of Harvard Square, maintained and staffed by **Cambridge Discovery, Inc.** (☎ **617/497-1630**), open Monday through Saturday from 9am to 5pm (to 6pm in summer) and Sunday from 1 to 5pm. Walking tours of Old Cambridge leave from the kiosk four times daily between late June and Labor Day; call for details and schedules.

WHAT TO SEE & DO

Harvard Square is the heartbeat of Cambridge, a place where all styles of life commingle in a wild, busy carnival atmosphere.

   In addition to the guided walking tours mentioned above, Cambridge Discovery, Inc. (☎ 617/491-1630) also supplies maps for **self-guided walking tours** and other informative literature about the rest of Cambridge.

Around Boston

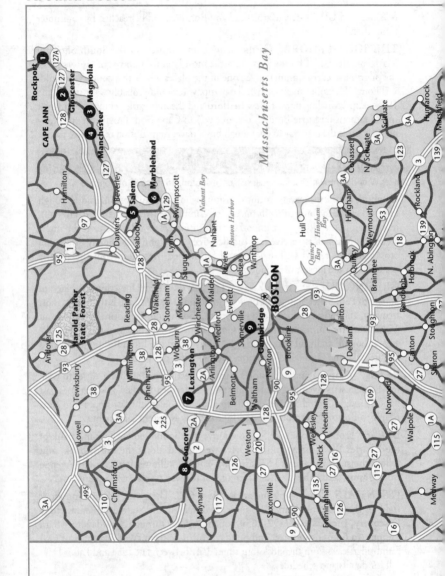

Massachusetts Bay

BOSTON

NEW ENGLAND

Cambridge 9
Concord 8
Fall River 12
Gloucester 2
Lexington 7
Magnolia 3
Manchester 4
Marblehead 6
New Bedford 11
Plymouth 10
Rockport 1
Salem 5

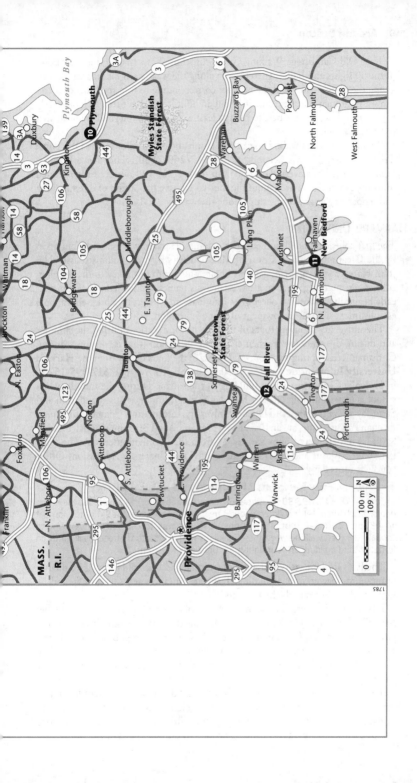

The "Old Cambridge Walking Guide" brochure has a map and a description of the 30 sights and buildings to be seen along the walk, each marked with a sign giving the place's name and the number corresponding to it in the brochure. You can walk through the tour route in about an hour if you don't stop to look closely at any one place, but it's best to plan at least a few hours, for you'll want to visit some of the buildings.

If you'd rather not walk, you can also climb aboard a trolley for an **Old Town Trolley Tour,** 329 W. Second St. (☎ **617/269-7150**). They leave Harvard Square on the hour every day from 9am to 4pm for 100-minute fully narrated tours of Cambridge. Throughout the tour you'll have the option of disembarking and reboarding at any of the stops along the way.

HARVARD UNIVERSITY

The first college founded in the British colonies, Harvard was established in 1636 by the Great and General Court of Massachusetts Bay, the colonists' assembly. John Harvard, a clergyman, gave his library and a sum of money to the fledgling college, a generous gesture that has earned his name worldwide fame. From that early beginning, Harvard College grew into Harvard University, a huge educational establishment with an endowment of over $5.5 billion.

The university sponsors tours of its most historic sections during the summer and during the school year when classes are in session (that is, no tours during Christmas recess, spring vacation, etc.). Most of the tours depart from the **Harvard University Information Center,** 1350 Massachusetts Ave. (☎ **617/495-1573**), in Holyoke Center, the tallest building in the square. During the months when school is in session, tours depart Monday through Friday at 10am and 2pm and Saturday at 2pm from the Harvard University Information Center. From June through August, tours are at 10 and 11:15am and 2 and 3:15pm Monday through Saturday and 1:30 and 3pm Sunday, all from the information center. The tours last about an hour and are free. Additionally, the University Admissions Office conducts tours daily.

Harvard University Museums of Cultural and Natural History

24 Oxford St. ☎ **617/495-3045**. Admission (covers all museums) $4 adults, $3 seniors and students, $1 children 3–13, children under 3 free; free for everyone Sat 9–11am. Mon–Sat 9am–4:30pm, Sun 1–4:30pm. Directions: Ask your way to the Science Center and Memorial Hall, then walk between these buildings to get to Oxford Street. Walk north on Oxford; the third building on your right is the University Museums.

The Harvard University Museums of Cultural and Natural History are a quartet of museums located in one building. There are entrances at 24 Oxford St. and 11 Divinity Ave. Here are the high points of each:

Botanical Museum: The world-famous collection of glass flowers is the big attraction here. The incredibly delicate and detailed glass replicas of flowers that grow all over the world were made in the days before color photography allowed a botanist to make teaching aids easily and cheaply with only a camera. The variety of "flowers" on view and the artistry that it took to make them are truly amazing.

The Botanical Museum has other displays and dioramas on the stair landing as you enter the building. These change from time to time, but may include such things as an exhibit of crossbreeding in the cultivation of corn or the various narcotic substances used by primitive peoples in different parts of the world.

Museum of Comparative Zoology: Despite its forbidding name, this museum is a favorite with children, for it's loaded with stuffed animals of all kinds, from a tiny hummingbird to a towering giraffe. Sharks, ostriches, hippopotamuses, and zebras abound, as do the exotic beasts from exotic places: tapirs, lemurs, quetzals, and aardvarks. The museum is a product of the 19th-century rage for natural history, which sent Harvard men all over the world in search of specimens to use in scientific teaching. Don't miss the full-size whale skeletons, in the same high-ceilinged room that houses the giraffe.

Peabody Museum of Archeology and Ethnology: The collections here were gathered by adventurers, explorers, archeologists, and scholars. The museum's strong suit is the indigenous peoples of North America; its great hall of the North American Indian reopened in 1990 after having been closed for 10 years. The Maya civilization is particularly well represented, with statues (authentic as well as fiberglass copies); wall-size photographs of jungle scenes; copies of the giant stelae and zoomorphs from Quirigua, Guatemala, and Copan, Honduras; gold jewelry; and household artifacts. Notes and extracts from diaries posted here and there give you an idea of what it was like being one of the first archeologists to discover and study these fascinating works of art.

Other exhibits cover the tribal art of Oceania, and 19th-century photographs and objects from Japan. The Peabody Museum Shop is one of Cambridge's most fascinating places. Handcrafts and folk art from all over the world are on display and on sale, at reasonable prices.

Mineralogical and Geological Museum: This museum houses an internationally important collection of rocks, minerals, ores, and meteorites. Exhibits include an unusually comprehensive systematic mineral collection, minerals from New England, gems, and meteorites.

Busch-Reisinger Museum

32 Quincy St. ☎ **617/495-9400.** Admission (also good for the Fogg Art Museum and Arthur M. Sackler Museum): $5 adults, $4 seniors, $3 students, free for children 18 and under; free for everyone on Sat morning. Mon–Sat 10am–5pm, Sun 1–5pm. Closed holidays. Subway: Red Line to Harvard.

The Busch-Reisinger Museum specializes in the arts of German-speaking Europe. It showcases one of North America's leading collections of German expressionist art, with famous pieces by Klee, Nolde, Kandinsky, Beckmann, and others. It also houses an impressive collection of constructivist, Vienna Secession, and Bauhaus pieces. The museum is located in the recently completed Werner Otto Hall, which adjoins the Fogg Art Museum.

Fogg Art Museum

32 Quincy St. ☎ **617/495-9400.** Admission (also good for the Busch-Reisinger Museum and Arthur M. Sackler Museum): $5 adults, $4 seniors, $3 students, free for children 18 and under; free for everyone Sat morning. Mon–Sat 10am–5pm, Sun 1–5pm. Closed holdiays. Subway: Red Line to Harvard.

The Fogg Art Museum ranks as one of the more important collections of painting and sculpture in the Boston area. Founded in 1891, the Fogg has long served as the center of art study at Harvard. The Fogg is on Quincy Street between Harvard Street and Broadway, east of Harvard yard. As you enter, the mood for your visit to the galleries is set by the interior court, copied in Italian travertine from an Italian building. The museum's permanent exhibits include a fine collection of English silver, drawings, photographs; Italian, Dutch, and American art;

and 19th- and 20th-century French art. Shows of other works from the museum's holdings are set up periodically and are very well done.

Arthur M. Sackler Museum

485 Broadway. ☎ 617/495-9400. Admission (also good for the Busch-Reisinger Museum and Fogg Art Museum): $5 adults, $4 seniors, $3 students, free for children under 18; free for everyone Sat morning. Mon–Sat 10am–5pm, Sun 1–5pm. Closed holidays. Subway: Red Line to Harvard.

The Arthur M. Sackler Museum opened late in 1985. Housed here are the university's collections of ancient, Asian, and Islamic art, including the world's most extensive collection of ancient Chinese jades, plus important collections of Persian miniatures and Japanese prints.

A HISTORIC HOUSE

Longfellow National Historic Site

105 Brattle St. ☎ 617/876-4491. Admission $2 adults, free for children under 16 and senior citizens over 62. Wed–Sun 10am–4:30pm; tours (the only way to see the house) are at 10:45 and 11:45am and 1, 2, 3, and 4pm. Directions: From Brattle Square (a few steps from Harvard Square), take Brattle Street, and after about five blocks, look for the big yellow house on the right-hand side.

Those interested in 19th-century Cambridge will want to see this house, which is now a National Historic Site. Although the house was built by Maj. John Vassall in 1759 and was for a time Washington's headquarters (he and Martha celebrated their 17th wedding anniversary here), most of the furnishings are left from the time of Henry Wadsworth Longfellow, who lived here for 45 years. Mrs. Andrew Craigie took in boarders (mostly Harvard professors), and Longfellow was one, starting in 1837. Soon after he and Fanny Appleton were married, Fanny's father bought the house for the young married couple, and the poet lived here until his death in 1882. Virtually all of his belongings and furnishings are still here, as he left them when he died, for the house was occupied by his descendants until the early 1970s. It's an elegant and beautiful house, and yet still warm and homey, a treat to walk through. The National Park Service guides who take you through are friendly and knowledgeable.

Longfellow House sponsors several free concerts in the summer, on the lawn, which are open to the public. Other special events include the February birthday anniversary celebration, and the Christmas open house.

WHERE TO STAY

There's no reason you shouldn't plan to stay in Cambridge during the length of your Boston visit. In fact, Cambridge is a good choice for those of you who want access to downtown Boston but prefer a quieter location. Keep in mind that bed-and-breakfast organizations serving the Boston area serve Cambridge as well. See "Accommodations," in Chapter 4, for details.

EXPENSIVE

✪ Charles Hotel

1 Bennett St., Cambridge, MA 02138. ☎ **617/864-1200** or 800/882-1818. Fax 617/864-5715. 296 rms, 44 suites. A/C MINIBAR TV TEL. $239–$259 double; $325–$1,400 suite. Children under 18 stay free in parent's room. Weekend packages available. AE, CB, DC, DISC, ER, JCB, MC, V. Parking $16. MBTA: Harvard Square (Red Line).

In Charles Square, the upscale shopping, dining, and office complex just a stone's throw away from Harvard's halls of ivy, this hotel creates a special niche of its own with its award-winning jazz bar, European-style Le Pli Day Spa, the city's only four-star restaurant, and distinctive guest rooms. Antique blue-and-white New England quilts, handcrafted between 1865 and 1885, hang in the Charles's great oak staircase as well as at the entrance to each guest-room floor.

The updated country style of the guest rooms is bright and airy, with custom-designed adaptations of early American Shaker pieces. The light wood tones of the armoires, apothecary chests, and four-poster beds are accented with homespun fabrics. Bathrooms are equipped with hairdryers, scales, and terry-cloth robes. All rooms have large windows that can be opened, and are equipped with dataports. A novel service includes a tie-in with the nearby Words Worth discount bookstore. A Charles staffer will purchase books for you and even have them gift wrapped. The tab is added to your bill.

There are five great weekend packages, including a workout weekend for two with a full day of pampering at the spa for about $500. In addition there is a $1,000 spa weekend with spa and salon treatments and gourmet low-calorie meals.

Dining/Entertainment: The new Henrietta's Table serves breakfast, lunch, dinner, and Sunday buffet brunch. The highly acclaimed Rialto emphasizes French, Italian, and Spanish cuisine by award-winning chef, Jody Adams (see my recommendation in "Where to Dine").

Services: 24-hour room service; twice-daily maid service, evening turndown with bottle of iced mineral water. Pets can be accommodated.

Facilities: Glass-enclosed pool, Jacuzzi, sun terrace, and exercise room at the new Well Bridge Health and Fitness Center. Beauty treatments are available at Le Pli Day Spa. Facilities for teleconferencing. Seven floors for nonsmokers, 13 rooms for the disabled, rooms with special amenities for women travelers.

Doubletree Guest Suites Hotel

400 Soldiers Field Rd., Boston, MA 02134. ☎ **617/783-0090** or 800/222-8733. Fax 617/783-0897. 310 suites. A/C MINIBAR TV TEL. $159–$209 suite Sun–Thurs, $109–$149 suite Fri–Sat. AE, CB, DC, DISC, MC, V. Parking $12 Sun–Thurs, free Fri–Sat. Directions: See below.

The Doubletree Guest Suites Hotel is a good choice if you're in search of more space and convenience for the same money as a standard hotel room. Though the address is Boston, this 15-story building is as close to Harvard Square and MIT as it is to Boston University and downtown. Each suite consists of a bedroom with a king-size bed, AM/FM radio, writing desk, living room with full-size sofa bed, and dining table.

Coming from Boston, take Storrow Drive westbound, follow the signs for Newton and Arlington, and exit at the Central Square/Mass. Pike exit; at the set of lights, take a wide left U-turn. From Harvard Square, take Storrow Drive eastbound (toward Boston) and take the Mass. Pike exit, but instead of turning right to the Mass. Pike entrance, go straight ahead to the hotel.

Dining/Entertainment: Scullers Grille serves breakfast, lunch, and dinner and specializes in New England seafood. Scullers, the hotel's jazz club, is one of the city's best.

Services: Room service, free van shuttle to Cambridge and Boston for weekend guests.

Facilities: Indoor pool, whirlpool, sauna, exercise room.

Hyatt Regency Cambridge

575 Memorial Dr., Cambridge, MA 02139. ☎ **617/492-1234** or 800/233-1234. 469 rms, 18 suites. A/C MINIBAR TV TEL. $109–$239 double; $400–$575 suite. Weekend discounts available. Additional person $20 extra. AE, CB, DC, DISC, ER, JCB, MC, V. Parking $18 per day. Directions: Take Memorial Drive eastbound from Harvard Square about two miles.

The most dramatic hotel in town is the Aztec-pyramid Hyatt Regency Cambridge. True to the Hyatt design tradition, it has a grand interior space rising from ground floor to top floor, planted with trees and hanging vines and surrounded by mezzanine walkways to the well-appointed, modern guest rooms. Families are especially welcome here. There are special reduced room rates for parents who choose to have their children sleep in a separate room, and there are also adult and children's bicycles available for guest use. It's not easily reached by public transportation, so plan to use taxis, bicycles, or your car. There's a complimentary shuttle to local points of interest.

Dining/Entertainment: Jonah's Seafood Café serves breakfast, lunch, and Sunday brunch. The Pally Sadoe Bar, just off this mezzanine, features billiard tables, dart boards, board games, and sports TV. Take one of the crystal-shaped glass elevators that slide up the wall to reach the revolving Spinnaker Italia restaurant on the top floor. It's open for lunch and dinner and offers a panoramic view that includes Boston, Cambridge, and the Charles River.

Services: Concierge, free shuttle van to Harvard Square and downtown Boston.

Facilities: Pool, health club, children's playground, nonsmoking rooms.

The Inn at Harvard

1201 Massachusetts Ave., Cambridge, MA 02138. ☎ **617/491-2222** or 800/458-5886. Fax 617/491-6520. 113 rms. A/C TV TEL. $155–$249 double. Parking $18. Ask about special packages. AE, CB, DC, DISC, MC, V. Subway: Red Line to Harvard.

Step into the lobby of the rather impersonal, red-brick, Georgian-style Inn at Harvard and you'll feel as if you've stepped into a university library. Indeed, this fairly new hotel has an academic air about it and feels as if it's an extension of the university. The glass-roofed main lobby—known as the atrium—is four stories high and is surrounded by guest rooms and balconies. There's a library stocked with books as well as current periodicals, newspapers, and Harvard Press publications. Individual guest rooms are simply but tastefully decorated in earth tones, and each one has a lounge chair or two armchairs around a table, windows that open, and an original painting from the Fogg Art Museums. Phone systems feature computer dataports and a voice-mail message service. The inn is adjacent to Harvard Yard, at the intersection of Massachusetts Avenue, Harvard Street, and Quincy Street.

Dining/Entertainment: The Atrium restaurant serves seasonal New England fare.

Services: Business services with fax, courier, typing, copying, and package shipping and receiving. Complimentary newspaper delivery; free shoe shine; limited room service.

Facilities: Nonsmoking and handicapped-accessible rooms.

Royal Sonesta Hotel

5 Cambridge Pkwy., Cambridge, MA 02142. ☎ **617/491-3600** or 800/766-3782. Fax 617/661-5956. 400 rms, 28 suites. A/C TV TEL. $185–$235 double; $275–$635 suite. AE, CB, DC, MC, V. Parking $15 per day. Directions: Follow Route 3 across the Charles River Dam on the Msgr. O'Brien Highway, pass the Museum of Science, and turn left onto Land Boulevard. Subway: Green Line to Science Park or Lechmere.

Although it's in Cambridge, the Royal Sonesta is actually closer to downtown Boston than to Harvard Square. A short trundle from the hotel across the Charles River Dam by the Museum of Science brings you right to Beacon Hill. Located right on the Charles River, the rooms have spectacular views of the Boston skyline. Original contemporary artwork is displayed throughout public spaces as well as in some guest rooms. Across the street from the hotel is the new CambridgeSide Galleria, which houses many shops and restaurants.

Dining/Entertainment: Davio's Ristorante and Café is the hotel's Italian restaurant and is more formal than the hotel's other restaurant, the Gallery Café.

Services: Room service (Sun–Thurs 6am–1am, Fri–Sat 6am–2am), babysitting, courtesy van service to downtown Boston and Cambridge.

Facilities: Health club, gift shop, indoor/outdoor pool.

Sheraton Commander

16 Garden St., Cambridge, MA 02138. ☎ **617/547-4800** or 800/325-3535. Fax 617/868-8322. 176 rms, 20 suites. A/C MINIBAR TV TEL. $135–$295 double; $225–$375 suite. Children under 18 stay free in parents' room. AE, CB, DC, DISC, JCB, MC, V. Free parking. Subway: Red Line to Harvard Square.

Located in the most interesting and historic district of Cambridge, this hotel, situated just across Cambridge Common from Harvard University, first opened in 1927. It stands just a few feet from the elm tree, where, on July 3, 1775, General George Washington took command of the American troops, and for years it has been the hotel of choice for this country's politicians. In fact, in 1952, the Sheraton Commander hosted John F. Kennedy. The decor in the public rooms tends to the high-brow colonial, and a bronze statue of General Washington (the commander for whom the hotel was named) stands in the entry garden, to the right of the doors. The New England colonial decor extends to the guest rooms with their tall four-poster beds, pine desks, Boston rockers, and "oil" lamps. Although there is free parking at the hotel, the lot is small and you may have to leave your keys at the desk so the doorman can jockey the cars around to best advantage.

Dining/Entertainment: 16 Garden Street Restaurant serves breakfast, lunch, dinner, and a splendid Sunday brunch. The 16 Garden Street Cafe serves lighter fare throughout the afternoon and evening.

Services: Room service, concierge, limited business services.

Facilities: Fitness center; sundeck.

MODERATE

Ⓢ Best Western Homestead

220 Alewife Brook Pkwy., Cambridge, MA 02138-1102. ☎ **617/491-8000** or 800/528-1234. Fax 617/491-4932. 69 rms. A/C TV TEL. Jan–Mar, $84–$114 double; Mar–May, $110–$143 double; June–Aug, $114–$154 double; Sept–Oct, $124–$144 double; Nov–Dec, $74–$114 double. Rates may be higher during special events. Additional person or a rollaway bed $10 extra. Children under 12 stay free in parents' room. AE, DISC, MC, V.

The family-owned and -operated Homestead stands head and shoulders above other Best Western hotels I've stayed in. You'll feel at home in the elegant yet comfortable lobby, which has an inviting sitting area in front of a carved mahogany fireplace. Guest rooms in this four-story hotel are attractively furnished and decorated with deep wine-colored carpeting and light floral-print bedspreads and draperies, plus reproduction furnishings. The baths are modern and spotlessly clean. Hotel facilities include an indoor pool and whirlpool and rental-car pickup and dropoff. Guests may also take advantage of the scenic $2^1/2$-mile jogging trail across from the hotel (it circles Fresh Pond) and a Nautilus facility one block away (for a nominal fee). Same-day dry cleaning is available during the week, and the hotel's 99 Restaurant offers American cuisine at moderate prices. The Homestead is within walking distance of a 10-screen movie theater.

Howard Johnson Hotel
777 Memorial Dr., Cambridge, MA 02139. ☎ **617/492-7777** or 800/654-2000. 205 rms. A/C TV TEL. $88–$145 double. Additional person $10 extra. Weekend discounts available with advance notice. AE, MC, V.

The Howard Johnson is a 14-story establishment, and the higher rooms have better views; some have small balconies. Views are of Boston and the Charles, straight across the Charles, up the Charles River to Harvard, and a city view of Cambridge. The hotel has a year-round pool, a restaurant and bar, and a pleasant brick-and-dark-wood interior. Harvard special events (freshmen registration, Harvard-Yale game, homecoming, graduation, and the like) can fill the hotel, and rooms should be reserved well in advance. The hotel is one mile east of Harvard Square; a car or taxi must be used to get to and from Harvard Square or downtown Boston.

BUDGET

A Cambridge House Bed & Breakfast Inn
2218 Massachusetts Ave., Cambridge, MA 02140. ☎ **617/491-6300** or 800/232-9989 in U.S. and Canada, 800/96-2079 in the United Kingdom. Fax 617/868-2848. 16 rms (13 with bath). A/C TV TEL. $99–$225 double. All rates include breakfast. Extra person $30. AE, DISC, MC, V. Free parking. MBTA: Porter Square (Red Line).

A Cambridge House is a beautifully restored 1892 colonial home listed in the National Register of Historic Places. Each room is warmly decorated with Waverly fabrics and antiques. Most of the rooms have fireplaces and four-poster canopy beds, which are covered with Fieldcrest linens and plush down comforters. Complimentary beverages and freshly baked pastries are served by the fireplace in the library or parlor. And a full breakfast, also complimentary, prepared by a professionally trained chef, is available every morning. There's something different each day—omelets, crepes, waffles, or fresh fruit. Every evening, complimentary wine and cheese are also offered.

WHERE TO DINE

Cambridge is even more cosmopolitan than Boston, and this is well demonstrated in its restaurants. Cannelloni to couscous, wonton to Weisswurst, Cambridge has it. Some of the best places to have a good, inexpensive lunch or a light supper are Cambridge's coffeehouses, almost all of which serve food as well as a wide selection of hot and cold coffee and tea drinks. And finally, there are the ice-cream shops of Harvard Square, worthy of a list unto themselves.

EXPENSIVE

Harvest
44 Brattle St. ☎ **617/492-1115.** Reservations required Fri–Sat; not accepted in the cafe. Main courses $7.50–$12 at lunch; $21.50–$28 at dinner; dinner in cafe $7.50–$18.50. AE, DC, DISC, MC, V. Mon–Fri 11:30am–2:30pm; Mon–Thurs 6–10pm, Fri–Sat 5:30–10:30pm. Sat–Sun brunch 11am–3pm. Subway: Red Line to Harvard. AMERICAN.

The Harvest, hidden away down the passageway that penetrates the four-story glass building which houses the Crate and Barrel on Brattle Street, is one of Cambridge's best. The restaurant's location allows it to have the most pleasant outdoor luncheon area in all Cambridge, and it's a favorite gathering spot of the literati as well as Harvard professors and young professionals. Harvest offers meticulously prepared dishes: A sample dinner may start with potato-wrapped filet of sole with spinach, chanterelles, and a mint-and-orange vinaigrette. An excellent main-course choice might be the vegetarian tagliatelle with porcini mushrooms, fresh peas, and bell peppers with parmesean in a light-cream sauce. The dessert menu might include chocolate truffle cake on a praline crème anglaise or an apple-apricot compote. There's also a cafe on premises, which offers lighter meals and is less expensive than the main dining room, but equally interesting. Sunday brunch is excellent.

✪ Rialto

One Bennett St., in the Charles Hotel. ☎ **617/661-5050.** Reservations are recommended. Main courses $17–$29. AE, MC, V. Sun–Thurs 5:30–10pm, Fri–Sat 5:30–11pm. Bar is open Sun–Thurs 5pm–1am, Fri–Sat 5pm–1:30am. Subway: Red line to Harvard Square. FRENCH/ ITALIAN/SPANISH.

In the past many people have avoided hotel restaurants as a rule, but today you'll find some of the country's best restaurants tucked away within hotels. Rialto is one of those places. The dining room with floor-to-ceiling windows, gold-colored walls, rich wood trim, and plush banquettes is comfortable and inviting. Walls are hung with artwork on loan from Gallery Naga as well as some works collected by restauranteur, Michaela Larson (formerly of Michaela's Caffe). Chef Jody Adams is, simply put, a wizard with food. The way she combines taste and texture is brilliant, and you have to taste it to believe it. It was a difficult choice, but I started with the *soupe de poisson* (Provençal fisherman's soup with rouille, gruyère, and basil oil); I wasn't disappointed. I followed that with grilled mackerel with a tomato-caper vinaigrette and crab, asparagus, and swiss chard bundles, and couldn't have been happier. Finally, I had the chocolate mousse pyramid with caramel sauce and pistachio praline—fantastic! No matter what you do in Boston or Cambridge, you should make Rialto a first-choice stop.

Upstairs at the Pudding

10 Holyoke St. ☎ **617/864-1933.** Reservations recommended, especially on theater evenings. Main courses $17–$27; dinner $30–$40. AE, DC, MC, V. Ask about the pre-theater meal. 11am–2:30pm; 6–10pm; brunch Sun 11:30am–2:30pm. Subway: Red Line to Harvard. CONTINENTAL/NORTHERN ITALIAN.

Located on the third floor of the building that houses Harvard's famous Hasty Pudding Club, this is about as "Harvardy" as a place can get. There's always a low hum of satisfaction in the grandly accoutred main dining room (complete with brass service plates) and Secret Garden terrace (during fair weather months). The menu, which changes daily, includes a fine selection of northern Italian dishes and desserts. You might start with the roasted asparagus soup with chive crème fraîche, followed by skillet-seared Atlantic salmon with a mixed grill of corn, leeks, red and yellow peppers, and garlic mashed potatoes. For dessert, try the pear bread pudding with bourbon cream; it's an unusual twist on a traditional dish.

MODERATE

Border Café

32 Church St. ☎ **617/864-6100.** Reservations not accepted. Main courses $6–$11. AE, MC, V. Mon–Thurs 11am–1am, Fri–Sat 11am–2am, Sun noon–11pm. Subway: Red Line to Harvard. MEXICAN/CAJUN.

The Border Café, a mock-stark Mexican cantina with rough-hewn wood tables and naive murals of favorite Mexican bottles, is popular partly because of its tongue-in-cheek decor, but more because the food is surprisingly inexpensive. The cuisine here borrows from Cajun, Tex-Mex, and Caribbean cooking, and you'll love it. Try the enchiladas, tacos, Caribbean shrimp (in a spicy coconut batter), or fajitas done in the traditional way and served with all the fixings. You might also have a sandwich and Corona (beer), or blackened redfish (which in my experience has always been light, flaky, and adequately moist). The restaurant is at the corner of Church and Palmer Streets.

Casa Portugal

1200 Cambridge St. ☎ **617/491-8880.** Reservations recommended on weekends. Main courses $7.95–$13.95. AE, DISC, MC, V. Daily 4:30–10pm. Subway: Red Line to Harvard Square, then take the Lechmere bus to Inman Square/Cambridge Square. PORTUGUESE.

The locals like this casual bistro for its hearty, inexpensive Portuguese fare and warm, inviting, casual atmosphere. Soup of the day, rice, and Portuguese fried potatoes come with all entrées. The tureens, which combine several types of shellfish, are quite popular, as is the *bacalhau assado a cuca* (codfish, garlic, peppers, and potatoes baked with olive oil). There are four items on the menu singled out as "spicy," including *grelha mista* (grilled bits of veal, pork, liver, and *linguica* served on a skewer). Casa Portugal is a lovely place.

Cottonwood Café

1815 Massachusetts Ave. ☎ **617/661-7440.** Reservations recommended. Main courses $9–$16 at lunch, $12–$16 at dinner. Sun–Fri noon–3pm; Sun–Thurs 5:45–10pm, Fri–Sat 5:30–11:30pm. Subway: Red Line to Porter. SOUTHWESTERN.

Located in the Porter Exchange building at Porter Square, the Cottonwood is a cozy, attractive, upscale southwestern place with an inventive menu that might best be described as "Modern Southwest Cuisine." The original creations here are a blend of Native American, Spanish, and European cuisines. A lot of the cooking is done on an open grill, and the chef uses spices and chiles indigenous to the Southwest. Among the specials you might find Rocky Mountain lamb (four superb little chops arranged on red raspberry chipotle sauce and green cilantro pesto) and salmon Colorado (a grilled fillet with smoked tomato sauce and cilantro-garlic cream). Many dishes are pretty spicy, so ask. Authentic, carefully chosen crafts enliven the decor.

Grendel's Restaurant and Bar

89 Winthrop St. ☎ **617/491-1160.** Reservations recommended. Main courses $5–$18. AE, DC, DISC, MC, V. Sun–Thurs 11am–11pm, Fri–Sat 11am–midnight. (Bar, daily 4pm–1am.) Subway: Red Line to Harvard. INTERNATIONAL.

Every college student reads about Grendel, the dragon that threatens the hero of the ancient English epic *Beowulf,* but anyone in Harvard Square—student or not—can frequent Grendel's, a restaurant noted for its reasonable prices and large portions. Grendel's is behind a tiny patch of grass off John F. Kennedy Street at Mount Auburn Street, one block south of Harvard Square toward the Charles River. A huge sign on the roof leads the way. The cellar of the red-brick building is the bar, furnished with a fireplace for cold winter nights, and dark-wood tables. Upstairs is the restaurant, with two fireplaces and a glassed-in terrace overlooking busy John F. Kennedy Street. The menu tells of international specialties, such as spinach pie, fettuccine, chicken curry, shish kebab, quiche, omelets, burgers, and sandwiches. There's a good salad bar. Alcoholic beverages are served. As for the desserts, they're a list in themselves, but suffice it to say that they include sour-cream fudge cake.

⊙ Henrietta's Table

One Bennett St., in the Charles Hotel. ☎ **617/661-5005.** Reservations are recommended. Main courses at breakfast $2.25–$9.50; $7.50–$10 at lunch; $9–$12.50 at dinner. AE, MC, V. Mon–Fri 6:30–11am, Sat 7–11:30am, Sun 7–10:30am; brunch Sun 11:30am–3pm; Mon–Sat noon–3pm; Sun–Thurs 5:30–10pm, Fri–Sat 5:30–11pm. Market hours Mon–Fri 6:30am–10pm, Sat–Sun 7am–10pm. Subway: Red line to Harvard Square. NEW ENGLAND.

The creators of Henrietta's Table describe the food as "fresh and honest country cooking." Indeed, you'll feel like you're in the country when you enter this charming place. There's a farmstand market filled with fruits, vegetables, and fresh breads adjoining the white-walled dining room. Mission-style chairs surround white-clothed tables, and there's an open kitchen. The short menu changes daily to accommodate the freshest produce, but on a recent visit for dinner I had the herb-crusted rotisserie chicken (moist and tender) and the apple-wood smoked Maine salmon with a beach plum vinaigrette (the fish was flaky and flavorful, and the vinaigrette added an unexpected twist). The lunch menu features sandwiches, Yankee pot roast, and baked scrod, among other items. And at breakfast you can get hotcakes, waffles, cereals, and farm fresh eggs. Incidentally, in case you were wondering, Henrietta's Table is named after the hotel owner's 1,000-pound pet pig who lives on Martha's Vineyard.

House of Blues

96 Winthrop St. ☎ **617/491-2583.** Reservations accepted for Sunday brunch only. Main courses $4.95–$14.95. AE, MC, V. Sun–Wed 11:30am–1am, Thurs–Sat 11:30am–2am. Subway: Red Line to Harvard. CAJUN/PIZZA/INTERNATIONAL.

Located in a blue clapboard house just outside the center of Harvard Square, the House of Blues is one of Boston's hottest restaurants. Everything is blue here, and the walls and ceilings are dotted with whimsical pieces of folk art by various artists. On the ceiling near the bar area are plaster bas-reliefs of great blues musicians. Above the bar is a poster of the Blues Brothers and a sign that reads "THE WAGES OF SIN IS DEATH."

The menu offers a variety of interesting dishes. You might begin with the buffalo legs (they're much bigger than your average buffalo wings) and follow with jambalaya or a burger. There's a long list of pizzas available—try the one topped with feta cheese and garlic—that are baked in a wood-fired pizza oven. Barbecue ribs and chicken are also house favorites.

The House of Blues features live blues entertainment during the week and on weekends. The Sunday Gospel Brunch requires reservations at least two weeks in advance.

La Groceria

853 Main St. ☎ **617/547-9258** or 876-4162. Reservations are not accepted. Main courses $3.95–$7.95 at lunch, $9.95–$15.95 at dinner. Early-bird special $9.95. Children's menu $4.95–$5.95. AE, DC, DISC, MC, V. Mon–Fri 11:30am–4pm; Mon–Thurs 4–11pm, Fri–Sat 4–11pm, Sun 1–10pm. Subway: Red Line to Central Square. ITALIAN.

With its stucco archways, tile floors, and colorful artwork, this restaurant off Central Square could easily be off a main square in Bologna. For lunch, start out with the antipasto fantasia (an assortment of hot and cold vegetables, baked clams, salami, and cheese). Salads play a large role on the lunch menu. The *insalata di pollo con pesto* (sliced rotisserie chicken breast with pesto served over romaine lettuce, radicchio, string beans, and potatoes and drizzled with creamy Italian dressing) is quite good. Sandwiches, such as the sirloin strip sandwich (grilled marinated sirloin with roasted tomatoes, peppers, onions, and provolone cheese) and the vegetarian (grilled eggplant, tomatoes, artichokes, and zucchini topped with pesto and Giardiniera salad), are served on focaccia bread, with a light tomato-and-cucumber salad and potatoes topped with a vinaigrette. The dinner menu is more substantial, featuring everything from homemade pasta to fish, chicken, and veal. Start with the simple but tasty garlic bread Groceria (topped with tomatoes, red onions, olive oil, and fennel seed). I'm a big fan of fettuccine Alfredo, which is good here, but better is the tortelloni al forno (baked tortellini suffed with shiitake and porcini mushrooms), and prociutto tossed with sautéed ground veal, onions, bread crumbs, parmigiano cheese, and fresh tomatoes topped with mozzarella cheese. Another favorite is the chicken *con carciofi,* sautéed in white wine with mushrooms, roasted peppers, and artichoke hearts. If you have room, top off your meal with homemade cannoli (filled to order) and a freshly ground cappuccino. Check out the pasta machine at the entrance to La Groceria. The noodles you see may be rushed upstairs to be part of your dinner. Early-bird specials, served until 6:30pm Sunday through Friday, include a main course, salad, and cannoli.

S&S Deli and Restaurant

1334 Cambridge St., Inman Sq. ☎ **617/354-0777.** Reservations are not required. Main courses $2.95–$10.95. No credit cards. Mon–Sat 7am–midnight, Sun 8am–midnight. Sat–Sun brunch 8am–4pm. Subway: Take the Red Line to Harvard Square and then bus no. 69 to Lechmere which goes by Inman Square and along Cambridge Street. DELI.

Back in the good old days when nobody watched calories, Jewish mothers would show their hospitality by urging guests to "Es and es"—Yiddish for "Eat and eat." This spot, founded in 1919 by the great-grandmother of the current owners, gives you an opportunity to do just that. On the outskirts of Cambridge (actually in Somerville), it is close enough to be listed here. You can find the traditional deli items on the menu: corned beef, pastrami, tongue, and Reuben sandwiches; potato pancakes, blintzes, knockwurst and beans (Boston baked beans no less!), and lox and whitefish. Also chopped liver, borscht, chicken soup, and, naturally, bagels and cream cheese. But S&S is also a full-service restaurant with entrées of beef, chicken, and fish, plus quiche and croissants! What would grandma say to that?

S&S serves breakfast anytime during restaurant hours. Brunch, served Saturday and Sunday, is quite popular—plan to arrive before 10am to avoid the long lines.

Wursthaus

4 John F. Kennedy St., at Harvard Sq. ☎ **617/491-7110.** Reservations are not required. Main courses $8–$14.25.AE, DC, DISC, MC, V. Mon–Fri 7:30–11am; Sat–Sun 9am–2pm; Mon–Sat 11am–3pm; Mon–Sat 4pm–midnight, Sun 11:30am–9pm. Subway: Take the Red Line to Harvard Square. GERMAN/AMERICAN.

This famous spot is very German and always very crowded. The bar with an attached eating counter is always jammed with university teachers, students, politicians, passersby, and occasional businesspeople. The Wursthaus claims to have the world's largest selection of foreign beers (128 in all) and specializes in such items as bratwurst, knockwurst, sauerbraten, and imported wieners. More than 30 varieties of sandwiches are also available.

BUDGET

An intellectual center will have its coffeehouses, dedicated to serving the beverage that stimulates thought and aids conversation. Harvard Square has a good selection of coffeehouses, all of which serve light meals, desserts, ice cream, and beverages besides coffee. Each draws a special clientele (particularly those on a budget), and you can spend a very pleasant day or two hopping from one to another of these, testing them to find the one that suits you best. The ones that follow are, in my opinion, the best places in Cambridge.

Algiers Coffeehouse

40 Brattle St. ☎ **617/492-1557.** Reservations not accepted. Main courses $2.25–$7.95. No credit cards. Mon–Thurs 8am–midnight, Fri–Sat 8am–1am. Subway: Red Line to Harvard. MIDDLE EASTERN.

For those of us who remember the Algiers Coffeehouse when it was a dark, smoke-filled literary hangout, the "new and improved" version (a historical renovation) is a little shocking, but extremely pleasant nonetheless. Located in Brattle Hall, it's still one of the favorite hangouts of the literati of Cambridge, and it still serves delicious soups, sandwiches, pizzas, omelets, falafel, and hummus. It's a great stop for a snack, a light meal, or just a cup of coffee or tea (there's a rather long list of beverages available). In a way, a trip to Cambridge would be lacking without even the quickest stop at Algiers Coffeehouse.

⑤ Blacksmith House Bakery and Café

56 Brattle St. ☎ **617/354-3036.** Reservations not required. Beverages 70¢–2.50; desserts $1.20–$3.75; salads and sandwiches $5.95–$8.75; main courses $6.95–$8.75. MC, V. Mid–Sept to mid–June, Mon–Wed 9am–4pm, Thurs–Sat 9am–5pm, Sun (brunch) 11am–3pm. Mid–June to mid–Sept, Tues–Sat 9am–8pm, Sun (brunch) 11am–3pm. Subway: Red Line to Harvard. CAFE.

It's said that Longfellow, who lived only six blocks away, wrote his famous poem about a Cambridge blacksmith whose shop was on Brattle Street: "Under the spreading chestnut tree/ The village smithy stands;/ The smith, a mighty man is he,/ With large and sinewy hands." The spot the smithy occupied is now taken by the Blacksmith House, a cafe/bakery, just 1½ blocks up Brattle Street from Harvard Square. In summer the large terrace in front of the house is set with tables; in winter coffee lovers have to settle for a nice upstairs room in the house, furnished with small wood tables and spindle-back chairs. Hot main dishes include nasi goreng (sautéed shrimp and chicken tossed with rice, peanuts, raisins, spices, and herbs) and mussel pasta (steamed mussels in white wine, garlic, and cream sauce with linguine and parmesan cheese) when available. There's also a selection of salads and cold dishes. The coffee is good, and refills are cheap, but the stars of the show are the German- and Austrian-style pastries, such as Wiener torte, Sacher torte, Mozart torte, Linzer torte, and apple torte. Other types of *kuchen,* and also brioche and croissants, are made daily, too. The Blacksmith House does as big a business selling cakes (especially wedding cakes) and pastries to go as it does selling coffee to stay.

✪ Café Pamplona

12 Bow St. No phone. Reservations not accepted. Coffee $1–$3.75; pastries and sandwiches $2.50–$6.50. No credit cards. Mon–Sat 11am–1am, Sun 2pm–1am. Subway: Red Line to Harvard. CAFE.

Harvard Square's woolliest of intellectual coffeehouses is the Café Pamplona. Nothing disturbs the current of conversation here, for there's no telephone, no music, and no live entertainment. Various kinds of coffee are served, from the inexpensive espresso to the mocha, a rich coffee-and-chocolate blend topped with real whipped cream. Most coffees start from a very dark-roast bean and are therefore quite strong. From 11am to 3pm, gazpacho, toasted sandwiches, and other light-lunch items are prepared, and in summer the tiny terrace beside the Pamplona's entrance stairway is furnished with tables, chairs, and umbrellas (the indoor cafe is in a basement). In winter the atmosphere is that of a group of high-brow troglodytes, and invariably the table next to yours will be occupied by someone writing poetry or music, or translating some abstruse language. The Pamplona is tiny, and you may have to wait for a seat.

Coffee Connection

36 John F. Kennedy St. ☎ **617/492-4881.** Reservations not accepted. Coffee $1.25–$4; pastries $2–$5. AE, MC, V. Mon–Thurs 6:30am–11pm, Sat 7:30am–midnight, Sun 9am–11pm. Subway: Red Line to Harvard. CAFE.

It's generally agreed that the finest and most delicious coffee in Harvard Square—and the widest selection—is to be had at the Coffee Connection. Although light meals are served here—such as breakfast of fresh-squeezed juice, granola, and coffee—the star of the show is the coffee. The different characteristics of the various brews are described in the menu. Some coffees are very strong and hearty, others are smooth and mild—but the flavor in all is well rounded and delicious. The cheapest way to have good coffee here is to order the coffee of the day; cappuccino and other coffee specialty drinks are more expensive. Black and herbal teas are also available. The surroundings here are modern and attractive, light and airy, with a raised sitting area and a nearby counter where coffee beans and teas can be bought in bulk to take home.

Passim

47 Palmer St. ☎ **617/429-7679.** Reservations not accepted. Coffee $1.50–$3; pastries $2–$5; light lunch $4–$9. MC, V. Tues–Sat noon–4:45pm. Subway: Red Line to Harvard. CAFE.

Passim is a Harvard Square institution, known in the world of jazz, blues, and folk music as a place where numerous nationally known performers first thrilled an audience. Drop in for a beverage, snack, tea, and cake, or a light meal, and then spend some time at the small gallery, which displays the work of local artists, or look for a bauble among the glass cases of interesting objets d'art from all over the world that are on sale here. While you're here, check out the schedule of performers, then come back in the evening in plenty of time to get a good seat. Palmer Street runs between the Harvard Coop's main store and bookstore. The gift shop is open Tuesday through Saturday from noon to 5:30pm.

ICE CREAM

From a short study of Harvard Square shops, it might appear that the two most valued commodities hereabouts are the photocopy and the ice-cream cone. Ice cream, at $1.65 to $3.75 for a "small" (actually, huge) cone, is almost a cult food in Cambridge, and the virtues of the various shops and their selections of flavors are a frequent topic of debate, and even fierce loyalty. The eating of ice cream is by no means limited to the summer months, and in fact only one or two people thought it unusual that cones should be seen along Massachusetts Avenue during the bitter days of a blizzard. Herewith, a guide for the discriminating connoisseur:

Once upon a time, a local fellow decided to open an ice-cream parlo
only ice cream made from cream and things like vanilla beans, frui
natural ingredients. He set up shop in Somerville, and the lines o
devotees soon stretched around the block.

That's the legend behind the legendary Steve Herrell, founder of Steve's Ice
Cream. He later sold the business and retired to the mountains for a breather, but
then returned to franchise a new line of stores called **Herrell's,** with one at 15
Dunster St. (☎ 617/497-2179), along similar lines. Just around the corner from
the Cambridge Savings Bank in Harvard Square, Herrell's is the ultimate of
Harvard Square ice-cream shops. It's located in a former bank building, and you
can devour your cone or dish in the vault, now walled with mirrors. Flavors change
somewhat from day to day, and all cost the same. Take special note of Chocolate
Pudding, a supercharged chocolate ice cream that leaves chocoholics in ecstasy.
There's also their own frozen yogurt, made right here, and No-Moo, a nondairy
ice cream, as well as Vitari, another ice-cream alternative. Herrell's is open until
1am on Friday and Saturday during the summer months.

Steve's Ice Cream is now famous from coast to coast, still producing top-quality
treats, still attracting hordes of faithful devotees. The Harvard Square location,
at 31 Church St. (☎ 617/491-0254), has been added to the original shop at
191 Elm St. (Davis Square) in neighboring Somerville. The solution to unhappi-
ness on any hot summer day is a cone from Steve's—or on winter days, too, for
that matter.

Baskin-Robbins Ice Cream Store, 1230 Massachusetts Ave. (☎ 617/
547-3131), at the corner of Bow Street, several blocks east along Massachusetts
Avenue from Harvard Square proper, sells good ice cream in more than 50 flavors,
plus frozen yogurt. They'll make you an ice-cream cake, sundae, shake, sandwich,
freeze, or banana split if you like, anytime daily from 6am to 12:30am.

CAMBRIDGE AFTER DARK

For full listings of clubs in the Boston/Cambridge area, see "Boston After Dark"
in Chapter 4.

THEATER

Harvard's Loeb Drama Center
64 Brattle St. ☎ 617/547-8300. Tickets $10–$42, depending on the show.

The touchstone of theater in Cambridge is Harvard's Loeb Drama Center, located
at the corner of Hilliard, home of the American Repertory Theatre. This resident
professional company performs a variety of works year-round in a rotating repertory. For six weeks in the autumn and spring, the ART steps aside as Harvard/
Radcliffe undergraduates take the stage.

FILMS

Although Boston has a lively movie nightlife, Cambridge has its own group of
movie theaters, many of which tend to be slightly more "far out" than some of the
mass-market houses downtown. If you're staying in Boston but want to go to a
cinema in Cambridge, take the Red Line to Harvard. Check the *Boston Globe* for
listings of what's currently being shown. Here are Cambridge's major movie
houses:

Brattle Theater, 40 Brattle St. (☎ 617/876-6837), not far from the Harvard subway station, specializes in nostalgia and American and foreign classics.

Janus Cinema, 57 John F. Kennedy St. (☎ 617/661-3737), two blocks from the Harvard subway station down toward the river, usually has one of the hotter big films of the season, playing to a packed house.

Harvard Square, 10 Church St. (☎ 617/864-4580), is right around the corner from the subway station. In this multiscreen complex, two screens are reserved for first-run showings and the others feature the most popular films with the college crowd that have been released in the past few years; they're repeated at intervals of a few weeks. This is where you go to see it if you missed it two or three years ago or didn't want to pay the high price when it was a first-run hit. Seats are low priced, especially before 6pm (call for exact screening times).

To find out about **free films,** get hold of a copy of the *Harvard Gazette* (free) from the Harvard University Information Office or call the events line at ☎ 617/495-1718, Holyoke Center, just across the street from Harvard Yard. The *Gazette,* published regularly when Harvard is in its fall and spring semesters, sporadically at other times, lists all the university activities, including quite a few films for free or for a very low price.

2 Lexington

6 miles NW of Cambridge, 9 miles NW of downtown Boston, 6 miles E of Concord

Lexington was the home of the first Minutemen to die from British bullets in the Revolutionary War. Although they weren't the first Americans to die for their country (victims of the Boston Massacre hold that honor), nor even the first to offer spirited resistance as the Minutemen of Concord did, the eight Minutemen who fell on Lexington Green served their country well. For without the battle at Lexington, the Concord Minutemen might not have been determined to offer strong resistance to the British force.

American colonists had been virtually independent of their mother country and so, when the government in London tried to levy taxes the colonists didn't approve of, their anger was aroused. To show who was boss, the government sent troops from England and quartered them in the homes of the colonists, further stirring up their anger. As it looked more and more likely that a direct confrontation might occur, the colonists, led by Samuel Adams and John Hancock, began stockpiling arms and ammunition—especially cannons. Hearing rumors of these stockpiles, General Gage, the British commander in Boston, prepared to send out a body of troops to scour the countryside and destroy the stockpiles so as to nip armed resistance in the bud. But the colonists' spy network caught wind of the plan and, as the troops mustered late at night in preparation for the expedition, Paul Revere and William Dawes galloped through the darkness to alert the patriots.

The "alarm system" was so efficient that the Lexington Minutemen, led by Capt. John Parker, turned out shortly after Revere arrived at midnight, but there were no British troops in sight. The patriots returned home or retired to the Buckman Tavern near the Green, ready to appear again the minute they heard the sound of the drum.

About daybreak the British column finally arrived in Lexington, and the 100 or so Minutemen drew themselves up in soldierly order on the Green. Nobody knew what would happen. The Minutemen knew only that a much larger force of some 600 soldiers was coming to search their homes, and although it would have been folly to try to stop them, they could still show that they didn't like it and perhaps worry the British a little. The British soldiers knew only that men with rifles were waiting in a position of defiance to keep the soldiers from doing their duty. When the forces finally came face to face at the Lexington Green, officers on both sides seemed to think it would be just as well if everybody kept calm. Captain Parker ordered, "Stand your ground! Don't fire unless fired upon! But if they mean to have a war, let it begin here." However, not a shot was fired. Parker, perhaps fearing capture of his men, then told them to disperse peaceably; yet this only encouraged the British to try and round them up, and some of the soldiers took after the Minutemen. Somehow the running added a sense of alarm to the situation, and a shot rang out. Whether it was a patriot defending himself and his friends or a British soldier "out to get the rebels" and excited by the chase, no one knows, and the identity of the man who fired the first shot remains a mystery. Other shots quickly followed, and soon eight Minutemen lay dead. Ten others were wounded.

The "battle" was more like a troop riot, and once the British officers regained control of their troops, they started marching them out of town. The Minutemen took their wounded to Buckman Tavern to treat them. It all took less than half an hour. Word was rushed to Concord, where Minutemen assembled for the later events of the day, knowing that they might be the next in the line of fire.

GETTING THERE   While public transportation to Lexington is good, note that it's not possible to go directly between Lexington and Concord by public transportation.

By Car   Coming from Boston in a car, take U.S. 3 to Mass. 2 to Mass. 4/225, into the center of Lexington. An alternative route subject to tolls is the Mass. Pike west to I-95 (Mass. 128) north, exiting at Exit 44, "Bedford Street," for Lexington.

By Train   You can take a commuter train (☎ 617/722-3200 for schedules) from Boston's North Station or Cambridge's Porter subway station to Waltham (every 20 minutes during rush hours, every 1 1/2 hours during the day, every hour in the evening, every 2 hours or more on weekends), and then bus no. 525, "Lexington-Waltham," to your destination—buses run every hour during the day (no evening or Sunday service).

By Bus   To get to Lexington from Cambridge, the easiest way is to take bus no. 528, "Hanscom Field-Harvard," which leaves Harvard Square for the 45-minute ride every hour during the day, every half hour during rush periods (no night or Sunday service).

ESSENTIALS   The **telephone area code** is **617.** The first thing to do is to go to the **Lexington Visitors' Center,** 1875 Massachusetts Ave. (☎ **617/862-1450**), just off the Green near the Minuteman statue and next door to Buckman Tavern. Here, every day between the hours of 9am and 5pm (10am and 4pm from October to June), you can pick up a sketch map of the town, and brochures and information on the sights. More important, you can inspect the diorama, or scale model, of the Battle Green and the events of April 19, 1775: the Minutemen in their farmers' clothes scattering before the long files of crack troops dressed in brilliant colors. The diorama is well worth seeing (it's free, too); historical accounts and explanations of the battle accompany the display.

The National Park Service has organized most of the interesting historical sites in Lexington and Concord into **Minute Man National Historical Park,** and those with their own car can pick up the park service's Minuteman brochure, which has a sketch map of Battle Road and most of the sights to see.

WHAT TO SEE & DO

When you approach Battle Green and come up to the Minuteman statue (erected in 1900), you'll feel the great historic significance of the spot. **Battle Green** is really where it all began: The ivy-covered monument on the southwest part of the green marks the burial spot of seven of the eight Minutemen killed on the memorable day, April 19, 1775. The boulder that sits incongruously on the soft grass of the green marks the place where the Minutemen drew up in a double rank to face the British grenadiers.

The Lexington Green looked much different in the 1770s than it does today. The meeting house, or church building, was located near where the Minuteman statue stands; since it was mid-April and the green was in the center of town traffic, it may have been pretty muddy rather than "green." The best time to visit Lexington's historic sights is, of course, at dawn on April 19, when the townfolk reenact the famous confrontation with festivities, real musket fire, and fife-and-drum corps. But any day from April 19 to the end of October will do; note that most of the happenings and places mentioned below are closed from November to April 18.

Besides the Battle Green, several early buildings figured significantly in the battle, and they are today maintained by the **Lexington Historical Society** (Buckman Tavern, Munroe Tavern, and Hancock-Clarke House), Lexington (☎ **617/862-1703**).

Of the houses, **Buckman Tavern** (1709), facing Lexington Green, is the most important. Here, in the taproom, many of the Minutemen waited out the time between that first midnight call to muster and the final arrival of the British forces at daybreak. After the battle, the wounded were brought here and laid out on the tables for treatment. The tours are given by costumed historic interpreters well versed in their subject, which not only encompasses the events of the battle but also ranges much more widely, covering a great number of topics on life in the colonies at the time of the Revolution. They'll tell you about the construction of the tavern; about the people who came there to stay, or to have a drink, or for a reception or tea; what and how they ate and drank; how they cooked, slept, and kept warm in unheated rooms. The tavern has an excellent collection of utensils, tools, and implements from the period—"time- and labor-saving devices" that show a good deal of Yankee ingenuity. The tour is well worth the price of admission. The tavern is located opposite the Common and has a gift shop.

The **Munroe Tavern** (1695), 1332 Massachusetts Ave., was the site of a temporary field hospital for the British during their retreat to Concord through Lexington. Earlier on the day of the retreat, two Munroe family members had fought at the Battle on the Green. Today the Munroe Tavern is furnished with Munroe family items and artifacts from the Revolution. It's a walk (or a short drive) from Battle Green, seven blocks southeast along Massachusetts Avenue; the tavern will be on your right. Its garden of colonial flowers and its wildflower garden are open to the public daily free of charge. The tavern is open Monday through Saturday from 10am to 5pm and Sunday from 1 to 5pm.

The third significant house is the **Hancock-Clarke House** (1698), 36 Hancock St., which was the parsonage of the Rev. Jonas Clarke at the time of the battle, and it was with Clarke that John Hancock and Sam Adams, the two "rabble-rousers" most wanted by the British authorities, hid themselves during the uncertain days before the battle. Clarke's house was the first place Paul Revere headed for when he heard of the British plan to march out into the countryside. Revere actually came to Clarke's house twice to warn Adams and Hancock: on April 15, just after hearing that the British were about to do something, and again on April 18, the night the British troops moved out. It's located only about a block north of Battle Green.

Admission and a guided tour cost $3 for adults, $1 for children 6 to 16 (free for children under 6), at each house; an adult combination ticket, good for all three houses, can be purchased at the Buckman Tavern gift shop for $7 for adults, $2 for children. It's open mid-April to October, Monday through Saturday from 10am to 5pm and Sunday from 1 to 5pm.

Several other sights in Lexington are worth a look. Gravestone-rubbers will want to head for **Ye Olde Burying Ground,** just off Battle Green by the church, on its western side. The oldest stone dates from 1690. Another way to get into the spirit of the day of battle is to visit **Cary Memorial Hall,** several blocks southeast of the green along Massachusetts Avenue, between the town offices and the police station. Here you can see Sandham's famous painting *The Battle of Lexington,* and also statues of John Hancock and Samuel Adams.

Lexington has a handsome modern gallery for historical displays of Americana, the **Museum of Our National Heritage,** at 33 Marrett Rd. (☎ **617/861-6559**), near the intersection of Mass. 2A and Mass. 4/225, a short way from the center of Lexington on the road to Boston. Built by the Scottish Rite Masons in 1975 are four galleries of changing exhibitions on unique topics in American history and popular culture. Lectures and films are scheduled frequently as well. An exhibit entitled *Lexington Alarm'd* explains the town's crucial role in the American quest for independence. Call for details of current exhibits. The museum is open Monday through Saturday from 10am to 5pm and Sunday from noon to 5pm; closed Thanksgiving Day, Christmas Eve, Christmas Day, New Year's Eve, and New Year's Day. Admission and parking are free.

WHERE TO STAY

Although Lexington will most likely be a day trip for you, here are two lodging suggestions in case your itinerary indicates a night in the Minutemen's town:

Battle Green Motor Inn

1720 Massachusetts Ave., Lexington, MA 02173. ☎ **617/862-6100** or 800/343-0235, 800/ 322-1066 in Massachusetts. 96 rms. A/C TV TEL. Summer, $65 room with one bed; $72 room with two beds. Winter, rates are lower. AE, DC, DISC, MC, V.

Whether you are driving or busing, the Battle Green Motor Inn, located three blocks east of the Lexington Green, is a convenient place to stay. The modern and comfortable units are grouped around a long central court dotted with young trees and potted plants. Room cable TVs have HBO, and you can park your car in a covered lot. From the inn, you can easily walk to the green and all the historic sites.

Sheraton Tara Lexington Inn

727 Marrett Rd. (off I-95), Lexington, MA 02173. ☎ **617/862-8700** or 800/325-3535. Fax 617/863-0404. 119 rms. A/C TV TEL. $119–$150 double depending on the season. AE, DC, DISC, MC, V.

If you're looking for a full-service hotel in the Lexington area, the Sheraton Tara is where you should look first. The rooms are attractively decorated in varying shades of blue, and all have sitting areas with wingback chairs or couches. Cable TV and digital clocks are standard amenities for all rooms. Some of the more expensive rooms have balconies. Guests have use of the outdoor pool (seasonal) and fitness room, and for nightly entertainment the hotel has a formal dining room as well as a bar and lounge.

WHERE TO DINE

Hartwell House

94 Hartwell Ave. ☎ **617/862-5111.** Reservations recommended. Main courses $12.95–$22.95. AE, DC, DISC, MC, V. Bistro 11:30am–10pm; main dining room, Mon–Fri 11:30am–2:30pm (last reservation at 2pm), Mon–Sat 5:30–10pm. AMERICAN.

One of the loveliest restaurants in the area, Hartwell House is found at Exit 31B off Mass. 128. Start your meal with scallops Rockefeller (fresh sea scallops baked with seasoned spinach, mornay sauce, and bacon) or Caribbean chicken fingers with a coconut/sesame-seed crumb coating and served with pineapple dipping sauce. As a main course, try the Oriental stir-fry or one of the fresh fish dishes. There's also a variety of pasta and meat dishes. For dessert you shouldn't miss the cappuccino ice-cream sundae. Try to get a table out on the terrace with a view of the pond. You may dine downstairs in the main dining room (for which reservations are highly recommended at lunch and dinner) or in the upstairs bistro.

Peking Garden

27 Waltham St. ☎ **617/862-1051.** Reservations recommended. Main courses $5.95–$28; lunch buffet $5.25; dinner buffet $10.50 adults, $6 children under 10; Special House Dinner $14.95 per person. AE, DC, DISC, MC, V. Sun–Thurs 11:30am–9:30pm, Fri–Sat 11:30am–10:30pm. Directions: From Massachusetts Avenue in the center of the commercial district, turn onto Waltham Street and the restaurant is one block away, on the right. CHINESE.

The best value in a full restaurant is, believe it or not, Chinese. It's the Peking Garden, several doors down from the intersection of Massachusetts Avenue and Waltham Street, right in the main shopping district. The special bonus is the Chinese buffet served Monday through Thursday evening from 6 to 9pm, and the food is delicious and varied. Two or more can order the Special House Dinner at other times and receive a varied and bounteous selection of dishes. Besides the evening buffet, the Peking Garden hosts a luncheon buffet Monday through Friday from 11:30am to 2:30pm. Wine, beer, and drinks are served. Special Mandarin dim sum is served every Saturday and Sunday from 11:30am to 2:30pm.

3 Concord

18 miles NW of Boston, 15 miles NW of Cambridge, 6 miles W of Lexington

Once strictly a farming town, Concord today is part Boston suburb, part farm town. It's a beautiful place filled with old trees, graceful houses, and a rich history that goes beyond the events of the Revolution. Besides the historic sites encompassed by Minute Man National Historical Park, Concord offers a look at the lives and times of America's great 19th-century writers and philosophers: Emerson, Thoreau, Hawthorne, and Louisa May and Bronson Alcott.

GETTING THERE   By Car   The most interesting route is via Lexington along Mass. 2A, following the signs reading BATTLE ROAD; this is the route taken by the British troops going out to Concord to search for arms stockpiled illegally by the colonials. The fastest route, however, is Mass. 2. At the traffic signal at the bottom of the steep hill, the highway turns left; continue straight on along the Cambridge Turnpike to reach the center of Concord.

By Train   On weekdays, 20 trains a day leave Boston's North Station for the 40-minute trip to Concord; on Saturday there are 12 trains, and on Sunday, 8. The train can also be boarded at the Porter Square subway station in Cambridge. Call ☎ **617/722-3200** for the latest detailed schedule information. The train arrives at Concord's Depot, which is about five blocks from Monument Square.

By Bus   By public transportation, there's no way to travel along Battle Road unless you're in a sightseeing tour bus.

ESSENTIALS   The **telephone area code** is **508.** The Minute Man National Historical Park's **Battle Road Visitors' Center** (174 Liberty St.; ☎ **617/862-7753**) is just off Marrett Road (Mass. 2A) half a mile west of I-95 (Mass. 128)—take I-95 Exit 30B. This is the place to get a map and brochure of Battle Road.

The **Concord Chamber of Commerce** (☎ **508/369-3120**) operates an information center kiosk on Heywood Street. It's open April through October daily from 9:30am to 4:30pm. One-hour tours are available at 1pm every Saturday, Sunday, and on Monday holidays. It's also open April through October on weekdays by appointment.

The chamber of commerce also operates an **information kiosk** on Heywood Street, one block east of Concord Center. It's open April 11–30, Monday through Friday from 10am to 3pm and Saturday and Sunday from 9:30am to 4:30pm; May to October, daily from 9:30am to 4:30pm. Historic tours are available by appointment.

WHAT TO SEE & DO

Begin your walk around Concord at the town green, officially called **Monument Square,** complete with obelisk inscribed FAITHFUL UNTO DEATH. The little church facing Main Street, **St. Bernard's** (Roman Catholic), is particularly pretty when seen from a short distance down Main Street. Of the other buildings on the green, the most historically noteworthy is the **Wright Tavern,** which, being right on the road from Boston, was one of the first places the British stopped to search for arms. Several shops and firms' offices are located in the tavern today, and you're welcome to walk in and look around during business hours. The **Colonial Inn** has been facing the square since colonial times; it's a good place for a refreshing drink, a meal, or a bed for the night.

MINUTE MAN NATIONAL HISTORICAL PARK

The Minute Man National Historical Park, Monument Street (☎ **508/369-6993**), encompasses many of the most important sites having to do with the first Revolutionary War battle at Concord. There's a **visitors center** located on

Liberty Street in the Buttrick Mansion, north of the center of Concord, on the other side of North Bridge. A large parking lot near North Bridge is often full during the summer, and if you have a good parking spot in town and a few extra minutes, walk the half mile to the bridge and admire Concord's lovely old houses as you go.

After the events in Lexington, the British officers headed their men quickly off to Concord, afraid that since shots had been fired and men killed, there'd be a great deal more trouble coming. The Minutemen in Concord kept an eye on the British as they entered the town, waiting for whatever was to happen. When a force of regulars was sent to stand guard over Concord's North Bridge, the Minutemen retreated before them, crossing the bridge and taking up a position on a hilltop nearby, where they awaited reinforcements from nearby towns.

Meanwhile, in Concord a polite and not-too-thorough search was being carried out; some arms were found, in particular a number of gun carriages, which were brought out and burned. The Minutemen saw the smoke, assumed the British were burning the town, and began to advance in revenge. The regulars retreated across the bridge and began firing at the Minutemen, who fired back and pursued them until they fled. It was here at the North Bridge, then, that the Minutemen fired the "shot heard 'round the world."

Soon afterward the British troops began the return to Boston, but Minute-men kept up a constant sniper fire on them all the way back, which enraged the regulars and goaded them to murder some of the innocent people they met along the way of their march. The bitterness left on both sides by the events of this April 19 would soon bring war to all the British colonies in North America.

Walk across the placid Concord River on the Old North Bridge (a modern reproduction of the kind of bridge that spanned the river in colonial times) and it's easy to imagine, even to half see, the way things happened on the day of the battle. At the far (western) end of the bridge is Daniel Chester French's famous *Minuteman* statue, the pediment inscribed with Emerson's famous poem. On the near (east) side of the bridge, take a look also at the plaque on the stone wall commemorating the British soldiers who died and are buried here.

Admission to the park is free, and it's open daily year-round (except major holidays).

THE OLD MANSE

After visiting the bridge and the visitor center on the far side, turn back toward town. Right next to North Bridge, slightly nearer to the center of town, is the Old Manse, Monument Street at the North Bridge (☎ **508/369-3909**), Concord's most famous house. It was built in 1769 by the Rev. William Emerson and was lived in by his descendants for 169 years, except for a three-year period when young Nathaniel Hawthorne and his bride, Sophia, lived here. Hawthorne's residence here gave him material for several later stories. The house today is filled with the spirit and the mementos of their short stay, and those of the Emerson clan. Admission includes a guided tour and costs $5 for adults, $4 for students and seniors, $3 for children 6 to 16, free for children under 6; $12 for families (three to five people). The Old Manse is open from mid-April through October, Monday and Wednesday through Saturday from 10am to 5pm and Sunday and holidays from 1 to 5pm.

SIGHTS OF THE TRANSCENDENTALISM MOVEMENT

Concord was the center of a philosophical and social movement that, although small in scope, had important effects on American thought and literature. Emerson, Thoreau, Bronson Alcott, and others were all friends living in Concord from about 1836 to 1860. They were aware of the philosophical upheaval going on in Europe at this time and were encouraged to break away from the Unitarianism that had been their belief. Although they never published a manifesto detailing their beliefs, their creed at this time was that each person has a part of God within himself and, by being sensitive to the dictates of that part, can do what is good and right. Nature also played a large role in their beliefs, for the transcendentalists thought true harmony in life could be achieved only by communing closely with nature and coming to understand it. This, perhaps, was the basis for Thoreau's period of retreat at Walden Pond.

The transcendentalists got together and tried out their beliefs by buying a farm and communing with nature there (1841–47). The Brook Farm experiment, although it failed, has been an example down to our own times. (The farm was in West Roxbury, now a suburb of Boston.) Hawthorne lived on Brook Farm for a while, and he and his friend Herman Melville were both affected by transcendentalism.

The best way to learn about the transcendentalist movement is to read Ralph Waldo Emerson's works. While you're here in Concord, you can visit his house and those in which other adherents of the movement lived, and also go out to **Walden Pond** and see the place where Thoreau had his cabin from 1845 to 1847. Drive out Walden Street (Mass. 126), which leaves the center of Concord from Main Street near Monument Square. After crossing Mass. 2, look for signs on the right not far from the intersection; park and walk to the site of his hut, marked by a pile of stones. The path circling the pond provides an interesting and refreshing walk; fires and alcoholic beverages are not permitted at any time. The main parking lot (which you are required to use) by the public beach costs $8 per carload in summer; the beach itself is free.

On your way back from the Old Manse, by Old North Bridge, take a detour up the hill, east off Monument Street before you reach the town green, to get to **Sleepy Hollow Cemetery.** Author's Ridge, on top of the hill, has the graves of Hawthorne, Thoreau, the Alcotts, and Emerson. Emerson's grave, you'll notice, is marked by a great uncarved boulder, very natural and without religious symbolism.

Starting from Monument Square, most of the transcendentalists' homes are east along Lexington Road; Thoreau sites and memorabilia are, appropriately, off by themselves, in another direction.

House of Ralph Waldo Emerson

28 Cambridge Tpk. ☎ **508/369-2236.** Admission $4.50 adults, $3 children 6–17, free for children under 6. Tours $4 adults, $2.50 students. Mid–Apr to Oct, Thurs–Sat 10am–4:30pm, Sun 2–4:30pm.

Located at the intersection of Lexington Road and Cambridge Turnpike, a 10-minute walk from the green, the house was a center for meetings of Emerson and his friends, and still contains original furniture and Emerson's memorabilia.

Concord Museum

Lexington Rd. and Cambridge Tpk. ☎ **508/369-9763.** Admission $6 adults, $5 seniors, $3 students and children 15 and under; $12 for families. Apr–Dec, Mon–Sat 10am–5pm, Sun 1–5pm; Jan–Mar, call for hours. Closed New Year's Day, Easter, and Christmas Day.

The Concord Museum, across the street from Emerson's house, transports the visitor back in time to the early 17th century when the town of Concord was founded. The museum contains numerous period rooms and galleries, and vividly depicts the growth and evolution of Concord. The collections of documented decorative arts and domestic artifacts were either owned by Concord-area residents or made by Concord-area artisans.

Period rooms and galleries provide an introduction to Concord's history from Native American habitation and European settlement to the 1775 battle at North Bridge and through the days of Emerson, Thoreau, the Alcotts, and Hawthorne. On exhibit are one of the lanterns that signaled Paul Revere's famous ride; Ralph Waldo Emerson's entire study arranged as in 1882, when the author, poet, and philosopher died; as well as the largest collection of Thoreau's possessions in the world. There are changing exhibitions in the New Wing throughout the year.

Orchard House

399 Lexington Rd. ☎ **508/369-4118.** Admission (including the requisite tour) $5.50 adults, $4.50 seniors and adult students, $3.50 youths 6–17, free for children under 6; $16 for families. Apr–Oct, Mon–Sat 10am–4:30pm, Sun 1–4:30pm; Nov–Mar, Mon–Fri 11am–3pm; Sat 10am–4:30pm, Sun 1–4:30pm. Closed Jan 1–15, Easter, Thanksgiving, and Christmas.

Continuing east along Lexington Road, a short drive will bring you to home of the Alcotts during the period 1858–77. Bronson Alcott's life passion was the reform of traditional educational methods. His open and natural approach to education was not appreciated in cosmopolitan centers such as Boston but was perfectly congenial to transcendentalist Concord. Here he was ultimately commissioned as superintendent of schools, and he opened a "School of Philosophy" in a building in his backyard. This is also the house in which Louisa May Alcott wrote *Little Women.*

Wayside

455 Lexington Rd. ☎ **508/369-6975.** Admission fees vary. Call for current hours. Tours are limited to 10 people.

One mile east of Monument Square and just a few steps east of Orchard House is the house described by Louisa May Alcott in her famous book, although today most of the furnishings are those of Margaret Sidney, who wrote *Five Little Peppers.* There are several exhibits dealing with the house's famous former residents; Hawthorne also lived here.

CANOEING ON THE CONCORD RIVER

After you've taken the standard walking tour of Concord, see the town again, adventurously, by renting a canoe for a paddle up the Concord River. The **South Bridge Boat House** (☎ 508/369-9438), west of the center of town at 496 Main St. (Mass. 62), will rent you a canoe for $8.50 per hour, $38 per day (students get lower rates on weekdays only). In two hours or so, you should be able to make your way down to Old North Bridge and back, depending on the strength of your paddling muscles. The grand houses and gardens that grace the riverbanks alternate with patches of field and wild shrubbery to make a serene and lovely landscape. You can also rent a small boat with an outboard motor for $25 an hour. The boat house is open from the beginning of April into November, until the first snowstorm.

A VISIT TO A WINERY

You've heard of Concord grapes, a variety developed here by Ephraim Bull and now used to make grape juice, jelly, and sweet wines. You might think the **Nashoba Valley Winery,** 100 Wattaquadoc Hill Rd., Bolton, MA 01740 (☎ **508/779-5521**), only a dozen miles west of Concord, would use Concord grapes. But you're in for a delightful surprise.

Nashoba pursues the old New England tradition of making delicious wines from fruits other than grapes: apples, peaches, pears, blueberries, cranberries. They've taken this art one step further and now make premium varietal dry table wines from fruit. The wines are intriguing, satisfying, and delightful. The tart, dry cranberry-apple goes especially well with Thanksgiving turkey, and the "After Dinner Peach" has an exquisite sweet-dryness like good sauterne. Clear your palate and drop in for a free tasting any day of the week, until 6pm. Winery tours cost $1 and are conducted on Saturday and Sunday from 11am to 5:30pm. Leave time for a self-guided walking tour through the orchards, with a picnic at one of the tables, all of which enjoy fine country views. From June through October, you can come out and "pick-your-own" fruit.

To get here, take Mass. 62 west from Concord through Maynard to Stow, then Mass. 117 west to Bolton, just west of I-495 (Exit 27). Take Mass. 117 west to the blinking yellow light in the center of Bolton. Turn left onto Wattaquadoc Hill Road; the winery is a quarter of a mile up the hill, on the left-hand side.

LONGFELLOW'S WAYSIDE INN

The country inn made famous by Henry Wadsworth Longfellow's poem "Tales of a Wayside Inn" is still serving the public and is still an interesting place to visit. For details on this historic inn in the neighboring town of Sudbury, see "Where to Stay," below.

WHERE TO STAY
CONCORD INNS

Colonial Inn
48 Monument Sq., Concord, MA 01742. ☎ **508/369-9200** or 800/370-9200. Fax 508/369-2170. 49 rms. A/C TV TEL. Main inn, $125–$150 double; Prescott wing, $85–$ double; The Cottage, $150–$200 double. AE, DC, MC, V.

The main building of the Colonial Inn dates from 1716 and is quite small, but several new and modern additions make it significantly larger. Only 12 original colonial-era rooms are available to guests, and as you might imagine, these are the ones most in demand. So, if you're interested in staying in the main inn, make your reservations as early as possible. Housekeeping rooms are also available should you be planning to stay a while. The inn faces Monument Square in the center of Concord.

In addition to overnight accommodations, the Colonial Inn has a restaurant offering an eclectic selection of items, including jumbo prawns, and a grilled chicken burrito at lunch. Dinner is primarily surf and turf. Jackets are required for men at dinner.

Hawthorne Inn
462 Lexington Rd., Concord, MA 01742. ☎ **508/369-5610.** Fax 508/369-5610. 7 rms. TV. $102–$181 double. All rates include continental breakfast. Additional person $15 extra.

AE, DISC, MC, V. Directions: From Monument Square, follow Lexington Road east one mile to the inn, on the right.

Concord's coziest place to stay is the Hawthorne Inn, located directly across the road from The Wayside, Nathaniel Hawthorne's house. The location is convenient to Orchard House, the Alcotts' home, as well. The inn has pleasant gardens with a tiny fountain, and the rooms are decorated with period pieces, antique beds, original works of art, and nice homey touches such as hooked rugs. There are only seven rooms here, so reserve early.

A SOUTH SUDBURY INN

Wayside Inn (1700)

Wayside Inn Rd., South Sudbury, MA 01776. ☎ **508/443-1776.** 10 rms. TEL. $96.60 double. All rates include full breakfast. AE, DC, MC, V. Directions: Drive 13 miles along Sudbury Road (which starts from Main Street in Concord), and U.S. 20 West will take you to the inn.

The Wayside Inn was made famous by Longfellow's "Tales of a Wayside Inn" and now boasts that it's the oldest operating inn in the country. Bought by Henry Ford in the early 1920s, it is now a private, nonprofit operation and all proceeds from the guest rooms and restaurant are put toward its upkeep and restoration. Rooms 1 through 8 are of modern construction and traditional decor; Rooms 9 and 10 are in the old, original part of the inn and are very quaint. These latter two rooms are the ones most in demand, particularly from April to December. Should you want to stay at the inn, it's wise to make reservations as far in advance as possible, even a month or two; but if you can't make them, call up in any case and see what vacancies they might have.

A fire around 1955 caused heavy damage to the inn (as you can see in the old kitchen), but restoration work was done well and the rooms are worth seeing even if you don't plan to stay for the night. A short self-guided tour is available. Lunch is served Monday through Saturday from 11:30am to 3pm; dinner, Monday through Saturday from 5 to 9pm and Sunday from noon to 8pm.

Besides the inn itself, you should explore the grounds and surroundings: the beautiful formal garden near the inn, the reconstructed barn across the road, and the Grist Mill, a short (15-minute) walk away, farther down the road. The Grist Mill, a pretty and romantic stone building, is a replica of the mills that used to dot the New England rivers and streams. It's in a beautiful spot, with a copse of pines nearby, and although it's not 100% authentic (the mill wheel is made of heavy-gauge steel instead of wood), it's worth a look and a walk around. The flour ground here is used in the Wayside Inn's kitchens and is for sale at the inn's shop. By the way, the Martha-Mary Chapel, on the road between the inn and the Grist Mill, is a typical New England meeting house that Ford had built to be rented out for weddings. The chapel and the Wayside Inn are very popular with wedding parties and honeymooners.

WHERE TO DINE

Wayside Inn

Wayside Inn Rd., South Sudbury. ☎ **508/443-1776.** Reservations recommended. Lunch $7.50–$14.50; dinner $15–$27. AE, DC, MC, V. Mon–Sat 11:30am–3pm; Mon–Sat 5–9pm; Sun and holidays noon–8pm. Directions: Drive 13 miles along Sudbury Road (which starts from Main Street in Concord), and U.S. 20 West will take you to the inn. NEW ENGLAND.

If you can't stay in this historic inn (see "Where to Stay," above), at least have a meal here. In addition to a main dining room, there are four smaller dining rooms, all beautifully furnished with antiques. Absolutely every inch is filled with history. There are wood beams, old brick fireplaces, even the bar that has been welcoming wayfarers since 1716. Specialties include roast duckling, Indian pudding, and a deliriously good deep-dish apple pie.

4 Salem

17 miles NE of Boston, 4 miles NW of Marblehead, 16 miles SW of Gloucester, 22 miles SW of Rockport

Think of Salem, think of witches. Although the fame of Salem's witch trials has spread around the world, the town's place in New England history comes from its maritime industries—shipbuilding, warehousing, chandlery, and trade. In the late 1700s, ships from Salem sailed the world, many dealing in trade from the Far East, especially spices, silks, and other luxury goods. The wealth of the Indies brought great prosperity to the town, which enabled its citizens to build and decorate fine mansions and impressive museums.

As for the witches, it has never been proved that there were any in Salem. The witch-hunt took place in only one year (1692), and the score of people executed met that fate because they would *not* admit to being witches—many of the less courageous "admitted" to being witches so they wouldn't be executed. The whole witch-calling affair reached the point of absurdity and then fizzled out. Salem would like to forget it all, no doubt, but the rest of the world enjoys remembering this bizarre episode.

GETTING THERE   By Car   The fastest way from Boston to Salem is the least direct: Take I-93 north to I-95 north (Mass. 128 east), and take the exit marked for Mass. 114 and Salem. A more direct route, via U.S. 1, is not faster. The most direct route, via Mass. 1A, is slowest because it passes through many towns (and many traffic signals) along the way. Mass. 1A North becomes Lafayette Street in Salem.

Note that street and highway signs on the North Shore are particularly bad. Routes are filled with turns, and signs are confusing or missing—you'll probably find yourself lost more than once. Resign yourself to stopping and asking the way, not once but several times.

By Bus   Salem is served by MBTA bus nos. 450 and 455, which leave from the parking garage next to the Haymarket subway station in Boston; the trip, under good traffic conditions, takes 40 to 50 minutes. Buses leave every 20 to 30 minutes during rush hours, every hour during the day Monday through Saturday, every hour on Sunday.

By Train   Commuter trains run from Boston's North Station to Salem, Beverly, Gloucester, and Rockport. The trip to Salem takes about 30 minutes; trains run about every 20 minutes during rush hours, every half hour during the day, every hour at night and on weekends. Call ☎ 617/722-3200 for schedules.

ESSENTIALS   The **telephone area code** is **508**. The **Salem Chamber of Commerce,** 32 Derby Sq. (☎ **508/744-0004**), maintains an information booth in Old Town Hall at 32 Derby Sq. It is open Monday through Saturday from 9am to 5pm and Sunday from noon to 5pm. The **National Park Service Visitor**

Center at 2 Liberty St. (☎ **508/741-3648**) has exhibits on early settlement, the maritime age, and the leather and textiles industries, as well as a free film on Essex County. It's open daily from 9am to 6pm in the summer and until 5pm the rest of the year.

WHAT TO SEE & DO

Salem today is a very interesting town, with many of its old houses (dating back to the 1600s) and 19th-century mansions intact and in good repair. Try to visit at least one of the **17th-century houses** to see what life was like in one of the earliest towns in the United States. Part of the downtown section has been restored and closed to traffic as a fine pedestrian mall. Additionally, the waterfront area— **Pickering Wharf**—has been restored and colonized by several restaurants, gift shops, antiques shops, crystal shops, a new-age bookstore, and the like.

At the National Park Service Visitors Center (Essex Street side) you can board the **Salem Trolley** (☎ 508/744-5469) for a one-hour narrated sightseeing tour and shuttle service to the historic attractions. (You can also board at any of the 12 stops along the way.) Get off for shopping, sightseeing, or dining, and reboard for only one all-day ticket. The cost is $8 for adults, $4 for children age 5 to 12. In December, during Salem Trolley's Holiday Happenings Celebration, the Salem Trolley Players present Ebenezer Scrooge in a traveling presentation of *A Christmas Carol* on board the trolley. Special performances leave from Pickering Wharf; advance reservations are suggested.

Though you could keep yourselves busy for days seeing the town's most celebrated historical sights below, take time to visit some of its newer attractions, including **Harbor Sweets,** 85 Leavitt St. (☎ 508/745-7648), where you can buy sailboat-shaped almond-butter-crunch chocolates right where they're made (you get to sample the selections). Tours of the chocolate factory are offered, but it's necessary to call for an appointment. By the way, if you plan to take home boxes of these outrageously good chocolates, they'll pack them in cold packs. In the fall of 1995, Harbor Sweets introduced two new sugar-free chocolates (The Starfish™ and the Sea Horse™).

Crows Haven Corner, 125 Essex St. (☎ 508/745-8763), is another must-see nonhistorical attraction in Salem. This tiny witch shop is owned by Laurie Cabot, Salem's most illustrious witch. Here you can buy all sorts of herbs, powders, and seeds to ward off evil or attract love, luck, and money. Also for sale are gargoyles and unicorns, witch books, crystals, moonstones, black cat candles, crystal balls (just like the one in *The Wizard of Oz*), magic wands—you get the picture. You can also make an appointment to have a tarot card reading with Laurie Cabot.

Finally, while poking around the shops on Pickering Wharf, make a point of going into the **Pickering Wharf Antiques Gallery** (☎ 508/741-3113). When you first step in, it looks like any other antiques shop. Wander around to the back, turn the corner, and all of a sudden you'll find yourself in an enormous theater-in-the-round where over 40 dealers display their collections. So much for "a quick look around" an antiques gallery.

Salem Witch Museum
19¹/₂ Washington Sq. ☎ **508/744-1692.** Admission $4 adults, $3.50 seniors, $2.50 children 6–14, free for children under 6. Sept–June, daily 10am–5pm; July–Aug, daily 10am–7pm.

Housed in a 19th-century stone building at the intersection of Brown Street and Hawthorne Boulevard, the Salem Witch Museum offers a historically correct, audiovisual re-creation of the witch trials of 1692, using life-size figures, a sound track, and special lighting. Presentations take place every 30 minutes.

Witch House

310¹/₂ Essex St. ☎ **508/744-0180.** Admission $5 adults, $4 seniors, $1.50 children 5–16, children under 5 free. Mid-Mar to June and Labor Day to Dec 1, daily 10am–4:30pm; July–Labor Day, daily 10am–6pm

The home of Magistrate Jonathan Corwin, one of the judges in the witch trials, stands at the corner of Essex and North Streets. Preliminary examinations of those accused of witchcraft were held in the house, which is now nicely restored.

The House of the Seven Gables

54 Turner St. ☎ **508/744-0991.** Guided tours of the Gables and Hawthorne's birthplace, $7 adults, $4 children 13–17, $3 children 6–12, children under 6 free. July–Oct, daily 9am–6pm; Nov–June, daily 10am–4:30pm. Free parking.

The House of the Seven Gables, which served as the setting for Nathaniel Hawthorne's novel of the same name, is the centerpiece of a historic site with period gardens on Salem Harbor. The attractions here include the House of the Seven Gables (1668), the Hooper-Hathaway House (1682), Hawthorne's birthplace (ca. 1750), and the Retire Becket House (1655). The Garden Café is open from May through October, and there's a new, enlarged visitor center with a unique interactive video that documents the 300-year history of the Gables.

Pioneer Village: Salem in 1630

Forest River Park. ☎ **508/745-0525** or 508/744-0991. Admission $4.50 adults, $3.50 children 13–17 and seniors, $2.50 children 6–12, children under 6 free. Late May–Oct, Mon–Sat 10am–5pm, Sun noon–5pm.

For a look at 17th-century Salem, tour this "living history museum" built in 1930 and recently restored. Costumed "interpreters" will guide you through the village, past dugout houses, wigwams, thatched cottages, and the governor's house, through gardens such as the colonists might have cultivated and species of animals that they may have raised. Demonstrations of yarn spinning, building, and open-hearth cooking are here to see; children love the opportunities for hands-on participation. Pioneer Village, adjacent to a beach and picnic area, is off West Street.

✪ Peabody/Essex Museum

East India Sq. ☎ **508/7459500** or 800/745-4054. Admission to galleries and libraries or historic houses, $7 adults, $6 seniors and students, $4 children 6–18, free for children under 5. Families $18 (2 adults and one or more children). Free for everyone the first Thurs of the month 5–8pm. Mon–Sat 10am–5pm, Sun noon–5pm. Closed Mondays from November 1 to Memorial Day and New Year's, Thanksgiving, and Christmas Days.

When a group of Salem sea captains and world travelers formed the East India Marine Society in 1799, their charter included provisions for a "museum in which to house the natural and artificial curiosities" brought back from their travels. This was the genesis of the Peabody Museum, America's oldest museum in continuous operation.

In 1824 the society and its collections moved to larger quarters at East India Marine Hall. Since then, five annexes have been added. The most recent, the highly acclaimed Asian Export Art Wing, is dedicated to decorative art made in Asia for Western use from the 14th to 19th centuries.

Now part of the Peabody Museum, the **Essex Institute** was founded as a museum/historical society dedicated to the preservation, study, and exhibition of historical works and artifacts dealing with Essex County. The artifact collection ranges from rare early newspapers to entire houses, restored and furnished with authentic antiques. Just about anyone who comes to Salem finds something of interest here: Historians of American trade and culture can use the library, nautical buffs will want to see the relics of the China trade, and those interested in architecture and decoration can take the tour through one or more of the institute's half-dozen houses, which date as far back as 1684. Children are fascinated by the unique collection of dolls, doll furniture, and toys from earlier times.

There's a lot more here than you can see on a day trip to Salem, but an hour spent in one of the institute's 13 buildings, particularly in the main building and the adjoining houses, is a must for any Salem visitor. Here's a list of some of the special collections you can look over: clocks, ceramics, military uniforms and weapons, dolls and toys, glassware, buttons, silver and pewter, lamps and lanterns, sculpture, tools, costumes from earlier centuries, and bits and pieces from the China trade, as well as a very good collection of work by Massachusetts artists, including paintings and furniture. Several galleries and exhibition rooms have changing shows, so the return visitor should check to see what's new.

Salem Maritime National Historic Site
174 Derby St. ☎ **508/740-1660.** Free admission. Daily 9am–5pm.

In 1938, the National Park Service took over the **Custom House,** where Nathaniel Hawthorne once worked, and nearby Derby Wharf, one of the city's busiest trade centers, as a basis for the maritime site. The first thing to do is to pick up free copies of the National Park Service's materials about the site, which have a sketch map and directory of the buildings as well as short histories of the prominent Derby merchant family and of the adventures of several famous Salem vessels, both merchantmen and privateers. These accounts are very well written and are just the thing to get you in the mood for a tour of the Custom House, wharves, and warehouses.

The site also contains the **Derby House,** built in 1762 for shipping magnate Elias Derby by his father, Capt. Richard Derby; and the **West India Goods Store,** right next to Derby House, open for business and selling teas, coffee (beans and brew), spices, and other treasures from the East. Daily house tours are given; hours vary.

Witch Dungeon Museum
16 Lynde St., near Washington St. ☎ **508/741-3570.** Admission $4 adults, $2.50 children. Daily 10am–5pm.

Just half a block from the western end of the East India Marine Mall, this museum offers live reenactments of a witch trial, a re-created dungeon, and a replica of Old Salem Village, among other exhibits.

WHERE TO STAY

Coach House Inn
284 Lafayette St., Salem, MA 01970. ☎ **508/744-4092** or 800/688-8689. 11 rms and suites (9 with bath). TV. $65–$72 double without bath, $72–$95 double with bath; $125–$155 suite with kitchenette. All rates include continental breakfast. Lower off-season rates available. AE, MC, V.

A 10-minute walk from the center of town and two blocks from the water, the Coach House Inn is a large Victorian house built in 1879 by E. Augustus Emmerton, sea captain, merchant, and banker. The Victorian decor (some rooms even have antique fireplaces) has been updated with private bathrooms; several rooms have kitchenettes. The Coach House Inn is nonsmoking.

Hawthorne Hotel

18 Washington Sq. W., Salem, MA 01970. ☎ **508/744-4080** or 800/729-7829. Fax 508/745-9842. 89 rms and suites. A/C TV TEL. $95–$132 double. Additional person $12 extra. Children under 16 stay free in parents' room. AE, DC, DISC, MC, V.

The Hawthorne, on Salem Common, a major Salem landmark in the middle of town, is within easy walking distance of all the sights in town. It's a good-size hotel, restored with lots of fine wood paneling and brass chandeliers. The lobby and public rooms (including the tavern and the restaurant, called Nathaniel's) use these elements to achieve a simple but very elegant atmosphere; it's echoed in the rooms with the use of smaller brass chandeliers and wingback chairs. Otherwise, the rooms are modern and decorated in solid colors.

Salem Inn

7 Summer St., Salem, MA 01970. ☎ **508/741-0680** or 800/446-2995. Fax 508/744-8924. 31 rms. A/C TV TEL. Jan 1–Sept 30, $109–$159 double; Oct 1–Oct 7, $119–$169 double; Oct 11–Nov 2, $140–$175 double; Nov 3–Dec 29, $99–$149. Special Package Rates Dec 30–Dec 31. All rates include continental breakfast. Additional person $15 extra. AE, DC, DISC, MC, V. Free parking two blocks away in a city lot, with validation.

The Salem Inn, near the intersection with Essex Street, is only half a block from the Witch House and two blocks from the Peabody/Essex Museum. It's comprised of two restored sea captain's homes with large, beautiful, and comfortable rooms. Rooms have queen- or king-size beds and fireplaces. The price differential for rooms depends on plumbing: All rooms have private bathrooms, but the baths for the less expensive rooms are across the hallway from the rooms themselves. Many rooms have working fireplaces, canopy beds, and antique furnishings. Some rooms have Jacuzzis, and all have in-room coffeemakers. There's a restaurant on the premises, as well as a gift shop.

WHERE TO DINE

The Grapevine Restaurant

26 Congress St. ☎ **508/745-9335.** Reservations recommended, especially on weekends. Main courses $5.95–$8.25 at lunch, $11–$15.95 at dinner. AE, DISC, MC, V. Mon–Sat 11:30am–10pm, Sun 5–10pm. NORTHERN ITALIAN/AMERICAN GRILL.

During the warm-weather months, choose to sit in the courtyard out back, and you'll feel as if you've been transported to Tuscany. Both lunch and dinner menus include a wonderful selection of Italian cuisine along with some creative American dishes. The menu changes seasonally, but some specialties of the house include duck spring rolls or crab cakes as appetizers. Main courses include swordfish breaded with cornmeal and served with tequila-lime sauce, and eggplant wrapped around ricotta and seasoned with basil. If you don't want to settle in for a long drawn-out meal, you can always sit at the bar and order a bowl of linguine tossed with pesto and topped with sautéed vegetables—or, for that matter, anything else from the menu. You'll undoubtedly find yourself sitting next to locals in for their weekly Grapevine fix.

Lyceum Bar & Grill

43 Church St. ☎ **508/745-7665.** Reservations recommended. Main courses $9–$18. AE, DISC, MC, V. Mon–Fri 11:30am–3:30pm; 5:30–10pm; Sun brunch 11am–3:30pm. AMERICAN.

One block from the pedestrian mall, near the corner of Church and Washington Streets, the Lyceum was once at the center of the city's cultural life, and Alexander Graham Bell, who once lived in Salem, gave the first public demonstration of the telephone in its halls. Today the Lyceum is an attractive restaurant–bar and grill. The menu is heavy with local seafood, plus grilled meats and poultry. You might try the grilled butterflied whole baby chicken with a maple glaze, or the cracked-black-pepper and lemon-rubbed grilled pork tenderloin (served with Yankee cranberry chutney and garlic mashed potatoes). In good weather, find your way to the terrace out back in the courtyard.

⑤ Red's Sandwich

15 Central St. ☎ **508/745-3527.** Reservations not accepted. Breakfast $1.25–$3.75; lunch $1.25–$5.75. No credit cards. Mon–Sat 5am–3pm, Sun 6am–1pm. DINER.

Located in the 18th-century Old London Tea House behind the Peabody/Essex Museum, Red's has been popular with locals and out-of-towners alike for more than 37 years. Here you'll find the townies crowded around two horseshoe-shaped bars and in adjacent tables and booths every morning from 5am (6am on Sunday). It's the kind of place where you sit down for breakfast and the waitress immediately plunks down a heavy mug and asks, "Coffee?" It's also the kind of place where you can fill up on all the breakfast foods you'd only dare eat while on vacation, like Belgian waffles piled high with whipped cream and the fattest French toast you've ever seen. For lunch, you'll find all your diner favorites, including burgers and club sandwiches. In warmer months, Red's has an outdoor cafe.

Stromberg's

Rte. 1A. ☎ **508/744-1863.** Reservations not accepted. Seafood platters $9–$14. AE, DISC, MC, V. Tues–Thurs 11am–9pm, Fri–Sat until 10pm.

On the bridge between Salem and Beverly, Stromberg's is one of the most popular seafood restaurants on the North Shore. The draw is the combination of top-quality fish and low prices. Flounder comes straight from the fishing boats, and there are always daily specials in addition to the regular menu. Stromberg's is located on the spot where Roger Conant and his followers landed in 1686 and founded the town of Salem.

5 Marblehead

4 miles SE of Salem

What Salem was to merchant ships a century ago, Marblehead is to yachts today. Summer and winter, the beautiful, perfectly sheltered harbor is full of white boats bobbing on the water, or in dry dock, or heading out to sea. But it's not only yachters who come to Marblehead. This is without doubt one of the prettiest and best-kept towns in the country, and people love to come up from Boston on the weekend just to walk the streets, window-shop, or have a bowl of chowder in one of several good restaurants. They also come for a look at *The Spirit of '76*, the famous painting made even more famous during the Bicentennial celebrations, which is hung in Abbot Hall, Marblehead's Town Hall. If you plan to go to Salem, make the detour to Marblehead for at least an hour or two, or for a meal or even overnight.

GETTING THERE   By Car   See "Salem," above. From Mass. 1A North, take Mass. 129 in Swampscott and follow it right into Old Town, Marblehead.

By Bus & Train   The commuter trains between Boston and Salem (see "Salem," above) stop at Lynn, and bus nos. 441 and 442 run between Marblehead and Boston's Haymarket Square about every half hour during rush hours, every hour other times, but note that only bus no. 442 runs in the evening and on Sunday.

ESSENTIALS   The **telephone area code** is **617.** For information, contact the **Marblehead Chamber of Commerce**, 62 Pleasant St. (P.O. Box 76), Marblehead, MA 01945 (☎ **617/631-2868**).

WHAT TO SEE & DO

Walking around, window-shopping, and admiring the buildings and the rugged coast are the best things to do in Marblehead's Old Town section. Here are some landmarks to seek out as you go:

DOWNTOWN

Abbot Hall

Washington St. ☎ **617/631-0528.** Free admission; donations appreciated. Nov–May, Mon–Fri 9am–1pm; June–Oct, Mon–Tues, and Thurs–Fri 9am–4pm, Wed 9am–8pm, Sat 9am–6pm, Sun and holidays 11am–6pm.

Abbot Hall (home of the Marblehead Historical Commission) dominates the town from a hilltop, readily visible as you ride into Marblehead. You can hardly miss its brick clock tower. Go to the hall and ask the way to the Selectmen's Meeting Room to find that marvelous patriotic painting, *The Spirit of '76.* While you're there, take a look at the deed by which the Native Americans transferred ownership of the land to European newcomers in 1684. The new Marine Room is now open to the public.

Jeremiah Lee Mansion

Near the intersection of Hooper and Washington Sts. ☎ **617/631-1069.** Admission $4 adults, $3 students and children 10–16, children under 10 free. Mid-May to Columbus Day, Mon–Sat 10am–4pm, Sun 1–4pm.

In the center of the town's historic district, the Jeremiah Lee Mansion is owned by the Marblehead Historical Society and is one of two historic Marblehead homes open to the public. Built in 1768 by a prominent merchant, it's an outstanding example of pre-Revolutionary Georgian architecture, with original rococo carving and architectural features, period furnishings, and the only example of hand-painted 18th-century English wallpaper still on the walls of its original home. Collections of children's furniture and toys, nautical items, military memorabilia, and folk art are all housed inside.

King Hooper Mansion

8 Hooper St. ☎ **617/631-2608.** Free admission for exhibits in gallery and ballroom, donation requested for house tours. Mon–Sat 10am–4pm, Sun 1–5pm. There are often private parties; tours are not held on those days. Call ahead to be sure it's open to the public when you're in town.

Located more or less across the street from the Lee Mansion (see above), the King Hooper Mansion was built in 1728 (a Georgian addition was added in 1747). It was home of merchant prince Robert Hooper, known as "King" because of his generosity to the town. Splendidly decorated and furnished, it includes a ballroom and wine cellar. Now the headquarters of the Marblehead Arts Association, it offers tours of four floors. Art exhibits change each month.

THE WATERFRONT & CROCKER PARK

After a walk in the "downtown" part of the historic district, make your way down to the waterfront and **Crocker Park,** on a hill at the western end of Front Street. Relax on one of the benches and admire the panoramic view of the harbor and the town. Bring or buy a sandwich and have a picnic here. The view is unforgettable.

From Crocker Park, walk east along Front Street, past its little restaurants, boatyards, and houses built on the rocks, to **Fort Sewall.** The fort is an earthwork fortification built in the 1600s and "modernized" in the late 1700s to include barracks and half-buried buildings, which still remain. The fort is right at the mouth of the harbor and offers a commanding view of the water and of Marblehead Neck, at the other side of the harbor's mouth, dominated by a light. This is another good picnic place, and it's great for children, who will love playing in the fort (where there's little risk of falling into the water).

When you're ready to leave Fort Sewall, walk back along Front Street, turn right on Franklin, then right again on Orne Street to get to **Fountain Park** and **Old Burial Hill,** where the town's first church meeting house was built (it's gone now) and where ancient gravestones mark the places of many of Marblehead's earliest inhabitants and Revolutionary War dead. Orne Street east of Fountain Park leads to the beach.

If you're traveling by car, be sure to drive the loop around **Marblehead Neck.** This quiet residential community is made up of several grand ocean- and harborfront homes surrounded by handsome lawns and gardens. Along the way there's an **Audubon Bird Sanctuary** (on Ocean Avenue), **Castle Rock** (from which the ocean views are staggeringly beautiful), and—at the tip—**Chandler Hovey Park,** which is home to the Marblehead Light and several benches where you can sit and look out at the boat-filled harbor. This is one day not to leave the camera in your hotel room.

WHERE TO STAY

Should you really want to get into the spirit and soul of this beautiful seacoast town, you'll have to spend the night. Possibilities are limited but very attractive. I suggest that you try to plan your visit for a weekday, and that you call ahead for reservations, especially in July and August. In addition to the places listed below, you can get information through Bed & Breakfast Marblehead & North Shore/Greater Boston & Cape Cod. Contact them at P.O. Box 35, Newtonville, MA 02160 (☎ 617/964-1606 or 800/832-2632 outside MA; fax 617/332-8572).

Harbor Light Inn

58 Washington St., Marblehead, MA 01945. ☎ **617/631-2186.** 20 rms and suites. A/C TV TEL. $95–$150 double; $160–225 suite. All rates include continental breakfast. AE, MC, V. Directions: See below.

Located between Pearl and Pickett Streets, the Harbor Light Inn is made up of two 18th-century Marblehead houses right in the center of the historic district. The inn is attractive from the outside but even better inside. Each of the guest rooms has either a four-poster or a canopied queen-size bed; some have views of the harbor. One room has its own large private deck with a fine view, and all have antique furniture and modern private baths. Four rooms have Jacuzzis, and 11 have working fireplaces. Most of the rooms also have VCRs, and use of the videos in the inn's video library is free. There's a beautiful formal parlor, an observation deck on the roof, and an outdoor pool. Here you're only steps from shopping and two blocks from the waterfront. The continental breakfast includes fresh baked breads, muffins, coffee cake (baked on premises), and rolls and pastry (from a local bakery), fresh fruit, coffee, and tea.

To get here, take Washington Street into the historic district until you see the yellow Old Town Hall on its own little "island" in the middle of the road; just behind the town hall is the corner of State Street, and just beyond that, on Washington Street, is the inn.

The Nautilus
68 Front St., Marblehead, MA 01945. ☎ **617/631-1703.** 4 rms (none with bath). $75 double. No credit cards. Directions: See below.

The recommendable guest house on the waterfront is the Nautilus, run by Ethel Dermody. This small Marblehead house is in great demand because of its waterfront location and its proximity to some of Marblehead's finest antiques and gift shops, so it's advisable to call ahead for reservations, particularly on weekends in summer. Bathrooms are not in the rooms but are nearby, and a small refrigerator is in the hall for guests' use. One or two rooms have sea views. Parking is a problem downtown, but Mrs. Dermody will recommend places without danger of towing or tickets. The Nautilus is right across the street from the Driftwood Restaurant, which is by the municipal parking lot on the water at the end of State Street.

To get to the Nautilus, take Washington Street into the historic district, until you see the yellow Old Town Hall on its own little "island" in the middle of the road; just behind the town hall, turn right on State Street, follow it to the waterfront, and turn right; the Nautilus is on the right.

Spray Cliff
25 Spray Ave., Marblehead, MA 09145. ☎ **617/631-6789** or 800/626-1530. 4 rms. Memorial Day weekend to mid-Oct $159–$199 double; lower rates off-season. Additional person $15 extra. All rates include full breakfast and evening refreshments. MC, V.

Spray Cliff, a large Victorian Tudor located on a cliff overlooking the ocean, changed management in 1994. Innkeepers Roger and Sally Plauché have tastefully redecorated the mansion. It's Marblehead's only oceanfront bed and breakfast, and rooms offer mesmerizing views of ever-changing ocean activity. The setting is relaxing and peaceful, and Spray Cliff is just a one-minute walk to the beach and a five-minute drive into town. Smoking is not permitted.

WHERE TO DINE

The first three dining recommendations below can be reached by taking Washington Street into the historic district until you see the yellow Old Town Hall on its own little "island" in the middle of the road. Just behind the town hall, turn right on State Street, and you'll find these restaurants either on State Street or near its end at the waterfront.

⑤ Driftwood Restaurant
63 Front St. ☎ **617/631-1145.** Reservations not required. $1.50–$7.50. No credit cards. Summer, Mon–Thurs 5:30am–2pm, Fri–Sun 5:30am–3 or 4pm; winter, daily 5:30am–2pm. Directions: See above. DINER.

In spite of its magnet-for-tourists location, the Driftwood is a part of the real Marblehead full of hearty fishers and boatbuilders. Its barn-red clapboard exterior is matched inside with red-and-white-checked tablecloths and a long lunch counter. At 5:30am the fishers troop in for coffee, eggs, and ham; later in the day they may return for a bowl of chowder or a portion of "fried dough," a Driftwood specialty served with butter and maple syrup. Breakfast, clam chowder, sandwiches, and fish or seafood plates are the hot items here.

King's Rook

12 State St. ☎ **617/631-9838.** Reservations not required. Main courses $7–$12. MC, V. Mon–Fri noon–2:30pm; Tues–Fri 5:30–11:30pm, Sat–Sun noon–11:30pm. Directions: See above. CAFE.

The literary-minded in Marblehead who have a free hour in the evening spend it at the King's Rook, a European-style coffeehouse and wine bar located not far from the intersection with Washington Street. Coffee drinks are in the $1.50 to $4 range, and the atmosphere—provided by captain's chairs, small wood-plank tables, low-beamed ceiling, tin lamps, and watercolors on the walls—is yours at no extra charge. Beers, over 40 wines by the glass, light entrées, pizzas, and a long list of rich desserts are also served. Many couples find it a romantic place.

The Landing

81 Front St., on Clark's Landing. ☎ **617/631-1878.** Reservations recommended. Lunch $6.95–$9.95, dinner $13.95–$19.95. AE, DISC, MC, V. Daily 11:30am–midnight. SEAFOOD.

The Landing, about the largest and most elaborate of Marblehead's restaurants, caters to the boating crowd, which includes early-morning amateur scallop and lobster hunters. Here you'll find an English-style pub and dining rooms with a view of yacht-filled Marblehead Harbor. Come for a simple lunch of fish and chips or something fancier. At dinnertime there's mesquite-smoked duck or mahimahi. The setting, a semiformal dining room right over the water, is excellent. The Landing's pub section, popular with the younger boating set, offers burgers and beer.

EN ROUTE TO GLOUCESTER AND ROCKPORT

When Bostonians tell you they're taking a trip to the Cape, they mean they're heading south to Cape Cod. But there's another cape that attracts weekend and summer visitors from the metropolis: **Cape Ann,** just over an hour's drive or train ride north of the city.

Though few out-of-towners are familiar with Cape Ann, many have heard of Gloucester and Rockport, the picturesque seaport towns with a fascinating, almost legendary, history of struggle and communion with the sea.

If you look closely at the map, you'll notice that Cape Ann is in fact an island connected by bridges to the mainland (as is Cape Cod, since construction of the Cape Cod Canal). The bays, inlets, harbors, and coves of Cape Ann lend a variety to the landscape and shoreline, which has long attracted vacationers, especially in the summertime. The best way to appreciate the scenic beauties of the North Shore and Cape Ann is to drive north along the coast through Manchester and Magnolia to Gloucester.

Manchester is a tidy little North Shore town peopled by old New England types and many professionals who commute into Boston by train. Should you visit during the summer, you can take advantage of **Singing Beach,** half a mile from the train station (center of town) along Beach Street. If you drive, you'll have to pay a parking fee; if you walk, you swim for free. **White Beach,** off Ocean Street, has the same arrangement and the same facilities: bathhouse and snack bar.

A drive three miles northeast of Manchester along Mass. 127 brings you to **Magnolia.** Once a humble fishing village, Magnolia is now a lush and wealthy town. Lavish "summer cottages" built by the rich during the 19th century have had insulation and heating installed so that they can be used as year-round principal residences.

The town center is quite pretty, and less than a mile past it lie two natural features you may want to inspect: **Rafe's Chasm,** a dramatic cleft in the shoreline rock, is just opposite the reef of **Norman's Woe,** which figured in Longfellow's poem "The Wreck of the Hesperus." Should you want to spend some time in this lovely setting, there are two good places to stay the night.

GETTING THERE

For a visit to Cape Ann, I'd suggest that you tour by private car. Coming from Boston, take I-93 North to I-95 North (Mass. 128 east), and take the exit for Manchester. From Salem, follow Mass. 1A to Beverly, then Mass. 127 north to Manchester. The drive up the coast on Mass. 127 from Salem is of exceptional beauty.

The **telephone area code** is **508.** For information, contact the **Cape Ann Chamber of Commerce,** 33 Commercial St., Gloucester, MA 01930 (☎ **508/ 283-1601** or **800/321-0133**). They'll have information on Manchester and Magnolia, as well as the towns covered below.

WHAT TO SEE & DO

North of Magnolia along Mass. 127, signs will point to the right, down Hesperus Avenue, to the **Hammond Castle Museum,** 80 Hesperus Ave. (☎ **508/283-2080** for a recorded announcement). The castle-mansion was built by inventor, electrical engineer, and collector Dr. John Hays Hammond Jr. (1888–1965), whose creations included radio remote control, and aspects of radar and sonar, including torpedo-guidance systems. Despite his name and his interest in things electric, J. H. Hammond Jr. was not related to Laurens Hammond, inventor of the electric organ.

The castle builder's father, John Hays Hammond (1855–1936), was a mining engineer who helped Cecil Rhodes open up South Africa's hugely rich gold mines. He took part in the Boer War and was captured, ransomed, and returned to the United States.

His son grew up in a cosmopolitan and wealthy household, and did a lot of traveling himself, as you'll see from exhibits in the castle. The younger Hammond grew rich on government defense contracts and the proceeds from his inventions, became a director of RCA, and spent his wealth on his obsession: European history. His castle is built in four sections, each made to epitomize a distinct period of European architecture. The Great Hall is Romanesque, the interior courtyard is fitted out as a medieval town square, and the living quarters are Gothic and Renaissance French. The guide who takes you on the obligatory 45-minute tour will explain Dr. Hammond's passion for collecting and his macabre sense of humor. You come away from the tour marveling at the house's lovely setting, amused by its half-treasure-chest, half-gimcrack planning and construction, and puzzled by Hammond's genius, romanticism, and sheer weirdness. In any case, you don't want to miss it.

While you're waiting for the tour, you can explore the Tower Galleries, with various exhibits and artifacts, and you can pick up a flyer listing the museum's many concerts, lectures, and special programs. There are recitals on the Great Hall's fabulous 8,200-pipe organ, which got a brand-new console in 1987. Other concerts have included Scott Joplin rags, chamber music, and guitar music. There are special-theme evenings as well (call for details).

The museum costs $6 for adults, $5 for seniors and students, and $4 for children 4 to 12; children under 4 enter free. It's open May through October daily from 10am to 5pm, weekends only November through April.

WHERE TO STAY
Old Corner Inn

2 Harbor St., Manchester by the Sea, MA 01944. ☎ **508/526-4996.** 9 rms (6 with bath). $65–$125 double (lower rates are for rooms with shared bath). AE, MC, V. Directions: From Rte. 128, take Manchester's Pine Street exit, turn left at the end of the ramp, and follow that road approximately three miles; turn right onto Mass. 127, go half a mile, and the inn is on the left.

This aptly named inn is indeed on a corner and is indeed old; the building was erected back in 1865. It's also the only inn in Manchester, so reservations made well in advance are a must. Guest rooms are located on three floors; the lower-level rooms are the loveliest. Rooms 1 and 2 have four-poster feather beds, working fireplaces, and ball-and-claw bathtubs. The inn is within easy reach of beaches (including Singing Beach) and the village.

White House

18 Norman Ave., Magnolia, MA 01930. ☎ **508/525-3642.** 16 rms (13 with bath). TV. $75 double without bath; $75–$95 double with bath. All rates include continental breakfast. DISC, MC, V. Directions: Take Raymond Street off Mass. 127 and follow it as it turns into Norman Avenue; the White House is at the corner of Lexington Avenue, near the town's shops.

Centerpiecing a stately lawn and surrounded by gardens and rhododendrons, the White House is a fine old Magnolia Victorian house with an unobtrusive residential wing attached. In the house are six charming rooms, three with private bath; in the wing are 10 recently renovated motel-style rooms with complete facilities: private bath, TV set, and air conditioning. Guests receive passes for the use of a private beach; Rafe's Chasm, Norman's Woe, and the Hammond Castle (see above) are all close by. Right across Mass. 127 is Lexington Avenue, a short and interesting shopping street.

6 Gloucester

33 miles NE of Boston, 16 miles NE of Salem, 7 miles S of Rockport

The Pilgrims founded Plymouth in 1620, and three years later fishermen founded Gloucester. The marvelous natural harbor and the plentiful fishing grounds made that early settlement a fisher's paradise. Almost four centuries later, it still is.

Gloucester, at one time an important shipbuilding town, prides itself on being the birthplace of the schooner (1713). Like many other communities on the New England coast, it profited from the wealth of forests inland, the plentiful fish, and the richness of trade. Over the years, Gloucester lost so many of its sons to the ravages of the sea that the town thought it fitting to set up a memorial to them. The *Gloucester Fisherman* (also known as "The Man at the Wheel") is one of

New England's most famous statues, with a plaque that reads "THEY THAT GO DOWN TO THE SEA WITH SHIPS, 1623–1923."

The sea is still Gloucester's provider, and the "fishing boats out of Gloucester" still head for open water early each morning. You'll see some of these sturdy little boats, festooned with all sorts of nets and rigging, down in the harbor. Fish-packing plants at quayside process the catch as soon as it's brought in.

Another maritime industry has become important in recent years: whale-watching tours (see below). You might want to take yours from here.

GETTING THERE   By Car   Leaving from Boston and heading directly for Cape Ann, you'll save time by taking I-93 North to I-95/Mass. 128. Follow I-95 North/Mass. 128 east, and when the highway divides, stay on Mass. 128 (I-95 will head north, toward Maine) all the way into Gloucester. For the scenic coastal drive, follow Mass. 128 to the exit for Manchester. In Manchester, take Mass. 127 north.

By Train   Commuter trains run from Boston's North Station to Salem, Beverly, Gloucester, and Rockport. Trains run about every 20 minutes during rush hours, every half hour during the day, every hour at night and on weekends. Call ☎ 617/722-3200 for schedules. From the station in Gloucester, it's about a mile to the "Man at the Wheel" statue. The beaches and some other attractions are several miles away.

By Bus   CATA, the Cape Ann Transportation Authority (☎ 508/283-7916), runs local buses among the towns and villages of Cape Ann.

ESSENTIALS   The **telephone area code** is **508.** The **Cape Ann Chamber of Commerce** (☎ **508/283-1601** or **800/321-0133**) provides information at two locations. The downtown headquarters at 33 Commercial St., Gloucester, MA 01930, has a spacious information center furnishing maps, brochures, special-events bulletins, listings of accommodations, restrooms, and a rack of restaurant menus. Not far from the statue of the *Gloucester Fisherman,* across the drawbridge, at the intersection of Mass. 127 and Mass. 133, is the chamber's little tourist information booth. Guides at either of these locations will be happy to provide information on any town on Cape Ann.

WHAT TO SEE & DO

Signs direct motorists along Gloucester's **Scenic Tour,** covering the Harbor Cove, Inner Harbor, and Fish Pier, as well as to the famous statue of the *Gloucester Fisherman* by Leonard Craske.

If you're lucky enough to be in Gloucester late in June, ask about the **Festival of St. Peter,** the high point of which is the Blessing of the Fleet. Several hundred boats make up Gloucester's important fishing fleet, and the blessing pays tribute to them.

A great "summer cottage" turned museum, **Beauport,** the Sleeper-McCann House, is at 75 Eastern Point Blvd. (☎ 508/283-0800), on Eastern Point, the peninsula across the bay from downtown Gloucester. The house, now under the care of the Society for the Preservation of New England Antiquities, was built by Henry Davis Sleeper, a prominent interior decorator and antiquarian of the 1920s. Sleeper worked for 27 years to make Beauport a showplace. You can take the hour-long tour May 15 to October 15, Monday through Friday from 10am to 4pm; also on weekends mid-September through mid-October, from 1 to 4pm.

Admission costs $5 per adult, $4.50 for seniors, $2.50 for children 6 to 12; children under 6 enter free.

On your excursion down to Beauport, you'll want to stroll through East Gloucester's **Rocky Neck Art Colony.** The winding streets offer interesting glimpses of the harbor, and every other house seems to be an artist's studio. You'll see signs asking you to park *before* you enter the narrow streets. Take advantage of the lot next to the signs.

Beaches Gloucester's favored place for a hot summer afternoon is **Good Harbor Beach** in East Gloucester, on Mass. 127A toward Rockport. It may be crowded if the day is really hot, and parking will be tight. Alternatives are **Long Beach** and **Pebble Beach,** just a bit farther along Mass. 127A, within the bound-aries of Rockport. **Wingaersheek Beach** is on Ipswich Bay to the northwest (head back down Mass. 128 south and watch for signs). **Coffin Beach** is just northwest of Wingaersheek.

Whale-Watching Cruises There are a number of boats offering whale-watching cruises out of Gloucester Harbor from April to November. Cruises usually last between four and five hours and thus take up a full morning or afternoon. Bring warm clothing, even on a warm day, because the maritime breezes out on the water will make the ambient temperature at least 10° cooler than on land, and the windchill factor might make it feel even colder. Also, remember your sunglasses to ward off the glare from the water; and sunscreen, because that same glare, combined with the bright sun, can really give you a burn. Wear rubber-soled shoes if you have them. You can buy soft drinks and snacks on board.

Once out on the water, keep your eyes peeled for humpback whales, 30-ton creatures usually about 50 feet long, which seem to love their briny habitat, breech-ing and playing for hours, accompanying themselves with their own curious songs. A cousin of the humpback is the finback, about twice as heavy and up to 80 feet long, making it second in size to the great blue whale. Long and slender, it's a super-fast swimmer, propelling its great bulk through the deep at speeds of 20 knots or even more. The minke whale is "small," weighing only 11 tons and grow-ing to 30 feet in length. Minke whales have a well-developed sense of curiosity and may snoop around your boat just to see what's up. In addition, you may see right whales, dolphins, pilot whales, seals, sharks, and seabirds such as petrels, shear-waters, gannets, and gulls.

Capt. Fred Douglass and his sons pioneered whale-watching cruises out of Gloucester with their Daunty Fleet of boats, and now they operate **Cape Ann Whale Watch** (☎ 508/283-5110), with daily departures at 8:30am and 1:30pm from Rose's Wharf, at 415 Main St., across from the Old Colony gas station. A research naturalist accompanies every cruise. Whale sightings are guaranteed (Captain Douglass has had a 99% record since 1979); if you don't see a whale, you'll receive a free pass for a future cruise. Reservations are requested, and tickets can be purchased from the ticket office on Rose's Wharf daily from 7am to 6pm. Daytime cruises cost $21 for adults, $15 for seniors over 60, and $12 for children under 16, and other discounts are given for AAA members, military personnel, and college students.

Seven Seas Whale Watch, Seven Seas Wharf (☎ 508/283-1776, or 800/238-1776), operates two cruises daily (one at 8:30am, the other at 1:30pm) Fares are $21 for adults (if you're a member of AAA, you get a $2 discount), $16 for seniors, and $12 for children 16 and under. Be sure to reserve in advance, especially for the afternoon cruise, because they sell out early. In high summer, there are also sunset cruises with entertainment.

WHERE TO STAY

Best Western Bass Rocks Ocean Inn

107 Atlantic Rd., Glouster, MA 01930. ☎ **508/283-7600**. 48 rms. A/C TV TEL. Apr 15–June 16, $85 first-floor double, $99 second-floor double; June 17–Sept 5, $110 first-floor double, $125 second-floor double; Sept 6–Oct, $105 first-floor double, $115 second-floor double. All rates include buffet breakfast. AE, MC, V. Closed Nov–Apr 15.

The last place you'd expect to find a Best Western is in this oceanfront, late 19th-century Colonial Revival mansion. Built in 1899 by hotelier George O. Stacy as a wedding gift for his wife, the Bass Rocks Ocean Inn never served as their home because Mrs. Stacy refused to live in such a remote location. The house was then rented to a prominent New York publisher until 1928, when George Stacy died and the mansion was sold. In 1946 the house was purchased by the Muller family, who opened it as a guesthouse that summer. Over the next 40 years the house had nine different incarnations as a tourist operation while in the hands of the same family. Today the inn is run by Tracey Muller, who has refurbished and redecorated it while maintaining its 19th-century feeling. The guest rooms (all located in the motel, not in the Stacy House) are modern and feature standard amenities such as color TVs, modern baths, and sliding glass doors that open onto patios or balconies. There's a games room complete with a billiard table and board games. In good weather, guests may enjoy the gardens, pool, or rooftop observation deck. A complimentary cold buffet breakfast is served every morning.

Gray Manor

14 Atlantic Rd. (Bass Rocks), Gloucester, MA 01930. ☎ **508/283-5409**. 9 units. A/C TV. Summer, $55–$60 double; $425 efficiency apartment per week for two people. Off-season (May 1–June 22 and after Labor Day), $40–$45 single, $50 efficiency double. Additional person $8 extra. Spring and fall discounts available. MC, V. Closed Winter. Directions: Take Exit 9 off Mass. 128 North, and turn left onto Bass Avenue, then right onto Atlantic.

Robert and Madeline Gray have operated this guesthouse for 34 years; the Gray Manor is up the hill, only a few minutes' walk from Good Harbor Beach. Guest rooms have private baths, and some even have their own decks.

WHERE TO DINE

The Gull

75 Essex Ave. (Mass. 133). ☎ **508/283-6565**. Reservations recommended. Main courses $5.95–$11.95 at lunch, $6.95–$20.95 at dinner. MC, V. Daily 5am–9:30pm. Directions: Take Mass. 133 less than two miles west of the "Man at the Wheel" statue, or approach along Mass. 133 eastbound from Mass. 128. SEAFOOD.

Among my favorite dining places in Gloucester is The Gull, located at the Cape Ann Marina on Mass. 133, a mile or so from the center of town right next to where the Yankee Whale Watch boats depart. The Gull is a big, friendly, fairly simple but attractive restaurant overlooking the Annisquam River, usually packed with boaters, whale-watchers, families, couples, and sailors. Seafood is the forte here, and you can have the huge, succulent lobster sandwich or a full clambake with steamers, corn on the cob, coleslaw, and a lobster, or you can settle for fish and chips. In addition to seafood, the menu also offers prime rib and steak selections. The Gull has a full bar.

Halibut Point

289 Main St. ☎ **508/281-1900.** Reservations not accepted. Main courses $7–$13. DISC, MC, V. Daily 11:30am–11pm. SEAFOOD.

Halibut Point is the name of a state park near Rockport and also of this publike restaurant in downtown Gloucester. The atmosphere is of a friendly neighborhood tavern, not fancy but fun. The menu is short and to the point, with sandwiches, salads, burgers, and several popular seafood items, but the blackboard always bears interesting special dishes. Swordfish is usually a good bet. The soup-and-sandwich special, with a mug of beer, is a particularly good bargain, and you must have the Italian fish chowder, the specialty of the house.

✪ The Rudder Restaurant

73 Rocky Neck Ave., East Gloucester. ☎ **508/283-7967.** Reservations required for weekends. Main courses $12.95–$19.95. DISC, MC, V. Mid-Apr to Nov, daily noon–10:30pm. SEAFOOD/INTERNATIONAL.

A meal at the Rudder is not just a meal—it's a party! This wildly imaginative restaurant—smack dab on the water in the heart of the Rocky Neck Art Colony—not only has some adventurous cooks in the kitchen (try the shrimp farcis for an appetizer) but is literally crammed floor-to-ceiling with gadgets, gizmos, colored lights, antiques, cards, photos, menus from around the world, and other collectibles. On top of that, there's entertainment, including a woman who does an invisible flaming baton twirling act. Incidentally, main-dish offerings run the gamut from baked stuffed sole to fried clams and chicken picatta. Brunch is served Friday through Sunday.

White Rainbow Restaurant

65 Main St. ☎ **617/281-0017.** Reservations recommended. Main courses $17.95–$21.95. AE, DC, MC, V. Tues–Fri and Sun 5:30–9:30pm (and Mon in summer), Sat 6–10pm. CONTINENTAL.

Gloucester's fanciest and best is the White Rainbow Restaurant in the basement of a 19th-century brick office building (go by the street numbers, as the sign is small and difficult to spot). There are two places to dine here: the formal dining room and the less formal cafe. Both have dusky brick walls, low lights (tables are lit by candle), and modern paintings. Waiters and waitresses are dressed in black and white, friendly but professional, and after you've been seated they'll take your order for an opener like pâté, Maui onion soup, or baked Brie; then you can go on to roast duck, grilled beef, or homemade pasta. Fresh fish specials are offered daily. Desserts are heavily biased in favor of chocolate. The wine list gives you plenty of room for making your selection, and prices are just slightly higher than the moderate range.

7 Rockport

40 miles NE of Boston, 7 miles N of Gloucester

North of Gloucester is the small seacoast town of Rockport, famed as an artists' colony and, well, just as a very picturesque place. Winslow Homer, Childe Hassam, and Fitz Hugh Lane came here to paint the fishermen working on their vessels and the quarrymen cutting and moving granite.

It has been a long time since Rockport was a village of hearty, independent fishermen and their families, living by their daily struggle with the sea, and today you're likely to see 10 times as many day-trippers as you are to see colorful village types. But the Rockport Art Association is active—the town is dotted with galleries holding paintings and crafts both pleasing and awkward, and amateur daubers test their skill at capturing daily life all over town. The Rockport Art Association's headquarters is also the venue for musical performances during the month-long annual Rockport Chamber Music Festival.

Rockport's popularity means that there are lots of good places to stay and to dine, and if you decide to remain overnight here, you'll notice that as the evening wears on, the streets become calmer and the village resumes something of its slow, antique pace.

GETTING THERE   By Car   Between Gloucester and Rockport are two loop roads. Mass. 127 takes you to Rockport through the middle of Cape Ann, then loops around the northern and western shores to return to Gloucester. Mass. 127A, on the other hand, takes you up the eastern shore of the cape before reaching Rockport. If you get lost, don't worry—in a short while some loop will bring you back to one or the other town.

By Train   Commuter trains run from Boston's North Station to Salem, Beverly, Gloucester, and Rockport. The trip to Rockport takes about 1 1/4 hours; trains run about every 20 minutes during rush hours, every half hour during the day, every hour at night and on weekends. Call ☎ 617/722-3200 for schedules.

By Bus   CATA, the Cape Ann Transportation Authority (☎ 508/283-7916), runs local buses among the towns and villages of Cape Ann.

ESSENTIALS   The **telephone area code** is **508.** The **Rockport Chamber of Commerce** (☎ **508/546-6575**) maintains a seasonal information booth on Upper Main Street (Mass. 127) on the outskirts of town, coming from Gloucester. In season you'll get help finding a room for the night, if there's one available. Stop at the booth for this free service. The chamber's office at 3 Main St. is open year-round.

Parking conditions downtown are sure to be very tight anytime in summer, so if you drive, find a nice back street or use the town-supported parking lot on the outskirts rather than getting snarled in the press of traffic downtown. The town lots charge several dollars per day for parking, but they offer a free shuttle bus from the lot to downtown Rockport. This isn't a bad deal, considering the gasoline you'll waste and the frustration you'll feel trying to find a legal spot to park downtown.

WHAT TO SEE & DO

The first thing every visitor does after arriving in Rockport is take a stroll down **Bearskin Neck,** the narrow peninsula jutting into the water off Dock Square, the town's main square. Here you'll find lots of quaint shops and art galleries to draw your attention, and many good views of the water and of the town.

Other strolls in town are also rewarding, and local brochures will urge you to take a photograph of the red fisherman's shack called "Motif No. 1," apparently named for its popularity among the first picture painters who moved to Rockport. Actually it should now be named "Motif No. 2," as the original shack was swept away in the great storm of 1978 and a new one was built from scratch. In the interest of originality, try to be the first person to visit Rockport *without* seeing this unimportant landmark; frankly, the thing is now famous because it's famous.

Rather, spend your time looking at the **local granite.** It was cut at the town's Swan Quarry (now flooded) and shipped out, giving the town its name. Curbstones, markers, pavements, foundations, piers, even whole buildings were made of the durable stone during the town's quarrying heyday. Now if "Motif No. 1" were a fisherman's shanty made of granite, that would be something to see!

For swimming, walk along Beach Street north to **Front Beach** and **Back Beach,** or wander (in your car or on your bike) north along the coast to **Pigeon Cove,** about two miles north (a half-hour walk).

You can go farther than Pigeon Cove by car or bike. In fact, you can make a loop of Cape Ann on Mass. 127 via Pigeon Cove, Folly Cove, Plum Cove, Annisquam, and Lobster Cove, ending in Gloucester.

If you love chamber music, plan your visit to coincide with the **Rockport Chamber Music Festival.** Recitals are given during the summer; for exact dates and details, call ☎ 508/546-7391.

WHERE TO STAY
IN TOWN

Addison Choate Inn

49 Broadway, Rockport, MA 01966. ☎ **508/546-7543** or 800/245-7543. 6 rms, 1 suite, 2 apartments. Mid-June to Labor Day, $91–$118 double; early May to mid-June and Oct 31–Dec 31, $80–$101 double; mid-June to Labor Day, Stable House/Cottage $645 per week. All rates include continental breakfast. DC, MC, V. Directions: Coming from Gloucester on Mass. 127, you enter Rockport on Broadway; the inn is on the right.

Rockport's most charming place to stay is the Greek Revival Addison Choate Inn. Its new owners have proudly taken charge of this meticulously restored 1851 house. Interior furnishings include modern and antique furnishings. You'll have a choice of rooms. You might just want a double room with a private bath or, if it's a special occasion, the two-room suite with an ocean view. For families with children over 12, the post-and-beam cottage with a furnished apartment is a good choice. The suites have TVs, and some rooms are air-conditioned. Breakfast is served buffet style and includes cereal, yogurt, cheeses, coffee cake, muffins, breads, seasonal fresh fruit, juice, coffee, and tea. Afternoon tea and coffee are available on request. The inn is within walking distance of the center of town, and there's a pool on the property.

Captain's Bounty Motor Inn

1 Beach St., Rockport, MA 01966. ☎ **508/546-9557.** 24 rms and efficiencies. TV TEL. Apr 1 to May 11, $65 oceanfront room, $68 oceanfront efficiency, $70 oceanfront efficiency suite; May 12 to June 15, $77 oceanfront room, $80 oceanfront efficiency, $85 oceanfront efficiency suite; June 16 to Sept 3, $95 oceanfront room, $100 oceanfront efficiency, $110 oceanfront efficiency suite; Sept 4 to Oct 31, $78 oceanfront room, $80 oceanfront efficiency, $86 oceanfront efficiency suite. Additional person $10 extra. Rollaway $5 extra. MC, V. Directions: From Dock Square, go east on Mass. 127 toward Annisquam, but turn right onto Beach Street.

For those who want modern hotel comfort and a beachfront location, this inn is the place. Ocean breezes provide natural air conditioning, since each room overlooks the water and has its own balcony and sliding glass door. Comforts such as sound-proofing and ceramic tile baths with tub and shower are provided. Kitchenette units are available.

Inn on Cove Hill

37 Mt. Pleasant St., Rockport, MA 01966. ☎ **508/546-2701.** 11 rms (9 with bath). A/C TV. $49 double without bath; $65–$101 double with bath. All rates include continental breakfast. No credit cards. Closed Nov to Mar. Directions: From Dock Square, follow Mass. 127A east for 100 yards; the inn is on the left.

The Inn on Cove Hill is only a few steps from the center of town on Mass. 127A. The charming house was built in 1791 with the proceeds (so they say) from cashing in some pirate gold found on Cape Ann. Today Marjorie and John Pratt, who lovingly restored the 18th-century Rockport home, keep the inn neat as a pin. Inside you'll find original pumpkin-pine floors, antique and reproduction furnishings, and paintings by Rockport artists. Breakfast is served in your room or by the garden during comfortable weather.

⑤ Linden Tree Inn

26 King St., Rockport, MA 01966. ☎ **508/546-2494.** 18 rms and efficiencies. $98–$107.50 double. All rates include continental breakfast. Folding bed $15 extra. MC, V. Closed mid-Oct to late Apr.

The Linden Tree Inn, located on a quiet street in the center of town three blocks from the train station, is a tidy inn run by friendly innkeepers Dawn and Jon Cunningham. The yard is shaded by an enormous old linden tree, as you'd expect. The inn has rooms in various sizes and styles. All rooms in the main house have private bath; half have air conditioning. In the modern carriage house, each efficiency has a double and twin bed, air conditioning, a cable color TV, a refrigerator, a toaster oven, a coffee maker, and a private deck. This is a nice place—homey, convenient, and friendly.

Peg Leg Inn

2 King St., Rockport, MA 01966. ☎ **508/546-2352,** or 800/346-2352. 33 rms. TV. Mid-June to Oct, $80–$125 double. All rates include continental breakfast. Off-season rates are lower. Additional person $10 extra. MC, V. Closed late Nov to Apr 1. Directions: From Mass. 127, turn left onto Railroad Avenue at the five-road intersection, then take the first right onto King Street.

Serenely situated on the edge of the sea, the Peg Leg Inn has been a haven for Rockport visitors for many years now. The original inn has been expanded to include five buildings, and most of the rooms have views of the water. The decor varies from room to room and building to building, but, as the houses of the inn are a century or two old, emphasis is on Early American, with modern luxuries added. The rooms are kept as neat as the white clapboard houses they're in, and the rates depend on the size of the room and its water view. The Peg Leg Inn is a short walk from the center of town, but the location makes it a good deal quieter than most in-town lodgings. The inn's full-service restaurant is next door.

ON THE OUTSKIRTS

Old Farm Inn

291 Granite St., Rockport, MA 01966. ☎ **508/546-3237.** 9 rms and suites, 1 cottage. TEL. In-season, $93–$125 double; off-season, $78–$115 double. Room with kitchenette $115; two-room suite $125. Two-bedroom housekeeping cottage $995 per week. Additional person $10 extra. Rollaway $15. Apr–June and Nov, lower rates available. All rates include buffet breakfast. AE, MC, V. Closed Dec–Mar. Directions: Follow Mass. 127 north and west from Rockport toward Annisquam, and watch for the inn on the right.

The Old Farm Inn is a 1799 saltwater farm with charming antique-furnished rooms in the inn, the barn guesthouse, and the fieldside cottage. Each room is uniquely decorated with country-style furnishings (many have beautiful quilts on the beds) and is equipped with everything you could possibly need to make your stay enjoyable and comfortable. The buffet breakfast here, which includes fresh fruit, homebaked breads, a selection of hot and cold cereals, yogurt, and juices, is excellent. All rooms, except one, have air conditioning.

Ralph Waldo Emerson Inn

Phillips Ave., Pigeon Cove, Rockport, MA 01966. ☎ **508/546-6321.** Fax 508/546-7043. 36 rms. A/C TEL. Summer, $100–$138 double. Add $23 per person for breakfast and dinner. DISC, MC, V. Closed Dec–Mar and weekdays in Apr and Nov. Directions: Follow Mass. 127 north from Rockport toward Annisquam for two miles, and watch for a sign on the right.

Somewhere in the old guest register of the Ralph Waldo Emerson Inn you might find the name of Emerson himself, for the distinguished philosopher was a guest in the old section of the inn in the 1850s. Of course, changes have been made since then in this lovely resort at Pigeon Cove, but it still retains the charm of a gracious era with furnishings such as spool beds and old-fashioned toilets. The view of the ocean from Cathedral Rocks is magnificent. Guests can enjoy the heated outdoor saltwater swimming pool or the indoor whirlpool and sauna, or go fishing, sightseeing, and shopping, or just relax in the comfortable chairs on the veranda. Recreation rooms include areas for playing cards, table tennis, or watching the wide-screen TV.

The dining room is open to the public on an availability basis. Breakfast is served from 8 to 10am, and dinner from 6 to 8pm.

Sandy Bay Motor Inn

173 Main St. (Mass. 127), Rockport, MA 01966. ☎ **508/546-7155.** 72 rms. A/C TV TEL. Summer, $92–$121 double. Fall–spring, lower rates available. AE, DC, MC, V.

For a modern hotel on the outskirts, try the Sandy Bay Motor Inn. The colorful rooms here, which include standard double rooms and efficiencies, are only the beginning of the story. Besides these, the motel has an indoor swimming pool, a whirlpool bath, saunas, tennis courts, a putting green, and a breakfast/lunch room. It's a good idea to make reservations in the busy summer months.

Yankee Clipper Inn

96 Granite St. (P.O. Box 2399), Rockport, MA 01966. ☎ **508/546-3407** or 800/545-3699. Fax 508/546-9730. 26 rms. TEL. Summer, $110–$239 double. All rates include full breakfast. Midweek and extended-stay packages available. AE, DISC, MC, V. Directions: At the end of Mass. Rte. 128 take Rte 127 left toward Rockport for 3 miles. Turn left on 127 toward Pigeon Cove and follow it for 1 mile to the hotel.

Two of the inn's four buildings occupy a waterfront site with excellent views; a third is a fine old house designed by none other than Charles Bulfinch, architect of the Massachusetts State House in Boston and (in part) of the Capitol in Washington. Grounds include several shady nooks and a heated saltwater swimming pool. The Bulfinch House is up the hill a bit and across the road. The fourth building is a three-bedroom cottage that's rented weekly (call for rates). An oceanfront dining room is open to the public, but reservations are essential. Main dishes, classic American and European, are $15.95 to $21.95 at dinner.

WHERE TO DINE

The first thing you should know is that Rockport is a dry town. No liquor, wine, or beer is served in its restaurants or sold in its inns or shops. You can drink in Rockport if you bring your own, and the restaurants will provide setups, corkscrews, ice buckets, and the like. But you must plan ahead and buy your booze in Gloucester, or in Lanesville, on Mass. 127 west of Rockport.

This all came about in 1856 when one Hannah Jumper, an outspoken leader of the temperance movement in Rockport, led a raid on the town's liquor supplies. In the four preceding years, sales of ardent spirits in Rockport had more than doubled, and many a fisherman and quarry worker spent on rum the wages that should have gone for family needs.

The town's Fourth of July bash in 1856 had gotten out of hand as usual, and on July 8 Hannah and other good citizens went to work. Casks and bottles stored in shops and warehouses—and even in private homes—were breached and broken, and though some people cried "Foul!" most people supported this radical solution. Hannah's early-morning direct action changed the history of Rockport, and it has been dry, by the active consent of a majority of its citizens, ever since.

Blacksmith Shop Restaurant

23 Mount Pleasant St. ☎ **508/546-6301.** Reservations recommended. Main courses $8.95–$15.95. AE, CB, DC, MC, V. May–Oct, daily 11am–10pm. SEAFOOD/TRADITIONAL AMERICAN.

Just off Dock Square, in the center of Rockport, the Blacksmith Shop Restaurant has something that Bearskin Neck restaurants don't have: lots of space and some sense of elegance. And yet the views of the harbor and of "Motif No. 1" from the Blacksmith Shop are as good as any in town, and better than most. There's so much space here that you enter through various old-time kitchen exhibits and memorabilia, then step down into the spacious waterside dining rooms to order from a menu heavy in seafood and traditional American favorites.

Brackett's Oceanview

27 Main St. ☎ **508/546-2797.** Reservations not required. Main courses $6.50–$12.25. AE, DC, DISC, MC, V. Tues–Sun 11am–closing. SEAFOOD/NEW ENGLAND.

An ocean view is exactly what you'll get at Brackett's. In fact, there are lovely views of the water from both sides of the simply furnished dining room. Open for lunch and dinner, Brackett's is a local favorite. Simple, traditional fare is what you should expect. There's something for everyone here—from chicken pot pie to scallop casserole and a deep-fried seafood platter. Codfish cakes are quite good here. For dessert, I'd recommend the French silk pie.

Ellen's Harborside

Just off Dock Sq., on T-Wharf. ☎ **508/546-2512.** Reservations not required. Breakfast $1.25–$4; lunch $1.50–$7.95; dinner main courses $7–$15; meals $12–$20. MC, V. Apr–Nov, daily 7am–9pm. Closed Dec–Mar. SEAFOOD.

Ellen's Harborside next to the firehouse is a tiny, crowded, but pleasant place that specializes in fresh seafood, "authentic" pit-barbecue cooking, and homemade desserts, and packs 'em in every night of the summer. Ellen's is especially popular with thrifty seniors, who like the freshness of the seafood and the hard-working waitresses as well as those delicious and abundant desserts. The seafood special usually costs about $6.95. The dining room and coffee shop are simple and functional (the rear dining room overlooks Rockport Harbor).

My Place-by-the-Sea

68 Bearskin Neck. ☎ **508/546-9667.** Reservations recommended for dinner. Main courses $2–$6 at lunch, $11–$18 at dinner; lunch $9–$13; dinner $20–$30. AE, CB, DC, DISC, JCB, MC, V. Apr–Nov, daily 11:30am–9:30pm. Call ahead for hours during the rest of the year. Directions: Walk out to the top of Bearskin Neck; it's on the left. SEAFOOD.

At the very end of Bearskin Neck is My Place-by-the-Sea, a small cedar-shingled building with the best outdoor oceanfront dining on Cape Ann. The moderately priced lunch menu features soups, salads, omelets, and sandwiches. Dinner—which is available throughout the day—features lots of fresh fish and seafood, including lobster prepared about half a dozen ways. My Place-by-the-Sea also boasts a wide selection of nonalcoholic drinks, which make perfect accompaniments for watching the sun set. Setups are also available at a small charge if you prefer to bring your own spirits.

Peg Leg Inn

18 Beach St. ☎ **508/546-3038.** Reservations are recommended. Main courses $7.95–$15.95. AE, MC, V. Daily 11:30am–2:30pm, 5:30–9pm. AMERICAN/SEAFOOD.

For lunch or dinner in a greenhouse, complete with hanging baskets, 5-foot geranium trees, and flowers all around, walk through town to the end of Main Street to Peg Leg, where both the food and the surroundings are well-above average. The greenhouse, with recessed spot lights and candles, is cozy and romantic in the evening. The main dining room is also lovely. Dinner entrées include chicken pie, a multitude of fresh fish, steaks, and the restaurant's specialty, lobster. Try the lobster broiled, baked and stuffed, à la Newburg (in a rich sauce served with toast points in a casserole), in a pie, or done Thermidor style (simmered in a sherry-and-mushroom sauce and then baked). All the baking is done on premises, and breadbaskets always include sweet rolls.

⑧ Portside Chowder House

Bearskin Neck. ☎ **508/546-7045.** Reservations not accepted. Chowders and appetizers $2–$7; sandwiches $3.50–$7.50; platters $6.50–$9.60. No credit cards. Late June to Labor Day, daily 11am–8pm; Labor Day to late June, lunch only, daily 11am–3pm. Closed Thanksgiving and Christmas Days. Directions: Walk out Bearskin Neck and look to the left. SEAFOOD.

Just want a bowl of chowder? The place to go is the Portside Chowder House, to the left off the main street on the neck. This is a tiny hole-in-the-wall of a place with low ceilings, wood beams, and a few tables in the back with partial views of the water. Chowder made from various seafoods is the specialty here, and it comes by the cup, the bowl, or the quart. Salads, sandwiches, and platters of fish, lobster, and crab are served, and there are also a few beefy items from the grill.

EASY EXCURSIONS

HALIBUT POINT   Head north out of Rockport on Mass. 127, toward Lanesville and Annisquam, and after a few miles you'll see a sign pointing off to the right (north) to **Halibut Point State Park,** just before the Old Farm Inn. Drive to the parking lot, leave your car, and then follow the path through the forest for 10 minutes, and you'll come to an old granite quarry, now flooded with water. The park's interpretive center is in the building that dominates the quarry. Exhibits demonstrate the flora and fauna of the reservation, and how granite quarrying contributed to the culture and economy of the region. A weird World War II concrete observation tower has been grafted onto the building, a typical clapboard Cape Ann house. From the tower during the war, sharp eyes kept a lookout for enemy submarines. The entrance fee is $2. Call ☎ 508/546-2997 for a schedule of edible-plant tours, bird walks, quarry tours, and tide-pool explorations.

Continue along the path to reach the **Observation Point** atop a cliff of granite quarry rubble. Far beneath, the Atlantic's waves roll in and crash on the smoothed granite bedrock below. You can make your way down to the water. Some people go swimming here, although it's not an ideal spot: The water is always chilly, the rocks difficult and slippery, the waves sometimes perilous. For additional information, write to the Halibut Point Association, P.O. Box 710, Rockport, MA 01966.

CASTLE HILL   Not far from Rockport is Castle Hill, the fabulous hilltop mansion built by Richard Teller Crane Jr., who made a fortune in plumbing and bathroom fixtures early in this century. The house is a Stuart-style mansion designed by David Adler. It's open for tours two Sundays during the year and on Tuesday, May to October. The Castle Hill Summer Festival begins in July with an Independence Day celebration and continues through August; it includes a circus, dressage, and a Reggae concert. Contact Castle Hill for information at P.O. Box 563, Ipswich, MA 01938 (☎ 508/356-4351).

8 Plymouth

39 miles SE of Boston, 38 miles NE of New Bedford, 37 miles NE of Fall River, 35 miles NW of Hyannis

Plymouth is famous because of a small and rather unimpressive boulder. But when visitors come to Plymouth Rock, they're coming not because the rock is much to look at—its only notable features are a crack and the date "1620" engraved on it— but because Plymouth, as the landing place of the Pilgrims, is a symbol for the ideal of religious freedom and the quest for a better life.

Besides the rock, which will take you about five minutes to inspect, Plymouth has lots of other sights and exhibits dealing with Pilgrim and Early American history: a collection of historic houses, a full-size replica of the Pilgrim ship *Mayflower,* an authentic re-creation of an entire Pilgrim village complete with living inhabitants, a wax museum, and still more. Many people make Plymouth a day trip, stopping here on their way from Boston to the Cape or vice versa, but should you want to stay overnight in the Pilgrims' town, there are several attractive lodging possibilities.

GETTING THERE   By Car   From Boston, follow the Southeast Expressway and Mass. 3 south. You might want to stop at the Regional Information Complex for Visitors on Mass. 3 at Exit 5.

By Bus   Plymouth is served from Boston and Hyannis by buses of the Plymouth & Brockton (P&B) Street Railway Company (☎ 508/746-0378). About two dozen buses a day run in each direction between Plymouth and downtown Boston and/or Logan Airport; about the same number of buses run from Hyannis to Plymouth and back. In Boston, buses leave from Park Square at Broadway or from the Peter Pan Trailways bus terminal, 555 Atlantic Ave. (☎ 617/482-5510), across the street from South Station, or from South Station itself.

Buses serving Logan Airport pick up and take on passengers at all airline terminals.

In Plymouth, the P&B terminal is in the Industrial Park, Mass. 3, Exit 7, North Plymouth (☎ 508/746-0378), but buses stop downtown in Plymouth as well. The express trip between Boston and Plymouth takes about an hour; the local route, stopping in downtown Plymouth and at Plimoth Plantation, takes 1 1/4 hours. From Plymouth to Hyannis is a 45-minute ride. In Hyannis, the P&B terminal is at 17 Elm St. (☎ 508/775-5524).

ESSENTIALS   The **telephone area code** is **508.** The town of Plymouth maintains a **visitors center** at 130 Water St., across from the town pier (☎ **508/ 747-7525** or **800/USA-1620**). They'll supply you with a current list of events and attractions for the area, and they'll also give you information about special-value lodgings packages.

WHAT TO SEE & DO

Sightseeing in Plymouth means Pilgrim lore: what the early settlers looked like, how they dressed, how they lived from day to day. The many exhibits here make it possible to get a very clear picture of what arrival in America meant to these pioneers.

At 5pm on Friday in August, a group of Plymouth citizens dressed as Pilgrims honor the memory of their ancestors by re-creating the **Pilgrims' procession to church.** The number of people, their sexes, and ages have been matched to the small group of Pilgrims who survived the first winter in the New World. When you see the procession, you may be amazed at the small size of the group that started it all.

If you're interested in guided tours of Plymouth, there are several companies that offer them, and you can go by land, by sea, or after dark. **Plymouth Rock Trolley Co.** (☎ 508/747-3419) has put together a narrated trolley tour with stops at Plymouth Harbor, the *Mayflower II,* and Plimouth Plantation, as well as over 30 others. You can disembark and reboard all day long for the price of one ticket ($6 adults, $3 children). Capt. John Boats, located at the Town Wharf (☎ 800/242-AHOY), offers 40-minute narrated harbor cruises. Departures are hourly, and the fares are $5 for adults, $4 for seniors, and $3 for children. Capt. John Boats also conducts deep sea fishing trips (ranging in price from $16.50 to $27 for adults) and whale-watch cruises for $22 for adults, $18 for seniors over 62, and $14 for children under 12. Call for current schedules.

A unique way to get a look at Plymouth is with New World Tours and Programs (P.O. Box 3541, Plymouth, MA 02361-3541, ☎ 508/747-4161) on one of their **Colonial Lantern Tours.** You'll be guided by lantern light (and a very knowledgeable tour guide) through Brewster Gardens and Town Brook. You'll also visit the site of the original plantation and Plymouth Rock, and you'll get to hear wonderful stories about 18th- and 19th-century Plymouth. There are two tours nightly, one at 7:30pm and the other at 9pm. The cost is $7 for adults, $5 for children 6 to 12. There is also a bargain family rate of $5 for a family of 4 or more.

After taking a tour or two and visiting the attractions and exhibits about the Pilgrims' life in Plymouth, visit **Cranberry World Visitors Center,** 225 Water St. (☎ 508/747-2350), and learn about these tart, juicy berries, the bogs where they're grown, and the products made from them. The Pilgrims found cranberries in abundance when they arrived, and cranberry harvesting and processing is still a big industry in and around Plymouth, on Cape Cod, and on the islands. Admission is free, and you can sample free cranberry refreshments. The center is open May to November, daily from 9:30am to 5pm.

If you'd like to try some alcoholic cranberry refreshments, take a trip to the **Plymouth Colony Winery** on Pinewood Road (☎ 508/747-3334), where you can taste Cranberry Grande (made from native grown cranberries) or Bog Blush (a blend of white wine and cranberry wine). Other varieties include peach, raspberry, and blueberry.

Plymouth Rock

Plymouth Rock State Park. ☎ **508/866-2580.**

From anywhere in Plymouth, road signs and residents will guide you to the rock on the waterfront.

Plymouth Rock is an American icon, a symbol of intrepid discovery, liberty, and freedom of conscience. The stone itself is granite, probably from a formation known as the Dedham granite, formed 680 million years ago (give or take a few million years). The rock was picked up from this formation at a spot south or west of Boston and transported by a glacier to Plymouth about 20,000 years ago. The spot it left was somewhere in the terrane (specific geologic area) called Atlantica, which surrounds Boston.

Geologists who study plate tectonics say that many millions of years ago there was a huge continent called Pangaea, which split into eastern and western parts, the eastern becoming Europe and Africa, the western part North America. The Dedham granite is found mostly in Africa, so it's surprising to consider that Plymouth Rock came over from another continent just as the Pilgrims did, only millions of years before.

When the Pilgrims arrived, they may or may not have stepped on the rock. If they did, they never mention it in their letters and written accounts. In any case, the rock was much larger in 1620, but erosion by sea and wind has reduced it to a mere fraction of its former self. Nature did wreak havoc on the rock, but humans did worse, chipping off small pieces for patriotic souvenirs, taking large pieces to put on display to build patriotic fervor, even using it as part of a wharf at one time. In 1774, 20 yoke of oxen came to move the rock and it split in the process. Half the rock was put on display at Pilgrim Hall from 1834 to 1867 but was then brought back here. In November 1989 the rock was repaired and strengthened to withstand the blows from the sea and the laserlike gazes of millions of affectionate visitors.

Today the rock is sheltered by a monumental enclosure, designed by McKim, Mead, and White and built in 1921, which stands in Plymouth Rock State Park.

Just as the rock marks the beginning of the Pilgrims' adventure in America, so it can serve as the beginning point for your tour of Plymouth. After your look at it, head for the attractions nearby.

Right next to Plymouth Rock is a replica of the sort of house the Pilgrims first built in the New World. Though there's not much to the interior, you can best imagine what it'd be like to live in so tiny a house by stepping inside. Remember that in the 1600s people were not as tall as average Americans today.

Plimoth Plantation

☎ **508/746-1622.** Admission (including Pilgrim Village, Wampanoag Indian Homesite, Carriage House Crafts Center, and *Mayflower II*) $18.50 adults, $11 children 5 to 12, free for children under 5. (Tickets for *Mayflower II* only, $5.75 adults, $3.75 children.) Apr–June and Sept–Nov, daily 9am–5pm; July–Aug, daily 9am–7pm.

Mention Saddam Hussein or even Michael Jackson to one of the roof-thatchers at Plimoth Plantation's Pilgrim Village and you'll get a totally baffled look. This is the year 1627.

In this Pilgrim village, all the buildings were built—and are always being improved upon by rebuilding—as they were in the 17th century. Houses have thatch roofs, wooden-frame chimneys, hand-hewn wood beams, and dirt floors. Well-versed in the history and culture of the time, role-players talk about life as it was after arriving on the *Mayflower* and other ships.

Adjacent to the Pilgrim Village is Wampanoag Indian Homesite, complete with houses made from bent saplings. And moored in nearby Plymouth Harbor is the *Mayflower II*, a meticulously detailed full-size reproduction of the *Mayflower*, with sails made of flax and sewn by hand (see below for complete details on the latter).

In 1992 a new exhibit center, called the Crafts Center, opened at Plimoth Plantation. Also a living exhibit, it explores the manufacture of goods as well as international trade relationships during the early 17th century. Visitors can watch artisans weave woolen cloth, create redware pottery, perform basketry, and demonstrate the crafting of fine furniture as it was done in England for export. Reproductions are for sale in the gift shop.

Mayflower II

☎ **508/746-1622.** Admission $5.75 adults, $3.75 children under 12. This includes free parking, a visit to the ship, and an outdoor exhibit. A special combination ticket ($18.50 adults, $11 children under 12) admits you to the *Mayflower II* and to Plimoth Plantation. Apr–June and Sept–Nov, daily 9am–5pm; July–Aug, daily 9am–7pm.

The suffering that the Pilgrims underwent to get to America will be brought home more forcefully when you tour the *Mayflower II*, a reproduction of the original ship, built in England in 1955 and sailed across the Atlantic to Plymouth in 1957. How, you are sure to ask yourself, was it possible for 102 passengers—even small ones—to fit themselves and all their baggage for setting up a new town into the tiny rooms and onto the tiny decks of this little ship? And how could they live on board for as long as two months? The only answer that comes to mind is "by courage and dedication," and it's for those virtues that the Pilgrims are admired and remembered. Guides on the *Mayflower II* will tell you about the ship's workings and will answer questions; display panels on the dock and an excellent leaflet given to you as you enter will explain other details of nautical lore. The *Mayflower II* is only a few steps from Plymouth Rock. Two museum shops, a restaurant, and a picnic area are here as well.

Pilgrim Hall Museum

75 Court St. ☎ **508/746-1620.** Admission $5 adults, $4 seniors and students, $2.50 children 6–15, children under 6 free. Daily 9:30am–4:30pm. Closed Jan and Christmas Day.

Seeing how the Pilgrims lived in the earliest period of America's colonization is what Plymouth is all about. You can see exhibits like the *Mayflower II* and the early huts to give you an idea, or you can see the actual Pilgrim furniture and huge oil paintings featured in Pilgrim Hall, at the corner of Chilton and Court Streets (Court, Main, and Sandwich are all names for different sections of the same street).

The oldest continually operating public museum in the United States, Pilgrim Hall was built in 1824 to house artifacts the Pilgrims used, a library for research into Plymouth's early history, and galleries for the monumental paintings depicting important events in Pilgrim history. In the main hall, you can see 19th-century paintings interpreting the Pilgrim story, the remains of the 17th-century ship *Sparrowhawk*, Wampanoag artifacts, and books and maps of the Pilgrims. The Lower Hall houses domestic possessions, tools, furniture, and decorative pieces of Plymouth Colony. Highlights of the collection include the wicker cradle of the first English child born in New England, Capt. Myles Standish's sword, and chairs that belonged to Elder William Brewster and Gov. William Bradford.

Plymouth National Wax Museum

16 Carver St. ☎ **508/746-6468.** Admission $5.50 adults, $4.50 seniors, $2.50 children 5–12; children under 5 free. Mar–June and Sept–Nov, daily 9am–5pm; July–Aug, daily 9am–9pm.

Even more lifelike than Pilgrim Hall's paintings are the tableaux at the Plymouth National Wax Museum, at the top of the hill across the street from Plymouth Rock. The hill is Cole's Hill, where the first Pilgrim cemetery was established and where the first victims of the frigid New England winter were laid to rest. The museum's scenes trace the history of the Pilgrims from persecution in England through the move to Holland to the trip across the Atlantic and the foundation of the settlement at Plymouth. There are more than 180 life-size figures in 26 different scenes. Sound tracks add to the vividness of the scenes.

The Forefathers' Monument
☎ **508/746-1790.**

The national monument to the forefathers is the sort of grand statue-and-pedestal one would expect to see on a central boulevard in a world capital. Instead it stands in a small park on Allerton Street, off Samoset (U.S. 44), near the junction with Mass. 3A. Follow the signs on the road. First proposed in 1820, the monument was designed by Hammet Billings of Boston in 1855 and dedicated in 1889.

The composition is figurative, with a great granite statue of Faith surrounded by smaller figures of Liberty (with Peace and Tyranny Overthrown), Law (with Justice and Mercy), Education (with Wisdom and Youth), and Morality holding the Decalogue (Ten Commandments) in the left hand and the scroll of Revelation in the right. Between the statues, bas-reliefs remember the most significant events of Pilgrim history: the departure from Delft Harbor in the Netherlands, the signing of the Mayflower Compact at Provincetown, the landing at Plymouth Rock, and the treaty with Massasoit, sachem of the Wampanoags.

The monument, 81 feet high, is impressive, and it's interesting to speculate about the times and people's thoughts through its history: when it was planned (only 44 years after the signing of the Declaration of Independence), when the cornerstone was laid (1859, on the eve of the Civil War), and when it was dedicated (a year after the invention of the Kodak box camera and the electric motor). The view from the little park, by the way, is very fine; a small cast-iron outline map near the base of the monument traces the outline of Cape Cod, which you can see on a clear day.

Richard Sparrow House
42 Summer St. ☎ **508/747-1240.** $1 donation requested. Thurs–Tues 10am–5pm.

Built in 1640 by one of the original colonists, Richard Sparrow, to endure tough New England winters, this is the oldest house in Plymouth. The Sparrow home is now a museum and is one of the only places in the United States where you'll be able to see how the earliest colonists lived. The house overlooks Town Brook Park, and there's a craft gallery with pottery made on the premises; the gallery stays open through Christmas.

Howland House
33 Sandwich St. ☎ **508/746-9590.** Admission $2.50 adults, $2 seniors and students, 50¢ children 6–12, free for children under 6. Tours given, late May to Oct, daily 10am–4:30pm.

The Howland House dates from 1667 and is the only Plymouth house still standing that was known to have been occupied by Pilgrims. The parents of Jabez Howland (the owner), Elizabeth Tilley and John Howland, came over on the *Mayflower*. It is presumed that they wintered here and, after John's death in 1673, Elizabeth remained in residence until 1680.

Plymouth Antiquarian Society
☎ **508/746-0012.** Admission $3 adults, 75¢ children 6–16, free for children under 6. Memorial Day–June and Sept–Columbus Day, Wed–Sat noon–4:30pm; July–Aug, Tues–Sun noon–4:30pm. Call ahead to be sure the houses are open when you visit.

At three historical homes, interpreters trace three centuries of Plymouth life. These include the **Harlow Old Fort House,** 119 Sandwich St., which was built in 1677 and offers a hands-on look at life for Plymouth's second generation of settlers; the **Spooner House,** 27 North St., which was built in 1747 and occupied by the Spooner family of Plymouth for over 200 years (there's a wealth of original furnishings and heirlooms); and the **Hedge House,** 126 Water St., a handsome Federal building built by a prosperous merchant family in 1809 and furnished with objects from around the world. Hedge House is also the site of changing exhibits of the society's extensive textile and decorative arts collections.

Mayflower Society Museum

4 Winslow St. ☎ **508/746-2590.** $2.50 adults, 25¢ children under 12. July to early Sept, daily 10am–4:15pm; June and early Sept to mid–Oct, Fri–Sun 10am–4:15pm. Also open two weekends prior to Thanksgiving, Thanksgiving Day, and the Fri and Sat that follow it.

The Mayflower Society Museum was once the elegant home of Edward Winslow (grandson of Pilgrim Edward Winslow). Part of the house was built in 1754 and the other part in 1898. Besides the furnishings, a primary attraction is a daring flying staircase, which looks as though it really should fall down but doesn't. It's double the size it was in 1754. The formal gardens are nice as well. On the first weekend in December, "Christmas on North Street" is observed and the museum is decorated for the season. Various musicians show up to perform during the Christmas event.

WHERE TO STAY
HOTELS/MOTELS
Blue Anchor Motel

7 Lincoln St., Plymouth, MA 02360. ☎ **508/746-9551.** 4 units. A/C TV. $48–$60 double. Rates include morning coffee. MC, V. Directions: From the center of town, go south on Sandwich Street from the post office; the third street on the left is Lincoln.

The tiny Blue Anchor Motel has only four units; thus there's a good chance it'll be full in busy periods, but it's worth considering because the motel is on a quiet street next to Plymouth's town hall and only a short walk from the center of town. It's very much a mom-and-pop place, informal and friendly, with comfortable rooms. Accommodations range from a room with one double bed to a two-room unit with a living room (with day beds) and a full bath/shower combination. The rates depend on the unit and the number in your party.

Cold Spring Motel

188 Court St., Rte. 3A, Plymouth, MA 02360. ☎ **508/746-2222.** 31 rms. A/C TV TEL. $41–$76 double, $61–76 cottage. Lower rates in the spring and fall. Extra person $5. AE, DISC, MC, V. Closed mid-Oct to Apr.

Convenient to all historic sites, this pleasant, quiet motel has rooms with wall-to-wall carpeting and private baths. In operation since 1946, the Cold Spring Motel has been a local favorite for years. There's parking at your door.

Governor Bradford Inn

98 Water St., Plymouth, MA 02360. ☎ **508/746-6200** or 800/332-1620. Fax 508/747-3032. 94 rms. A/C TV TEL. In season, $76–$120 double. Additional person $10 extra; children under 14 stay free in parents' room. AE, DC, DISC, MC, V.

One of the finest hotels in Plymouth, this inn is beautifully situated right on the waterfront and only one block from Plymouth Rock, the *Mayflower II,* and the center of town. The rooms are attractive in the modern style, each with two double beds, wall-to-wall carpeting, a refrigerator, and coffee maker. There's a small heated outdoor pool.

John Carver Inn

25 Summer St., at Town Brook, Plymouth, MA 02360. ☎ **508/746-7100** or 800/274-1620. Fax 508/746-8299. 79 rms. A/C TV TEL. In season, $79–$99 double. Rates vary with season. Passport to History Packages available. Senior discount available. AE, CB, DC, DISC, MC, V.

This impressive colonial-style building offers comfortable modern accommodations, a large pool, free cribs, and all the amenities. It's also within walking distance of the main attractions and is located on the site of the original Pilgrim settlement. A Hearth 'n' Kettle restaurant is on the premises.

Pilgrim Sands Motel

150 Warren Ave. (Mass. 3A), Plymouth, MA 02360. ☎ **508/747-0900** or 800/729-SANDS. Fax 508/746-8066. 64 rms. A/C TV TEL. Summer, $90–$120 double; spring and Indian summer, $70–$95 double; fall, $60–$80 double; winter, $50–$70 double. AE, DC, DISC, MC, V.

Down near Plimoth Plantation, $2^{1}/_{2}$ miles south of the center of Plymouth, is the Pilgrim Sands. The bonus here, besides proximity to the plantation, is its private beach. There are also two pools. The units here have individually controlled heating and air conditioning, wall-to-wall carpeting, and modern furnishings. Most rooms have two double or queen-size beds, many rooms have refrigerators, and some have spectacular views. In addition to the beach and pools (one indoor, one outdoor), there is a whirlpool spa.

WHERE TO DINE

Plymouth has a number of snack places, sandwich shops, and restaurants, and although it's not noted for a wide range of culinary styles, the town will be able to fill your needs.

Isaac's

114 Water St. ☎ **508/830-0001.** Reservations are recommended. Main courses $6.95–$10.95, burgers and sandwiches $3.95–$5.95, Sun brunch $7.95. AE, MC, V. Mon–Sat 11:30am–10:45pm; Sun brunch 8am–noon, lunch and dinner 1–10:45pm. AMERICAN.

Isaac Allerton was the first assistant governor of the colony that later became Massachusetts. His keen business sense made him a legend in the early 1600s. This excellent restaurant, located on the waterfront and bearing his name, is also becoming a legend in its own way. It has great food, great values, and a grand view of the harbor. The prices may be moderate, but everything else is top line. And there's something for almost everyone: charcoal-broiled sirloin; fettuccine; specialties stir-fried in a wok; baked, broiled, and fried seafood; and deli and turkey sandwiches.

The dining room is on two levels separated by a brass rail, and large windows overlook the harbor. The decor is striking, with red tablecloths, accents of black, and glass walls that visually enlarge the room. Isaac's is on the second floor of a renovated building.

Lobster Hut

Town Wharf. ☎ **508/746-2270.** Reservations not accepted. Main courses $1.75–$12.95. MC, V. Summer, daily 11am–9pm. Winter, daily 11am–7pm. SEAFOOD.

A favorite self-service place on the waterfront is the Lobster Hut, which serves up steaming bowls of clam chowder, lobster bisque, fried clams, fish and chips, and lobsters, plus wine and beer (with your meal only). Order a huge portion of fish and chips, or fried clams, and with a soft drink you'll pay less than $10. Dine inside or at one of the picnic tables overlooking the bay. It's north of Plymouth Rock.

McGrath's Harbour Restaurant

Town Wharf. ☎ **508/746-9751.** Reservations recommended. Lunch and dinner $9.95–$14.95. AE, MC, V. In season, daily 11:30am–10pm. Closed: Mon in winter. SEAFOOD.

McGrath's is big, busy, and the choice of many families and tour groups. In addition to fish and seafood dinners, the menu features chicken, prime rib, sandwiches, and a special children's menu. Check out the clambakes, too. McGrath's has been a waterfront favorite for about 50 years.

IN NEARBY SOUTH CARVER

Crane Brook Restaurant

Tremont St., South Carver. ☎ **508/866-3235.** Reservations are required. Main courses $8.95–$14.95 at lunch, $18.50–$29 at dinner. AE, MC, V. Wed–Fri 11:30am–2:30pm; Wed–Sun 5:30–9pm; Sun brunch (Sept–June only) 11:30am–2:30pm. AMERICAN.

Crane Brook is a charming restaurant with a wood-beamed, candlelit dining room, a lounge with a wood-burning stove, and a deck with gazebo overlooking a pond for outdoor dining. Entrées include a nice selection of meat, chicken, and fish and are served with homemade rolls. Crane Brook was formerly a tea room, but now it serves afternoon tea only for groups of 15 or more. Currently, there is live piano music on Friday and Saturday evenings. The restaurant can be reached from Route 495 and from Route 3. Ask for directions when you phone for reservations.

EN ROUTE TO CAPE COD

If you're headed to Cape Cod (see Chapter 6) from Plymouth, or even from Boston, two towns worth stopping in for a visit (though I wouldn't recommend an overnight stay) are New Bedford and Fall River.

New Bedford is located 57 miles south of Boston and 38 miles southwest of Plymouth; Fall River is 51 miles S of Boston; and 15 miles W of New Bedford.

GETTING THERE Fall River is easy to reach by car, as it stands at the confluence of several major highways, including I-195, Mass. 24, and U.S. 6. To get to New Bedford from I-95, take the exit for I-495 and follow 495 until you see signs for Rte. 21. You'll see the exits for New Bedford.

American Eagle (☎ **508/993-5040**) operates frequent buses daily between New Bedford and Boston, and if you're going by car, New Bedford is one mile south of I-95, on U.S. 6. From Boston, take Mass. 128 to Mass. 24 south, then Mass. 140. From Plymouth, take Mass. 3 south to U.S. 6 south and west, but pick up I-495 and I-195, when possible, to save time.

If you're heading for Fall River, **Bonanza Bus Lines** (☎ **617/423-5810** in Boston) operates frequent daily buses between Boston's Greyhound Terminal and Fall River, and runs buses between Fall River and other points as well.

ESSENTIALS The **telephone area code** for both New Bedford and Fall River is **508.** Right in the middle of the restoration area is the **New Bedford Office of Tourism,** 47 N. 2nd St., New Bedford, MA 02740 (☎ **508/991-6200**). Here you can pick up brochures, maps, and other information on the area. There are also hour-long guided walking tours of the historic area (donations accepted) daily in the summer (tours at 9:30am, 11:30am, and 3pm Monday through Saturday and at noon Sunday). The office is open Monday through Saturday from 10am to 4pm and Sunday from noon to 3pm. A satellite historic **Waterfront Visitors Center** (Wharfinger Building-Pier #3, New Bedford, MA 02740. ☎ **508/979-1745** or

800/508-5353) recently opened on Pier #3. Guided tours of the waterfront are available from 10am to 2:30pm during July and August, and open hours are the same as for the 2nd Street office. To get there, take Exit 15 off I-195 and follow Rte. 18 to the downtown exit. For information about Fall River, contact the **Bristol County Convention and Visitors Bureau,** 70 N. 2nd St. (P.O. Box 976), New Bedford, MA 02741 (☎ **508/997-1250**). There's also an **information center** in Heritage State Park, 200 Davol St. W., at Battleship Cove (☎ **508/ 675-5759**), where you can pick up maps and brochures. The **state park visitors center,** located at 47 N. 2nd St. in New Bedford (☎ **508/991-6200**), is open daily from 9am to 5pm.

NEW BEDFORD

Due south of Boston on Buzzards Bay is New Bedford, one of the region's best-known towns during the whaling era. The **Whaling Museum** and **the ferry to Martha's Vineyard** are the big attractions in New Bedford today.

New Bedford, like Fall River, owed part of its living to textiles, but its fame rests on its history as a whaling port. Herman Melville set his American classic, *Moby-Dick*, in New Bedford as the logical spot to begin a whaling epic, and so it was. During the heyday of whale-oil lamps, New Bedford had about 400 ships out scouting the seas for the monster denizens. A ship might be at sea for several years, and when it returned to port it could have thousands of barrels of whale oil in its hold. The story of what whaling was all about—how the ships were staffed and equipped, how the search was carried out, how the men pursued and killed the whale, and then butchered and rendered it to get the oil—is all told in New Bedford's famous Whaling Museum on Johnny Cake Hill.

New Bedford's **historic waterfront downtown section** has undergone extensive renovation and restoration. The centerpiece of the restoration is Melville Mall, a pedestrian shopping street complete with trees, benches, and music in the air. East of the mall, going down to the water's edge along cobblestone streets, the Custom House and many merchants' buildings are being restored. The center of the city is taking on an appearance much as it had during its 19th-century heyday.

What to See & Do

✪ **Whaling Museum**
18 Johnny Cake Hill. ☎ **508/997-0046.** Admission $5 adults, $4 seniors, $3.50 children 6–14, free for children under 6. Daily 9am–5pm (until 8pm on Thurs). Closed New Year's, Thanksgiving, and Christmas Days.

In the heart of the historic waterfront district, the New Bedford Whaling Museum is a complex of seven buildings that form the block between William and Union Streets. The museum is dedicated to the history of New Bedford, with particular emphasis on the story of whaling in the age of sail.

The first exhibit to confront you is the largest ship model in the world: a replica of the bark *Lagoda* made to exactly one-half the ship's original size. Rigging, tryworks, whaleboats, and other equipment are all in place, and you can walk about the model at will. On the wall of the *Lagoda* room is a 100-foot-long mural showing sperm whales. The family who owned and operated the *Lagoda* donated the model, and the building to house it, to the museum. Around the walls of the museum are old photographs and drawings explaining the whaling industry, and many other rooms in the museum hold collections of other whaling lore:

cooperage and chandlery; records of the countinghouse, brokerage, banking, and insurance; and articles of glass, china, and pewter manufactured in the New Bedford area or owned by leading citizens.

Perhaps the most beautiful exhibit besides the *Lagoda* is the scrimshaw— delicate, intricate articles of carved whalebone and tooth that the whalers made to while away their long hours at sea. The artistry displayed is almost breathtaking, and the ingenuity very revealing of quick and sensitive minds. It wouldn't be far wrong to say that without understanding whaling, one couldn't understand 19th-century New England; and the place to find out about whaling is certainly New Bedford.

Seamen's Bethel

Johnny Cake Hill. ☎ **508/992-3295.** Free admission; donations requested. May–Columbus Day, Mon–Sat 10am–4pm, Sun noon–4pm.

Across the street from the Whaling Museum, the Seamen's Bethel is a chapel (still functioning) constructed in 1832 "for the moral improvement of sailors," and immortalized in *Moby-Dick*. And several blocks away, at Pleasant and William streets, the **public library** has displays of whaling books and pamphlets.

New Bedford Fire Museum

Bedford St. at 6th St. ☎ **508/992-2162.** Admission $2 adults, $1 children 6–16, free for children under 6. Summer, daily 9am–4pm. Hours vary during rest of year—call ahead.

Anyone interested in the history of firefighting in America will want to take a look at the New Bedford Fire Museum. The museum's beginnings date back to 1890, and it's situated appropriately next to New Bedford's Fire Station No. 4, a building dating from 1867 that is still in active use. Come any day in summer to see the restored antique fire trucks and other firefighting equipment, displays of old uniforms, working models of pumps and fire poles, and other memorabilia.

Rotch-Jones-Duff House and Garden

396 County St. ☎ **508/997-1401.** Admission $3 adults, $2 seniors, $1 children under 12. Sept–May, Tues–Fri 10am–4pm; June–Aug, Mon–Sat 10am–4pm, Sun 1–4pm.

A beautiful example of Greek Revival architecture as practiced by New Bedford's wealthy whaling merchants, the Rotch-Jones-Duff House was designed in 1834 by Richard Upjohn, founder of the American Institute of Architects. The period gardens include a wildflower walk.

DEPARTING NEW BEDFORD   If you'd like to go directly to Martha's Vineyard from New Bedford, the **Ferry to Martha's Vineyard**, MV *Schamonchi,* operated by **Cape Island Express Lines, Inc.,** P.O. Box 4095, New Bedford, MA 02741 (☎ **508/997-1688**), carries passengers (no cars) from New Bedford to the town of Vineyard Haven on the island of Martha's Vineyard three times daily in summer for $16 same-day round trip, $9 one-way (if you're not returning the same day) for adults, $7.50 same-day round trip, $4.50 one-way for children. Call for up-to-date schedules and information. You might, however, wish to go to Fall River first and then go back to New Bedford to catch the ferry.

FALL RIVER

In the mid-19th century Fall River was a boom textile town. Because of its natural harbor, ample waterpower, and a moist climate ideal for working thread, it became a world textile-weaving center. Huge mills made from blocks of the local granite were built everywhere, making an awesome scene of industry and wealth. But in the 20th century the textile business began moving to the southern states and Fall River's industry foundered.

Prosperity has returned to Fall River, and now many of the impressive granite mills produce finished apparel; others turn out rubber products, foods, and paper. The town's Government Center, built on the airspace over I-195, is a symbol of Fall River's resurgence and adds its impressive appearance to that of the great mills. Today most visitors come to Fall River to shop in the many factory-outlet stores and to visit the battleship and submarine docked at Battleship Cove.

Fall River's other claim to fame is the celebrated 1892 Lizzie Borden murder trial, in which Lizzie, a young Fall River girl, was tried for chopping up her father and stepmother with an ax. Although Lizzie was acquitted, there is still much speculation as to whether she truly did the deed. What's your verdict?

What to See & Do

Battleship Cove

Fall River. ☎ **508/678-1100** or 800/533-3194. Admission $8 adults, $4 children 6–14, free for children under 6. Daily 9am–5pm. Closed New Year's, Thanksgiving, and Christmas Days.

Most people pass through Fall River on their way from Providence to Cape Cod or from Boston to Newport, and when they do, the sight they stop to see is Battleship Cove, the permanent berth of a number of impressive craft. In 1965 the battleship USS *Massachusetts* came to Fall River and was the catalyst in the formation of Battleship Cove and the revitalization of the waterfront. Battleship Cove is the home of one of the world's premier exhibits of historic naval ships of the World War II period, and each is a National Historic Landmark. Visitors can board and explore the *Massachusetts*, the destroyer *Joseph P. Kennedy, Jr.*, and the submarine *Lionfish*, and inspect the only two PT boats on exhibit anywhere in the world. A landing craft, mechanized (LCM), Japanese special attack motorboat, North American T-28 trainer plane, and a Patriot missile are also on display. Ships house the official state memorials for World War II, Korea, Vietnam, and the Gulf War.

○ Fall River Carousel

Battleship Cove. ☎ **508/324-4300**. Admission $1. Memorial Day to Labor Day, daily 10am–10pm; Labor Day to Memorial Day, Fri–Sun 11am–4pm.

Also located at Battleship Cove is the Fall River Carousel. Built in the 1920s, the carousel was once located at Lincoln Park (where, incidentally, I spent many a summer afternoon throughout my childhood), but after the park's closure in 1992, the carousel was moved to its new dockside location. It has been beautifully restored and is a great place to take the kids.

Marine Museum at Fall River

70 Water St. ☎ **508/674-3533**. Admission $3 adults, $2.50 seniors, $2 children 6–14, free for children under 6. Summer daily 9am–5pm.; winter, Wed–Fri 9am–4pm, Sat–Sun noon–4pm.

The Marine Museum at Fall River, past the battleship and the State Pier, on the left, has a number of fascinating shipping exhibits, including lots of *Titanic* lore. Certainly the most popular is the one-ton, 28-foot-long scale model of the *Titanic*, created in 1952 for 20th Century–Fox's movie about the *Titanic* tragedy. Other beautiful ship models and maritime artifacts detail the history of the Fall River Line, which ran luxury steamers between Fall River and New York from 1847 to 1937. Yet another exhibit follows the history of steam power at sea. Nautical buffs from around the world, many of them famous collectors, have donated exhibits to the museum.

Shopping

Fall River is a mecca for those who love **factory-outlet shopping,** because the revival of apparel manufacture here has led to the opening of dozens of huge factory-outlet stores. Billboards on I-195 trumpet that it's the "largest factory-outlet center in New England!" Signs lead you off the highway to the "Heart of Fall River's Factory-Outlet District," with more than 70 outlet stores. If you follow the signs, will you really save money? Yes, a definitive yes!

What can you find here? When it comes to clothing, everything! Shoes, sweaters, raincoats, accessories, designer labels, coats, handbags, jewelry, children's clothing, cosmetics, luggage. Branch out a bit and you'll find kitchenware, gifts, furniture, braided rugs, curtains, crystal, candy and nuts, greeting cards and giftwrap, toys, towels, linens, baskets, brass—even wallpaper. This is definitely a town in which you can shop till you drop.

The outlets are located in abandoned mills. For information or a brochure, contact the Fall River Factory Outlet District Association at 683 Quequechan St., ☎ 800/424-5519.

Cape Cod 6

This 70-mile-long arm of sand curled into the Atlantic was formed by glacial action and was given its name by an early (1602) visitor to the New World, Bartholomew Gosnold. The Pilgrims landed in the New World at Provincetown and drew up the Mayflower Compact before heading on to the mainland at what would become Plymouth.

Strictly speaking, Cape Cod is an island, separated from the rest of Massachusetts by the Cape Cod Canal, a deep waterway built from north to south across the base of the Cape in the early part of this century. Two graceful bridges span the canal—one at Bourne to the south (Mass. 28), the other at Sagamore to the north (U.S. 6)—and both are very busy in the warm months. Just before crossing either bridge, look for the little information sheds run by the Cape Cod Chamber of Commerce, open daily from 9am to 7pm in summer. Maps, booklets, motel brochures, and tabloid newspaper "current listings" are all yours for free. The chamber of commerce will also help you make room reservations.

SEEING CAPE COD

GETTING THERE   Cape Cod was once a seafarers' domain, and although it's still possible to get there by boat, the rail, bus, air, and road routes make it easy to get there any way you choose.

By Plane   Business Express (☎ **800/345-3400**), a Delta Connection carrier, provides service to Hyannis and Nantucket from Bridgeport (Conn.), Baltimore, Boston, New York, and Philadelphia; **Cape Air** and **Nantucket Airlines** (☎ **508/790-0300** or **800/352-0714**) has service to Hyannis, Martha's Vineyard, Nantucket, and also Provincetown from Boston several times a day throughout the year. Most flights are non-stop. **Colgan Air** (☎ **800/272-5488**) has three flights a day between Newark (N.J.) and Hyannis; **Island Airlines** (☎ **508/775-6606**) flies between Nantucket and Hyannis eleven times a day; and **Northwest Airlink,** a regional airline associated with Northwest Airlines (☎ **800/225-2525**) flies between Boston and Hyannis three times a day throughout the year.

By Car   Coming from New York or Providence, take I-195 to Mass. 25/28 South, and cross the Bourne Bridge if you're heading for Falmouth and Woods Hole; if you're going to Sandwich, Hyannis, or other Cape points, don't take the Bourne Bridge, but

What's Special About Cape Cod

Museums
- Heritage Plantation of Sandwich, a 76-acre estate with outstanding collections of Americana.
- Sandwich Glass Museum, where the town's renowned glass industry lives on.

Nature Reserves
- Monomoy National Wildlife Refuge, south of Chatham, rich in birdlife.
- Cape Cod Museum of Natural History in Brewster, with its own nature walks.
- Cape Cod National Seashore, with miles of hiking and bike trails, and excellent beaches.

Picturesque Towns
- Sandwich, "the oldest town on Cape Cod."
- Falmouth, with a picture-perfect New England Village Green.
- Chatham, with its graceful old trees and sturdy lighthouse.
- Provincetown, with whole neighborhoods of galleries and cozy inns.

Especially for Kids
- New England Fire and History Museum in Brewster, with 35 highly polished fire engines.
- Railroad Museum in Chatham, with a wonderful wooden caboose.
- Schooner cruises out of Provincetown, for a real taste of life at sea.
- Whale-watching cruises from Provincetown, with their excellent record of whale sightings.

After Dark
- Provincetown Playhouse, an old-time favorite, active all summer.
- Cape Cod Melody Tent in Hyannis, featuring top-name popular vocalists in concert.
- Cape Playhouse in Dennis, with famous actors in timely productions.
- Monomoy Theater in Chatham, with a stock company from Ohio University.

Historic Monuments
- Pilgrim Monument, Provincetown, near where the Pilgrims first stepped onto American soil.
- French Cable Station Museum, Orleans, where the first transatlantic telephone cable came ashore.
- Marconi Station site, near South Wellfleet, where the great Italian physicist established a transatlantic wireless station in 1902.

take U.S. 6 East just before the Bourne Bridge, and this will take you north and east to the Sagamore Bridge, where you cross the canal.

Coming from Boston, you can take the Southeast Expressway (I-93) right to Mass. 3, which goes straight to the Sagamore Bridge. If you're on your way to Falmouth and Woods Hole, stay on I-93 past the intersection with Mass. 3 and take Exit 66 for Mass. 24 South, then I-495 South to Mass. 28, before taking you right over the Bourne Bridge.

Keep in mind that as wonderful as the Cape may be, driving there during the summer months can be a bit trying at times. Do yourself a favor: Before setting

Cape Cod & Vicinity

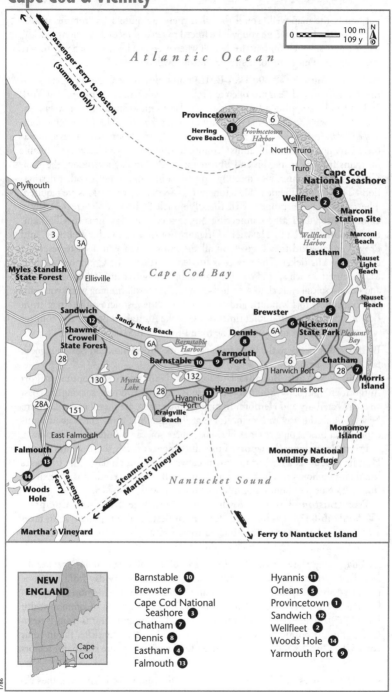

Atlantic Ocean

Passenger Ferry to Boston (Summer Only)

Provincetown ①
Herring Cove Beach
Provincetown Harbor
North Truro
Truro
Cape Cod National Seashore ③
Wellfleet ②
Marconi Station Site
Wellfleet Harbor
Marconi Beach
Eastham ④
Nauset Light Beach
Nauset Beach

Plymouth

3
3A

Myles Standish State Forest
Ellisville

Cape Cod Bay

Orleans ⑤
Brewster ⑥
Nickerson State Park
Pleasant Bay

Sandwich ⑫
Shawme-Crowell State Forest
Sandy Neck Beach
6A
Dennis ⑧
6A
28
6
Barnstable Harbor
Barnstable ⑩
Yarmouth Port ⑨
130
132
6
Chatham ⑦
Harwich Port
28
Morris Island
Mystic Lake
28
Hyannis ⑪
Hyannis Port
Dennis Port
28A
151
Craigville Beach
East Falmouth

Monomoy Island

Falmouth ⑬
Monomoy National Wildlife Refuge
Woods Hole ⑭
Passenger Ferry
Steamer to Martha's Vineyard
Nantucket Sound

Martha's Vineyard
Ferry to Nantucket Island

NEW ENGLAND
Cape Cod

Barnstable ⑩
Brewster ⑥
Cape Cod National Seashore ③
Chatham ⑦
Dennis ⑧
Eastham ④
Falmouth ⑬

Hyannis ⑪
Orleans ⑤
Provincetown ①
Sandwich ⑫
Wellfleet ②
Woods Hole ⑭
Yarmouth Port ⑨

1786

out, study the map well. You'll find that there are quite a few rotaries (traffic circles) on the Cape, where you will be forced to make direction decisions quickly. These rotaries, which work perfectly well when everyone knows which way they're going, can be dangerous for confused out-of-towners.

By Train   Amtrak (☎ **800/USA-RAIL**) runs trains to the Cape during the summer months only. The trains operate Friday through Sunday between New York and Hyannis, stopping at major New England cities (Stamford, New Haven, Providence) and several Cape destinations along the way. The Friday-afternoon *Cape Codder* leaves New York's Penn Station in the afternoon and arrives approximately six hours later in Hyannis. Connections to the *Cape Codder* are available on trains from Washington and Philadelphia. On Sunday afternoon, the *Cape Codder* leaves Hyannis, also meeting up with connecting trains to other destinations. The round-trip fare is $170 (one-way is $85), and reservations are required. The railroad has arranged with the Plymouth & Brockton Street Railway Company for dedicated connecting bus service from Hyannis to Chatham, Dennisport, Eastham, Harwich, Orleans, South Yarmouth, Wellfleet, and Provincetown, and they'll give you all the information you need to reserve a connecting bus ticket. The service is funded in part by the Commonwealth of Massachusetts. Such special contracts are subject to governmental budgetary ups and downs, so call Amtrak to see whether the service is still running when you want it. Connection to Plymouth and Brockton buses is just across the street from Boston's South Station. Other times of year, take Amtrak to Boston and connect with an Amtrak bus to Hyannis. The round-trip fare is $109.

By Bus   Bus service to the Cape from New York, Providence, and Boston is good, fast, and frequent.

From New York: Bonanza (Adirondack Trailways ticket counter in Port Authority terminal; ☎ **800/556-3815**) runs buses via two routes, along the coast and via Waterbury and Hartford. In high summer, there are three buses a day from New York all the way to Provincetown at the tip of the Cape and a good number of other buses going as far as Hyannis, where you can transfer for other points.

From Providence/Newport: From Providence, catch the Bonanza bus to Hyannis (about six a day) or to Provincetown (about four a day). The trip takes less than two hours to Hyannis. The Bonanza Bus Line Terminal is off Exit 25 from I-95 North or South. For information, call **800/556-3815.**

From Boston: The Plymouth & Brockton Street Railway Company (☎ **508/746-0378**) has buses that leave from Boston. The trip to Hyannis takes 1¹/₂ hours. The one-way fare from Boston to Hyannis is $10; from Boston to Provincetown, $19; and from Plymouth to Hyannis, $6.

By Boat   Bay State Cruises (☎ **617/723-7800** or **508/487-9284**) operates the MV *Provincetown II* on a run from Boston to P-town every day from late June through Labor Day and on Saturday and Sunday between Memorial Day and Columbus Day. There's one daily sailing, which leaves Boston's Commonwealth Pier at 9:30am and arrives in P-town at about 12:30pm; it returns from P-town (at 3:30pm) to Boston (arriving about 6:30pm). A round-trip ticket for an adult costs $29, $24 for seniors and kids under 12. The one-way fare is $16; for seniors and kids, $13.

GETTING AROUND THE CAPE   U.S. 6, the Mid-Cape Highway, is the fastest way to travel from the "Upper Cape" (the part you first come to by land) to the "Lower Cape" (the narrow portion north of Orleans to Provincetown). But U.S. 6 is not necessarily the prettiest way to go; if you have the time, travel one of the smaller, scenic roads instead.

Bus transportation on the Cape is provided by the **Plymouth & Brockton Street Railway Company,** Elm and Centre Streets, Hyannis (☎ **508/775-5524**). You can take a Plymouth & Brockton bus from Hyannis to Provincetown via Orleans, Eastham, and Wellfleet.

Transportation to the islands of Martha's Vineyard and Nantucket is covered in the sections on Woods Hole and Hyannis.

A Suggested Route You'll need several days to tour the Cape, and at least a week to explore it thoroughly. The northern and western shores, facing Cape Cod Bay, are the more peaceful and bucolic ones. The southern shore has the more commercial towns; most of the eastern shore is part of Cape Cod National Seashore (see below).

On **Day 1,** take a leisurely drive along Mass. 6A through Sagamore, Sandwich, Barnstable, Yarmouth Port, Dennis, Brewster, and Orleans, staying the night in one of these towns. On **Day 2,** explore Cape Cod National Seashore, Wellfleet, and Provincetown, returning to your first night's lodging for the night. (Off-season, you can safely plan a second-night stay in Provincetown, but call ahead for reservations.) **Day 3** can be spent along Mass. 28 west, enjoying Chatham and the towns on the way to Hyannis. On **Day 4,** make your way to Mashpee, Falmouth, and Woods Hole; or make a day-long excursion from Hyannis to Nantucket, or from Woods Hole to Martha's Vineyard (see Chapter 7 for Martha's Vineyard and Nantucket).

BED & BREAKFAST INFORMATION Bed & Breakfast Cape Cod, **Nantucket, and Martha's Vineyard,** P.O. Box 341, West Hyannisport, MA 02672-0341 (☎ **508/775-2772** or **800/686-5252;** fax 508/775-2884; Internet http://www.ccsnet.com./bbcc/), will find you a room on Cape Cod (and on Martha's Vineyard or Nantucket for that matter) in one of 100 historic inns and host homes for $45 to $70 single, $60 to $203 double, breakfast and tax included. Get in touch with them in plenty of time and you'll be sent a free brochure listing a variety of accommodations that might interest you.

1 Falmouth

37 miles S of Plymouth, 37 miles SE of New Bedford, 15 miles S of the Bourne Bridge, 23 miles SW of Hyannis, 50 miles SW of Provincetown

Falmouth is a pretty town that has grown rapidly in recent years but has managed to preserve a lot of rural New England community charm. A city park next to the library, a well-preserved village green (used as a military training ground in the 1700s), and magnificent tall trees along Main Street make the downtown section attractive. Manicured lawns and white clapboard houses dress up the side streets. The town has a few pleasant historic inns and several good beaches.

A few miles past Falmouth to the south is Woods Hole, home of the world-famous Woods Hole Oceanographic Institute; car-ferries depart from Woods Hole for Martha's Vineyard several times daily in summer.

GETTING THERE See "Getting There" under "Seeing Cape Cod," at the beginning of this chapter.

DEPARTING   Ferry from Falmouth to Martha's Vineyard   Falmouth's own *Island Queen*, Falmouth Heights Road (☎ 508/548-4800), operated by Island Commuter Corp., carries passengers and bicycles only (no cars) from Falmouth Harbor to Oak Bluffs on the island. The ferry does not operate year-round, but sails twice a day in each direction during early June and mid-September (five times a day on weekends), and seven times a day in each direction from mid-June through the first week in September. Adults pay $10 round-trip, $6 one-way; children under 13 are charged $5 round-trip. Bicycles are taken at a charge of $6 round-trip. The voyage takes about half an hour and is usually quite smooth and comfortable. A refreshment bar on board serves snacks, sandwiches, soft drinks, beer, and cocktails.

For car-ferries to the islands, you'll have to go to Woods Hole or Hyannis (see those sections for details).

ESSENTIALS   The **telephone area code** is **508.** The **Falmouth Chamber of Commerce,** P.O. Box 582, Falmouth, MA 02541 (☎ **508/548-8500** or **800/ 526-8532;** fax 508/548-8521), operates an information office downtown off Main Street in the Lawrence Academy building as well as a summer information office at 322 Palmer Ave. If the chamber can't answer your question, it's probably not about Falmouth. Call or write for the free Falmouth guidebook.

WHAT TO SEE & DO

Walks along Falmouth's beaches, through the older sections of town, and across the village green, or a bike ride on the scenic Shining Sea bikepath (4 miles) that takes you from Falmouth's main village to the village of Woods Hole, are musts. For a detailed map, or for other information, send for the visitors information guide from the **Falmouth Chamber of Commerce,** P.O. Box 582, Falmouth, MA 02541 (☎ **508/548-8500**).

Aside from fishing, boating, and beach sitting, a prime Falmouth activity is **renting a bicycle** and following the Shining Sea Bicycle Path down to Woods Hole (see below). The **Bikeways Committee of Falmouth** publishes a pamphlet-map that shows bike routes and beaches and gives the addresses of shops that rent bicycles. Ask at the information office, or call the chamber of commerce. By biking to a beach, you avoid paying the several dollars for parking.

Besides bike trips down to Woods Hole, Falmouth's greatest outdoor attraction is its many miles of coastline. The **Town Beach** is down at the end of Shore Street (best to walk, as parking can be a problem). The water can be very chilly except in July and August, but otherwise the beach is fine, and it has a view of Martha's Vineyard in the distance.

The best **swimming and sunning** spot in the area is **Old Silver Beach,** several miles northwest of downtown Falmouth. If you have more energy than money, bicycling is the way to go, even though it's a distance, as the entrance fee at Old Silver is $10 per car for the day. Old Silver is a favorite with windsurfers.

A headland and several jetties set the beach off into sections; the town runs a clam bar, which sells sandwiches, fried clams, and soft drinks, and offers changing rooms.

The town of Falmouth sponsors free **band concerts** down at Falmouth Marina on Thursday evening at 8pm during the months of July and August. Try to make it to at least one concert; it's a real old-time event. Bring your own chair.

The Falmouth Historical Society has interesting displays pertaining to Falmouth's history in its lovely old mansion, the **Julia Wood House,** 55–65 Palmer Ave. (☎ 508/548-4857), located just off the village green. For the price of admission ($2 for adults, 50¢ for children under 12), you also get to see the adjacent Hallett Barn, with displays of early tools and farm implements, and the historical society's shop, as well as Conant House, next door, with more historical collections. The Katharine Lee Bates Room holds memorabilia of Falmouth's poet, who wrote the words to "America the Beautiful." The cordial staff at the historical society will be sure to point out that the white Congregational church on the green is equipped with a bell cast by Paul Revere. It's open mid-June to mid-September, Monday through Friday from 2 to 5pm (the tour lasts approximately an hour, so try to arrive by 4pm).

WHERE TO STAY

Although Falmouth has dozens of motels, mostly expensive and somewhat sterile (though modern and comfortable), the best way to spend a week or two by the sea, at moderate cost, is to rent a room in a private home—or in one of the small inns or guesthouses. During off-season, when inquiring about room prices, be sure to ask about reductions for stays of a few days or more. A room costing $70 for one night may well cost $65 per night if you stay two or three days.

Lots of houses in **Falmouth Heights,** southeast of the center of Falmouth proper, are devoted to renting rooms with shared bathrooms for low rates. If you request it, your room may have a view of the sea. You should also be aware that this is the most boisterous section of town.

DOWNTOWN

Elm Arch Inn

26 Elm Arch Way, Falmouth, MA 02540. ☎ 508/548-0133. 24 rms (12 with bath). Summer, $55–$70 twin or double without bath, $65–$80 twin or double with bath. Additional person $10 extra. Off-season, rates are lower. No credit cards.

The Elm Arch Inn, located off Main Street, was originally a whaling captain's house, but it has been taking paying guests for over a century—almost 70 years of which it has been under the present management. The location couldn't be better: right in the center of town, a few steps from the green, and yet back off Main Street in peace and quiet. The inn's rooms are furnished with colonial-style pieces, many handmade, and are just plain charming. Several have private baths; others share a bath. In Richardson House, the addition to the inn, there are private baths, air conditioning, and television throughout. No meals are served, but the inn offers free coffee in the mornings, in season. Although you're a 15-minute walk from the beach here, the inn has its own small pool, bordered by a lush lawn and large trees, and a big screened patio for summer evenings.

Mostly Hall Bed & Breakfast Inn

27 Main St., Falmouth, MA 02540. ☎ 508/548-3786 or 800/682-0565. 6 rms. A/C. May–Oct, $95–$125 double; Nov–Apr, $85–$95 double. All rates include breakfast. AE, DISC, MC, V.

Mostly Hall is only steps from Falmouth Green and the beginning of the bicycle path to Woods Hole. The plantation-style house (complete with wraparound porch) was built in 1849 as a wedding present for the New Orleans bride of Capt. Albert Nye. The guest rooms are attractively furnished with queen-size canopied beds, exquisite Oriental rugs, floral wall coverings, and antique and reproduction furnishings. Breakfast here is such a treat that the inn's recipes have been compiled in a cookbook, *Mostly Hall Breakfast at 9*. Entrées might include eggs Benedict soufflé, cheese blintz muffins, or stuffed French toast, to name a few. Rates include the use of bicycles. For getting the real flavor of Falmouth, Mostly Hall can't be beat. Note that it's a nonsmoking bed-and-breakfast inn.

The Palmer House Inn

81 Palmer Ave., Falmouth, MA 02540. ☎ **508/548-1230** or 800/472-2632. Fax 508/540-1878. 12 rms, 1 suite. Peak season, $90–$135 double; $165 suite. Off-season, from $65 double; $135 suite. Discounts available for extended stays. All rates include breakfast. AE, CB, DC, DISC, MC, V.

A few steps from the Falmouth Historical Society near Falmouth Green is the Palmer House Inn, located very near the center of town. The innkeepers, Ken and Joanne Baker, have decorated each of the guest rooms in this turn-of-the-century Victorian house with antiques and authentic period pieces. The suite, located in a separate cottage, has a Jacuzzi, living room, and kitchenette, and the newly renovated carriage house (known as the Guest House) holds four large corner rooms. Two rooms in the Guest House have jacuzzis, and one is handicap accessible. The Bakers serve a wonderful gourmet breakfast (*pain perdu* with orange cream, Finnish pancake, and strawberry soup). If the perfect location doesn't get you, the lovely stained glass, antique furnishings, beautiful woodwork, and romantic laces will. Bikes are available to guests at no charge. A proper English tea is served, at an extra charge, on weekends from October to April.

Village Green Inn

40 W. Main St., Falmouth, MA 02540. ☎ **508/548-5621**. 4 rms, 1 suite. TV $85–$110 double; $110–$135 suite. All rates include full breakfast. Directions: From Mass. 28 heading south, turn left at Queen's Byway, right on Hewins Street, and right on Main Street.

Located on the Village Green, this stately white Victorian-colonial house is a small inn with four lovely guest rooms, two of which have working fireplaces, and a two-room suite. All the rooms are large and thoughtfully decorated in soft colors, and all have ceiling fans. There's a formal parlor stocked with books, magazines, and games, as well as a front porch lined with white wicker chairs and red ivy geranium in hanging pots. One of the highlights of every stay is the full gourmet breakfast: a tasty selection of specialty dishes, including fruit dishes, homemade muffins, breads, and rolls. Seasonal beverages and home-baked goods are served in the afternoon, and complimentary ten-speed bicycles, sand chairs, and beach towels are available for guest use.

ALONG GRAND AVENUE

The guesthouses on Grand Avenue in Falmouth Heights differ only slightly from one another in price, accommodations, sea views, and charm. During the summer season your selection may well have to be made on the basis of availability.

Head down Falmouth Heights Road, which skirts the eastern side of Falmouth Harbor, and soon you'll see Grand Avenue bearing off to the right. It then makes a loop south and east, running along Falmouth Heights Beach before heading back to rejoin Falmouth Heights Road. From Mass. 3, exit onto U.S. 6 west to the Bourne Bridge Circle (a rotary). Take Mass. 28 over the Bourne Bridge and go south into Falmouth. Turn left onto Jones Road to Worcester Court, then turn right onto Grand Avenue.

Gladstone Inn

219 Grand Ave. S., Falmouth Heights, MA 02540. ☎ **508/548-9851.** 14 rms (4 with bath), 1 apt (with bath). $66 double without bath; $93.50–$104.50 double with private bath; $109 studio apartment. All rates include full breakfast. MC, V. Closed mid-Oct to mid-May. Directions: See above.

The Gladstone Inn, owned by Jim and Gayle Carroll, is at the corner of Montgomery Avenue, across from the beach. A glassed-in veranda shares the sea view, and this is where you have your buffet breakfast or cool afternoon drink. The apartment over the garage has been newly renovated.

Grafton Inn

261 Grand Ave. S., Falmouth Heights, MA 02540. ☎ **508/540-8688** or 800/642-4069. Fax 508/540-1861. 11 rms. A/C. Peak season, $95–$139 double. Low-season discounts available. All rates include buffet breakfast. MC, V. Closed Jan. Directions: See above.

The Grafton Inn is right across the street from the main beach area, with snack stands and restaurants located conveniently nearby. Rates include a fine buffet breakfast, an enclosed porch, sufficient parking, use of bicycles, and a very comfortable, simple atmosphere. All rooms have queen-size beds, and all have ceiling fans. Special treats are fresh flowers, homemade chocolates, and afternoon wine and cheese. No smoking, no children, and no pets.

Inn on the Sound

313 Grand Ave. (P.O. Box 201), Falmouth, MA 02541. ☎ **508/457-9666** or 800/564-9668. 10 rms. Mid-June to mid-Sept, $95–$140 double; Apr to mid-June and mid-Sept through Oct, $75–$115 double; Nov to mid-Apr, $60–$100 double. Additional person $30 extra. All rates include breakfast. AE, DISC, MC, V. Directions: See above.

Romantically poised on a bluff overlooking Martha's Vineyard Sound, Inn on the Sound offers spectacular views. Most rooms have views of the ocean and tasteful country furnishings (two have fireplaces). A full gourmet breakfast—homemade muffins and pastries, fresh fruits, and specialties, such as banana-stuffed French toast and the Inn's own eggs Florentine—is served daily.

OUT OF THE TOWN CENTER

Coonamessett Inn Cape Cod

Jones Rd. and Gifford St., Falmouth, MA 02540. ☎ **508/548-2300.** 25 rms, 1 cottage. A/C TV TEL. $90–$115 sitting room/bedroom combo; $105–$140 living room/two-bedroom combo; $126–$153 cottage. Additional person $10 extra. Lower rate applies to midweek; higher rate, weekend. AE, DC, MC, V.

A venerable red farmhouse, barn, and sheds make up the Coonamessett Inn Cape Cod. It may sound like a farm, but what you see when you arrive is a beautifully maintained resort hotel with extensive grounds. The rear of the property is landscaped beautifully and slopes gently down to a pond where a gaggle of geese makes its home. Favored by a mature clientele, the Coonamessett is also noted for its dining room (see "Where to Dine," below).

WHERE TO DINE

Coonamessett Inn Dining Room

Jones Rd. and Gifford St. ☎ **508/548-2300.** Reservations recommended. Main courses $14.95–$22.95. AE, DC, MC, V. Mon–Sat 11:30am–2:30pm, Sun noon–3pm; daily 6–9pm (to 10pm Fri–Sat in season). CONTEMPORARY REGIONAL.

This restaurant, at the corner of Gifford Street, has casual elegance and service that's attentive yet not overbearing. Start with the napoleon of salmon (medallions of steamed salmon and spinach layered between puff pastry and served with a chablis cream sauce with a hint of chervil) or the white-truffle-and-chèvre ravioli in a roasted lobster sauce. Follow that with shrimp scampi or the pan-seared filet mignon. The herb-crusted Chatham cod with a tomato-and-lemon vinaigrette is also quite good. Save room for a side of homemade fresh pasta of the day, and then linger over coffee and the inn's deservedly famous Indian pudding.

Eli's, a separate dining area that's a more casual alternative, serves the dining-room lunch menu throughout the day; try a chicken club ($6.95) or the seafood pappardelle ($14.95). Before you leave, check out the *Legend of the Mermaid* paintings that hang in the dining room.

Domingo's Olde Restaurant

856 Main St. (Mass. 28A), West Falmouth. ☎ **508/540-0575.** Reservations recommended. Main courses $9.50–$17.25. AE, DC, MC, V. Daily 5–11pm. Directions: Follow Mass. 28A to West Falmouth. SEAFOOD.

Domingo's Olde Restaurant is an excellent restaurant, offering moderately priced seafood (with Italian overtones) in an unassuming converted old home. Chef-owner, Domingo and his brother began their business in a fresh fish market where they started offering cooked fish specialties that became so popular Domingo decided to open his own restaurant. I can assure you that this man knows his fish, and he personally selects items daily from a local fish market. Choose from traditional dishes like broiled or fried scallops, bouillabaisse, baked stuffed haddock, fried clams, shrimp scampi, fish and chips, or baked stuffed lobster. There are also several meat dishes, like veal picatta, New York strip steak, or chicken français, are available. Simple desserts include ice cream, mud pie, cheesecake, and fresh fruit (in season).

The Regatta of Falmouth by the Sea

217 Clinton Ave. ☎ **508/548-5400.** Reservations recommended. Main courses $18–$30. AE, MC, V. Daily 4:30–closing. Closed Oct–May. FRENCH/AMERICAN.

Falmouth's finest place to dine from late May through September is undoubtedly the Regatta, located at the corner of Scranton and Clinton Avenues, overlooking the entrance to Falmouth's long harbor. You'll want to be dressed neatly, if informally. Start with the sautéed Maryland soft shell crabs with a cilantro-and-lime vinaigrette and a fried angel-hair-pasta nest or the wild-mushroom strudel with a five-mushroom sauce; then proceed to the seared lemon-chive-encrusted swordfish filled with a farci of baby shrimp and scallops, in a caramelized lemon vinaigrette, or the seared loin of lamb with a cabernet sauce. Finish your meal with the crème brûlée with macadamia nut liqueur.

2 Woods Hole

6 miles SW of Falmouth

When Emperor Hirohito of Japan visited the United States in 1976, the only scientific center he wanted to visit was Woods Hole. Being a marine biologist himself, he was interested in seeing one of the world's great centers for the study of sea life, especially the **Marine Biological Laboratory.** Besides the laboratory, Woods Hole is home to the **Woods Hole Oceanographic Institution (WHOI),** the **Northeast Fisheries Science Center,** and the **U.S. Geological Survey's Branch of Atlantic Geology.** Marine science is the lifeblood of the town, for the scientific buildings take up most of the space at the tip of a tiny peninsula, leaving room for only a few streets of fine old houses, a few small boatyards, a handful of restaurants, and the car-ferry dock to Martha's Vineyard.

GETTING THERE   See "Getting There" under "Seeing Cape Cod," at the beginning of this chapter; see below for information on ferries to Martha's Vineyard.

DEPARTING   Ferry from Woods Hole to Martha's Vineyard   The **Woods Hole, Martha's Vineyard and Nantucket Steamship Authority,** 509 Falmouth Rd., Mashpee, MA 02649 (☎ **508/477-8600**), operates car-carrying ferries between the points listed in its name, and also Hyannis. Schedules change several times a year, so it's best to call in advance for full current information. In fact, if you plan to ship your car, you must have a car reservation. You can get one by calling the number above. Ferries from Woods Hole to Vineyard Haven or Oak Bluffs on Martha's Vineyard leave about 6 times a day in winter, 14 times a day in summer, on the 45-minute trip. Fares are $9.50 round-trip for adults, half price for kids 5 to 12, free for kids under 5. Bikes go for $6 one-way. Autos cost $76 round-trip in season (that's in addition to the regular per person fare). You can't get to Nantucket from Woods Hole or Falmouth, but you can from Hyannis (see below).

Parking Fees at the Docks   If you don't plan to ferry your car over and you don't ride a bike or take the bus to Woods Hole, figure on paying $10 to park your car for each *calendar* day ($20 if you leave your car overnight). It's virtually impossible to find a free, legal parking place in Woods Hole in summer or for overnight unless you stay at a motel and use its lot. The Steamship Authority has a dockside lot charging these fees, and also two large lots in Falmouth (if one is full, you'll be directed to the other), with free shuttle-bus service to the Woods Hole docks. In late July and all of August, the dockside lot is almost always full, so you'll save yourself some time by planning to park in a Falmouth lot. The Woods Hole ferry docks are served by Bonanza bus lines to Boston, Providence, and New York.

Note: Although bus schedules leaving Woods Hole are designed to work in conjunction with ferry arrivals, connections are not guaranteed because weather can make the ferry late, and *the bus doesn't wait.* Don't take the last ferry of the day from the islands to Woods Hole (or to Hyannis) and count on getting the last bus out—you may in fact be able to do it, but it's not dependable. Take an earlier ferry.

ESSENTIALS   The **telephone area code** is **508.** The nearest **visitors center** is the Cape Cod Chamber of Commerce, at U.S. 6 and Mass. 132, Hyannis, MA 02601 (☎ **508/362-3225**), open Monday through Friday from 8:30am to 5pm and Saturday and Sunday from 10am to 4pm.

WHAT TO SEE AND DO

The **Woods Hole Oceanographic Institution** at 15 School Street has an exhibit center (☎ **508/457-2000,** ext. **2663**) where visitors can see displays featuring a deep-diving submersible, oceanographic instruments, WHOI research vessels and tools, discoveries from the *Titanic* and *Bismarck,* and educational videos. There's a suggested donation of $1 per person, and the center is open year-round except for January, Easter, and Christmas. Hours are 10:30am to 4pm Tuesday through Saturday, and from noon to 4:30pm on Sunday in high-season, but may vary during the rest of the year, so call ahead.

The U.S. Department of Commerce's National Marine Fisheries Service maintains **an aquarium** (☎ **508/548-7684**), on Water Street (the town's main street) down at the end of the peninsula. Follow Water Street through the town; just after it turns right, the aquarium is on your left. It's open mid-June to mid-September, daily from 10am to 4pm; the rest of the year, Monday through Friday from 9am to 4pm. Admission is free. During summer months, they feed the seals in the outdoor pool daily; times are posted. Call ahead.

WHERE TO STAY

Sands of Time Motor Inn & Harbor House

Woods Hole Rd. (P.O. Box 106), Woods Hole, MA 02543. ☎ **508/548-6300** or 800/841-0114. Fax 508/457-0160. 33 rms. A/C TV TEL. Summer, $85–$125 double. All rates include continental breakfast. Off-season discounts available. Children under 18 $5 extra. AE, DC, MC, V. Closed Nov–Mar. Directions: Turn right onto Woods Hole Road from Mass. 28 in Falmouth, and the Sands will be on your right as you enter Woods Hole.

The Sands of Time Motor Inn, just out of town on the road to Falmouth, has a fine view of the harbor and is only a short walk from the ferry docks. Rooms are in a modern motel unit and a grand Victorian house, both of which overlook the harbor. A small garden and swimming pool are fitted into the hillside between the two. Most rooms have two double beds, and several have king-size beds. Those in the motel are modern and comfortable; the ones in the house have nice old touches like crystal doorknobs, fireplaces, bright new paint, and sparkling bathrooms. A grandfather clock inhabits the attractive entranceway.

WHERE TO DINE

Fishmonger's Café

56 Water St. ☎ **508/548-9148.** Reservations not accepted. Main courses $3.75–$14.95 at lunch, $6.50–$17.95 at dinner; breakfast specials $3.20–$6.25. MC, V. Wed–Mon 7am–11pm, Tues 11:30am–11pm. SEAFOOD.

I recommend a light lunch at the Fishmonger's Café, on Woods Hole's main street just before the little drawbridge on the left. Lunch and dinner specials are written on the blackboard, and sandwiches are available at lunch. There are also many burgers and vegetarian main courses from which to choose, but most people go for the fish and chips and the good clam chowder. Dinner specials might include salmon, swordfish, tuna, halibut, or mahi mahi dishes. Wine and beer are served with meals. The atmosphere is rustic, with rough wood tables, board floors, and sea breezes wafting in through the windows. Heavily patronized by local people and visitors to the institute, the cafe may echo with Japanese or Spanish as foreign biologists discuss their countries' marine problems and opportunities. Service is fast (there's a take-out window, too), which is what you need if you have to catch a ferry.

Shuckers

91A Water St. ☎ **508/540-3850.** Reservations not accepted. Main courses $9.95–$15.95. AE, MC, V. Daily 11am–11pm. SEAFOOD.

Located right on the docks, Shuckers is famed for its raw bar and its home-brewed beer, Nobska Light. Try to get one of the tables outside, where you can sit under an umbrella and watch the boating activity on Eel Pond. In addition to the raw bar, you'll find a satiating selection of seafood offerings, including broiled scrod, haddock au gratin, and mesquite-grilled swordfish, as well as jerk chicken or teriyaki chicken for non–seafood lovers. Their lobster roll is almost prohibitively good.

3 Sandwich

4 miles SE of the Sagamore Bridge, 22 miles SE of Plymouth, 16 miles NW of Hyannis, 15 miles W of Yarmouth Port, 62 miles SW of Provincetown

Sandwich, calling itself "the oldest town on the Cape" (incorporated 1639), is certainly one of the most beautiful and serene. Much of the vacation traffic to the Cape rushes past it on the way to Provincetown, leaving Sandwich to those few who appreciate it. The town holds its appeal both winter and summer, for although it has beaches, its antiques stores and gracious old houses also draw visitors. Other attractions are Heritage Plantation, Dexter Mill, and the Sandwich Glass Museum, which holds a fine collection of the exceptional glassware once made here.

GETTING THERE   See "Getting There" under "Seeing Cape Cod," at the beginning of this chapter.

ESSENTIALS   The **telephone area code** is **508.** For information, contact the **Cape Cod Chamber of Commerce,** U.S. 6 and Mass. 132, Hyannis, MA 02601 (☎ **508/362-3225**). It's open Monday through Friday from 8:30am to 5pm and Saturday and Sunday from 10am to 4pm.

WHAT TO SEE & DO

Sandwich is an old-fashioned town true to its traditions, a very pleasant place to live or visit. A walk downtown will give you clues to its character right away: backyard shops for artisans working in wood, leather, wrought iron, clay, or oil-on-canvas; graceful church steeples; small, well-groomed parks; comely old houses, many with the date of construction posted over the front door.

The town's beaches include **Town Beach,** the most westerly, and then, in order heading east, **Spring Hill Beach, East Sandwich Beach,** and over the line in Barnstable, **Sandy Neck Beach.** They all have toilets and places to park, and the bay side of the Cape has generally warmer swimming than the ocean side. Look for signs to the beaches on the side roads left (north) off Mass. 6A between Sandwich and Barnstable.

Dexter Grist Mill

Near Main and Grove Sts. ☎ **508/888-4910.** Admission $2 adults, $1 children 12–16, free for children under 12; combination ticket good for Dexter Grist Mill and Hoxie House. Weekends Memorial Day–Columbus Day, Mon–Sat 10am–5pm; mid-June to Sept, Mon–Sat 10am–5pm, Sun 1–4:45pm.

Dexter Mill is located at the end of a lovely mill pond (complete with ducks) and next to a cool, splashing mill race and an old pump. The mill (1654) was fully restored in 1961 and is not just a picturesque attraction, although you can go in and see the wooden mechanisms at work; the mill actually grinds corn, and you can buy bags of fresh meal the same day it's ground.

Heritage Plantation of Sandwich

Grove St. ☎ **508/888-3300.** Admission (grounds, exhibits, shows, concerts, etc.) $8 adults, $7 seniors, $4 children 6–18, free for children under 6. Mid-May to late Oct, daily 10am–5pm.

Perhaps the most famous local attraction is the Heritage Plantation of Sandwich, one mile from town on Grove Street. Another of the museums in which New England abounds, Heritage Plantation does not specialize in any one era but has exhibits from all periods of American history. The automobile collection, 34 cars dating from 1899 to 1936, is one of the most popular sights in town.

Another collection features firearms and military miniatures, and still others show American crafts and Currier & Ives prints. The buildings and grounds of the plantation are an attraction in themselves: All are reproductions of early-style buildings set in gardens and nature areas covering 76 acres.

There are picnic areas; a cafe where you can have continental breakfast, light lunches, or snacks; and a museum store that features unique gift items.

Hoxie House

Mass. 130. ☎ **508/888-1173.** Admission $2 adults, $1 children; combination ticket good for Hoxie House and Dexter Mill (see above) available. Mid-June to Sept, Mon–Sat 10am–5pm, Sun 1–5pm.

Sandwich has several old houses open to the public for a fee. The best known is Hoxie House, located along the shore of Shawme Pond (the millpond). The house dates from the end of the 1600s and has been restored and furnished with articles of that period.

Pairpont Crystal

Mass. 6A, Sagamore. ☎ **508/888-2344** or 800/899-0953. Free admission. Gift shop, 9am–6pm Mon–Sat, 10am–7pm Sun; glassblowing demonstrations, Mon–Sat 1–5pm.

In nearby Sagamore, on the shores of the Cape Cod Canal, you'll find Pairpont Crystal, America's oldest glassworks. Here you can watch skilled glassblowers create exquisite crystal items, using tools and techniques that were developed over a century ago.

Sandwich Glass Museum

129 Main St. ☎ **508/888-0251.** Admission $3 adults, $1 children 6–16, free for children under 6. Apr–Oct, daily 9:30am–4:30pm; Feb–Mar and Nov–Dec, Wed–Sun 9:30am–4pm. Closed Jan.

Across from Sandwich's Greek Revival town hall is the Sandwich Glass Museum. Sandwich was a major glass-producing town from 1825 to 1888, and although it specialized in the new process of pressing glass in a mold, it produced blown, cut, etched, and enameled works as well. A brilliant collection of this American glassware is on display, and dioramas, videos, and pictures show how it was made. Glassmakers' tools and other articles of Sandwich memorabilia are also part of the museum's collection. The glass museum is the only one of its kind on the Cape. Special exhibits are installed each year. Call ahead to see what's on when you're planning to be in town.

Yesteryear's Doll and Miniature Museum

Main and River Sts. ☎ **508/888-1711.** Admission $3 adults, $2.50 seniors, $1.50 children under 12. Mid-May to Oct, Mon–Sat 10am–4pm.

Sooner or later your walk will bring you by Yesteryear's Doll and Miniature Museum, in what was once the First Parish Meetinghouse. Literally hundreds of fascinating antique dolls, dollhouses, and toys as well as many other domestic articles are on display, and exhibits change from time to time. The museum is nonprofit but charges admission to defray expenses.

WHERE TO STAY

Captain Ezra Nye House

152 Main St., Sandwich, MA 02563. ☎ **508/888-6142** or 800/388-2278. Fax 508/833-2897. 6 rms (all with bath). $71–$82 standard double, $83–$93 twin room, $82–$104 queen-bedded room. All rates include full breakfast. AE, DISC, MC, V. Directions:

At the fork at Mass. 130 and Main Street, go right onto Main Street; the house is the fourth on the right.

The Captain Ezra Nye House is a lovely 1829 Federal-style home that was once the residence of a clipper-ship captain. Choose your bedroom according to color preference—green, yellow, blue, peach, or rose. The Blue Room has a working fireplace, the Peach Room holds two one-hundred-year-old Jenny Lind spool beds, and the Rose Suite has a queen-size gold-leaf bed as well as a small sitting area with a sofa and television. Hand-stenciling decorates the upstairs floors and walls. The two common rooms have a piano, TV, VCR, and fireplace.

Dan'l Webster Inn

149 Main St. Sandwich, MA 02563. ☎ **508/888-3622** or 800/444-3566. Fax 508/888-5156. 37 rms, 9 suites. A/C TV TEL. $89–$325 double. Additional person $10 extra; children under 12 stay free in parents' room. AE, DC, DISC, MC, V.

Ask anyone how to get anywhere in Sandwich and they'll inevitably include the Dan'l Webster Inn in their directions. "Go past the Dan'l Webster. . . ." Indeed, it's one of the town's most significant landmarks. Its 37 rooms and nine suites are decorated in a colonial motif. Many have canopy beds, and more than half a dozen offer whirlpool tubs. In addition to the rooms in the main building, suites with working fireplaces are available in the Fessenden House, an old sea captain's house located on the property, and in the Quince Tree House, just down the street. The Dan'l Webster Inn is a good choice if you want all the conveniences of a fine hotel, such as room service, pool, gift shop, meeting rooms, and health club privileges. There are three dining rooms at the inn, all serving the same menus (see "Where to Dine," below). Friday and Saturday evenings and at Sunday brunch there is live music.

Isaiah Jones Homestead

165 Main St., Sandwich, MA 02563. ☎ **508/888-9115** or 800/526-1625. 5 rms. Summer, $95–$155 double. Winter, $75–$124 double. All rates include breakfast. AE, DISC, MC, V.

The Isaiah Jones Homestead in the center of town is a small, no-smoking bed-and-breakfast. The rooms (two with whirlpool baths) have a comfortable elegance to them and are furnished with Victorian antiques. Oriental rugs, chintz fabrics, alcove sitting areas, triple sheeting on the beds, and fresh flowers are all the norm here. Each room is named after an important local person from the town's early days. A candlelit breakfast of fruit juices, baked goods, and a hot entrée, set at one long table, and afternoon tea, are included in the room rates.

Seth Pope House 1699

110 Tupper Rd., Sandwich, MA 02563. ☎ **508/888-5916** or 800/699-SETH. 3 rms (all with bath). A/C Apr–Oct $65–75 double. Memorial Day–Labor Day, two-night minimum stay on weekends. All rates include full breakfast. MC, V. Directions: From Sagamore Bridge, take Mass. 6A to the Sandwich Cooperative Bank (Tupper Road), turn right, go a quarter of a mile to Moody, and turn right; the driveway is on the left.

Propped up on a knoll overlooking a salt marsh, the Seth Pope House is listed on the Sandwich Town Hall Square National Register of Historic Homes. It's a very welcoming bed-and-breakfast lovingly run by Beverly and John Dobel. Throughout, you'll find the couple's collection of antiques, wonderful stenciling on the walls, and a total of seven fireplaces. Guest rooms include the Victorian Room, which has a queen-size bed piled high with pillows, and marble-topped furniture; the Pineapple Room, with two four-poster twin beds and braided rugs; and the Colonial Room, with exposed beams, wide wood floors, and a queen-size pencil-post bed. Each morning a full breakfast is served by candlelight in the "keeping" room.

The Summer House

158 Main St., Sandwich, MA 02563. ☎ **508/888-4991.** 5 rms (1 with bath). Nov–May 1, $55 double without bath, $65 double with bath; May 25–Oct 31, $65 double without bath, $75 double with bath. All rates include full breakfast and afternoon tea. AE, DISC, MC, V. Directions: From Sandwich Village off Mass. 130 North, bear right onto Main Street for a quarter of a mile.

Built around 1835 in Cape Cod Greek Revival style popular at that time, the entire front of the house is set aside for guests. One double room, on the first floor, has a private bath, and the four bedrooms on the second floor share two baths. Four of the guest rooms have working fireplaces, and all are decorated with antique furnishings, hand-made quilts, and heirloom linens. English-style afternoon tea is included in the room rates. You'll enjoy the porch, lawn, patio, and garden here.

Village Inn at Sandwich

4 Jarves St., Sandwich, MA 02563. ☎ **508/833-0363** or 800/922-9989. 8 rms (6 with bath). $90–$105 double. All rates include breakfast. AE, MC, V. Closed Jan–Mar. Directions: Go east on Mass. 6A to Jarves Street and turn right; the inn is on the left before Main Street.

This restored home is now one of the most cared-for bed-and-breakfasts on the Cape. Much of the furniture has been made by the owner, a German carpenter by trade whose work belongs in an expensive furniture showroom. I particularly like the pickled hardwood floors and the central staircase. Breakfast is served in an elegant dining room with striped wallpaper and French drapes. Two fireplaces warm the Victorian double parlor. You can relax on the wraparound porch in front of the house. Two guest rooms have fireplaces, and appointments include pine armoires, crisp linens and comforters, queen-size beds, and matching wallpaper and fabrics. You won't find anyone smoking at the inn or any children under 12.

WHERE TO DINE

✪ Dan'l Webster Inn

149 Main St. ☎ **508/888-3623.** Reservations recommended. Main courses $13.95–$23; early-evening special starts at $9.95. AE, DC, DISC, MC, V. Daily 8–11:15am; 11:45am–4pm; 4:45–9pm. CONTINENTAL.

Those who are not watching their budgets but who still value their dollar will want to know about the dining room at the Dan'l Webster Inn, located right in the heart of Sandwich Village. There's a grand solarium with a high ceiling, known as the conservatory, which offers views of the grounds and is filled with lush greenery. You can also dine in the Inn's Heritage Room, complete with an old working fireplace, grand piano, and historic artifacts; or the smaller, elegant Webster Room. A bounteous menu is offered, with lots of beef and seafood choices. For the early-evening special, you must be seated by 5:45pm and order by 6pm. On Friday and Saturday evenings and at Sunday brunch, there is live entertainment.

Marshland

Mass. 6A. ☎ **508/888-9824.** Reservations not required. Breakfast special $2.75–$4.95; dinner special $5.95–9.95. No credit cards. Mon 6am–2pm, Tues–Sat 6am–8pm, Sun 7am–noon. DINER/BAKERY.

Marshland is almost always packed—both with local regulars and visitors who crowd around the twin horseshoe-shaped bars or into the surrounding booths. Here you'll find a mainstream menu, plus several blackboards full of "specials" that are more creative and health-conscious. Best are the breakfasts where you can take your pick of homemade muffins (orange poppyseed, blueberry, corn with peaches, dark bran—you name it). If you want dinner, try to arrive before 6pm to avoid waiting in line.

⑤ Sagamore Inn

1131 Mass. 6A, Sagamore. ☎ **508/888-9707.** Reservations not accepted. Main courses $7.50–$13.25. AE, MC, V. Apr to late Nov, Wed–Mon 11am–9pm. Directions: Take Mass. 6A, just past the Sagamore Bridge. ITALIAN/SEAFOOD.

The Sagamore Inn isn't fancy—wooden booths, a stamped-tin ceiling—but neither are its prices. The clientele are local families, and the food is hearty, savory, and delicious, with huge portions and low prices. The cook's inspiration is Italian cuisine; you can find spaghetti, seafood, sandwiches, and that hot summer-weather favorite, an antipasto plate. Everyone here is friendly and pleasant and out to make you happy.

4   Hyannis

16 miles SE of Sandwich, 23 miles NE of Falmouth, 50 miles SW of Provincetown

Hyannis gained national fame during the presidency of John F. Kennedy because of his summer home in nearby Hyannisport. Some of the town's growth and perhaps a good portion of its honky-tonk date from that time, and although curious or devoted fans of the late president still stop to look at the town or to visit its memorial to J.F.K., the attractions in Hyannis these days are commercial. Should you need the services of an airline or a department store, supermarket, or foreign auto-parts warehouse while on the Cape, Hyannis is the place to come. If you don't need these things, there are many nicer places on the Cape to spend precious vacation time.

GETTING THERE   By Plane   Hyannis's **Barnstable Municipal Airport** (☎ **508/775-2020**) is the busiest airport on Cape Cod, with regular flights to Boston, Nantucket, and Martha's Vineyard, and connecting flights through those points. For details, see "Getting There" under "Seeing Cape Cod," at the beginning of this chapter. The airport is just on the northern outskirts of town on Mass. 132 a short taxi ride from the bus stations or the center. Several companies based here offer small planes for charter.

By Car, Train, or Bus   See "Getting There" under "Seeing Cape Cod," at the beginning of this chapter.

By Boat   Hyannis has two main docks, at the foot of Ocean Street for **Hy-Line passenger ferries** (☎ **508/477-8600**) to Nantucket, and at the foot of Pleasant Street for the passenger and car-ferries operated by the **Steamship Authority** (☎ **508/477-8600**). The docks are about five blocks from the bus stations. (Many buses connecting with ferries take passengers right to the dock.) For details on both these ferries, see below.

DEPARTING   Ferries from Hyannis to Martha's Vineyard & Nantucket Two companies operate ferries from Hyannis to the islands of Martha's Vineyard and Nantucket, and each sails from a different dock. Here are the details:

   The Woods Hole, Martha's Vineyard, and Nantucket Steamship Authority (☎ **508/477-8600**) runs car and passenger ferries from Hyannis's Pleasant Street docks (follow the signs in town). No direct service is run between Hyannis and

Martha's Vineyard by this company—you have to go via Nantucket or, preferably, direct from Woods Hole to Martha's Vineyard. The Steamship Authority's boats run six times daily to Nantucket in summer, less frequently off-season; the trip takes less than 2¹/₂ hours and costs $20 for adults, $10 for children under 12, round-trip. Car-ferry space must be reserved in advance; in high summer it costs $180 to ship a car round-trip from Hyannis to Nantucket. In high summer, one passengers-only boat is run in each direction daily between Martha's Vineyard and Nantucket, taking about two hours. The ferries are large, comfortable, and equipped with lunch counters and bars. Note that if you park in the dockside lots, you'll have to pay $10 per *calendar* day for the privilege, and that you should arrive at the lot 45 minutes prior to the ferry's departure time.

Note: When returning to Hyannis from Nantucket, don't plan on taking the last ferry of the day and meeting the bus to Boston or New York, for the ferries are often delayed and *the bus does not wait.* To be safe, catch a ferry well ahead of the last bus trip scheduled from Hyannis. If you find yourself in a jam because of ferry mixups, you can always take another line (see below) or fly.

Hy-Line Cruises (☎ **508/778-2600**) has several swift (two-hour) passengers-only boats, which depart from Hyannis's Ocean Street docks for Nantucket or Martha's Vineyard; the fare is $11 for an adult, $5.50 for a child, to either island. Although no cars are carried on the Hy-Line's boats, you can take your bicycle over for $4.50 one-way. These boats operate May through October only. By the way, if you sign up for a same-day round-trip, you'll have to decide which boat you plan to return on, and your ticket will be stamped with the boat's departure time. Reservations are accepted with an additional nominal charge (☎ **508/778-2602**). Otherwise, parking is $6 to $9 per *calendar* day, depending on the season.

ESSENTIALS   The **telephone area code** is **508.** For information, contact the **Cape Cod Chamber of Commerce,** U.S. 6 and Mass. 132, Hyannis, MA 02601 (☎ **508/362-3225**), open Monday through Friday from 8:30am to 5pm and Saturday and Sunday from 10am to 4pm.

WHAT TO SEE & DO

Many visitors to Hyannis stop to see the **memorial to President Kennedy,** a stone monument bearing the presidential seal and a small fountain, on Ocean Street right along the water. Hyannisport and the "Kennedy compound," noted in news stories while the late president vacationed here, are not far from the monument. The Kennedy compound is not visible from the street and is not open to the public.

Also along Ocean Street are **Kalmus Park** and **Veteran's Park,** with their respective beaches, bathhouses, and snack bars. Go down to the south end of Sea Street for none other than **Sea Street Beach.** Besides swimming facilities, Sea Street Beach has a little platform on top of a dune from which you can take a look at the sweep of the beach.

Big-name stars and bands perform at the **Cape Cod Melody Tent,** at the West Main Street Rotary in Hyannis (☎ **508/775-9100**). The season goes from early July through Labor Day, and runs the gamut—Peter, Paul, and Mary, Patti Labelle, Jay Black and the Americans, and Dion played at the Melody Tent in the summer of 1995. Tickets are priced differently depending on the show, but most run in the $19 to $40 range. Most shows take place between Wednesday and Sunday nights. Children's shows are Thursday mornings at 11am. Tickets can be charged by calling the box office.

WHERE TO STAY

Inn on Sea Street

358 Sea St., Hyannis, MA 02601. ☎ **508/775-8030.** Fax 508/771-0878. 9 rms (7 with bath), 1 cottage. $75–$103 double; $115 cottage. All rates include breakfast. AE, DISC, MC, V.

The Inn on Sea Street is the kind of place guests return to year after year. It consists of two Victorian buildings, one a Greek Revival house that was built in 1849, the other a grand Victorian (built in 1899) with a French mansard roof and a wraparound porch. Between the two, there are nine guest rooms, all crisply decorated with antiques and Oriental rugs. Those in the newer building have remote-control TVs (discreetly hidden away in armoires). The cottage is furnished with wicker. Every morning, breakfast—a feast of fruit, eggs, cheese, cake, granola, and the usual hot drinks—is served in the sun porch as well as the formal dining room. The inn is full of thoughtful details, such as goose-down pillows and umbrellas in guest rooms.

Sea Breeze Inn

397 Sea St., Hyannis, MA 02601. ☎ **508/771-7213.** 13 rms (all with bath). A/C TV. Mid-June to mid-Sept $65–$95, rest of the year $49–$69. Rates include expanded continental breakfast. AE, MC, V.

If being near the beach is a top priority, the Sea Breeze Inn is a good choice. It's a 3-minute walk away. It's also a good choice if you're planning to take a ferry over to one of the islands; the docks are about 15 minutes away by foot. All the rooms in this romantic Victorian inn are furnished with antiques, and many feature canopy beds. A couple of the rooms have ocean views. Breakfast includes fresh fruits, cereals, muffins, bagels, coffee, tea, and juice.

The owners of the Sea Breeze Inn now offer accommodations (week-long reservations only in season) in three cottages, located at 256 Ocean Avenue. Rates for the three-bedroom cottage are $1,200 to $1,600 per week in-season, $850 to $1,000 during the rest of the year. One-room efficiency cottages (one with a jacuzzi) run $590 to $690 per week in season, $300 to $350 during the rest of the year. All cottages have fully equipped kitchens and a washer and dryer.

WHERE TO DINE

Hyannis is full of restaurants specializing in cuisines from around the world. So whether you crave a slice of oven-baked pizza, a chimichanga, or a bowl of sesame noodles, you're sure to find it here. You'll also find a good selection of restaurants specializing in dishes that the Cape is famous for, such as chowders dense with clams, lobsters, and fish and chips. There's also a **Ben & Jerry's,** at 352 Main St. (☎ **508/790-0910**).

Fazio's Trattoria

586 Main St. ☎ **508/771-7445.** Reservations recommended. Main courses $8.95–$18.95; pizza $8.95–$11.50. MC, V. Daily 11:30am–2:30pm, 5pm–closing. ITALIAN.

The owners of Fazio's hail from San Francisco's North Beach area—and it shows. Offering traditional Italian specialties, Fazio's is probably the best and most reasonably priced Italian restaurant in the area. You shouldn't pass up the delicious minestrone soup. You can't go wrong with your main dish—try anything. Fazio's now features excellent Italian-style pizza from the wood-burning brick oven. Breads as well as chicken, fish, and veal dishes are also done in the wood-burning oven.

All the ingredients are fresh and homemade—even the sausages. Each night a homemade pasta is featured on the specials board. Don't miss the homemade cannoli for dessert. It's a small restaurant, and because the food is so good it's usually full; call ahead so you won't be disappointed.

Mildred's Chowder House

290 Iyanough Rd. ☎ **508/775-1045.** Reservations recommended. Main courses $8–$22. AE, MC, V. Mon–Thurs 7am–10pm; Fri–Sat 7am–11pm; Sun buffet 9am–noon, dinner noon–9:30pm. Closed Thanksgiving and Christmas Days. SEAFOOD.

For the ultimate bowl of chowder, you have to go to Mildred's. This famed chowder house first opened in 1949 and to this day uses Mildred's original recipe. It's a busy spot, all decked out in nautical decor. In addition to chowder, there are seafood and other popular New England dishes, including the lobster boil. The most expensive item on the menu is a stuffed twin lobster.

✪ The Paddock

W. Main St. at West End Rotary. ☎ **508/775-7677.** Reservations recommended. Main courses $14.95–$23.95. AE, DISC, MC, V. Daily 11:45am–2:30pm; 5–10pm. Closed mid-Nov to Apr. NEW ENGLAND.

For fine dining, the Paddock is a good choice. It's located beside the Melody Tent, which makes it the perfect place for a before-show dinner or after-show dessert. Attractively furnished in Victorian decor, The Paddock has been owned and run by the same family for 27 years. To start, try the chilled raspberry soup or steamed mussels *à la grecque*. Follow your appetizer with grilled salmon, the daily pasta special, or grilled marinated twin veal chops served with pesto. The menu also features several items for the health conscious, like baked sole, Thai scallops (with garlic, ginger, and lime), and a vegetarian platter.

Penguins Sea Grill

331 Main St. ☎ **508/775-2023.** Reservations recommended. Main courses $10.95–$19.95. AE, CB, DC, MC, V. Daily 5pm–closing. ITALIAN/SEAFOOD.

If you're in the mood for good seafood in a slightly formal, romantic atmosphere, Penguins Sea Grill is just what you're looking for. You'll know the restaurant by the tuxedoed penguin outside. Candlelit tables, exposed brick and paneled walls, and soft music set the scene inside. A glass of wine (or a bottle) from the extensive wine list is the first order of business. You'll enjoy the fresh bread while you wait for your appetizers and main courses. Seafood choices range from lobster to Wellfleet oysters or a fresh fish of the day. If you love pasta, try the scampi and Portuguese mussels. Seafood stews and paella are house specialties. Black Angus steaks and lamb chops are grilled over a hardwood fire. All breads and desserts are made on the premises.

✪ Up the Creek

36 Old Colony Rd. ☎ **508/771-7866.** Reservations recommended. Main courses $3.95–$6.95 at lunch, $8.50–$10.95 at dinner; brunch $7.50. AE, DC, DISC, MC, V. Mon–Sat 11:30am–2:30pm; daily 4:30–10pm; brunch Sun 11am–2:30pm. Closed Tues–Wed Nov to mid-May. Directions: Turn left off Sea Street onto Gosnold Street, then take the first left (you can't miss the jammed parking lot). AMERICAN.

Follow your nose and the locals' toes to Hyannis's value-for-money eatery: Up the Creek. Expect a cozy, tasteful interior. Try a fish, chicken, or sirloin lunch for $5 to $6. For dinner, choose from the seafood, veal, chicken, and beef specials, or try the special seafood strudel (lobster, shrimp, scallops, crab, and cheese wrapped in pastry) at $8.50.

5   Barnstable

3¹/₂ miles N of Hyannis, 2¹/₂ miles W of Yarmouth Port

The stretch of Mass. 6A between Sandwich and Dennis is a lush panorama of bogs and marshes, distant views of dunes and the sea, birds calling and fluttering, the winding road dotted with antiques shops, craft shops, art galleries, and other businesses—including lots and lots of real estate offices. The road leads through the villages of Barnstable, Cummaquid, Yarmouth Port, Yarmouth, and Dennis before heading eastward to Brewster.

Visitors may be surprised to know that Barnstable, the largest incorporated town on the Cape, actually includes within its boundaries the busy commercial center of Hyannis, its airport, and several small historic villages on the wide salt marshes along the shores of Cape Cod Bay. The village of Barnstable proper is little more than a namesake for the much larger township.

As you wend your way eastward along Mass. 6A, the village of Barnstable offers several good choices for lodging. In Barnstable, as well as Yarmouth Port, Mass. 6A becomes Main Street, also called the Old Kings Highway.

GETTING THERE   See "Getting There" under "Seeing Cape Cod," at the beginning of this chapter.

ESSENTIALS   The **telephone area code** is **508.** The nearest **visitors center** is the Cape Cod Chamber of Commerce, at U.S. 6 and Mass. 132, Hyannis, MA 02601 (☎ **508/362-3225**).

WHAT TO SEE AND DO

Whale-watching excursions depart from Barnstable Harbor daily, April through October. On these excursions, you are taken to the feeding grounds of the great baleen whales. Sightings have included 40- to 60-ton humpback whales with their calves, finbacks, minke, and right whales, as well as other marine mammals. All cruises are narrated by a naturalist and sightings are guaranteed. Summer sailings depart at approximately 8am, 12:45pm, and 5pm. In the spring and fall, there are two departures, one leaving at 9am and the other at 2pm. Rates are $22 for adults, $19 for seniors over 62, $15 for children 4 to 12, free for children under 4. Advance reservations are necessary; contact Hyannis Whale Watcher Cruises, P.O. Box 254, Barnstable Harbor, Barnstable, MA 02630 (☎ **508/362-6088** or **800/287-0374**).

WHERE TO STAY

Ashley Manor

3660 Old Kings Hwy. (P.O. Box 856), Barnstable, MA 02630. ☎ **508/362-8044.** 6 rms and suites, 1 cottage. $126–$148 double; $175–$191 suite. AE, MC, V. Directions: Take Rte. 6 east over the Sagamore Bridge to Exit 6. Make an immediate left onto Rte. 132 North and follow it to the end. Turn right and head east on Mass. 6A. Go three miles through Barnstable Village to the light. Go straight through the light for six-tenths of a mile. The inn will be on your left.

A stay at Ashley Manor is a lesson in leisurely living. Innkeepers Donald and Fay Bain will encourage you to linger over afternoon cocktails, evening conversations, and a full gourmet breakfast on the backyard brick terrace, enjoying the inn's two-acre grounds (or in the winter months by the fire in the formal dining room). The six spacious suites and guest rooms in the main manor house all have private baths, Oriental rugs, country furnishings, and antiques, and all but one have a working fireplace. The cottage has a freestanding fireplace and an efficiency. Ashley Manor has its own tennis court, as well as bicycles, beach chairs, and croquet. Children 14 and older are welcome at the inn. Pets are not welcome.

Beechwood

2839 Main St., Barnstable, MA 02630. ☎ **508/362-6618** or 800/609-6618. Fax 508/362-0298. 7 rms. $115–$150 double. All rates include breakfast. AE, MC, V. Directions: Head east on Mass. 6A; it's on your right.

This gabled-roof Victorian house takes its name from the big old beech trees that shade the veranda. Don't let the staid parlor mislead you—it's not at all in keeping with the light and airy guest rooms. Period antiques, colored glass, marble-topped dressers, unique bathrooms, and tall shuttered windows make this place special. The garret room in the attic is very private and has angled walls and eaves. Bicycles are available for guest use, and there's a wonderful porch glider. Beechwood is set on Old Kings Highway (also known as Mass. 6A and Main Street) within walking distance of the beach, antiques and art galleries, restaurants, and hiking and biking trails.

Charles Hinckley House

Old Kings Hwy. (P.O. Box 723), Barnstable Village, MA 02630. ☎ **508/362-9924.** 4 rms. $129–$169 double. All rates include breakfast. No credit cards. Directions: Take U.S. 6 to Exit 6, go left at the stop sign, then make a right onto Mass. 6A; the inn is 1^1/$_2$ miles down on the left.

With only four rooms (all with working fireplaces), the Charles Hinckley House is very special and welcoming. This Federal-colonial house is a historic landmark and has been painstakingly renovated. Flowers from the profuse bank of wildflower gardens fill the interior. The innkeepers keep their distance, but will spoil you if you give them half a chance.

6 Yarmouth Port

2^1/$_2$ miles E of Barnstable, 4^1/$_2$ miles SW of Dennis

Yarmouth is a town with a serious split personality. In the south, along Mass. 28, there is one motel and fast-food store after another built along crowded beaches. In the north, in the area of the Old Kings Highway, is the Cape just as you pictured it: dignified old Cape Cod houses, lofty trees, and the calm waters of Cape Cod Bay. You won't find any neon lights in the latter. Nor will you find malls, movie theaters, or motels.

Yarmouth Port, a very old community (incorporated 1639), has managed to preserve its history beautifully. You can glimpse its beauty by driving along Mass. 6A, which started life as an Indian path and later became known as the Kings Highway before Massachusetts declared its independence. Today it's known as Main Street and nicknamed the Captains' Mile because of its profusion of captains' houses. At one point, over three dozen sea captains lived in the town.

GETTING THERE See "Getting There" under "Seeing Cape Cod," at the beginning of this chapter.

ESSENTIALS The **telephone area code** is **508.** The **Cape Cod Chamber of Commerce** is at U.S. 6 and Mass. 132, Hyannis, MA 02601 (☎ **508/362-3225**).

WHAT TO SEE & DO

One of the highlights of any visit to Yarmouth Port is following the **nature trails of the Historical Society of Old Yarmouth.** The trails are open during daylight hours seven days a week year-round; 50¢ admission for adults, 25¢ for children. Note that these are not formal "botanical gardens" but rather trails through particularly beautiful wild areas of Yarmouth's land and marshes. Local flowers and trees, plants, and geological features are on view, and maps and trail booklets available at the gatehouse where you pay admission will tell you all about what there is to see.

Down Centre Street lies **Gray's Neck Beach** right on Bass Hole, a small cove. Here you'll find a boardwalk that stretches across a marsh (a rewarding spot for birdwatching) and a lovely patch of beach. According to legend, the Norsemen landed in this very spot back in 1003. The beach is free and open to the public.

Back on Main Street, at the corner of Summer Street, you'll find the **village pump and watering trough,** which dates back to 1866. Nearby is the **Parnassus Book Store** (☎ 508/362-6420), in a building that started life as a church and later became the local incarnation of the A & P grocery chain. Shelves of used books always stand outside, even when the store is closed. Feel free to help yourself by putting the posted price in the box.

Bangs Hallet House

Mass. 6A. ☎ **508/362-3021.** Admission $3 donation adults, 50¢ children under 12. July–Aug, tours Thurs–Fri and Sun 1:30 and 2:30pm; June and Sept, tours Sun 1:30 and 2:30pm.

The Captain Bangs Hallet House is the headquarters of the Historical Society of Old Yarmouth. This Greek Revival (circa 1840) house museum was the home of Capt. Bangs Hallet following his retirement from the Indo-China trade and is furnished in the manner in which a prosperous 19th-century sea captain would have lived. Ship models, ship paintings, and other maritime memorabilia are on display.

Winslow Crocker House

240 Rte. 6A. ☎ **508/362-4385.** Admission $4 adults, $3.50 seniors, $2 children 5–12, children under 5 free. June to mid-Oct: Tues, Thurs, and Sat–Sun noon–4pm.

The Winslow Crocker House is owned and maintained by the Society for the Preservation of New England Antiquities. The rooms in this Georgian house are furnished with 17th- to 19th-century collections.

WHERE TO STAY

Many of the former sea captains' homes of Yarmouth Port have become bed-and-breakfasts. Here, you'll find my favorites. For a complete list, contact the **Yarmouth Area Chamber of Commerce,** P.O. Box 479-F, South Yarmouth, MA 02664 (☎ **508/778-1008** or 800/732-1008).

Liberty Hill Inn

77 Main St., Yarmouth Port, MA 02675. ☎ **508/362-3976** or 800/821-3977. 5 rms. Summer, $120–$150 double. Off-season discounts available. Additional person $20 extra. All rates include breakfast. AE, MC, V.

Atop Liberty Hill, set back from Mass. 6A at the corner of Willow Street, is the Liberty Hill Inn. The classical pillars are a giveaway: Greek Revival architecture, built in 1825. The Liberty Hill is perhaps Yarmouth Port's best bargain: You get a double room (private bath) in the lovely house furnished with authentic Early

American pieces, a full breakfast, and a convenient location. Each room is uniquely decorated—for instance, Roscommon features white eyelet and lace, and Normandy has a French country feel to it. Innkeepers Beth and Jack Flanagan see to it that your stay is an enjoyable one. They'll get you theater or whale-watching tickets, and they'll even get tee times for golfers. For business travlers who prefer a bed and breakfast inn to a chain hotel, photocopy and fax services are easily arranged. You save money if you come in spring or fall, especially on a weekday.

One Centre Street Inn

1 Centre St., Yarmouth Port, MA 02675. ☎ **508/362-8910.** 7 rms, 1 suite. TEL. $65–$110 double. All rates include breakfast. AE, DISC, MC, V.

Despite its name, the One Centre Street Inn is on Old Kings Highway; the entrance is around to the side, on Centre Street, right in the middle of Yarmouth Port. For simple good taste, the inn is first choice in this town. Innkeeper, Karen Iannello will make your visit nothing short of pleasant and enjoyable. All rooms are small and thoughtfully furnished (with an understated elegance), and a full gourmet breakfast is served in the formal dining room or in the screened porch. The inn is within walking distance of sights and other activities. Picnic lunches and complimentary bikes are available. The inn is just one mile from Gray's Neck Beach.

○ Wedgewood Inn

83 Main St., Yarmouth Port, MA 02675. ☎ **508/362-5157.** 6 rms. A/C. Peak season, $115–$160 double. Off-season discounts available. All rates include breakfast. AE, DC, MC, V. Directions: Head east on Mass. 6A; it's on your right.

Poised on a knoll right on the Old Kings Highway, the Wedgewood Inn is as pretty as a picture. Indeed, this nearly 200-year-old house did grace the cover of *Colonial Homes* magazine in April 1992, and in 1995 it was featured in a cable television show entitled, "Great American Homes." Here you'll find half a dozen guest rooms, all individually decorated in a formal country style, except one that is very Victorian. Four rooms have working fireplaces; two have screened-in sun porches. Throughout the inn, there are conversation-piece antiques, some hand-stenciled floors, and an overall make-yourselves-comfortable feel.

WHERE TO DINE

Abbicci

43 Main St. (Mass. 6A). ☎ **508/362-3501.** Reservations recommended. Main courses $5.95–$10.95 at lunch, $15–$25 at dinner. AE, CB, DC, DISC, MC, V. Daily 11:30am–2:30pm; 5–10pm; brunch Sun 11:30am–2:30pm. CONTEMPORARY ITALIAN.

If you're looking for something "Cape-y," Abbicci is not it. This sophisticated Italian restaurant is far more contemporary and cosmopolitan (in spite of the fact that it's located in an historic 1755 Cape Cod cottage). Try the seafood stew (assorted fish and shellfish in a spicy tomato, leek, and saffron broth on garlic crostini) or the pistachio crusted rack of lamb with shallot compote, or if it's available as a special, the roast duck (with a honey, balsamic vinegar, and apricot sauce) and you'll have to agree. There is a quartet of small dining areas, each set up with fresh white linens and sturdy bottles of Pellegrino water. A map-mural of the Mediterranean area graces the walls. The restaurant is near the corner of Willow Street and Mass. 6A.

7   Dennis

4¹/₂ miles NE of Yarmouth Port, 5¹/₂ miles W of Brewster

The town of Dennis is much like Yarmouth. Here, it is claimed, the commercial cranberry-harvesting industry began, and salt works flourished for a period.

GETTING THERE   See "Getting There" under "Seeing Cape Cod," at the beginning of this chapter.

ESSENTIALS   The **telephone area code** is **508.** For information, contact the **Dennis Chamber of Commerce,** 242 Swan River Rd. (P.O. Box 275), South Dennis, MA 02660 (☎ **508/398-3568,** or 800/243-9920).

WHAT TO SEE & DO

As you enter the center of Dennis, start looking for a cemetery and a white church, and as you come to them, look for Old Bass River Road. Turn right onto this road and follow signs for eight-tenths of a mile to the **Scargo Hill Tower.** Park at the base of this stone structure surrounded by oak and pine, and climb the iron staircase inside to the top (not far) for a view that will tell you what the Cape is all about. On a clear day you can easily see Provincetown, the white blade of the Cape beaches cutting the deep blue of Cape Cod Bay. The Cape itself appears like a huge green scimitar, a sea of green trees with little white or silver-gray shingled houses poking through here and there. At the foot of the hill that holds the tower is Scargo Lake, and west is the outline of Barnstable Harbor. The tower was given to the town of Dennis in 1929 by the Tobey family, who had had ancestors living in Dennis since 1678. Follow the same road back to Mass. 6A.

More pretty scenes, including those cranberry bogs and salt marshes, await you in Dennis. If you get off Mass. 6A to wander and explore, expect to get lost. This is a confusing, if beautiful, place. For instance, though the village of East Dennis is actually east of Dennis, the village of South Dennis is due north of West Dennis, and these two are due south of East Dennis—got it? The **Cape Playhouse,** Mass. 6A (☎ **508/385-3911**), is the place to go on the Cape if you want to see a famous actor or actress in a well-known play. The plays (and performers) usually change every week, so call to see what's current. The season runs from late June through early September, with performances Monday through Saturday evenings at 8:30pm, plus matinees on Wednesday and Thursday at 2:30pm. Tickets are priced from $13 to $25. The playhouse has its own restaurant, open for lunch on matinee days, dinner, Sunday brunch, and after-theater snacks. Also here is the **Cape Cinema,** which specializes in foreign and independent American films. It's open from Memorial Day through the third weekend in September, and it has a brand-new, noiseless air-conditioning system (something for which many here are grateful). For information, call ☎ **508/385-2503.**

WHERE TO STAY

The Four Chimneys Inn

946 Main St. (Mass. 6A), Dennis, MA 02638. ☎ **508/385-6317.** 8 rms (all with bath). Summer $75–$120 double; the rest of the year, $70–$110 double. All rates include continental breakfast. Extra person $15. AE, DISC, MC, V.

The Four Chimneys Inn in Dennis Village is located across from beautiful Scargo Lake, and it holds some of the most spacious rooms on the entire Cape. The newly renovated 1881 Victorian home has a beautiful decor, which accentuates the high ceilings with medallions, marble fireplaces, French doors, and hardwood or painted floors found throughout. In fact, owners Russell and Kathy Tomasetti recently won an award for restoration in a Capewide contest. Guests may relax in the living room by the fireplace or in the library which is equipped with a VCR. All rooms are impeccable, and recently renovated bathrooms feature new fixtures, including pedestal sinks. Russell and Kathy are currently in the process of relandscaping the gardens, and have recently uncovered an old stone wall, which adds even more charm to the property. Continental breakfast is served in the dining room or on the screened porch.

Isaiah Hall B&B Inn

152 Whig St., (P.O. Box 1007) Dennis, MA 02638-1917. ☎ **508/385-9928** or 800/ 736-0160. Fax 508/385-5879. 11 rms (10 with bath). Mid-June to Labor Day, $62 double without bath, $82–$112 double with bath. Off-season discounts available. All rates include breakfast. AE, MC, V. Closed mid-Oct through Mar. Directions: Take U.S. 6 to Exit 8, go left 1¹/₄ miles to Mass. 6A, turn right, and go 3¹/₂ miles to Hope Lane (opposite the church and cemetery); turn left onto Hope Lane and at the end turn right onto Whig Street; the inn is a short distance on the left.

The Isaiah Hall B&B Inn is a gem of a bed-and-breakfast run by Marie and Dick Brophy. Good old-fashioned, homespun country comforts prevail in this 1857 Greek Revival farmhouse built by builder and cooper, Isaiah B. Hall. Public spaces and guest rooms in the main house feature large, solid antiques, like the 12-foot long cherry table in the dining room, or the Victorian parlor stove in the living room. Beds, many of which are iron and brass, are covered with hand-made quilts. The cathedral-ceilinged carriage house has guest rooms furnished with white wicker and knotty pine. The house abuts a cranberry bog. Isaiah's brother, Henry cultivated the first cranberry bogs in this country just a short distance from the inn, and Isaiah created and patented the original cranberry barrel. The inn is a 10-minute walk to Corporation Beach and is right behind the Cape Playhouse.

8 Brewster

5¹/₂ miles E of Dennis, 5 miles W of Orleans

Brewster is another of the picturesque little towns along Mass. 6A. A country store, several fine churches, and a town hall make it look like many other pleasant Cape towns, but Brewster's different in the number of noteworthy museums and exhibitions situated in the town or nearby. It also has one of the best French restaurants on the East Coast.

GETTING THERE See "Getting There" under "Seeing Cape Cod," at the beginning of this chapter.

ESSENTIALS The **telephone area code** is **508.** For information, contact the **Cape Cod Chamber of Commerce,** at U.S. 6 and Mass. 132, Hyannis, MA 02601 (☎ **508/362-3225**). It's open Monday through Friday from 8:30am to 5pm and Saturday and Sunday from 10am to 4pm.

WHAT TO SEE & DO

Brewster is proud of its **Old Grist Mill** and **Herring Run** at the Stony Brook Mill Sites, on Stony Brook Road near the intersection with Satucket and Run Hill Roads. The water wheel, still in good working order, powers the grinding machinery inside the mill. You can watch the whole process at work, and buy freshly ground cornmeal, from 2 to 5pm on Wednesday, Friday, and Saturday afternoons in July and August. Upstairs is a small museum with artifacts from the "Factory Village" that occupied this site more than 100 years ago.

The mill is now part of a park owned by the town of Brewster. Wander around the millpond, certainly one of the most romantic and picturesque locales on all of Cape Cod. If your visit falls during mid-April to early May, watch for the run of alewives (herring), which surges upstream from the ocean to freshwater spawning grounds.

New England Fire and History Museum

1439 Main St. (Mass. 6A). ☎ **508/896-5711.** Admission $4.75 adults, $4.25 seniors over 62, $2.50 children 5–12, free for children under 5. Memorial Day to mid-Sept, Mon–Fri 10am–4pm, Sat–Sun noon–4pm; Mid-Sept to Columbus Day, Sat–Sun noon–4pm.

The New England Fire and History Museum has one of the world's largest (35 engines) and most varied collections of early firefighting equipment and memorabilia, plus gardens both herbaceous and ceremonial, and a picnic area. Firefighting paraphernalia dates as far back as the 17th century and includes the world's only known 1929 Mercedes-Benz fire truck. Other exhibits include the Arthur Fiedler memorabilia collection, a historic apothecary, a blacksmith shop, and an award-winning animated diorama of the Great Chicago Fire of 1871. The museum's newest exhibit, entitled *Firefighters Thru the Centuries,* is a display of life-size mannekins dressed in firefighting gear, from Rome 226 B.C. to present. Guided tours are given; related movies are shown.

Cape Cod Museum of Natural History

Mass. 6A. ☎ **508/896-3867.** Admission $4 adults, $2 children 6–14, free for children under 6. Mon–Sat 10am–4:30pm, Sun 12:30–4:30pm.

Those interested in Cape Cod's flora, fauna, and ecology will want to visit the Cape Cod Museum of Natural History. The museum organization was founded in 1954 to preserve the wildlife and plant life in the area around Stony Brook and its marshes and beaches, to study this land, and to teach others about it. Nature walks, lecture programs, field trips, and adult and children's classes are held year-round. In summer, museum naturalists lead trips to Nauset Marsh and Monomoy Island to observe birds and wildlife and will take visitors on canoe trips around the Cape. Also in summer, live musical entertainment is offered on Wednesdays beginning at 7:30pm.

WHERE TO STAY

Ocean Edge Resort and Golf Club

Mass. 6A, Brewster, MA 02631. ☎ **508/896-9000** or 508/896-2774 or 800/343-6074. Fax 508/896-9123. 280 units. A/C TV TEL. $95–$475 double. AE, CB, DC, DISC, MC, V. Directions: From U.S. 6, take Exit 10 and turn left onto Mass. 124 and then right onto Mass. 6A; the mansion is 1.6 miles ahead on the left.

Ocean Edge is a complete resort and conference center. The main resort features an 1890 estate known as Fieldstone Hall that was once part of a grand 1,800-acre estate. Today, a few hundred villas and guest rooms are scattered over the grounds, which include an 18-hole golf course, a tennis complex with a pro, jogging paths, a beach, basketball court, a fitness room, and two indoor and four outdoor pools. The main mansion houses The Oceanfront, a fine-dining restaurant, as well as a pub. In addition, there are two more casual restaurants, Mulligans and the Reef

Café. Accommodations include hotel rooms or more elaborate villas, which are fully equipped with kitchen and laundry facilities.

Old Manse Inn

1861 Main St. (P.O. Box 839), Brewster, MA 02631. ☎ **508/896-3149.** 9 rms. A/C TV. $75–$110 double. All rates include breakfast. AE, DISC, MC, V. Directions: At the end of Mass. 134, take Mass. 6A; the inn is 4^1/$_2$ miles down on the left side.

Just west of the intersection of Mass. 6A and Mass. 124 South in Brewster is the Old Manse Inn, a lovely old white building surrounded by tall trees. Like so many other gracious Brewster houses, this one was built in the early 1800s by a captain in the China trade, one William Knowles. Many of the rooms here have queen-size canopy beds with patchwork quilts, hand-braided or Oriental rugs, and old-fashioned print wallpapers. One room has a working fireplace. If you just want to relax and not wander out for all your meals, you'll be happy to know that dinner (which has been highly praised by several food critics) is served in the inn's dining rooms. The menu features traditional items such as roast rack of lamb, steamed lobster, and country-style duck pâté. Reservations are recommended.

Old Sea Pines Inn

2553 Main St., Brewster, MA 02631. ☎ **508/896-6114.** Fax 508/896-8322. 21 rms and suites (16 with bath). June–Oct, $48 double without bath; $70–$104 double with bath; $150 suite with fireplace. Nov–May, discounts available. Additional person $16 extra. All rates include full breakfast. AE, DC, DISC, MC, V. Directions: Head east on Mass. 6A; the inn is on your left.

The Old Sea Pines Inn is a pleasant surprise. Built in 1907 as the Sea Pines School of Charm and Personality for Young Women, it retains its turn-of-the-century grace beneath the shade of several old oaks. The spacious, comfortable common rooms have hardwood floors and a working fireplace, and the wraparound porch is furnished with green cane rockers. The highest-priced room has a fireplace and four-poster bed. The family suite is for four people; the suite with a fireplace can accommodate two, three, or four people, and a bottle of champagne is included. The Old Sea Pines Inn is smoke-free.

WHERE TO DINE

The Bramble Inn & Restaurant

Mass. 6A. ☎ **508/896-7644.** Reservations required. Fixed-price four-course dinner $38–$48. AE, MC, V. Apr–Jan 1, Tues–Sun 6–9pm. NEW ENGLAND.

Located in a building that dates back to 1861, the Bramble Inn & Restaurant, located just east of the intersection of Mass. 6A and Mass. 124, is a wonderful old Cape Cod restaurant. It is, in fact, considered one of the top three restaurants on the Cape. There are five small dining rooms, each decorated with antique furnishings and unmatched vintage place settings. The restaurant is very conscientiously run by the Manchester family. You'll have a choice of several hot or cold appetizers, such as pan-sautéed cotuit oysters with roasted corn chowder, pancetta, and pepper confetti; or country-style pâté made with chicken liver, morel mushrooms, green tomato, and deviled almonds, served with honey mustard. As an entrée, the grilled farm-raised Atlantic salmon filet with spinach-and-crab-rissotto timbale, summer-savory-and-lemon zabaglione, and a Seville-orange-and-vidalia-onion relish is really quite wonderful. I also enjoyed the grilled marinated boneless breast of duckling with roast spring vegetables, foie-gras-and-white-bean ravioli, served in a double-rich duck consommé. Different desserts are featured daily, and there is a nice selection of wines by the glass available.

Brewster Fish House ✓

Mass. 6A. ☎ **508/896-7867.** Reservations not accepted. Main courses $5.75–$9 at lunch, $12.50–$21 at dinner. MC, V. Mid-Apr to mid-Nov, daily 11:30am–3pm and 5–9:30pm. Directions: Head east on Mass. 6A; it's on your right. SEAFOOD.

One look at the lunch or dinner menu at the Brewster Fish House and you're thrown into a tizzy. They offer all the standard seafood dishes, from grilled sea scallops to steamed lobster, but with their own special twists. For example, the grilled Atlantic salmon is prepared with spinach, prosciutto, and a mild Dijon-mustard sauce. The cod is served with a cranberry-and-ginger relish. If the sautéed cornmeal flounder (with lime, olive oil, and capers) is offered as a special, order it. For non-seafood eaters, there are usually some lamb, veal, beef, and duck specials available. The Brewster Fish House is a good casual choice for a leisurely lunch or dinner. If you happen to pass it between meals, however, you can always stop in for Billi Bi or lobster bisque.

Chillingsworth

2449 Main St. ☎ **508/896-3640.** Reservations recommended. Main courses $8–$13.50 at lunch; à la carte bistro dinner main courses $9.50–$22.50; table d'hôte seven-course dinner for two $100–$120. AE, DC, MC, V. Mid-May to mid-June and mid-Sept to Thanksgiving, Fri–Sun 11:30am–2:30pm; Fri–Sat seatings from 6–6:30pm or 9–9:30pm; brunch Sun 11am–4pm. Mid-June to mid-Sept, Tues–Sat 11:30am–2:30pm; Tues–Sun seatings from 6–6:30pm or 9–9:30pm. Casual bistro dinner, Fri–Sun from 6pm–closing; brunch, Sun 11:30am–2:30pm. Directions: Go one mile east of the intersection of Mass. 6A and Mass. 124; it's on the left. CONTEMPORARY FRENCH.

Chef-owner Robert Rabin's Chillingsworth is one of the loveliest restaurants on the Cape. The fare is contemporary French cuisine; the atmosphere is a delightful blend of modern and traditional, cozy and spacious. The luncheon menu includes crab cakes with a lemon/sour-cream sauce and golden caviar to start. You might follow it with a duck-breast salad with a sun-dried-cranberry–raspberry vinaigrette. If you've still got room after that, go for the chocolate nemesis with English cream. There are two seatings for the seven-course dinner (6 to 6:30pm and then again at 9 to 9:30pm). Recent offerings for the fixed-price dinner included grilled marinated shrimp on red-pepper pancake, with avocado salsa, corn relish, and cilantro as an appetizer; and rack of lamb with roasted tomatoes and potatoes, pepper mousse, and fava beans. For dessert, the mango crème brûlée or the white-chocolate-and-raspberry mousse Toulouse are my choices. Chillingsworth now also serves an à la carte bistro dinner in the greenhouse, a more casual setting. Bistro dinner items include a grilled pork chop with fresh fruit salsa, grilled potato, and a rosemary sauce; and grilled salmon in a lemon-chive-butter sauce served with a tomato-and-cucumber salad. If you have a special celebration for a party of two to four, request the separate library room.

The owners of Chillingsworth also have three antique-appointed rooms available for rent.

9 Chatham

9¹⁄₂ miles S of Orleans, 19 miles E of Hyannis

Chatham was once the railhead for Cape Cod, and the trains that brought vacationers in and took fish, salt, and shoes out also brought the opportunity for wealth. Chatham is therefore a graceful community with many big old homes and inns, an easy pace, friendly people, and pleasant vistas all around.

GETTING THERE   See "Getting There" under "Seeing Cape Cod," at the beginning of this chapter.

ESSENTIALS   The **telephone area code** is **508.** During the summer season, there's an **information booth** at 533 Main St. in the center of town. It's run by citizens who know the town inside and out, and offers brochures on places to stay, copies of menus from local restaurants, and information on activities. You can contact them before your arrival at the **Chatham Chamber of Commerce,** P.O. Box 793, Chatham, MA 02633 (☎ **508/945-5199**). There are public restrooms next door, in the rear of the town hall.

WHAT TO SEE & DO

Chatham Light is the first place to go. Go east on Main Street and turn right (south) on Shore Road to the light. The lighthouse is right next to the Coast Guard Station; on the other side of the street is a place to park while you look at the view through some coin-operated telescopes, and down below, a fine beach. The first light was erected on this point of land in 1808, and the present lighthouse dates from 1878.

The view is very pleasant, looking out to sea across Nauset Beach (the sand bar, actually a peninsula, you see out in the water). The cool sea breeze in summer and the nautical blast in winter make it incredible that Rome is at almost exactly the same latitude (but 4,200 miles away) as Chatham. To get to the **Fish Pier,** take Main Street east to Shore Street, then go left (north). The pier is operated by the town for licensed Chatham fishers. Chatham is very proud of its fishing fleet of small boats, which the townspeople boast bring in the freshest fish around. The boast has some truth to it, for the use of little boats means that the catch must be brought home every day; larger boats often stay out to sea for several days, refrigerating their catch on board.

The time to go down to the pier is between 3 and 6pm (aim for 4). You'll see the fleet come in and unload, and you can buy the day's catch right after it comes off the boat. Those who like to do it themselves can rent a boat at Fish Pier for a day's hunting for bass, bluefish, and tuna out at sea.

The town of Chatham has **public beaches** at Oyster Pond, only a few blocks from the center of town south on State Harbor Road from Main Street; and a bit farther out at Harding's Beach—follow Main Street (Mass. 28) west from the center of town for about two miles and turn left (south) onto Barn Hill Road to Harding's Beach Road. Lifeguards and toilets are at both beaches, but no bathhouses.

Chatham is a particularly good place for seeing birds, for **Monomoy Island,** south of the town, has been a National Wilderness Area since 1970. More than 300 different species of birds have been spotted on Monomoy. May is the best time to see birds in their mating plumage, and starting in late July many birds begin to be seen in winter plumage. The only way to get to Monomoy is by boat from Chatham. Full details on current offerings are available from the town's information booth on Main Street. For wildlife-tour information, call ☎ **508/349-2615.**

Another place to visit is the **Chatham Winery** (☎ **508/945-0300**), where interesting wines (like cranberry) are bottled in unique lobster-shaped bottles.

One of the nicest things about Chatham in July and August is the schedule of **band concerts** every Friday evening at 8pm in Kate Gould Park, just past the Wayside Inn on Main Street. Everybody comes to the concerts, and on a typical

Friday evening the crowd may reach into the thousands. Most of the musicians in the town band are year-round residents of Chatham who live and work in the town and enjoy providing a little free entertainment for their fellow citizens and visitors once a week.

The **Monomoy Theater,** 776 Main St. (☎ **508/945-1589**), not far west of the intersection with Old Harbor Road, is the summer-stock operation of Ohio University and offers a different play each week from mid-June through August. Performances are given Tuesday through Saturday (curtain rises at 8:30pm), and the current play is advertised on flyers around town and in the local newspapers. Season tickets are available, should you be spending the summer in Chatham. The last week of July features classical music concerts by the Monomoy Chamber Ensemble. Call for details.

Atwood House Museum

347 Stage Harbor Rd. ☎ **508/945-2493.** Admission $3 adults, $1 students, free for children under 12. Mid-June to Sept, Tues–Fri 1–4pm.

Housed in one of Chatham's oldest houses, this museum, operated by the Chatham Historical Society, features more than 2,000 exhibits, including an outstanding collection of shells, antique tools, maritime artifacts, J. C. Lincoln memorabilia, Parian ware, Sandwich glass, and a large selection of local scenes painted by well-known artists, sea captains, and townspeople. It takes about an hour to see the museum, so try to arrive by or before 3pm.

Railroad Museum

Depot Rd. Admission free; donations accepted. Mid-June to mid-Sept, Tues–Sat 10am–4pm.

Chatham's Railroad Museum is located in the old station on Depot Road (take Old Harbor Road north off Main Street, and Depot Road is a short distance up on the left). The station was built in 1887 by the Chatham Railroad Company and was turned into a museum in 1960. Among the railroading exhibits is a completely restored 1910 wooden caboose, used by the New York Central until that company gave it to the museum. The museum is staffed by volunteer guides.

Grist Mill

Shattuck Place. Admission free; donations accepted. July–Aug, Sat–Sun 10am–4pm.

Chatham also has an old Grist Mill open to the public. Sometimes corn is ground between the mill's stones if the wind is sufficient. To find it, take Cross Street south off Main Street to Shattuck Place, which winds down to the mill.

WHERE TO STAY
A RESORT HOTEL

Chatham Bars Inn

Shore Rd., Chatham, MA 02633. ☎ **508/945-0096** or 800/527-4884. Fax 508/945-5491. 150 rms and cottages. TEL. Summer (until July 25) $170–$320 double; $385 suite. Summer (July 26–Sept. 1) $190–$340 double; $405 suite; 2-bedroom cottage $1,000 per night. Rest of the year $90–$650 double. All rates include breakfast and service. AE, DC, MC, V. Directions: Take U.S. 6 East to Mass. 137, proceed three miles and turn left onto Mass. 28 South; go three more miles, through the traffic circle, to the end of Main Street; take a left on Shore Road and the inn is half a mile down on the left.

The Chatham Bars Inn is a true bit of old Cape Cod, a huge, rambling, gracious resort complex with 26 attractive cottages (no kitchens) on the property. As you approach the motor entrance of the inn, bear to the right, and you'll enter the parlor, with its high-arched ceiling, lots of windows looking onto a shady veranda, and wicker furniture for cool sitting on warm summer days. The lobby is also grand, large, and spacious, and a stairway out the front door tumbles down the hillside to the road and beyond it to the inn's private beach.

The staff is friendly, well trained, and soft-spoken. If the rates look high, remember that, on the average, a luxury inn or motel room costs around $140, plus two breakfasts and two good dinners, which often brings a normal vacation day's expenses to around $300 per couple daily. The Chatham Bars Inn is a bit of history brought up to modern standards of comfort and service.

Dining/Entertainment: The elegant main dining room serves contemporary New England cuisine. The North Beach Tavern serves more casual fare in a clublike setting. You can dine al fresco at the Beach House Grill. Jacket and tie requested in the main dining room after 6pm.

Services: Children's program July–Aug; guest services director on hand.

Facilities: Private beach, outdoor heated pool, four outdoor tennis courts; adjacent nine-hole golf course; fitness center.

INNS

Bradford Inn and Motel

26 Cross St. (P.O. Box 750), Chatham, MA 02633. ☎ **508/945-1030** or 800/562-4667. Fax 508/945-9652. 25 rms. A/C FRIDGE TV TEL. June 23–Sept 3 $120–$189 double; May 26–June 22 $105–$165 double. Rest of the year (except some holiday weekends) $79–$139. Single rates are available all year except June 23 to Sept 3. All rates include full breakfast. AE, DISC, MC, V. Directions: From the town center, take Main Street and turn right onto Cross Street.

The Gray family's Bradford Inn and Motel is right at the center of town. This extremely neat and tidy complex has 25 guest rooms (11 in a motel annex), a patio, outdoor heated pool, and silk flowers in many of the rooms. All rooms have refrigerators and some have full kitchen facilities. Eight of the rooms feature working fireplaces. This should be your first motel choice in Chatham. The restaurant, Champlain's, serves lunch and light dinners in season, breakfast year-round. Fax service is available.

Captain's House Inn

369–377 Old Harbor Rd., Chatham, MA 02633. ☎ **508/945-0127.** Fax 508/945-0866. 16 rms. A/C TEL $125–$225 double. All rates include continental breakfast and afternoon tea. AE, MC, V.

The Captain's House is one of Chatham's most charming inns. New owners Jan and Dave McMaster are taking the Captain's House to the next level of elegance and graciousness. Jan and her staff, which includes British and other European university students, prepare homemade gourmet breakfasts and English afternoon high tea. The two-acre estate's gardens and lawns have been restored to reflect genteel days of quiet luxury. There you can play lawn croquet or relax in an Adirondack chair while sipping lemonade. The guest rooms in this 1839 sea captain's house hold period furnishings, fine antiques, and canopy beds, and some even have fireplaces and sitting rooms. Courtesy bicycles are available for guest use.

Carriage House Inn

407 Old Harbor Rd., Chatham, MA 02633. ☎ **508/945-4688.** 6 rms. A/C. Summer $135–$160 double; spring and fall $120–$150 double; winter $75–$125 double. Package rates are available during the fall, winter, and spring. All rates include an extended continental breakfast. MC, V.

The Carriage House Inn, boasting the tallest flagpole (and a 200-square-foot flag) in Chatham, is one of the area's newest bed-and-breakfasts. Innkeepers Pam and Tom Patton have created an oasis in one of New England's most popular vacation spots. The inn's ground floor has a comfortably furnished living room where you can relax by the fireplace while watching TV (there's also a VCR for guest use). In warm weather you might choose to spend time on the outdoor deck (overlooking the well-manicured grounds) or open porch. The guest rooms are well furnished and airily decorated with country chintzes; all have queen-size beds and private bathrooms. An extended continental breakfast of fresh fruit, homemade muffins and breads, and a hot entrée is served each morning in the dining room or, in warmer weather, in the adjacent sunroom. In the afternoon guests are treated to homemade cookies and tea or soft drinks.

In addition to the three rooms in the main house, the inn has three new rooms in the recently renovated carriage house which is connected to the main building by a covered walkway. All have fireplaces and sliding glass doors with access to private patios. Courtesy bicycles are available for guest use.

Chatham Town House Inn

11 Library Lane, Chatham, MA 02633. ☎ **508/945-2180** or 800/242-2180. Fax 508/945-3990. 26 rms. A/C MINIBAR TV TEL. July–Sept, $155–$200 double, $2,100 per week cottage (up to four people); May–June and Oct–Dec, $135–$185 double, $300 cottage (per night); Jan–Apr, $100–$165 double, $275 cottage (per night). Additional person $25 extra. All rates include full breakfast. AE, DC, MC, V.

Another downtown inn, at the corner of Library Lane and Main Street, the Chatham Town House has 26 rooms, plus a six-room lodge and several cottages. All the rooms are decorated differently, but with taste and thoughtfulness; hand-hooked rugs rather than wall-to-wall carpeting are used so that the beautiful old floors can be seen. Honeymoon rooms have canopy beds, and two two-bedroom cottages have fireplaces. All have individual thermostats.

The Two Turtles restaurant serves breakfast, lunch, and dinner from mid-May to October. Reservations are recommended. The inn has a swimming pool and a spa which are open during the summer months.

Cranberry Inn at Chatham

359 Main St., Chatham, MA 02633. ☎ **508/945-9232** or 800/332-4667. 18 rms. A/C TV TEL. Summer, $155–$210 double. Off-season, $85–$160 double. All rates include continental breakfast buffet. AE, MC, V.

A few minutes' walk from downtown is the Cranberry Inn at Chatham, operated by Jim and Debbie Bradley. Before taking over operations at the Cranberry Inn, the Bradleys worked for a major hotel chain and have brought their years of experience to Chatham. The circa-1830 inn has been meticulously restored, and all rooms are decorated with antique and 19th-century reproduction furnishings. Special touches—like triple sheeting and feather pillows—make staying at the Cranberry Inn a delightful experience. Many of the rooms have fireplaces, and beautiful art and artifacts from around the world are scattered throughout. Children 8 and over are welcome. Smoking is permitted outdoors.

Cyrus Kent House Inn

63 Cross St., at Kent Place, Chatham, MA 02633. ☎ **508/945-9104** or 800/338-5368. 10 rms. TV TEL. Memorial Day–Oct, $95–$165 double; Mar–Memorial Day and Nov–Dec, $75–$120. Additional person $22 extra. All rates include breakfast. AE, MC, V.

Located within steps of Chatham's restaurants and shops, and within walking distance of the water, this former sea captain's house is ideally situated. Guests can stay in the main house in an antique brass or canopy bed or in a fireplaced room in "The Carriage House." Common rooms include a large inviting living room stocked with area brochures and local newspapers, a sundeck out back, and a breakfast room, where a homemade continental breakfast is served every morning. Many of the home's original features, like plaster mouldings, ceiling rosettes, and wainscoting have been left intact. Bay and Palladian windows and French doors fill rooms with bright sunlight. Between Labor Day and Memorial Day, complimentary afternoon tea and wine and cheese are also served. All the rooms are freshly decorated with thoughtfully selected fabrics, original art, and antique furnishings.

Moses Nickerson House Inn

364 Old Harbor Rd. (Mass. 28), Chatham, MA 02633. ☎ **508/945-5859** or 800/ 628-6972. 7 rms. $119–$169 or double. Off-season discounts available. AE, MC, V.

Most people describe this white clapboard country bed-and-breakfast with one simple word—warm. The Moses Nickerson House has been splendidly renovated. Well-kept wide-board pine floors, antiques, and individually decorated guest rooms make this one of the area's most comfortable bed-and-breakfasts. All the rooms have queen-size beds and private baths (most with showers only), and if you're lucky you'll have your pick of rooms. Perhaps you'd like a canopied four-poster bed, or maybe you'd be more comfortable in a more masculine atmosphere—one that features Ralph Lauren designs and a green leather wingback chair. Of course, then you'll have to decide whether or not you want a fireplace. Breakfast is served on fine china in the glass-enclosed breakfast room. Deciding on your room might be difficult, but staying here will be easy.

Mulberry Inn

44 Cross St. (P.O. Box 212), Chatham, MA 02633. ☎ **508/945-2020** or 800/562-4667. Fax 508/945-9652. 3 rms. A/C TV TEL. June 23–Sept 3, $159–$179 double. May 26–June 22 and Sept 4–Oct 14, $125–$155 double. Rest of the year $100–$129 double. All rates include full breakfast. AE, DISC, MC, V. Directions: From the town center, take Main Street and turn right onto Cross Street.

Right next door to the Bradford Inn and Motel (see above) is the Mulberry Inn, also managed by the Gray family. They've restored this historic house with turn-of-the-century furnishings, including canopy beds, and have added private bathrooms and other modern amenities.

Old Harbor Inn

22 Old Harbor Rd. (Mass. 28), Chatham, MA 02633. ☎ **508/945-4434** or 800/ 942-4434. 8 rms. Summer, $120–$200 double. Off-season, $90–$175 double. All rates include extended continental breakfast. CB, DC, DISC, MC, V. Directions: From the rotary in the center of Chatham, follow Mass. 28; the inn sits behind the church.

This is a perfect base for exploring Chatham. You can walk everywhere, including to the town's beach area. This new (early 1930s) gray clapboard home is set on finely landscaped grounds. Inside is a warm and inviting living room with a fireplace and a breakfast room overlooking the lawns. The guest rooms are marvelous; each room has a style of its own—for instance, one room is done completely in red and white, while another is decorated with Laura Ashley fabrics and wicker furnishings. In 1995 the Old Harbor Inn was extensively renovated and expanded. There is a new library/sitting room, a new second-floor has been added to a first-floor wing, and a sunny breakfast room has been added.

Breakfast includes two types of muffins or scones, a fruit entrée, yogurt, granola, cereals, juices, coffee, tea, or hot chocolate. In winter breakfast might also include a hot entrée. Afternoon tea is served Thursday through Saturday by reservation only. The inn is smoke-free.

Queen Anne Inn

70 Queen Anne Rd., Chatham, MA 02633. ☎ **508/945-0394,** or 800/545-4667. Fax 508/945-4884. 30 rms, 2 studios. TV TEL. $147–$300 double. Package rates are available in the late fall, winter, and spring. All rates include full breakfast. AE, EU, MC, V. Directions: Take U.S. 6 East to Mass. 137 South to Mass. 28 toward Chatham; at the first traffic light, bear right onto Queen Anne Road and the inn will be in sight immediately on your right.

The Queen Anne Inn is just a few blocks from the center of Chatham and has been a favorite hostelry here for well over a century. The graceful, shingled, gabled inn is authentic 19th-century Cape Cod, but has many of the amenities of a resort hotel. Several of the rooms have fireplaces, private balconies (some look onto the Oyster Pond), and whirlpool baths. In 1994 the inn's 100-year-old garden cottage was renovated, adding two luxury studios to the property. Each studio features a fireplace, and one has a Jacuzzi, the other a private outdoor patio and hot tub. Guests can enjoy excursions to Monomoy Island to see the seals, shore birds, and deer. The inn also has a new heated outdoor pool, located in the garden behind the inn.

Elegant dinners are available Wednesday through Monday at the inn's Earl of Chatham restaurant from 6:30 to 10pm. Facilities include tennis courts (with a resident pro for lessons and clinics), bicycles, and an indoor spa. The Queen Anne Inn is a member of Romantik Hotels International.

A GUESTHOUSE

⊗ Bow Roof House

59 Queen Anne Rd., Chatham, MA 02633. ☎ **508/945-1346.** 6 rms. $60–$70 double. All rates include breakfast and are based on a stay of three or more nights. No credit cards. Directions: Take U.S. 6 East to Mass. 137 South to Mass. 28 toward Chatham; at the first traffic light, bear right onto Queen Anne Road and the house is on the left.

The Bow Roof House has been run by the Mazulis family for more than 20 years now. A pleasant guesthouse, it's located not far from the water, and only a few minutes' walk from the center of town and a shopping center. The main house is that of an old sea captain, and many rooms still have the original fireplaces (not working now). A large living room with rough-timbered ceiling and large fireplace is available for guest use, and just through the door from it is a terrace with tables and umbrellas for a glass of wine (BYO) or tea in the evening. If you go in summer, the bank in front of the house will be a riot of wildflowers, and the two yuccas by the door may be in bloom.

MOTELS

The Moorings Bed & Breakfast Motel

326 Main St., Chatham, MA 02633. ☎ **508/945-0848** or 800/320-0848. 15 units. A/C TV. $95–$115 double; $140–$195 one-, two-, or three-bedroom efficiency. All rates include buffet continental breakfast. MC, V.

Close to the downtown area and just steps to the beach, this grand old Chatham house has a guesthouse with a motel annex and efficiency apartments. The complex once belonged to a retired admiral and now serves well as a hostelry, owned by Jan and Earl Rush. Furnishings and styles of rooms vary with the building you stay in: The guesthouse is traditional Victorian; the motel annex and efficiencies are modern but decorated in colonial style. Bikes (and helmets), barbecue facilities, and a playground are available for guest use.

Pleasant Bay Village Resort Motel

Mass. 28 (P.O. Box 772), Chatham, MA 02633. ☎ **508/945-1133** or 800/547-1011. Fax 508/945-9701. 58 rms. A/C TV TEL. June 24–July 22, $145–$185 double; July 22–Labor Day, $155–$195; May 7–June 24, rest of Sept, and Oct, $135–$155. Closed Nov–May 6. AE, MC, V. Directions: Turn left onto Mass. 137 from U.S. 6 and then, after a short distance, turn left onto Pleasant Bay Road; continue to the end until you reach Mass. 28; turn right and Pleasant Bay Village is one mile ahead.

The Pleasant Bay Village, on Mass. 28 several miles north of town in the section called Chathamport, is accessible only by car. The motel is about as pleasant as you'll find, located on six acres of very skillfully landscaped grounds, with evergreen hedges, trees, bushes, and roses, plus a waterfall and pond. The motel's buildings are scattered through the grounds, and there's a heated pool, shuffleboard, and Ping-Pong, besides just lounging in the sun, to keep you occupied. The motel has a breakfast room (light lunches served as well). Rooms are modern, with wall-to-wall carpeting.

WHERE TO DINE

The Bistro

595 Main St. ☎ **508/945-5033.** Reservations are recommended. Main courses $10.95–$18.95. MC, V. Daily 5:30–9pm (10pm on busy evenings). CREATIVE INTERNATIONAL

Located in the Galleria shopping center, The Bistro is one of Chatham's most popular eateries. High ceilings and large windows give this casual restaurant an open, airy feeling. The chef's creativity shines through in generous portions of dishes like the lobster taco (in a soft tortilla served with spinach and jalapeño jack cheese). Other items of interest include a vegetable curry with a North African influence and Thai chicken satay. There's also an incredible pasta tossed with Scotch bonnet peppers, spicy sausage and smoked chicken (it's served with an interesting guava-banana ketchup. A large number of menu items are prepared over aromatic woods on the open grill. There is a short wine list and a substantial list of beers.

Christian's

443 Main St. ☎ **508/945-3362.** Reservations required downstairs. Main courses $18–$26. AE, DC, DISC, MC, V. Summer, daily 11:30am–10pm. Hours vary during rest of year—call ahead. AMERICAN.

Lodged in an old Chatham house in the middle of town, Christian's has a cocktail bar and light menu served upstairs on a pretty deck (open at 4pm) and several dining rooms within the house itself. The dinner menu, which changes every month, is the most original and creative in the area. Appetizers might include Oriental dumplings served with ponzu sauce or crab buerrecks (flaky pastry filled with crabmeat and a bit of curry). As an entrée, the seafood melange (lobster, shrimp, and scallops) is a good choice if it's on the menu, and the roast duck served with a fresh fruit sauce, is one of the specialties of the house (when I tried it, it was served with a kiwi sauce). Upstairs at Christian's is available for coffee and an after-dinner drink. There's a piano bar and a beautiful oak bar. In the summer there's entertainment nightly; in spring and fall the music is on weekends only. A bistro menu that focuses on burgers, salads, pizzas, and a selection of entrées is served on the rooftop deck or upstairs.

Cookie Manor

499 Main St. ☎ **508/945-1152.** Reservations not required. Main courses $4–$5. No credit cards. Memorial Day–Labor Day, daily Mon–Thurs 7am–9pm, Fri–Sat 7am–10pm, Sun 7am–6pm Labor Day–Memorial Day, daily 7am–5pm. ICE CREAM/FAST FOOD.

When you get a craving for ice cream, make your way to the Cookie Manor, located right in the center of town. Here you'll find more than 18 flavors plus a great selection of sandwiches (try the honey-baked ham and cheese), salads, and house specialties like homemade carrot cake and chocolate zucchini cake, which has been featured in food magazines. The Cookie Manor also serves breakfast (bagels and egg dishes) from 7 to 11am, for under $5.

The Impudent Oyster

15 Chatham Bars Ave. ☎ **508/945-3545.** Reservations recommended. Main courses $15.50–$22.50. AE, MC, V. Mon–Sat 11:30am–3pm, Sun noon–3pm; daily 5:30–10pm (5–9pm off-season). Closed Thanksgiving Day, Christmas Eve, and Christmas Day. INTERNATIONAL.

The Impudent Oyster, located just off Main Street, has a long and eclectic menu. Chinese, French, Italian, and Mexican-style dishes, each with a different local touch; sandwiches and elegant main courses; seafood and meats—all share the menu. Maybe you're in the mood for scrod with feta and fennel, Portuguese mussels (mussels and chourico sausage steamed in a spicy tomato diablo sauce), or even scallops Kaanapali (Cape sea scallops broiled en casserole with a toasted macadamia-nut breading and a lemon-butter sauce). The oysters, by the way, are freshly shucked. Be forewarned, this is not the place to go for an intimate romantic dinner—The Impudent Oyster is always packed and the crowd can get quite boisterous at any hour. The menu changes often, and there is always a list of daily specials. Dress neatly, but not formally.

Sea in the Rough

1077 Main St. (Mass. 28). ☎ **508/945-1700.** Reservations not accepted. Main courses $9–$15. DISC, MC, V. Apr–Oct, daily 11:30am–9pm. SEAFOOD.

If you don't mind driving a couple of minutes from the center of town, head out to Sea in the Rough. It's a good, hearty, informal family place with red-vinyl chairs, basic service, and generous servings. Fried clams are a favorite here. In nice weather, sit outside on the side patio under the shade of umbrellas. Specials are available at lunch and dinner. Sea in the Rough is a nonsmoking restaurant.

10 Orleans & Eastham

Orleans: 8 miles S of Wellfleet, Eastham: 10 miles S of Wellfleet

Orleans owes its name and its fame to French connections. Known as Nauset since its earliest settlement in 1644, the town was renamed Orleans in 1797 when it was separated from neighboring Eastham and incorporated. The duc d'Orléans had made a visit to Cape Cod and the townspeople chose the name in the French nobleman's honor.

Orleans's other French connection was as close as can be without moving continents. In 1879 Orleans was physically connected by underwater telegraph cable with the town of Brest in France, almost 4,000 miles away. You can still see the telegraph station where the cable came ashore before continuing overland to New York.

In its day, Orleans has made its living through fishing and shellfishing, clothing manufacture, agriculture, and the production of salt from seawater, not to mention trade in contraband. During the Revolutionary War, Orleans sent men and supplies to aid the colonial forces. In the War of 1812, the town refused to pay $1,000 "protection money" demanded by the British enemy. A landing force was sent ashore from HMS *Newcastle,* and the town militia quickly convinced the redcoats that it was probably a good idea to return to the ship, which they did. Needless to say, Orleans kept its $1,000. When a German submarine broke the surface off Nauset Beach during World War I, the townspeople again demonstrated their coolness in the face of danger. The sub released a few torpedoes at some coal barges and everybody turned out to watch the show.

Nearby Eastham also has a few attractions worth stopping for.

GETTING THERE   See "Getting There" under "Seeing Cape Cod," at the beginning of this chapter.

ESSENTIALS   The **telephone area code** is **508.** For local travel information, you can contact the **Orleans Chamber of Commerce,** P.O. Box 153, Orleans, MA 02653 (☎ **508/255-1386** or **800/865-1386**), or the **Eastham Chamber of Commerce,** P.O. Box 1329B, Eastham, MA 02642 (☎ **508/255-3444**).

ORLEANS
WHAT TO SEE & DO

Orleans has a rare sight: a museum in the building erected to house the American terminus of a transatlantic cable from Brest, France. Laid in 1879, the cable came to Orleans in 1891, and the **French Cable Station Museum,** Mass. 28 and Cove Road (☎ **508/240-1735**), remains much as it was when the cable was still in use. Among other important messages, the cable, which remained in use until 1959, transmitted word of Lindbergh's arrival in Paris. It's open from late June or early July through Labor Day, Monday through Saturday from 10am to 4pm.

Several good beaches are a short distance from Orleans. Remember that Atlantic-side beaches will invariably be cooler for swimming than the beaches on Cape Cod Bay.

Nauset Beach, a stretch of wide, flat sand 10 miles long, is a town beach of Orleans, and therefore subject to a parking fee; the use of bathhouse and other facilities is included. Permits for a week or more are also available at reduced prices. The surfing's not bad at Nauset, and a section of the beach is reserved for it.

Skaket Beach, on Cape Cod Bay, has less surf but warmer water and a gently sloping beach. It's operated by the town, with lifeguards, parking places, and a bathhouse, and there's a charge. This is an especially good beach for families with young children.

A short detour to Fort Point off Mass. 6A will reveal a breathtaking **view** of the surrounding marshlands. There are also some nice trails you can take down to Nauset Marsh.

Orleans is home to a store that's quickly becoming a major Lower Cape attraction. The **Bird Watcher's General Store,** Mass. 6A (☎ **508/255-6974** or **800/562-1512**), is exactly as its name implies: a general store devoted to wild birds for bird lovers. Here you'll find birds on everything from postcards to mailboxes, as well as bins of corn, thistle, and sunflower and a good selection of birdhouses. If you're having trouble keeping the squirrels out of your birdfeeder, Bird Watcher's General Store has several squirrel-proof feeders available.

WHERE TO STAY

The Cove

Mass. 28 (P.O. Box 279), Orleans, MA 02653. ☎ **508/255-1203** or 800/343-2233. 47 rms. A/C TV TEL. Summer, $91–$163 double; the rest of the year, $49–$119 double. AE, DC, DISC, MC, V.

The Cove is a motel and then some. What separates it from the average motel is its landscaped grounds (complete with gardens, patios, and a heated pool) and its attention to detail. You'll find that all rooms have the customary motel amenities, but they also have special extras, such as small refrigerators, coffee makers, and hair dryers (most even have microwaves), and all are individually decorated. Suites have kitchens, and some units even have fireplaces. All guests are treated to a cruise on The Cove's float boat.

Nauset House Inn

Beach Rd. (P.O. Box 774), East Orleans, MA 02643. ☎ **508/255-2195.** 14 rms (8 with bath). $65–$85 double without bath, $105–$115 double with bath. MC, V. Closed Nov–Mar.

Absolutely every inch of the Nauset House Inn seems to have been touched by somebody with good taste. From the gardened grounds to the antique-furnished rooms, this family-owned inn is obviously very loved. One of the highlights of every stay is the country breakfast prepared by innkeeper Diane Johnson (so many guests have asked for the recipes that she has printed them up in a booklet). Another highlight is taking time out to relax in the Conservatory, a greenhouse garden centerpieced by a weeping cherry tree. Each room is a conversation piece, with hand-painted stenciling, hooked rugs, and truly unique antiques. It's no wonder the inn is so well kept—in addition to Diane Johnson, there are three others: Al Johnson and Cindy and John Vessella. On top of all that, the Nauset House Inn is just half a mile from the beach.

Orleans Holiday Motel

Mass. 6A (P.O. Box 386), Orleans, MA 02653. ☎ **508/255-1514** or 800/451-1833. 46 rms. A/C MINIBAR TV TEL. Summer (through Labor Day) $87–105 double. The rest of the year, rates vary; call for details. All rates include continental breakfast. AE, DC, DISC, MC, V.

The Orleans Holiday, just past the intersection of Mass. 6A and Mass. 28 as you head northeast, has contemporary newly redecorated motel rooms, all with tile bath and shower, picture windows, and a balcony-walkway. There's a fine large pool surrounded by lounge chairs and equipped with a backyard garden and picnic area with a gas barbecue. Several rooms in the unit behind Heathers (open for breakfast, lunch, and dinner) are larger than normal, newer, and a bit more luxurious.

The Parsonage Inn

202 Main St. (P.O. Box 1501), East Orleans, MA 02643. ☎ **508/255-8217.** 8 rms. June–Sept $75–$100 double; Oct–Nov $70–$90 double; Apr–May $65–$85 double; Dec–Mar $65–$75 double. Additional person $10 extra. All rates include breakfast. AE, MC, V. Directions: From Boston take Rte. 3 South. From central Massachusetts take Rte. 495 South. Cross Cape Cod Canal and take Rte. 6 to Exit 12. Bear right onto Rte. 6A, make the first right onto Eldredge Park Way. At the second set of lights turn right onto Main Street. The Parsonage is 1 mile on the left.

Once an 18th-century parsonage, this lovely inn is an authentic full-Cape house (with some additions). Conveniently located just one and a half miles from the beach, The Parsonage Inn is the creation of innkeepers, Ian and Elizabeth Browne. Guest rooms are furnished with country antiques and are individually decorated.

All rooms (except one) have queen-size beds, and two have an additional twin bed. The Barn Room also has a sofa bed, sitting area, TV and refrigerator, and the Willow Room is a studio apartment with a kitchenette, TV, and a private entrance. A hearty breakfast is served on the patio outside, in the sunny dining room, or in your room. In winter months you can relax in front of a blazing fire in the parlor.

Ship's Knees Inn

186 Beach Rd. (P.O. Box 756), East Orleans, MA 02643. ☎ **508/255-1312.** Fax 508/ 240-1351. 22 rms (11 with bath), 1 efficiency, 2 cottages. May–Oct, $55–$80 double without bath; $85–$100 double with bath; $650–$775 per week efficiency or cottage. Off-season rates lower. All rates include continental breakfast. MC, V. Directions: Take Exit 12 off U.S. 6; at the bottom of the ramp, turn right onto Eldredge Parkway and go one mile to the second set of traffic lights at Main Street; turn right and go 1 1/2 miles and bear left at the fork in the road onto Beach Road; the inn is one mile ahead.

Propped up on a sunny knoll a five-minute walk from Nauset Beach, the Ship's Knees is a restored 170-year-old sea captain's house. The name "Ship's Knees" comes from the fact that when the house was built, it was held together by ship's knees—the blocks of wood that connect deck beams to ship frames. The inn's rooms are done in a colonial decor, some with water views, and with either private or shared bath; the nearby Cove House has more rooms, each with private bath, cable color TV, and water view. Two rental cottages and one efficiency are right at the water's edge, with private bath and cable color TV. A tennis court and swimming pool are on the grounds.

WHERE TO DINE

The Arbor & Binnacle Tavern

Mass. 28. ☎ **508/255-4847** for the Arbor, 255-7901 for the Binnacle Tavern. Reservations required for the Arbor only. Main courses $12–$20. AE, MC, V. May–Oct, daily 5–10pm. Nov–Apr, Fri–Sun 5–10pm. ECLECTIC.

Serving creative cuisine in more eclectic surroundings, the Arbor combines just the right ingredients to make a person relax. Perhaps it's the yellow toy truck and the antique tins, or maybe it's the sincere service. At any rate, for starters you'll get an extensive assortment of vegetables, dips, and crackers, followed by home-made biscuits. Proceed to a main course of veal, beef, fowl, or fish. The Cajun swordfish is good, and the grilled duckling served on a bed of rice with a raspberry-peach sauce is terrific. If you dine before 6:25pm and pay cash, your dinner will cost 20% less. In the adjacent Binnacle Tavern, the fare is less formal and more family-oriented, and includes rich and elaborate pizzas and homemade pastas. The Binnacle Tavern stays open until 11:30pm.

Joseph's Lighthouse Restaurant

Mass. 6A ☎ **508/420-1742.** Reservations recommended. Main courses $9.95–$20. CB, DC, MC, V. Sun–Thurs 4–10pm, Fri–Sat 4–11pm; brunch Sun 9am–1pm. SEAFOOD/ NEW AMERICAN.

One of Orleans's newer restaurants, Joseph's offers a wide selection of healthy and innovative dishes. Consider the seafood fettuccine (with shrimp, scallops, clams, and lobster, served in a basil cream); the chicken and shrimp stir-fry is also excellent. You'll not be sorry no matter what you try. There's a brunch buffet on Sunday.

Kadee's Lobster & Clam Bar

212 Main St., East Orleans. ☎ **508/255-6184.** Reservations not accepted. Main courses $10–$22. MC, V. Daily 11:30am–9pm. Directions: Follow Beach Road east toward East Orleans; Kadee's will be on the left. SEAFOOD.

Kadee's Lobster & Clam Bar is a gem of a restaurant. The seafood here is fresh (and wonderfully affordable). Favorites include the Kadee's Clambake (a 1¼-pound lobster served with steamers and corn on the cob), charcoal-grilled swordfish, and a selection of fruity drinks (try the cranberry bog or the apricot sunset). You can sit outside in the sun or under a shady umbrella, or step inside to one of the cheery dining areas hung with fish nets and buoys. Kadee's also has a take-out window (where you can get everything from chowder to boiled lobster) and a gift shop full of T-shirts, visors, and other items emblazoned with the restaurant's logo.

Lobster Claw

Mass. 6A. ☎ **508/255-1800.** Reservations not accepted. Main courses $9–$15; lobsters $17–$25; daily specials $12. AE, MC, V. Apr–Nov, daily 11:30am–9pm. SEAFOOD.

If you're itching to have the experience of rolling up your sleeves, wearing a bib, and feasting on lobster, the Lobster Claw is the place to do it. Though unquestionably geared for tourists and downright kitschy, this place is a lot of fun. The atmosphere is family-friendly with buoys, fish nets, and lobster traps, with marine murals providing the backdrop. The menus, in the shape of lobster claws, list fish and seafood plates, lobsters, and daily specials, such as soft-shell crabs with french fries and coleslaw. The lobster rolls here are the fattest and tastiest you'll find in the area.

EASTHAM
WHAT TO SEE & DO

Eastham's main attraction is the **Salt Pond Visitor Center** of the Cape Cod National Seashore (see below). Right across the street from the center is the quaint and attractive **Eastham Historical Society Museum.** Look for the curious gateway, made from the jawbones of a huge whale. The museum, once a schoolhouse, dates from 1869.

Just south of the Salt Pond Visitor Center on U.S. 6 is the **oldest windmill** on Cape Cod (1793), a favorite place to stop and take a photo. From the windmill, take a side trip west to **First Encounter Beach,** where the Pilgrims first met the Native American inhabitants of the Cape back in 1620. A plaque on a boulder up the hill just north of the parking lot commemorates the meeting, which apparently was anything but cordial. You can visit the boulder plaque for free, but if you want to park and use the beach during the summer, you'll have to pay the town's beach-use parking fee.

WHERE TO STAY

Whalewalk Inn

220 Bridge Rd., Eastham, MA 02642. ☎ **508/255-0617.** 7 rms, 1 studio, 4 suites. $95–$145 double; $160–$175 suite. All rates include full gourmet breakfast. MC, V. Closed Dec–Mar. Directions: At the Orleans rotary, go about three-quarters around if you're headed east on U.S. 6 (there's a sign for the courthouse), get off and take a quick left, then turn right on Bridge Road; the inn is on the right about 100 yards ahead.

The Whalewalk is the kind of place you bring someone very special: The rooms will seduce you, the atmosphere will let you unwind, and the breakfasts will make it hard to push away from the dining table. The inn with its Georgian architecture dates back 150 years, when it was owned by a whaling master. The gravel driveway adds to the lovely look of the grounds. The main inn has six rooms, including one with a private entry off the patio. In the adjoining barn are upper and lower suites with living rooms and kitchens; one has a deck overlooking the grounds. There are also three other designer units in two separate buildings, one a saltbox and the other a guesthouse. The saltbox cottage is a delightful studio arrangement with a fireplace, while the guesthouse has two suites, both charming, each with bleached hardwood floors and a fireplace. One has a queen-size bed; the other has both a queen-sized bed and a twin-bedded loft. Children over 12 are welcome. This is one of the best inns in Massachusetts, and possibly all New England.

11 Cape Cod National Seashore

Established by President Kennedy in 1961 to protect the area from commercialization, the Cape Cod National Seashore encompasses nearly 44,000 acres. It protects much of the Cape's "forearm," including some of its most beautiful ocean beaches. In addition to the beaches (six are run by the federal government and have lifeguard services and related facilities, and several towns also have public beaches), there are picnic areas, bicycle trails, bridle paths, and self-guided nature trails. Visitors may surf and windsurf outside lifeguarded beaches and surf-fish from many of the beaches away from swimmers. Within the national seashore area, which stretches 40 miles from the southern tip of Nauset Beach all the way to Provincetown, there are four developed areas for visitors. (Keep in mind that there's a parking fee at all the beaches.)

ESSENTIALS The national seashore includes virtually all of the eastern shore of Cape Cod, from Chatham to Provincetown. For information, send a stamped, self-addressed, business-size envelope to: Superintendent, Cape Cod National Seashore, South Wellfleet, MA 02663, or call ☎ **508/349-3785.** Once in the area, you'll find two extremely efficient visitor centers: the **Salt Pond Visitor Center,** on U.S. 6 in Eastham (☎ **508/255-3421**), and **Province Lands Visitor Center,** on Race Point Road in Provincetown (☎ **508/487-1256**). Each contains exhibits, an audiovisual presentation, maps, pamphlets, and information services. There are several activities that take place throughout the spring, summer, and fall, including guided walks, talks, and evening programs. The centers are open from spring until early winter, daily from 9am to 5pm.

NAUSET AREA If you're driving out on the Cape, this is the first part of the national seashore you'll reach. Stop at the **Salt Pond Visitor Center** on U.S. 6A in Eastham. Here, you can pick up maps and pamphlets and get an overall orientation to the seashore. Inquire about the summer evening programs.

There are two beaches in the Nauset Area, including **Nauset Light Beach** (at the end of Cable Road in Eastham), which is one of the Outer Cape's most attractive. The other beach is **Coast Guard Beach,** which has taken somewhat of a beating from winter storms. Parking is restricted at the latter, but a free shuttle bus is provided from a parking lot near Nauset Light Beach. The bus runs from late June to early September.

In addition to the beaches, there are several nature trails, including the mile-long **Nauset Marsh Trail,** which takes you around Salt Pond and Nauset Marsh, and **Buttonbush Trail,** a quarter-mile-long trail that's part boardwalk. Both originate at the visitor center. The **Nauset Bike Trail** (1¹/₂ miles) winds its way from the visitor center to Coast Guard Beach.

MARCONI STATION AREA   Here's where you'll find the seashore's head-quarters (in South Wellfleet). There's also an interpretive shelter at the site of Marconi's wireless station, the first in the United States. Marconi Beach is a lovely stretch of sand located behind the National Seashore headquarters. There are two self-guided nature trails to follow, including the Atlantic White Cedar Swamp Trail (1¹/₄ miles long) and the Great Island Trail, a 4-mile-long (one-way!) trail that takes you through some of the seashore's most densely scenic shoreline.

PILGRIM HEIGHTS AREA   This area between North Truro and Province-town on the Outer Cape has an interpretive shelter dealing with the Pilgrims and Native Americans, a picnic area, several nature trails, a bike trail, the **Head of the Meadow Beach** (follow Head of the Meadow Road in Truro to the end), and the picturesque **Highland Light** (also known as the Cape Cod Light). Make a point of seeing the lighthouse: It was the very first one in Cape Cod, built in 1797 to warn sailors of the notorious stretch known as "the graveyard of ships." It was rebuilt in 1857 and converted to electric power in 1932.

Nature trails in the Pilgrim Heights area include the **Cranberry Bog Trail,** a half-mile-long path that's part boardwalk; **Small Swamp Trail** (three-quarters of a mile); and **Pilgrim Spring Trail** (three-quarters of a mile), which leads to the site of a spring where Pilgrims may have drunk their first water in the New World. The **Head of the Meadow Bike Trail** spans a two-mile distance from the bay side to the ocean side of the Cape.

PROVINCE LANDS AREA   A **visitors center** outside Provincetown on Race Point Road provides information and exhibits on the seashore. There are audio-visual programs, an amphitheater, and evening programs in summer months. There are two excellent beaches in the area. **Race Point** (at the end of Race Point Road in Provincetown) is a spectacularly scenic beach backed by dunes that look like whipped egg white. **Herring Cove** (on Province Lands Road in Provincetown) is a bayside beach and *the* place to go to watch the sunset.

Throughout the Province Lands Area is a network of bicycle paths that take you over dunes, through pine groves, and alongside the sea. These include the **Loop Trail** (5¹/₄ miles), **Herring Cove Beach** spur (1 mile), **Race Point Beach** spur (half a mile), **Bennett Pond** spur (a quarter mile), and **Race Point Road** spur (a quarter mile).

Beech Forest Trail is a one-mile-long self-guided nature trail that takes you through a consistently scenic part of the Province Lands scenery. There's also a picnic area.

12   Wellfleet

10 miles N of Eastham, 12¹/₂ miles SE of Provincetown

Cooking lobsters and corn on the cob at a beach picnic, meeting friends down-town at the lunch counter for a mid-morning's lazy second cup of coffee, running errands barefoot or in rubber thongs—if you've enjoyed that sort of an easy summer atmosphere, Wellfleet will bring it back to you. Although a number of motels on U.S. 6 take in travelers heading for Provincetown, Wellfleet is mostly a town of "steadies," people who come every summer for the whole summer. But it does have a few inns and restaurants worth a look should you decide to stop here.

GETTING THERE   See "Getting There" under "Seeing Cape Cod," at the beginning of this chapter.

ESSENTIALS   The **telephone area code** is **508.** The **Wellfleet Chamber of Commerce,** P.O. Box 571, Wellfleet, MA 02667 (☎ **508/349-2510**), operates an information booth just off U.S. 6 on the way into town. It's open from late June through Labor Day, daily from 10am to 6pm; Memorial to mid-June and Labor Day to Columbus Day, Friday through Sunday from 10am to 4pm.

WHAT TO SEE & DO

As most of Wellfleet's crowd is permanent for the summer, not as many things are available for the transient visitor. Note the **town clock** in the steeple of the First Congregational Church, which is supposedly the only church clock in the world that rings ship's time.

Most **beaches** are reserved for permanent or all-summer residents (you need two different permits to swim there, and if you're passing through it's not worth getting them), but White Crest Beach and Cahoon's Hollow Beach, off U.S. 6 on the Atlantic coast, are open to day visitors for $12. And you can always go south on U.S. 6 a short distance from Wellfleet and turn left (east) to the **Marconi Beach** in the national seashore. At the beach is an ocean overlook and an interpretive shelter explaining the activities of the **Marconi Wireless Station,** the first in the United States, which was on this site. The Atlantic White Cedar Swamp nature trail starts from here as well.

The Massachusetts Audubon Society operates the **Wellfleet Bay Wildlife Sanctuary,** P.O. Box 236, South Wellfleet, MA 02663 (☎ **508/349-2615**), 1,000 acres of woods, salt marshes, moors, freshwater pond, and sandy beach. A year-round program of hikes, birding trips, canoe expeditions, boat cruises, workshops, and speakers is offered. There are also birding tours to **Monomoy National Wildlife Refuge.** In July and August there's a natural-history daycamp for children; July through September there are field schools for adults. Trails are open year-round, from 8am to dusk. Sanctuary admission is $3 for adults and $2 for children.

A REFUELING STOP IN TRURO   If you want to head straight to the beach, but you're starving from the long drive and don't want to deal with traffic in P-town, turn off Mass. 6A into downtown Truro for a quick stop. **Jams, Inc.** (☎ **508/349-1616**), in addition to carrying standard grocery items, stocks an impressive assortment of pâtés, spreads, meats, cheeses, breads, imported crackers, and the like (even an authentic baklava). They also have a cappuccino bar where you can get a lattè, iced cappuccino, or some other delectable drink to go. If you need a beach umbrella, a picnic basket, or a pair of flip-flops, you'll find them all here as well. It's open long hours from Memorial Day through Labor Day.

WHERE TO STAY

Holden Inn

P.O. Box 816, Wellfleet, MA 02667. ☎ **508/349-3450.** 28 rms (16 with bath). $60 double without bath, $70 double with bath. No credit cards. Closed Oct–Apr. Directions: From U.S. 6, take a left at the WELLFLEET CENTER sign and another left at the sign to the pier; the inn is on the right.

Not far from the center of Wellfleet, the Holden Inn consists of three buildings of very nicely kept rooms, all different, some with water views, and with double or twin beds. One room, for instance, is paneled all in cedar and is quite handsome. No meals are served, and rates vary with the plumbing. Several of the rooms are furnished with antique pieces. No children under 14 or pets allowed.

WHERE TO DINE

✪ Aesop's Tables

Main St. ☎ **508/349-6450.** Reservations recommended. Main courses $15.75–$22.75. AE, DC, MC, V. Mid-May through Aug Wed–Sun noon–3pm, daily 5:30–9:30pm, Sept to mid-Oct Wed–Sun noon–3pm, Wed–Sun 5:30–9:30pm. Hours may vary, call ahead to confirm. NEW AMERICAN.

For fine New American cuisine, Aesop's Tables is the place to go. Once the summer mansion of a Massachusetts governor, it now has six welcoming dining rooms, all busy on any summer night, so call for reservations. You might start dinner with the tri-color terrine, a nice combination of grilled vegetables, goat cheese, and pesto; or The Curious Oysters, Wellfleet oysters on the half shell with a mignonette sauce. Then go on to the chicken Mexicano (half a roasted chicken in a mole sauce of mild chiles, toasted pumpkin seeds, cilantro, and cinnamon) or the salmon baked in parchment (served with a julienne of ginger, green onions, carrots, and cilantro sauced with toasted sesame and soy). There's always lobster and the day's freshest fish, as well as a vegetarian dish at dinner. A tavern menu, which features many of the same dishes on the dinner menu along with a selection of barbecued items, is available throughout the day. Finish with Aesop's trademarked Death by Chocolate dessert (Belgian chocolate mousse in a deep brownie crust topped with whipped cream) and watch your diet pass away happily. The second-floor lounge is an enjoyable place for a pre- or postprandial drink (you can take dinner, the tavern menu, or dessert here, too). Dining rooms on the first floor are smoke-free, but smoking is permitted in the upstairs bar or outside on the terrace. Live music is featured Thursday nights (usually) from 9pm to midnight in the upstairs bar.

Bayside Lobster Hutt

Commercial St. ☎ **508/349-6333.** Reservations not accepted. Main courses $8–$20. No credit cards. Memorial Day–June and Sept, dinner only, daily. July–Aug, daily noon–3pm; 4:30–9pm. Directions: From U.S. 6, take the road to Wellfleet Harbor and look for the giant lobster on an old oyster shack. SEAFOOD.

You can't miss the Bayside Lobster Hutt; on the roof of this big white building is a lobster dory complete with a statue of a lobsterman, a net, and an enormous lobster. Wellfleet regulars and visitors come into this old oyster shack for a summer picnic-style self-service dinner consisting of live boiled lobster—you pick 'em from the tanks—corn on the cob, steamed clams, and the like. A 1½-pound lobster, easily a plentiful meal for one person, comes with corn on the cob; or have a huge plate of fried clams. Informal, fun, and good food, the Lobster Hutt is on the way to the town dock. Bring your own wine or beer.

Captain Higgins' Seafood Restaurant

Commercial St. ☎ **508/349-6027.** Reservations recommended. Main courses $6.95–$12.95 at lunch, $10.95–$20.95 at dinner. MC, V. Mid-June to Sept, daily noon–9:30pm. SEAFOOD.

Down by the town dock is Captain Higgins', overlooking the marina. You can dine inside or outside on the large deck. Start your meal with the Wellfleet oysters on the half shell or the fried spiced calamari. Among the entree offerings are seafood lasagne and grilled seafood specialties, like scallops DeJonge (baked in white wine, butter, and garlic, topped with breadcrumbs) and grilled shrimp brochette served with a tomato mayonnaise. There is a children's menu available.

13　Provincetown

62 miles NE of Sandwich, 50 miles NE of Hyannis

Provincetown is separated from the rest of the Cape by sand, forest, and marsh, and thus it has something of an island ambience, a feeling accentuated by the town's compact size. Out of season, the inhabitants are mostly fishers, descendants of hardy Portuguese sailors who came here for the whaling trade a century ago. In season, Provincetown is a carnival constantly alive with all sorts of people from all around: New York, Boston, Montréal, Québec, and also Podunk. Artists and writers, the successful and the hopeful, college sophomores and sophisticates, dowagers and down-at-heelers all mix and mingle in the evening along P-town's narrow streets. The town is at the same time quaint and sophisticated, elegant and tawdry, depending on where you look and how you look at it.

Of all things, the most important when planning a visit to P-town in late July and August is to *have a room reservation without fail.* It's just not possible to find a room in Provincetown for the six weeks of hectic high season unless you reserve ahead. If you have no reservation, it's best to plan to stay in Orleans or Wellfleet, or along U.S. 6 some distance from P-town, and to drive up for the day.

Like San Francisco and Key West, Provincetown hosts a large **gay community** on vacation during the summer. The great majority of establishments—hotels, inns, guesthouses, restaurants, cafés, bars, and nightclubs—welcome all customers regardless of sexual orientation, regardless of whether the proprietor is gay or straight.

GETTING THERE　By Plane　Cape Air has daily service year-round between Provincetown Airport and Boston's Logan Airport. Call ☎ **508/771-6944** for more information and reservations.

By Car　U.S. 6 is a divided highway all the way to P-town, where it ends and brings you face to face with a parking problem. Don't try to park in the center of town. Get a space in one of the municipal lots (follow the signs) if you can.

By Train　See "Getting There" under "Seeing Cape Cod," at the beginning of this chapter.

By Bus　In summer, **Bonanza Bus Lines** (☎ 800/556-3815) has regularly scheduled service between New York's Port Authority terminal and Hyannis. From Hyannis, it's necessary to transfer to a **Plymouth & Brockton** bus (☎ 508/775-5524) to reach Provincetown. The complete trip takes about 8 hours from Manhattan, $3^{1}/_{2}$ hours from Providence.

Bonanza also runs buses from Albany and Springfield, Mass., to Hyannis, where you connect for P-town. Plymouth & Brockton runs four buses daily in summer from Boston to Provincetown. Connections are arranged for buses coming from Montréal via Boston to the Cape (two buses daily in summer, with additional services on weekends). Note that the bus will drop you off near or right at your hotel, if it's out of the center of town, if you ask the driver to do so. This is a normal service, so feel free to ask.

Provincetown

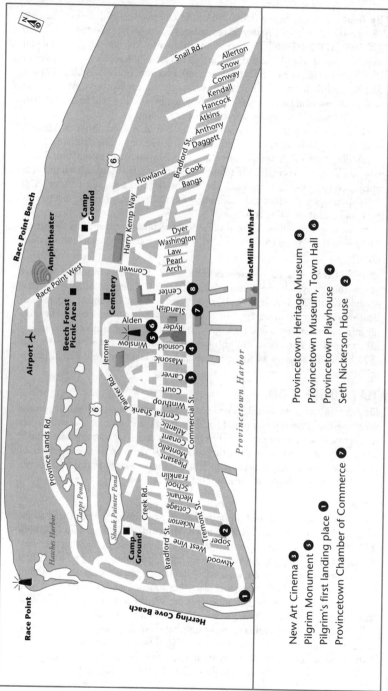

New Art Cinema ❸
Pilgrim Monument ❺
Pilgrim's first landing place ❶
Provincetown Chamber of Commerce ❼

Provincetown Heritage Museum ❽
Provincetown Museum, Town Hall ❻
Provincetown Playhouse ❹
Seth Nickerson House ❷

1787

By Boat   You can take a delightful cruise to Provincetown aboard the MV *Provincetown II,* operated by **Bay State Cruises,** 66 Long Wharf, Boston, MA 02110 (☎ 508/617/723-7800). The three-hour cruise costs $16 one-way, or $29 if you make the round-trip all in one day. The ship leaves from Boston's Commonwealth Pier: Take the subway's Blue Line to Aquarium Station, or the Red Line to South Station, and then cross the Fort Point Channel. Ask for Northern Avenue, and walk southeast along it for a few blocks; Commonwealth Pier will be on your left. The walk from either subway stop takes about 15 minutes.

Here's the schedule: Leave Commonwealth Pier at 9:30am, arrive at P-town's MacMillan Wharf, right in the middle of town, at 12:30pm. The return trip leaves MacMillan Wharf at 3:30pm to arrive at Commonwealth Pier by 6:30pm. Breakfast, lunch, snacks, cocktails, and refreshments are on sale aboard; a band provides music, and the captain describes the landmarks and sights in passing. The 1,100-passenger, 195-foot *Provincetown II* has three decks providing open, covered, and enclosed seating areas.

By the way, MacMillan Wharf is where intercity buses begin and end their runs, and where the Provincetown Chamber of Commerce operates its information office.

ESSENTIALS   The **telephone area code** is **508.** The **Provincetown Chamber of Commerce** operates an information office at 307 Commercial St. near MacMillan Wharf (☎ 508/487-3424), open April through December. Boats from Boston arrive at this wharf, and behind the chamber office is also the stop for intercity buses from New York, Providence, and Boston. Bus and boat schedules are posted here. You can also get information on the new shuttle bus (50¢ for senior citizens, $1 for everyone else) that takes you to different points in P-town.

WHAT TO SEE & DO

Provincetown is an interesting small town to browse around. Although people-watching could keep you amused for days, below are some of P-town's other highlights. *Provincetown* magazine hits the streets every Thursday; it's free and it has plenty of suggestions for things to do. Or drop in at the chamber of commerce's information office and pick up the Provincetown Historical Society's pamphlet which tells you all the historical sights in town.

SIGHTS

For the best view of the town in both physical and historical terms, head to the **Pilgrim Monument** and **Provincetown Museum,** High Pole Hill (☎ 800/247-1620). The museum is an interesting potpourri of old firefighting gear, costumes, a whaling-ship captain's quarters on board, primitive portraits, World War I mementos, arctic lore, and a sequence of displays on the activities of the Pilgrims in Provincetown, for this is the first place they touched land in the New World. After seeing these, you can continue with the Wedgwood, the model of a Thai temple, antique dolls, and other arcana. Then head for the tower.

The Pilgrim Monument is copied from the Torre del Mangia in Siena, Italy, and is all granite and a little over 252$^1/_2$ feet high. The cornerstone was laid in 1907 with President Teddy Roosevelt in attendance, and the structure was completed three years later, when President William Taft did the dedicating. You may think that there's an elevator in it. Well, there's not, and you'll have to *climb* to the top—the equivalent of going up the steps in a 20-story building—to see the view. Most of the climb is on a ramp, not steps, and you can take your time and read the commemorative plaques from New England cities, towns, and civic groups which line the granite walls. The view is worth the climb: 45 miles of Provincetown and all Cape Cod spread out like the maps you've been following.

The manicured grounds and picnic area provide a respite from the downtown bustle, and from the hilltop you can see all of Provincetown. The monument is also the focal point for the town's annual "Lighting of the Monument," when the tower is decorated with over 5,000 lights every Thanksgiving Eve.

Admission costs $5 for adults and $3 for children 4 to 12; children under 4 free. It's open from mid-April to October, from 9am to 5pm; off-season hours vary, so call ahead. *Note:* Tower climbing stops 45 minutes before closing.

Check out the **Pilgrims' first landing place,** the monument commemorating the signing of the Mayflower Compact (America's first democratic "constitution"), and the 12-room **Seth Nickerson House,** the oldest dwelling in town (1746), at 72 Commercial St.

The **Provincetown Heritage Museum**—actually the municipal museum—at Commercial and Center Streets (☎ **508/487-7098**), preserves the town's heritage in its wide-ranging displays. Relics of the fishing industry, Victoriana, and many other items capture Provincetown's history. Especially exciting for children are the antique fire engine and the *Rose Dorothea,* the world's largest half-scale fishing schooner model. Admission is $3 for adults, free for children under 12. The museum is open from mid-June to September, daily from 10am to 6pm.

GALLERIES, CINEMAS & THEATER

The latest schedules for galleries, cinemas, and theater are published in the local newspaper, the *Provincetown Advocate.* Galleries dot the downtown streets (especially on the east end of town), often open until late in the evening. The **Provincetown Playhouse** (☎ **508/487-0955**) is active all summer; call for current information. The **New Art Cinemas,** across from the post office downtown at 212 Commercial St. (☎ **508/487-9222**), plays both foreign and domestic first-run films.

WHALE-WATCHING CRUISES

It's a great thrill when you see one of the monster denizens break the surface, spout, sport, and play. You can sight whales from the Coast Guard Station on Race Point Beach, and even with the naked eye you can see them spouting and rolling. But to see them up close is something else, and for that you need to sign up for a whale-watching cruise. Several boats leave on morning and afternoon runs, and give you several hours in which to find and watch the whales. Call the **Dolphin Fleet** (☎ **800/826-9300**), which by the way has a 99.7% sighting record; **Portuguese Princess Excursions** (☎ **508/487-2651,** or **800/442-3188**); or the *Ranger V* (☎ **508/487-1582,** or **800/992-9333**) for times, prices, and reservations. Boats leave from MacMillan Wharf and charge around $20 for adults; children are charged several dollars less, and some companies offer a family rate. By the way, the whales—which seem to perform expressly for the appreciative crowds on the boats—enjoy the trip as much as you do.

OTHER ACTIVITIES

Bicycling in the Provincetown area is perhaps the best way to get around—especially in mid-summer in town, when traffic can be dense. In addition to exploring the town's warren of narrow streets, you'll find a wonderful webwork of paved trails that take you through the dunes of the national seashore. Even these can get congested, however, so take care in riding. Avoid speeding, keep to the right, and be careful not to brake abruptly when you hit sand. In town, it's necessary to be 100% alert at all times—there are lots of pedestrians, roller skaters, cars, and other bicyclists moving about. **Arnold's Bicycle Shop,** 329 Commercial St. (☎ **508/487-0844**), rents bikes by the hour, the day, and the week. It also provides free maps of the national seashore trails.

If you want to try something new and exciting, consider taking a **beach buggy tour** through the national seashore area. **Art's Dune Tours** (☎ **508/487-1950**) runs trips throughout the day, from 9am to sunset. The trip starts at the head of Town Wharf in a comfortable "Dunes Mobile," and wends its way through the streets to the dunes. In addition to the astonishingly beautiful dune scenery, it takes in several highlights of the area, including the stretch of coast called the "Graveyard of the Atlantic" and Pilgrim Lake. The $1^1/4$-hour narrated tour costs $10 for adults and $7 for children under 12.

You can also take an **aerial tour** of the seashore. **Cape Air** offers both helicopter and small plane sightseeing flights. Call **508/771-6944** for rates and reservations.

Another way to enjoy the area is to take a sail on a **schooner.** The 73-foot-long *Bay Lady II* has four two-hour sailings every day in the summer months, including a sunset cruise. You'll find the *Bay Lady II* berthed at the end of MacMillan Pier in the heart of town. Tickets vary according to which sailing you take, but range from $10 to $13 for adults and $5 for children under 12. Reservations are recommended; contact Capt. Bob Burns, c/o Schooner *Bay Lady II,* MacMillan Wharf, Provincetown, MA 02657 (☎ **508/487-9308**). Those who want more action on their cruise can go out with one of the two daily deep-sea fishing voyages that leave from MacMillan Wharf; whale-watching boats also leave from here, especially from mid-April to mid-June.

Should you want to do nothing more active than sit, you can have a local artist do **your portrait** in pastels while you're sitting. Shops are along Commercial Street and inside Whalers' Wharf near the town wharf (MacMillan Wharf), and prices start at $70 for a front view, $40 for the side, $40 and $20 if it's to be charcoal; frames and glass are extra and cost $35 and up. The portrait can be done, framed, and wrapped to take home in a surprisingly short time.

You can also sit back and see the sights of Provincetown by taking a narrated sightseeing tour aboard the **Provincetown Trolley** (☎ **508/487-9483**). Tours leave from the town hall on Commercial Street every half hour from May through October from 10am to 4pm and also at 5, 6, 7, and 8pm. The 40-minute trip costs $7 for adults, $6 for senior citizens, and $5 for children under 13.

But biking, schooner sails, deep-sea fishing, and portrait sitting can't equal the sense of freedom you get if you sail your own boat out onto Cape Cod Bay. You don't have to own a boat, of course, because Provincetown has **Flyer's Boat Rental,** 131A Commercial St. (☎ **508/487-0898**), behind Gallerani's Restaurant. Little Sunfish, larger (18- to 20-foot) sailboats, dinghies with outboard motors, and large horsepower speedboats are all for rent. Flyer's will even teach you how to sail if you don't already know. It's open May 15 to October 15, daily from 8am to 6pm.

WHERE TO STAY

Provincetown's streets are lined with guesthouses, inns, and motels, and in the six weeks from mid-July to Labor Day every room in every one will be rented. Outside of that time you have a chance of finding a room by arriving in town by late morning or early afternoon.

A special note is in order concerning credit and charge cards. Demand for services is so great here that very many hotels and restaurants don't accept credit or charge cards. Also, most lodging places require some minimum stay during the peak-season period, usually from three or four days (at least, on weekends) to a full week. And you won't be able to fudge it: You'll probably have to pay the full amount for your stay when you check in.

When you set out to hunt for accommodations or to find your reserved room, remember that P-town is about three miles long from one end of Commercial Street (the main street) to the other.

WEST END GUESTHOUSES & INNS

The West End—west of MacMillan Wharf, that is—has the richest concentration of inns and guesthouses.

Captain and His Ship

164 Commercial St., Provincetown, MA 02657. ☎ **508/487-1850.** 8 rms (6 with bath). A/C TV. Summer, $70 single or double without bath, $105–135 double with bath. Apr to mid-June and mid-Sept to Oct, from $50 double. Minimum stay, four nights on Memorial Day weekend; five nights for visits that include a Fri or Sat night, seven nights for July 4. All rates include continental breakfast. MC, V. Parking $10 per day (two blocks from the inn). Closed Nov–Mar.

The Captain and His Ship sounds like the title of a Cape Cod novel, but in fact it's a handsome guesthouse located just far enough from the heart of town to keep the noise level low. Provincetown's shipboard tidiness characterizes the house. Its small front lawn is complete with bench. Each room is different, furnished with Victoriana, and each has a different price: The more expensive ones are those with water views. All rooms have refrigerators and clock radios; most also have VCRs.

Captain Lysander Inn

96 Commercial St., Provincetown, MA 02657. ☎ **508/487-2253.** Fax 508/487-7579. 13 rms (7 with bath), 1 apartment, 1 carriage house. High season, $75 room without bath, $85 room with bath. Off-season, room rates $10–$20 less. Additional person $15 extra. Minimum stay four nights over holidays, three nights on weekends. All rates include continental breakfast. MC, V.

The ancestral home of Dr. Vannevar Bush, this inn was built by Capt. Lysander Paine in 1852. The rooms feature a blend of antique and traditional furnishings. Enjoy breakfast in the front parlor or outside on the spacious front deck or sun porch.

1807 House

54 Commercial St., Provincetown, MA 02657. ☎ **508/487-2173.** E-mail PTOWN1807@AOL.COM. 8 rms (5 with bath). Summer, $68–$108 double. Off-season, $58–$75 double. Additional person $10 extra. Three-day minimum stay required on Memorial Day, July 4, and Labor Day weekends. AE, MC, V.

Bright, cheerful, comfortable, and well equipped—that describes this Provincetown west end inn. The original 1807 cedar-shingled main house faces the beach and the bay; the addition joining it to the carriage house, and the separate secluded garden cottage, each contain studios and apartments with kitchens. All share the quiet location and grassy lawns. The owners will be happy to describe each room for you.

Masthead

31–41 Commercial St., Provincetown, MA 02657. ☎ **508/487-0523** or 800/395-5095. Fax 508/487-9251. 21 units. A/C TV TEL. July–Labor Day, $69–$239 double; $893–$1,550 per week, cottage, suite, or efficiency for two. Labor Day–June, rates are lower. AE, DC, DISC, MC, V.

The Masthead lists cottages, apartments, and motel rooms among its accommodations, but you must see the place to appreciate it. All these overnight possibilities are contained in a collection of cozy little cottages that look across flawless green lawn to a private boardwalk, a beach, and the water. Write for the descriptions of the 21 types of accommodations, from modern rooms through efficiency studios to cottages for up to seven people. All rooms have refrigerators and coffee makers. Valet laundry service is available, and beach towels are provided daily. If you can't find the sort of room you want at the Masthead, you're probably looking for a tent.

EAST END GUESTHOUSES & INNS

The eastern reaches of Provincetown, along Commercial Street, Bradford Street, and the small cross streets between them, hold dozens of small inns and a few guesthouses. Generally speaking, these are more expensive than the majority of West End places. The location is roughly the same in terms of convenience.

Anchor Inn

175 Commercial St., Provincetown, MA 02657. ☎ **508/487-0432.** 24 rms. TV. $95–$135 double. Off-season discounts available. AE, MC, V.

The Anchor Inn is a gracious, expansive, turn-of-the-century house, and as with most inns and guesthouses in P-town, every room is decorated differently. Most have a deck, balcony, or porch, and several have sea views. The simple, bright, airy decor and furnishings make the rooms pleasantly inviting. The rooms are not air-conditioned (chances are you wouldn't need it anyway), but all have ceiling fans.

Asheton House

3 Cook St., Provincetown, MA 02657. ☎ **508/487-9966.** 2 rms (with shared bath), 1 suite. Summer, $86.40 double; $113.40 suite. Off-season, rates 20%–30% lower. No credit cards.

Absolutely every inch of Asheton House is attractive—from the double staircase that leads to the front door to the imaginatively decorated guest rooms. Guests can choose The Suite, which has a fireplace and a view of the harbor, The Captain's Room, with a grand four-poster bed, or The Safari Room, decorated with artifacts from Africa. Out back is a deck where you can sit among the Japanese Temple trees. Asheton House is half a mile from the center of town.

Bradford Gardens Inn

178 Bradford St., Provincetown, MA 02657. ☎ **508/487-1616** or 800/432-2334. 17 rms. TV. Summer, $138–$168 inn double; $750–$1,710 cottage double (by the week only). Rates are lower during rest of year. Additional person $20 extra. All rates include breakfast. AE, MC, V.

The Bradford Gardens is near the corner of Miller Hill Road and is certainly one of Provincetown's most charming and serene places to stay. Every room in the century-and-a-half-old inn is different, and each has a name rather than a number. Alternative arrangements include nine apartments, a Swiss chalet–type cottage, and a six- to eight-person lodge. Rates include a big breakfast and (for rooms with facilities to use it) firewood as well (the inn has 15 working fireplaces). And speaking of gardens, the Bradford has half an acre of rose beds and perennials set with cushioned wooden chairs and even a garden swing for your enjoyment.

White Horse Inn

500 Commercial St., Provincetown, MA 02657. ☎ **508/487-1790.** 12 rms (8 with bath), 6 apartments. June 15–Sept 15 and Memorial Day weekend, $60–$70 double without bath, $70 double with bath. The rest of the year, $40 double with bath; $110 ocean-view studio apartment ($700 per week with a 3-night minimum in season); $100 other apartments ($650 per week). Additional person $15 extra. No credit cards.

Located in the quiet East End of town, the White Horse is a lovely 150-year-old captain's house. Inside, lots of quaint old pieces picked up in the area are used as decoration to keep the period feeling, and every room contains original paintings. Studio apartments have kitchen facilities. The beach is right across the street (guests have beach rights), and the inn has backyard lawn chairs.

WHERE TO DINE

Wander around the streets of Provincetown and you'll smell garlic, fish, bread—you name it. Here you'll find a wonderful selection of restaurants, from Portuguese-owned bakeries to fine restaurants that have been featured in magazines such as *Gourmet* and *Bon Appétit.* Seafood, of course, is a big specialty. Keep in mind that during the summer months (and weekends off-season), it's imperative to have a reservation at most restaurants.

IN TOWN

Front Street

230 Commercial St. ☎ **508/487-9715.** Reservations recommended. Main courses $5.95–$24.95; dinner for two $60–$75. AE, MC, V. Apr–Dec, daily 6–11pm (bar remains open until 1am). Closed Tuesdays Apr to mid-May and mid-Sept to Dec. CREATIVE CONTINENTAL/ITALIAN.

In the very hub of Provincetown is Front Street, located in the lower level of a Victorian house. This chef-owned restaurant has a loyal clientele who, when asked, will recommend the smoked duck or the herb-crusted rack of lamb. Both dishes are offered regularly along with an excellent selection of seafood and continental dishes. The innovative menu changes every Friday, but recent offerings have included coconut shrimp with black-bean confit and salmon and roasted shallot croustade. Desserts like raspberry Chambord cheesecake and truffled chocolate-orange torte are worth waiting around for. In 1992 and 1993, Front Street won the Award of Excellence from *The Wine Spectator* for its extensive wine list, and in 1994 it won an award of excellence in the *Boston Magazine* Readers Poll.

Napi's

7 Freeman St. ☎ **508/487-1145.** Reservations recommended. Main courses $11.95–$21.95. AE, DC, DISC, MC, V. Daily 5pm–closing. Free limited parking available at 5 Freeman Street. INTERNATIONAL.

Located on the corner of Freeman and Bradford Streets near the center of town, Napi's is one of Provincetown's most interesting and eclectic restaurants. Inside, you'll find exposed-beam ceilings, stained-glass windows, and scores of live plants. Once you're seated in the dining room, take time to observe the displays of local artwork, including a "brick mural" by Conrad Malicoat, sculptures, cartoons, and some beautiful paintings. The wide variety of art reflects the equally varied menu at Napi's. You might start with Portuguese soup, hummus, or Chinese dumplings. Your main course might consist of a Brazilian steak, the Portuguese bouillabaisse, or, my personal favorite, the coconut curry. If you're a vegetarian, don't worry, Napi's offers several vegetarian dishes, including a tofu-and-vegetable stir-fry or a Syrian falafel melt. Save room for dessert!

Sal's Place

99 Commercial St. ☎ **508/487-1279.** Reservations recommended. Main courses $9–$18. MC, V. Summer, daily 6–10pm. Spring and fall, Fri–Sat 6–10pm. ITALIAN.

Want to have a good dinner at small, intimate candlelit spot with interesting and delicious food at moderate prices? The place to go is Sal's Place, where the food is Italian and all cooked to order. It has tiny wooden tables, chianti bottles hanging from the ceiling, and a small dining room both simple and romantic; there's also a newer, larger room on the water, and outdoor dining. Specialties are brodetto (served on Friday); Wellfleet mussels, scallops, clams, and fish in a wine broth; and *bistecca alla pizzaiola*, prime rib-eye steak with mushrooms and olives in a red-wine marinara sauce. Try one of the homemade desserts like chocolate mousse pie. On Tuesday several special veal dishes are featured. Sal's, which has been here since 1963, is past the Coast Guard station in the West End.

OUT OF TOWN, ON THE MOORS

Moors Restaurant

5 Bradford St. W. ☎ **508/487-0840.** Reservations required on weekends. Main courses $9–$19 at dinner; fixed-price dinner $14–$16. AE, DC, DISC, MC, V. Apr to mid-May, Fri–Sun 5:30–10pm. Mid-May to Oct, Wed–Mon noon–3pm; daily 5:30–10pm; brunch Sat–Sun from 10:30am. PORTUGUESE/SEAFOOD.

At Moors Restaurant, at the end of the Bradford Street at the junction with Mass. 6A, the dining rooms are positively fraught with nautical paraphernalia—on the walls, on the ceiling, adorning the bar. The cuisine is Provincetown seafood with Portuguese accents. At lunchtime you can eat for as little as $7 if you can be contented with a *linguica* roll (a mildly spicy Portuguese sausage in pastry) and a beer; or you can spend a few dollars more for sea-clam pie or broiled Cape scallops. The daily special dinner includes soup, salad, dessert, and coffee. Besides the standard fresh fish and lobster casserole, you might find *lagosta vieira a moda de peniche* (lobster and crabmeat in a casserole, made with wine, brandy, and tomato sauce). There's live entertainment most evenings in the Smuggler's Lounge.

SPECIALTY DINING
Outdoor Cafes

Café Blasé

328 Commercial St. ☎ **508/487-9465.** Reservations not accepted. Main courses $6.50–$11.95 at lunch, $9.50–$13.95 at dinner. AE, MC, V. Memorial Day–Sept, daily 9am–1am. INTERNATIONAL.

Located just east of the center of town, Café Blasé is a seaside outdoor cafe and a fine perch from which to watch the steady colorful parade of tourists and

Provincetown characters. The menu describes an equally varied menu of burgers, quiches, pasta, gourmet individual pizzas, salads, and sandwiches, plus a selection of dinner specials, the most expensive of which is the clambake. If you just want to sit and sip, you can take your pick of an astounding array of drinks, including beer, wine, tropical drinks, and several nonalcoholic specialties.

Euro Island Grill and Café

258 Commercial St. ☎ **508/487-2505.** Reservations recommended. Main courses $4.50– $17. AE, DC, MC, V. Early May to early Oct, daily 11:30am–1am. CAFE/ITALIAN/CARIBBEAN.

During the day, the al fresco Euro Island Grill and Café serves a good selection of cafe dishes. Come night, however, it turns into a full-blown dinner restaurant with Sicilian and Caribbean specialties (including conch chowder and conch fritters). Day and night, you can get the stone-hearth baked pizza, which is to die for. There's always a good selection of local seafood, plus homemade desserts, including a delectable key lime pie. The Euro Island Grill and Café is next to the town hall, upstairs.

Breakfasts

For not just fresh coffee in the morning, but also fresh bread and rolls, find the **Portuguese Bakery,** right down by MacMillan Wharf at 299 Commercial St.— follow the coffee and fresh-bread smells. Not only is breakfast the freshest here, it's the cheapest. Put it together yourself, take it out to the wharf to consume, and you can do it for $2.50 easily.

Another favorite breakfast spot is the **Café Edwige,** 333 Commercial St. (☎ **508/487-2008**), which has a strong emphasis on natural healthy foods, including a wide selection of vegetarian dishes.

Quick Meals

A real institution in P-town for a do-it-yourself lunch or quick dinner is the **Cheese Market,** 225 Commercial St. (☎ **508/487-3032**), which offers a multitude of different sandwiches, both hot and cold, and soups and salads from $3 to $7. The Cheese Market now serves espresso and cappuccino; it is open from 9am to 11pm daily from Memorial Day through October, and until 7pm the rest of the year.

EVENING ENTERTAINMENT

Throughout the summer months, the hub of Provincetown (along Commercial Street, the town hall being the center) always has a sparkly air of carnival. But nighttime is when it's at its most glittery. Start with a satiating seafood dinner in one of the many restaurants or a sunset picnic on the beach at Herring Cove and then do as everyone who goes to Provincetown does: Stroll along Commercial Street. Within the span of one or two blocks, you're likely to see more characters (and character) than some people see in a lifetime. Among them will be cabaret barkers, portrait artists, female impersonators, salty old fishermen with toothy grins, and spandex-clad roller skaters whizzing through the crowds at alarmingly high speeds.

Many of P-Town's shops remain open late into the evening—especially on weekends. Among them you'll find several selling very hip clothes, one that specializes in kites and wind socks, another devoted to cat things (cat mugs, cat bumper stickers, cat earrings), and a couple selling fudge and penny candy.

Most of P-town's galleries also stay open late (to 10 or 11pm). In many of them, you'll find excellent works by contemporary Provincetown and Lower Cape artists.

If you feel like resting your feet a bit, take time out to people-watch from Café Blasé, 328 Commercial St., a centrally located outdoor cafe. Later, dance till you drop at the **Surf Club,** 315A Commercial St. (☎ **508/487-1367**), to the lively tunes of the Provincetown Jug Band or another band that happens to be spotlighted.

If you're interested in hearing some great jazz, reggae, or perhaps gospel music, check who's performing at **Club Euro at Euro Café.** This nightclub is located in a 152-year-old Congregational church. Tickets are sold at the door. For schedules and tickets, call ☎ **508/487-2505.**

Many Provincetown restaurants also spotlight musicians in their lounges, including the **Café Mews,** 429 Commercial St. (☎ **508/487-1500**).

A word of warning to motorists: If you're planning to drive into town at night, be prepared to move as if in a marching parade. The traffic, as one local put it, is "traffic, but 'friendly' traffic."

Martha's Vineyard & Nantucket

7

Martha's Vineyard and Nantucket are among the eastern seaboard's most attractive and most visited resorts. There's something special about vacationing on an island, a particular feeling of isolation, of being apart from the schedules and worries of city life, and this is truly relaxing and therapeutic.

1 Martha's Vineyard

5 miles S of Cape Cod

To Bostonians and denizens of Cape Cod, it's simply "the Vineyard." The island got its odd name in the early 1600s, when mariner and explorer Bartholomew Gosnold stopped here. It's said he found wild grapes, and it's thought he had a daughter named Martha. Voilà! Today, the island actually has a commercial vineyard and a winery producing fine vintages that you can sample and buy.

Although it's in the same legislative district, the Vineyard is not a part of Cape Cod. Vineyard residents are proud that the island is the County of Dukes County, not part of some mainland county, and they guard the anachronistic redundancy of that title very closely. For a long time the Vineyard had its own representative in the General Court (state legislature), and when redistricting made the island a part of the Cape Cod legislative district, the islanders threatened to secede from Massachusetts and become part of another state, one that would allow them their own representative.

Islanders get their exceptional sense of independence from a history of struggle with and mastery of the sea, from the days when whaling brought great wealth to an otherwise poor island. And just about the time the whaling industry declined, the tourist industry began, and Martha's Vineyard found its place in the modern world. Today, the ferries are packed with visitors every day in summer, and are also crowded on weekends in spring and fall.

A special note: You will undoubtedly learn it for yourself when you disembark from the boat, but let me be the first one to tell you: The best value on the Vineyard is a $2.50 homemade ice-cream cone at Mad Martha's. Prime locales in Vineyard Haven, Oak Bluffs, and Edgartown will ensure that no matter where you are, a Mad Martha's will never be very far. Keep your eyes peeled for the wild antique ambulance that zips between stores.

What's Special About Martha's Vineyard & Nantucket

Island Ambience
- That particular feeling of "being away from it all" on a breezy island out to sea.

Museums
- The Thomas Cooke House in Edgartown, dating from the 1760s, now a historical museum of Vineyard life.
- The Nantucket Historical Association's fascinating museums, including one on whaling, another on Nantucket history, and a still-functioning windmill built in 1746.

Outdoor Activities
- Bicycling on both islands—bike paths are well maintained and rentals are reasonably priced.
- The many beaches, some very suitable for children.
- Schooners, sloops, and a variety of other sailing vessels available for excursions.

Charming Towns
- Oak Bluffs, once a tent camp for summer Methodist church meetings, with lots of fine Victorian gingerbread architecture.
- The stately ship captains' houses of Edgartown, many of which are now inns.
- The beautiful town and fine buildings of Nantucket—thanks to the great wealth brought to the island by whalers.

GETTING THERE   By Plane   Year-round, there are scheduled flights to Martha's Vineyard Dukes County Airport from Boston, Hyannis, Nantucket, and New Bedford. The airport is located in the center of the island within easy reach of all points. There are plenty of taxis available for scheduled arrivals.

Cape Air and Nantucket Airlines flies between Boston, Hyannis, Nantucket, New Bedford and Martha's Vineyard throughout the year; for information and reservations, call ☎ **508/771-6944. Direct Flight, Inc.,** provides charter service for up to five passengers from airports all over New England; call ☎ **508/693-6688** for more details.

By Ferry   For ferries to Martha's Vineyard, see the information in the sections on Woods Hole, Falmouth, Hyannis (all in Chapter 6, "Cape Cod"), and New Bedford (in Chapter 5).

Hy-Line Cruises, Ocean Street Dock, Hyannis (☎ **508/778-2600**), operates three daily passenger boats (morning, noontime, and afternoon) in each direction between Martha's Vineyard and Nantucket islands from early-June to mid-September. The voyage takes $2^{1}/_{4}$ hours and costs $11 for adults, $5.50 for children 5 to 12 (children under 5 travel free). Buy tickets in Oak Bluffs, Martha's Vineyard (☎ **508/693-0112**), and on Straight Wharf, Nantucket (☎ **508/228-3949**). Hy-Line Cruises has also just finished building a high-speed catamaran that crosses to Nantucket in less than an hour. Departures from Hyannis begin at 6:30am and run every $2^{1}/_{2}$ hours after that. Round-trip fares are $52 for adults, $39 for children 12 and under. If you're taking your bike, it will cost you an additional $4.50 each way.

ESSENTIALS   The **telephone area code** is **508.**

Martha's Vineyard

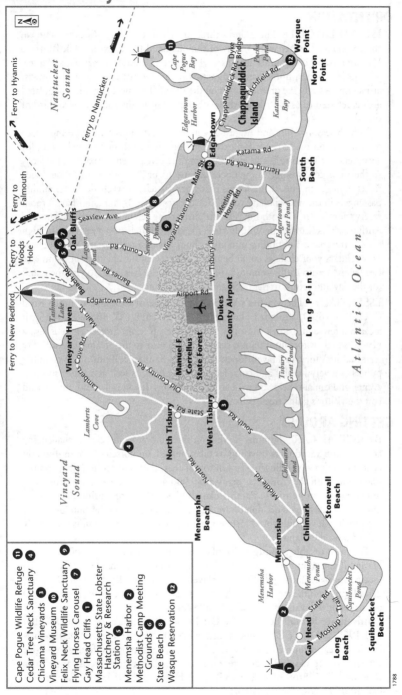

Cape Pogue Wildlife Refuge ⑪
Cedar Tree Neck Sanctuary ④
Chicama Vineyards ③
Vineyard Museum ⑩
Felix Neck Wildlife Sanctuary ⑨
Flying Horses Carousel ⑦
Gay Head Cliffs ①
Massachusetts State Lobster Hatchery & Research Station ⑤
Menemsha Harbor ②
Methodist Camp Meeting Grounds ⑥
State Beach ⑧
Wasque Reservation ⑫

1788

ORIENTATION

ISLAND LAYOUT   The island's three principal towns are **Vineyard Haven,** the commercial center where many of the mainland ferries dock; **Oak Bluffs,** a Victorian resort community of ornate "gingerbread" houses, a marina, and a few grand old wooden hotels; and **Edgartown,** the county seat and main tourist attraction—clearly the prettiest town on the island. The more rural, less populated area is referred to as Up Island; these are the towns in the southwestern third of the island.

In high season—July and August—you need reservations for everything: space for your car on the ferry (or for a rental car on the island), for a hotel room, for a weekend mainland-to-island flight. You can't reserve passenger space on the ferry, so the thing to do is get to the docks at least 15 or 20 minutes early, buy your ticket, and get in line. If the ferry's passenger capacity is reached, the remaining passengers in the line will have to wait for the next boat. If you don't have a room reservation in an island hotel, use the direct-line telephone in the Steamship Authority ticket office in Woods Hole for island hotels. On weekends in high season, the chances of finding a room without advance reservations are not great; on weekdays your chances could be much better. Call the chamber of commerce (see below) for up-to-the-minute availability. If all else fails, plan to visit the island for the day and return to the mainland in the evening.

ESSENTIALS   The **Martha's Vineyard Chamber of Commerce,** Beach Road (P.O. Box 1698), Vineyard Haven, MA 02568-1698 (☎ **508/693-0085**), is located a few doors down from the Tisbury Inn off Main Street. There is also a new seasonal visitors information center located next to the Steamship Authority terminal in Vineyard Haven (open daily from 8am to 5:30pm). The chamber publishes a very helpful and complete visitor's guide, as well as a list of summer events, and can also help you with accommodations. If you call ahead, they'll send you the visitor's guide free of charge.

GETTING AROUND

BY RENTAL CAR   Summer driving on the Vineyard can be a bit challenging at times with vacationers traveling by bike, moped, on horseback, or on foot, on generally narrow, winding roads. On top of that, there are no stop lights on the island and, with the crowds (as many as 80,000 people visit every year), four-way intersections can be tricky. Parking can also be challenging during the summer months. Whatever you do, don't leave a car in a lot longer than the amount of time for which you've paid; you'll instantly be ticketed. Also, speed limits are strictly enforced on the island.

The most reliable is **Budget** (☎ **508/693-1911**) in Oak Bluffs and Vineyard Haven. If you want to ride around in high style, call **Vineyard Classic Car Rental** located in Oak Bluffs and Vineyard Haven (open daily May through October). They'll find you the perfect specialty or classic car with rates beginning at $59.99 per day. For reservations, call ☎ **508/693-5551.**

Adventure Rentals and Thrifty Car Rental of Martha's Vineyard (☎ **508/ 693-1959** and also a direct line from the Woods Hole Ferry Terminal) specializes in offbeat equipment, such as dune buggies, vans, mopeds, four-wheel-drive vehicles, and trucks, but it does rent cars as well. Other firms are **Atlantic Auto Rentals** (☎ **508/693-0480**) in Vineyard Haven and **All-Island Rent-a-Car** (☎ **508/693-6868**) at the airport.

BY BUS   Island Transport Bus Service (☎ **508/693-0058**) operates school bus–type vehicles between the Vineyard's various settlements every half hour or so, with stops near the various ferry docks. (Trips to Gay Head from Vineyard Haven are much less frequent, though.) Prices vary according to distance traveled; round-trip tickets are always sold at a discount over the normal two-single-trip fare, so ask for a round-trip if that's what suits your needs. The cheapest trip is Vineyard Haven to Oak Bluffs, and fares can be several dollars for longer trips. Don't plan on being in a hurry, as the buses frequently run behind schedule.

BY BICYCLE & MOTORBIKE   Rental agencies abound, and you can barely descend from the ferry without coming across one. Prices are all competitive, and a 10-speed mountain bike should cost around$15 for a day's rental. You'll also have to leave a small deposit. The island and the bicycle were made for each other, and islanders have even helped this relationship along: There's a fine bike path between Oak Bluffs and Edgartown, right along the beaches. No need to reserve bikes in advance, for there are always plenty to go around. Mopeds cost $40 to $50 a day, but are also a great way to see the island. Call **Ride On Mopeds & Bikes** (☎ **508/693-2076**) for rental information and prices. They're located in Oak Bluffs and offer free pick-up or drop-off at most island locations.

WHAT TO SEE & DO

The most delightful thing about Martha's Vineyard is that it is its own entertainment, and one can often be fully satisfied just strolling along past picket-fenced houses, swimming at the many beaches, or biking past the marshes, forests, and island heath. But should you wish a little directed, purposeful activity, you won't be at a loss. First thing to do is to find out what's on currently in the way of festivities and special events. There's an information desk in the Steamship Authority's dockside ticket office in Woods Hole, so you can find out some things even before getting to the island. But once on the Vineyard, pick up a copy of "This Week on Martha's Vineyard" (a pull-out section of the paper). Here you'll discover a list of the church-sponsored white-elephant sales, music concerts (many free), lectures, dances, movies, tournaments (kite flying, fishing, table tennis), community sings, and the like. **Vineyard Summer,** a free paper published by the **Martha's Vineyard Times** can be picked up at the ferry dock and in most shops. The island's most important to-do is the annual Regatta and Around-the-Island Race, held on a weekend in late July (hotels are extra-full then).

The **Gay Head Sightseeing Company** (☎ **508/693-1555**) operates daily sightseeing bus tours of the island, including the Vineyard's six towns, and features a stop at the multicolored cliffs at Gay Head. The fully narrated trip takes about two hours, covers 56 miles, and costs $11.50 for adults and $3 for children. Tours leave the ferry wharves after the arrival of the ship (in season only, call for information at other times of the year), and tickets may be purchased on board the ship or on the sightseeing bus.

SPORTS & RECREATION

BEACHES & BIKE TRIPS   The **State Beach** on the road between Oak Bluffs and Edgartown is probably the first beach you'll see. It's a fine long stretch of white sand, free and open to the public, with parking along the road. South of Edgartown, the County Beach at Katama Bay, also called **South**

Beach, has surf swimming, and is likewise free. The three major towns all have town beaches open to everyone, but the smaller towns and villages reserve their beaches for local property owners, or charge a beach-use fee. Two other public beaches are **Menemsha Beach** in Chilmark (a good sunset point) and **East Beach** on Chappaquiddick (a five-minute ferry ride from Edgartown).

Bicycle riding is one of the most enjoyable ways to get around Martha's Vineyard since the island is fairly flat. The island maintains many miles of paved bike paths between Vineyard Haven, Oak Bluffs, Edgartown, and West Tisbury. Keep in mind that Massachusetts law requires riding on the right-hand side of the road in single file. For after-dark bicycling, your bike must be equipped with a working headlight and rear and side reflectors. At all times, hand signals are required.

In addition to cycling to the Vineyard's beaches and attractions, consider taking a bike over to the island of Chappaquiddick ("Chappy" to locals). The five-minute ferry ride from the docks in Edgartown costs $2.50 for both the bike and rider, round-trip.

There are several **wildlife preserves** you can cycle to, including Felix Neck Wildlife Sanctuary between Edgartown and Vineyard Haven (woods, salt marshes, and meadows), Cedar Tree Neck (more than 250 acres of headlands on the island's north shore), Long Point (a 580-acre preserve on the Atlantic shore), Manuel F. Corellus State Forest (a 4,000-acre preserve of forests in the center of the island), and Cape Poque Wildlife Refuge and Wasque Reservations, two adjacent wilderness areas on the island of Chappaquiddick.

You can also ride out to **Gay Head** to see the amazingly colorful cliffs that plunge into the sea. Make certain you're up for the journey; it could take up the better part of the day. You can view the cliffs for free. As with all tourist spots, you'll find a colony of souvenir and snack shops crowning the cliffs, where you can buy the customary postcards, T-shirts, and a Mad Martha's ice-cream cone. If you're not up for pedaling out to Gay Head, you can drive or take a bus tour.

On the way to or from Gay Head, take time to visit **Menemsha Harbor** (take Cross Road at Beetlebung Corner in Chilmark up to North Road, turn left, and you'll run right into it). This tiny working harbor is about as picturesque a harbor as you'll find, complete with shingled boathouses crowded around the water's edge, buoys and fishing nets, soaring seagulls, and boats with names like *Wannakum II.* There's not exactly anything "to do" except stroll and while away a couple of peaceful hours. Take time out to have a lobster roll on the back porch of the Galley (☎ **508/645-9819**), a snack shack from which you can watch the harbor activity and hear nothing but the sound of mastheads clinking as boats rock with the tide.

BOATING   One of the best ways to enjoy Martha's Vineyard is to get out on the water in a boat. After all, as a fishing and whaling center, this is an island with a long seafaring history. You can take your pick of boating options from small Jetskis to multimasted schooners. You'll find a variety of charter boats available in Vineyard Haven, Oak Bluffs, Edgartown, and Menemsha; sailboats for rent in Vineyard Haven and Edgartown; powerboats in Edgartown and Oak Bluffs; and windsurfers in Vineyard Haven.

Sights

Edgartown

The Vineyard Museum (of the Dukes County Historical Society)

Cooke and School Sts. ☎ **508/627-4441**. Admission $5 adults, $3 seniors and youth 12–17 years of age; children under 12 are admitted free. July 5–Labor Day, Mon–Sat 10am–4:30pm, Sun noon–4:30pm; Labor Day–July 4, Wed–Fri 1–4pm, Sat 10am–4pm.

Here you'll find a collection of buildings devoted to preserving and interpreting the island's history. The Capt. Francis Pease House (ca. 1845) has an exhibition called "Early Man on Martha's Vineyard" on permanent display, along with temporary exhibitions. The Gale Huntington Research Library and Francis Foster Museum contain a maritime exhibition. A replica watch tower houses the Fresnel First Order lens that was used in the Gay Head lighthouse from 1856 to 1952. The Carriage Shed houses a collection of antique vessels and vehicles. The Thomas Cooke House (ca. 1765) is a 12-room home used as a museum of Vineyard history (tours are held daily).

Oak Bluffs

The Flying Horses Carousel

33 Oak Bluffs Ave. ☎ **508/693-9481**. Admission $1 for carousel rides. Summer, daily 10am–10pm; spring and fall, Sat–Sun 10am–10pm.

Whether you're traveling with or without children, a visit to this antique carousel is a must. Listed on the National Register of Historic Places, this merry-go-round is the nation's oldest. Along with the cavorting horses (which, by the way, have real horse hair and were hand-carved in New York back in 1876), you'll find a combination platter of video games and pinball machines, plus the customary popcorn and cotton candy vendors.

Massachusetts State Lobster Hatchery and Research Station

Shirley Ave. ☎ **508/693-0060**. Admission free. Mon–Fri 9am–noon and 1–3pm. (Contact the director, Michael Syslo, for additional information and visiting hours.)

Here, thousands of tiny lobsters are raised on pieces of shrimp meat to keep them from devouring one another until they're judged capable of fending for themselves in the chilly waters of the Atlantic. This is the oldest operating lobster hatchery in the world, and a fascinating stop for anyone interested in the life and times of New England's tastiest crustacean. The state lobster hatchery is just outside the town of Oak Bluffs on Lagoon Pond.

✪ Methodist Camp Meeting Grounds

Off Circuit Ave. Admission to grounds free, $1 donation requested for museum. Grounds, daily 24 hours; museum, mid-June to Sept, daily 10:30am–3:30pm.

Walk around this web of gaily painted cottages and you'll feel as if you're at an amusement park—without the rides, the cotton candy, and the crowds. It's a carnival spirit that pervades this community of summer residences that began as a religious retreat in 1835. Back then, many groups would come and camp out in tents summer after summer, returning to the same spot each year. Eventually they replaced the tents with wooden cottages modeled after the Victorian styles popular in Newport, but added many Revival elements. Today, more than 300 cottages—in a unique "Carpenter Gothic" style (gabled roofs and filigree trim)—stand like contestants in a beauty contestant just off Circuit Avenue. The cottages radiate out from the **Tabernacle,** where sing-alongs, concerts, and religious services are held. On the grounds, you'll also find the **Cottage Museum,** at 1 Trinity Park, a cottage decorated as it would have been 100 years ago, with hooked rugs, rocking chairs, and bric-a-brac. If you happen to be on the island in July, don't miss Illumination Night, in which hundreds of paper lanterns from Asia are hung throughout the campgrounds and in the Tabernacle.

VINEYARD HAVEN
Elsewhere on the Island

Chicama Vineyards
Stoney Hill Rd., West Tisbury. ☎ **508/693-0309.** Admission free. Mon–Sat 11am–5pm, Sun 1–5pm. The vineyard is open two days a week in winter; call for details. Closed July 4 and Labor Day.

Martha's Vineyard has its own real vineyard: The 33 acres are planted in vinifera varieties such as cabernet, chardonnay, and chenin blanc. The vineyard has been in operation since 1971. Free tours are offered every hour on the hour beginning one hour after opening.

WHERE TO STAY

Martha's Vineyard has a wide range of places to stay available, including basic motel-like accommodations, country inns and bed-and-breakfasts, and resort hotels. The highest concentrations of accommodations are in Edgartown, Vineyard Haven, and Oak Bluffs.

EDGARTOWN
Expensive

Captain Dexter House
35 Pease's Point Way (P.O. Box 2798), Edgartown, MA 02539. ☎ **508/627-7289.** Fax 508/693-8448. 11 rms. Apr to mid–June $65–$130 double; mid–June to mid–Sept $120–$195 double; mid–Sept to Dec $85–$180. AE, MC, V. Closed Jan to early May.

The Captain Dexter House (ca. 1840) is the kind of inn you discover and then hesitate to tell anyone about for fear of its becoming too popular. Evidently the word is out. A flip through the guestbook revealed that visitors from around the globe (New Zealand, Sweden, Japan) have had the pleasure of staying here. Its rooms are thoughtfully decorated with the kind of big comfortable beds you never want to leave (in several rooms, you have to climb bed steps to get into bed). Some of the rooms have air conditioning, and four have working fireplaces. Common areas include a garden and a parlor complete with a fireplace and the daily papers. The continental breakfast includes homemade muffins and breads. The Captain Dexter House in Edgartown is the sibling to the well-established Captain Dexter House in Vineyard Haven.

Charlotte Inn
27 S. Summer St. (P.O. Box 1056), Edgartown, MA 02539. ☎ **508/627-4751.** 25 rms. Mid-June to mid-Oct, $250–$650 double; late Oct to Apr, $150–$450 double; May to mid-June and mid- to late Oct, $165–$550 double. Rates Mon–Sat include continental breakfast. AE, MC, V.

Built in 1860 as the home of a sea captain, the Charlotte Inn sits amid beautiful flowerbeds, well-kept lawns, and tall, shady trees. On the grounds are also the lovely Carriage House and the beautifully restored Summer House. Also part of the Charlotte Inn is the 1705 Garden House, located across the street. Rooms in the Carriage House have wonderful fireplaces, and the Summer House features a full-length porch. Fine English antiques are found throughout the inn, as are original paintings and engravings from the on-premises art gallery. Fresh-cut flowers make the atomosphere all the more pleasant. Each room is uniquely furnished and decorated. Breakfast is served on the open-air terrace. The Charlotte Inn is also home to L'Etoile restaurant (see below for description), offering fine French cuisine. The inn is located less than a half a block from Main Street, and the public beach is only five minutes away by car. If you're planning to make a reservation at the Charlotte Inn, call or write well in advance because this place fills up early.

Colonial Inn

38 N. Water St. (P.O. Box 68), Edgartown, MA 02539. ☎ **508/627-4711** or 800/627-4701. Fax 508/627-5904. 42 rms. A/C TV TEL. Spring and fall, $89–$139 double. Summer, $140–$220 double. All rates include continental breakfast. Additional person $15 extra; children under 16 stay free in parents' room. Off-season and midweek rates available. AE, MC, V. Closed mid-Dec to mid-Apr.

This inn in the center of town looks like Edgartown's answer to the huge rambling Victorian hotels of Oak Bluffs and elsewhere, although to keep with tradition on North Water Street, this one is covered in cedar "shakes" (shingles), and many windows have shutters like those of the sea captains' houses. The advantages at the Colonial, besides its central location, recent renovations (rooms are refurbished annually here), shops, hairstylist, and sea views, are its large number of rooms and varied rates—rooms with harbor views are more expensive, but for your extra dollars you not only get a great view but a refrigerator and a big brass bed. The Colonial's restaurant, Chesca, is open for breakfast, lunch, and dinner. Continental breakfast consisting of fresh fruits, muffins, orange juice, coffee, tea, and assorted breads is served in the beautiful solarium.

Daggett House

59 N. Water St. at Daggett St. (P.O. Box 1333), Edgartown, MA 02539. ☎ **508/627-4600** or 800/946-3400. 22 rms, 4 suites. $150–$195 double; $240–$395 suite. AE, MC, V. Directions: Take Main Street down to the water, turn left on North Water, then go three blocks on the right.

Located at the waterfront, the Daggett House is comprised of three buildings—the main inn (built in 1750), the Captain Warren House located across the street, and the garden cottage. The rooms are all furnished with numerous antique pieces, and walls are hung with interesting pieces of art. Many of the rooms are quite large, and some have good water views—the larger rooms and those with views are the more expensive ones. All rooms have king-size, queen-size canopy or four-posters, double, or twin beds. Some are arranged in suites (including two luxury suites with private hot tubs), and there are even lodgings with kitchen facilities. The garden cottage has three rooms and is located down by the water. Some rooms have telephone, air conditioning, and television. A full country breakfast is available at an additional cost. The main house has its own dock, and a chimney room (ca. 1660), said to have been Edgartown's oldest tavern, now used as a dining room for breakfast and dinner (open to the public). Three of the dining room's most interesting and delightful features are the original beehive fireplace, the secret staircase room (accessed by a book panel in the dining room), and a mural painted by the same artist who has illustrated books for Carly Simon. The intimate dining room seats only 40 people. Appetizers might include salmon gravlax or crab cakes, and main courses run the gamut from pan-fried breast of duck to rack of lamb and linguine with lobster. The raspberry mascarpone tart is an excellent dessert.

Governor Bradford Inn

128 Main St., Edgartown, MA 02539. ☎ **508/627-9510.** Fax 508/693-8611. 16 rms. TV. In season, $95–$230 double. Off-season, $60–$155 double. All rates include full breakfast and afternoon tea. Two-night minimum stay in season. AE, MC, V. Directions: Follow the signs to Edgartown Center, head down Main Street, and watch for the sign.

This is a handsome white clapboard New England Gothic house with high-peaked roofs and bright windows. The atmosphere in the common rooms is one of restrained elegance rather than frilliness. The guest rooms are comfortably furnished, all with ceiling fans and brass or four-poster king-size beds. Most rooms have televisions. After a day of sunbathing or sightseeing, guests may retire to the library for a glass of complimentary sherry. Breakfast consists of homemade muffins, scones, breads, juice, coffee, and tea. Afternoon tea, accompanied by a variety of sweets, is also served.

Moderate

The Edgartown Inn

N. Water St. (P.O. Box 1211), Edgartown, MA 02539. ☎ **508/627-4794.** 20 rms (16 with bath). May 26–Sept 23 $115–$175 double in the inn, $75–$175 double in the garden house, $80–$140 double in the barn; Apr 6–May 25 and Sept 24–Oct 29 $80–$115 single or double in the inn, $60–$115 double in the garden house, $45–$90 double in the barn. Additional person $20 extra. Midweek (Sun–Thurs) discounts available Apr–June and Sept–Oct. No credit cards. Closed Nov–Mar.

The Edgartown Inn has been hosting famous guests for well over a century, including Daniel Webster, Nathaniel Hawthorne (who wrote *Twice Told Tales* here), and John F. Kennedy (during his days in the Senate). The inn is thus a place of contrasts: In the rooms, 19th-century decor competes with the modern tile baths, and in the parlor, a portrait of Hawthorne hangs glowering at the color TV. Two rooms in the remodeled garden house have king-size beds, TVs, balconies, and private baths; another room shares a bath with an employee. Also, there are rooms in the barn on the grounds. The inn serves country breakfasts (which might include homemade breads, pancakes, waffles, and eggs) in its quaint, cozy breakfast room, old-fashioned and neat as a pin: a deer head, a fine ship's model, and "colonial" ceiling fans add to the decor. Whether a guest at the inn or not, you can have the full breakfast here for $7, or a continental breakfast of homemade cakes and breads baked every day for $4.25.

Point Way Inn

104 Main St. (P.O. Box 5255), Edgartown, MA 02539. ☎ **508/627-8633.** Fax 508/627-8579. 15 rms. July–Aug, $140–$255 double; Apr–June and Sept–Oct, $95–$215 double; Nov–Mar, $85–$140 double. All rates include continental breakfast. Additional person $22 extra. AE, MC, V. Directions: Take Main Street to the corner of Pease's Point Way.

Once a 14-room whaling captain's house, this place has been converted to a cozy, charming 15-room inn with a satisfying variety of accommodations. The garden, gazebo, and croquet lawn belie the loveliness of the Point Way Inn, which has a real family feel to it. There are small rooms, large rooms, 11 rooms with fireplace or deck, even a luxury two-room unit, all with private bath; four rooms have balconies and are air-conditioned, and all rooms have recently been redecorated. The remodeled garden room overlooks the croquet lawn. The inn has a complimentary guest car available to guests for island touring.

Shiverick Inn

Pease's Point Way and Pent Lane (P.O. Box 640), Edgartown, MA 02539. ☎ **508/627-3797** or 800/723-4292. 10 rms. $175–$235 or double. Suites $260. All rates include extended continental breakfast. AE, MC, V.

A night at the Shiverick Inn is money well spent. Built in 1840 by the town doctor, Dr. Clement Shiverick, the inn is a Victorian beauty complete with cupola and mansard roof. Inside, you'll find equally impressive details like the original mahogany staircase, crystal chandeliers, and beautiful Oriental rugs. Furnishings that date from the 18th and 19th centuries decorate the house, and bedrooms have four-poster or canopy beds. Six rooms have working fireplaces. Breakfast consists of cereal, granola, yogurt, fresh fruits, pastries, coffee and tea. Afternoon refreshments are complimentary.

OAK BLUFFS

Expensive

The Oak House

Seaview Ave., Oak Bluffs, MA 02557. ☎ **508/693-4187.** Fax 508/696-7385. 8 rms, 2 suites. TEL. All rates include continental breakfast and Victorian tea: mid-May 12–June 23, $85–$160 double; June 24–Sept 5, $135–$230 double; Sept 6–mid-Oct, $110–$185 double. All rates include continental breakfast. AE, DC, MC, V. Closed mid-Oct to mid-May.

Overlooking the water, The Oak House is full of dark oak: oak ceilings, oak floors, oak paneling, oak furniture, and oak bannisters. The living rooms and dining rooms are dark and rich in contrast to the white, glass-enclosed sun porch. Guest rooms are antique-appointed and are done up with colonial- or country-style fabrics. Three of the rooms have private balconies and two are suites. Most have air conditioning and televisions. There's a three-night minimum stay on summer weekends. The Oak House is located on the corner of Seaview and Pequot Avenues, and free on-street parking is available. This inn is particularly popular with European travelers.

Moderate

The Admiral Benbow Inn

508 New York Ave. (P.O. Box 2488), Oak Bluffs, MA 02557. ☎ **508/693-6825.** 7 rms. Summer, $100–$160 double; the rest of the year, $65–$100 double. All rates include full breakfast. Additional person 13 and over, $20 extra; ages 3–12, $15; babies in cribs stay free in parents' room. AE, MC, V. Closed Jan.

If you arrive at The Admiral Benbow Inn carrying the weight of your job on your shoulders, you'll leave well-rested and completely relaxed. Dating back to the 1870s, the former private home (now owned by the people who own the Black Dog Tavern) is a stately building within walking distance of the center of town. Its rooms are attractively furnished, some with floral wallpapering, antique pieces, and cooling ceiling fans. Common areas include a parlor (complete with a TV, an assortment of books, and a fireplace surrounded by intricate woodwork and relief tiles) and a breezy veranda so attractive that it was once the setting for a wedding.

The Oak Bluffs Inn

Circuit Ave. (P.O. Box 2477), Oak Bluffs, MA 02557. ☎ **508/693-7171** or 800/955-6235. 9 rms and suites. May 13–June 20 and Sept 8–Oct 12, $110–$120 double, $145 suite; June 20–Sept 7, $115–$150 double, $160–$200 suite; Oct 13–May 16, $75–$90 double, $110–$125 suite. All rates include continental breakfast. 10% discount for singles and seniors. AE, MC, V.

Conveniently located in town at the corner of Pequot Avenue, within minutes of all the shops, restaurants, and ice-cream parlors, The Oak Bluffs Inn is a notice-me blue-and-pink Victorian building topped by a cupola. Guest rooms have antique furnishings. The breezy front porch with its white wicker furniture is a perfect place to settle in and watch the world. For a 360° view of town and the surrounding environs, climb the ladder up to the widow's walk.

Wesley Hotel

1 Lake Ave. (P.O. Box 2370), Oak Bluffs, MA 02557. ☎ **508/693-6611.** Fax 508/693-2216. 82 rms and suites (62 with bath). Low season, $50 double without bath, $75–$85 double with bath, $100 suite; high season, $70 double without bath, $120–$150 double with bath, $160 suite. Additional adult $25 extra in summer, $15 in winter. AE, MC, V. Closed Oct to Apr. Directions: From the Steamship Authority docks, walk straight inland toward the marina; the Wesley is a few blocks down on the left.

Built in 1870, this big, rambling wooden place dominates the lodging market in town. The lobby is country formal, and the hallways are papered with a pretty floral design. The rooms, while not in keeping with the gracious common area, are still clean and have standard motel furnishings; most are equipped with televisions. The rooms in the Wesley Arms building are less desirable. A big plus here is the harbor view from the old-time rocking chairs on the wraparound porch. The Wesley Hotel is popular with families.

Inexpensive

Attleboro House

11 Lake Ave. (P.O. Box 1564), Oak Bluffs, MA 02557. ☎ **508/693-4346.** 8 rms (none with bath). $49–$77 double. All rates include continental breakfast. MC, V. Free on-street parking. Closed Oct–May. Directions: From the Steamship Authority docks, walk straight inland toward the marina; the Attleboro is a few blocks down on the left.

This is in that marvelous row of gingerbread houses next to the old Wesley Hotel, which faces the sheltered harbor. If you arrive by Hy-Line boat, you'll be able to spot the Attleboro House even before you debark. The wide verandas are well furnished with rockers and fine views. Many rooms have porches over-looking the harbor. The rooms are spartan but tidy, and fully in the spirit of Oak Bluffs; in fact, the house is on land owned by the Methodist Campmeeting Association, so guests must agree to refrain from "rude or loud behavior." Only a few rooms have washbasins, none has private bath, and though there are plenty of clean sheets and towels, chamber service is strictly do-it-yourself. Here, and at the Wesley, you're living right within Oak Bluffs's history.

VINEYARD HAVEN

Lothrop Merry House

At Owen Park (P.O. Box 1939), Vineyard Haven, MA 02568. ☎ **508/693-1646.** 7 rms (4 with bath). In season, $115–$125 double without bath, $165–$175 double with bath; off-season, $105–$115 double without bath, $155–$165 double with bath. All rates include breakfast. MC, V. Directions: Turn off Main Street toward the ocean at Owen Park.

Protected on both sides, the lawn slopes gently down to a little beach on the quiet side of the harbor, which makes the location of John and Mary Clarke's Lothrop Merry House special. It's a three-minute walk along the shoreline right to the boat dock. And if that's not enough, the sunrise sends reflections from the bay waters into most of the guest rooms. The ambience in this 18th-century house is coun-try ofortable. Braided rugs and uneven door frames add some charm. There are rooms with private baths and working fireplaces on the first floor, and smaller rooms, two of which have harbor views, all share baths on the second floor. You can while away the morning with the complimentary breakfast served on the patio overlooking the harbor. Ask about a sail on the innkeepers' 54-foot alden ketch *Laissez Faire*. There's also a canoe and a Sunfish (small sailboat) for guests' use. The Lothrop Merry House is open all year.

Thorncroft Inn

Main St., Vineyard Haven, MA 02568. ☎ **508/693-3333** or 800/332-1236. Fax 508/693-5419. 13 rms. A/C TV TEL. Late June to Labor Day, $179–$349 double; Labor Day to late June, $129–$309 double. All rates include breakfast. AE, CB, DC, DISC, ER, MC, V. Directions: Take Main Street one mile from the center; the inn is on the left.

The Thorncroft Inn may have started as a bed-and-breakfast, but it has evolved into a wonderful four-star country inn described by the owners as a "first-class, exclusively couples-oriented" establishment. Set on 3¹/₂ acres, the inn manages to convey a colonial and Renaissance flavor with a slight mix of Victorian thrown in for good measure. A neatly trimmed lawn surrounds the main house, which features a fireplace in the lobby. There's a minibar and TV in the sun room, while the dining room has another fireplace. You'll enjoy accommodations in the main inn or the carriage house. Nine rooms feature fireplaces (all of which are wood-burning and prepared "match ready" by the inn's staff on a daily basis), four have whirlpools (including one with two whirlpools—one in the bath and another on a private deck), and four rooms have furnished balconies. Most rooms have canopy beds, and all have cable TVs, irons and ironing boards, and hairdryers. The *Boston Globe* is delivered to each room daily, and if guests would rather have breakfast in their rooms, they can choose the "continental breakfast in bed" option. Afternoon tea and pastries is a daily event.

UP ISLAND

The best place to get away from the crowds and to begin to feel the serenity of island living is to spend time "up island"—in the towns and areas around West Tisbury, Chilmark, Menemsha, and Gay Head. The scenery here resembles parts of the English countryside; you'll find stone walls, forested roads, and plenty of space.

Beach Plum Inn & Restaurant

Beach Plum Lane (P.O. Box 98), Menemsha, MA 02552. ☎ **508/645-9454**. 11 rms. TEL. June 10–Sept 21, $155–$300 double; May–June 9 and Sept 22–Oct, $100–$250 double. All rates include full breakfst. AE, DISC, MC, V. Closed Nov–Apr.

A long dirt road leads to this inn, which is propped up on a hill overlooking Menemsha Harbor, Vineyard Sound, and the Elizabeth Islands. The scenic flower-dotted grounds have been the site of several weddings (ask to see the inn's photo album). Rooms are located in the main house (many with views of the water) and in cottages. Three rooms have air conditioning. The inn has a tennis court, an ocean beach, and a living room complete with cable TV (including the Disney Channel for the kids). The Beach Plum restaurant is highly regarded for both its cuisine and its sunset views (see "Where to Dine," below). Additionally, the inn can provide full-time nanny service.

WHERE TO DINE

The dining situation is both helped and hurt by Vineyard Haven's status as a "dry" town. You don't have the convenience of ordering wine with dinner, but if you remember to bring your own from Edgartown or Oak Bluffs, you'll save the normal (substantial) restaurant markup on beverages. Plan ahead and save.

EDGARTOWN

Edgartown—like the island in general—can boast a large number of eateries, plain and fancy. I couldn't possibly list them all in the limited space here, and in fact an all-inclusive list would be more bewildering than helpful. Although I can heartily recommend the establishments below as delivering good value for the money, you will no doubt want to do some exploration of your own. By the way, Edgartown is one of the Vineyard's two "wet" towns.

David Ryan's Restaurant

11 N. Water St. ☎ **508/627-3030.** Reservations required for parties of six or more on weekends. Main courses $13.95–$21.95 at dinner. MC, V. Daily 11:30am–11pm. (Bar, daily 11:30am–12:30am.) CONTEMPORARY AMERICAN/ITALIAN.

Walk into David Ryan's and you feel as if you've found the hippest place in town. You've also found a good, casual dining choice for both lunch and dinner. On the street level you'll find a bar area with good jazz music playing and tanned vacationers crowded around the high tables and stools. Upstairs is more sedate, with quiet tables and booths. You can have your meal in either place. For lunch, there's a good selection of pita pizzas, burgers (with guacamole, cheddar cheese, or other toppings), and sandwiches. Dinner main courses include grilled rosemary chicken, fresh grilled swordfish, and some creative pasta dishes.

✪ L'Etoile

In the Charlotte Inn, 27 S. Summer St. ☎ **508/627-5187.** Reservations required. Fixed-price dinner $48–$58. AE, MC, V. Summer, daily 6:30–9:45pm. Spring and fall, Fri–Sun 6:30–9:45pm. Closed Jan–Feb 14. CONTEMPORARY FRENCH.

In the garden and glassed-in terrace of the Charlotte Inn, the white tables and chairs set out among the trees, vines, and flowers on a patio surrounded by trelliswork provide the perfect place for a warm-weather evening's repast; in bad weather the terrace room is just as pleasant, with lots of windows and skylights. The menu reads like a list of ambrosias: pastrami smoked salmon and grilled shrimp on mesclun; Long Island duck breast with pan-fried quinoa and vegetable croquette in a pinot-noir-and-blackberry sauce; roasted lamb noisettes with goat cheese, toasted walnut-filled baby eggplant, and apple-wood-roasted tomato in a rosemary au jus; and roasted farm-raised striped bass fillet in a crisp potato paupiette on sautéed artichoke hearts with a pinot noir fumet and tomato concasse. Desserts might inlude a frozen chocolate and Godiva liqueur souffle or a coeur de crème with berry coulis and strawberry and mint salad. There is a well-selected wine list available. Be sure to call ahead for reservations.

✪ Savoir Fare

14 Church St., Old Post Office Sq. ☎ **508/627-9864.** Reservations required for dinner, not accepted at lunch. Main courses $19–$30. AE, MC, V. Mon–Sat 11:30am–2:30pm; daily 6–10pm. Closed mid-Oct to mid-Mar. CREATIVE TUSCAN.

Follow your nose to the courtyard behind the Dukes County Court House and Savoir Fare if you're in the mood for some good Italian food. This all-white restaurant (white tables, walls, floors, linens, and candles) has been featured in *Gourmet* and several other magazines—and deservedly so. The food (and wine list) is nonpareil. Top dinner choices on my list include seared sashimi tuna with braised baby artichokes and olive-lemon reduction, polenta-crusted salmon, veal osso buco, and seared halibut with stir-fried lobster in a lobster vinaigrette. The wine list offers a good selection of California and Italian wines (including some super Tuscans). A favorite dessert is tiramisu. Try to get a table in the patio/garden.

OAK BLUFFS

Jimmy Seas Pan Pasta Restaurant

32 Kennebec Ave. ☎ **508/696-8550.** Reservations not accepted. Main courses $11.75–$16.75. No credit cards. Breakfast (summer only) 7–11am; daily 5–10pm. ITALIAN.

One whiff of the garlic outside Jimmy Seas and you'll know that the food is good. Young chef-owner Jimmy Cipolla is a master in the kitchen, whipping up all sorts of flavorful Italian meals. All hot dishes are generously proportioned and served in a pan. The decor is budget-minded in this old Victorian home, but it's more than compensated for by the celestial food. To start, try the roasted red peppers—marinated in olive oil, balsamic vinegar, and roasted garlic. Follow it with ziti bolognese, gamberetto chicken, or lobster fra diavolo. The linguine puttanesca was especially delicious. All dinners include a house salad. The breakfast menu features a variety of frittatas (including a wonderful one with goat cheese and pesto and another with lobster meat, tomato, and crushed red peppers), as well as a variety of eggs served in the pan. By the way, don't even think of asking Jimmy to change the Frank Sinatra music—it's his passion.

Oyster Bar

162 Circuit Ave. ☎ **508/693-3300.** Reservations recommended. Main courses $28–$44. AE, MC, V. May–Nov, daily 6pm–12:30am. SEAFOOD.

The Oyster Bar is very trendy and upscale, something you'd expect to find in New York or San Francisco. The solitary strip of hot-pink neon, high on the back wall, sets the tone. The general decor is pink and green with soft lighting; the ceiling is high (it's tin, so the noise level is a bit high, too), and the Doric pillars are green, painted to look like marble. The dinner menu (as well as the wine list and dessert menu) is quite extensive: Oysters galore from the raw bar or as a cooked appetizer, striped bass or mahi-mahi, and a peach, papaya, and passionfruit cobbler make a superb supper.

VINEYARD HAVEN

The Black Dog Tavern

Beach St. Extension. ☎ **508/693-9223.** Reservations not accepted. Main courses $2.95–$10.95 at lunch, $17.95–$24.95 at dinner; breakfast dishes $2.25–$7.25. AE, DISC, MC, V. May–Oct, Mon–Sat 7–11am; daily 11:30am–2:30pm; daily 5–10pm; brunch Sun 7am–1pm. Nov–Apr, Mon–Sat 7–11am; Mon–Sat 11:30am–5pm, Sun 1–5pm; daily 5–9pm; brunch Sun 7am–1pm. Directions: Go to the water end of Beach Street (Beach Street Extension), right down next to the Coastwise Marina. AMERICAN.

Ask anyone on the Vineyard what restaurants are recommended and he or she will inevitably include The Black Dog Tavern in the response. Set on the water, it's famed for its food, especially breakfast and dinner. It's always a lively spot, with crowds of fanatical regulars as well as visitors seated in a screened porch overlooking the harbor and in the rustic dining room. There's always a great selection of innovative dinner items, such as warmed smoked island bluefish salad with capers and red onions or baked chèvre on organic mixed greens to start. A main course I enjoyed was the pan-fried shrimp with spicy ginger sauce, and the grilled tuna with a lemon vinaigrette was light but filling. For lunch, try the tortellini with smoked salmon cream sauce; hummus melt; stir-fried summer squash and zucchini with a spicy peanut sauce; or a hamburger or B.L.T. The nearby Black Dog Bakery is the place to go for take-out sandwiches and homemade desserts. *Note:* As this book goes to press, the owners of The Black Dog Tavern were opening The Black Dog Bakery & Cafe at 157 State Road in Vineyard Haven.

Le Grenier

Main St. ☎ **508/693-4906.** Reservations recommended. Main courses $16–$29. AE, DC, MC, V. Mar–Dec, daily 6–10pm. Directions: Walk up the street from the ferry and turn right to the cobble-studded porch of Le Grenier. FRENCH.

The menu, as you might guess, tends toward classical French, but stresses local ingredients. Chef-owner Jean Dupon, who hails from Lyons, France, offers nearly 30 main dishes. Relax on the elegant, candlelit porch or in the latticework-decorated main dining room under a pitched ceiling. Try the stuffed mushrooms to start, and follow it with either steak au poivre flamed with cognac at your table or quail with red/white grapes. For dessert, try the banana flambé or the mousse cake.

Louis' Tisbury Café & Take-Out

102 State Rd. ☎ **508/693-3255.** Reservations not accepted. Main courses $12.75–$23. AE, MC, V. Mon–Sat 11am–9pm, Sun 4–9pm. AMERICAN/ITALIAN.

Not quite a mile out on State Road toward Gay Head is Louis'. The name of the game here is pasta, great homemade pasta. Try a hot and spicy linguine lobster diavolo for $19.95, or perhaps mussels steamed with garlic and sherry for $15.25. (Knock $2 off if you want any main dish as an appetizer; everything on the menu is also available for take-out.) There are numerous vegetarian and egg-free vegetarian offerings on the menu. A low-key, casual atmosphere reigns here. Expect to wait if you arrive after 7pm; there's a terrific following among the locals—Louis' really packs 'em in here.

Tisbury Inn Café

Main St. ☎ **508/693-3416.** Reservations recommended. Main courses $8–$22. AE, MC, V. Mid-Mar to mid-Nov, daily 11:30am–3:30pm; daily 5:30–10pm. MEDITERRANEAN.

The specialty here is Mediterranean cuisine featuring local seafood, pastas, steaks, and nightly specials. Some of the best dishes are the spicy, smoked, grilled andouille sausage or the eggplant fritters to start; and grilled lemon-pepper chicken with cranberry-lime chutney or grilled peppered swordfish with a honey dill sauce as entrées. There are also several good pasta offerings, and theres a lite menu for those watching cholesterol. Outdoor dining is available.

UP ISLAND

Beach Plum Inn & Restaurant

Beach Plum Lane, Menemsha. ☎ **508/645-9454.** Reservations required. Prix-fixe dinner $50. AE, DISC, MC, V. Mid-May to mid-Oct, daily 6–10pm. NEW ENGLAND.

It's hard to say what you'll like best about the Beach Plum Inn: the New England cuisine, the sunset views, or the pianist who plays Gershwin, Cole Porter, and Nat King Cole on a white grand piano. The four-course prix fixe menu—which changes nightly—has some lovely selections, including roast boneless duck with a honey-curry sauce and salmon baked in a puffed pastry. For dessert, hope they'll be serving crème brûlée—it's one of the best I've ever had.

✪ Home Port

North Rd., Menemsha Harbor. ☎ **508/645-2679.** Reservations strongly recommended. Prix fixe $15–$27. AE, MC, V. May–Oct, daily 5–10pm. SEAFOOD.

There's no better seafood platter (baked, broiled, or fried) on the island than at Home Port, on the harbor. It's not an intimate place—it's a family place—and the decor is rather plain, but the sunset harbor views from here will bring out the romantic in anyone. At first, prices may seem high, but they include an appetizer of your choice, salad, beverage, and dessert—and their wonderful fresh-baked breads. Bring your own wine. There's an outdoor raw bar on the patio.

2 Nantucket

27 miles S of Cape Cod

More difficult of access than Martha's Vineyard (at least in terms of time and price), Nantucket draws an elite crowd. But the crowd is no smaller for it; prepare for your visit in advance by booking reservations.

To its year-round inhabitants, Nantucket is not just another resort island off Cape Cod but a special seagoing world of its own. All the brochures and booklets handed out on the island seem to bear the legend THIRTY MILES AT SEA. With its history of whaling, its choppy Native American name, and its people's reputation for hardiness, you might expect to find clusters of peasant dwellings and strong-armed shipwrights making rough island boats, but in fact the opposite is true: Nantucket's Main Street is lined with gracious buildings and towering elms, and the rest of the town boasts street after street of charming and dignified houses from the 18th and 19th centuries. This is to be expected when you think of the money that whaling brought to Nantucket. Before the oil sheiks, there were the whale-oil magnates, for whale oil fired the lamps of all New England, whalebone provided the stays for the corsets then in style, and ambergris was the base for perfume, a luxury item.

In 1659 the first colonists came ashore to settle the island, already inhabited by four tribes of Native Americans. The Jethro Coffin House, the first fine house to be built, went up in 1686, almost 20 years after the first whale had been claimed off Nantucket's shores. By the time of the Revolution, Nantucket was already wealthy from the whale-oil trade and contributed greatly to the Revolutionary cause, losing more than 100 whaling ships and 2,000 Nantucketers in the war. Before the island could recover fully, the War of 1812 again interfered with its prosperity. In another 50 years, the age of the sail-rigged whaling ship was at an end, but the same device that put an end to that era—the steamship—brought the beginning of a new era for Nantucket as a vacation destination. In summer, the cobblestones of Main Street are worn down by visitors from Boston, New York, and even farther away, and in winter the islanders go about their business getting ready for the next summer season.

Nantucket is well organized and well governed, and local residents have various regulations that they want visitors to observe, such as not wearing bathing suits on Main Street, obeying all traffic rules when riding a bicycle, and not camping—whether in a vehicle or a tent or under the stars—anywhere on the island.

GETTING THERE   By Plane   Flights to Nantucket's Memorial Airport are operated by several national carriers and by various local air services. Except at the

Nantucket

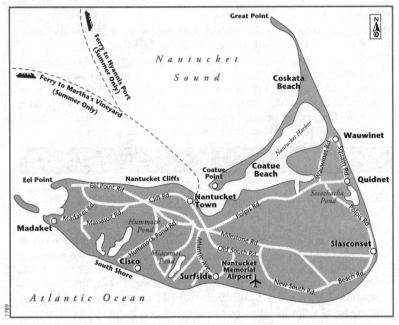

evening rush hour, or on weekends, you should be able to show up at Hyannis's Barnstable Municipal Airport or New Bedford Municipal Airport, buy a ticket, and be in the air, bound for Nantucket, within half an hour, even without advance reservations.

By the way, parking at the New Bedford airport is free of charge.

Business Express, a Delta Connection carrier, operates flights to Nantucket from New York (LaGuardia) and Boston (Logan), with connections from many cities in the region, including points as far away as Albany; Baltimore; Burlington, Vt.; Montréal; Philadelphia; Presque Isle, Me.; Toronto; and Washington, D.C. For reservations and information, call ☎ **800/345-3400.**

Cape Air and Nantucket Airlines flies between New Bedford, Hyannis, Martha's Vineyard, and Nantucket. For reservations and information, call ☎ **508/771-6944** or **508/790-0300.**

Ocean Wings and Coastal Air Services, with offices at at Nantucket Memorial Airport (☎ **508/228-3350**), provides air-charter and aircraft rentals. If you don't want to charter the entire plane, you can join an open charter with a few other people who want to fly to the same point at the same time.

Continental Express (☎ **800/525-0280**) has daily flights between Newark, N.J., and Nantucket, and twice-weekly flights between Martha's Vineyard and Nantucket.

Island Airlines (☎ **800/248-7779**) has round-trip flights between Hyannis and Nantucket daily. It's a 20-minute flight.

Northwest Airlink, a regional airline associated with Northwest Airlines (☎ **800/225-2525**) and operated by Northeast Express Regional Airlines, flies between Boston and Nantucket several times daily from mid-May to mid-September.

Charter service is available with **Westchester Air, Inc.,** from the Tri-State area (New York, New Jersey, and Connecticut). Flights carry six passengers at a time. For more details, call ☎ **914/761-3000,** or **800/SKY-AWAY.**

By Ferry   In summer, ferryboats carrying both cars and passengers run to Nantucket from Hyannis (see Chapter 6) and Martha's Vineyard. When taking a ferry, note which island port—Oak Bluffs or Vineyard Haven—the ferry operates from or to.

The **Steamship Authority** makes six trips a day both ways, between Hyannis and Nantucket from mid-May through mid-September. The trip is 2¼ hours and costs $20 round-trip for adults, $10 for children 5 to 12; children under 5 free. Bicycle fares are $6 one-way. Round-trip auto rates are $180. Rates for cars may be lower from mid-Oct to the end of December. For reservations (which are a must during summer months and should be made far in advance) and more information, call ☎ **508/477-8600.** Be prepared to be put on hold for a while, especially if you're calling just before or during the summer months. You can also send away for a schedule by writing to the Martha's Vineyard and Nantucket Steamship Authority, P.O. Box 284, Woods Hole, MA 02543.

Hy-Line Cruises, Ocean Street Dock, Hyannis (☎ **508/778-2600**), takes passengers only between Hyannis and Nantucket six times a day from June 23 to September 4 and at least once a day in the spring and fall. The one-way adult fare is $11; children 12 and under, $5.50. The round-trip fare for adults is $22; children, $11. Children 4 and under ride for free. The bicycle rate each way is $4.50. Buy tickets (credit cards are accepted) in Oak Bluffs, Martha's Vineyard (☎ **508/693-0112**), and on Straight Wharf, Nantucket (☎ **508/228-3949**).

ESSENTIALS   The **Nantucket Cottage Hospital,** at South Prospect Street and Vesper Lane (☎ **508/228-1200**), is a modern accredited facility. You can contact the **Massachusetts State Police** at their office on North Liberty Street (☎ **508/228-0706**), and the **Nantucket Town Police** on East Chestnut Street (☎ **508/228-1212**). The emergency number for police, firefighters, and ambulance service is **911.** The **telephone area code** for the entire island is **508.**

TOURIST INFORMATION

The **Nantucket Island Chamber of Commerce** (☎ **508/228-1700**) and its Public Relations Committee have done a lot to organize the tourist industry on the island, and information about rooms, tours, and sights is surprisingly easy to get. The chamber is open Monday through Friday from 9am to 5pm. The **Nantucket Visitor Services and Information Bureau,** 25 Federal St. (☎ **508/ 228-0925**), is the place to get daily information on room availability, activities, and island services and businesses. The bureau is not far from Main Street and the ferry docks, and it's open daily year-round. Call for exact hours.

GETTING AROUND

BY RENTAL CAR   Rental cars are available from several companies, including **Nantucket Windmill Auto Rental,** Nantucket Airport (P.O. Box 1057), Nantucket, MA 02554 (☎ **508/228-1227,** or **800/228-1227**), which rents cars, vans, and four-wheel-drive vehicles at the airport. Elsewhere on the island, you'll find **Nantucket Car Rental,** at 4 Broad St. (☎ **508/228-7474**); **Nantucket Jeep Rental,** 3 Square Rigger Rd., P.O. Box 117 (☎ **508/228-1618**); and **Young's Car and Jeep Rental,** on Steamboat Wharf (☎ **508/228-1151**).

Nantucket Town

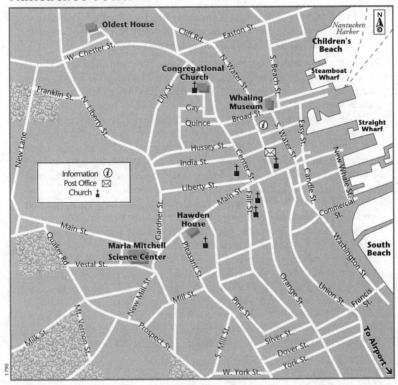

BY BUS **Barrett's Tours,** 20 Federal St. (☎ **508/228-0174**), runs daily bus tours (in summer) from their office in Nantucket town. The tour will take you to the windmill, the cranberry bogs, and to the town of 'Sconset, making three stops along the way. The tour takes 1¹/₂ hours. Round-trip tickets cost $10 for adults, half price for children.

BY TAXI Taxis abound on Nantucket (especially during the summer). Fares are charged on a per person basis and are fixed within town limits. For trips that cover a greater distance, rates are posted in the cab. Incidentally, almost any taxi driver will be glad to give you a tour of the island, with rates depending on how much ground you want to cover and time you want to spend. Call **All Points Taxi** (☎ **508/228-5779**) or **Atlantic Cab** (☎ **508/228-1112**).

BY BICYCLE & MOPED Traveling around Nantucket by bicycle or moped is one of the best ways to see the island. However, keep the following in mind: If you're riding a bike, obey all traffic laws (especially one-way streets), use bike paths, and always lock up your bike. If you're renting a moped, you must have a valid driver's license, wear a helmet, and drive on the road only, following the rules of the road that cars must follow. Take care when driving on beach roads that are sandy—mopeds skid very easily.

Bikes generally rent for between $18 and $20 a day; you can also rent bikes by the hour or by the week. Mopeds cost between $40 and $60 per day.

Both bicycles and mopeds can be rented at **Nantucket Bike Shop,** at Steamship Authority Dock (☎ **508/228-1999**), and **Young's Bicycle Shop,** on Steamboat Wharf, (P.O. Box 1229) (☎ **508/228-1151**).

WHAT TO SEE & DO

Once on Nantucket, you'll find that your activity schedule will take care of itself. In good weather everyone takes off to the beaches, by taxi, bus, or bike. For variety, the island offers tennis, golf, horseback riding, movies, antique stores, and art galleries. Sports fishers should wander down to Straight Wharf to talk to one of the charter-boat captains about a day's run for bluefish or striped bass. Those who just like being in a boat can rent a sailboat and take sailing lessons at one of the establishments on Washington Street Extension or Steamboat Wharf. There are also sea kayaks available for rent and for tours. The island's information office on Federal Street will be able to help you out with details.

TOURS

BIKE & MOPED TRIPS   Between the cobblestones and the summer crowds, riding bikes and mopeds in town can be quite annoying. Elsewhere on the island, however, you'll find it's easy and very enjoyable to travel via two wheels. Here are some destinations to head for:

Surfside Area   Located within easy riding distance of town (about three miles) on the island's south shore, Surfside is a popular spot for beachgoers. There's a lunch bar, lifeguards, and a changing facility. The surf here is substantial and the beach wide and white.

Hummock Area & Cisco Beach   Also on the south shore is Cisco Beach, which is a popular swimming and surfing spot. The trip out takes you through some of the island's most scenic farmland.

Madaket   A six-mile ride on paved bike paths from town, Madaket is as far west as you can go on Nantucket. The big attractions here are the beaches and sunsets.

'Sconset Area   A bike path connects Nantucket with 'Sconset, the island's east-ernmost town, $7^1/_2$ miles away. Back in the 18th century, this area was colonized by a group of fishermen who built little cottages. Today, it's a summer resort area with long sandy beaches and Atlantic waves. The tiny town is home to a handful of restaurants, a post office, and a collection of gray-shingled cottages. Bikers customarily stop at **Claudette's** (☎ **508/257-6622**) for box lunches to take to the beach ($6.50). En route to 'Sconset, you can turn off (about six miles out of town) to the right and head for **Tom Nevers Head.** This is a bluff (about 65 feet high) overlooking the ocean.

Wauwinet   This small village is located on that skinny strip of land you see curving to the north on any map of Nantucket. About nine miles from Nantucket town, it's wedged between the ocean and the harbor. You'll need a four-wheel-drive vehicle to travel beyond the village—or strong legs and stamina. It's a protected area, home to many rare and endangered birds.

BUS TOURS   Tour buses meet some ferryboats at Steamboat Wharf or Straight Wharf, ready to take you on a $1^1/_2$-hour tour of the island. There's no better way to get your bearings, and the short time spent will help you better organize the few precious days you'll have on the island.

Nantucket Island Tours (☎ **508/228-0334**), with offices on Straight Wharf, offers five island tours daily in summer, charging $10 per adult, $5 per child.

Barrett's Tours, 20 Federal St. (☎ **508/228-0174**), operates six daily tours between Nantucket town and 'Sconset. The 1¹/₂-hour tour costs $10 for adults, half price for children. Senior citizens get discounts on all tours departing from Barrett's office.

CRUISES

Nantucket Harbor Cruises, Straight Wharf (☎ **508/228-1444**), operates the most original cruises: morning trips to pull up live lobsters from the company's own traps (with explanations and descriptions of the whole lobstering process), afternoon ice-cream voyages, evening and harbor lights cruises. Fares range from $10 to $25 for adults, $7.50 to $20 for children. Call for reservations.

Friendship Sloop *Endeavor,* Slip 15, Straight Wharf (☎ **508/228-5585**), makes four or five voyages daily from May 1 to November 1. Cruises last 1, 1¹/₂, or 3 hours and cost $15 to $25 per person, depending on the time and length of the cruise. The three-hour cruises are much more pricey and have to be specially arranged.

MUSEUMS

Maria Mitchell Science Center

2 Vestal St. ☎ **508/228-9198** or 508/228-0898 (summers only). Admission varies according to activity; call for details. Center and library, June 15 to the last Sat in Aug, Tues–Sat 10am–4pm; library only, Sept–June, Mon–Fri 1–4pm.

This is a group of buildings organized and maintained in honor of Nantucket's foremost astronomer, Maria Mitchell (1818–89). Born on Nantucket to an astronomer-teacher father and teacher-librarian mother, Mitchell became interested in the stars at an early age. Out here on Nantucket she studied the heavens and in 1847 discovered a hitherto uncharted comet. Her scientific feat earned her a gold medal from the king of Denmark and membership in the American Academy of Arts and Sciences (the first woman so honored), and led to a distinguished career as a professor at Vassar College. Founded in 1902, the Nantucket Maria Mitchell Association seeks to preserve a fitting memorial to the island's famous astronomer and to make available science facilities to residents and visitors. The science center consists of astronomical observatories, with children's science seminars, and stellar observations if the sky is clear; the **Hinchman House** at 7 Milk St., with its Museum of Natural Science, birdwatching, marine ecology, wildflower and nature field trips, and children's nature classes; the **Mitchell House** at 1 Vestal St., birthplace of Maria Mitchell, with a children's history series, adult artisans seminars, and its wildflower and herb gardens; the **Science Library** at 2 Vestal St.; and the **Aquarium** at 28 Washington St. Check with the center for current activity schedules.

Nantucket Historical Association

2 Whalers Ln. ☎ **508/228-1894.** Special museum pass for all sites, $8 adults, $4 children 5–14, children under 5 free; admission to individual buildings, $2–$5 each (total of $18) if purchased separately. In season, Thomas Macy Warehouse, daily 10am–5pm; all other buildings, daily 10am–5pm. Off-season, hours as posted. The tour begins on Straight Wharf, three wharves south of ferry landing.

Nantucket's history can keep you occupied for days. To run the gamut, buy a special visitor's pass to the 12 buildings filled with the exhibits of the Nantucket Historical Association. These buildings include the famous Whaling Museum, the Thomas Macy Warehouse (Nantucket history museum), the Jethro Coffin House—oldest on the island, and a windmill built in 1746 and still functioning. Individual admissions to all buildings would cost much more, and the pass gives you the advantage of being able to browse in a museum for a while, go to the beach, and return to another museum later in the afternoon. You can get your pass at the Whaling Museum on Broad Street, or at any of the other association buildings.

CHAMBER MUSIC & THEATER

In the past few years Nantucket has supported chamber music concerts and theater productions at various times, particularly in the weeks of high summer. Ask at the information bureau, or look for notices of upcoming events. A calendar of events is provided in *Nantucket Vacation Guide,* published monthly (available at the information bureau).

WHERE TO STAY

Nantucket Island harbors nearly 100 places to stay, but the real character of the place is best captured in the old whaling merchants' and ship captains' houses converted to inns and guesthouses. Many of these are carefully restored, luxuriously appointed, and staffed with professionals; others are run by one person or a couple and are modest but warm and friendly.

Rooms may be hard to find in July and August unless you reserve well in advance, and while you'll have a chance of finding a room for a day or two during the week, on weekends it's virtually impossible.

Although some lodging establishments on Nantucket stay open all year, many operate only between May and October. Any place will give you an off-season discount on room rates if you come in spring or autumn, although the dates vary from one place to the next. In high season (roughly mid-June to mid-September), you'll certainly have to send a substantial deposit to hold your room reservation. Minimum-stay requirements may be imposed during the high season as well. Some lodging and dining places may not accept credit or charge cards.

EXPENSIVE

Centerboard Guest House

8 Chester St. (P.O. Box 456), Nantucket, MA 02554. ☎ **508/228-9696.** 7 rms. A/C MINIBAR TV TEL. $160–$275 double. All rates include continental breakfast. AE, MC, V.

If romance is what you have in mind, try the Centerboard Guest House, located just a short distance from the center of town. The building dates from the 19th century and holds a treasure trove of antiques and is the realization of a fantasy for owner Marcia Wasserman. Oriental rugs cover pickled wood floors, and there is a lovely window seat in the living room. Victorian elegance reigns supreme in the upstairs guest rooms, which have queen or two double beds and are decorated in pastel tones. The downstairs suite has burgundy walls, a fireplace, and an incredible green marble bathtub. Additionally, there is a studio apartment in the basement. All rooms have ceiling fans. The inn is entirely nonsmoking, and children and pets are not welcome.

Chestnut House

3 Chestnut St., Nantucket, MA 02554. ☎ **508/228-0049.** 5 rms and suites, 1 cottage. Mid-June to mid-Oct, $130 double; $165–$195 suite; $245 cottage. All rates include full breakfast. Off-season rates available. Minimum stay three nights in summer. AE, MC, V.

Innkeepers Jeannette and Jerry Carl open their home to visitors. There's a common room with television available to all guests (although all suites and the cottage have TVs and VCRs), and rooms are furnished in the style of Nantucket's heyday with original details—hooked rugs, stained glass, and handmade quilts. A connecting cottage sleeps four and has a private bath. Chestnut House is next to the Quaker House Inn, where full complimentary breakfasts are served each morning in season; or guests may choose to have breakfast at Arno's on Main Street anytime throughout the year.

Cliff Lodge

9 Cliff Rd., Nantucket, MA 02554. ☎ **508/228-9480.** 12 rms. TV TEL. June–Sept, $125–$165 double; Oct–May, $130 double. All rates include continental breakfast. MC, V. Directions: From the ferry, take the second right onto North Water Street; cross over Easton and North Water becomes Cliff Road; Cliff Lodge is the third house on the right.

Built in 1771, the house has been redecorated in English Country style, with spatter-painted floors, white linens, and pine furniture. There are marvelous views from the guest rooms, the garden patio, and the widow's walk. Some rooms have king-size beds and fireplaces. Use of the pantry, refrigerator, kitchen utensils, and beach towels is included. There is an apartment with a working fireplace, bedroom, living room, and full kitchen and private deck, located at the rear of the house ($1,350 per week in season). Other apartments are available at Cliff Lodge's twin facility, Still Dock (for information, call ☎ **508/228-6071**).

Four Chimneys

38 Orange St., Nantucket, MA 02554. ☎ **508/228-1912.** 10 rms. High season, $150–$250 double. All rates include continental breakfast. Off-season rates lower. AE, MC, V.

At one time there were 126 whaling captains living in the mansions on Orange Street. Capt. Frederick Gardner commissioned the building of what is now the elegant and charming Four Chimneys in 1835. Located only a few minutes' walk from the town center and only about 15 minutes from the area's beaches, the Four Chimneys is exquisitely furnished with 19th-century period pieces and Oriental rugs. Each of the rooms is individually decorated, and five have canopy beds, working fireplaces, and harbor views. The inviting double parlor has two fireplaces and a TV, and there's a well-maintained Japanese garden for guests to enjoy. Breakfast consists of coffee, tea, fruit juices, and homemade breads and muffins, which can be taken in the guest rooms or out on the porch. Complimentary cocktails and hors d'oeuvres are served every evening.

Great Harbor Inn

31 India St., Nantucket, MA 02554. ☎ **508/228-6609** or 800/377-6609. 9 rms. TV. Summer, $120–$185 double. Spring and fall, $107–$132 double. Winter, $67–$97 double. All rates include continental breakfast. Additional person $20 extra. MC, V. On-street parking. Directions: From the ferry dock, take Broad Street, turn right onto Center Street, then right again onto India Street; it's three blocks down.

This is an 18th-century sea captain's home now restored and furnished in 19th-century style, with patchwork quilts and four-poster or canopy beds. All rooms have modern facilities. The continental breakfast (which includes fresh fruit and home-baked goods) can be served in your room, in the parlor, or on the pretty terrace. The inn, about a five-minute walk from the town center, is open all year.

Harbor House

S. Beach St. (P.O. Box 359), Nantucket, MA 02554. ☎ **508/228-5500.** 112 rms. TV TEL. Summer, $210–$250 double (plus a $25 surcharge Fri–Sat); spring and fall, $165–$210 double;

winter (except for holidays) $105–$140 double. Additional person $25 extra. AE, DC, MC, V. Directions: From the ferry wharf, take Broad Street and turn right on South Beach Street.

Set on a private street amid groves of shade trees, this modern hotel looks just like a small group of old Nantucket clapboard and shingled houses. The nine buildings of the Harbor House give you a choice of staying in the Town House (which has six town houses holding a total of 57 large and luxurious rooms), in the main hotel, in the neighboring Garden Cottage, or in the Springfield House. All rooms are modern and have every comfort, despite the Federal-inspired decor. The location is good—walking distance from the center of town and not far from Children's Beach and Brant Point. There is a dining room as well as a cocktail lounge with live entertainment as well on weekends. There's also an outdoor pool, with poolside food and beverage service.

✪ Jared Coffin House

29 Broad St. (P.O. Box 1580), Nantucket, MA 02554-1580. ☎ **800/248-2405** (reservations Mon–Fri 9am–5pm), **508/228-2400** (hotel operator). Fax 508/228-8549. 60 rms. TV TEL. Jan 1–Mar 30, $85–$100 double; Mar 31–May 11 and Oct 15–Oct 28, $100–$135 double; May 12–June 29 and Oct 1–Oct 14, $135–$160; June 30–Sept 30, $150–$200 double; Oct 29–Dec 31, $95–$110 (excluding holidays) double. All rates include breakfast. Additional person $15 extra. AE, DC, DISC, MC, V. Directions: Walk straight up Broad Street from the ferry dock.

Built in 1845 by a wealthy shipowner (just before he decided to move to Boston), this impressive Federal-style brick house was the first three-story mansion to be built on the island. The shipowner and his family lived in the house for only a few months, after which it became, and still is, an inn.

Since its conversion to an inn in 1846, additions have been built, and neighboring houses bought and converted to lodgings, so the hotel now has rooms in six different structures. The Jared Coffin House proper and its Eben Allen wing of the building have 25 rooms with single, twin, or double beds. The attached Swain House, dating from the 1700s, has three rooms, each with a queen-size canopy bed. Similar beds are in the rooms of the Federal-style Henry Coffin House (1821), and also in the rooms of the Greek Revival Harrison Gray House (1842). The Daniel Webster House (1964) is a recent building in a Federal-inspired style, with canopy-bed guest rooms and a conference room. No matter which building you choose, you'll enjoy the elegant public rooms of the several buildings. Most rooms have televisions.

Jared's has two restaurants worthy of consideration. One of them, the Tap Room, is recommended below (see "Where to Dine") and it's open for lunch and dinner. The other Jared's is open for breakfast and dinner.

Seven Sea Street

7 Sea St., Nantucket, MA 02554. ☎ **508/228-3577.** Fax 508/228-3578. 8 rms and suites. A/C TV. Summer, $145–$175 double; $185–$215 two-room suite; $225–$245 suite with kitchen. All rates include continental breakfast. Additional person $20 extra. MC, V. Off-street parking available. Directions: Sea Street is only one block long, running between North Water Street and South Beach Street; from the ferry landing, go up Broad Street, right on North Water, then right on Sea Street two blocks up.

Operated by Matthew and Mary Parker, the publishers of *Nantucket Journal* magazine, this is among Nantucket's best small lodging places. Though built fairly recently, it follows the canon of post-and-beam construction and is furnished in colonial style, so you'll feel Nantucket all around you. The guest rooms have queen-size canopy beds, exposed beams, and lots of colonial touches, but also cable color TVs and small refrigerators. The theme of modern comforts in a colonial atmosphere continues in the public spaces. You can relax in a full-size, heated whirlpool bath and then sit by the fireplace or go up to the widow's walk to take in the view. The location, just a few blocks from Steamboat Wharf and the center of town, couldn't be better. Continental breakfast is served in bed if you wish.

✪ The Wauwinet Inn

Wauwinet Rd. (P.O. Box 2580), Nantucket, MA 02584. ☎ **508/228-0145** or 800/ 426-8718. Fax 508/228-6712. 35 rms. A/C TV TEL. Spring and fall, $190–$550 double. Summer, $250–$690 double. Cottage suites also available. All rates include full breakfast and use of sporting facilities. AE, DC, MC, V. Closed Nov to mid-May.

Off in a world of its own on the northeastern corner of the island, the Wauwinet offers the ultimate getaway vacation. Here you'll find all the luxuries of a grand resort (sports, fine dining, elegantly appointed guest rooms and common rooms) in a scenic setting (right on the bay, within view of the ocean). However, the inn is not a huge hotel, and it has a wonderful country-club feel to it. Rooms are attractively decorated and full of handmade quilts, antiques, a selection of hardcover books, his and hers robes, and Crabtree & Evelyn toiletries. Some have bay views.

Dining/Entertainment: Topper's Restaurant is one of the island's finest restaurants. There's also a small bar with a bar menu served throughout the afternoon and into the evening.

Services: Concierge, daily bay cruises, complimentary jitney service to and from Nantucket town, natural history excursions (four-wheel-drive safaris), evening housekeeping service, early risers' coffee service; afternoon cheese, sherry, and port in the library.

Facilities: Two beaches (private bay beach and access to ocean beach), two Har-Tru tennis courts, sailboats, rowing sculls, surf fishing, bicycles, beach chess, croquet, library, videocassette library.

The White Elephant

Easton St. (P.O. Box 359), Nantucket, MA 02554. ☎ **508/228-2500** for reservations, or 800/475-2637. 50 rms, 32 cottages. $245–$475 double; $235–$675 cottage (higher prices water views). Additional person $25 extra. Three-night minimum stay July 1–Labor Day. AE, DC, MC, V. Closed Columbus Day–Memorial Day (except for Christmas stroll).

The White Elephant is under the same ownership as the Harbor House and is equally well run. This elegant old hotel near the center of town has fine views of the harbor and is comprised of quite a few buildings, including the main inn, the cottages, and The Breakers. All rooms are bright and airy. The restaurant and bar have fine harbor views, as do some guest rooms (ask for one when you reserve). Rooms in the main building are simplest, and those in The Breakers building the most luxurious (complimentary wine and cheese and fresh flowers are provided); cottages (some with kitchens) with or without harbor views are also available and are a good choice for families.

Dining/Entertainment: The Regatta dining room serves New American and continental cuisine; the view of boat traffic from the bar is delightful.

Services: 24 Concierge service in The Breakers.

Facilities: Beautifully kept grounds, harborside pool; tennis courts and two nine-hole putting greens.

MODERATE

Anchor Inn

66 Center St., Nantucket, MA 02554. ☎ **508/228-0072.** 11 rms. Mid-June to mid-Sept (as well as certain holidays and special events), $95–$145 double; late-May to mid-June and mid-Sept to late-Oct $75–$110; rest of the year $55–$90. All rates include continental breakfast. Directions: From the dock, walk up the street and take a right onto Center Street.

Currently owned by Charles and Ann Balas, the Anchor Inn is aptly named, considering that it was built (1806) by Archaelus Hammond, the first man to strike a whale in the Pacific Ocean. The location is good—close enough to the center to be convenient, far enough away to be quiet. Pass through the white picket fence onto the well-manicured grounds, then into house, which has many of its original features, including old floorboards and a working fireplace in the common room. The guest rooms are done in Federal style, and some have four-poster beds. Continental breakfast, which includes fresh-made muffins, is served on the porch. Ann is a member of the garden club and participates in a house and garden tour in August.

Brass Lantern Inn

11 N. Water St., Nantucket, MA 02554. ☎ **508/228-4064** or 800/377-6609. 17 rms (10 with bath). Summer, $120–$175 double. Spring and fall, $90–$132 double. Winter, $60–$112 double. All rates include continental breakfast. Additional person $20 extra. MC, V. Parking on the street. Closed Jan–Mar. Directions: From the ferry, walk up Broad Street and turn right onto North Water Street just after South Beach Street.

This attractive old Nantucket house, only a few blocks from downtown, has not only the traditional rooms but also a more modern annex with larger, lighter rooms that still carry 19th-century touches in their decor. You can have breakfast in your room, on the patio, in a small grassy yard, or in the sunny breakfast room. Afternoon hors d'oeuvres are served as well.

Fair Gardens

27 Fair St., Nantucket, MA 02554. ☎ **508/228-4258** or 800/377-6609. 10 rms. Summer, $105–$170 double. Spring and fall, $90–$127 double. Winter, $60–$87 double. All rates include continental breakfast. Additional person $20 extra. MC, V. Closed Jan–Mar. Directions: From Main Street, go south on Fair Street. Parking is on the street.

Fair Gardens is a lovely 18th-century house located in the historic district of Nantucket town. Behind the house is an English-style garden, complete with a Shakespearean herb plot (with plants mentioned in the Bard's plays), carefully tended flowers and lawns, and a patio for breakfast or an afternoon cup of tea. Each room is uniquely decorated with antique furnishings and handmade quilts. There are two deluxe rooms in the Garden House. Breakfast includes freshly baked bread or muffins and fresh fruit, and is served in the garden in good weather.

Fair Winds Guest House

29 Cliff Rd., Nantucket, MA 02554. ☎ **508/228-1998.** 9 rms. 2-room apartment. $110–$175 double. All rates include continental breakfast. MC, V. Directions: From Main Street, follow Center Street to Cliff Road.

Cliff Road has many guesthouses, and Fair Winds is one of the most pleasant and comfortable of all. Built between 1830 and 1860, it stands on high land and commands some good views of the harbor. The guest rooms at the back of the house have lovely water views. Kathy and George Hughes worked hard to restore the house and provide a warm welcome for their guests. Kathy redecorates the guest rooms often, and a large deck at the back of the house affords guests harbor views while they relax at breakfast and at other times throughout the day. The extended continental breakfast buffet includes a variety of freshly baked breads and muffins, 'Sconset sweets, fruits, coffee, tea, and juice.

House of Orange

25 Orange St., Nantucket, MA 02554. ☎ **508/228-9287.** 4 rms. $120–$160 double. No credit cards. Directions: Follow Orange Street south from Main Street.

One of the owners of the House of Orange is a painter, and the inn is decorated with an artist's eye for color and harmony. The rooms are as lovingly furnished and as carefully kept as is the little garden. Some rooms have fireplaces, although, as is often the case, local regulations prohibit guests from using them.

Nantucket Landfall

4 Harbor View Way, Nantucket, MA 02554. ☎ **508/228-0500.** 7 rms. Mid-June to Sept, $95–$170 double; Apr to mid-June and Oct, $80–$130 double. All rates include continental breakfast. No credit cards.

This is an inn full of conversation pieces. Each room is filled with antiques and centerpieced by beds festooned in beautiful lace and linens. Four rooms have views of the water. It's right near the center of town and on the water. There's a little lawn out front, and a porch with white rocking chairs where you can sit and watch boats puttering around the harbor. For cold or rainy days, the inn's common room has a fireplace and a library.

Periwinkle Guest House

7 and 9 N. Water St. (P.O. Box 1436), Nantucket, MA 02554. ☎ **508/228-9267** or 800/ 837-2883. 18 rms (13 with bath). Summer, $85–$95 double without bath, $145–$175 double with bath; off-season, $50–$75 double without bath, $60–$95 double with bath. All rates include continental breakfast. Call about special off-season packages. Additional person $40 extra; crib $10 extra. AE, DISC, MC, V. Directions: From the ferry landing, turn right onto North Water Street from Broad Street.

A tasteful old Nantucket house run by Sara Shlosser-O'Reilly, the Periwinkle has newly renovated rooms of various shapes, sizes, sleeping capacities, and bath facilities. Most rooms feature canopy beds, and some offer harbor views. The location is excellent, on a charming street only a few short blocks from Main Street. The Periwinkle—which is the name of a spiral-shaped saltwater snail— is open all year.

Quaker House Inn

5 Chestnut St., Nantucket, MA 02554. ☎ **508/228-0400.** 8 rms. A/C. $110–$150 queen; all rates include $8 value per person for breakfast each day. AE, MC, V. Parking available on the street. Closed mid-Oct to Apr. Directions: From Broad Street, go up to Center Street and turn left onto Chestnut.

This inn was built in 1847, and the huge tree out front may date from the same year, or even earlier. Located right in the heart of the historic district, just a few steps from shops and restaurants, the Quaker House is something of an anomaly in Nantucket. Because Caroline and Bob Taylor and their family do much of the work at the inn, and because they own the building, their costs are kept down, and so are yours. Their restaurant (see "Where to Dine," below) is justly famous for providing excellent dinners in attractive surroundings at moderate prices, and a similar level of quality is found in the inn's guest rooms. Each room is different, but all have queen-size beds: in one a brass bed, in another a carved four-poster. Dressers and wardrobes also echo the era when the inn was built, and tab curtains are a reminder of even earlier colonial days. Rooms are simple but comfortable and attractive, as befits an inn with a Quaker name.

INEXPENSIVE

Beachway Guests

3 N. Beach St., Nantucket, MA 02554. ☎ **508/228-1324.** 7 rms (5 with bath). $75 double without bath, $100 double with bath; $115 cottage room. All rates include continental breakfast. MC, V. Directions: From the ferry, take your first right onto South Beach and follow it around to North Beach; Beachway will be on your right.

Having served the traveling public for more than two decades, the Beachway has added some very comfortable rooms in the renovated cottage; these have TV and refrigerator as well as private bath. The shared-bath rooms, however, offer the best bargains.

⑤ Hungry Whale

8 Derrymore Rd., Nantucket, MA 02554. ☎ **508/228-0793.** 2 rms (1 with bath). $65 double without bath, $70 double with half-bath. All rates include breakfast. No credit cards. Directions: Leaving the Steamship Authority, walk up Broad Street and take the first right onto N. Water. Go left on Chester and left again on West Chester. Take a right onto North Liberty and then a left on Derrymore.

The Hungry Whale is exceptional in several ways. Mrs. Johnson, the smiling and hospitable owner, charges several dollars less than most other houses and includes a hearty breakfast to boot! The residential location is extremely quiet, the 10-minute walk to town a pleasant tour through Nantucket's neighborhoods. There's a sunny deck for sitting and enjoying a cooling afternoon drink.

Nesbitt Inn

21 Broad St., Nantucket, MA 02554. ☎ **508/228-0156.** 13 rms (none with bath). Mid-June to mid-Sept, $71 double. Off-season, $60 double. All rates include continental breakfast. MC, V.

Despite its appellation and downtown location, the Nesbitt Inn is one of the island's lodging bargains (rates have gone up only once in the last 6 years) and is a nice big mansard-roofed Victorian house (1872) located three blocks from the wharf. All rooms have sinks, and many have original Victorian furnishings, including brass beds and marble-topped tables. Guests have use of a refrigerator and of the common rooms with fireplace. The innkeepers, Dolly and Nobby Noblit, are the third generation of a Nantucket innkeeping family that has been welcoming guests here since 1914.

WHERE TO DINE

All of Nantucket's dining places are surrounded by waters full of fish, lobsters, crabs, clams, scallops, and squid. But visitors do not live by seafood alone. Island restaurants offer many wonderful meat and fowl dishes as well as the occasional vegetarian platter. The range of cuisines includes French, Italian, New England, and New American, with the occasional Mexican main course. On weekends in July and August, dinner reservations are advisable.

EXPENSIVE

✪ Company of the Cauldron

7 India St. ☎ **508/228-4016.** Reservations required. Fixed-price dinner $42–$44. MC, V. Tues–Sun at 7pm and 9pm. NEW AMERICAN.

The Company of the Cauldron, in the center of town, serves only dinner, at one or two sittings—and you must have a reservation. The menu changes nightly (but is decided a week in advance), and there are no choices, so call ahead to make sure the menu suits you before you make a reservation. The staff is happy to read the night's menu over the phone. You might have chilled cracked lobster to start, followed by an interesting salad, and then almond- and hazelnut-crusted salmon served with a beurre blanc, ginger carrots, and saffron rice. The dining room is small, with kitchen and wine racks in the rear. A harpist plays Wednesday, Friday, and Sunday. An antique-fancier's collection of old tubs, buckets, and cauldrons serves to show off a cascade of flowers. As you walk to the restaurant, look for the old copper tub (cauldron?) hanging above the entrance; that's the sign.

De Marco

9 India St. ☎ **508/228-1836.** Reservations recommended. Main courses $17–$28. AE, MC, V. Daily 6–10pm. NORTHERN ITALIAN.

One block away from Main Street, the rooms of this old Nantucket house are furnished as simple but elegant dining rooms offering a variety of classic Northern Italian dishes. The appetizers I would recommend are the timbale of prosciutto and Paglietta with a pear and dried-cherry salad, and the *insalata di Granchia* (Maine crab in a red-pepper remoulade, marinated tomato, and green bean salad). My personal choice for a main course is the fettuccine d'Anatra (fettuccine with grilled duck breast, porcini mushrooms, sundried tomato, and arugula). The *vitello* (grilled pillard of veal chop with herb-and-roast-garlic cheese in a balsamic-vinegar sauce, served with wilted spinach and polenta croutons) is also excellent. All the pasta, baked goods, and desserts are made on the premises daily.

Le Languedoc

24 Broad St. ☎ **508/228-2552.** Reservations not required for bistro; required for dining rooms. Main courses $19.75–$32, bistro dishes $9–$15.50. AE, MC, V. Daily 11:30am–2:30pm, 6–10pm. Closed Feb to mid-Apr. NEW AMERICAN/CONTINENTAL.

Right in the heart of Nantucket's Old Historic District, Le Languedoc offers two dining styles. Downstairs and on the terrace, bistro fare is served at tables covered with checked cloths; upstairs, fine dining is offered in five small dining rooms pleasantly decorated in peach tones. Walls are hung with works from a local art gallery. Two of the most popular main dishes are noisettes of lamb with a rosemary sauce, and the fennel-crusted salmon served with spaghetti squash. Desserts always include something chocolate and a pie made with fresh seasonal fruit. A meal in the bistro would include equally interesting dishes at lower prices. You may dine outside.

Obadiah's Native Seafood

2 India St., between Center and Federal Streets. ☎ **508/228-4430.** Reservations recommended. Main courses $9–$18; dinner $20–$30. MC, V. Early June to mid-Oct, daily noon–3pm; 5–10pm. SEAFOOD.

You can start your meal here with clam chowder, then go on to any of 20 main courses, including all the fresh seasonal fish and dishes like baked yellowtail sole stuffed with lobster scallops. Obadiah's, in operation for 19 years, has some of the best lobster recipes around. You can eat lunch with appetizer, main course, and beverage for under $10. Dining areas include the cozy main room in the cellar of the building and the cool, shady porch and patio behind it.

Topper's at the Wauwinet

Wauwinet Rd., Wauwinet. ☎ **508/228-8768.** Reservations recommended. Main courses $11–$16 at lunch, $19–$31 at dinner. AE, MC, V. May–Oct, daily noon–2pm; 6–9pm; brunch Sun 10:30am–2pm; bar menu daily 2–8:30pm. Transportation: Complimentary jitney service from the Information Bureau on Federal Street, a 25-minute trip; call for exact times. NEW AMERICAN.

Expect perfection at Topper's—this highly acclaimed restaurant won't let you down. Everything seems to conspire to please you—the artwork in the dining rooms (take a look at the portrait of Topper, the owner's dog and restaurant's namesake), the view (at dinner you can watch the sun melt into the water), the service (attentive, but not fawning), and the food (main courses such as grill-seared tuna with sesame eggplant and wasabi, and rack of lamb with wilted radicchio relish and a potato-and-fennel brandade are deliriously good). Topper's also offers a complimentary bay cruise to the restaurant aboard the *Wauwinet Lady* for Topper's patrons. The trip lasts 50 minutes and is available daily during the summer season. A reservation is required for the cruise.

The Woodbox

29 Fair St. ☎ **508/228-0587.** Reservations recommended. Main courses $17–$25; breakfast $9–$10. No credit cards. Tues–Sun 8:30–10:30am; Tues–Sun at 6:30pm and 9pm. Closed Nov–May. Directions: Turn onto Fair Street (at the Pacific National Bank on Main Street); it's 1¹/₂ blocks away. CONTINENTAL/GOURMET.

This is the kind of restaurant you imagine people propose marriage in (in fact, it was voted "most romantic dining room on Nantucket" by *Cape Cod Life* three years in a row). There are three small dining rooms; each has a fireplace and is lighted by candle in the evenings. The building itself is an utterly romantic old sea captain's house that was built circa 1709. Specialties include beef Wellington, rack of lamb, and grilled breast of duck, plus whatever kind of fresh seafood and fish the chef gets that day (clams, swordfish, scallops). Homemade popovers accompany each meal. Renowned desserts include bananas Foster and crème brûlée.

The Woodbox Inn, also located at 29 Fair Street (☎ **508/228-0587**) offers accommodations in nine guest rooms (some are suites with working fireplaces), which are furnished with period antiques. Room rates range from $125 to $205 per night.

MODERATE

American Seasons

80 Centre St. ☎ **508/228-7111.** Reservations are recommended. Main courses $14–$22. AE, MC, V. Daily 6–10pm. Closed some Weds and Jan–Mar. CREATIVE AMERICAN.

Chef/owner Everett G. Reid III and his wife, Linda, have outdone themselves in this fancifully decorated establishment. Tabletops are painted to look like game boards, and unusual murals grace the walls. The food and its presentation are equally creative. The corn tortilla flutes filled with pork and topped with black bean sauce and guacamole are a good choice if they're on the menu, or you might prefer something that hails from east of the Mississippi, like a traditional New England dinner. Desserts here are quite beautiful.

Tap Room

In the Jared Coffin House, 29 Broad St. ☎ **508/228-2400.** Reservations not accepted. Main courses $12.50–$18.75. AE, DC, DISC, MC, V. Daily 11:30am–9pm. Directions: From the ferry wharf, head straight up Broad Street away from the water. AMERICAN.

Informal counterpart to the main dining room at the Jared Coffin House (see "Where to Stay"), this 19th-century tavern has a wonderful verdant terrace shaded by lofty elms. The food is hearty and traditional, from baked sole Florentine to sirloin steak or codfish cakes served with baked beans. You can also get soups, salads, and burgers. Prices are reasonable, and there's entertainment most evenings in summer.

INEXPENSIVE

Espresso Café
40 Main St. ☎ **508/228-6930.** Reservations not accepted. Menu items $3–$7. No credit cards. Summer, daily 7:30am–11pm. Winter, daily 7:30am–5:30pm. CAFE/BAKERY.

Perhaps the best coffee in town can be found at Espresso Café on Main Street, in the center of town. Try the "Nantucket Blend" or the "Harvard Blend," two local favorites. The cafe is a pleasant spot for breakfast, lunch, midafternoon snack, or dinner. Breakfast, served from 7:30am to 11am, features scrambled eggs, omelettes, bagels, homemade granola, and cereal. After 11am sandwiches like a pesto, plum tomato, and four-cheese melt served on French bread, or a hamburger served on a multigrain roll, are available. There's also a stew of the day. The Espresso Café offers an eclectic selection of dinner specials, with such items as pan-seared tuna steak, and spinach lasagne. There are all sorts of goodies to choose from in the bakery, including scones, cinnamon twists, cookies (seriously chocolate are my favorite), biscotti, and carrot cake. In addition to the marble-topped tables inside, there's a sun-splashed garden patio out back. A "White Bag Special," which includes your choice of sandwich, Cape Cod Potato Chips, a giant chocolate chip cookie, and a small bottle of Poland Spring Water, is available at any time of day and costs only $7.95. Pick one up before heading off to the beach.

ⓢ Quaker House Restaurant
31 Center St. ☎ **508/228-9156.** Reservations are accepted. Fixed-price dinner $17.95–$24.95. AE, MC, V. Daily 8–11:30am; 6–9pm. Directions: From Broad Street, turn left onto Center Street and walk to the corner with Chestnut Street. AMERICAN.

The simple but charming dining rooms in this inn have fireplaces, lace curtains, crisp tablecloths, antique accent pieces, and candlelight in the evening. At breakfast, try the baked apple pancakes, baked German pancakes, waffles or pancakes made with blueberries or pecans, fresh vegetable omelets, and fresh-squeezed orange juice. At dinnertime, order one of the 10 main courses—such as pasta with lobster, shrimp, and scallops; fresh fish of the day steamed and served with a mango beurre blanc; swordfish with banana salsa; or tournedos béarnaise—and you get a choice of starters (clam chowder, organic field greens, pâté, or melon) and a choice of desserts (chocolate mousse, fresh fruit tart, ice cream truffle, or sorbet) all included in the price. Beer and wine by the glass, carafe, or bottle are available at moderate prices. Note that the Quaker House has room for only 40 diners at a time, so reserve a table in advance.

White Dog Café
1 N. Union St. ☎ **508/228-4479.** Reservations not accepted. Lunch $6–$11; dinner $8–$18. No credit cards. Daily 11am–5pm; 5–closing. Closed early Oct to mid-May. AMERICAN/SEAFOOD.

Just off Main Street, this cafe is on the terrace of the Gaslight Theatre. The tiny patio is usually crowded with diners having lunch or dinner, perhaps before attending the show, or perhaps just because of the excellent people-watching possibilities. Burgers, seafood, and fancier items, such as grilled tuna steaks and lobster, are offered. There is nightly entertainment on the patio, and there's an outdoor bar as well.

BUDGET

Henry's Sandwiches

Steamboat Wharf. ☎ **508/228-0123.** Reservations not accepted. Sandwiches $3–$4.50. No credit cards. Mid-May to mid-Oct, daily 9am–10pm. SANDWICHES.

Everyone should pick up a mammoth sandwich from Henry's, on Steamboat Wharf at the foot of Broad Street, before getting on the boat. Henry's huge sandwiches are made in the best Italian sub/grinder/hoagie/po'boy tradition. Soft drinks are available, and everything can be wrapped to go or consumed post-haste at small tables on the premises (either inside or outdoors). Remember Henry's if you're planning a picnic, or are down to your last $3 plus your ticket home.

AN EXCURSION TO 'SCONSET

Almost everyone who gets to Nantucket for a few days has a chance to ride a bike to 'Sconset on the other side of the island. The village of Siasconset is called nothing but 'Sconset by islanders—the contracted name is hallowed by tradition. The village consists of Post Office Square, a rotary (traffic circle) from which you can see the tennis courts, post office, 'Sconset Café, Claudette's, and various houses. To the right of Claudette's is the road to the beach, only 100 yards away.

The rest of 'Sconset is residential, notably with narrow streets of doll-like, rose-covered Welsh fishermen's cottages dating from the 18th and 19th centuries that seem determined to stare down the threat of violent winter storms.

Though there are several daily buses to 'Sconset, the best way to go is by bicycle along the bike path from Nantucket town. The journey from the center of Nantucket to the center of 'Sconset is seven miles. If you make the trip in late July or early August, watch for the carpet of low-bush blueberries. Maybe you'll be in luck and find the bushes full of tangy fruit, yours for the picking.

Once in 'Sconset, have something to eat, go to the beach, take a walk or bike ride around, and in the evening drop in at the Siasconset Casino (on the opposite side of the tennis courts from Post Office Square) for a movie or a show. Just across the street from the casino is the Chanticleer Inn, founded in 1909, and still 'Sconset's prime spot for elegant dining (see below for details).

WHERE TO DINE

At the **Siasconset Market,** just around the corner from the post office, you can choose the makings of a sandwich or picnic lunch, and the clerk will put it all together for you so that all you have to do is the eating.

✪ Chanticleer Inn

9 New St. ☎ **508/257-6231.** Reservations required well in advance. Full dinner $80–$85. AE, MC, V. May to mid-Oct, Daily noon–2pm; 6:30–9:30pm. FRENCH.

The Chanticleer, owned by chef Jean-Charles Berruet, is noted for its elegant French cuisine and for the charm of its dining area, which at lunchtime in the summer is a courtyard surrounded by rose-covered trellises under which tables are set. At dinnertime, you can sit in one of three lovely indoor rooms. Order à la carte to get whole sea bass grilled with roasted peppers or Nantucket bay scallops in a madeira sauce. There's a bar and lounge called the Grille Room. The menu changes seasonally. This is 'Sconset's—perhaps Nantucket's—most elegant spot, and a meal here becomes a nice memory. Jackets are required for men in the evening, except in the Grille Room. The wine list here is phenomenal.

'Sconset Café

Post Office Sq. ☎ **508/257-4008.** Reservations not accepted. Main courses $4–$12 at lunch; dinner $16–$21. No credit cards. Daily 8:30–11am, noon–3pm, 6–9:30pm. ECLECTIC.

'Sconset's all-purpose eating place is light and pleasant, with walls hung with local artists' works and offering a tempting array of edibles, such as breakfast pancakes made with blueberries and cranberries, and a soup-and-salad special at lunch. The fare at dinnertime is fancier and includes homemade pastas, confit of duck, and fresh grilled seafood. Bring your own liquor to the 'Sconset Café.

Central & Western Massachusetts

8

West of Boston spreads a landscape familiar to the early pioneers: a beautiful land of clear lakes and glacial ponds, cool forests, and massive granite outcrops. Farming, forestry, and light industry occupy the people of central and western Massachusetts; there are also textile and paper mills dotted along the region's many rivers. Amid this bucolic scenery you'll also find several of America's finest colleges, posh 19th-century mountain resorts, and New England's premier summer music festival.

Wealthy 19th-century vacationers who loved the sea would get away to Newport, Cape Cod, or Bar Harbor; but those who loved the mountains would head for Saratoga Springs, N.Y., or for the storybook New England towns scattered through the low mountains known as the Berkshires in western Massachusetts. This chapter covers those areas as well as some interesting surrounding towns like Sturbridge, home of the famed living museum of the same name; Springfield, where steel-blade ice skates were invented; and South Hadley, home of Mount Holyoke College; among others.

SEEING CENTRAL & WESTERN MASSACHUSETTS

Thanks to the major east-west highways Mass. 2 and the Massachusetts Turnpike (I-90), traveling to central and eastern Massachusetts is easy. Worcester is about an hour's drive west of Boston, Sturbridge just over an hour, and Springfield less than two hours. In three hours you can be amid the cool Berkshire hills.

If you are coming from New York City, choose the Taconic State Parkway for its beauty and directness.

GETTING THERE By Car From New York City, the Taconic State Parkway provides a very pleasant route to the Berkshires; from other points, I-90 (the Massachusetts Turnpike) and I-91 are the fastest routes to the area.

By Train Amtrak's *Lakeshore Limited* runs daily between New York/Boston and Chicago, one section leaving Boston (South Station) in midafternoon and another leaving New York City in early evening. The two sections link up in Albany-Rensselaer and continue on to Chicago. The section from Boston passes through Worcester and Springfield, and then Pittsfield, Mass., in the evening. The *Adirondack,* traveling between Montréal and New York City,

What's Special About Central & Western Massachusetts

Museums
- Old Sturbridge Village, an authentic re-creation of a New England town in the early 1800s.
- Worcester Art Museum, home of Hicks's famous *Peaceable Kingdom* and Mary Cassatt's *Woman Bathing*.
- Springfield's Museum of Fine Arts, with its fine collection of impressionist paintings, and the Smith Art Museum, with art objects from around the world.
- The Norman Rockwell Museum in Stockbridge, with an outstanding collection of works by this beloved illustrator/painter.
- Chesterwood, the Stockbridge estate of sculptor Daniel Chester French, who made the statue of Lincoln in the Lincoln Memorial.
- Clark Art Institute in Williamstown, with 18 significant collections of European and American artists, including Fragonard, Gainsborough, the impressionists, Cassatt, Homer, and Sargent.

Impressive Views
- Mount Greylock, highest mountain in Massachusetts, topped by a war memorial originally designed as a lighthouse.

Events & Festivals
- Tanglewood Music Festival in Lenox, with symphony and chamber music, solo recitals, and even jazz, from July through August.
- The "Big E," or Eastern States Exposition, in Springfield in mid-September, New England's largest state fair.
- Jacob's Pillow Dance Festival in Lee, from late June through August.

Cool for Kids
- Higgins Armory Museum in Worcester, with more than 100 suits of medieval armor, even for children and dogs.
- Naismith Memorial Basketball Hall of Fame in Springfield, with lots of video displays and hands-on exhibits.

passes through Albany-Rensselaer as well. From that point, you'll have to get to your destination by bus.

In addition, Amtrak's Inland Route trains traveling between Boston and New York pass through Wellesley, Framingham, Worcester, and Springfield, Mass., as well as Hartford and New Haven, Conn. There are at least two trains daily on this route (call Amtrak ☎ **800/USA-RAIL**).

By Bus   Greyhound   (☎ **800/231-2222**) provides direct service between Boston and Albany via Worcester, Sturbridge, Springfield, Lee, Lenox, and Pittsfield, Mass., with several buses a day. In addition, there's direct Toronto–New York service with a stop in Albany, where transfers can be made to a Lenox-bound bus.

Vermont Transit (☎ **800/451-3292**) operates buses between Montréal and New York City, stopping in Albany at the Greyhound terminal, where transfers can be made for the trip to Lenox. There are also direct buses between Montréal and Pittsfield, Mass., passing through Williamstown; in Pittsfield the transfer can be made for Lenox.

Central & Western Massachusetts

1791

292

100
109

NEW ENGLAND

Central &
Western Massachusetts

Bonanza Bus Lines (☎ **800/556-3815,** or **617/720-4110** in Boston) has direct Providence–Albany service, with stops in Pittsfield, Lenox, and Lee, and also direct buses between New York City and Great Barrington, Stockbridge, Lee, Lenox, and Pittsfield. There is direct service from Boston's Greyhound terminal to Springfield, Pittsfield, Greenfield, North Adams, and Williamstown.

Peter Pan Trailways (☎ **800/237-8747,** or **413/781-2900** in Springfield), which operates from its terminal near Boston's South Station, provides service from Boston to Amherst, Northampton, Holyoke, South Hadley, Worcester, and Springfield, Mass., and thence to Pittsfield, Lee, and Lenox.

By taking a Greyhound bus from Hartford or New York City to Springfield, you can connect with the Bonanza or Peter Pan buses to reach just about anywhere in western Massachusetts.

Local buses connect Berkshire County towns and resorts with one another.

1 Worcester

43 miles W of Boston, 51 miles E of Springfield

Massachusetts's second-largest city has much to recommend it, and only one serious drawback (which is not its own fault): Worcester is only an hour's drive west of Boston. What this means is that people consider Boston the Massachusetts metropolis, and they simply forget about the neighboring city so close at hand.

Worcester's claims to fame are considerable: It's the home of the American Antiquarian Society (founded in 1812), the famed Worcester Art Museum, and the Higgins Armory Museum. If you're searching for documents dating from America's early years, Edward Hicks's famous painting *The Peaceable Kingdom,* or rare suits of medieval armor, you've come to the right place.

GETTING THERE   See the beginning of this chapter.

ESSENTIALS   The **telephone area code** is **508.** The **Worcester County Convention and Visitors Bureau,** 33 Waldo St., Worcester, MA 01608 (☎ **508/753-2920**), can answer your questions.

WHAT TO SEE & DO

Worcester is very pleasant; there are spacious parks and gardens, several academic institutions of note (Clark University, College of the Holy Cross, and Worcester Polytechnic Institute), and many attractive buildings—the evidence of Worcester's active manufacturing days during the mid-1800s. The city was the birthplace of ingenious machines that were the first to weave carpets, fold envelopes, and turn irregular shapes on a lathe. You can still see many of the old mill buildings in town. Some have been converted to office or retail centers, others lie abandoned, and many are still turning out products: men's and boy's clothing, raincoats, sportswear, winter coats, shoes, and dozens of other items. Worcester kept its spirit of Yankee ingenuity right into the 20th century. Dr. Robert Goddard, the father of modern rocketry, was a Worcester native.

Most of Worcester's products can be bought at a discount in the **factory outlets** sprinkled across the city—you'll see them. **Spag's,** at 193 Boston Turnpike (Mass. 9) in neighboring Shrewsbury, could be considered the L. L. Bean of discount houses. Vast quantities of discount merchandise are trucked in and sold out each day to a horde of loyal customers.

A Suggested Itinerary   Get to Worcester and take a turn through the center of town, stopping at the fine town common and impressive city hall, and perhaps at the modern shopping, dining, and entertainment complex called Worcester Common Fashion Outlet. Then visit the historic Mechanics Hall (1857), 321 Main St., as you make your way to the Worcester Art Museum. Spend the morning at the museum and nearby sights, perhaps have a bite of lunch in the museum's cafe (see below), go on to the Higgins Armory, and then head for Sturbridge (18 miles) to spend the night. Don't plan this tour for a Monday, when many of Worcester's museums are closed.

Worcester Art Museum

55 Salisbury St. ☎ **508/799-4406.** Admission $5 adults; $3 students, seniors, and youths 13–18; free for children under 13; free for everyone Sat 10am–noon. Tues–Fri 11am–4pm, Sat 10am–5pm, Sun 1–5pm. Closed New Year's Day, Easter, July 4, Thanksgiving Day, and Christmas Day.

Founded in 1896, the Worcester Art Museum is the second-largest art museum in New England. Often regarded as a "jewel among museums," the Worcester houses one of the nation's most distinguished collections. More than 30,000 objects span 5,000 years of art and culture—from Egyptian antiquities and Roman mosaics to impressionist painting and pop art. Besides Hicks's *Peaceable Kingdom,* you'll see Paul Gauguin's famous *Brooding Woman,* Rembrandt's *St. Bartholomew,* and Mary Cassatt's *Woman Bathing.*

The museum has a pleasant cafe serving an interesting menu of soups, salads, and specials, as well as lots of desserts. Wine and beer are served. Lunch can cost as little as $4 or as much as $12 per person. The cafe is open Tuesday through Saturday from 11:30am to 2pm for luncheon.

Worcester Historical Museum

30 Elm St. ☎ **508/753-8278.** Admission free; $2 suggested donation at both the historical museum and Salisbury Mansion. Museum, Tues–Sat 10am–4pm, Sun 1–4pm; library, Tues–Sat 10am–4pm; Salisbury Mansion, Thurs–Sun 1–4pm.

Chartered in 1877, the Worcester Historical Museum serves to record and interpret the city's industrial and societal achievement and community progress for those who visit Worcester every year. There are several permanent and changing exhibitions as well as special events, educational programs, and library services. In addition, you can trace Worcester's history from town to city at the **Salisbury Mansion,** 40 Highland St. (☎ 508/753-8278), which is owned and operated by the historical museum. The home of leading businessman/philanthropist Stephen Salisbury, this historic house was built in 1772 and has been restored to its 1830s' appearance.

American Antiquarian Society

185 Salisbury St. ☎ **508/755-5221.** Free admission. Public tours Wed at 2pm.

An independent research library, founded in 1812, with the largest single collection of printed source materials relating to the history, literature, and culture of the United States from 1640 through 1876.

✪ Higgins Armory Museum

100 Barber Ave. ☎ **508/853-6015.** Admission $4.75 adults, $4 senior citizens, $3.75 children 6–16, free for children under 6. Tues–Sat 10am–4pm, Sun noon–4pm. Closed holidays.

That Worcester should have one of the world's great collections of medieval armor is not as odd as it may seem. The ingenious Yankees who lived here in the 1800s were fascinated by machinery and thus deeply involved with metallurgy.

John Woodman Higgins wanted to know how medieval armorers made such excellent steel, so he collected their work. Now more than 70 magnificent suits, true works of art, are arranged in the museum. You'll even see armor made for kids, and for dogs. Among the museum's most popular exhibits is the Quest Gallery, with hands-on exhibits, including replica armor and "castle clothing" you can try on for size.

2 Sturbridge

18 miles SW of Worcester, 32 miles E of Springfield

The creators of Old Sturbridge Village couldn't have chosen a better spot for their "living museum." It's set in the beautiful hills of east-central Massachusetts right where the Massachusetts Turnpike (I-90) intersects with I-84, a major route to Hartford and New York City. Anyone who passes should certainly stop to see Old Sturbridge Village, and perhaps to spend the night.

GETTING THERE   By Car   Take Exit 9 from the Massachusetts Turnpike, or Exit 3B from I-84, to U.S. 20 West.

ESSENTIALS   The **telephone area code** is **508.** For more information, contact the **Tri-Community Area Chamber of Commerce,** 380 Main St., Sturbridge, MA 01566 (☎ **508/347-2761**), open Monday through Friday from 9am to 5pm; or the **Sturbridge Area Tourist Information Center** (☎ **800/628-8379**), open daily from 9am to 5pm.

WHAT TO SEE & DO

Besides the obvious headline attraction in Sturbridge, you might want to have a picnic in **Wells State Park,** a few miles north of Sturbridge (take U.S. 20 East, then Mass. 49 north and follow the signs). Swimming and camping are available here as well.

Don't miss the chance to pore over junk and treasures at the **Brimfield Antiques Fair,** in nearby Brimfield (seven miles west along U.S. 20). Up to 2,000 antiques dealers fill several fields near town in mid-May, with similar fairs in early or mid-July and mid-September. If Brimfield is not in session, you can still do some browsing in the many shops on U.S. 20 between Brimfield and Sturbridge.

✪ Old Sturbridge Village

U.S. 20. ☎ **508/347-3362** (TDD 347-5383). Call ☎ 800/SEE-1830 for winter hours. Admission $15 adults, $13.50 seniors, $7.50 youths 6–15, free for children under 6. Apr–Oct, daily 9am–5pm.

Old Sturbridge Village, off U.S. 20, is one of America's first outdoor museums, and it is the largest outdoor history museum in the northeast. It's a re-creation of an early 1800s New England town actually formed with the artifacts: Buildings and tools, machines and methods of work were all collected and brought together in this beautiful part of the Massachusetts countryside to show everyday life 50 years after the Revolution. Like Plimoth Plantation and Mystic Seaport, Old Sturbridge Village is peopled with authentically dressed "interpreters," folks who perform the tasks of the village's daily life and celebrations, and explain to visitors how things are done. Plan on taking at least a few hours, or perhaps a full day, to get into village life.

The admission fee entitles you to a map/guide to exhibits in the village, and re-admission the following day at no extra charge. Within the village are several varied

places to eat: the Bullard Tavern, which serves a luncheon buffet fr
through October and operates a cafeteria year-round. During sum
snacks, light lunches, and soft drinks are served at locations th
village. Fresh baked goods are also available.

St. Anne Shrine

16 Church St., Fiskdale. ☎ **508/347-7338.** Admission free, but donations accepted.
Mon–Fri 10am–4pm, Sat–Sun 10am–6pm. Directions: Go one mile west from Old Sturbridge
Village along U.S. 20 and watch for a sign on the right (just before the junction with
Mass. 148); turn right on Church Street up the steep hill.

Those interested in Russian icons will want to stop at the St. Anne Shrine. The
icons were collected by Msgr. Pie Neveu, an Assumptionist bishop who served in
Russia from 1906 to 1936, and by other Assumptionist fathers who served as chap-
lains at the U.S. Embassy between 1934 and 1941. The collection of 60 treasured
icons is rare.

WHERE TO STAY

Motels abound in Sturbridge and nearby. Trade is brisk in summer, autumn, and
during the three annual Brimfield Flea Market weekends (in May, July, and September), when nearby Brimfield, a normally sleepy place eight miles west of
Sturbridge on U.S. 20, springs to life. As Brimfield has few hotels and motels itself, those in Sturbridge—and even in Springfield, 35 miles away—are packed with
people, so if you come at flea-market time, have ironclad reservations. During the
slow months of January through March, several Sturbridge inns and motels band
together to offer attractive discount "Winter Weekend" package plans. For details,
contact the Publick House (described below).

In summer, some visitors and music lovers actually stay as far east as Sturbridge,
where rooms are plentiful. With Sturbridge as a base, you can make a tour through
the Berkshires, including a stop at Tanglewood, a day's outing.

You should note that the village of Sturbridge, a bona-fide Massachusetts
colonial-era town, and Old Sturbridge Village, a "living museum," are actually two
different places in the same general area. They're only about a mile apart, but the
village of Sturbridge's Town Common, or center, is on Mass. 131, while the
entrance to Old Sturbridge Village is on U.S. 20.

AN INN

Publick House Historic Inn & Country Motor Lodge

On the Common (P.O. Box 187), Sturbridge, MA 01566-0187. ☎ **508/347-3313.** 117 rms,
12 suites. $55–$135 double, depending on season; $114–$155 suite. AE, CB, DC, MC, V.
Directions: From the Massachusetts Turnpike, take Exit 10 (I-84) to Exit 3B (Route 20 West).
Go left onto Route 131; the Publick House is 1 mile on the right.

Founded in 1771 by Col. Ebenezer Crafts, the Publick House is a local institution. The original building is comprised of 16 guest rooms and 10 dining rooms.
Each of the guest rooms in the main inn is furnished in colonial style with a double
or queen-size canopy bed. Adjacent to the Publick House is the Chamberlain

Impressions

*I went a hundred miles north into the Berkshires. It was April . . . .
Was I in England? Almost, but not quite.*
    —E. M. Forster, "The United States," in Two Cheers for Democracy, 1951

House, which offers four suites, each with a queen-size bed and cable television. The Country Motor Lodge, with 96 rooms, is located behind the Publick House. Each unit features modern conveniences, a private balcony, and cable television. There are smoking and non-smoking rooms available in the motor lodge.

At the summit of Fiske Hill, a mile from the Publick House, is the **Colonel Ebenezer Crafts Inn**. The fine old house was built by David Fiske in 1786 and later converted to an inn by the management of the Publick House. It's gracious, filled with antiques, and small, taking only about 20 people at one time. Continental breakfast and afternoon tea are included in the room rate.

Rooms in the Publick House and the Colonel Ebenezer Crafts Inn are smoke-free, but there are rooms available for smokers in the motor lodge and the Chamberlain House.

There are three restaurants—the Publick House (see "Where to Dine," below), Ebenezer's, and Charlie Brown's Steakhouse. All are open seven days a week. Facilities include an outdoor pool, tennis court, shuffleboard courts, horseshoes, volleyball, badminton, a children's playground, and running/walking trails.

MOTELS

Carriage House Inn at Sturbridge

U.S. 20 (P.O. Box 206), Sturbridge, MA 01566. ☎ **508/347-9000.** 73 rms. A/C TV TEL. May–Sept, $62–$95 double, depending on the season. AE, DISC, MC, V.

At the intersection of U.S. 20 and Mass. 131 is the modern and attractive Carriage House Inn, a brick-and-wood motel with an outdoor pool. It's comfortable and conveniently located.

Old Sturbridge Village Lodges and Oliver Wight House

Rte. 20., Sturbridge MA 01566. ☎ **508/347-3327.** Fax 508/347-3018. 59 rms. A/C TV TEL. $60–$120 double. AE, MC, V.

Another good choice in Sturbridge is the Old Sturbridge Village Lodges and Oliver Wight House. The Wight House, built around 1787, is listed on the National Register of Historic Places. Rooms are located either in the individual lodges that dot the well-manicured grounds or in the Wight House. Lodge rooms have colonial country-style decor, and those in the Wight House have canopy beds, wingback chairs, wall-to-wall carpeting, and modern facilities; some have fireplaces. The staff is friendly and very helpful.

Sturbridge Coach Motor Lodge

408 Main St., Sturbridge, MA 01566. ☎ **508/347-7327.** 54 rms. A/C TV TEL. $49–$76 double. Additional person $5 extra. AE, MC, V.

Although it's obviously a modern two-floor luxury hotel, situated atop a quiet hillside, the Sturbridge Coach, on U.S. 20, almost opposite Old Sturbridge Village, is colonial in both its design and decor. There's nothing colonial about the rooms, each quite modern and equipped with a dressing-room area separate from the bathroom. The hotel is located within walking distance of shops and restaurants. There's a seasonal outdoor pool.

Sturbridge Host Hotel

366 Main St., Sturbridge, MA 01566. ☎ **508/347-7393.** 241 rms. A/C TV TEL. $109–$148 double. Weekend packages available. AE, CB, DC, DISC, MC, V.

Prime among Sturbridge's modern hostelries and right across from Old Sturbridge Village is the Host Hotel. This lavish spread on the shores of Cedar Lake has its

own tennis and racquetball courts, health clubs, indoor swimr
iature golf course. Decor in the plush guest rooms is, of cours
standard hotel units, rooms with queen-size pull-out couch
rooms with king-size beds, sunken living rooms, and firepl
VIP rooms has its own private lounge and concierge services.

WHERE TO DINE

Oxhead Tavern

Rte. 20. ☎ **508/347-7393.** Reservations not accepted. Main courses $9.95–$16.95. AE, DC, DISC, MC, V. Mon–Sat 11am–10pm, Sun noon–11pm. AMERICAN.

The fare here is designed with transients in mind. It's not an elegant restaurant and doesn't try to be. Furnished in rustic colonial, it has an old-fashioned pub bar at one end and a big stone fireplace at the other. The fare includes New York sirloin and various meat and fish dishes; lots of sandwiches are cheaper and equally filling. The Oxhead is off U.S. 20, near the Sturbridge Host Hotel, with which it's associated.

✪ Publick House

On the Common, Mass. 131. ☎ **508/347-3313.** Reservations recommended. Main courses $12.50–$26.50. AE, CB, DC, MC, V. Mon–Thurs 7am–8:30pm, Fri–Sat 7am–9pm, Sun 8am–8:30pm. Directions: Follow Mass. 131 to Sturbridge's Town Common. AMERICAN.

This is a Sturbridge favorite, located right on the town common on Mass. 131. It's big: The several dining rooms can handle a large number of diners at once, yet the feeling of an old New England inn has not been lost. The lunch menu lists a few sandwiches but concentrates on hot main courses and cold meat or salad plates. Prices of main courses like omelets, chicken, and broiled fish include vegetable, potato, assorted relishes, and a bakery basket filled with freshly baked bread and rolls. Dinner is fancier and more expensive. You can get everything from a cranberry-orange shrub as an appetizer to broiled maple chicken or roast prime rib, or even a full turkey dinner. The Publick House has a new all-American wine list as well as an innkeeper's reserve wine list.

Rom's

Mass. 131. ☎ **508/347-3349.** Reservations recommended. Main courses $4.50–$12.50. AE, MC, V. Daily 11:30am–9pm. Directions: Follow Mass. 131 southeast from U.S. 20 and Sturbridge to the restaurant, across from a shopping center. AMERICAN/ITALIAN.

This Italian-American restaurant is an all-American success story. Started as a roadside sandwich-and-seafood stand, Rom's now seats up to 700 people in attractive, air-conditioned surroundings. What packs 'em in is Rom's unbeatable formula: good, plentiful food in pleasant dining rooms at low prices. A lunch of soup, broiled swordfish steak, potato, vegetable, and coleslaw costs less than $10. The menu features Italian dishes, steaks, seafood, and traditional meals. The original dairy bar–lunchstand is still here, by the way. Food to go, including Italian dishes, is even lower in price.

3 Springfield

89 miles W of Boston, 32 miles W of Sturbridge, 21 miles S of Northampton, 23 miles N of Hartford, 45 miles E of Lee

Springfield is Massachusetts's third-largest city, with a solid place in American history and life. The Springfield Armory produced weapons for American troops

.ne War of 1812, and Union soldiers in the Civil War used the famous
,pringfield rifle. The armory was a virtual cornucopia of small arms, many
examples of which you can still see in its museum.

Yankee ingenuity and technical prowess were lavished on weapons, yes, but
on other things as well. The monkey wrench was invented in Springfield, as were
steel-bladed ice skates and the first American planetarium.

Elegant as these things may be, they were not Springfield's finest products. This
honor is reserved for Duryea and Rolls-Royce automobiles. The Duryea brothers,
Charles and Frank, built the first practical internal-combustion engine automobile
(1894) on the top floor of the building at 41 Taylor St. And for a short time in
the 1930s, the world's most elegant auto, the Rolls-Royce, was assembled here
in Springfield.

Among all its inventions, only one has brought real world fame to Springfield:
basketball. Yes, this is the place where, in 1891, Dr. James Naismith, a physical
education instructor at Springfield's YMCA college, originated the game. The city
has a suitable memorial, the Naismith Memorial Basketball Hall of Fame, a place
that's fascinating and fun even if you're not sports-minded.

GETTING THERE By Car Located near the junction of the major east-west
artery, the Massachusetts Turnpike (I-90), and the major north-south artery, I-91,
Springfield is easily accessible.

By Train Amtrak's *Lakeshore Limited* runs daily between Boston and Chicago.
It leaves Boston (South Station) in midafternoon and passes through Springfield.

In addition, Amtrak's Inland Route trains traveling between Boston and New
York City pass through Springfield. There are at least two trains daily on this route.
Call Amtrak (☎ **800/USA-RAIL**).

By Bus Greyhound (☎ **800/231-2222**) provides direct service between Boston and Albany, N.Y., via Worcester, Sturbridge, Springfield, Lee, Lenox, and
Pittsfield, with several buses a day.

Bonanza Bus Lines (☎ **800/556-3815,** or **617/720-4110** in Boston) has
direct Providence–Albany buses, which stop in Springfield, Pittsfield, Lenox, and
Lee. There is direct service from Boston's Greyhound terminal to Springfield,
Pittsfield, Greenfield, North Adams, and Williamstown.

Peter Pan Trailways (☎ **800/237-8747,** or **413/781-2900** in Springfield),
which operates from its terminal near Boston's South Station, provides service from
Boston to Amherst, Northampton, Holyoke, South Hadley, Worcester, and
Springfield, and thence to Pittsfield, Lee, and Lenox.

By taking a Greyhound bus from Hartford or New York City to Springfield,
you can connect with the Bonanza or Peter Pan buses to reach just about anywhere
in western Massachusetts.

ESSENTIALS The **telephone area code** is **413.** The **Greater Springfield
Convention and Visitors Bureau,** 34 Boland Way, Springfield, MA 01103
(☎ **413/787-1548** or **800/723-1548**), can provide visitor services.

SPECIAL EVENTS Starting on the second Friday after Labor Day in September, for about 17 days, West Springfield hosts New England's great state fair,
The Big E or Eastern States Exposition. There's an admission fee to the grounds,
but all entertainment is free once you're inside. Call for exact dates and ticket
information. The fair is located on Mass. 147, at 1305 Memorial Avenue. For
24-hour information, call ☎ 413/787-0271.

WHAT TO SEE & DO

Located at the junction of I-90 (Mass. Turnpike) and I-91, Springfield is a city most people know only through the car window. Even if you're headed somewhere else, you should spend a few hours here. Exit from I-91 at State Street, go to Main Street, and you'll find Court Square, Springfield's heart, surrounded by fine buildings, including Symphony Hall, the First Congregational Church (1819), and the granite Hampden County Superior Courthouse, modeled somewhat on Venice's Palazzo Vecchio by H. H. Richardson. The statue in the square is of William Pynchon, who led the group of Puritans who settled here in 1636 and incorporated the town five years later.

Just northeast of Court Square is the Springfield Library (☎ **413/739-3871**), at **Museum Quadrangle,** corner of State and Chestnut Streets, open Monday and Wednesday from noon to 8pm, Tuesday and Thursday through Sunday noon to 5pm (closed weekends in summer only).

At the entrance to the quadrangle, in Merrick Park, is Augustus St. Gaudens's statue called *The Puritan.*

George Walter Vincent Smith Art Museum

Museum Quadrangle. ☎ **413/733-4214.** Admission (includes all four museums): $4 adults, $1 children 6–18, free for children under 6. Thurs–Sun noon–4pm.

The oldest building on the Quadrangle, the George Walter Vincent Smith Art Museum, built in 1895 in the style of an Italian villa, houses the vast collections of its Victorian namesake and his wife, Belle Townsley Smith. Avid collectors, the couple acquired an exotic array of Japanese arms and armor, screens, lacquers, textiles, and ceramics; exquisite Islamic rugs; and the largest collection of Chinese cloisonné in the Western world. A focal point of the collection is an elaborately carved Shinto shrine. An outstanding selection of 19th-century American paintings includes Frederic Church's early masterpiece, *New England Scenery,* and the largest number of paintings by J. G. Brown in a public museum.

Museum of Fine Arts

Museum Quadrangle. ☎ **413/732-6092.** Admission (includes all four museums): $4 adults, $1 children 6–18, free for children under 6. Thurs–Sun noon–4pm.

This museum has more than 20 galleries. Its collection is built on lesser masters, or lesser paintings of the great masters, but is a fine representation nonetheless. Pride of place—right above the main stairway—goes to Erastus Salisbury Field's *The Rise of the American Republic,* which can keep you busy for the better part of an hour. You'll see why. The impressionist and expressionist gallery includes a painting from Monet's *Haystacks* series, and works by Degas, Dufy, Gauguin, Pissarro, Renoir, Rouault, and Vlaminck. In the contemporary gallery, you'll find works by George Bellows, Lyonel Feininger, Georgia O'Keeffe, and Picasso, among others. Modern sculptors featured include Leonard Baskin and Richard Stankiewicz. The new American Gallery highlights works by 19th- and 20th-century American painters, including pieces by Winslow Homer, Maurice Prendergast, William Trost Richards, and Henry Rinehart.

Springfield Science Museum

Museum Quadrangle. ☎ **413/733-1194.** Admission (includes all four museums): $4 adults, $1 children 6–18, free for children under 6. Thurs–Sun noon–4pm.

At the Springfield Science Museum, visitors step into a world filled with the wonders of natural and physical science. Dominated by a huge African elephant, the multilevel R. E. Phelon African Hall reveals the diversity of the continent's wildlife and peoples. In Dinosaur Hall, a full-size replica of a *Tyrannosaurus rex* towers over visitors. In the Exploration Center, children and families are encouraged to participate in the hands-on exhibits. Habitat groupings of mounted animals, a 100-seat planetarium, an aquarium, a 1937 Springfield-built Zeta airplane, Native American artifacts, and interactive life-science exhibits fascinate children and adults alike. The Springfield Science Museum recently opened the Monsanto Eco-Center, an aquarium and live-animal center designed to accommodate creatures in their natural habitat. Some of the more unusual animals featured are fish that walk on land, turtles that resemble leaves, and poisonous frogs.

Connecticut Valley Historical Museum

Museum Quadrangle. ☎ **413/732-3080.** Admission (includes all four museums): $4 adults, $1 children 6–18, free for children under 6. Thurs–Sun noon–4pm.

The history and traditions of the Connecticut River Valley are preserved at the Connecticut Valley Historical Museum. Built in 1927, the stone Colonial Revival building houses artifacts and documents that tell the story of the region from 1636 to the present. Changing exhibitions highlight various aspects of the Pioneer Valley's rich 360-year history, much of it documented in the museum's collection of handcrafted furniture, pewter, silver, and portraits by itinerant artists. The museum also has a genealogy and local history library, which holds, among many other things, the Ellis Island passenger records and the largest collection of French-Canadian genealogical information outside Québec. The newest exhibit here shows the significance of the role greater Springfield played in the development of this country's firearms industry.

Springfield Armory National Historic Site

1 Armory Sq. (Federal St. at State St.). ☎ **413/734-8551.** Admission and parking are free. Memorial Day–Labor Day, daily 10am–5pm; Labor Day–Memorial Day, Tues–Sun 10am–5pm. Closed New Year's, Thanksgiving, and Christmas days.

The Springfield Armory, just 10 minutes from Museum Quadrangle, was where, from 1794 to 1968, a sizeable portion of our national defense budget was spent. The arsenal at Springfield, established in 1777, became the first National Armory in an act signed by President George Washington in 1794. There's an awful lot of firepower here—not just the Springfields and Garands that were made in the armory, but even some weapons dating from the 1600s, and lots of Remingtons, Colts, and Lugers. It's thought to be the world's largest such collection of weaponry, and it's mighty impressive. The collection is unique for its large number of experimental and one-of-a-kind arms. Don't miss the Organ of Rifles, immortalized in Henry Wadsworth Longfellow's poem. Here you'll also find exhibits on women ordinance workers. The museum is the last armory to remain in continuous operation.

Naismith Memorial Basketball Hall of Fame

W. Columbus Ave., at Union St. ☎ **413/781-6500.** Admission $7 adults, $4 seniors and children 7–15, free for children under 7. July–Aug, daily 9am–6pm; Sept–June, daily 9am–5pm. The Hall of Fame is located off I-9 (going north, take Exit 4; going south, take Exit 7).

The Hall of Fame is no stuffy museum but a very active place—this is where you'll have some fun. The light, spacious structure is decorated with elements relating to the sport: One whole wall is made of those tiny strips of hardwood used on courts. Video displays abound, telling the history of the sport and recalling its most exciting games and players. Here you can play against a Hall of Famer in a virtual reality game, and you can also interact with basketball stars (past and present) in the Wilson Imagymnation Theater. In another exhibit, you step onto a conveyor belt from which you can shoot balls at baskets that vary in height and distance from you. At the end of the belt, try your skill at jumping to touch one of the tapes hanging from the ceiling, suspended at heights from 7 to 11 feet. You can see and do a lot here in less than an hour, but you could also spend an entire morning.

WHERE TO STAY

Motel 6

Burnett Rd., Chicopee, MA 01020. ☎ **413/592-5141.** 88 rms. A/C TV TEL. $42 double. AE, DC, DISC, MC, V. Directions: From I-90 (Massachusetts Turnpike), take Exit 6 (I-291).

Among the best bargain lodgings in the area is this modern motel. The conveniences include ice machine, coin-op laundry, outdoor swimming pool, and free HBO and ESPN channels on the TV. Complimentary coffee is available, and there are several restaurants nearby.

Susse Chalet Inn

1515 Northampton St., Holyoke, MA 01040. ☎ **800/5-CHALET** or 413/536-1980. 52 rms. A/C TV TEL. $51.70–$56.70 double. All rates include continental breakfast. AE, DC, DISC, MC, V. Directions: Take I-91 to Exit 17 or 17A; the motel is seven miles from downtown Springfield.

Look for the Susse Chalet on the right-hand side, behind a Howard Johnson's restaurant, as you head south from Northampton on U.S. 5. Susse Chalet Inn rooms are comfortably furnished with all the usual services, yet they cost a lot less than "standard" motel rooms. Here you get an outdoor pool, nonsmoking rooms, and free HBO and ESPN channels on the TV. Several restaurants are nearby.

EN ROUTE TO NORTHAMPTON

On the way to Northampton, you might like to make a stop in **South Hadley,** which is 15 miles N of Springfield and 7 miles S of Amherst. From the Mass. Turnpike, follow I-91 and U.S. 202 and Mass. 116 north to South Hadley.

The **telephone area code** is **413,** and the **chamber of commerce** is at 10 Harwich Place (☎ 413/532-6451). South Hadley is a small town most famous as the home of one of New England's most highly respected women's colleges.

Mount Holyoke College in South Hadley bears the distinction of being one of the country's oldest women's colleges, founded in 1837. The lovely campus was originally designed by Frederick Law Olmsted, who fashioned many beautiful parks and forests during the 19th century. The campus now boasts a $9-million sports complex, an equestrian center, a Japanese teahouse and meditation garden, and a unique handcrafted classical organ (one of the last designed by Charles B. Fisk) in the chapel. The College Art Museum is open year-round to campus visitors, and the Summer Theatre offers plays in a tent on campus Tuesday through Saturday nights. The enrollment at Mount Holyoke is about 1,900 women. For a campus tour, call ☎ 413/538-2023.

On the way from South Hadley to Northampton on Mass. 47 (a gorgeous drive, especially in the spring and fall), take a detour to **Skinner State Park** at the top of Mt. Holyoke (the mountain, not the college). On a clear day, from the Summit House, you'll have a great view of the winding Connecticut River, the fertile valley's patchwork of farmland, various church and college steeples, and distant mountain ranges.

4 Northampton

21 miles N of Springfield, 16 miles S of Deerfield, 7 miles W of Amherst

A beautiful little town located about a half-hour drive north of Springfield, Northampton is perhaps best known as the home of Smith College. The town was founded in 1654 and is listed in the National Register of Historic Places. Among the Northampton's claims to fame are that Calvin Coolidge had a law practice here and served as town mayor from 1910 to 1911.

GETTING THERE   By Car   Go north on I-91; from South Hadley, go north on Mass. 116 to Mass. 47, then west on Mass. 9.

By Train   See "Springfield," above.

By Bus   See "Springfield," above.

ESSENTIALS   The **telephone area code** is **413.** The **Greater Northampton Chamber of Commerce,** on State Street (☎ 413/584-1900), will answer your questions.

WHAT TO SEE & DO

The pretty campus of **Smith College,** founded in 1871, is worthy of a stroll. You can arrange for a tour of the campus by contacting the Office of Admissions, Garrison Hall, Northampton, MA 01063 (☎ 413/585-2500). But the handy campus guide folder available at the college switchboard in College Hall, and from the Office of Admissions, may well satisfy your needs. The botanic gardens and the College Art Museum are two high points. Smith's enrollment is about 2,700 women.

Historic Northampton

46 Bridge St. ☎ **413/584-6011.** Mar to Dec Wed–Sun noon–4pm. Call for admission prices.

Historic Northampton is a non-profit organization dedicated to preserving and interpreting the history of Northampton as well as the upper Connecticut River Valley. A variety of changing exhibits is offered each year, and the museum sponsors tours of eight rooms in three historic houses. In the Parsons House, built c. 1730, visitors will see samples of surviving original wallpapers and interior finishes; the Shepherd House (c. 1796) houses Shepherd family (in residence from 1856 to 1969) heirlooms; and the Damon House (c. 1813) has one room designed to look like an early 19th-century parlor room and another that is used as an education center and for special exhibitions.

WHERE TO STAY

Accommodation in the area is very much geared to college life. Most visitors come on college business, and when big college events—such as homecomings and graduations—draw big crowds, rooms are scarce throughout the area. Try to reserve well in advance if you think you'll arrive at a busy time.

Autumn Inn

259 Elm St., Northampton, MA 01060. ☎ **413/584-7660.** Fax 413/586-4808. 30 rms and suites. A/C TV TEL. $96 double; $110 suite. Additional person $12 extra; children 3–11 charged $6. AE, DC, MC, V.

This is the closest thing in Northampton to the traditional college inn. From the street, you see an attractive brick house, which fronts comfortable motel units and a small, pretty swimming pool. Special attention is given to good-quality furnishings and equipment here; a lounge and dining room provide sustenance. It's conveniently located within walking distance of the college.

Hotel Northampton

36 King St., Northampton, MA 01061. ☎ **413/584-3100**. 70 rms, 5 suites. A/C TV TEL. $79–$160 double; $211–$350 suite. AE, CB, DC, DISC, MC, V.

The grand Georgian Revival Hotel Northampton, built in 1927, is the most prominent place to stay in town. Commpletely restored and refurbished, the rooms and suites have been furnished with classic pieces (including some four-poster beds) and Laura Ashley fabrics. Suites feature jacuzzis and sitting areas, and many of the rooms have balconies.

Wiggins Tavern is an authentic colonial restaurant serving traditional American fare. The Coolidge Park Café dishes up lighter items and drinks; customers spill out onto the patio for dining in warmer months.

WHERE TO DINE

Curtis and Schwartz

116 Main St. ☎ **413/586-3278**. Reservations not accepted. Breakfast $2.50–$7.50; main courses $3.50–$7.95. AE, DC, MC, V. Mon–Sat 7:30am–3pm, Sun 8am–3pm. INTERNATIONAL.

This is the place for breakfast and lunch (and I do mean breakfast *and* lunch—some devotees come with the newspaper at breakfast, do some shopping, and return for lunch). There's much to love here: pecan waffles with fresh fruit, crème fraîche, and real maple syrup; salad niçoise with mixed greens, tomatoes, cucumbers, red potatoes, green beans, hard-boiled eggs, tuna, olives, capers, anchovies, and a mustard-tarragon vinaigrette; and a cheesy herb omelet served with a warm scone. The Jewish specialties, like latkes, blintzes, and challah bread, are especially good. In a town with many breakfast places, this one reigns. There's always a line, but the wait never seems too long.

✪ La Cazuela

7 Old South St. ☎ **413/586-0400**. Reservations recommended for parties of five or more. Main courses $7.25–$10.75. AE, DISC, MC, V. Mon–Thurs 5–9pm, Fri 5–10pm, Sat–Sun 3–10pm. SOUTHWEST/MEXICAN.

Good Mexican and southwestern cooking in Northampton? You bet, at La Cazuela (it means "earthen cooking pot"), off Main Street. The dining room accented with regional artwork is pleasant, but in the warmer months, if the mosquitoes aren't too fierce, you might prefer eating outside on the terrace. A complimentary basket of corn chips and salsa was hastily dispatched before I settled into *ceviche* (fresh bay scallops in a citrus marinade with jalapeño chiles, tomatoes, red onions, and cilantro) followed by *pollo en adobo* (chunks of chicken breast marinated in New Mexican chile-and-garlic paste, charbroiled with sweet peppers and onions, served over rice with tortillas, guacamole, and Pico de Gallo sauce). Portions of food and drink are generous; a frosty margarita costs $3.75 to $5, depending on its ingredients, and there's a wonderful non-alcoholic, award-winning sangria available. Buen provecho!

Paul and Elizabeth's

150 Main St. ☎ **413/584-4832.** Reservations recommended on weekends. Main courses $7–$16. MC, V. Sun–Thurs 11:30am–9:15pm, Fri–Sat 11:30am–9:30pm (sometimes later). NATURAL FOODS.

On Northampton's main street is Paul and Elizabeth's, a natural-foods restaurant. There's a second entrance on Old South Street, above Herrell's Ice Cream. In the pleasant dining room, you'll see a cross-section of Northampton society dining on fresh fish, salads, tempura, tofu, rice, and noodle dishes, fresh-baked breads, and desserts. Prices are quite moderate. Wine and beer are served.

5 Amherst

7 miles E of Northampton, 16 miles SE of Deerfield

Amherst is a college town, through and through. Though Amherst College is perhaps its best-known institution of higher learning, the University of Massachusetts has a larger presence here. It is also the site of Hampshire College.

GETTING THERE   By Car   Follow Mass. 9 east from Northampton, or I-91 and Mass. 116 north from the Mass. Turnpike.

By Train   See "Springfield," above.

By Bus   See "Springfield," above.

ESSENTIALS   The **telephone area code** is 413. There's an **information booth** right on the town common across the street from the bus depot, or you can look to the **Amherst Area Chamber of Commerce,** 11 Spring St., Amherst, MA 01002 (☎ 413/253-0700), open Monday through Friday from 9am to 3:30pm.

WHAT TO SEE & DO

You'll want to take a tour of **Amherst College,** founded in 1821. The information booth on the town common in Amherst can furnish you with a handy map and guide. The college is all around you. Want more information about the college? Contact Amherst College, Converse Hall (☎ 413/542-2000).

One of the major points of interest near the Amherst College campus is the **Emily Dickinson Homestead** (at 280 Main Street), the poet's birthplace and residence for all but 15 years of her life. The Federal-style house was built in 1813 by Dickinson's grandparents, Samuel Fowler and Lucretia Gunn Dickinson. Although they were a well-to-do family (Samuel was a founder and benefactor of Amherst College), in 1830 they found themselves in a bit of financial trouble; to help out, their son, Edward, moved into the western half of the homestead with his wife, Emily Norcross Dickinson, and their son, Austin. Within a short time, the now-famous poet was born.

Today the homestead is owned by the college and is a faculty residence. Portions of the house—including Emily's bedroom, where she wrote most of her poems—are open to the public by appointment for $3 per person. Hours in May to October are Wednesday through Saturday from 1:30 to 3:45pm; hours in early spring and late fall are Wednesday and Saturday only from 1:30 to 5:30pm. The homestead is closed from December 15 to March 1. Call ☎ 413/542-8161 for an appointment, or write in advance to the Emily Dickinson Homestead, 280 Main St., Amherst, MA 01002.

The sprawling campus of the **University of Massachusetts** takes more time to see, but there's a free PVTA bus line you can use, and an excellent campus map. Ask at the information booth on the common, or at the information desk in the

Campus Center (east end of second-floor concourse; ☎ **413/545-0111**). U. Mass., by the way, was founded in 1863 as Massachusetts Agricultural College. Present enrollment on the Amherst campus is about 24,000—compare that to Amherst College's 1,500.

The roads between Amherst, Northampton, and South Hadley form a triangle and are some of the prettiest in the area. Mass. 116 between Amherst and South Hadley passes **Hampshire College,** the newest and most unconventional of the area's colleges. Farther along the road, you may want to stop at **Atkins Farms** (☎ **413/253-9528**). Cider, pumpkins, apple picking, maple sugar products, and locally grown produce are all here. Atkins has grown so large from its humble beginnings as a farm stand that it now stays open daily, year-round. Continuing along, you'll climb into the Holyoke Mountain Range, a tiny range of mountains that runs east to west. Well-marked hiking trails begin from the visitors center here. Once over "the notch," you'll coast down toward South Hadley.

WHERE TO STAY

Accommodation in the area is very much geared to college life. Most visitors come on college business, and when big college events such as homecomings, graduations, and major football matches draw big crowds, rooms are scarce throughout the area. Try to reserve well in advance if you think you'll arrive at a busy time.

✪ Campus Center Hotel

Murray D. Lincoln Campus Center, U. Mass., Amherst, MA 01003. ☎ **413/549-6000.** Fax 413/545-1210. 116 rms. A/C TV TEL. $76 double or quad. AE, DC, DISC, MC, V. Parking $2.50 a night in the underground garage. Directions: Head north on North Pleasant Street, enter the U. Mass. campus, and follow signs to Campus Center Parking, an underground lot right next to the hotel.

U. Mass. has its own major lodging facility for out-of-towners. Within the Murray D. Lincoln Campus Center, a modern tower, is the Campus Center Hotel. Besides the standard amenities, most rooms have wonderful, panoramic views of the campus, the town, and the surrounding farmland.

Howard Johnson Lodge

401 Russell St., Hadley, MA 01035. ☎ **413/586-0114** or 800/654-2000. 100 rms. A/C TV TEL. $57–$104 double. All rates include continental breakfast. Additional person $10 extra; children under 18 stay free in parents' room. MC, V.

Even though it's very close to Amherst—only a few miles from the town common—its mailing address is Hadley. Rooms are of the high Hojo standard, some with cathedral ceilings and balconies, and in addition the lodge has a nice big outdoor pool and lots of deck chairs for sunning. All rooms are newly renovated and have two double beds. VIP, handicapped-accessible, nonsmoking, and adjoining family rooms are also available. Local phone calls are free.

Northampton Road is the highway (Mass. 9) between Amherst and Northampton. The road starts at the southern end of the town common, and exactly one mile later, after crossing the Amherst town line, it enters a commercial zone. A little farther along Mass. 9 toward Northampton is the local Howard Johnson Lodge.

✪ Lord Jeffery Inn

30 Boltwood Ave., Amherst, MA 01002. ☎ **413/253-2576.** 48 rms, 8 suites. A/C TV TEL. $108–$138 suite. AE, DC, MC, V.

Every college town has its college inn, usually a gracious old place with a refined atmosphere and very comfortable—often plush—accommodations. Amherst is no exception, and the Lord Jeffery, named for Lord Jeffery Amherst, stands right on the town common. The Lord Jeff is cozy, colonial, and collegiate, but with modern conveniences in the comfortable guest rooms. Ask for a room overlooking the garden courtyard. A tavern, lounge, and dining room provide food and refreshment from morning to night (see below).

WHERE TO DINE

Judie's

51 N. Pleasant St. ☎ **413/253-3491.** Reservations not accepted. Main courses $6.50–$9.95 at lunch, $7.95–$14.95 at dinner. AE, DISC, MC, V. Sun–Thurs 11:30am–10pm, Fri–Sat 11:30am–11pm. CONTEMPORARY AMERICAN.

Among the longtime favorites is Judie's, on the town's main street. The eclectic menu has something for everyone, from steaks to salads, from beer-batter potato skins to gooey desserts. For lunch, you might try a cup of seafood bisque and a three-cheese bacon burger. Many people come just for a light meal of soup and a popover with apple butter (a specialty). Or try something from the stuffed popover section of the menu. At dinner you dine in one of several small, attractive rooms in this converted house or on the glassed-in streetside porch. Try the Rockefeller scallops and shrimp or the vegetarian primavera pasta. Go early to get a porch table for lunch. Liquor is served, and there's a great children's menu as well.

Lord Jeffery Inn

30 Boltwood Ave. ☎ **413/253-2576.** Reservations recommended. Main courses $13–$24. AE, DC, MC, V. Daily 7–9:30am; noon–1:30pm; 5–9pm; brunch Sun 11:30am–2pm. CONTINENTAL.

The Lord Jeffery, facing the town common, offers an interesting if mostly traditional menu (steaks, seafood, chicken) in elegant colonial-style formality. Chandeliers provide soft light; in winter a fireplace adds visual as well as thermal warmth.

6 Deerfield

16 miles N of Northampton, 16 miles NW of Amherst, 3 miles S of Greenfield

GETTING THERE By Car From Boston, follow Mass. 2 west, then U.S. 5/Mass. 10 south. From Springfield and the Mass. Pike, follow I-91 north, then Mass. 116 east and U.S. 5/Mass. 10 north.

By Train The closest service you can get is Springfield; see that section, above.

By Bus See "Springfield," above. The closest service is to Greenfield.

ESSENTIALS The **telephone area code** is **413.** The **information desk,** at the museum across from the Deerfield Inn, has maps, brochures, information, and a short audiovisual show that gives you an overview of the village. For information in advance, contact **Historic Deerfield,** P.O. Box 321, Deerfield, MA 01342 (☎ **413/774-5581**). The **Greater Springfield Chamber of Commerce,** 34 Boland Way, Springfield, MA 01103 (☎ **413/787-1555**), also has information on the area.

About 15 miles north of Northampton and Amherst on U.S. 5 and Mass. 10 is **Historic Deerfield,** a mile-long stretch of road lined with well-preserved 18th-century houses. Unlike Old Sturbridge Village or Mystic Seaport, Historic Deerfield is a "gateless museum" where visitors can walk through the old village at any time of day or night. Fourteen historic houses are open as museums displaying more than 25,000 objects made or used in America from 1650 to 1850. Each museum is shown on 20-minute guided tours. Admission tickets to all buildings are $10 for adults and $5 for children 6–17; children under 6 are admitted free. Tickets are valid for two full days. Guided village walking tours are included in the general admission. Single museum house tickets are $5 for adults and $3 for children. You can visit Historic Deerfield daily from 9:30am to 4:30pm every day of the year (with the exception of Thanksgiving, Christmas Eve, and Christmas Day). Throughout the year Historic Deerfield offers lecture series, antique forums, hearth cooking demonstrations and classes, and special events for families.

The **Wright House** (1824), beautiful in itself, holds collections of Chippendale and Federal furniture, American paintings, and Chinese export porcelain. The **Flynt Textile Museum** (1872) houses a large collection of textiles, costumes, and needlework from America, England, and continental Europe. The **Henry N. Flynt Silver and Metalwork Collection** (1814) holds the museum's collection of silver, pewter, and other base metals. The **Allen House** (1720) is furnished with items made in Boston and the Connecticut River Valley. The **Stebbins House** (1799–1810) is a wealthy landowner's residence, with rich period furnishings. The **Barnard Tavern** (1740–95) is a favorite with children because some of its rooms have exhibits that are okay to touch. The **Wells-Thorn House** (1717–51) has a series of period rooms extending from the frontier to the Federal periods. The **Dwight House** (1725) was actually built in Springfield, and moved to Deerfield in 1950. Local furniture and a period doctor's office are the attractions. The **Sheldon-Hawks House** (1743) was home to the same family during two centuries. The Sheldons, rich Deerfield farmers, were able to buy the best available land at the time. The **Ashley House** (1730) was the minister's residence in old times, and by the look of it, this wasn't such a bad life.

One of the most fascinating exhibits is the **Ebenezer Hinsdale Williams House** (1816), which is open to view as a restoration-in-progress. The tour fills you in on the technical and historical work being done to re-create the house as it may have been between 1816 and 1838.

Besides the exhibits of Historic Deerfield, you should see the **Memorial Hall Museum,** at the corner of Memorial Street and U.S. 5 and Mass. 10 (☎ **413/ 774-7476**), open May through October, daily from 10am to 4:30pm. Admission (separate from the other buildings of Historic Deerfield) is $5 for adults, $3 for students, $1 for children 6 to 12, free for children under 6.

Memorial Hall (1798) was the original home of famed Deerfield Academy, still one of New England's most prestigious private schools. Less than a century after its construction, the building became a historical museum of Pocumtuck Valley life, both Native American and Puritan. Local furniture, pewter, tools, textiles, decoration, and tribal artifacts, arranged in period rooms, make up the collection. There are special collections for carved and painted chests, local embroidery, musical instruments, and glass-plate photographs (1880–1920) by the Allen sisters, Deerfield's talented early photographers.

But no exhibit here is more memorable than the **Indian House Door.** Old Deerfield survived two Native American massacres and numerous other battles in its early days on the New England ferry. It was the night of February 29, 1704, during the French and Indian Wars, when the Sheldon House (now gone) was attacked, its door suffering the punishment of tomahawk chops and bashes. The attackers finally hacked a hole in the center, through which they got at the inhabitants. This door brings American history to life.

For a closer look at the Connecticut River, climb aboard the *Quinnetukut II* riverboat, Mass. 63 North (☎ **413/659-3714**), for a 12-mile, 1¹/₂-hour interpretive **boat cruise.** Geology, ecology, and history of the river are the featured subjects, but the scenery alone is worth the fee: $7 per adult ($6 for seniors), $3 per child 14 and under. Call for schedules so that you're sure to get the cruise you want. Reservations are required. Buy your tickets at the Northfield Mountain Recreation and Environmental Center, on Mass. 63 to the north of Mass. 2, due east of Greenfield (take I-91 north to Exit 27, then Mass. 2 east, then Mass. 63 north). It's open Wednesday through Sunday from 9am to 5pm.

WHERE TO STAY
IN DEERFIELD
Deerfield Inn

The Street, Deerfield, MA 01342. ☎ **413/774-5587,** or 800/926-3865 outside MA. Fax 413/773-8712. 23 rms. A/C TV TEL. $140.50 double. Additional person $43.50 extra. All rates include breakfast and service. AE, DC, MC, V. Closed Christmas.

Built in 1884 and modernized in 1981 after a fire, the Deerfield Inn, in the center of town, has rooms inspired—shall we say—by the 18th century, but constructed with 20th-century materials and comforts. They're decorated with period pieces and good replicas to put you in the mood of two centuries ago. There's a fine restaurant, coffee shop, bar, and two living rooms; on the front porch, rocking chairs are all set to take in the view of Historic Deerfield, with its 14 museum houses. The inn is open all year (except for several days at Christmas). Jane and Karl Sabo are your innkeepers here. The inn is now entirely nonsmoking.

NEARBY
1797 House

Charlemont Rd., Buckland, MA 01338. ☎ **413/625-2975.** 3 rms. $80 double. All rates include breakfast. No credit cards.

In Buckland, on the green, stands the 1797 House, run by a very hospitable hostess named Janet Turley. The house (built guess when?) has immaculate guest rooms with down quilts; there are numerous fireplaces, a screened porch for warm-weather breakfast or relaxation, and interesting nooks and corners. The full country breakfast is juice, fruit, eggs, breakfast meats, French toast (or other main dish), and a hot beverage. Buckland is a few miles southwest of Shelburne Falls, just off Mass. 112.

7 The Berkshires

The grand residences and hotels of the wealthy remain in Stockbridge, Lenox, Williamstown, and other Berkshire communities, adding to the romance and interest of the area. Today, the lure of the Berkshires is enhanced by the Berkshire Music Festival at Tanglewood, near Lenox. Williamstown, in the northern Berkshires, the home of Williams College since 1785, continues to draw crowds attracted to its beauty and educational opportunities. Whatever your reason for going, you can't fail to enjoy the lush countryside, the picturesque towns with rows of fine houses, and the acres of manicured greenery.

LEE

45 miles W of Springfield, 134 miles W of Boston, 5 miles SE of Lenox, 11 miles NE of Great Barrington

The Berkshires

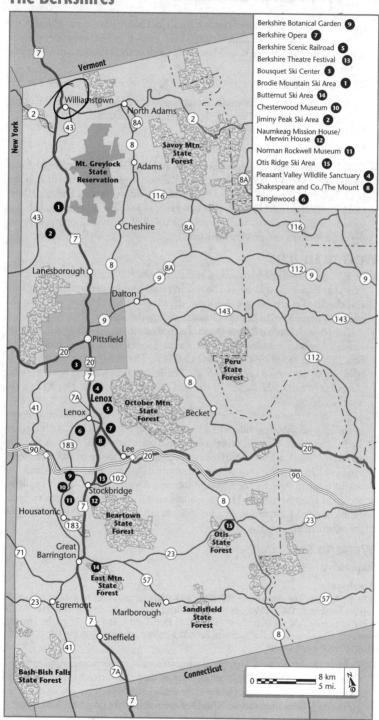

Berkshire Botanical Garden **9**
Berkshire Opera **7**
Berkshire Scenic Railroad **5**
Berkshire Theatre Festival **13**
Bousquet Ski Center **3**
Brodie Mountain Ski Area **1**
Butternut Ski Area **14**
Chesterwood Museum **10**
Jiminy Peak Ski Area **2**
Naumkeag Mission House/
Merwin House **12**
Norman Rockwell Museum **11**
Otis Ridge Ski Area **15**
Pleasant Valley Wildlife Sanctuary **4**
Shakespeare and Co./The Mount **8**
Tanglewood **6**

Vermont

New York

Williamstown

North Adams

Savoy Mtn.
State
Forest

Mt. Greylock
State
Reservation

Adams

Cheshire

Lanesborough

Dalton

Pittsfield

Peru
State
Forest

Bousquet

Lenox

October Mtn.
State
Forest

Becket

Lee

Stockbridge

Housatonic

Beartown
State
Forest

Otis
State
Forest

Great
Barrington

East Mtn.
State
Forest

Egremont

New
Marlborough

Sandisfield
State
Forest

Sheffield

Bash-Bish Falls
State Forest

Connecticut

0   8 km
     5 mi.

N

Lee is famous for its summer dance festival, and many people pass through the town on their way to the Tanglewood Music Festival in Lenox. By the way, the hamlet named **South Lee** is on Mass. 102, south of the Massachusetts Turnpike (I-90) and Lee proper.

GETTING THERE   By Car   Take the Mass. Turnpike (I-90) to the Lee exit.

By Train   Coming from Boston, trains stop in Pittsfield, 11 miles to the north. If you are coming from New York City and Montréal, the nearest station is Albany-Rensselaer.

By Bus   See the beginning of this chapter.

ESSENTIALS   The **telephone area code** is **413.** The **Lee Chamber of Commerce** (☎ 413/243-0852) is located on Railroad Street in the Airoldi Building (P.O. Box 345), Lee, MA 01238. The **Berkshire Visitors Bureau,** Berkshire Common, Pittsfield, MA 01201 (☎ **413/443-9186,** or **800/237-5747** in the U.S. and Canada), can provide you with information on all of Berkshire County, covering the entire western end of Massachusetts.

WHAT TO SEE & DO

In 1932, a dilapidated barn served as the birthplace of a major American dance festival in Becket. Bought by Ted Shawn and renovated for performances, the barn and the festival grew larger and more important over the years, enlisting the talents of Mark Morris, Martha Graham, and similar lights.

The 10-week **Jacob's Pillow Dance Festival** season begins in late June and runs through August. For a season brochure, contact Jacob's Pillow Dance Festival, P.O. Box 287, Lee, MA 01238 (☎ **413/243-0745**). The performance center is eight miles east of downtown Lee, off U.S. 20. Performing groups change weekly. Ticket prices range from $27 to $42 in the Ted Shawn Theatre and cost $12 in the Studio/Theatre.

Besides the dance festival, the most notable sight in Lee is not in Lee at all but in the tiny neighboring village of Tyringham, five miles south of Lee along the Tyringham Road. It's the **Tyringham Art Galleries** (known by many as the Gingerbread House), a curious thatched cottage built as a studio by sculptor Henry Hudson Kitson at the turn of the century. Kitson's most famous statue is the one of Captain Parker (*The Minute Man*) on Lexington Green. The art galleries are open from Memorial Day to Columbus Day, daily from 10am to 5pm. Admission is $1 for adults, free for children under 12. Call ☎ 413/243-3260 for information.

WHERE TO STAY
Expensive

Applegate
279 W. Park St., Lee, MA 01238. ☎ **413/243-4451.** 6 rms. A/C. Nov–May, $85–$150 double weekdays, $107–$190 weekends; June–Oct, $100–$190 double weekdays, $120–$210 weekends. MC, V. Directions: Take I-90 to Exit 2 and follow U.S. 20 to the first stop sign; go straight through the stop sign for half a mile; Applegate is on the left, across the street from the golf course.

Built in the 1920s by a New York surgeon as a summer home, Applegate is a Georgian colonial home built on six acres of land and surrounded by apple and pine trees. Nancy and Rick Cannata, the innkeepers, will escort you to one of six individually decorated rooms. Several of the rooms have fireplaces, and Room 1 has a sauna/steam shower. Room 6 has grandma's evening cape and topper on the nightstand. Most of the beds are antiques or reproductions, and all have down comforters. Room colors vary from white to peach to forest green, and brandy and chocolates await your arrival. There is now a separate sitting room with a TV and VCR for those rainy days, and guests have full use of the pool and can borrow bicycles. Also available at Applegate is a fully equipped carriage house apartment complete with a Jacuzzi, a TV/VCR, a dining room, two bedrooms, and a kitchen. It is a long-term rental ($950 per week, with a two-week minimum in summer).

Candlelight breakfast (with silver candelabras), served in the dining room, might consist of orange scones and sour-cream loaf, cereal, yogurt, freshly squeezed orange juice, coffee, and tea. Wine and cheese are served every evening at 5pm. Be on the lookout for Ray, the resident cockatiel.

Chambéry Inn

199 Main St. Lee, MA 01238. ☎ **413/243-2221** or 800/537-4321. Fax 413/243-3600. 2 rms, 6 suites. A/C TV TEL. July–Sept 4 and Oct: $85–$95 double weekdays, $125–$150 weekends; $135 suite weekdays, $195 weekends. The rest of the year: $55 double weekdays, $85–$125 weekends; $95 suite weekdays, $145 weekends. AE, DISC, MC, V. Directions: From I-90, take Exit 2 to U.S. 20; the inn is one mile from I-90.

Constructed in 1885, the Chambéry Inn was once Saint Mary's School, a parochial school run by the teaching order Sisters of Saint Joseph, who came to the United States from Chambéry, France (hence the name). Originally located only a block away, the building was scheduled to be demolished in 1988 but was saved by the current owners, Joe and Lynn Toole, and moved to its present location. The inn is a luxury hostelry with a unique twist—the schoolhouse chalkboards still remain in the rooms. You are, of course, supplied with chalk and erasers, and you can read all the wonderful things people have written on the boards about their stay at the inn. Also, because it was a schoolhouse, the rooms are extraordinarily large and have 12-foot ceilings. Each suite has two queen-size or one king-size canopy bed, a sitting area, a fireplace, and a whirlpool tub.

A continental breakfast of granola or breakfast pastries with coffee, tea, or juice, will be delivered to your door at the time you specify on the card you hang on your door at night. There's a library for quiet reading or small meetings. The inn is nonsmoking. No children under 16 are admitted.

Federal House

Main St., South Lee, MA 01260. ☎ **413/243-1824.** 6 rms. A/C. High season, $155 double. Off-season, $75–$95 double. All rates include breakfast. Three-night minimum stay July–Aug. AE, MC, V. Directions: Follow Mass. 102 south to South Lee; Federal House is on the right-hand side in the center of town.

Thomas O. Hurlbut had the brick Greek Revival mansion built in 1824 when he was head of the Owen and Hurlbut Paper Company here. Owned by the original family for 124 years, it was just recently converted to an inn. The guest rooms have many original touches and furnishings. The Federal House is famous for its cuisine (wine and cheese are served in the inn every afternoon) as well as its rooms (see "Where to Dine," below).

Moderate

Historic Merrell Inn

1565 Pleasant St., South Lee, MA 01260. ☎ **413/243-1794** or 800/243-1794. Fax 413/243-2669. 9 rms. A/C TEL. Summer–fall, $75–$95 double weekdays, $115–$135 weekends;

Nov–June, $55–$85 weekdays, $65–$95 weekends. All rates include breakfast. Additional person $15 extra. MC, V. Directions: Follow Mass. 102 south to South Lee; the inn is on the left-hand side in the center of town.

Right on village main street and along a riverbank is Charles and Faith Reynolds's elegant and authentic inn. "Authentic" describes it well, for this house, built in 1794, has been an inn since 1817. From 1947 to 1981 it belonged to the Society for the Preservation of New England Antiquities. Preservation of the inn's character, including a nonfunctioning but historic birdcage bar and authentic period furnishings, has obviously been of paramount importance. The guest rooms have recently been redecorated and include finer touches like designer-print sheets, beautiful wall hangings, and an extensive array of Gilchrist and Soanes amenities. Full cooked-to-order breakfasts are served by the fire in cool weather. In warm weather, guests enjoy a screened gazebo located at river's edge.

Inexpensive

Lee has numerous guesthouses. They're not furnished with antiques like Lenox's inns, and many don't have dining rooms, but they offer good lodging value in the Berkshires. Exactly what you pay depends on the particular room in the particular private home, but the price will easily be less than half that for a room in Lenox. As the rooms are scattered around town, the **Lee Chamber of Commerce,** Railroad Street, in the Airoldi Building (P.O. Box 345), Lee, MA 01238 (☎ **413/ 243-0852**), handles reservations. An after-hours phone number is placed in the window of the information booth when it's closed.

WHERE TO DINE

Federal House

Main St. ☎ **413/243-1824.** Reservations required, especially on weekends (taken 5:30–6:30pm). Main courses $16–$24. AE, MC, V. Daily 6:30pm–closing. Directions: Follow Mass. 102 south to South Lee; the Federal House is on the right-hand side in the center of town. CONTINENTAL.

The Federal House is among the Berkshires' more acclaimed restaurants. Elegantly set tables are arranged in the mansion's original dining room, front parlor, and billiards room. To get a table on Friday or Saturday evening you must reserve well in advance for one of the two seatings. The fare is continental and classic, with innovative touches: ravioli stuffed with goat cheese, medallions of pork sautéed with Granny Smith apples, duck with maple-pecan bourbon sauce, or salmon with saffron-leek cream sauce. Desserts might include profiteroles, lime mousse with raspberry sauce, or bittersweet-chocolate torte.

Sullivan Station Restaurant

Railroad St. ☎ **413/243-2082.** Reservations are recommended. Main courses $10.95–$14.95. MC, V. Daily 11:30am–closing. AMERICAN.

You won't be surprised to learn that the owner of the Sullivan Station Restaurant is the same person who owns the Chambéry Inn, located just across the street. This old railroad passenger depot, built in 1893 to accommodate travelers on the New York, New Haven, and Hartford Railroad, has been converted into a casual eatery. The menu changes frequently but always includes a soup of the day, sandwiches, and salads at lunch. At dinner you might find traditional dishes, like roast rack of lamb or baked scrod. There is also a variety of pasta selections.

LENOX

5 miles NW of Lee, 7 miles S of Pittsfield, 23 miles S of Williamstown

In the 1700s, pioneers spreading through the lands west of Boston came to settle among the fertile fields of the Berkshires. At first the settlement at Lenox was called Yokuntown, after a Native American chief, but the name was later changed to honor an English lord—Charles Lenox, Duke of Richmond—who was sympathetic to the American Revolutionary cause. Although small industries have at times appeared in the town, it has been predominantly rural and agricultural, and has remained unspoiled. In the 19th century, business tycoons (including Andrew Carnegie) came to admire the tidy farms and streets of Lenox as the perfect place for a summer's retreat, and many of them bought up farms for this purpose. The houses are still standing for visitors to admire.

GETTING THERE   By Car   Take the Mass. Turnpike to the Lee exit, then follow U.S. 20 West. From Williamstown, follow U.S. 7 South. Mass. 183 goes right to Tanglewood. See also the beginning of this chapter.

By Train   Coming from Boston, trains stop in Pittsfield, seven miles to the north. If you are coming from New York City or Montréal, the nearest station is Albany-Rensselaer.

By Bus   See the beginning of this chapter.

ESSENTIALS   The **telephone area code** is **413.** For information, apply to the **Lenox Chamber of Commerce,** Lenox Academy Building, 75 Main Street, Lenox, MA 01240 (☎ **413/637-3646** or **800/25-LENOX**). The **Berkshire Visitors Bureau,** Berkshire Common, Pittsfield, MA 01201 (☎ **413/443-9186,** or **800/ 237-5747** in the U.S. and Canada), can provide you with information on all of Berkshire County, covering the entire western end of Massachusetts.

SPECIAL EVENTS   For information on **Tanglewood,** see below. In nearby Pittsfield, **South Mountain Concerts** (☎ **413/442-2106**) specializes in chamber music, and concerts begin in August and last into October. South Mountain Concerts was started in 1918 in a lovely old hall located a mile south of Pittsfield on U.S. 7 and 20. For a printed schedule of concerts, drop a line to the South Mountain Association, P.O. Box 23, Pittsfield, MA 01202.

WHAT TO SEE & DO

✪ Tanglewood

The number-one activity in Lenox is, of course, Tanglewood, the summer home of the Boston Symphony Orchestra. Since 1934, concerts have been held in July and August on the grounds of Tanglewood, a fine estate about a mile from the center of Lenox out in the Berkshire Hills. More than 50 concerts—by full orchestra, chamber groups, and soloists in recital—take place during the Tanglewood season, including the famous weekend BSO concerts. In addition to the seasoned musicians from the Boston Symphony, there are performances by the young and extremely promising musicians who attend the Tanglewood Music Center for study and advanced training. Maestro Seiji Ozawa, now music director of the BSO for 21 years, was once among this young up-and-coming elite.

In 1994, Tanglewood opened a new performance hall, completing the seven-year expansion plan that was begun in 1987. It has been named for Seiji Ozawa, who began his career at Tanglewood in 1960 when he was a conducting fellow at the tender age of 24. Its opening marked Mr. Ozawa's 20th-anniversary season as music director of the Boston Symphony Orchestra. The gala opening concert featured Yo-Yo Ma, Peter Serkin, Leon Fleisher, John Williams, and Jessye Norman.

Programs of the concert series are available from the information booth in Lenox, or by mail from Symphony Hall, 301 Massachusetts Ave., Boston, MA 02115. For recorded concert information, call the Tanglewood Concert Line (☎ 413/637-1666) in July and August. For other information, call Symphony Hall (☎ 617/266-1492) until early June; from early June until the end of the season, call Tanglewood (☎ 413/637-5165).

Seats in the Music Shed ($13.50 to $70) are bought up early, but lawn tickets ($12 to $15, depending on the concert) are easy to find at Tanglewood. Concert hall tickets range in price from $21 to $36; lawn tickets for the recitals in the concert hall range from $11 to $12. Tickets (except for lawn tickets) can be bought by phone through **Ticketmaster** (☎ 617/931-2000 in Boston, **212/ 307-7171** in New York City, **413/733-2100** in Western Massachusetts, or **800/347-0808** elsewhere); you'll pay a small service charge for this convenience. You may also book tickets through **Symphonycharge** in Boston by calling ☎ **800/274-8499.** In addition, tickets may be purchased in person at the Tanglewood Box Office. Children under 12 can attend free of charge. Up to four free children's tickets can be obtained at one time by a parent or guardian and can be picked up at the Tanglewood Box Office the day of the performance.

Tanglewood also sponsors a series of popular, folk, and jazz concerts in addition to the more lofty Tanglewood Music Festival series. When you call ☎ **413/ 637-5165,** ask about what's coming up in the **Popular Artists' Series.**

Special excursions to Tanglewood concerts are offered by various tour companies, including, in New York City, **Biss Tours** (☎ 718/426-4000) and **Parker Tours** (☎ 718/428-7800). From Boston, **K & L Tours** (☎ 617/ 267-1905) will take you there, or you can catch a bus run by Peter Pan Trailways (☎ 617/426-7838).

Tips   If you drive to Tanglewood, here are some tips to make things easier. First, expect heavy highway traffic. Plan to get to Tanglewood proper at least two hours before the concert begins. Bring your picnic—everyone does, and that's why the parking lots fill up early.

Now you can also order a picnic through the **Tanglewood Functions Office** (☎ 413/637-5165). The boxed supper consists of two vegetables, a salad, croissants, cheese, chocolates, and an entrée. You might have a choice of cold salmon with a vinaigrette sauce, sliced tenderloin with a Dijon sauce, spiced raspberry chicken, jumbo shrimp, or lobster. Prices range from $8 to $25 per person, depending on your order. If you're in the mood for a special treat, order one of the more extensive picnic baskets ($35 to $65) 24 hours in advance. Call the Functions Office for more details.

If you don't feel like bringing or ordering a picnic, you can always grab a bite at Tanglewood's new cafe, which serves gourmet coffees, beers, and wine and cheese, and has an international grill.

Expect a tremendous jam of traffic when you leave at the end of the concert. The flood is ably directed by Tanglewood staff, but the exodus takes time nonetheless.

Other Attractions

What do William Shakespeare and Edith Wharton have in common? **The Mount** (☎ 413/637-1899) is a house and gardens planned by Wharton, a Pulitzer Prize–winning author. You can tour the house and watch a salon drama based on Wharton's life and works, June through October, Monday noon to 3pm and Tuesday through Sunday from 10am to 2pm.

You can see Shakespeare under the stars or under the sun at the Mount, the regal home in a pastoral setting of Shakespeare & Company, Lenox, MA 01240 (☎ 413/637-3353 for the box office). As many as eight performances daily of both Shakespearean and modern plays are presented May 26 through September 4 in two outdoor and two indoor theaters (closed Monday). Performances begin at noon (10:30am on Saturday and Sunday) and continue through the evening. Shakespeare in the open air on a warm summer evening is definitely among the finer things in life!

The Mount is located just south of Lenox, at the junction of U.S. 7 and Mass. 7A.

Lenox is also home to the **Berkshire Scenic Railway Museum,** Willow Creek Road (☎ 413/637-2210), where you can find out about local railroad lore, poke around in a New Haven Railroad caboose, watch model railroads run, and see railroading videos; there's a gift shop, too. Nostalgic excursion trains take visitors on a 15-minute ride over yard tracks. There's also a locomotive cab tour for the kids. (Tours are available on Saturday, Sunday, and holidays from Memorial Day through October.) Drop by, or call, for the latest information on the trains.

In Lenox proper, be sure to walk to the top of the hill on Main Street (U.S. 7), north of the center of town, to see the **Church on the Hill,** a very fine New England Congregational church building erected in 1805.

Otherwise, long walks or a drive around the "back streets" and lanes of Lenox can turn up unexpected sights: tremendous mansions, even small castles, nestled in fine parks and copses of trees, once occupied for a few months in summer by commercial and industrial magnates and their immediate families. Many of the mansions are still in private hands, enjoyed by an ever-widening circle of the descendants of the original builders. Most are not open to the public, so you must settle for tantalizing looks from the sidewalk.

For a beautiful hike through 1,000 acres of the Berkshire countryside, find your way to the **Pleasant Valley Sanctuary,** northwest of Lenox. Follow the signs, or take Mass. 7A north to West Dugway Road, then West Mountain Road. Pay the admission fee ($3 for adults, $2 for children 3 to 16; children under 3 are free), and set out on the seven miles of nature trails to explore native Berkshire flora and fauna. It's open Tuesday through Sunday from dawn to dusk. The Pleasant Valley Sanctuary also sponsors 1½-hour bat walks twice in the summer; call ☎ 413/637-0320 for dates and information.

WHERE TO STAY

The overnight lodging situation in Lenox is not the best. Proprietors of inns and motels bemoan the short season and the incredible press of traffic on Tanglewood weekends, which thins out to less-than-capacity during the week. For most lodging places, rooms are in great demand. Some Tanglewood travelers stay as far east as Springfield and drive to the concert, then back to Springfield. In any case, have reservations for weekends.

During the off-season, though, all that's missing from Lenox is Tanglewood and the crowds. The same gorgeous rooms are still here, but at a fraction of the price. More and more travelers are realizing this value and making the Berkshires a year-round destination.

If you'd like to stay in a bed-and-breakfast, contact **Berkshire Bed-and-Breakfast,** P.O. Box 211, Williamsburg, MA 01096 (☎ **413/268-7244**). They publish a directory of homes scattered throughout the Berkshires, eastern New York State, Greater Springfield, the Pioneer Valley, and Sturbridge. Write for a copy, or call between 9am and 6pm weekdays.

Very Expensive

Canyon Ranch

91 Kemble St., Lenox, MA 01240. ☎ **413/637-4100** or 800/742-9000. Fax 413/637-3245. 120 units. A/C TV TEL. $4,100–$5,700 double per week. Daily rates are available, but there is a three-night minimum requirement. All rates include three meals per day. AE, DC, DISC, MC, V.

You'll pass through a rather foreboding gate on your way into Canyon Ranch, but don't be put off—this resort spa lacks pretention in almost every aspect. Rooms are standard throughout and are furnished with desks, upholstered chairs, and armoires (televisions hidden within). Hunter-green wall-to-wall carpeting is complemented by the bedspreads. Bathrooms are large. The most formal part of Canyon Ranch is the main building, built in 1897 of brick and marble (part of the Bellefontaine estate), in which are housed the dining and beauty treatment rooms. All meals are low in fat and calories, alcohol is not served, and true to spa fashion, smoking is not allowed. There are plenty of outdoor activities available on this 120-acre estate. Bicycles, cross-country skis, and canoes are available for guest use; and there are racquetball, squash, tennis, and basketball courts, as well as weight-training facilities, a pool, an indoor track, and an aerobics studio. Children under 14 are not welcome.

Gateways Inn

51 Walker St., Lenox, MA 01240. ☎ **413/637-2532.** Fax 413/637-1432. 12 rms. A/C TV TEL. June 28–Oct 30, $120–$215 double weekdays, $165–$295 weekends; Oct 31–June 27, $85–$185 double weekdays, $125–$260 weekends. All rates include continental breakfast. Three-night minimum stay July–Aug Thurs–Sun. AE, DC, DISC, MC, V.

The rather formal Gateways Inn is a fine place to stay and an even finer place to dine. Quite near the center of Lenox, the Gateways is a grand old dove-gray mansion built by Harley Procter of Procter & Gamble in 1912. Accommodations are large—in fact, the Fiedler Suite is almost cavernous. Some rooms have working fireplaces for use in winter. The main courses at dinner cost between $12.50 and $21.50 and may include médaillons of beef or rack of lamb. Lunch is offered July through October.

Kemble Inn

2 Kemble St., Lenox, MA 01240. ☎ **413/637-4113** or 800/353-4113. 12 rms. A/C. July–Oct, $90–$225 double weekdays, $125–$295 weekends; Nov–June, $75–$175 double weekdays, $100–$195 weekends. All rates include continental breakfast. Three-night minimum during Tanglewood season, two-night minimum during the fall and on holiday weekends. MC, V.

The Kemble Inn would likely bring a smile to the face of its namesake, the legendary 19th-century American actress Fanny Kemble, who spent four decades making the residents of the Berkshires laugh out loud. Built in 1881 by Secretary of State Frederick T. Frelinghuysen, the smoke-free Kemble Inn is owned today by Richard and Linda Reardon, who purchased it in late 1993. They opened their doors to the public in February 1994 and have been delighting guests with their hospitality for well over two years now. The home's beautiful wraparound staircase sets the stage for a vacation filled with elegance and beauty, and the sweeping mountain view is the backdrop that completes the scene. Guest rooms (each named for an American author who was associated with the Berkshires at one time or another) are spacious and individually decorated. You'll find rooms with hardwood floors covered with Oriental rugs or wall-to-wall carpeting throughout. Each room also has floral fabric draperies and bed coverings, as well as high-quality reproduction furnishings. The master room boasts a fireplace in both the bedroom and the bathroom, as well as a Jacuzzi. Some rooms have four-poster beds. Children over 15 are welcome.

Wheatleigh

W. Hawthorne Rd. (P.O. Box 824), Lenox, MA 01240. ☎ **413/637-0610** or 800/321-0610. Fax 413/637-4507. 17 rms and suites. A/C TEL. $155–$525 double. AE, DC, MC, V. Directions: From the monument intersection in Lenox, go down the hill on Old Stockbridge Road and turn right onto Hawthorne Street; at Hawthorne Road, turn left.

Of the Berkshire inns, none is more dignified (perhaps even somewhat stuffy) than Wheatleigh. At the center of the vast estate is the tawny brick mansion in the style of a 16th-century Florentine villa, which once belonged to the American-born Contessa de Heredia. The gracious turn-of-the-century, top-of-the-heap lifestyle has been preserved in the airy public rooms, the porticoed and balconied guest rooms, and the sweeping lawns. There are Tiffany windows and beautiful views. Full payment is required for a confirmed reservation. The restaurant is comparable to New York's finest; dinner is served daily. The inn also has tennis courts and an outdoor pool.

Expensive

Apple Tree Inn and Restaurant

334 West St., Lenox, MA 01240. ☎ **413/637-1477.** 34 rms and suites (32 with bath). A/C. High season, $150–$300 double. Off-season, $75–$240 double. All rates include continental breakfast. AE, DC, MC, V. Directions: Just past Tanglewood's main gate, bear right at fork and look for the inn's sign.

"Across the road from Tanglewood" is how the owners describe the Apple Tree Inn and Restaurant. The name suits, for the century-old mansion is indeed in the midst of an apple orchard. Perched high on the hill directly opposite Tanglewood's West Street entrance, the gracious restaurant and public rooms, and many of the guest rooms, look out on a gorgeous panorama. Some rooms in the main house have a fireplace, most have private bath, and some have televisions. There are also 20 modern rooms in the nearby guest lodge. The inn has a heated swimming pool and a clay tennis court.

Cliffwood Inn

25 Cliffwood St., Lenox, MA 01240. ☎ **413/637-3330** or 800/789-3331. Fax 413/637-0221. 7 rms. A/C. High season, $100–$200 double. Off-season, $72–$140 double. All rates include continental breakfast. No credit cards.

The Cliffwood is a vast 1889 mansion set back from the street on its own crescent-shaped drive. As you pass through the curious split Dutch front door into the spacious foyer, you'll be surprised to learn that there are only seven bedrooms (six with fireplace) for rent—the huge place looks as if it should hold many more. Each of the bedrooms is named for an ancestor of innkeepers Joy and Scottie Farrelly, and holds a picture and biography of its namesake. In five minutes you can walk to town. There's a pool.

Rookwood Inn

19 Stockbridge Rd. (P.O. Box 1717), Lenox, MA 01240. ☎ **508/413/637-9750** or 800/ 223-9750. 19 rms, 2 suites. A/C. June 30–Sept 1, $85–$150 double weekdays, $140–$225 double weekends; Sept 2–22 and Nov 1–June 29, $75–$130 double weekdays, $80–$160 double weekends; Sept 23–Oct 31, $90–$140 double weekdays, $130–$180 double weekends. All rates inlcude breakfast and afternoon tea. AE. Directions: From the statue at the town center, take a left onto Stockbridge Road; Rookwood is the first building on the left.

Just a short walk down the hill from the monument intersection in Lenox is the Rookwood Inn, a charming Victorian place with a well-kept lawn and formal gardens. It can accommodate up to 35 guests. Seven rooms have working fireplaces, a few rooms have a small screened-in porch, and one has a multiwindowed turret. Spaces in this gracious turn-of-the-century "cottage" are larger than normal. Rookwood is entirely nonsmoking.

Walker House

64 Walker St., Lenox, MA 01240. ☎ **413/637-1271** or 800/235-3098. 8 rms. A/C. $60–$190 double. All rates include breakfast. Additional person $15 extra. No credit cards. Directions: After the stop sign in Lenox Village, turn left and the Walker House is on the left.

This spacious house, right in the heart of town, was built in 1804. Each room is named after a composer, some have fireplaces, and many look onto the three acres of lawn, gardens, and woods. Common rooms are decorated with modern art and attractive antiques, creating gracious eclectic spaces. There's also a 100-inch television for screening movies or watching regular programs. Walker House is smoke-free.

Moderate

Brook Farm Inn

15 Hawthorne St., Lenox, MA 01240. ☎ **413/637-3013** or 800/285-POET. 12 rms. July–Sept 7, $100–$120 double weekdays, $110–$175 weekends; Sept 5–21, $65–$90 double weekdays, $95–$110 weekends; Sept 22 to Oct 31, $75–$110 double weekdays, $95–$135 weekends; Nov–June, $65–$100 double weekdays, $80–$115 weekends. All rates include breakfast. MC, V. Directions: Go down the hill from the monument intersection on Old Stockbridge Road, and turn right onto Hawthorne Street.

About two blocks from the center of town is the Brook Farm Inn, run by Joe and Anne Miller, with a cozy, authentic Victorian atmosphere and a swimming pool. The brochure claims "there is poetry here," and there is: Hundreds of volumes are carefully organized on shelves, and there are poetry readings on Saturday afternoon. In the library, an unfinished jigsaw puzzle tempts you to add a piece, or you can just read a book and sit by the fire.

You might like Room 5, a bright room with butterfly-and-flower wallpaper and a pastel-colored quilt, a wicker rocker, and a white dresser. Room 8, which is under the eaves, has deep mauve wallpaper, rose carpeting, oak furnishings, and a skylight. Six of the rooms have fireplaces.

Breakfast is served buffet style at a formal dining table and includes granola, fresh fruit and juices, bread pudding, or an egg dish. In the afternoon, tea and scones are served. Additionally, coffee and tea are free and available throughout the day at the new butler's pantry.

Candlelight Inn

35 Walker St. (P.O. Box 715), Lenox, MA 01240. ☎ **413/637-1555.** 8 rms. A/C. July–Aug and Oct, $160–$160 double; Nov–June and Sept, $90–$135 double. AE, MC, V.

The Candlelight Inn, at the corner of Church Street in the center of town, is best known for its restaurant, but there are rooms for rent in the big and graceful old house. The location is excellent. Call early for July, August, or October reservations.

The Gables Inn

81 Walker St., Lenox, MA 01240. ☎ **413/637-3416.** 19 rms. A/C. $60–$195 double. All rates include breakfast. DISC, MC, V.

Built in 1885, The Gables, in the center of town, is a Queen Anne–style Berkshire "cottage." Once owned by the family of Edith Wharton's husband, this was her home for two years while she waited for her own cottage, the Mount, to be built. The present innkeepers have re-created the famous eight-sided library where Mrs. Wharton wrote many short stories. Stay at The Gables to surround yourself with all this grace and history (as well as a swimming pool and tennis court).

Garden Gables Inn

135 Main St. (P.O. Box 52), Lenox, MA 01240. ☎ **413/637-0193.** Fax 413/637-4554. 18 rms. TEL. June–Oct, $70–$200 double. All rates include full breakfast. Nov–May, rates dramatically lower. Three-night minimum on weekends July–Aug and on holiday weekends. AE, MC, V.

The Garden Gables Inn, at the bottom of Church Hill down its own private road, is very near the center of town. The inn's name is appropriate, as you'll see when you drive or walk down the road through the gardens to the large white house with three sharply triangular gables set in its roof. The shape of the house gives you a clue that all the rooms are of different shapes and sizes, with lots of interesting nooks, crannies, and angles. All are furnished differently; some have working fireplaces, TVs with VCRs, whirlpool tubs, and private balconies or porches. Downstairs are two cozy low-ceilinged living rooms with rows of books and fireplaces as well as a rare Steinway grand piano. The lowest price is for a small room in midweek, and the highest price for a large room on a weekend. The inn has its own 72-foot pool out back.

Village Inn

16 Church St. (P.O. Box 1810), Lenox, MA 01240. ☎ **413/637-0200** or 800/253-0917. Fax 413/637-9756. 32 rms. A/C TEL. Summer, $90–$195 double; fall, $80–$165 double; winter, $70–$150 double; spring, $60–$130 double. AE, DC, MC, V.

Right downtown is the Village Inn, a charming old landmark built in Federal-style in 1771. All rooms are individually furnished with country antiques and are decorated with stenciled wallpapers and Oriental rugs. Six of the rooms have fireplaces, and many have four-poster beds. One Sunday a month the inn features an afternoon tea accompanied by chamber music. The Village Inn Restaurant is good for breakfast (Belgian waffles, a farmer's omelette, or eggs Benedict) English tea (with homemade scones and Devonshire cream), and dinner; and the tavern features English ales and a light menu.

WHERE TO DINE

Most of the inns mentioned above have excellent dining rooms. For a change of pace, try this place:

Church Street Café

65 Church St. ☎ **413/637-2745.** Reservations required. Main courses $15.95–$19.95. MC, V. Daily 11:30am–2pm; Sun–Thurs 5:30–9pm, Fri–Sat 5–9:15pm. Closed Sun–Mon in winter. AMERICAN/ECLECTIC.

This very successful "American bistro" serves lunch and dinner daily and Sunday brunch in small, cozy dining rooms or out on pleasant covered decks. Service is personal and informal, and prices are quite moderate for Lenox. Try the grilled garlic sausage served with a French green lentil salad, cornichons, mustard, and peasant bread to start; then follow with Jamaican spiced grilled pork loin with rice, black beans, and watercress salad with a mango vinaigrette; and finish with lemon-almond tart and espresso. The pasta and the country pâté are homemade here. Luncheon includes sandwiches and a few good southwestern items.

STOCKBRIDGE

6 miles S of Lenox, 4 miles SW of Lee, 7 miles N of Great Barrington

Any way you look at it, Stockbridge is a beautiful town. Its wide Main Street is lined with grand houses and other buildings each set apart in its own lawns and gardens. Stately trees fill the skyline. Stockbridge is the center of many Berkshire activities, including the Berkshire Playhouse (details below); it was also once the home of famed painter Norman Rockwell. It's rich in historical and cultural attractions.

In addition to the sights listed below, it's also worth taking a look at a sumptuous estate atop Eden Hill in Stockbridge. From its beginning as a Native American mission in 1734, the estate has seen many additions over the years. Having served as a mansion for the wealthy and as a private school, it's now a monastery for the **Marian Fathers,** and visitors are welcome to stroll the grounds and take in the impressive buildings and the views of the Berkshire Hills.

The town of **West Stockbridge** is a different municipality altogether, four miles west of Stockbridge and Lenox. The dilapidated town was bought up by developers some years ago and reconstructed, expanded, and spruced up as a real-life Disneyland for shoppers, browsers, and sightseers. Purists may say that the town is now like a movie set, but most visitors enjoy their time here, meandering along the short streets, peering in windows and shops, having a meal or a cool refresher. It's all pretty commercial, it's true, but that's the attraction.

GETTING THERE   See "Getting There" under "Lee," above, and the beginning of this chapter.

ESSENTIALS   The **telephone area code** is **413.** The Stockbridge Kiwanis Club maintains an **information booth** open 24 hours on Main Street right in the center of town. There you can pick up brochures and pamphlets. Write or call the **Stockbridge Chamber of Commerce** at P.O. Box 224, Stockbridge, MA 01262 (☎ 413/298-5200) in advance of your trip for further information.

The **Berkshire Visitors Bureau,** Berkshire Common, Pittsfield, MA 01201 (☎ **413/443-9186,** or **800/237-5747** in the U.S. and Canada), can provide you with information on all of Berkshire County, covering the entire western end of Massachusetts.

SPECIAL EVENTS   In the **Berkshire Playhouse** (☎ **413/298-5536 for information; 298-5576 for tickets**) and in a big red barn close by, the Berkshire Theater Festival hosts a series of performances now in its second half-century. From late June through August, plays are staged Monday through Saturday evenings and on Thursday and Saturday afternoons. The classic plays with name performers are in the playhouse proper. The Unicorn Theater Company puts on experimental and new plays in the barn, and throughout July and August special children's theater performances are held outside, under a tent, Thursday through Saturday at 11am.

WHAT TO SEE & DO
Sights
Berkshire Botanical Garden
Rtes. 102 and 183. ☎ **413/298-3926.** Admission $5 adults, $4 seniors, free for children under 12. Daily mid-May to mid-Oct 10am–5pm.

A great place to visit in Stockbridge is the Berkshire Botanical Garden. There, from spring to early fall you'll find 15 acres of flowering gardens filled with roses, delphiniums, primrose, dogwood, and scores of other natural beauties (all are labeled). In addition, there are vegetable and herb gardens. There is a gift shop.

Norman Rockwell Museum
Mass. 183. ☎ **413/298-4100.** Admission May–Oct, $8 adults, $2 children 6 and older; Nov–Apr, $7.50 adults, $2 children 6 and older, free for children under 6. May–Oct, daily 10am–5pm; Nov–Apr, Mon–Fri 10am–5pm, Sat–Sun 11am–4pm. Closed Thanksgiving, Christmas Day, New Year's Day.

In a new building just outside the center of Stockbridge is a large permanent collection of Norman Rockwell paintings. Rockwell, the famed American illustrator who did many pictures for magazine covers and posters, lived in Stockbridge for 25 years, up to his death in 1978. In fact, the museum has the world's largest collection of his work. You can also visit his last studio. The original building was moved to a place within walking distance of the museum. The museum also offers a variety of exhibitions, programs, and art classes for all ages.

Mission House
Main St. ☎ **413/298-3239.** Admission $5 adults, $2.50 children 6–12, free for children under 6. Memorial Day–Columbus Day, Tues–Sun and Mon holidays, 11am–4pm.

Owned by the Trustees of Reservations, Mission House (1739), in the center of town, is worth a visit. It was built by the Rev. John Sergeant to carry out his Christian mission to the Stockbridge Native Americans. The house is a National Historic Landmark, and is furnished in colonial and Early American pieces. Guided tours are offered.

Naumkeag
Prospect Hill, Prospect St. ☎ **413/298-3239.** Admission $6.50 adults, house and garden; $5 adults, garden only; $2.50 children 6–12, free for children under 6. Memorial Day weekend–Columbus Day, Tues–Sun and Mon holidays, 10am–5pm. Closed Tues after Mon holidays. Directions: Take Pine Street from the Red Lion Inn, then turn onto Prospect Hill to reach Naumkeag.

The palatial Naumkeag was built by Stanford White for Joseph Choate, a New York City attorney, in 1886. Many of the sumptuous furnishings are still in place, and there are extensive formal gardens.

✪ Chesterwood
Williamsville Rd. ☎ **413/298-3579.** Admission $6 adults, $3 children 13–18, $1 children 6–12, free for children under 6; grounds only, $5 adults, $4 children 13–18, $2 children 6–12, free for children under 6. May–Oct, daily 10am–5pm. Directions: Drive west on Mass. 102 and follow the signs.

Just a few miles from Stockbridge is Chesterwood, the former summer estate of Daniel Chester French, sculptor of the statue of Lincoln that graces the Lincoln Memorial and also of *The Minute Man* at Concord North Bridge. French (1850–1931) summered here from 1897 until 1931 and used the studio (built in 1898) near the house for his work. You can visit both the mansion and studio as well as an 1800s barn which has been converted to a gallery featuring exhibits on French's life and work. A lovely country garden, a woodland walk laid out by French himself, a panoramic view of Monument Mountain, and a museum store are unexpected extras to a Chesterwood visit. Admission fees go toward the upkeep of the property, which is maintained by the National Trust for Historic Preservation.

✪ Hancock Shaker Village

U.S. 20. ☎ **413/443-0188.** Admission $10 adults, $5 children 6–17; $25 family of two adults and children under 18; free for children under 6. Apr and Nov, daily 10am–3pm (guided tours only); May–Oct, daily 9:30am–5pm. Directions: Drive north of West Stockbridge nine miles along Mass. 41, then west on U.S. 20 to the outskirts of Pittsfield and Hancock Shaker Village.

Hancock Shaker Village is one of the most fascinating sights in the Berkshires. Up until 1960, the village was home to members of a religious sect noted for their quiet, simple lives, hard work, and quality handcrafts.

"The United Society of Believers in Christ's Second Appearing" or "The Millennial Church," more readily known as the Shakers, was a movement begun in 1747 in England as an offshoot of Quakerism. It gained momentum when Ann Lee, "Mother Ann," proclaimed that she had received the "mother element" of the spirit of Christ. After being imprisoned for her zeal, Mother Ann and eight followers immigrated to the American colony of New York and founded a settlement near Albany in 1774. After Mother Ann died in 1784, her followers founded other Shaker communities based on the principles of communal possessions, celibacy, pacifism, open confession of sins, and equality of the sexes. The communities were organized into "families" of 30 to 90 people. Work was a consecrated act, reflected in the high quality of workmanship and design in Shaker furniture and crafts: In effect, every product was a prayer.

Shakers, named for the trembling that came upon them from their religious zeal, believed that God had both a male and a female nature. The male was embodied in Jesus, the female in Mother Ann. Though converts devoted themselves and all their possessions to the community, they were free to leave at any time. Celibacy and the onslaught of the 20th century's complex lifestyle almost put an end to Shakerism after more than two centuries; there are only a handful of the faithful left now, living in a small community in Maine.

One cannot help but admire a lifestyle based on kindliness and hard work. Shaker products are still copied and admired because these good people treated even daily tasks as an art. Twenty of the original Shaker buildings at Hancock have been restored, furnished with artifacts of Shaker life, and staffed with men and women who can explain and demonstrate the customs of the Shaker life to you. Don't miss it.

Stockbridge Cemetery

At the corner of Main and Church Sts.

This cemetery has become one of Stockbridge's main attractions of late. You can visit the gravesites of notables like Gertrude Robinson Smith (founder of Tanglewood) and Norman Rockwell. If you want in-depth information about those who have made Stockbridge Cemetery their final resting place, call the Berkshires Visitors Bureau (☎ 800/237-5747) and they'll tell you how you can purchase a cassette driving tour of Stockbridge (by Gordon Hyatt) that will take you into the cemetery. Gravestone rubbings are allowed.

SKIING

There are at least six well-known downhill ski areas in the Berkshires. Call to get information on ski conditions and year-round activities: **Butternut** (☎ 413/528-2000) has 22 trails and 8 lifts, and rises to an elevation of 1,800 feet; **Bousquet** (☎ 413/442-8316) offers 21 trails and 5 lifts, and has an elevation of 1,875 feet; **Catamount** (☎ 413/582-1262) has 24 trails and 5 lifts, and at its summit reaches 2,000 feet; **Brodie** (☎ 413/443-4752) has 30 trails and 6 lifts, and rises to 2,700 feet; **Jiminy Peak** (☎ 413/738-5500) maintains 28 trails and 7 lifts, and peaks at an elevation of 2,390 feet and **Otis Ridge** (☎ 413/269-4444) is the smallest of all, with 11 trails and 5 lifts, and an elevation of 1,700 feet.

WHERE TO STAY

In Stockbridge

Red Lion Inn

Main St., Stockbridge, MA 01262. ☎ **413/298-5545.** Fax 413/298-5130. 111 rms (85 with bath). $72 double without bath weekdays, $87 weekends; $108–$350 double with bath weekdays, $108–$350 weekends. AE, CB, DC, DISC, MC, V.

The Red Lion Inn located right on Main Street is a town institution. The huge white four-story Victorian hotel with a wide front porch was established as an inn in 1773, and it is known to have hosted Henry Wordsworth Longfellow and Nathaniel Hawthorne at one time. All rooms here are individually decorated with period furnishings and attractive wallpapers. In keeping with the Stockbridge theme, guest room walls are hung with Norman Rockwell prints. Some rooms have sitting areas. Accommodations are either in the main building or in one of the five outbuildings. Vintage photographs dot the hallways, and public spaces are done up with American furnishings and Oriental rugs. By the way, the building dates from 1897, when it was constructed on the site of an earlier inn that was completely destroyed by fire.

Dining/Entertainment: The Red Lion is also Stockbridge's premier place for dining. Besides the formal dining room, there's the Widow Bingham Tavern, a rough-hewn and woody place in colonial style. The Lion's Den, downstairs, serves a pub-style menu that offers soups to sandwiches to delicious desserts. There is entertainment there every night, and there's never a cover charge. Plan to spend about $35 to $45 per person for a luxurious New England style dinner in the dining room and the Widow Bingham Tavern. In warmer weather the Red Lion Inn opens the flower-filled courtyard for outdoor dining.

In West Stockbridge

West Stockbridge harbors several establishments offering lodging and meals at lower rates than in Stockbridge proper. These are well worth a look.

Williamsville Inn

Mass. 41, West Stockbridge, MA 01266. ☎ **413/274-6118.** Fax 413/274-3539. 16 rms. Summer, $140–$185 double. Off-season, $105–$160 double. All rates include full breakfast. AE, MC, V. Directions: From West Stockbridge, follow Mass. 41 south four miles.

Many places call themselves country inns these days, even though they have down-town locations, Muzak, and cable color TV, bus tours, and whirlpools. The Williamsville, however, is a true country inn. It's out in the country. Four rooms have woodstoves, and some have four-poster beds; all have fine old furnishings. Ten rooms are located in the main house, and six are out back in a renovated barn and a cottage. The inn, built in 1797, has 10 acres of grounds, a swimming pool, a clay tennis court, woodland trails, and a seasonal outdoor sculpture garden. The dining room is well known and well regarded (in winter, the story telling on Sun-day night makes dining extra-special). A three-night minimum stay is required in July and August, a two-night minimum on holiday weekends.

WHERE TO DINE

Shaker Mill Tavern

Rte. 102, West Stockbridge Village. ☎ **413/232-8565.** Reservations not necessary. Main courses $3.95–$15.50. AE, DISC, MC, V. Daily 11am–10pm; brunch Sun 10:30am–2pm. AMERICAN/INTERNATIONAL.

Billing itself as the "most entertaining restaurant in the Berkshires," Shaker Mill Tavern was a stagecoach stop in the early 19th-century and was once the home of inventor Anson Clark. Today it's popular with residents for its pizzas, huge burger platters, and dinner specials like chicken Oriental, veal parmesan, barbecue ribs, and shrimp scampi. If you order a dinner special, a trip to the salad bar is included in the price of your entrée. A great dessert is the mile-high sour-cream cheesecake; I also enjoy the raspberry–chocolate-mousse cake. Dining is available inside or outside on the deck. Nine rooms decorated with contemporary furnishings are available for overnight stays.

Truc Orient Express

Harris St. ☎ **413/232-4204.** Reservations recommended in summer. Main courses $11.50–$24. AE, DISC, MC, V. Daily 11:30am–10pm. Closed Mon in winter. VIETNAMESE.

If you are over in West Stockbridge for the day, one of the very best things you can do is have a meal at the Truc Orient Express. Light and airy, with wicker furniture, it's an exceptionally attractive place, and a welcome change from the antique-packed dining rooms hereabouts. The cuisine is Vietnamese: appetizers such as *mien cua* (crab and bean-thread soup) or *ga nuong chanh* (skewered lemon chicken), with a main course of sautéed squid with bamboo shoots or fresh flounder in a spicy sweet-and-sour sauce. For dessert, the customary lychee or not-so-customary flan finish up nicely. Accompany everything with a glass of saké or plum wine. There are lots of vegetarian dishes, too. Don't miss it.

GREAT BARRINGTON

7 miles S of Stockbridge, 11 miles SW of Lee, 4 miles NE of South Egremont

Although it's certainly not a city, Great Barrington is the largest town in the south-ern Berkshires, a major crossroads and commercial center. Supplies and services that you might not find in Stockbridge or Lenox will be available here.

Great Barrington was an important town even before the Revolution. The citi-zenry, angered at Britain's denial of the colonials' rights, prevented the king's judges from convening in the courthouse here in 1774. In the 19th century, Mr. and Mrs. Edward Searles became the town's benefactors, establishing many pub-lic buildings and constructing for themselves an immense mansion in a 100-acre park which nudges right into the center of town.

GETTING THERE   See "Getting There" under "Lee," above, and the beginning of this chapter.

ESSENTIALS   The **telephone area code** is **413.** There's a little **information kiosk** in the center of town, by the Berkshire Motor Inn and Searles' Castle, on Main Street. It's operated by the **Southern Berkshire Chamber of Commerce,** 362 Main St., Great Barrington, MA 01230 (☎ 413/528-1510). You'll get help finding a room if you need one. Donations are accepted to defray expenses. The **Berkshire Visitors Bureau,** Berkshire Common, Pittsfield, MA 01201 (☎ 413/443-9186, or 800/237-5747 in the U.S. and Canada), can provide you with information on all of Berkshire County, covering the entire western end of Massachusetts.

WHAT TO SEE & DO

Great Barrington and South Egremont are the antiques collector's towns par excellence. Everyone here, it seems, deals in **antiques** and old stuff. Browsing the shops is the daily passion, but several excursions out of town to nature spots provide an antidote to buying-and-selling.

Take U.S. 7 south from Great Barrington for about 10 miles, and turn onto Mass. 7A for Ashley Falls. Your destination, a mile from Ashley Falls along Rannpo and Weatogue Roads, is **Bartholomew's Cobble,** bordering the Housatonic River. A "cobble" in this case is a high knoll of limestone, marble, or quartzite, 500 million years old, and covered with a rich and varied collection of native flora: trees, ferns, mosses, wildflowers. The nature reservation, open year-round, is owned by the Trustees of Reservations (☎ 413/229-8600), and has six miles of hiking trails. A naturalist is on duty from mid-April to mid-October, Wednesday through Sunday from 9am to 5pm, to answer your questions and point out highlights.

Another pretty nature nook, good for a picnic, is **Bash Bish Falls,** 12 miles southwest of South Egremont, right on the New York state line. Take Mass. 41 south out of town, and turn right onto Mount Washington Road (signs for Catamount ski area). Follow signs to the falls, taking East Street, then West Street, and finally Bash Bish Falls Road, deep in the Mount Washington State Forest. You'll plunge into the valley carved by the Bash Bish Creek, and finally come to a parking area from which a steep trail leads to the falls. Stay on the road a bit farther and you'll come to another parking place, and an easier—but longer—trail. Stay on the road any longer and you'll end up in New York.

At the end of the trails, deep in the forest, is the 50-foot Bash Bish Falls, cascading into a chilly pool. A half hour's relaxation here on a hot summer's day is pretty close to nirvana.

If mountain hiking is more to your taste, head north out of Great Barrington on U.S. 7 and after 4¹/₂ miles you'll see signs for **Monument Mountain.** There are two trails to the summit, one easier but slightly longer than the other. The hike to the top, a rest, and back down will take between two and three hours. The view at the summit is very fine.

WHERE TO STAY

In Great Barrington

Seekonk Pines Inn

142 Seekonk Cross Rd., Great Barrington, MA 01230. ☎ 413/528-4192, or 800/ 292-4192 (for reservations only). 6 rms. High season, $75–$105 double; additional person $20 extra. Off-season, $70–$85 double; additional person $15 extra. All rates include full

breakfast. MC, V. Directions: From the center of Great Barrington, follow Mass. 23/41 southwest 2¹/₂ miles to the inn.

Linda and Chris Best are your hosts at the Seekonk Pines, and their inn features a nice pool, a garden from which they will sell you fresh produce, bicycles for rent, and a full breakfast; and in winter, a fireplace in the large living room. Its clean, neat rooms are decorated with antiques, old quilts, and Linda's watercolors. There's also a "suite" (one large room) with a sitting area that sleeps four (perfect for a family or couple on a longer visit). Discounts are given on stays of five days or more.

Windflower

684 South Egremont Rd., Great Barrington, MA 01230. Tel. **413/528-2720** or 800/ 992-1993. 13 rms. $170–$230 double. Extra person $35–$50. Ski packages are available. All rates include breakfast and dinner. AE.

Windflower, situated on 10 acres of land in the Berkshire Mountains, is a comfortable, antique-filled Federal-style inn built in the late 19th century. Public spaces are restful, and guest rooms feature grand antique beds, floral bed coverings, and rich print wall coverings. There is an outdoor pool surrounded by colorful flower gardens, and golf and tennis are available across the street at the Egremont Country Club. A full dinner (included in the room rate along with breakfast) includes an appetizer, salad, an entrée (there are always three from which to choose), dessert, and coffee and tea.

Nearby

New Boston Inn

101 N. Main St., Sandisfield, MA 01255. ☎ **413/258-4477.** 8 rms. May 24–Dec 1, $95 double; Dec 2–May 23, $75–$85 double. Additional person $25 extra. All rates include breakfast. AE, MC, V. Directions: Take 1-90 East to Mass. 8 south to the inn, which is at the junction of Mass. 8 and Mass. 57.

The New Boston Inn is "Berkshire County's oldest Publick House, faithfully serving travelers since 1737." The inn, which has uniquely decorated rooms and a pub, is a good deal for the price. Some of the rooms are located in the main house, which is more formal, and therefore a bit more pricey, while the others (in the carriage house) are less formal and might fit a tighter budget. The inn is entirely nonsmoking and has some handicapped-accessible rooms.

✪ The Old Inn on the Green & Gedney Farm

Star Rte. 70, New Marlborough, MA 01230. ☎ **413/229-3131** or 413/229-7924. 16 rms and suites (12 with bath). Inn on the Green, $90–$140 double. Gedney Farm, $160–$245 suite. AE, MC, V.

You'll get your money's worth at The Old Inn on the Green & Gedney Farm. The Old Inn houses several rooms with private or shared bath that are decorated with antique or country furnishings—they are lovely rooms, but they're similar to those you'd find in any other country inn. However, the rooms in the Gedney Farm building (which is a converted dairy barn) are extraordinary and quite special. In the barn you'll find two-level suites with a bedroom and bathroom upstairs and a sitting area downstairs. You'll be charmed by the rich colors (which lend almost a southwestern touch to the country inn), exposed beams, Turkish kilim rugs, French tapestry, down sofas, whirlpool tubs, and indoor balconies. Some of these rooms even have fireplaces. Everything here is meant to please the eye and ease the spirit—all the way down to the 80 acres of land on which the inn is situated. The restaurant at the inn is open daily in summer, weekends only in winter.

Orchard Shade

Maple Ave. (P.O. Box 669), Sheffield, MA 01257. ☎ **413/229-8463.** 8 rms (1 with bath). $55–$125 double. All rates include breakfast. AE, DISC, MC, V. Directions: Take U.S. 7 to Maple Avenue; Orchard Shade is about 200 yards down the road.

Orchard Shade, a white clapboard house built in 1840, has been operating as a guesthouse since 1888. As you enter, you'll see the living room on your right, which is filled with interesting little knickknacks, a grand piano, family portraits, a lacquered desk, books, sculpture, and a comfortable sitting area. To the left is the dining room, where each morning you'll dine at a Georgian table in front of a brick fireplace on a breakfast of bread, muffins, sticky buns, fruit, and cereal. The rooms share bathrooms (except for one room that has a separate entrance to the garden) and are brightly decorated with floral wallpapers, wicker, and painted cottage furnishings, and some antiques. Children are welcome. The inn is nonsmoking and has 10 acres of grounds, which are well landscaped and feature a lovely pool.

WHERE TO DINE

✪ Castle Street Café

10 Castle St. ☎ **413/528-5244.** Reservations recommended. Main courses $9–$20. AE, DISC, MC, V. Daily 5–10pm. NEW AMERICAN.

The Castle Street Café is one of Great Barrington's hottest restaurants, and it offers good food in a casual yet cosmopolitan atmosphere. The restaurant consists of a large room with exposed brick on one side and a white wall decorated with paintings and food ads. While relaxing with a drink and listening to the soft jazz playing in the background, you might consider ordering the grilled shiitake mushrooms to start (they're wonderful!), and then move on to the roast duck with black-currant sauce and wild rice or eggplant roulade stuffed with three cheeses. As a side dish, try the grilled peasant bread with garlic, olive oil, and tomato. Dessert is a must—they're famous for their chocolate-mousse cake, but if you'd rather have something lighter, try the frozen lemon soufflé with raspberry sauce. There's a small bar at the back of the restaurant, and there's an award-winning wine list. This is a great place for a romantic dinner.

EGREMONT

4 miles SW of Great Barrington

The first thing you must know is that Egremont actually consists of two towns. North Egremont is a tiny place on Mass. 71, due west of Great Barrington. It has a country store, an inn/restaurant, and a few houses. South Egremont is a much bigger place, with several inns and restaurants, shops, churches, and more antiques dealers than you've ever seen in one place before. South Egremont, on Mass. 23 and Mass. 41, is four miles southwest of Great Barrington.

GETTING THERE   See "Getting There" under "Lee," above, and the beginning of this chapter.

ESSENTIALS   The **telephone area code** is **413.** The **Berkshire Visitors Bureau,** Berkshire Common, Pittsfield, MA 01201 (☎ **413/443-9186,** or **800/ 237-5747** in the U.S. and Canada), can provide you with information on all of Berkshire County, covering the entire western end of Massachusetts.

WHERE TO STAY

In South Egremont

Egremont Inn

Old Sheffield Rd., South Egremont, MA 01258. ☎ **413/528-2111** or 800/859-1780. Fax 413/528-6133. 21 rms. A/C TEL. In summer $80–$175 double; rest of the year $75–$140 double. Additional person $15 extra. AE, MC, V.

A block off the highway in South Egremont (follow the signs) is the Egremont Inn, sometimes called the 1780 Egremont Inn. A stagecoach inn since the early days of the Republic, the inn's guest rooms now are fitted out with period furnishings. A pool and tennis courts provide entertainment the stagecoach never had. All of the village is within walking distance. Weekends in July and August there's a two-night minimum stay.

In Sheffield

Staveleigh House

59 Main St. (P.O. Box 608), Sheffield, MA 01257. ☎ **413/229-2129.** 5 rms (1 with bath). $85–$100 double. All rates include breakfast. No credit cards.

Five miles south of Great Barrington on U.S. 7 in Sheffield is the Staveleigh House, a homey bed-and-breakfast run by two women who enjoy the slower pace of life in this quiet corner of the state. The mood is reflected in their comfortable living room and simple but lovely guest rooms. Antiques are used here, not doted over. Innkeepers Dorothy Marosy and Marion Whitman enjoy chatting with the guests, suggesting outings, and making sure repeat guests aren't served the same breakfast twice.

WHERE TO DINE

In North Egremont

Elm Court Inn

Rte. 71. ☎ **413/528-0325.** Reservations are recommended. Main courses $17.75–$24.50. AE, MC, V. Dinner only Wed–Sat 5–9pm, Sun 4–8:30pm. INNOVATIVE CONTINENTAL.

Built in 1790 the Elm Court Inn was originally known as the Tuller Tavern. Today, though it has undergone many changes, it maintains its original charm. The bar area has a lovely rustic quality about it. Chef Urs Bieri, once Executive Chef at the United Nations in New York City, creates interesting and flavorful dishes for which the inn serves as an elegant backdrop. Begin with the wild-mushroom-filled ravioli (served with fresh sage butter) or the Swedish matjes herring. For an entrée try the grilled swordfish with wasabi soy sauce, the sautéed breast of pheasant with papardelle pasta, or the rack of lamb provençale. There is an extensive wine list.

8   Williamstown

145 miles W of Boston, 165 miles NE of New York City, 23 miles N of Lenox, 14 miles S of Bennington

The town was founded in 1753 as West Hoosuck, but its life and its name were soon affected by the career of Ephraim Williams, Jr., a soldier in the British colonial army. Born in 1714, Williams surveyed several townships in these parts, then took command of fortifications that demarcated the frontier between the British and French North American empires. Among these defenses was Fort Massachusetts, which stood in North Adams.

Williams led a column of troops from Massachusetts toward the French positions on Lake George and died in the fighting (1755). His will provided for the founding of a school in West Hoosuck, but only if the town took his name. It did, and Williams College enrolled its first students in 1793. The college celebrated its 200th anniversary in 1993.

Williams College, with an annual freshman class of 2,000, is the reason the town of 8,500 exists. It's a beautiful, delightful example of the New England rural college town.

GETTING THERE   By Car   Take U.S. 7 or Mass. 2 in Massachusetts or New York.

By Bus   If you're coming directly from Boston or New York City, contact **Bonanza Bus Lines** (☎ **800/556-3815**). You may have to change buses in Springfield or Pittsfield. From Montréal, take Vermont Transit (see the beginning of this chapter). Local buses connect Berkshire County towns and resorts with one another.

ESSENTIALS   The **telephone area code** is **413.** During the summer months, the town operates an **information booth** in the middle of town at the intersection of Mass. 2 and U.S. 7, a short distance from the Williams Inn. Contact the **Williamstown Board of Trade** (P.O. Box 357) for information. They also run a staffed tourist booth in the summer (☎ 413/458-9077). The **Berkshire Visitors Bureau,** Berkshire Common, Pittsfield, MA 01201 (☎ **413/443-9186,** or **800/237-5747** in the U.S. and Canada), can provide you with information on all of Berkshire County, covering the entire western end of Massachusetts.

SPECIAL EVENTS   The big draw from late June through the end of August is the **Williamstown Theatre Festival,** P.O. Box 517, Williamstown, MA 01267 (☎ **413/597-3399** for information, **413/597-3400** for the box office). The **Main Stage** company puts on five principal productions in the 500-seat Adams Memorial Theatre on Main Street, and the smaller (96-seat) **Other Stage** next door is the scene for new works by both young and established playwrights. There are special dramatic events at the **Clark Art Institute,** and even an open-air Free Theatre literary adaptation staged at twilight in a meadow near the town (bring a picnic dinner). After June 10, call the box office to charge tickets on your credit card.

The **Williams College Department of Music** arranges numerous concerts when college is in session. Call the **Concertline** (☎ 413/597-3146) for information. In the summer, **Williamstown Chamber Concerts** (☎ 413/458-8273) organizes several chamber music performances at the Clark Art Institute.

WHAT TO SEE & DO

Stop by the information booth and pick up the brochure entitled "Williamstown: A Walk Along Main Street," which gives details on the interesting buildings lining Main Street (Mass. 2 East), many of them now part of Williams College.

IN TOWN

✪ Sterling and Francine Clark Art Institute

225 South St. ☎ **413/458-9545.** Free admission. Tues–Sun (also Memorial Day, Labor Day, and Columbus Day) 10am–5pm. Open Mon 10am–5pm in July and Aug. Closed New Year's, Thanksgiving, and Christmas Days. Directions: From the information booth, follow South Street for less than a mile to the museum.

This is perhaps the most famous of Williamstown's cultural attractions. The institute's marvelous collections are the achievement of Robert Sterling

1956), a Yale engineer whose forebears had been successful in the ...chine industry. Clark began collecting works of art in Paris in 1912, ... a French woman named Francine, and eventually housed his masterpieces ...lassic white-marble temple here in Williamstown.

The pristine original museum was greatly expanded in 1973, and now has strong collections of paintings by the impressionists, their academic contemporaries in France, and the mid-century Barbizon artists, including Millet, Troyon, and Corot. Of the Americans, there are significant works by Cassatt, Homer, Remington, and Sargent. Earlier centuries are represented by well-chosen pieces of Piero della Francesca, Memling, Gossaert, Jacob Van Ruisdael, Fragonard, Gainsborough, Turner, and Goya. There are some sculptures, including Degas's famous *Little Dancer of Fourteen Years,* as well as prints, drawings, and noteworthy collections of silver and porcelain.

Williams College Museum of Art   *Wonderful museum*
Main St. ☎ **413/597-2429.** Free admission. Tues–Sat 10am–5pm, Sun 1–5pm.

The museum is in Lawrence Hall, the Greek Revival octagonal building (with modern additions), on Main Street. Call to ask about current exhibits, which are lively, timely, and well displayed in the museum's galleries and dramatic open spaces.

NEARBY

Five miles east of Williamstown along Mass. 2, in North Adams, a road goes off to the right, climbing the slopes of **Mount Greylock** (3,491 feet), the highest point in Massachusetts. If the weather is clear, drive the several miles to the top, where you'll find marvelous views, the AMC Bascom Lodge (see "Where to Stay," below), and a curious, imposing 92-foot-tall war memorial that was originally designed as a lighthouse. The memorial is open to the public.

Other roads approach the summit from the south, starting from U.S. 7 at New Ashford or Lanesboro.

While you're up here, explore some of the 40 miles of **hiking trails** (including part of the Appalachian Trail) which thread through the forest of the Mount Greylock State Reservation's 11,000 acres.

WHERE TO STAY

Far enough from Tanglewood to avoid the crush of its summer crowds, Williamstown is favored with a fine selection of small guesthouses and inns, two full-service hotels, and several moderately priced motels. You should have little trouble finding the sort of room you want in this charming Berkshire town. But do reserve early for dates in September (classes begin), October (foliage season), and early June (graduation).

SMALL INNS & GUESTHOUSES

✪ Field Farm Guest House

554 Sloan Rd., Williamstown, MA 01267. ☎ **413/458-3135.** 5 rms. $99 double. All rates include breakfast. No credit cards. Directions: Follow U.S. 7 south four miles to junction of Mass. 43; turn right onto 43, then immediately right onto Sloan Road; Field Farm is one mile up Sloan Road.

A guesthouse in the country near historic Williamstown conjures up images of a quaint Berkshire farmhouse or exuberant Victorian inn, so Field Farm comes as a surprise, almost as a shock. Set on 294 acres, the house was the country villa of Lawrence H. and Eleanore Bloedel, noted art collectors, who built it in 1948 in the clean, spare, understated style that came to dominate in the 1950s. Field Farm was bequeathed to The Trustees of Reservations in 1984, and today 20 pieces of art from the Bloedel collection—including a Laren MacIver and a Wolf Kahn—have been loaned back to Field Farm by the Williams College Museum of Art and adorn the house and grounds. Four guest rooms face the sunny lawns (three have their own decks), and two have fireplaces. The huge, airy living room and dining room, tennis court, swimming pool, and hiking and skiing trails are yours to enjoy. Field Farm is open all year.

✪ River Bend Farm

643 Simonds Rd. (U.S. 7 N.), Williamstown, MA 01267. ☎ **413/458-3121.** 4 rms (none with bath). $80 double. All rates include breakfast. No credit cards. Directions: Go north on U.S. 7 a mile from Williamstown's information booth in the center of town; turn left onto the private drive immediately after crossing a bridge over the river.

My favorite place in Williamstown is the River Bend Farm, open May to October. This 1770 roadside inn and tavern-turned-farmhouse has been lovingly restored and run with an engaging low-key, unpretentious style that makes guests immediately feel at home. True country-inn feeling is provided by the hosts' warm welcome, the variety of interesting old furnishings at the inn, and the bounteous, delicious breakfast included in the price.

FULL-SERVICE HOTELS

✪ The Orchards

222 Adams Rd., Williamstown, MA 01267. ☎ **413/458-9611** or 800/225-1517. Fax 413/458-3273. 47 rms. A/C TV TEL. Late May–Oct, $160–$225 double; Nov–late May, $125–$180 single or double. AE, DC, MC, V. Directions: Head one mile east of the center of campus on Mass. 2.

The Orchards is the top-of-the-line hostelry in Williamstown. Don't be put off by the bland exterior. Though it's a fairly simple modern stucco building on the outside, the inn's interior is an eclectic gallery of English antiques, Oriental carpets, and furnishings of classic design. The owners are especially proud of the 18th-century carved oak mantelpiece in the lounge, a nice little army of Victorian tin soldiers, and a fine collection of silver teapots. The courtyard has a quiet garden; there's also a swimming pool and exercise room. Standard guest rooms are done in traditional English country style and have thick carpets, his-and-hers washbasins, tub and shower trimmed in marble, and all the expected luxury-hotel touches. Superior rooms are larger, and some have a four-poster bed, fireplace, and little refrigerator. All rooms have one or two antique accent pieces (armoire, desk, or dresser). The dining room is the fanciest in town (see "Where to Dine," below). There's live music on Friday and Saturday nights from 8:30pm to 12:30am.

Williams Inn

On the Green, Williamstown, MA 01267. ☎ **413/458-9371.** Fax 413/458-2767. 100 rms. A/C TV TEL. Apr–Oct, $110–$140 double; Nov–Mar, $5–$20 less. Package plans available. Children under 14 stay free in parents' room. AE, DC, DISC, MC, V.

The Williams Inn, at the junction of U.S. 7 and Mass. 2, is the town's largest hostelry, with rooms equipped with colonial-style furniture and the amenities expected in a comfortable full-service hotel. This is the "college hotel," a very comfortable place with a good dining room, a less formal tavern lounge, a heated indoor pool, men's and women's saunas, and a spa. You can walk to any point on campus from here. Pets are welcome in first-floor rooms.

A Hikers' Lodge

The Appalachian Mountain Club operates **AMC Bascom Lodge,** P.O. Box 1800, Lanesboro, MA 01237 (☎ **413/743-1591**), in the Mount Greylock State Reservation atop Massachusetts's highest peak. Bascom Lodge is one of those substantial, well-designed rustic hostelries built by the Civilian Conservation Corps in the 1930s; it's open from mid-May through late October. The simple accommodations here benefit from the mountain air and the closeness of the park's hiking trails, not to mention the panoramic views. Four co-ed bunkrooms sleep six to eight people each. Linens, a towel, and a wool blanket are provided. Bunks cost $30 per adult, $19 per child under 12, excluding tax; the four private rooms go for $70 double. These nonmember rates are for Sunday through Friday during most of the season; prices are $5 higher on Saturday and during August. Simple but hearty, wholesome meals are served from an open kitchen in the spacious dining room overlooking the mountains; dinner costs $10 and an all-you-can-eat breakfast is $5 for adults, $3 for children. Call first, then write for reservations.

WHERE TO DINE

You can easily find a good meal in town, and during the summer months when the Williamstown Theater Festival is in progress, cabaret troupes offer song-and-dance revues in some local restaurants after the curtain has fallen on the festival's main evening performance. When you've exhausted all the dining possibilities in Williamstown, try one of the places in Bennington, Vt., a mere 13 miles to the north along U.S. 7.

EXPENSIVE

Le Country

101 North St. ☎ **413/458-4000.** Reservations recommended. Main courses $13.95–$22. AE, MC, V. Tues–Fri 11:30am–1:30pm; Tues–Sun 5–9pm. AMERICAN.

Le Country, located 100 yards down the hill from the information booth, has a long-standing reputation for good, standard fare in pleasant surroundings. Rough boards accent the dining room's white walls, and hunting prints add a note of country gentry life. The menu is short and to the point, listing such longtime favorites as coquilles St-Jacques, chicken provençal, filet mignon, coq au vin, and veal cazadora. Start with escargots bourguignons or shrimp cocktail, and end with cheesecake, pecan pie, or baba au rhum. The wine list, too, is short, but well selected, and prices are surprisingly moderate. Service is slow (you're warned on the menu) but competent and friendly.

The Orchards

222 Adams Rd. ☎ **413/458-9611.** Reservations required. Main courses $19.50–$28. AE, DC, MC, V. Daily noon–2pm, 6–9pm; brunch Sun 8–11am. Directions: From the information booth, go two miles east along Mass. 2 to the hotel, on the right. CONTINENTAL.

Williamstown's fanciest is The Orchards. The dining room here is divided into two parts, one of which looks out onto the courtyard, and well-spaced tables are set with German china. Breads arrive in silver baskets, and the service staff is well-informed, friendly, and efficient. The menu, in spite of its length, changes frequently. On a recent visit, I started with the shrimp wrapped in rice paper with bean sprouts, a wine-ginger sauce, and glazed julienne of leeks. For a main course, I chose the chestnut-crusted duck breast with black current sauce and stewed polenta. Both dishes were excellent. The paupiette of sea bass in a beaujolais sauce, served with a nest of vegetable confetti, was also quite good. The dessert menu is equally interesting and substantial. There was a nice peach soup served with a trio of sorbets, and a wonderful Venetian tiramisú between chocolate disks served with espresso sauce.

MODERATE

For moderately priced meals, seek out **Water Street** (Mass. 43). Turn south off Mass. 2 by the Methodist church in the midst of the campus.

Specialty Dining

For a quick breakfast, sandwich, pizza, snack, or ice-cream cone, the place to go is **Spring Street,** one long block west of Water Street in the midst of the campus. This short commercial street is crowded with good places, like the **Colonial Pizza** (☎ 413/458-8014) and a bakery called the **Clarksburg Bread Co.,** 37 Spring St. (☎ 413/458-2251).

9

Rhode Island

Just because Rhode Island is the smallest state in the Union, many people assume that the variety of things to see and do in this corner of New England is limited. Not so. The state's beaches are famed throughout the region, sites and structures of historical importance abound, the cities are pleasant and of manageable size, and then there's Newport—a world apart. In fact, the only real effect the state's small size seems to have is to make the residents feel that they're a part of a very special place and to make everything easily accessible to the visitor.

In the 1600s, when New England was being colonized by Europeans, the best solution to a community conflict was for the weaker of the conflicting parties to shove off into the wilderness and found and develop their own community. To save his skin and freely express his beliefs, Roger Williams left Puritan Salem in 1636 and came to Narragansett Bay, followed soon afterward by others who shared his views, or at least knew they would be allowed to disagree. Williams was ahead of the times in his political, religious, and ethical thinking, and his contribution to the American democratic tradition is very important: In his new community of Providence, citizens could think and say what they liked. In the years that followed the founding of Providence, Williams persuaded Parliament to include the settlements of Portsmouth and Newport on Rhode Island with his own Providence Plantation under the same charter— these towns had also been founded by dissenters who desired freedom of thought and speech—thus securing for the colony as a whole the right of absolute liberty in matters of belief. The official name of the state to this day remains "Rhode Island and Providence Plantations."

Today, Rhode Island is a manufacturing center and a maritime state, with a lot of rich agricultural land and several important industries. But the summer vacationers who come to Rhode Island— beginning with the very wealthy socialites who started the custom in the 19th century—are also an important part of the economy, and the state government does a lot to see that "Little Rhodie" retains the lure it had for those discriminating types who built palatial mansions in Newport, Watch Hill, and other coastal towns.

One event not to miss, if you take your vacation at the right time, is **May Day Breakfasts.** May is officially celebrated as Heritage

What's Special About Rhode Island

Museums
- The Rhode Island School of Design's Museum of Art, in Providence.
- The International Tennis Hall of Fame and Tennis Museum, in Newport.

Architectural Highlights
- Rhode Island's harmonious white-marble State House in Providence.
- Touro Synagogue, in Newport, designed by Peter Harrison and built in 1763.

Events & Festivals
- "May Day Breakfasts," celebrating Rhode Island's patriotic heritage.
- The Newport Music Festival, bringing together well-known artists each July to perform in the great mansions.
- Block Island Race Week, in late June, featuring boat races and parties.
- Newport Folk Festival & JVC Jazz Festival in August.

Houses & Gardens
- The palatial mansions of Newport, bringing to life the resort's turn-of-the-century opulence.

Especially for Kids
- The 1883 Carousel in Watch Hill, one of the oldest merry-go-rounds in the nation.

Beaches
- Narragansett Bay and Rhode Island's southern shore, known for their broad swaths of sand.

Month in Rhode Island, commemorating that "Little Rhodie" was the first colony to declare independence from British rule (May 4, 1776). On May 1 or thereabouts, **May Day Breakfasts** are held by all sorts of church, civic, and fraternal organizations across the state, and the public is invited to most of them. These can be pretty lavish affairs, and you're sure to get your money's worth.

Rhode Island is known for its beaches, and some of the finest are along the state's southwestern shore: Wonderful names such as Misquamicut, Weekapaug, and Quonochontaug identify the built-up areas along the strand. The buildings are usually private homes, or snack bars and restaurants, and much of the waterfront land is privately owned and fiercely guarded. But the state beaches dotted along the shore are open to all at a fee of $3 per car with Rhode Island plates, $5 per car with out-of-state plates during the week, a dollar more on weekends and holidays.

SEEING RHODE ISLAND

I-95 connects Rhode Island to the Connecticut coast and Boston. From Cape Cod, take I-95 via New Bedford to Fall River (where you turn south for Providence), or to Providence.

Car-ferries connect Block Island with the mainland at Galilee year-round. In summer, passenger ferries operate to Block Island from Providence and Newport, R.I., and New London, Conn.

ESSENTIALS   For Rhode Island tourist information, call ☎ **800/ 556-2484** from the United States and Canada. You can also write to the **Rhode Island Economic Development Corporation** , which issues brochures, maps, lists of festivals and special events, and other useful materials, at 7 Jackson Walkway, Providence, RI 02903 (☎ **401/277-2601**). The state's free "Vacation Kit" has a complete list of Rhode Island events and attractions and accommodations.

The statewide **room tax** is 5%. The **sales tax** is 7%. Both will be added to your hotel bill. The **telephone area code** for all of Rhode Island is **401**.

1   Providence

32 miles NW of New Bedford, 45 miles SW of Boston, 55 miles NE of New London, 30 miles N of Newport

Providence is an attractive city. Its downtown area is compact enough that a visitor can get off the train or park the car and walk to just about everything there is to see and do. The State Capitol crowns a hilltop on the edge of the downtown section. College Hill rises from the east bank of the Providence River, which runs through downtown; Brown University, the Rhode Island School of Design, and a collection of exceptionally beautiful and interesting houses from the 17th, 18th, and 19th centuries give College Hill its character.

The city was founded in 1636 by Roger Williams (1603–83), who had been minister of the church at Salem, Mass., but whose freethinking religious ideas had made the General Court banish him from Massachusetts Bay. (He held that the Massachusetts Bay charter was not legal, that the Puritans should face the fact that they had really separated from the Church of England, and that in matters of conscience no civil authority had any power—no wonder the powers-that-be thought him a dangerous man!) He dedicated his new settlement of Providence to the proposition that all people should have freedom of conscience. A good number came from Massachusetts, and others came directly from England, to the new colony. Williams had bought the land for the town from the Narragansett tribe, and he remained on very good terms with them, even writing a book on their language that was published and sold in England.

Rhode Island became the first colony to declare independence from England, in May 1776. After the Revolutionary War, it took over from Newport the position as the state's most important seaport. It's still an important port, and its industries of textiles, machine tools, rubber, jewelry, and boatbuilding also contribute to its prosperity.

GETTING THERE   **By Plane**   Rhode Island is so compact that one airport handles all the important national flights. T. F. Green State Airport in Warwick is just a few miles south of Providence. From the airport, you'll have to take a taxi to the center of Providence.

By Car   I-95 goes right through the center of Providence on its way between New York and Boston; right downtown, I-95 branches off to go through Fall River (the turnoff for Newport), New Bedford, and then on to Cape Cod.

Note: Street parking in Providence is scarce and meters are checked frequently. The center of town has lots of private pay lots, which it's best to use if you need to be downtown. Otherwise, park on a side street on College Hill, where there's plenty of shade and no time limit.

Rhode Island

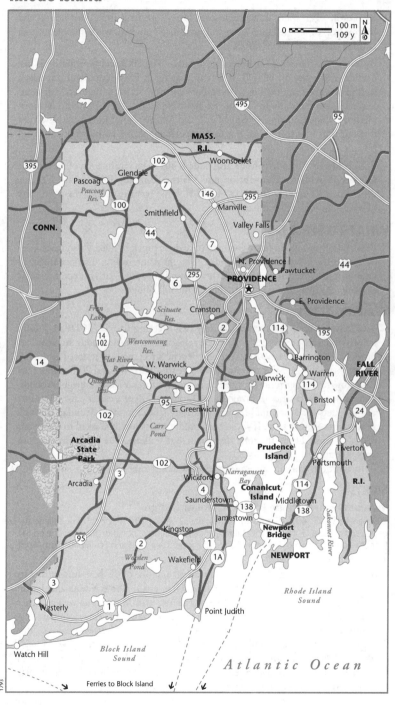

0 — 100 m
109 y

N

MASS.
R.I.

Woonsocket

495

95

395

102

Glendale

Pascoag
Pascoag
Res.

7

146

295

100

Smithfield

Manville

Valley Falls

44

7

CONN.

6

295

N. Providence

Pawtucket

44

PROVIDENCE

Fresh
Lake

Scituate
Res.

Cranston

E. Providence

14
102

Westconnaug
Res.

2

114

195

Flat River
Res.

Barrington

14

Quidnick
Res.

W. Warwick

Warren

FALL
RIVER

Anthony

3

Warwick

114

95

1

Bristol

E. Greenwich

24

Carr
Pond

102

4

Prudence
Island

Tiverton

Arcadia
State
Park

Wickford

Narragansett
Bay

Portsmouth

3

102

4

Conanicut
Island

114

R.I.

Arcadia

Saunderstown

Middletown

138

95

Kingston

Jamestown

138

Sakonnet River

2

1

Newport
Bridge

Wakefield

1A

NEWPORT

Worden
Pond

3

Rhode Island
Sound

Westerly

1

Point Judith

Watch Hill

Block Island
Sound

Atlantic Ocean

Ferries to Block Island

1793

By Train   Ten trains a day each from New York (trip time: four hours) and Boston (trip time: one hour) arrive in Providence's modern, white-marble Amtrak railroad station (☎ 800/USA-RAIL).

By Bus   The terminal for Bonanza (☎ 401/751-8800) and Greyhound is just outside of the city off of I-95. If you are staying in Providence, you can take a shuttle or a taxi from the bus terminal into the city. Shuttles run every half hour. Several buses run daily to Providence from New York City, Boston, Newport, Hartford, Cape Cod, Springfield (Mass.), and Albany. Travel time from New York is about four hours; from Boston or Newport, about one hour; from Cape Cod (Hyannis), about 1¹/₂ hours.

ESSENTIALS   The **telephone area code** is **401**. The information office is at the **Greater Providence Convention and Visitors Bureau**, 30 Exchange Terrace, Providence, RI 02903 (☎ **401/274-1636**). Drop by or telephone them with any of your questions about the city.

WHAT TO SEE & DO

Preservation and urban redevelopment have done much to make Providence a delightful place in which to walk today. The most interesting districts are small enough that you can make your way around on foot. For an expert look at Providence's historical treasures, consider the following.

WALKING TOURS

The **Providence Preservation Society**, 21 Meeting St. (☎ **401/831-7440**), offers two audiocassettes and seven self-guided walking-tour booklets of historical areas in the city. Areas include Benefit Street, with its restored 18th- and 19th-century houses, the downtown section with its 19th- and 20th-century architecture, the waterfront, Brown University, and three Victorian neighborhoods, named Armory District, Elmwood, and Broadway. Rent a cassette for $5 or buy the booklets for a nominal fee at the society's headquarters Monday through Friday from 9am to 5pm. If you rent the audio tapes, you'll be asked to leave your driver's license during the time that you're out walking. The audio-cassette tour lasts 90 minutes.

In addition, you can take the suggested walking tour, below.

SIGHTS

Museum of Art, Rhode Island School of Design

224 Benefit St. ☎ **401/454-6500**. Admission $2 adults; 50¢ senior citizens, college students, and children 5–18; free for children under 5; voluntary donation for everyone on Sat. June 30–Labor Day, Wed–Sat noon–5pm; Sept–June, Tues–Wed and Fri–Sat 10:30am–5pm, Thurs noon–8pm, Sun 2–5pm.

The museum is among New England's finest, and one of the best museums of its size in the country, with collections from Greece and Rome, China and Japan; paintings by Manet, Monet, Degas, Cézanne, and Matisse, as well as other masters; and an excellent collection of ethnographic artifacts, American painting, furniture, costumes, and modern works of art. Of the choicest pieces in this impressive collection, Rodin's famous statue of Balzac ranks high, as does Monet's *Bassin d'Argenteuil* and the collection of Townsend/Goddard furniture in Pendleton House. The Daphne Farago Wing is a center dedicated to the display and interpretation of contemporary art in all media.

John Brown House

52 Power St. ☎ **401/331-8575.** Admission (including guided tour): $5 adults, $3 seniors and college students, $2 children 7–17. Combination tickets for John Brown and Aldrich House available. Mar–Dec, Tues–Sat 11am–4pm, Sun 1–4pm; Jan–Feb, Mon–Fri by appointment only. Closed holidays.

One of the fanciest historic houses on College Hill, the late-Georgian mansion constructed in 1786 is now owned and operated by the Rhode Island Historical Society. Proclaimed by John Quincy Adams to be "the most magnificent and elegant private mansion that I have seen on this continent," this restored house-museum reveals the prosperity of post-Revolutionary Providence and houses an outstanding collection of furnishings and decorative arts. John Brown was a merchant whose ships plied the seas both east and west out of Narragansett Bay and ultimately made him a wealthy man. The Brown family, by the way, had been prominent in Providence commerce and industry since the early 1700s. John's brother, Moses, joined with Samuel Slater to set up the first water-powered cotton-spinning mill in America in 1790, now known as Slater Mill (see below). One of his nephews, Nicholas Brown, was a graduate of Rhode Island College, which was later renamed Brown College (and later, University) in honor of the Brown family.

The State House

82 Smith St. ☎ **401/277-2357.** Free admission. Mon–Fri 8:30am–4:30pm (last tour at 3:30pm). Directions: From I-95, take Smith Street (U.S. 44) west; from I-195, take South Main Street (U.S. 44) north.

Overlooking downtown Providence, Rhode Island's State House is the center of state government. It is built of white Georgia marble and has one of the four self-supporting marble domes in the world. It is the fourth largest after St. Peter's in Vatican City, the Taj Mahal in India, and the Minnesota State Capitol in St. Paul. Constructed between 1895 and 1904, this important architectural landmark was entered in the National Register of Historic Places in 1971.

The building houses the Rhode Island House and Senate, along with the administrative offices of four of the state's five general officers: the Governor, Lieutenant Governor, Secretary of State, and General Treasurer. A number of historical artifacts are located in the building, including the Royal Charter of 1663 and an original copy of the Declaration of Independence. There are also portraits of Rhode Island's governors, including well-known Civil War General Ambrose E. Burnside. When you enter the building through the portal on Smith Street (U.S. 44), you'll see a Civil War cannon that was damaged during the battle and remained loaded for more than a hundred years, until it was taken from the State House and discharged in the 1960s.

There are tours of the building throughout the year. Volunteers direct tours for groups of interested individuals, providing insight into the construction of the building and its many historical treasures.

NEARBY ATTRACTIONS

Two more places to visit lie a few minutes outside the center of town. **Roger Williams Park** is a beautifully kept 19th-century Victorian masterpiece, conveniently located beside I-95 (Exit 17). It boasts the Museum of Natural History and Planetarium, Carousel Village, Greenhouses, and its gem—the **Roger Williams Park Zoo**. The Museum of Natural History (☎ 401/785-9457) houses nearly 250,000 items collected from sites around the world. The museum provides quality programming, interactive exhibits, and hands-on activities. The newest exhibit, *All Things Connected: Native American Creations,* features Native American ceramics, clothing, and textiles and includes baskets and beadwork. The museum also houses the Cormack Planetarium, Rhode Island's only public planetarium. The museum is open daily from 11am to 5pm. The Roger Williams Park Carousel (☎ 401/781-8008) is one of the most beautiful in New England. Other attractions include pony rides and a miniature golf course. Open hours are 11am to 6pm. In 1993 the *Boston Globe* declared Roger Williams Park Zoo (☎ 401/785-3510) "New England's great zoo," and with over 600 animals on display in their natural habitats (including cheetahs, elephants, polar bears, sea lions, giraffes, and zebra), the Roger Williams is a major player in the international wildlife conservation movement. The zoo is open year-round from 9am to 5pm on weekdays and 9am to 6pm on weekends and holidays. Admission is charged.

Water-powered cotton and textile mills changed all of New England in the 19th century, and it all started in Pawtucket, a few miles from downtown Providence. In 1793 three enterprising men named Slater, Almy, and Brown set up the first water-powered cotton-spinning factory in America, on the Blackstone River. Today the early mills and the **Sylvanus Brown House** (1758), home of the skilled artisan, make up the **Slater Mill Historic Site.** The mills have many of their old machines in working order, such as the water wheel, shafts, and pulleys in **Wilkinson Mill** (1810), and you can see them in action. Earlier handcraft devices for doing the same jobs are also on display to show you what a breakthrough the machine-filled **Slater Mill** (1793) was. Besides the permanent exhibits, traveling and temporary displays are set up from time to time, and guided tours interpret the history of the textile industry and the impact of factories on working conditions. Admission is $5 for adults, $4 for seniors, and $3 for children 6 to 12; children under 6 are free. Group rates are available. The site is open in summer, June to Labor Day, Tuesday through Saturday from 10am to 5pm and Sunday from 1 to 5pm; in spring and fall, weekends from 1 to 5pm; closed January and February. Call ☎ **401/725-8638** or write P.O. Box 696, Pawtucket, RI 02862-0696, for information. To get there, take I-95 North from Providence, get off at Exit 28, and turn left (under the highway) onto School Street. Cross the Blackstone River and turn right into Roosevelt Avenue; the site is on your right. From I-95 South, take Exit 27 and follow the signs to the mills.

WALKING TOUR
Providence

Start: Kennedy Plaza.

Finish: Prospect Terrace.

Time: About two hours, not including stops.

Best Times: Weekends, when there's less traffic.

Worst Times: Morning or evening rush hour.

Start your tour in

1. **Kennedy Plaza,** in the center of town. Shady trees and benches make the plaza an oasis in the middle of the city, and an equestrian statue of Gen. Ambrose

Burnside, the Civil War officer whose long side whiskers were the first "side-burns," watches over the eastern end of the plaza. At the western end is

2. City Hall, an agreeable Second Empire building completed in 1878 (go inside to see a wall display of other entries in the competition for the city hall design).

Go one block southeast from Kennedy Plaza to reach the Westminster Mall, a six-block section of Westminster Street closed to vehicles. The mall is a pleasant place to stroll or to sit and people-watch. Just past its eastern end, at 130 Westminster St., is

3. The Arcade, which looks like an imaginative bit of urban renewal but is in fact the creation of Russell Warren and James Bucklin, who designed the building in 1827. For a century and a half, some of Providence's better shops have operated in the Arcade. There are three levels of shops topped by a roof of glass panes; one modern addition to the Arcade is an elevator to take shoppers to the upper floors. Besides restaurants, the Arcade has stores selling antiques, jewelry, rare books, fine tobaccos, cosmetics, and other luxury items. Decorative cast-iron balustrades and stairways recall the Arcade's early 19th-century construction. Look at both facades—on Westminster Street and on Weybosset Street—which clearly show that each architect had his own idea of how the exterior should look. With two facades, each got his chance to do what he wanted.

Walk through the Arcade from Westminster Street to Weybosset Street, and turn right. Look for the golden dome, which marks Providence's historic

4. Round Top Church, officially known as the Beneficent Congregational Meetinghouse. It got its popular name because of its dome, which is a departure from the usual New England church spire. Finished in 1810, it was influenced by the classical revival then going on in Europe. The interior is as pleasant to look at as the exterior: Besides the gracious New England meeting house furnishings, the Round Top Church has a crystal chandelier consisting of almost 6,000 pieces. (Enter by the door on the side, around to the right.)

Now head northeast down Weybosset, past the Arcade, to the intersection of this street with Westminster and Exchange. Here in front of the Hospital Trust Bank, activities and shows are held during the warm months—perhaps a Boy Scouts' display of fancy marching or a small (but highly amplified) jazz combo giving a lunch-hour concert.

Walk two more blocks east, and you'll cross the Providence River to the foot of College Hill. The hill is the prettiest section of the city, its streets lined with 18th- and 19th-century houses, most of which have been well preserved or restored and many of which bear plaques, put up by the Providence Preservation Society, giving the builder's name and the date of construction.

At the bottom of College Hill, on South Main Street between Thomas and Waterman Streets, take a stroll past the

5. First Baptist Meeting House (☎ **401/454-3418**). Roger Williams founded the first Baptist congregation in the New World in 1638, but this building dates from 1775. The architect was Joseph Brown, and the steeple—designed from a plate in James Gibbs's *Book of Architecture* representing suggested steeples for St. Martin-in-the-Fields in London—rises to a height of 185 feet. It's one of the outstanding churches in New England. Admission is free, and the church is open year-round, Monday through Friday from 9am to 4pm. There are no guided tours in the winter, but a self-tour guide booklet is available. The front door of the church is locked, so go around to the right to the side (office) door.

To the left of the church, at 7 Thomas St., is a fantastic old building with half-timbering and stucco bas-reliefs on its facade. This is Sidney Burleigh's

6. **"Fleur de Lys" House,** built by this Providence artist in 1885 (the date is in the stucco). Thomas Street might be called "Artists' Row," because very near Burleigh's house is the Providence Art Club (☎ 401/331-1114), at no. 11. Open from 10am to 3pm (3 to 5pm on Sunday), the club has changing shows exhibited in its galleries. The club also runs the Dodge House at 10 Thomas St., which has contemporary shows from September through May.

At the intersection of Waterman and Benefit Streets, turn right and go south on Benefit for a block to the

7. **Museum of Art, Rhode Island School of Design** (see above). The Rhode Island School of Design, or RISD (known in Providence as "*riz*-dee"), is one of the country's best art, architecture, and design schools. Founded in 1877, it shares College Hill with Brown University.

You can also visit the

8. **Bayard Ewing Building,** at 231 S. Main St., which houses RISD's architectural division. Exhibits here change frequently, and feature architectural and industrial design.

Also up here on College Hill is Brown University (☎ 401/863-1000), a member of the Ivy League and the seventh-oldest university in the country. Founded in 1764, Brown's first building was

9. **University Hall,** used as a barracks for colonial and French soldiers during the American Revolution. It's now a National Historic Landmark. To get to it, walk up the hill (east) on Waterman Street, cross Prospect Street, and turn into the gates on your right. If you want a full, free tour of the beautiful and historic campus, find your way to the College Admission Office, one block from University Hall at the corner of Prospect and Angell Streets. Tours are available from here; call for times.

There are several other historical buildings on College Hill. The Rhode Island Historical Society operates both the

10. **John Brown House** (see above) and the

11. **Museum of Rhode Island History** (☎ **401/331-8575**), in the Aldrich House, a Federal-style mansion (1822) at 110 Benevolent St. Changing exhibitions highlight various aspects of Rhode Island's history and citizens. It's open Tuesday through Friday from 9am to 5pm; closed holidays. Adults pay $2 for admission, seniors pay $1.50, and children under 17 are charged $1; families pay a maximum of $6.

Prospect Street is so named because it passes near

12. **Prospect Terrace** (go to Cushing Street and turn left). From the Terrace, a small park, you can see downtown Providence and the State Capitol, along with a famous but rather wooden statue of the founder, Roger Williams. His grave is here as well. Trees have grown up below and block a bit of the perspective, but the view is still panoramic and impressive.

WHERE TO STAY

Most people who visit Providence stay in motels on the outskirts of town; these offer the best value and the greatest selection, although staying out of the center entails driving and parking problems. Providence does have a choice place to stay

Walking Tour—Providence

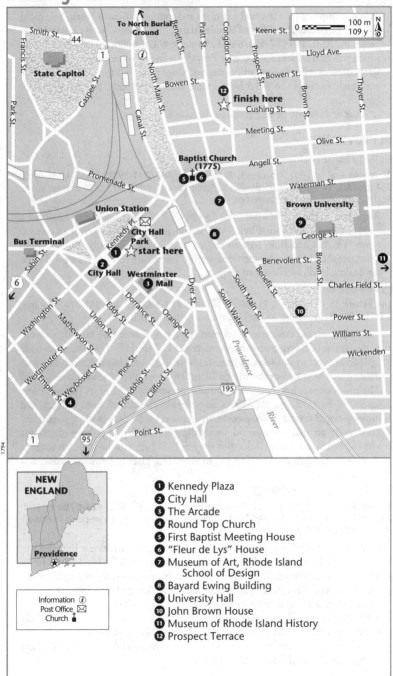

0   100 m
109 y

State Capitol

To North Burial Ground

Smith St. 44

Francis St.

Park St.

Gaspee St.

North Main St.

Benefit St.

Pratt St.

Congdon St.

Keene St.

Lloyd Ave.

Prospect St.

Bowen St.

Thayer St.

Bowen St.

Canal St.

❶❷ finish here

Cushing St.

Meeting St.

Olive St.

Baptist Church (1775)

Angell St.

❺ ❻

Promenade St.

❼

Waterman St.

Brown University

Union Station

City Hall Park

❾

George St.

Bus Terminal

Kennedy Pl.

City Hall

❶ start here

❷

❽

Benevolent St.

Brown St.

⓫

➔

Sabin St.

City Hall

Westminster Mall

❸

Benefit St.

Charles Field St.

6

↙

Washington St.

Mathewson St.

Union St.

Eddy St.

Dorrance St.

Orange St.

Dyer St.

South Main St.

South Water St.

⓾

Power St.

Williams St.

Westminster St.

Empire St.

Weybosset St.

Pine St.

Friendship St.

Clifford St.

Providence

Wickenden

❹

195

River

1

95

↓

Point St.

1794

❶ Kennedy Plaza
❷ City Hall
❸ The Arcade
❹ Round Top Church
❺ First Baptist Meeting House
❻ "Fleur de Lys" House
❼ Museum of Art, Rhode Island School of Design
❽ Bayard Ewing Building
❾ University Hall
⓾ John Brown House
⓫ Museum of Rhode Island History
⓬ Prospect Terrace

right downtown, plus a few of the familiar and comfortable chain hotels. You could also opt for **Bed & Breakfast of Rhode Island,** 580 Thames St. (P.O. Box 3291), Newport, RI 02840 (☎ **401/849-1298** or **800/828-0000;** fax 401/849-1306), which will find a room for you near Providence or any other Rhode Island town. Rates depend on the room, of course, but range from $80 to $185 for a double with bath, from $45 to $110 for a double with shared bath. You can phone 24 hours a day.

A **tax** of 12% will be added to your hotel bill.

IN PROVIDENCE

Holiday Inn–Providence

21 Atwells Ave. (at I-95), Providence, RI 02903. ☎ **401/831-3900.** Fax 401/751-0007. 274 rms. A/C TV TEL. $105.95 double. Children 18 and under stay free in parents' room. AE, DC, DISC, MC, V. Free covered parking.

Right next to the Civic Center, this 13-story, handicapped-accessible hotel has a good restaurant called the Black Swan, an indoor pool, a Jacuzzi, and an exercise room. The bus and train stations are less than half a mile away, and the hotel offers free shuttle service to and from nearby Green State Airport. It's a good value for quality, price, location, and services.

✪ The Old Court

144 Benefit St., Providence, RI 02903. ☎ **401/751-2002** or 401/351-0747. 11 rms. A/C TEL. $85–$135 double. All rates include breakfast. MC, DISC, V.

This handsome old three-story brick mansion is only a short walk from downtown, at the corner of North Street, on the slopes of College Hill. The house was built in 1863 as a rectory but takes its name from the old Rhode Island Courthouse next door, which now houses the Rhode Island Historical Preservation Commission. The inn itself is a fine example of historic preservation: All of its Italianate features—12-foot ceilings, plaster moldings, crystal chandeliers, brass sconces, and ornately carved marble mantelpieces—are in place. Furnishings in the spacious, airy guest rooms are true to the period, with wallpapers sporting large flowered patterns and old-fashioned alarm clocks. But the full tiled bath attached to each room is thoroughly modern in plumbing and fixtures. This place is very nicely done, and quite charming.

Providence Biltmore Hotel

11 Dorrance St., Kennedy Plaza, Providence, RI 02903. ☎ **401/421-0700** or 800/ 294-7709. 217 rms. A/C MINIBAR TV TEL. $99–$154 double. Reduced weekend rates available. AE, CB, DC, MC, V. Parking $7.

Right on Kennedy Plaza in the center of Providence, the Providence Biltmore was the most elegant hotel in Providence when it was built in 1922, and after a $14-million renovation, it's Providence's poshest place to stay once again. More than 100 rooms have their own lounge areas; 8 are designed especially for the disabled. If you knew the Biltmore before, you'll hardly recognize it now, as much has been changed. The outstanding features of 1920s elegance have been carefully preserved, and even the facade has been redone. Now a glass-enclosed elevator starts from the hotel lobby, penetrates the three-story-high lobby ceiling, and glides up the side of the 18-floor hotel to the top.

✪ Westin Hotel, Providence

1 W. Exchange St., Providence, RI 02903. ☎ **401/598-8000** or 800/228-3000. 341 rms, 22 suites. A/C TV TEL. $170–$195 double; $350–$1,200 suite. AE, CB, DC, DISC, MC, V.

Directions: Take I-93 south to 128th Street, then take Exit 22 and continue into the hotel's grounds; or take I-95 north for nine miles to Exit 22, then continue onto the hotel's grounds.

Rhode Island's new prize—the Westin Hotel, Providence—has been open for just over a year now. This place is just what the city needs to attract new commercial and convention business and spruce up the downtown district. A 25-floor brick high-rise, the hotel features a handful of restaurants and lounges, plus a full health club on the top floor. Besides the first-class regular guest rooms, the Westin offers a club level with executive rooms. Special programs for children include passes to the nearby Roger Williams Park and Zoo.

NEARBY

Most of Providence's hotel capacity is on the outskirts of greater Providence, in the neighboring cities of Warwick near the airport to the south, Pawtucket to the north toward Boston on I-95, and Seekonk, Mass., on I-95, the road to Cape Cod. As most of these hotels and motels are right off the highway, it's a good idea to pick them according to your plans for tomorrow: If it's evening as you approach Providence, stay in Warwick and then see Providence the next day; if it's early in the day, tour through Providence and then head out I-95 to Pawtucket if your next stop is Boston, or I-195 to Seekonk if you're headed for Cape Cod. You can call for a reservation while you're seeing the sights in Providence.

Comfort Inn/Providence

2 George St., Pawtucket, RI 02860. ☎ **401/723-6700** or 800/221-2222. Fax 401/726-6380. 134 rms. A/C TV TEL. $65–$100 double. Additional person $10 extra. Children under 18 stay free in parents' room. AE, DC, DISC, MC, V.

In Pawtucket, a few miles north of Providence off I-95, this is your best bet. The inn has an outdoor heated pool, an adjacent Ground Round restaurant, and a billiard parlor.

Ramada Inn

940 Fall River Ave. (Mass. 114A), Seekonk, MA 02771. ☎ **508/336-7300** or 800/228-2828. Fax 508/336-2107. 128 rms. A/C TV TEL. $65–$90 double. Additional person $5 extra. AE, DC, DISC, MC, V. Directions: From I-195 take Exit 1 in Seekonk.

Part of the Ramada hotel chain, this one is priced very competitively. Aside from its modern, functional rooms, it has an indoor pool, sauna, whirlpool, tennis courts, lounge with live entertainment, and a children's playground.

WHERE TO DINE

Providence's sophisticated university crowd generates a need for good restaurants, and Providence has plenty. Not all of them, however, are up on College Hill.

Bluepoint

99 N. Main St. ☎ **401/272-6145.** Reservations not accepted. Main courses $14–$27. AE, CB, DC, MC, V. Daily 5:30–10:30pm. (Bar, daily 5pm–midnight.) SEAFOOD.

Providence consumes almost as much succulent seafood as Newport, and a lot of the best seafood in Providence disappears at this one-room restaurant, with the oyster-and-spirits bar on the right as you enter. Bluepoint is usually filled with a classy young clientele busy talking but mostly eating. The clam chowder comes provençal (with tomatoes) or New England (with cream and potatoes). Oysters of many varieties are available on the half shell, as are littleneck and cherrystone clams. The entire menu, which changes daily, is printed on the blackboard. The specials, whether they be squid, grilled prawns, swordfish, bluefish, or scallops, constitute the best and freshest seafood at the lowest price. It's an easy walk from downtown. Smoking is permitted only in the bar.

Hemenway's Seafood Grill & Oyster Bar

1 Old Stone Sq. ☎ **401/351-8570.** Main courses $14.95–$22.95. Daily noon–3pm, Mon–Thurs 5–10pm, Fri–Sat 5–11pm, Sun 5–9pm. SEAFOOD.

It isn't just Hemenway's riverfront location that packs them in at lunch and dinner, it's the fine-quality oysters and fish that's shipped in from all over the world. Try something new, or stick with the traditional New England clambake. Softshell crabs are particularly good here. The fish is of the freshest quality. The restaurant is enormous, which accounts for the high noise level, but don't let that deter you—this is an excellent restaurant.

✪ Il Piccolo Ristorante

1450 Atwood Ave., Johnston. ☎ **401/421-9843.** Reservations recommended. Main courses $10.95–$18.95. AE, MC, V. Mon–Fri 11:30am–2:30pm; Mon–Sat 5pm–closing. ITALIAN.

There are scores of Italian restaurants in the Providence area, but Il Piccolo, located just outside Providence in Johnston, stands out. Indeed, people seem to flock to this wonderful restaurant with, among other things, its unique wood-granite bar. I started dinner with *bruschetta del sud* (Italian bread with roasted mashed eggplant, fresh tomato, and pecorino cheese). Another excellent appetizer was the *prosciutto e portobello* (roasted portobello mushrooms served over prosciutto with garlic, roasted peppers, and olive oil). As a main course, the *scaloppine alessio* (veal scaloppine sautéed with shiitake mushrooms, pine nuts, and roasted peppers, topped with a sauce of cognac and two mustards) made the taste buds tingle. Among the pasta offerings my favorite was the tortellini Katiuscia (tortellini stuffed with mild bleu cheese and topped with "vodka-pink" sauce). If you can manage dessert, go for the tiramisú pie or *tartuffos* (ice-cream balls covered with something delectable, like white chocolate and raspberry). The wine list is award-winning. You won't regret a trip to Il Piccolo, but if you're making a special trip you should make reservations in advance.

Ristorante Pizzico

762 Hope St. ☎ **401/421-4114.** Reservations recommended. Main courses $10.95–$22.75. AE, MC, V. Mon–Fri 11:30am–2:30pm, 5pm–closing. ITALIAN.

Providence is riddled with Italian restaurants, but this is one of the better ones. The dining room, with its crisp white cloths and green accents, is warm and inviting. The cuisine here is basic Italian with a twist. You should try the focaccia toscana, flat Tuscan bread with roasted peppers, aged ricotta, rosemary, and olive oil, to start, and follow it with veal scaloppine. If you're in the mood for fish, I'd recommend the Norwegian salmon roasted with lentils, fresh tomatoes, lemon, and olive oil. There's an abundance of pasta as well—from fettuccine to ravioli. The restaurant's award-winning wine list offers 780 selections.

Rue de l'Espoir

99 Hope St. ☎ **401/751-8890.** Reservations recommended. Main courses $13.95–$19.95. AE, DC, MC, V. Tues–Fri 7:30–11am, 11:30am–2:30pm; Sun–Thurs 5–9pm, Fri–Sat 5–10:30pm; brunch, Sat–Sun noon–2:30pm. NEW AMERICAN/FUSION COOKING.

About 10 blocks from Brown University, on College Hill, this restaurant takes its name from a French translation of the street it's on. Its menu is an international collection of fare, light and hearty, minceur and gourmande. For breakfast, try the honey-oat French toast. At lunch and dinner there are soups, salads, and pastas; grilled pizza; and main courses such as rack of lamb, aged sirloin steak, lobster, jumbo shrimp, asparagus over red rice risotto, and roast salmon with pistachio, orange, and basil crust, finished with orange-chili essence, and served with julienne vegetables and couscous. Note especially the menu of "small plates"—chicken-and-cashew spring rolls or petite ravioli is just the thing to order with a glass of wine for a light lunch or supper. Items on the dessert tray are not to be missed.

SPECIALTY DINING

The place to go if you're just interested in an informal bite is the **Arcade,** 65 Weybosset St. (☎ **401/598-1199**). This National Historic Landmark was built in 1828—a Greek Revival shopping arcade running between Weybosset and Westminster Streets, with three stories of shops surmounted by a glass canopy. The Arcade's ground floor is nothing but food shops, including the China Inn; Bess Eaton Donuts; Café LaFrance (with a full sandwich menu and gourmet coffees); Howe's Things (which serves sandwiches, salads, and natural foods); Spike's (with a wide variety of hot dogs); Jensen's Great Soups; Le Greque (with a full menu of Greek dishes); the Providence Cookie Co.; Villa Pizza; J. Thibs (which has a wonderful selection of ice cream and candy); and McDonald's, of course.

2 Newport

30 miles S of Providence, 17 miles SW of Fall River

Whatever glittering reports you've had of Newport, they're probably true because Newport is a fascinating and diverse place. Palatial mansions, the wealthy yachting set, major naval and Coast Guard installations, tennis tournaments, cocktails on marble terraces in the soft air of a summer's evening, or succulent seafood served in a waterfront restaurant—Newport is all of these.

Newport has enjoyed prominence during two periods in American history. In colonial times it was an important trade center, and so, like Salem, Mass., it has a lovely colonial section right downtown, much of which has been restored authentically in the styles of centuries ago. In the mid-19th century it became a resort for the very wealthy, who built what were called "cottages" but are indeed palaces in another part of town. Newport preserves remembrances of this past while pursuing its future as one of New England's prime vacation destinations: People who own yachts and people who can only afford to look at yachts, people who play tennis and those who watch it, people who live in mansions and people who take guided tours through mansions—they all flock to Newport. Besides the visitors, Newport is home to tens of thousands of Rhode Islanders who take all the glamour and glitter for granted, and who live here year-round.

Several things are important to remember when you're planning a visit to Newport. First, it's crowded in summer, particularly on weekends, and when the important tennis tournaments and yacht races are being held. Second, prices tend to go up on weekends and when the yachters are around. Third, Newport prides itself on having style, and many visitors will be dressed like movie stars; many restaurants, cocktail lounges, and hotels require "proper" dress at dinner and perhaps even lunch: jacket, or jacket and tie, for men; skirt and top or pants suit, or similar attire, for women.

A LOOK AT THE PAST   Newport is at the southern tip of an island that the Native Americans called Aquidneck and the colonial settlers dubbed Rhode

Island. Just as Providence was settled by Roger Williams, dissident from Salem, so Newport was founded by one William Coddington, who decided to strike out on his own from Providence in 1639. The new town soon became famous for ship-building and, as soon as the ships were built in sufficient numbers, for trade. The famous "triangle trade," from Newport to ports in the West Indies and Africa, would later bring great wealth to the town from the buying and selling of slaves, rum, molasses, and other goods. Because Providence and Newport were founded by dissidents, they became places of refuge for others wishing to worship as they pleased: Quakers from England, Jews from Portugal and Spain, and Baptists all came to Newport in the mid-1600s to find religious freedom. They brought talent and a gift for hard work, and the settlement prospered so that it became the colony's most important town and one of the New World's busiest ports. The many beautiful colonial homes, the handsome Old Colony House (center of government), the Touro Synagogue, and other landmarks attest to the wealth and prosperity of Newport at the time.

During the American Revolution, the British occupied the town and its excellent harbor, and held it for three years. A British frigate, HMS *Rose,* did much to hinder the transport of supplies to the Americans and spurred them to found the U.S. Navy in retaliation. Despite a French naval blockade and an American siege, the British held onto Newport until 1779, but after this interruption in its social and economic life, it never regained its status as Rhode Island's prime trade center.

Several decades later, however, Newport achieved prominence in another fashion. Drawn by the beautiful woods and dramatic coastline, wealthy merchants from New York and Philadelphia began to come to Newport to spend their summers. In the mid-1800s the first of Newport's famous mansions, Château-sur-Mer, was built, and others followed until Newport's Bellevue Avenue and Ocean Drive could boast the highest concentration of summer palaces—and they are *palaces*—anywhere in the world.

Today the city's symbol is the pineapple, a sign of welcome left from Newport's great commercial era when traders back from West Indies with this fruit would put a pineapple outside their warehouses to invite customers to come in and look over the stock. Newport is used to welcoming visitors, and you should have no trouble having a good time.

GETTING THERE   By Plane   Several national and regional airlines fly into T. F. Green State Airport in Warwick, south of Providence, 30 miles northwest of Newport.

By Car   From I-195 in Fall River, take R.I. 24 south to R.I. 114. From western Rhode Island, follow U.S. 1 to R.I. 138 east, which crosses the Jamestown and Newport Bridges to reach Newport.

By Train   Amtrak trains between Boston and New York stop in Providence, and buses run from Providence to Newport.

By Bus   Bonanza Bus Lines serves Newport with a stop downtown at Newport Gateway Center, 23 America's Cup Ave. (☎ 401/846-1820). Bonanza operates seven nonstop trips from New York's Port Authority Bus Terminal to Providence, with connecting service to Newport via Rhode Island Public Transit Authority buses. Bonanza also serves Newport with six daily trips from Boston's Back Bay Railroad Station.

Newport

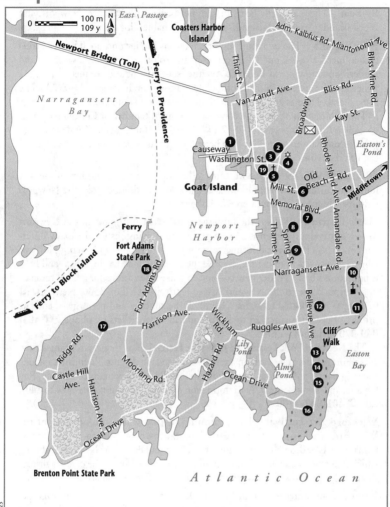

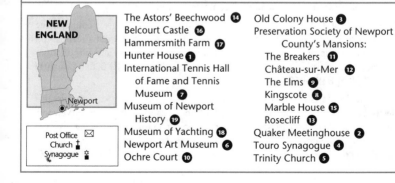

The Astors' Beechwood ⑭
Belcourt Castle ⑯
Hammersmith Farm ⑰
Hunter House ❶
International Tennis Hall
of Fame and Tennis
Museum ❼
Museum of Newport
History ⑲
Museum of Yachting ⑱
Newport Art Museum ❻
Ochre Court ❿

Old Colony House ❸
Preservation Society of Newport
County's Mansions:
The Breakers ⑪
Château-sur-Mer ⑫
The Elms ❾
Kingscote ❽
Marble House ⑮
Rosecliff ⑬
Quaker Meetinghouse ❷
Touro Synagogue ❹
Trinity Church ❺

Post Office ✉
Church ✝
Synagogue ✡

NEW ENGLAND

Newport

9323

By Boat   There are daily boats in summer between Providence, Newport, and Block Island. (See "Block Island," later in this chapter, for details.)

ESSENTIALS   The two most important streets in Newport are **Thames Street** (pronounced *thaymz,* not *temz*), center of the colonial section, the wharves, and modern downtown; and **Bellevue Avenue,** southeast of and parallel to Thames. Bellevue is the street with many of the old mansions on it. America's Cup Avenue is parallel to Thames and runs right along the water downtown.

The information office is the **Newport County Chamber of Commerce** office, 45 Valley Rd., Newport, RI 02842 (☎ **401/847-1600**), open Monday through Friday from 8am to 5pm. Get help here if you're stuck without a reservation and can't find a room.

SPECIAL EVENTS   Newport seems to have one festival or another all summer long. For current information on exact dates and offerings, contact the **Newport County Chamber of Commerce** (see above).

Music Festivals   Perhaps the biggest annual event in the town, the **Newport Music Festival** attracts great crowds to the grand mansions for the many different concerts. There are performances morning, afternoon, and evening for two consecutive weeks in mid-July. Because the capacity of all the mansions and halls is limited, it's best to order tickets—and to make reservations for a hotel room—in advance. Write to the Newport Music Festival, P.O. Box 3300, Newport, RI 02840 (☎ **401/846-1133**), for a list of all the concerts and performers, and the prices of tickets (usually $25 to $30). You can order tickets by phone (☎ **401/849-0700**) starting in June.

The **Newport Folk Festival & JVC Jazz Festival** draw thousands of music lovers to Fort Adams State Park on alternate weekends in August. Performers include such big names as Suzanne Vega, Judy Collins, Randy Newman, B. B. King, Ray Charles, and Tony Bennett. For information on schedules and tickets ($24 to $40), call ☎ **401/847-3700**.

Wickford Art Festival   The beginning of July marks the opening of the Wickford Art Festival in the nearby coastal town of Wickford (just across Conanicut Island on the other side of Naragansett Bay from Newport), during which 250 painters, sculptors, and photographers from around the country display their works outdoors. Call ☎ **401/295-5566** for more information.

Fishing Tournaments   From June to October, tournaments are organized periodically to see who can make a record catch of one of the familiar fish in the waters off Newport. The chamber of commerce can tell you more.

Tennis   Professional tennis championships are held on the grass courts at the International Tennis Hall of Fame/Newport Casino. These events feature top male and female pros and are usually held in July. For tickets and information, contact the Tennis Hall of Fame, 194 Bellevue Ave., Newport, RI 02840 (☎ **401/849-3990** or **849-6053**).

Taste of Rhode Island   If you're a foodie like me, you won't want to miss this festival at the end of September. About 50 Rhode Island chefs gather in Newport and serve up their specialties. It's a great way to get a taste of everything if you're only going to be in town a couple of days. There are arts and crafts tents displaying the work of local artisans as well. For more information, call ☎ **401/846-1600**.

WHAT TO SEE & DO

There's plenty to see in Newport, and during the summer there are also plenty of people here to see it. Parking places are at a premium, although the situation is certainly not hopeless. But why bother? If you're among the readers of this book who live close enough to arrive by car, why not bring a bicycle. If not, consider renting one when you get here? You can't really see the mansions by car—you always have to keep moving (the car behind you will make sure you do)—and Newport is small enough so that even an out-of-shape cyclist can see the town without much of a strain.

The **Newport Historical Society** (☎ **401/846-0813**) sponsors **walking tours** of historic Newport on Friday and Saturday from mid-June through September, departing at 10am (at 3pm on Fridays as well) from the Museum of Newport History at the Brick Market, Washington Square. If you plan on taking a walking tour, you should arrive at the museum a few minutes in advance of the start time. Tours last 2 hours. The cost for an adult is $5; children under 12 can come along for free. It's also free for anyone who has paid the cost of museum admission.

Should you want to get the "lay of the land" before heading out to see individual sights, take a bus tour of the town, Ocean Drive, Bellevue Avenue, and other districts. You don't necessarily have to take a tour that stops and goes through a mansion, although those are offered as well. **Viking Bus Tours of Newport,** in the Gateway Visitor's Center (☎ **401/847-6921**), will take you on a variety of tours through Newport for anywhere from $13 to $25 depending on the length of the tour and the number of mansions you visit. There is also a tour by land and by sea that lasts $4^1/2$ hours and takes you to the mansions as well as Hammersmith Farm ($25 for adults, $14 for children).Viking also has hour-long harbor tours from Goat Island for $7.50 (kids, $3). A harbor tour combined with a visit to Hammersmith Farm will cost you $14 for adults and $6 for children; it lasts $2^1/2$ hours.

THE MANSIONS

Newport boasts mansions of two types these days: those that are museums open to the public and those that are still private summer residences and are emphatically *not* open to the public. Believe it or not, many of these palatial houses are indeed still privately owned, maintained, and lived in. Interestingly, the wealthy people who live in private Newport mansions are often also responsible for opening others to the public. Through the efforts of the Preservation Society of Newport County, to which many of the owners belong, the marvelous houses we can tour today were preserved. To think that **The Elms**, perhaps the most graceful and charming of all the mansions, was to be torn down to make way for a housing development before the Preservation Society bought it is astounding.

Not all the mansions that are open to the public are owned by the Preservation Society, however. Several notable houses are privately maintained and open to visitors on terms similar to those of the society houses. When visiting the mansions, remember these two rules of thumb: First, figure on at least an hour per house to take it all in; second, don't try to see more than three or four houses in one day unless you have a tremendous capacity for absorbing glitter and magnificence. More than that in one day will leave you dizzy and exhausted. Also, try to visit the mansions on a weekday, when the crowds are smaller, saving Saturday and Sunday for Newport's other attractions. If you must go on Saturday, get there early.

❂ Preservation Society of Newport County's Mansions

118 Mill St. ☎ **401/847-1000.** Combination ticket for all seven buildings and the topiary garden, $35.50 adults, $10 children 6–11. Tickets for individual mansions cost $6.50 to $8 for adults, $3 to $3.50 for children, but since you'll probably be seeing more than one mansion, buy a "strip ticket" good for two mansions ($12), three ($17.50), four ($21), five ($24), six ($28), or seven mansions ($32). Children's prices are less than half of these. Tickets are on sale at any of the society's mansions. Admission to any mansion includes an informative tour through the rooms and the right to stroll about the grounds at your leisure. Tours are frequent, and the guides are usually well informed. From May to October, daily from 10am to 5pm (from July to September, The Breakers is open Saturday from 10am to 6pm). In April, the three fanciest mansions (The Breakers, Marble House, and Rosecliff) are open daily from 10am to 5pm; the rest, on Saturday and Sunday from 10am to 5pm. In November and from January through March, Marble House, The Elms, and Château-sur-Mer are open on Saturdays and Sundays from 10am to 4pm.

The Preservation Society of Newport County maintains six Newport mansions, plus **Hunter House** (a colonial house built in 1748) and **Green Animals** (a topiary garden with 80 sculptured trees and shrubs, many in the shapes of animals, in Portsmouth to the north of Newport). The Breakers, The Elms, and Château-sur-Mer are decorated for the holiday season in December.

The Breakers: Certainly the most grandiose of the mansions and most popular with visitors is The Breakers, an Italian Renaissance palace built for Cornelius and Alice Vanderbilt to replace the original Breakers, which burned down. It's nothing short of sumptuous, with lavish use of the finest marble. The marble columns in the two-story-high Great Hall have capitals carved of alabaster. Priceless tapestries, fine mosaic work, irreplaceable paintings, and ornate furniture testify to the wealth of The Breakers' owners. Designed by Richard Morris Hunt—who did a great many buildings, including several in Newport—The Breakers was built in only two years.

There's a children's cottage on the grounds (included in the price of admission to the mansion). Countess Szapary, a descendant of Cornelius Vanderbilt, maintains a private apartment at The Breakers.

The Elms: E. J. Berwind, son of a Philadelphia tradesman, got an appointment to the U.S. Naval Academy and served in the U.S. Navy until mustered out with high rank because of an injury. He soon made it big in the coal business and secured the contract to supply all navy ships with coal. With the profits, he built The Elms, perhaps the most gracious and pleasant of the Newport mansions. Although it's grand, it's also supremely harmonious, having been modeled on Asnières château in France (except for its three arched entrances, which were modeled after Buckingham Palace). The sunken formal garden at the far end of the spacious lawn was designed by a French landscape artist. The Elms is the masterpiece of Philadelphia architect Horace Trumbauer. It was threatened with destruction when a land-development firm bought it and planned to build a housing development on the site, but was saved by the zoning laws and the Preservation Society. Few of the original furnishings are left, but the mansion has been furnished with pieces from museum collections and private lenders.

Château-sur-Mer: The first stone mansion to go up on Bellevue Avenue was Château-sur-Mer (1852), built as a home for William S. Wetmore of New York. Wetmore's son, who met Richard Morris Hunt while on a tour of Europe, was responsible for bringing the American-born architect to Newport to rebuild his mansion, and later the mansions of others. (The senior Wetmore had lived in the mansion 10 years before he died, and upon his death his son took it over.) The Château is very rich Victorian Gothic, and to modern tastes it seems luxurious but dark and heavy. Château-sur-Mer has the feeling of being lived in and enjoyed—something that can't be said of some of the other mansions.

Marble House: Richard Morris Hunt threw himself into building this mansion for William K. and Alva Vanderbilt and finished it in 1892. It was modeled on the Petit Trianon at Versailles and is therefore decorated pretty much in the style of Louis XIV, which was, well, pretty grandiose—you'll see! As in The Breakers, the furnishings in Marble House are all original to the building. You'll see the Gold Room, a ballroom decorated with a king's ransom in gold; the kitchen; and the fascinating Chinese teahouse where Alva, an early feminist, held suffragette meetings.

Kingscote: Built in 1839, Kingscote is the type of "summer cottage" lived in by wealthy visitors to Newport before the great stone mansions were built. First built for G. N. Jones of Georgia by Richard Upjohn, it was later acquired by a merchant in the China trade called William H. King, who gave the house its name. A cottage it isn't, for no peasant lived here, but rather a man who appreciated Tiffany glass and an imposing dining room.

Rosecliff: Another famous New England architect, Stanford White, built Rosecliff in 1902 for Hermann and Tessie Oelrichs; Tessie's father had made a fortune in the Comstock Lode of Nevada. The building is modeled on the Grand Trianon, the larger of the two châteaux in the park at Versailles, but was meant to be even more lavish in layout and decor. Its ballroom is the largest one in Newport; the mansion is still used for summer entertainment and has been featured in several films, including *The Great Gatsby* (1974), with Robert Redford and Mia Farrow, and *True Lies* (1994), with Arnold Schwarzenegger and Jamie Lee Curtis.

Belcourt Castle

Bellevue Ave. ☎ **401/846-0669.** Admission $6.50 adults, $5 senior citizens or students with college IDs, $4 students 13–18, $2 children 6–12, children under 6 free. Feb–Memorial Day and mid-Oct to Nov, daily 10am–4pm; Memorial Day to mid-Oct, daily 10am–5pm. Hours may vary, be sure to call in advance.

Of the rest of the mansions in Newport, Belcourt Castle is the grandest. Another creation of Richard Morris Hunt, it was built in 1891. Oliver Belmont and his wife, Alva who had shockingly divorced William Vanderbilt (see "Marble House," above), had Hunt make them a castle in the style of Louis XIII (1610–43). Today the castle is filled with appropriate memorabilia: stained glass, armor, silver, and carpets. It even boasts a golden coronation coach. Well-informed guides escort the visitor through the beautiful period rooms and explain the collection. Tea or coffee is then served. Special parties can be arranged by calling the number above.

The Astors' Beechwood

580 Bellevue Ave. ☎ **401/846-3772.** Admission (including the show/tour) $8.50 adults, $7 for seniors and children. Daily 10am–5pm.

The house of William B. and Caroline Astor (*the* Mrs. Astor) was built in 1856. The "tour" here is quite different from what you'll find at any other Newport mansion. Here, Beechwood Theater Company actors and actresses play characters (tongue-in-cheek) who might have lived in such a summer cottage in 1891, during Newport's gilded age. It's all done in fun and with spirit, and it gives you quite another view of Newport life.

✪ Hammersmith Farm

Ocean Dr. ☎ **401/846-7346.** Admission $7 adults, $3 children. Apr to mid-Nov and "Christmas in Newport," daily 10am–5pm. Hours are extended in the summer, usually until 7pm. Call for hours before you set out because Hammersmith Farm sometimes closes early for private parties. Guided tours given daily.

Want to visit a summer White House? Hammersmith Farm was built by John W. Auchincloss in 1887 as his family's 28-room summer "cottage." After Jacqueline Bouvier, daughter of Janet Lee Bouvier Auchincloss, became Mrs. John F. Kennedy, the wedding reception was held at Hammersmith Farm. President Kennedy and his wife enjoyed visiting the farm when they could find the time, and no wonder. Beautiful rolling lawns and gardens, nature paths and copses of trees—not to mention the lovely old house itself—make the farm a seaside paradise. Mrs. Auchincloss sold Hammersmith Farm mansion in 1977, and it's now open to the public with many of the original furnishings. *Note:* At press time Hammersmith Farm was up for sale, so call to make sure it's still open to the public.

A WALK IN WASHINGTON SQUARE

Right downtown between Thames and Spring Streets, next to the new Brick Marketplace shopping mall, is Washington Square, the center of colonial Newport. At the western tip of the square is the **Brick Marketplace,** a Newport landmark, built in 1762 and designed by Peter Harrison. (Bricks were never sold here, the name simply refers to the construction of the market.) Having served variously as a town hall, theater, and crafts center, it's now occupied by shops.

At the other end of the square stands the **Old Colony House,** center of Newport governmental affairs from its construction in 1739 until the Rhode Island General Assembly (which met in Newport in the summer) last used it in 1900. It was from the Colony (later State) House's balcony that the Declaration of Independence was read to Rhode Islanders. In the assembly room is Gilbert Stuart's famous portrait of George Washington. You can get a free tour of the building July through Labor Day, Monday through Friday from 9:30am to noon and 1 to 4pm, and on Saturday and Sunday from 9:30am to noon.

OTHER ATTRACTIONS

Touro Synagogue

82 Touro St. ☎ **401/847-4794.** Free admission; donations accepted. Summer Mon–Fri, Sun 10am–5pm; rest of the year, Mon–Fri 2–3pm, Sun noon–3pm (and by appointment in winter). On Fri night and Sat morning, you may attend services.

The Touro Synagogue is the most famous and oldest Jewish synagogue in continental North America. Designed by Peter Harrison (it resembles his King's Chapel in Boston) and built in 1763, the temple was the spiritual center of Congregation Yeshuat Israel, an Orthodox Sephardic congregation. The synagogue and congregation prospered along with Newport, but after the British occupation of the town during the Revolutionary War, prosperity fled Newport and few of its erstwhile citizens returned. In the late 19th century Newport came to life again. The temple reopened in 1883 and has been used for services ever since. Throughout most of the year, short tours are conducted. You can see a copy of George Washington's historic letter on religious freedom to the congregation, written while he was president in 1790.

Quaker Meetinghouse

At the corner of Marlborough and Farewell Sts. ☎ **401/846-0813.** Free admission. Call for an appointment.

This was built in 1699 but was greatly modified in the early 1700s and again in the early 1800s. The congregation, founded in 1657, is the oldest of the Society of Friends in this country. The meeting house has been restored to look as it did in the early 1800s.

Trinity Church

At the corner of Spring and Church Sts. ☎ **401/846-0660.** Free admission; donations accepted. Late June to Labor Day, Mon–Sat 10am–4pm; Labor Day to late June, Mon–Fri 10am–1pm. Sun services at 8 and 10am in summer, at 8 and 11am in winter.

Newport, of course, has a beautiful old pre-Revolutionary (1726) church, and this one, recently renovated, is a real gem. It was designed and built by local master builder Richard Munday and is the first building in Newport for which we know the name of the builder. It still has the "bishop's mitre" weathervane, as it did before the Revolution. The church is full of history: Bishop George Berkeley gave the organ (1733), Washington was known to have worshiped here (pew no. 81), and its famous three-decker free-standing centralized "wineglass" pulpit is the only one of its kind that remains today. Handicapped accessible.

International Tennis Hall of Fame and Tennis Museum

194 Bellevue Ave. ☎ **401/849-3990.** Admission $6 adults, $3.50 seniors, $3 children 5–16, free for children under 5; $12 per family. Daily 10am–5pm. Closed Thanksgiving and Christmas Days.

This is sure to be of interest to anyone obsessed with the game or its history. It's housed in the Newport Casino, a National Historic Landmark, located across from the shopping center. The casino, built in 1880, is the perfect location for the tennis museum, as it was here that the first national tennis championships were held. Major professional tournaments are played here during summer. In addition, tennis history comes alive here at the world's largest tennis museum, which features tennis trophies, art, videos, and memorabilia from the game's origins through its evolution to the sport it has become today. Visitors can test their tennis savvy with new interactive video displays and walk through the enshrinee hall where plaques commemorate the approximately 160 legends so honored. The 13 grass courts are open to the public for play in season (May to October), so bring your racquet and call to make arrangements.

Museum of Newport History

At the Brick Market (Thames St. at Washington Sq.). ☎ **401/841-8770.** Admission $5 adults, $4 seniors, $3 children 6–12, free for children under 6; family rates available (maximum is $13). Mon and Wed–Sat 10am–5pm, Sun 1–5pm.

Newport's newest museum is a good place to begin your visit. The Newport Historical Society has designed the museum in such a way that it provides the whole family with an engaging introduction to Newport's history and the beauty of its architecture. Stories of those who have made significant contributions to the history and development of Newport—past and present—are told within the museum through historic objects, paintings, and images, as well as interactive computer and video displays. The museum also offers guided walking tours from May to October.

Museum of Yachting

In Fort Adams State Park, Ocean Dr. ☎ **401/847-1018.** Admission $3 adults, $2.50 seniors, free for children under 12. Mid-May to Oct, daily 10am–5pm.

As you might imagine, Newport has a Museum of Yachting; it's a short drive along Ocean Drive from the center of town. If you're at all interested in small wooden craft, boatbuilding, or yachting, you should make a visit. An exhibit highlighting the single-handed sailor is on the second floor.

Newport Art Museum

76 Bellevue Ave. ☎ **401/848-8200.** Admission $5 adults, $4 seniors and students, free for children under 12. July–Sept 7, daily 10am–5pm; Sept 8–June, Tues–Sat 10am–4pm, Sun 1–5pm.

Here you'll find changing exhibitions that highlight Newport's role in the creation of American art. Exhibits are featured year-round in the famous Griswold House (1862), which was designed by Richard Morris Hunt, and in the Cushing Gallery. Call for information on current shows.

Wanton-Lyman-Hazard House

17 Broadway. ☎ **401/846-0813.** Admission $5 per person. June 15–Sept 1, Thurs–Sat 10am–4pm, Sun 1–4pm.

Built circa 1675, the Wanton-Lyman-Hazard House is the oldest house in Newport and one of the finest examples of early colonial architecture in New England. The house is furnished with authentic period pieces. Tours are given.

SPORTS & RECREATION

OCEAN DRIVE & CLIFF WALK   Take a drive (or ride your bike, if you're in shape) along Newport's 10-mile Ocean Drive. The scenery is lovely, with low heath, evergreens, stretches of rugged coast, and several smooth, grassy lawns maintained as state parks. **Brenton Point State Park** has parking, walking, and picnic areas, and there's a public fishing area with parking nearby. Ocean Drive also gives you a look at some of the yachts sailing on Rhode Island Sound, and at the mansions around the end of the island.

For walkers, the pedestrian equivalent of Ocean Drive is Cliff Walk, a path that runs along the shore and along the edge of the "front yards" of the mansions on Bellevue Avenue. The official start of the hour-long walk is off Memorial Boulevard just before Newport Beach beneath the Cliff Walk Manor, but you can also get to the path by going east on one of the side streets off Bellevue Avenue. You needn't take the entire walk, but can head back to Bellevue Avenue at various points along the way.

FORT ADAMS STATE PARK   On a peninsula jutting into Newport Harbor, Fort Adams State Park (☎ **401/847-2400**) offers several attractions. The park is open from sunup to sundown all year, and picnic and fishing sites are open to all. The fort itself, named after President John Adams, is currently being restored, and tours may be offered by the time you read this, so call ahead for information. Boat-launching ramps, beach with lifeguard, picnic area, the Museum of Yachting (see above), and soccer fields are available for your enjoyment. The fort's defenses are some of the most impressive in the country—so impressive, in fact, that it rarely came under fire. Views of the town and the harbor from hills in the park are well worth the short climb.

BEACHES   Newport's beaches are of two types: public (open to everyone for a fee) or private (open to members only). Bailey's Beach, at the southern end of Bellevue Avenue, is definitely private, but **Newport Beach,** also called First Beach, is public and quite large. It's on the isthmus at the eastern reach of Memorial Boulevard. **Second Beach** is in Middletown, a bit farther along the same route where the street changes names to become Purgatory Road. Just around the corner from Second Beach is **Third Beach**, at the mouth of the Sakonnet River, facing east. It may be a bit chilly at any time except July and August.

Gooseberry Beach, on Ocean Drive, is an especially attractive beach, open to the public for a car-parking fee of $6 on weekdays, $1.50 for pedestrians and cyclists. It's framed by nice mansions on either side and has interesting rock formations.

JAI ALAI   An unusual spectator sport and game of chance in Newport is the fast-moving game of jai alai, familiar to those who have traveled to Latin America and Florida. The Newport Fronton is at 150 Admiral Kalbfus Rd., near the Newport end of the Newport Bridge. Betting is on which player or team will win, and is pari-mutuel as it is at horse and dog tracks. The game is fast and exciting, and the ball (harder than a golf ball) moves at murderous speeds approaching 188 miles an hour. If you've never seen it before (or bet before), you can get a brochure at the door explaining it all. For information call ☎ **849-5000** in Rhode Island, or **800/451-2500** out-of-state. Also located within are over 400 slot machines and simulcast horse racing. Admission is free. There's a moderately priced restaurant and a lounge that overlooks court action.

WHERE TO STAY

Newport has several large, comfortable hotels, a good number of charming small inns, and numerous bed-and-breakfast houses. Neighboring Middletown, which has many inexpensive motels and more guesthouses, is so close that many visitors to Newport stay in motels in Middletown and then drive the mile or two into Newport to see the sights. No matter what sort of accommodation you choose, it's a good idea to have reservations in advance, particularly in summer and especially on weekends. If you arrive in Newport on Friday from mid-July through Labor Day, you may well have to spend hours searching for that last hotel or inn room. On summer weekdays there may be more rooms, but you may not be able to find your preferred facilities and price unless you reserve in advance. The listings begin with some of Newport's fine inns, which are moderate in price but high in comfort and good looks, then go on to guesthouses (almost as charming, but cheaper), and hotels and motels.

The **Newport County Chamber of Commerce** (☎ **401/847-1600**) has a nice long list of bed-and-breakfast guesthouses and small inns. Send for it if you have the time; pick one up when you arrive if you don't; or call and ask for help in locating a room.

Anna's Victorian Connection, 5 Fowler Ave., Newport, RI 02840 (☎ **401/ 849-2489**) will help you find suitable lodgings in a bed and breakfast in Newport and other areas of Rhode Island.

Remember that Rhode Island has a **7% sales tax,** and a **5% room tax** is also applied to prices in establishments with three or more rooms.

INNS

Expensive

✪ Francis Malbone House
392 Thames St., Newport, RI 02840. ☎ **401/846-0392** or 800/846-0392. Fax 401/ 848-5956. 9 rms. A/C. May–Oct, $160–$295 double; Nov–Apr, $95–$175 double. AE, MC, V. Directions: Coming from the Newport Bridge, take a right onto America's Cup Avenue at the second set of lights; at the sixth set of lights, turn right onto lower Thames Street at the Perry Mill Market/Newport Bay Club; the Francis Malbone House is three blocks down on the left. To reach the parking area, turn left onto Brewer Street (the third left off Thames Street) into the first driveway on the right.

The Francis Malbone house was built in 1760 for shipping merchant Col. Francis Malbone by the same architect who designed Touro Synagogue and the Redwood Library. An elegant staircase with individually turned spindles graces the foyer, to the left of which is a formal gray, wood-paneled sitting room with a striped camelback couch, wingback chairs, and a gray marble fireplace. To the right you'll find a small library and, a bit farther back, a casual sitting room that houses the television, telephone, books, and a comfortable couch.

The guest rooms are comfortable and meticulously clean, with lovely fabrics and reproduction antiques throughout. For instance, the front room on the second floor is done in Wedgwood blue with white trim and holds a rice four-poster bed with a white-eyelet, lace-trimmed quilt; a highboy; pier mirror; window seats; an Oriental carpet; and two Martha Washington Queen Anne chairs in front of a marble fireplace with a wood mantel. The downstairs room holds a king-size bed, a Jacuzzi for two, and a double marble shower. Garden side rooms also have whirlpool tubs.

Innkeeper Will and his assistant, Mary Frances, tend to your every need and serve you breakfast every morning at the lace-covered dining room table in front of the hearth. The full breakfast might consist of eggs Florentine, raspberry/cream-cheese French toast, or pear-walnut pancakes in addition to scones, muffins, fresh fruit, and cereal, plus coffee and tea. You might like to take your final cup of coffee out to the beautifully maintained garden and sit in one of the Adirondack chairs on the flagstone patio. The Francis Malbone House is definitely one of the best places to stay in Newport.

Inn at Castle Hill

Ocean Ave., Newport, RI 02840. ☎ **401/849-3800.** 14 rms and suites (8 with bath), 6 harbor houses, 17 beach cottages. Dec–Mar, $40–$50 double without bath, $75–$90 double with bath, $130 suite; Apr–May and Nov, $50–$65 double without bath, $70–$135 double with bath, $180 suite; June–Oct, $65–$80 double without bath, $120–$190 double with bath, $230 suite. All rates include continental breakfast. AE, MC, V.

This marvelous Victorian summer mansion, perched on a hill at the southwestern tip of Rhode Island overlooking Narragansett Bay, is a Newport favorite. The house was built in 1874 for Alexander Agassiz (1835–1910), naturalist, industrialist, and great benefactor of Harvard. It has been authentically maintained and restored, and is a fine example of a wealthy family's Victorian summer cottage extravaganza: dark wood, ornate fireplaces, large-flower-pattern wallpaper (different in each room, of course), Oriental carpets, a sunny solarium—it's all here. The Harbor House (summer only), an unobtrusive motel-style structure, is next to the inn and just above the pebble beach. The inn also has a number of beach cottages capable of lodging two to four people. The cottages are rented by the week in summer ($750 to $850) and are booked very far in advance. There's a good dining room.

Wayside

Bellevue Ave., Newport, RI 02840. ☎ **401/847-0302.** 6 rms. TV. $115–$135 double. All rates include continental breakfast. No credit cards. Directions: Drive from the Newport Casino (International Tennis Hall of Fame) down Bellevue Avenue; pass The Elms on the right, then the Oakwood Healthcare Center on the left; the next building on the left is the Wayside, marked by a small marble plaque by the driveway.

For the full Newport experience, stay in the Wayside, a mansion right on Bellevue Avenue. This fine 1890s house of tawny brick is set back from the avenue with

its own little driveway and porte cochère. The interior spaces are ri[...]
but austere rather than fussy. The many parlors and bedrooms have b[...]
comfortable accommodations with private baths, and there's a pool o[...]

Moderate

Cliffside Inn

2 Seaview Ave., Newport, RI 02840. ☎ **401/847-1811** or 800/845-1811. 13 rms. A/C TV
TEL. $145–$325 double. Special winter rates are available. All rates include full
breakfast. AE, DC, MC, V. Directions: Take America's Cup Avenue to Memorial Boulevard
(R.I. 138A) and follow Memorial east to Cliff Avenue; turn right, go two blocks to Seaview
Avenue, and turn left onto Seaview; Cliffside is on the left.

Very near Cliff Walk and the beach is the Cliffside Inn, a 19th-century Victorian
"summer cottage" that was originally built for Gov. Thomas Swann of Maryland.
Later it was owned by Newport artist Beatrice Pasatorius Turner, who is said to
have painted more than 1,000 self-portraits while she lived here. Currently owned
by Winthrop Baker and operated by Stephan Nicolas, the Cliffside Inn is one of
the most elegant guesthouses in Newport. In keeping with the Victorian atmosphere, the color schemes are rich and vibrant, and the antique furnishings are
unique to each room. There are floor-to-ceiling bay windows, and seven rooms
have working fireplaces. One room even has a fireplace in the bathroom. Eight
rooms also have double Jacuzzis. A full gourmet breakfast (fresh-squeezed orange
juice, fruit, breads, muffins, and a hot entrée) is served each morning, and every
afternoon hot hors d'oeuvres are available. You can't go wrong here.

Melville House

39 Clarke St., Newport, RI 02840. ☎ **401/847-0640.** 7 rms (5 with bath). Late May to early
Oct, $85–$100 double without bath, $95–$110 double with bath. Early Oct to late May, rates
20%–40% less. All rates include breakfast. AE, MC, V.

"Where the past is present" is how innkeepers Vince DeRico and David Horan
describe their inn, on a quiet street only a few blocks up Historic Hill from
America's Cup Avenue and the Brick Marketplace. The inn couldn't be situated
better. It's not one of Newport's Victorian palaces but rather a beautiful old
colonial house dating from about 1750, and it's on the National Register of
Historic Places. The owners have been true to the period in their decorations, which recall colonial and Early American times, yet they've also catered to
guests' desires for modern facilities by installing up-to-date, if small, private
bathrooms. The mood here is one of antiques, good taste, quiet, and friend-
liness. Breakfast includes homemade granola, muffins, and breads, with items
like buttermilk biscuits, stuffed French toast, or fresh-fruit sourdough pancakes.
There is also a complimentary sherry hour in the evening. You'll love the Melville
House.

GUESTHOUSES

Many of the lodging establishments listed below are similar in ambience and
facilities to the inns listed above. The distinction between inn and guesthouse
is somewhat arbitrary. My feeling is that guesthouses have just a little more of
the feeling you get when you stay in someone's home.

The Covell House

43 Farewell St., Newport, RI 02840. ☎ **401/847-8872.** 5 rms. Mid-May to mid-Oct,
$105–$125 double or queen. Mid-Oct to mid-May, rates are lower. All rates include
continental breakfast. MC, V.

Built in 1805, this place was completely renovated in 1982, with antique-decorated guest rooms. The neighborhood is a quiet, residential one, but you're still only a short walk from the bustling waterfront.

Elm Tree Cottage

336 Gibbs Ave., Newport, RI 02840. ☎ **401/849-1610** or 800/882-3ELM. 6 rms. A/C. $125–$195 double weekdays, $165–$300 weekends. All rates include full breakfast. MC, V. Directions: Via Newport Bridge, exit at "Scenic Newport" and turn right off the exit ramp; at the second set of lights, turn right onto America's Cup Avenue and follow it to the seventh set of lights; stay to the left, proceed up the hill onto Memorial Boulevard toward First Beach, and cross over Bellevue Avenue; make a left onto Gibbs Avenue and proceed to the first stop sign; the Elm Tree Cottage is the third house on the right.

"Casual elegance" is the way Pricilla and Tom Malone describe their bed-and-breakfast inn, and it's a description that couldn't be more fitting. Once owned by the heiress to the Pennsylvania Rail Road, the house is full of interesting stories, in particular the one about the bar—ask Pricilla to tell you. The bar (not stocked, but available for use) is built like the interior of a ship and originally had 45, 1921 silver dollars imbedded in the top (some have since been stolen). Around the corner from the bar is a sun room with wicker furnishings. The living room holds a grand piano, a Victorian upright piano, a fireplace, and an enormous mirror that took four men to hang. There's stained glass all over the house—that's because Tom and Pricilla make stained-glass windows (they're definitely not your average innkeepers). They'll gladly take you down into the basement to show you how it's done.

The rooms are elegantly furnished with Louis XV beds, antique complementary pieces from England and France, and fine linens and fabrics. Most of the rooms have functional fireplaces. The light fixtures and Austrian crystal vanity in what is known to many as the Windsor Suite are original to the house. Every morning (as early as 7:30 if you wish), Pricilla has coffee and tea ready and then whips up a gourmet breakfast that might include crepes, French toast, orange waffles, or some other wonderful creation (never scrambled eggs).

Hydrangea House Inn

16 Bellevue Ave., Newport, RI 02840. ☎ **401/846-4435** or 800/945-4667. 6 rms. A/C. May–Oct, $89–$139 double; Nov–Apr, $55–$95 double. All rates include full breakfast.

The Hydrangea House Inn, built in 1876, has been beautifully but completely restored. The Rose Dutches Room overlooks Bellevue Avenue and is done in rose with floral chintz draperies. There's a queen-size bed, a Queen Anne flat-top desk, two cameo-back chairs, and a wingback chair. La Petite Rouge Chambre, located across the hall from the tiny sitting room, is the smallest of the rooms. The plum-red painted walls, hand-painted Edwardian chest of drawers, French cartoon prints, and fireplace (not working) make it one of the coziest spaces in the inn. The largest of the rooms is the Hydrangea Garden Room, which is located on the ground floor and faces the back garden. It can accommodate up to four people.

A breakfast of coffee, tea, juice, fruit, granola, and a hot main dish is available in the morning downstairs in the art gallery—yes, in the gallery. You can eat breakfast while admiring the original works by Rhode Island and New England artists. Much of the art in the inn is for sale. The Hydrangea House is non-smoking.

Ivy Lodge

12 Clay St., Newport, RI 02840. ☎ **401/849-6865.** 8 rms (7 with bath). A/C. Mid-May to mid-Nov, $100–$165 double; mid-Nov to mid-May, $100 double. Rates include full

buffet breakfast. AE, MC, V. Directions: Drive along Bellevue Avenue and watch for the Oakwood Healthcare Center on the left; turn left onto Parker Avenue just before Center, then right onto Clay Street; Ivy Lodge is on the left.

This huge shingled summer cottage, with its gables and chimneys, curving veranda with wicker furniture, and tidy carriage house, stands proudly even in the midst of the mansions. Its lofty entrance hall, done completely in glowing, artfully carved woodwork that rises all the way up to the third-floor roof, further proves the house's elegance. Staircases cascade in front of you and stained glass glows above. There's a fireplace and, to the right, a reading room with etched-glass windows. To the left is the formal dining room, where a full buffet-style breakfast is served. Guest rooms are similarly ornate and authentic. The hosts, Terry and Maggie Moy, will welcome you and then leave you pretty much to enjoy yourself as you please. Little extras include bicycles, coolers, and beach chairs.

Sanford-Covell Villa Marina

72 Washington St., Newport, RI 02840. ☎ **401/847-0206.** 8 rms (6 with bath), 2 apart-ments. $95–$225 double. All rates include continental breakfast. No credit cards. Directions: Follow Thames Street to America's Cup Avenue (on the left); continue to Long Wharf on the left, which turns right into Washington Street; the Sanford-Covell Villa Marina will be on the left.

Walking into the Sanford-Covell Villa Marina is like walking into a different era. In 1869, Milton Sanford, a New York industrialist, commissioned William Ralph Emerson, the cousin of Ralph Waldo Emerson, to build this stick-style Victorian building as a summer home. This commission is said to have been a catalyst of the famous Newport mansion wars. Today the rooms and hallways are filled with Victorian knickknacks, as well as toys, quilts, and antiques. Each room is unique. The Play Room, not the biggest or most elegant of the rooms but still very nice, was originally the Smoking Room. If you go into the Play Room and step out onto the balcony that overlooks the foyer, you'll be awed by the 35-foot drop to the ground floor, and you'll also be able to get a better view of the original lamp fixtures (which were converted to electricity in 1920) and the painting around the tops of the walls. It's not paper and it's not stenciled—the technique used to apply the paint is called "pouncing"—and it's not just painted on; it's actually pounded into the wall at the end of a lead weight. The most fascinating thing about the Play Room is the diaries of William King Covell (the third owner of the home) displayed on the bookshelf.

The house has a wraparound porch with porch swings and the most incredible view (since it's practically at water's edge) at the back. Here's where you'll head if you want to swim in the black-bottom saltwater pool or lounge in the saltwater Jacuzzi (open May to October). Beyond the pool and Jacuzzi there's a pier with a gazebo. You can't beat the Sanford-Covell Villa Marina for luxury, history, and a bit of adventure.

HOTELS & MOTELS

Besides these downtown hotels, there are many motels on the outskirts, in Middletown, particularly along West Main Road (R.I. 114). Prices are lower, but so are quality, convenience, and ambience.

Newport Islander Doubletree Hotel

One Goat Island, Newport, RI 02840. ☎ **401/849-2600** or 800/222-TREE. 235 rms, 18 suites. A/C TV TEL. $89–$290 double; $175–$500 suites. Additional person $15 extra. Children under 18 stay free in parents' room. AE, DC, MC, V.

Perched on an island in the midst of the yachts, the Islander has good views all around, comfortable modern rooms, lots of nautical decor, and many big-hotel services, including separate indoor and outdoor pools, a health center and sauna, a beauty salon, two racquetball courts, and two restaurants.

Newport Marriott

25 America's Cup Ave., at Long Wharf, Newport, RI 02840. ☎ **401/849-1000** or 800/ 228-9290. 317 rms. A/C MINIBAR TV TEL. $99–$244 double. AE, DC, MC, V.

The Marriott, one of Newport's newest hotels, is the prime place to stay if you like modern elegance and comfort. The many services include an indoor-outdoor pool, racquetball courts, health club, sauna, and three dining and drinking places, including the J.W. Sea Grill & Oyster Bar, which specializes in fresh seafood dishes. Many of the very comfortable rooms have water views. A concierge level is available in the summer and fall seasons.

WHERE TO DINE

Dining in Newport is anything you want to make it, from a seaside clambake on paper plates to an elegant dinner with candlelight, soft music, and polished service. **Bannister's Wharf/Bowen's Wharf** is the most charming of the waterfront redevelopment projects, and it has a selection of good restaurants. Bannister's Wharf is right next to the Treadway Inn, downtown on the waterfront, and would be West Pelham Street's extension if the wharf were still a street. On upper Thames Street, across from Memorial Boulevard, there are lots of places where you can get delicious seafood at very reasonable prices. Some restaurants allow you to bring your own wine or beer, which also helps to keep the price of a good seafood dinner in the reasonable range. You can pick up your favorite vintage or brew at **Thames Street Liquors,** 520 Thames St., or at one of several other stores in the area. The BYO restaurants can tell you how to find the nearest liquor store.

EXPENSIVE

Black Pearl

Bannister's Wharf. ☎ **401/846-5264.** Reservations required in summer. Main courses $17.75–$26.75. AE, MC, V. Commodore's Room, daily 6–11pm. Tavern, daily 11am–11pm. Closed Mid-Jan to mid-Feb. FRENCH/AMERICAN.

The Black Pearl, one of Newport's most well-established restaurants, is crowded for lunch and dinner, weekdays and weekends with members of the yachting set as well as tourists. There are actually three places to dine here. In the Commodore's Room, a jacket is required for men and similarly suitable dress for women. This is not the busiest of the Pearl's eating areas; rather, it's a refuge from the busy places. Quietly elegant table settings are lighted by a candle lantern. The decor is subdued, quite unlike the overdone or garish atmosphere characteristic of many waterfront restaurants. Next to the Commodore's Room is the Tavern, where a jacket is not required, and diners press in for a drink, a "Pearlburger," an omelet, or perhaps a daily special, such as fresh bluefish with lemon-caper butter. Outdoors, next to the Black Pearl, is the outdoor bar, a sort of waterfront cafe, with white metal tables and chairs set out on a patch of white gravel, shaded by brightly colored umbrellas. The Black Pearl is next to the Clarke Cooke House.

✪ Clarke Cooke House

Bannister's Wharf. ☎ **401/849-2900.** Reservations required. Main courses $21.75–$25.50. AE, MC, V. Daily 11:30am–10pm. TUSCAN/NORTHERN ITALIAN.

This is the poshest place on this very posh wharf, with an interesting Italian menu and two very different dining rooms. To your left at the top of the short flight of steps is the Dining Room, a very authentic-looking colonial room with rugged ceiling beams (original to the house, which is colonial), wood chairs and tables, gleaming crystal stemware, and tuxedoed waiters. Jackets and ties are required for this area. To the right as you enter, the Grill, a less formal room, overlooks the wharf and the water. Try the lobster ravioli, osso buco, pork tenderloin with herb crust, or swordfish with rosemary potatoes.

Le Bistro

Bowen's Wharf, at West Pelham St. ☎ **401/849-7778.** Reservations are required. Main courses $12–$26. AE, MC, V. Daily 11:30am–5pm, 5–11pm. CONTINENTAL/REGIONAL AMERICAN

Located on the second and third floors of a building on Bowen's Wharf, Le Bistro is a wonderful restaurant. Diners are treated to great harbor views from both dining rooms on the second floor and the bar on the third floor. For an appetizer I had the scallops and wild mushrooms in puff pastry and then moved on to the roast pheasant with apples and calvados. The grilled south Texas antelope steak with dried cherry poivrade and wild rice pancakes was interesting as well as tasty. In addition, there is a short list of French country classics, as well a list of heart healthy dishes. Each day brings a new group of specials to both the lunch and dinner menus. A lighter menu is available in the upstairs bar. For dessert I had the Creole bread pudding with bourbon sauce. The wine list is exceptional.

White Horse Tavern

At the corner of Marlborough and Farewell Sts. ☎ **401/849-3600.** Reservations required. Main courses $23–$33. AE, DC, MC, V. Wed–Mon noon–3pm; daily 6–10pm; brunch Sun noon–3pm. AMERICAN/CONTINENTAL.

Boasting that it's America's oldest tavern building, the White Horse, two blocks north of Washington Square, is certainly a Newport institution, having served the hungry and thirsty since about 1687. One family, the Nichols, ran the tavern for almost two centuries. Rescued from a period of neglect by the Newport Preservation Society in the 1950s, it's again in private hands and in excellent condition.

The old tavern is authentic and absolutely charming, with large fireplaces, huge exposed beams, and old oil paintings. Staff are formal in black and white, soft classical music wafts through the air, and the menu lists dishes that are a fascinating blend of the old and new: Duck breast is sesame grilled and served with a hoisin glazed duck leg, banana and pineapple, saffron-coconut rice and sautéed Oriental vegetables; beef Wellington with sauce périgourdine (Périgord is a region of France where geese are force-fed to produce foie gras); and grilled swordfish with fresh papaya salsa. Appetizers include gravlax brushed with dilled olive oil, and Peking raviolis filled with lobster mousse and shiitake mushrooms and served with basil pesto and a Thai curry aioli. Lunch includes a grilled swordfish sandwich made with foccaccia or grilled breast of duckling served in a flour tortilla with caramelized red onion and herbed Camembert and a fresh berry compote. Desserts are rich and delicious. Arrive well dressed.

MODERATE

ⓢ Anthony's Seafood & Shore Dinner Hall

Newport Harbor Marketplace, Waites Wharf, off upper Thames St. ☎ **401/848-5058.** Reservations not accepted. Main courses $6–$23. AE, MC, V. Daily 11am–9pm. Free parking. Closed Dec to mid-Apr. Directions: Turn right off lower Thames Street when you reach the upper 400 block; there's a small sign for the Shore Dinner Hall. SEAFOOD.

A shore dinner, an old New England custom, is a no-frills clambake, with clam chowder, steamed clams, boiled corn on the cob, steamed lobsters, and other simple but delicious dishes served on paper plates to diners seated at wooden picnic tables. Newport's most authentic shore dinner is served here, in a large, open warehouse-type building that has been nicely spruced up, painted, and hung with colorful flags. Pick up wine or beer on your way here, or decide on soft drinks with your dinner, then order any of the aforementioned items, or lobster rolls, clam rolls, mussels, hot dogs, french fries, or clam cakes. Try fish and chips, a large steaming plate of clams, or a steamed lobster weighing over a pound (price depending on the season). The view, through large, open doorways overlooking the bay, is among the best in Newport. The Shore Dinner Hall is operated by the SS *Newport* restaurant next door.

Brick Alley Pub and Restaurant
140 Thames St. ☎ **401/849-6334.** Reservations recommended. Main courses $5.95–$16.95. AE, CB, DC, MC, V. Daily 11am–1am. AMERICAN.

After a hot morning's sightseeing in Newport, this is just what you want: a cool, quiet place to sit down and have some refreshment. It's right across the street from the Brick Marketplace and right behind the block of shops housing the Newport Museum of History. Walk up the passage beside the restaurant and you'll come to a shady courtyard with tables set out. The selection of sandwiches, burgers, salads, and omelets is enormous, all costing about $6 to $8, and for a few dollars more you can have soup and a trip to the salad bar. The pub also has a wide choice of fresh seafood dishes. The Brick Alley has indoor dining rooms as well as an outdoor bar in the courtyard.

Dry Dock Seafood
448 Thames St. ☎ **401/847-3974.** Reservations not accepted. Main courses $1.50–$6.95 at lunch, $4.95–$9.95 at dinner. No credit cards. Daily 11am–10pm. SEAFOOD/SANDWICHES.

This attractive, clean, and modern eatery has lots of bright, cheerful wood and tile, a lunch counter, and tables with bentwood chairs. Ceiling fans keep you cool, and hanging plants add a touch of greenery. Order New England clam chowder for starters, and then a sandwich of fish, meatballs, or *chouriço* (spicy Portuguese sausage) and peppers. Or you can order a main-course dinner, such as fish and chips, a fisherman's platter, swordfish steak, or broiled scallops. You get about a pound of succulent sea scallops perfectly broiled in a light coating of crumbs, with an immense mound of french fries and a paper thimble of coleslaw, for a mere $10.95. One of the things that keeps prices reasonable here is that you bring your own wine or beer. Try a cup of soup and a sandwich, or a bowl of soup and a swordfish steak. This place is great!

⑤ Muriel's
58 Spring St. ☎ **401/849-7780**. Reservations recommended. Main courses $8–$16.95. MC, V. Mon–Sat 8–11:30am, Mon–Sat 11:30am–5pm, daily 5–10pm; brunch Sun 9am–2:30pm. Closed for dinner Mon–Wed in winter. INTERNATIONAL.

Muriel's is wacky and romantic. Inside you'll find Maxfield Parrish posters on the wall, banquettes, glass-topped tables with floral-and-lace–confetti covered cloths (under the glass), jade-colored walls, ficus trees, and two costumed mannequins. A guitarist and/or pianist plays classical or jazz music. One of the busiest times at

Muriel's is breakfast, when you can get huevos rancheros, eggs Benedict, French toast in spiced butter with walnuts and syrup, and waffles of all kinds. At lunch you'll find pasta dishes, sandwiches, salads, fish and chips, and burgers. The dinner menu changes with the seasons, but past menus have included items like scallops provençale, marinated lamb, grilled New York sirloin, chicken Bombay, fresh local seafoods, vegetarian entrées, and a variety of evening specials. Muriel's award-winning seafood chowder is served all day long. All desserts are made on the premises.

Music Hall Café

250 Thames St. ☎ **401/848-2330.** Reservations recommended for dinner. Main courses $10.25–$18. AE, DISC, MC, V. Daily noon–3pm; 5:30pm–"late." SOUTHWESTERN.

The Music Hall Café is identifiable by the green, yellow, and maroon awning and the glass-topped green tables and wooden chairs out front. Inside the historic Music Hall building (1894), you'll find exposed-brick walls, Spanish-style chandeliers, southwestern colors, a kiva ladder hanging on the wall, buffalo skulls, and wood tables. Latin music plays softly in the background, and you can order a drink from the full bar—perhaps a Music Hall Margarita. On the menu you'll find starters like southwestern crab cakes or Texas torpedoes (fried mild jalapeño peppers stuffed with cream cheese), plus entrées like grilled swordfish with jalapeño butter or blackened salmon with guava-ginger sauce. You'll also find some standard Mexican dishes like fajitas, quesadillas, tacos, burritos, and tamales on the lunch menu. There are a few vegetarian selections, like veggie fajitas and beans 'n' bananas (black beans, rice and fried bananas topped with a tomato vinaigrette). For dessert, the chocolate-mousse therapy and the chocolate-whiskey pecan pie are both excellent.

Puerini's

24 Memorial Blvd. W. ☎ **401/847-5506.** Reservations not accepted. Main courses $8.50–$13.95. No credit cards. Daly 5–10pm. ITALIAN.

Puerini's is a wonderful little Italian restaurant located just a few blocks from the waterfront. Instead of chianti bottles hanging from the ceiling and red-and-white-checked cloths on the tables, you'll find an interesting collection of black-and-white photographs of Italy hanging on the walls and black vinyl tablecloths with butcher paper and mismatched (even chipped—in a charming way) dishes on the tables. The bilevel restaurant is small but constantly bustling with a busy staff racing to and from the kitchen and patrons coming and going. The food is great, and the portions are large. To start, you might have garlic bread smothered with cheese and red sauce, or sweet roasted peppers in oil and garlic served with provolone cheese. If you like ravioli, try the spinach pasta ravioli stuffed with ricotta and Parmesan cheese (with just the right amount of cheese) and covered in a delicious pesto sauce. The menu includes a variety of excellent veal dishes. Also good are the vegetable lasagne and the *pollo al marsala*. You probably won't make it to dessert, but Puerini's does have a good selection. Puerini's has a beer and wine list.

Salas'

343 Thames St. ☎ **401/846-8772.** Reservations not accepted. Main courses $3.25–$13.95. AE, DC, DISC, MC, V. Dining room, dinner only, daily 5–10pm. Brasserie, dinner only, daily 6–11pm. SEAFOOD.

Salas' on lower Thames Street, half a block past the post office, actually consists of three establishments in one: a fish market and raw bar, a brasserie, and the dining room. For dinner you might try a stuffed quahog to start, followed by baked stuffed sole or surf and turf. The "No. 1 Clambake" includes a one-pound lobster, clams, corn on the cob, sausage, clam broth, and so forth. There are also several pasta dishes, as well as sandwiches for those who don't enjoy seafood. For dessert, try the carrot cake or the homestyle strawberry shortcake.

3   From Saunderstown to Point Judith

Narragansett Pier: 17 miles W of Newport, Galilee: 5 miles S of Narragansett Pier

At this point, if you're interested in visiting Block Island, take the scenic drive along Route 1A as outlined below to get to the ferry dock at Port Galilee. Along the way you'll find numerous reasons to stop, so you might want to start out early. The birthplace of portraitist Gilbert Stuart is a main attraction, as is the scenic Victorian resort town of Narragansett Pier. This coastline will also take you right by some lovely beaches, great for a quick stroll or a picnic before heading to Port Galilee to catch the ferry.

GETTING THERE   By Car   To get across Narragansett Bay from Newport, you will have to cross the Newport Bridge (toll) from Newport to Jamestown Island and then the Jamestown Bridge from Jamestown Island to Saunderstown (free). From Saunderstown, head south on U.S. 1A (Alternate U.S. 1).

ESSENTIALS   The **telephone area code** is **401**. The **Narragansett Chamber of Commerce** maintains a Tourist Information Office (☎ **401/783-7121**) in the base of the prominent stone Towers in Narragansett Pier (see below). The **South County Tourism Council,** 4808 Tower Hill Rd., Wakefield, RI 02879 (☎ **401/789-4422,** or **800/548-4662**), may be able to answer your questions as well. If you're approaching from the west along I-95, there's a state of Rhode Island **Visitor Information Center** at the state line.

Coming from Newport or Providence, take U.S. 1A south from R.I. 138. As you drive south along U.S. 1A to Saunderstown, look for signs off to the right (west) that point the way to the **Gilbert Stuart birthplace** (☎ **401/294-3001**). Stuart (1755–1828), America's most famous portrait painter after the Revolutionary era, did no fewer than three portraits of George Washington from life, perhaps the most famous of which is the so-called *Athenaeum Head,* model for the portrait of Washington on the dollar bill. (Look for the original of this in the Museum of Fine Arts in Boston.) Stuart was the son of a snuff-maker. Judging from the house, his father had a comfortable living, and the son was able to go to London to study painting with Benjamin West. Period furnishings, a water wheel–powered snuff mill, and copies of Stuart's portraits adorn the house. Open Saturday through Thursday from 11am to 4:30pm; closed November through March. Admission is $2 for adults, $1 for children.

U.S. 1A skirts the southwestern shore of Narragansett Bay passing through **Narragansett Pier,** a famous Victorian resort town, which is also the main town on the peninsula here. Although not quite so famous now, the town is still popular for the same reasons as in an earlier age: beautiful sea views, a fine waterfront promenade, and gracious old Victorian houses.

Passing through Narragansett on Ocean Road, you'll drive right under the last standing remnant of Stanford White's mammoth Narragansett casino, the **Towers,** built in 1882. The town's chamber of commerce maintains a tourist information office in the base of the seaward tower—park on either side of the underpass arch and walk to the door.

The main beach in Narragansett Pier is north of the Towers, about half a mile distant.

South of Narragansett Pier, U.S. 1A passes by the **Scarborough State Beach** facilities, very popular on hot summer days although never filled to capacity. Scarborough Beach, like all Rhode Island beaches, works on a system of parking/admission fees, charged *per car*.

Continuing along U.S. 1A south will bring you to the village of Galilee and the departure dock for ferryboats to Block Island.

POINT JUDITH/PORT GALILEE

Jutting southeast into the Atlantic Ocean and dividing Block Island Sound from Rhode Island Sound is Point Judith. The peninsula of Narragansett's southern extremity offers several things to travelers: The car and passenger ferry docks for boats to Block Island, located at Port Galilee; camping and picnic facilities at Fishermen's Memorial State Park, only two miles from Port Galilee; and good sand beaches along the southern and eastern shores of the peninsula. Port Galilee exists for the ferries to Block Island, the Wheeler Memorial Beach, several small fisheries, and a Coast Guard station.

THE BEACH & THE FERRY   First of all, be warned that Port Galilee has very few parking places on the street and these are usually taken up quickly by the people who work for the fishing companies. Parking for the beach is $3 a day ($4 on weekends and holidays) for Rhode Island residents, $5 a day ($6 on weekends and holidays) for out-of-state cars. This includes the entry fee to the beach for everyone in your party.

For the ferry, parking fees are of the same order, and the lot is across the street and down a few yards from the ferry dock. You might be tempted to park in restaurant and motel lots, but it's not advisable—you'll come back from Block Island and find your car missing.

4 Block Island

Sailing time to Block Island from Point Judith (Galilee) is 1¼ hours; from New London, 2 hours.

In 1614 a man named Adriaen Block visited a small island off the coast of Rhode Island, but his visit did little more than give the island its name. Slightly over 20 years later a colonist was found in a boat near the island, presumed murdered by the local Pequots, and this unhappy event precipitated a battle between Pequots and colonists that turned out to be very bloody.

A generation later, these events forgotten, settlers from the colony moved onto the island and the town of New Shoreham (incorporated in 1672) was built. For almost 200 years the people of Block Island lived their quiet lives, fishing in boats from the island's two natural harbors, growing what they could in the sandy and windswept soil. But in the mid-1800s the Age of Steam changed Block Island from a fishing outpost in the Atlantic to a summer excursion paradise, with regularly scheduled steamboats bringing residents of the sooty factory cities out for fresh air and bright sunshine. Late 19th-century frame hotels, huge and sprawling, went up to accommodate them, and the island's economy came to depend on tourism rather than fishing, and so it has remained. Most of the island's buildings—houses as well as hotels—date from the late 1800s or the turn of the century. The roads are rough and sandy (nobody has to be in a hurry to get quickly from one end of the island to the other—it's only seven miles); the pace is very relaxed; and the citizens of New Shoreham, which takes up all of the island, have a strong sense of community.

The boat trip is pleasant enough, with plenty of room to sun on the top-deck benches, and a small bar and snack counter on board. As you approach Block Island, the character of the place becomes clear: dunes and white cliffs, low shrubs and grass with a few trees, ponds, and hillocks (the highest point on the island is 211 feet above sea level). The big old hotels come right down to the harbor, most looking pretty weathered from the stiff breezes and salt air, not to mention the winter storms, that are the norm here. Several of the hotels have vans that will be waiting at the dock to pick up passengers who have reservations or those who want a room but have not reserved one.

GETTING THERE   By Plane   New England Airlines, Block Island's own airline, will fly you over from the State Airport in Westerly, R.I., on any of 14 daily flights year-round. The $34 flight one-way ($59 round-trip) takes 15 minutes. You must have reservations (☎ **401/596-2460** or 800/243-2460 outside Rhode Island); if you're on Block Island, dial **401/466-5881.** The airport is on Airport Road, Westerly, off R.I. 78.

Note: If you plan to fly, you should be aware that fog frequently causes the cancellation of flights. In the event of a cancellation, you can still opt to catch the ferry so that you won't have to lose your room deposit and your reservations.

By Boat   From Port Galilee: This is the port with the most frequent service, and there are six to nine daily sailings in each direction from mid-June to early September. The trip takes less than 1 1/4 hours and costs $6.60 per adult, one-way, or $10.50 for a same-day round-trip; children are charged half price. It costs $40.50 round-trip for a car (driver not included), and you must have reservations in advance. The Port Galilee agent is the **Interstate Navigation Co.,** Galilee State Pier, Point Judith, RI 02882 (☎ **401/783-4613**). Motorcycles and bikes are also carried. During spring, fall, and winter there are fewer trips: two daily in each direction in May and early June, and late September through October; in winter, there's one trip daily.

From New London: Mid-June to early September there's one trip daily (plus an additional Friday-evening boat) in each direction between New London and Block Island, leaving New London in midmorning, returning from Block Island in midafternoon. The trip takes about two hours and costs $13.50 for adults ($17.50 for same-day round-trip), and $9 for children over 5 ($11 for same-day round-trip). A car costs $50 round-trip. The fee for bikes is $7 round-trip. The boat leaves from Ferry Street, about an eighth of a mile from the railroad station. Advance reservations for cars is a must. For more information, contact the **Nelseco Navigation Co.,** P.O. Box 482, New London, CT 06320 (☎ **203/442-7891** or **203/442-9553** between 8am and 4pm). By the way, ferries from New London arrive at Old Harbor on Block Island, and you may have to take a taxi to reach hotel and restaurant choices.

From Providence: The **Interstate Navigation Co.** (see above) also runs a daily passenger boat from Providence via Newport to Block Island. Departure from Providence's India Street dock is at 8:30am, from Newport's Fort Adams dock at 10:30am, arriving at Block Island around 12:30pm. The return trip leaves Block Island at 3:45pm, leaves Newport at 5:30pm, and arrives in Providence at 7:45pm.

Block Island

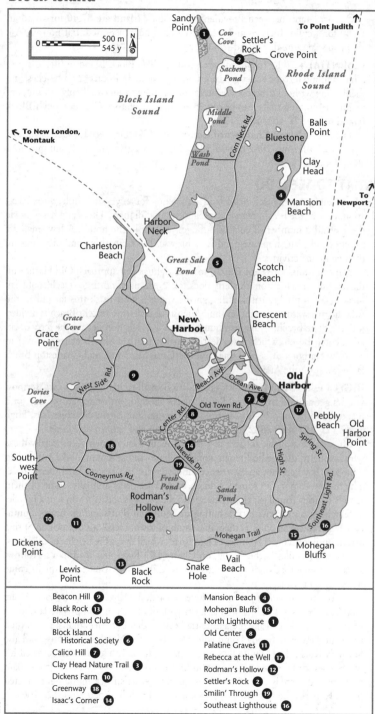

Sandy Point · **1**
Cow Cove
Settler's Rock · **2**
Grove Point
Sachem Pond
To Point Judith

Rhode Island Sound

Block Island Sound

Middle Pond

Balls Point

Corn Neck Rd.

Bluestone
Clay Head · **3**

To New London, Montauk

Wash Pond

To Newport

Clay Head

Mansion Beach · **4**

Harbor Neck

Charleston Beach

Great Salt Pond

Scotch Beach

Grace Cove

Crescent Beach

Grace Point

New Harbor

Old Harbor

West Side Rd.

Beacon Hill · **9**

Beach Ave.
Ocean Ave.

Pebbly Beach
Old Harbor Point

Dories Cove

Old Town Rd. · **7** · **6**

Calico Hill · **8**

17

Southwest Point

Greenway · **18**

Isaac's Corner · **14**

Center Rd.

Spring St.

Lakeside Dr.

Cooneymus Rd.

Smilin' Through · **19**

Fresh Pond

High St.

Southeast Light Rd.

Rodman's Hollow

Sands Pond

Dickens Farm · **10**

Palatine Graves · **11**

Rodman's Hollow · **12**

Mohegan Trail · **15**

Southeast Lighthouse · **16**

Dickens Point

Lewis Point

Black Rock · **13**

Snake Hole

Vail Beach

Mohegan Bluffs

Beacon Hill **9**
Black Rock **13**
Block Island Club **5**
Block Island Historical Society **6**
Calico Hill **7**
Clay Head Nature Trail **3**
Dickens Farm **10**
Greenway **18**
Isaac's Corner **14**

Mansion Beach **4**
Mohegan Bluffs **15**
North Lighthouse **1**
Old Center **8**
Palatine Graves **11**
Rebecca at the Well **17**
Rodman's Hollow **12**
Settler's Rock **2**
Smilin' Through **19**
Southeast Lighthouse **16**

1796

One-way fares between Providence and Block Island are $7.40 for an adult, $3.60 for a child. Bicycles and motorcycles can be transported, but no cars. Ask about special same-day round-trip fares.

ESSENTIALS   The **telephone area code** is **401.** Block Island ordinances prohibit camping (except Scout groups), sleeping overnight in cars or on beaches, and shellfishing without a license. Information on the Greenways Trails (25 miles of maintained hiking trails) can be obtained from the **Nature Conservancy's Block Island office** (☎ **401/466-2129**).

The **Block Island Chamber of Commerce,** P.O. Drawer D, Block Island, RI 02807 (☎ **401/466-2982** or **800/383-BIRI**), can answer many of your questions about local services.

WHAT TO SEE & DO

Most people coming to Block Island are looking for an easy schedule, quiet relaxation, time at the beach, bicycle trips, and seafood dinners. The island has a movie theater and a number of cocktail lounges, mostly in the hotels. A few small art galleries and craft shops are good for a browse. But sunbathing and bicycling are the two main activities.

You can't miss **Crescent Beach,** to your right as you approach Old Harbor on the ferry. It stretches from the ferry dock for several miles north to the cliffs of Clay Head. It's simply beautiful, although the water is a bit brisk this far out in the Atlantic (it's warmest in late July and August, of course). Crescent Beach is divided into the State Beach, with a bathhouse, which is the section nearest the ferry dock, and Scotch Beach, which is the section farther north. Other beaches are over in the New Harbor area, several small ones on Great Salt Pond, and Charleston Beach facing west on the Atlantic.

BICYCLE TOURING   Block Island is too small to handle many cars, so most visitors get around by bicycle. Rental places abound, with rates $8 per day for a 6-speed or $12 for a 15- to 21-speed. The rental shop at the **Seacrest Inn,** High Street (☎ **401/466-2882**), has good equipment and helpful personnel.

Mopeds are available for rent as well, but many local residents—especially those who belong to the medical rescue squad—advise visitors to rent a bike rather than a moped. If you're not an experienced motorcyclist, it's best to heed their advice: The medics respond to some six dozen moped accidents annually, some of them serious injuries. You'll get along better with the Block Islanders if you rent a bicycle.

Suitable goals for your bicycle outing are **Mohegan Bluffs** and the nearby **Southeast Lighthouse,** about 1 1/2 miles due south of town. Head out of town on Spring Street, until it becomes Southeast Light Road, which traces the heights of the bluffs.

About 2 1/2 miles farther along, on Cherry Hill Road, lies **Rodman's Hollow,** a glacial ravine that's now protected as a wildlife refuge. Binoculars might come in handy on this trip.

Three miles north of town, on the eastern shore off Corn Neck Road, is the **Clayhead Nature Trail,** as well as a network of other trails on private land once known as the Maze. Take the nature trail east to the shore (less than a mile), then north all the way to Sandy Point, where you'll see the **North Lighthouse** and also **Settler's Rock.** The granite lighthouse, dating from 1867, has been restored for use as a maritime museum. It's open in July and August only every day from 10am to 4pm, and there is a nominal admission fee. Settler's Rock monument, erected in 1911, marks the spot where the island's first English settlers landed in 1661.

Only about a mile northwest of town along Ocean Road and West Side Road is the island's **cemetery,** with headstones dating from the 1600s and 1700s. It's a pretty spot, and interesting to anyone intrigued with Block Island's history.

FISHING   Several marinas on the island have fishing boats for hire, and surfcasting for striped bass and other delicacies is popular. Even if you're alone, the marina hands may be able to get together a party to go out, thereby reducing your costs greatly. For details, drop by any one of the marinas. All the boat-rental and sport-fishing businesses operate out of the New Harbor.

WHERE TO STAY

Block Island is currently enjoying a tourist boom. Most of the large old Victorian hotels have been renovated and modernized, many small family guesthouses have been opened, and in general the lodging picture is good but pricey. Because demand for rooms is high, you should be sure to have reservations in advance during high season (from mid-July through Labor Day). You can save 10% to 20% on many lodging establishments by staying during the week (Monday through Thursday) instead of the weekend if your schedule allows it.

Most hotels on Block Island serve breakfast to their guests at no additional charge. Breakfast may be anything from pastries and coffee to a full all-you-can-eat buffet. Also, all hotel prices are subject to the Rhode Island **12% sales plus room tax,** and some hotels levy a service charge (usually 4% to 6%) in place of your tips to the staff.

VERY EXPENSIVE

Hotel Manisses

Spring St., Block Island, RI 02807. ☎ **401/466-2421** or 401/466-2063 or 800/MANISSES. Fax 401/466-2858. 17 rms. $148–$325 double (lower rates are available in the winter season). Rates include buffet breakfast, wine/nibble hour, and service. Third person in room $25 extra. AE, MC, V. Directions: Walk up the hill from the ferry dock, following the signs for Spring Street.

Operated by Block Island's premier hoteliers, the Abrams family, this is without a doubt Block Island's loveliest place to stay. The Manisses was built in 1870 as a small Victorian resort hotel. Restored by the Abramses in 1972, it's at least as fine a hotel as it was 100 years ago—probably better. The large-pattern floral wallpaper, white wicker and wrought-iron furniture, beveled mirrors, heavily carved and marble-trimmed parlor pieces, even the bubbling garden fountain, recall the best of a more gracious time. The guest rooms have double, queen-size, or king-size beds; some have Jacuzzis, and all have period furnishings. In the afternoon, wine and "nibbles" are served. The hotel's dining room (see "Where to Dine," below) is the best on the island. You'll love the Manisses.

♦ 1661 Inn & Guest House

Spring St., Block Island, RI 02807. ☎ **401/466-2421** or 401/466-2063 or 800/MANISSES. 21 rms (17 with bath). $60–$115 double without bath, $78–$325 double with bath. Rates include buffet breakfast and service. AE, MC, V. Directions: Walk up the hill from the ferry dock, following the signs for Spring Street.

Just up the hill from the Manisses is the Abramses' original establishment, a restored colonial inn that creates a mood of hospitality and luxury. Enjoy pleasant public spaces and decks with sweeping views of the Atlantic. Most of the rooms at the 1661 Inn feature a private deck and an ocean view. The Nicholas Ball Cottage offers three historically renovated rooms that feature fireplaces, Jacuzzis, and queen- or king-size beds. The Guest House has nine rooms. As at the Manisses, guests at the 1661 Inn find all the little touches for which the Abramses are famous: a full buffet breakfast, beach towels, and a decanter of brandy and dish of hard candy in each room. The 1661 Inn closes from mid-November through March, but the Guest House and Nicholas Ball Cottage stay open year-round. The 1661 Inn's dining room serves a full buffet breakfast as well as a cafe lunch on the canopy-covered deck with sweeping views of the Atlantic. For dinner, by reservation, you can stroll down the hill to the Manisses.

Blue Dory Inn

488 Dodge St. (P.O. Box 488), Block Island, RI 02807. ☎ **401/466-2254** or 800/992-7290. 11 rms, 3 cottages. Mid-June to early Sept, $139–$183 inn double with bath; $281 Cottage; $195 Tea House; $145 double in Doll House. Off-season rates available. All rates include continental breakfast and service. AE, MC, V. Directions: From the ferry dock, turn right and follow Dodge Street.

The Blue Dory, right next to the Surf Hotel and the National Hotel, is actually a guesthouse and several cottages perched right at the tip of Crescent Beach. The main building has guest rooms with Victorian furnishings, a living room, and a kitchen, which serves as the breakfast room. The Cottage can sleep up to six, has kitchen facilities, and is perfect for a family or for two couples traveling together. The Doll House is a one-room house good for couples who get along very well (it's tiny), and the Tea House sleeps two, and has its own kitchen, plus a porch overlooking the sea.

Inn at Old Harbour

Water St. (P.O. Box 994), Block Island, RI 02807. ☎ **401/466-2212** or 914/967-4670 off-season. Fax 401/466-2951. 10 rms (6 with bath). Summer $75–$150 double; rest of the year $65–$135 double. All rates include continental breakfast. Special weekday packages are available. AE, MC, V. Closed Columbus Day–Memorial Day. Directions: Walk from the ferry to Water Street, turn left, and walk half a block.

On a rise overlooking the ferry docks, facing the statue of *Rebecca at the Well*, is this three-story gambrel-roofed Victorian inn dating from 1882. What was once the lobby is now occupied by shops, but the guest rooms upstairs have all been totally renovated and fitted with modern fixtures and carpeting. Each room is different, the decor blending Victorian period pieces and a modern style. The inn has its own eating establishment, the Water Street Café, and a Ben & Jerry's ice cream.

The National Hotel

Water St., at Old Harbor. ☎ **401/466-2901** or 800/225-2449. Fax 401/466-5948. 45 rms. TV TEL. Mid-May to mid-June $69–$125 double; mid-June to Sept $149–$229; Oct–mid-Apr $49–$129. Closed Nov–Mar. AE, MC, V.

If you've stayed at the National in the past, you might be a little wary about making a return visit. The place was in terrible shape a few years back, but recent renovations have once again made this white clapboard landmark (built in 1888) a pleasant place to stay. It's located directly across from the harbor and ferry dock, so you couldn't really ask for a more convenient lodgings. Rooms are sparsely furnished, but they're clean, and there's an on-premises restaurant that offers limited room service. Note that rooms in the front can be quite noisy, so if you're a light sleeper you'll want to try to get a room in back.

The Rose Farm Inn

P.O. Box E, Block Island, RI 02807. ☎ **401/466-2021** or 401/466-2021. 19 rms (17 with bath). Mid-June to mid-Sept, $95–$175 double; Mar to mid-June and mid-Sept to Nov, $80–$140 double weekdays, $95–$175 weekends. All rates include light buffet breakfast. Additional person $25 extra. AE, DISC, MC, V. Closed Dec–Mar.

The Rose Farm Inn, a turn-of-the-century farmhouse, is inconspicuously tucked away behind the Atlantic Inn. The rooms here are exceptionally clean and tastefully furnished with Victorian antiques. Some of the most sought-after rooms feature king-size canopy or four-poster beds and ocean views. Some rooms also have double whirlpool baths. You can relax with a drink from the wet bar in the parlor, read on the stone porch, or sun yourself on the deck. In the morning, head for the sun-warmed breakfast room where you'll find coffee, fresh fruit, cereals, and muffins at the buffet. A bicycle rental shop is located on premises.

Seacrest Inn

207 High St., Block Island, RI 02807. ☎ **401/466-2882.** 17 rms. June 11–Sept 13, $90–$145 double; early May–June 10 and Sept 14–Columbus Day, $55–$100 double. All rates include continental breakfast. AE, MC, V. Closed Day after Columbus Day–early May. Directions: From the ferry docks, turn left and walk 100 yards.

Just a few steps from the statue of *Rebecca at the Well* is the Seacrest, renovated in 1982 and offering very comfy, modern guest rooms. The inn also has rooms that sleep up to four people. If I were you, I'd take some of my continental breakfast outside and sit in the cute little Victorian gazebo. The Seacrest is family-owned and operated, providing pleasant, comfortable lodging at moderate prices, with a smile and an honest welcome. It also has its own bicycle-rental shop ($5 to $12 a day) including mountain bikes, so you can be easily equipped for touring the island.

WHERE TO DINE

You probably will have had breakfast at your hotel, so here are recommendations on where to have lunch and dinner:

Harborside Inn

Water St. ☎ **401/466-5504.** Reservations recommended. Main courses $8–$18. AE, MC, V. Daily 7:30am–10pm. Closed Nov–Apr. SEAFOOD.

Block Island's most popular luncheon spot is definitely the front-terrace cafe of the Harborside. Take in the sun, or duck beneath one of the shady cafe-table umbrellas, and order something simple like a hamburger or club sandwich, or something fancier, like baked stuffed clams, broiled scallops, or sirloin steak. Wine, beer, and cocktails are served. At dinnertime the fare is somewhat fancier, but prices are still reasonable.

Hotel Manisses

Spring St. ☎ **401/466-2836.** Reservations recommended, especially on weekends in high season. Main courses $13–$25. AE, MC, V. Daily 6–10pm. Directions: Walk up the hill from the ferry dock, following the signs for Spring Street. AMERICAN.

As with lodging, this is the best place for dining. You can have dinner in one of the hotel's two cozy dining rooms, overlooking the farm and gardens, in the new gazebo, or on the glassed-in terrace overlooking the fountain. The varied menu includes things like an appetizer tart of puff pastry filled with goat cheese, roasted eggplant, and tomato with a roasted red pepper coulis and main courses such as boeuf au poivre. Desserts are beautiful as well as delicious. The peach-strawberry mousse served in a puff pastry shaped like a swan is delectable. Tableside flaming coffees, after-dinner drinks, and desserts are served in the upstairs parlor.

5   Watch Hill

6 miles S of Westerly; 10 miles SE of Stonington, Conn.; 17 miles SE of Mystic, Conn.

As a base for a day at the beach, you could choose no better place than Watch Hill, an old and genteel town at the end of a peninsula between the Atlantic Ocean and the Pawcatuck River. Watch Hill is a sort of Newport-in-miniature, with stately old homes (grand, but not palatial), yachts in the harbor (expensive, but not priceless), and a gentility still strongly felt if slightly faded.

GETTING THERE   By Car   From Westerly, go south on U.S. 1A to Avondale, then follow the signs to Watch Hill.

By Train   Most Amtrak trains on the run between New York City and Boston stop at Westerly.

ESSENTIALS   The **telephone area code** is **401**. The **Watch Hill/Westerly/ Misquamicut Chamber of Commerce,** 74 Post Rd. (U.S. 1) in Westerly (☎ **401/596-7761,** or **800/SEA-7636**), is open Monday through Thursday from 9am to 5pm, Friday 9am–7pm (Saturday and Sunday (9am to 2pm) also June through August).

WHAT TO SEE & DO

In Watch Hill, you spend time at the beach, you stroll along Bay Street and go window-shopping, you buy ice-cream cones early and often.

Children will jump at the chance to ride ($1) on the **1883 Carousel** at the end of Bay Street, one of the oldest in the nation.

In the little park across Bay Street from the Olympia Tea Room is a **statue of Ninigret,** Great Sachem of the Narragansetts, a noble man and friend of the local English colonists. The statue was erected in 1914.

Watch Hill is a place to start a romance or to pursue one; to read and relax or swim strenuously all day—to do as you please. There are no crowds, no neon signs, no plastic "lifestyles."

WHERE TO STAY

Inn at Watch Hill

118 Bay St., Watch Hill, RI 02891. ☎ **401/596-0665.** 16 rms. A/C TV. $155–$183 double. Weekly rates available. Additional person $26 extra; children stay free in parents' room. MC, V. Closed Nov–Apr.

Of Watch Hill's lodging places, the most comfortable and pleasant by far is this inn, in the commercial center of the village. Don't expect a great old Victorian palace, for the inn here is actually a suite of motel-style rooms perched above a block of shops on the main street. You enter by going around to the rear and up the hill, where there's a large parking lot and a little office cabin. After check-in, you proceed along a wooden walkway to your room. Rooms 1 to 12 have the best harbor views; Rooms 14 and 15 have some water views; Rooms 16 and 17 see a bit of the harbor, but mostly shops. The rooms themselves are very good, neat, and tidy, with contemporary furnishings, and each has a microwave oven and small table for breakfast or snacks; all rooms have separate kitchen sink. White-brick walls, natural-wood floors, and sliding glass doors opening onto little balconies overlooking the town make the rooms quite charming. Rates vary depending on the size and comforts of the room, and whether you rent on a weekday or on the more expensive weekend. Call for reservations early.

IN NEARBY WESTERLY

✪ Shelter Harbor Inn

10 Wagner Rd., Westerly, RI. ☎ **401/322-8883** or 800/468-8883. 23 rms. $88–$120 double. All rates include full breakfast. MC, V.

The main part of this excellent inn is a 19th-century farm house, in which there is a restaurant, a library, and nine guest rooms. Other rooms are located in the renovated barn and in the Coach House. Some rooms have phones and TVs; others have fireplaces. Guests have access to the rooftop deck and hot tub (the views are wonderful), and there are paddle courts and a croquet court. There is transportation available to and from the beach. The dining room is open to the public, and it serves breakfast (Mon–Sat), lunch daily, and dinner daily; brunch is offered on Sunday.

WHERE TO DINE

Olympia Tea Room

Bay St. ☎ **401/348-8211.** Reservations not accepted. Main courses $3.25–$8; lunch $7–$15; dinner $16–$25. AE, MC, V. Daily 8am–11:30am; noon–6pm; 6–9pm. AMERICAN.

In a row of shops at the center of town, across from the little park and the police kiosk, is Olympia, an authentic early 20th-century seaside-resort soda-fountain cafe, with black-and-white checkerboard floor tiles, well-used wooden booths, a few sidewalk tables, and waitresses in black dresses with white aprons. The atmosphere is refreshingly real, not "re-created." As for the food, there's plenty of it, and it's more up-to-date: sautéed shrimp with feta cheese, clam stew, chicken fajitas with hot tortillas and guacamole, bouillabaisse, and of course, lots of seafood, from clams and sausages on linguine to boiled lobster. The Olympia is a wonderful bit of old New England, lovingly preserved. Beer and wine are served.

10 Connecticut

Connecticut's landscape is sprinkled liberally with lakes, rivers, and streams. But the state's namesake is the mighty Connecticut River, which springs from the Connecticut lakes in northern New Hampshire, flows southward forming the boundary between New Hampshire and Vermont, cuts through Massachusetts and Connecticut, and finally empties into Long Island Sound. The great river is navigable as far north as Hartford, a significant fact that was not lost on the region's Native American inhabitants. They were the ones who gave it the name Quinnehtukqut, "the long tidal river."

Later inhabitants pasted different labels on the land. "The Nutmeg State" used to be a popular nickname, coming from the time when itinerant peddlers sold nutmeg from door to door. As often as not, the "nutmegs" were cleverly carved balls of wood. By the time a customer discovered the fakery, the peddler was gone.

For obvious reasons, the people of Connecticut prefer the moniker "Constitution State," which reminds one and all that Connecticut was the first American colony to have a written constitution.

Almost three-quarters of the territory in Connecticut is woodland, and drives along the back roads through these forests reveal rich fields of corn, grain, vegetables, and tobacco. But the state's wealth comes not from agriculture or tourism but rather from insurance and manufacturing. The capital city of Hartford is laden with tremendous buildings that are headquarters for dozens of insurance companies. As for manufacturing, Charles Goodyear, Eli Whitney, Seth Thomas, and Mr. Fuller (of Fuller Brush fame) were all Connecticut Yankees. In the old days the state's production of buttons, pins, doodads, and kitchenwares gave rise to the breed of men known as Yankee peddlers, who traveled from town to town in horse and buggy, spreading the products of Connecticut's industry far and wide. Today, the state's industries are a bit different: Sikorsky makes helicopters, General Dynamics makes atomic submarines, and the rubber companies turn out tires and products such as Naugahyde, the synthetic leather named after the Connecticut town of Naugatuck where it's made.

The **state tax** on rooms and meals is 8%.

What's Special About Connecticut

Museums
- Mystic Seaport, Connecticut's outstanding "living" museum of 19th-century New England maritime life.
- Yale University's outstanding museums, including the Center for British Art, the University Art Gallery, and the Peabody Museum of Natural History.
- Hartford's Wadsworth Atheneum's fine collection of more than 60,000 works of art.

Theater
- New Haven's several good theaters, including the Long Wharf and Yale Rep, the Shubert, and the Palace.
- Goodspeed Opera House in East Haddam, a Victorian gem mounting performances of American musical theater.

Literary Shrines
- Nook Farm, in Hartford, which contains the homes of Mark Twain, who wrote *Tom Sawyer* here, and also Harriet Beecher Stowe.
- In West Hartford, the home of Noah Webster, America's first great lexicographer.

SEEING CONNECTICUT

Although Connecticut has many historic houses and lovely New England villages, the places that are popular with tourists are mostly along the coast: New Haven, home of Yale University; Essex, a fine old town at the mouth of the Connecticut River; Groton and New London, submarine capital of the world; and, of course, Mystic Seaport, the exciting and attractive re-creation of an old Connecticut maritime village. Hartford, although not what one would think of as a tourist mecca, is a pretty and interesting city well worth a short visit. Besides the attractions of the city itself, it can be used as a base for excursions into the lush farm and woodlands of Litchfield County, in the northwest corner of the state among the Litchfield Hills, Connecticut's "Berkshires."

GETTING THERE   By Plane   The state is served by Bradley International Airport in Windsor Locks, 12 miles north of Hartford. There's direct one-plane service between Bradley and more than 60 other North American airports, operated by United, TWA, Delta, American, and USAir. Buses leave the terminal for downtown Hartford and for Springfield, Mass., periodically, and limousines shuttle from Bradley to most cities in Connecticut.

By Train   Amtrak runs trains daily from New York City to Boston along both the coastal route (via New Haven, Old Saybrook, New London, Mystic, and Providence) and the inland route (via Hartford, Windsor Locks, and Springfield). Stopovers are allowed at no extra charge on most trains, so if you buy a ticket from New York to Boston, the stops in New Haven, New London, and Mystic, or New Haven and Hartford, need cost no more. It's usually possible to catch a train from New York in the morning, be in Mystic by noon, tour the Seaport thoroughly, catch another train around 5pm, arrive in Providence by about 6pm and Boston by 8pm. The trip from New York to Hartford takes less than 3 hours; to New Haven, about $1^{1}/_{2}$ hours; to New London, about $2^{3}/_{4}$ hours; to Mystic, about 3 hours.

Besides the Amtrak trains, there are frequent and cheaper commuter runs operated on the Connecticut Department of Transportation's New Haven Line by Metro North. These trains depart New York City's Grand Central Terminal hourly from about 7am until after midnight on weekdays, with even more frequent runs during rush hours. Service on Saturday, Sunday, and holidays is almost as frequent, with trains at least every two hours. The trip by Metro North to New Haven takes 1²/₃ hours. For exact schedule information, call toll free ☎ 800/638-7646, or 212/532-4900 in New York City.

By Bus   Greyhound, Bonanza, and Vermont Transit all operate daily buses between New York City, New Haven, and Hartford. The trip to Hartford takes about 3 to 4³/₄ hours, depending on the line and the number of stops en route. Greyhound and Bonanza have services between New York and New London, and on to Providence and Cape Cod. The trip from New York City to New London takes about 3 or 3¹/₂ hours, depending on stops. It's difficult to take a bus to Mystic Seaport—the train's the best way to get there.

From Hartford, Bonanza has buses to Providence and Hyannis; Vermont Transit operates buses to Vermont, New Hampshire, Montréal, and Québec City. All the large lines have buses between Hartford and Boston. In Hartford, the bus stations and the railroad station are all within a block of one another close to downtown. The Hartford terminal for Greyhound, Vermont Transit, Bonanza, Peter Pan, and Connecticut Transit is Union Station (1 Union Pl., ☎ 860/727-1776).

1 Ridgefield

58 miles NE of New York City, 8 miles S of Danbury

Connecticut's extreme southwest corner is a busy maze of light industry, highways, and bedroom communities serving New York. But only a short drive to the north of the bustle along U.S. 7 lies Ridgefield, as tranquil and beautiful a town as one can find. Stately old trees shade the grassy lawns along its quiet streets, and huge old houses are well sited among the gentle rises and hollows of its topography.

GETTING THERE   By Car   From the north, take I-84 to Exit 3 near Danbury, and head south on U.S. 7. From the south, take I-95 or the Merritt Parkway to Norwalk, exiting to U.S. 7 north. From the west, take I-684 (the New York Thruway) to Katonah and head east on N.Y. 35, which becomes Conn. 35 at the state line, then leads straight into Ridgefield.

ESSENTIALS   The **telephone area code** is **203.** The **Ridgefield Chamber of Commerce,** 9 Bailey Ave. (☎ **203/438-5992**), is open Monday through Friday from 9am to 3pm, Sat 10am–3pm.

Impressions

The warm, the very warm, heart of "New England at its best," such a vast abounding Arcadia of mountains and broad vales and great rivers and large lakes and white villages embowered in prodigious elms and maples. It is extraordinarily beautiful and graceful and idyllic—for America.

—Henry James, letter to Sir T. H. Warren,
May 29, 1911, describing Connecticut

Connecticut

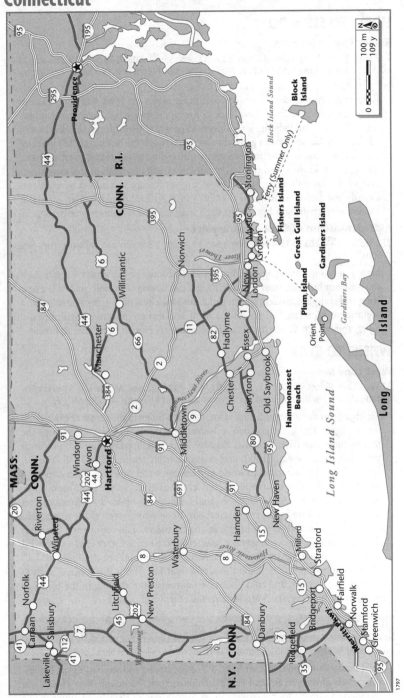

WHAT TO SEE & DO

Keeler Tavern Museum

132 Main St., at the junction of Conn. 33 and Conn. 35. ☎ **203/438-5485.** Admission $3 adults, $2 senior citizens, $1 children. Wed and Sat–Sun 1–4pm (last tour leaves at 3:30pm). Closed Jan.

Ridgefield's history dates from colonial times, when the town was a way station on the carriage road from New York to Boston. Carriage passengers needed inns for sustenance and lodging, and Ridgefield provided them. In the Keeler Tavern Museum, guides in colonial garb will take you through the historic (1715) building with its late 18th-century furnishings, pointing out the tap room, guest quarters, dining room, kitchen, and parlor. Despite the careful preservation and reconstruction of the tavern's early life, its most famous feature was added by accident. During the Battle of Ridgefield (1777) in the Revolutionary War, a British cannon sent a ball right into the Keeler's wall, where it remains to this day.

Aldrich Museum of Contemporary Art

258 Main St. ☎ **203/438-4519.** Admission $3 adults, $2 seniors and students. Tues–Sun 1–5pm.

Here you can see changing exhibits of work by contemporary artists. Even though the museum building itself is classic Ridgefield, having been built in 1783, a new wing and complete modernization make this an architectural gem. The museum's sculpture garden is a fine place for a stroll or a few precious moments of peace, quiet, and beauty. Concerts, films, and lectures are offered from time to time.

WHERE TO STAY

West Lane Inn

22 West Lane, Ridgefield, CT 06877. ☎ **203/438-7323.** 20 rms. A/C TV TEL. $140 double. All rates include continental breakfast. Additional person $10 extra. AE, DC, MC, V.

Set back from the street on a large lawn, off Main Street in the center of town (look for the signs), this is the grandest of Ridgefield's gracious old inns. Although the management advertises "colonial elegance," the building dates not from colonial times but from the early 1800s and was completely renovated in 1978. You enter the fine old house to find a world of gleaming wood paneling, thick carpeting, wingback chairs, fine old fireplaces, and a hushed quiet. In the guest rooms, furnishings are classic and comfortable, and facilities are up-to-date. Among other amenities, you'll find a radio in each room. Rooms come with either one or two queen-size beds, and several have working fireplaces. The continental breakfast includes fresh-squeezed orange juice, muffins, and pastries. Other services provided by the inn include babysitting, bicycle rental, laundry, and dry cleaning.

As for meals, the West Lane Inn serves light fare "from the pantry," such as sandwiches, desserts, and cold platters, from noon until evening in the breakfast room or on the long, spacious front veranda furnished in wicker.

2　New Haven

75 miles NE of New York City, 36 miles S of Hartford, 46 miles W of New London

This is a town of spires and steeples, of Gothic towers and steel-and-glass towers, very much of the present and very much of the past. Although New Haven was founded in 1638, the crucial year in its history was 1718, when Connecticut's

"Collegiate School" for the training of young men for the ministry decided to make its permanent and perpetual home in New Haven, ignoring the suits and blandishments of the other notable towns of Hartford and Saybrook. Perhaps the college came to New Haven because a local man offered a good deal of financial assistance, and in fact it was for this assistance that the school's name was changed to honor Elihu Yale.

New Haven has never been the same. Although today it's a town of business and industry—small arms, the telephone company, the county government—it's still more than anything the town where Yale is, and the presence of the great university dominates New Haven's social and cultural life.

GETTING THERE   By Car   New Haven is easily reached from New York City via I-95, but this road carries heavy truck traffic. A more pleasant alternative is to take the Hutchinson River Parkway to the Merritt Parkway and the Wilbur Cross Parkway. From Hartford, take I-91 south to Meriden, then the Wilbur Cross Parkway. From the east, I-95 is the only fast road.

By Train   Frequent and cheap commuter runs operated on the Connecticut Department of Transportation's New Haven Line by **Metro North** depart New York City's Grand Central Terminal hourly from about 7am until after midnight on weekdays, with even more frequent runs during rush hours. Service on Saturday, Sunday, and holidays is almost as frequent, with trains at least every two hours. The trip by Metro North to New Haven takes $1^2/_3$ hours. For exact schedule information, call toll free ☎ 800/638-7646, or 212/532-4900 in New York City.

Amtrak runs trains daily between New York City's Penn Station and Boston's South Station along the coastal route via New Haven. The trip from New York to New Haven takes about $1^1/_2$ hours; from New Haven to New London, about $1^1/_4$ hours; from New Haven to Mystic, about $1^1/_2$ hours; from Boston to New Haven, about 3 hours. An Amtrak ticket costs significantly more than a Metro North ticket.

By Bus   Greyhound, Bonanza, and **Vermont Transit** all operate daily buses between New York City, New Haven, and Hartford. Greyhound and Bonanza have services between New York and New London, and on to Providence and Cape Cod. The trip from New York City to New Haven takes about 1 or $1^1/_2$ hours, depending on stops.

Connecticut Transit (☎ 203/327-7433) also operates intercity buses in southwestern Connecticut.

ESSENTIALS   The **telephone area code** is **203.** The Greater **New Haven Convention & Visitors Bureau** has a seasonal (May to October) information center just off Exit 46 on I-95 (☎ **203/777-8550,** or toll-free **800/332-STAY**). Year-round information can be obtained at the GNHCVB Office at One Long Wharf Drive, Suite 7, New Haven, CT 06511 or by calling the above phone numbers. At no cost, guides will answer questions and give you maps of bus routes and streets and will supply information on suggested walking tours, the city's attractions, and recreational, cultural, and educational activities. For the most current information on special events, sports, concerts, and theater listings, as well as traffic and weather updates in the Greater New Haven area, call ☎ **203/498-5050** and enter code **1315.** This phone service is available 24 hours a day and is updated weekly by the Greater New Haven Convention & Visitors Bureau.

WHAT TO SEE & DO
SIGHTS & ATTRACTIONS
✪ Yale University

New Haven's prime attraction is Yale, almost three centuries old, founded in 1701 and moved to New Haven in 1718. Daily, Yale sponsors **free guided tours** of the campus (☎ **203/432-2300**). Tours start at 149 Elm Street across from the green at the Yale Visitor Information Center, which is housed in the oldest surviving residential building in New Haven. Tours are offered Monday through Friday at 10:30am and 2pm, Saturday and Sunday at 1:30pm only. The Information Center is open weekdays from 9am to 4:45pm and weekends from 10am to 4pm.

Yale's campus recalls England's Oxford and Cambridge, with its open grassy courts and flèched towers. Centerpiece of this English Gothic world is Harkness Tower, inscribed with the famous motto that has for generations admonished Yale students to move ever upward: FOR GOD, FOR COUNTRY, AND FOR YALE. Harkness Tower has a carillon, which is played daily throughout the academic year. You can also see the art galleries, the Beinecke Rare Book Library, the Georgian-style Connecticut Hall, and the Gothic-style Sterling Memorial Library.

CHURCHES

The churches on the green have illustrious heritages of design, for Gothic-style **Trinity Church** is said to have been modeled somewhat on England's York Minster; **Center Church** and **United Church** are both said to have sprung from early plans for London's famous St. Martin-in-the-Fields. Center Church, in Georgian style, is particularly interesting. It was built on an old burying ground and today has a crypt underneath where you can see more than 100 of the early gravestones. Guided tours of the church are offered Tuesday through Sunday.

Three blocks northeast of the green is **Grove Street Cemetery,** a beautiful final resting place for such eminent New Haven citizens as Eli Whitney, Noah Webster, and Charles Goodyear.

MUSEUMS & GALLERIES
Peabody Museum of Natural History

170 Whitney Ave. ☎ **203/432-5050.** Admission $5 adults, $3 seniors and children 3–15, free for children under 3; free for everyone Mon–Sat 10am–5pm, Sun noon–5pm. Closed New Year's Day, Easter, July 4, Labor Day, Thanksgiving, December 24, Christmas Day, and December 31.

The Peabody has one of those fine, turn-of-the-century collections assembled when American scientists were venturing into all the corners of the world to bring back specimens of terra, flora, and fauna for study and observation by university students. Dinosaur fossils, dioramas featuring North American animals in their habitats, exhibits on human origins and cultures, meteorites, and minerals are all on display, although what the museum can show is only a fraction of its vast holdings. Besides the permanent exhibits, the museum sponsors special events, lectures, and films. There's a museum shop that is open during museum hours.

✪ Yale Center for British Art

1080 Chapel St. ☎ **203/432-2800.** Free admission. Tues–Sat 10am–5pm, Sun noon–5pm.

The center, located on the corner of High Street, opened to the public in 1977. It has a fine collection of works by British artists from Elizabethan times to the present, and also features special exhibitions, lectures, films, and concerts. Check the *New Haven Register* listings for current exhibits.

Yale University Art Gallery

1111 Chapel St. ☎ **203/432-0600.** Free admission. Tues–Sat 10am–4:45pm, Sun 2–4:45pm. Closed New Year's, Independence, Thanksgiving, and Christmas days, as well as the month of August.

Yale's major art collection is housed in the oldest university art museum in North America. The Yale gallery, located between High and York Streets, is justifiably proud of its Garvan collection of American furniture and silver. Anyone interested in 18th-century American silver has got to see the Garvan—it's the best in the world. Along with Van Gogh's masterpiece *The Night Café*, there are paintings by Rubens, Hals, Manet, Picasso, and others. The university's collections form a substantial holding of European, African, pre-Columbian, American, ancient, and Asian art. Lectures, concerts, films, and special exhibits are always on when the university is in session; call the above number for current events.

Performing Arts

Because of Yale, New Haven has a rich cultural life in music, dance, and drama. Each academic year sees concerts and performances by more than a dozen excellent groups, including the New Haven Symphony Orchestra, the Yale Concert Band, Yale Glee Club, Yale Jazz Ensemble, the Bach Society, the New Haven Civic Orchestra, and the Community Choir. The Yale Repertory Theater and the Long Wharf Theater (a proving ground for New York–bound plays) get very good reviews each season, as does the Connecticut Ballet Company. New Haven also plays host to visits from the Boston Symphony Orchestra, major concert and popular performers, and groups. Several buildings in and around the campus are foci for these events. The listings recommended above have full information on the current season's performances. Most will be within a few blocks of the green. **Long Wharf** is a bit farther out, next to Howard Johnson's, in the wholesale market at 222 Sargent Dr. (Connecticut Turnpike (I-95) Exit 46; ☎ 203/787-4282).

Downtown theaters include the **Shubert** (☎ 203/624-1825) and the **Palace** (☎ 203/789-2120), across from one another on College Street between Chapel and Crown, half a block south of the green next to the Taft Apartments. The **Yale Rep** (☎ 203/432-1234) is in a former church building on Chapel Street at the corner of York, two blocks west of the green.

Evening Entertainment

New Haven must retain its dignity as the seat of Yale University. But that doesn't mean things are dead at night.

Boppers, at the corner of College and Crown Streets (☎ 203/562-1957), is a re-created 1950s diner, complete with half the body of a '56 Buick Special. Though you can dine here on burgers and pizza, the attraction is the 1950s music (recorded) for dancing.

WHERE TO STAY

New Haven is short on those cozy, charming lodging places (inns and bed-and-breakfasts) that are so densely scattered throughout the rest of New England. Most of the city's lodgings are to be found in modern hotels downtown and in motels on the outskirts.

The Colony Inn

1157 Chapel St., New Haven, CT 06511. ☎ **203/776-1234** or 800/458-8810. Fax 203/772-3929. 80 rms, 6 suites. A/C TV TEL. $98 double; $195 mini-suite. Additional person $10 extra. AE, DC, MC, V. Parking $3.

The Colony Inn is known to Yalies and their parents as a comfortable and convenient place to stay during campus visits. It's located just a block from the Yale Rep Theater and the Yale Art Gallery between Park and York. The spacious rooms in this modern five-story building are done in contemporary style, with colonial accents and reproduction pieces. Suites have one room with a queen-size bed that adjoins a sitting area. All the comforts are here, including free cable TV in your room and turn-down service. Other hotel services include indoor parking, a restaurant, and a lounge with live entertainment.

Holiday Inn–Downtown

30 Whalley Ave., New Haven, CT 06511. ☎ **203/777-6221** or 800/465-4329. Fax 203/772-1089. 160 rms. A/C TV TEL. $99 double. Rates may be higher on event weekends. Children stay free in parents' room. AE, CB, DC, MC, V.

The modern, comfortable Holiday Inn, just west of the Yale campus, is only a five-minute walk from the center of town. Rooms higher up in the hotel have better views and less traffic noise. The hotel has its own J. T. Ashley's restaurant and lounge, serving dishes from all over the world. The hotel also has an outdoor pool and a fitness room.

⊛ Hotel Duncan

1151 Chapel St., New Haven, CT 06511. ☎ **203/787-1273.** 90 rms (65 with bath). TV TEL. $60 double. Additional person $15 extra. Weekly rates available. AE, DC, MC, V. Parking available next door for $5 a day.

This old hotel boasts that it's "New Haven's oldest established hotel" and is certainly well established, having stood solidly on Chapel Street between Park and York for almost a century. To enter its Romanesque portal is to step back in time, right into a set for a black-and-white movie from the 1940s or 1950s. The Duncan's advantages are its location, just four blocks west of the green and even fewer blocks from the Yale campus; its prices; and the friendly, unpretentious, low-key staff and management. Except for cable TV, don't expect up-to-the-minute comforts in the guest rooms, for the Duncan is a true period piece. Expect basic, even worn, accommodations, but also basic cleanliness. The Duncan is a favorite with the young and the artistic, who love the fact that it's an honest, authentic echo of another time.

Inn at Chapel West

1201 Chapel St., New Haven, CT 06511. ☎ **203/777-1201.** 10 rms. $175 double. Additional person $15 extra. All rates include breakfast. AE, CB, DC, MC, V.

This well-located Victorian clapboard house fills a gap in New Haven's lodging market with its B&B service. The elegantly furnished rooms have period furniture, brass fixtures, four-poster beds, touches of lace, and down pillows. Some rooms have fireplaces. Breakfast includes homemade muffins and breads, fruit, yogurt, and cereals.

NEARBY MOTELS

Your best bet for a good, moderately priced motel room is at the cluster of hostelries near New Haven on the Wilbur Cross Parkway. The parkway is the scenic alternative to I-95. Passing several miles northeast of New Haven, the parkway provides access to the city at its Exits 57 (Conn. 34, Derby Avenue),

59 (Conn. 63, Whalley Avenue), and 60 (Conn. 10, Dixwell Avenue). Motels are grouped at each exit, but the best selection is at Exit 59, Whalley Avenue.

Staying at Exit 59, you'll be exactly 3¹/₂ miles from the greensward of Yale's Old Campus, the very center of the city. Bus B-1 ("Amity Road") will shuttle you between the motels and the center of town. A small shopping center and several restaurants are within walking distance of each motel.

You should be able to find what you want here.

WHERE TO DINE

New Haven's restaurants are spread throughout the metropolitan area, with no particularly rich concentration downtown such as one finds in Hartford or Boston. But if you're selective, it's not difficult to find the meal you're looking for, at the price you want to pay, within walking distance of the green. Some New Havenites who enjoy dining out belong to private clubs (the famed Mory's is one of these) and thus tend not to patronize restaurants that are open to the general public.

RESTAURANTS NEAR THE GREEN

Atticus Bookstore & Café
1082 Chapel St. ☎ **203/776-4040.** Reservations not accepted. Pastries $1.50–$3.50; light meals $2.95–$5.95. AE, MC, V. Daily 8am–midnight. CAFE.

Book lovers (and there are plenty of them in New Haven) congregate at Atticus, next to the entrance to the Yale Center for British Art. Sip tea and consume pastries while scanning the shelves from the comfort of your table, or browse through the store accompanied by the heavenly smell of coffee brewing. Come in the morning for croissants and coffee, at lunchtime for a substantial sandwich, or in the afternoon for cakes and tea. All menu items are made fresh daily—some in the Atticus kitchen, others in the kitchen of Atticus' sister company, Chabaso Bakery. To your cafe bill, add in the price of the book you'll discover.

Bruxelles
220 College St. ☎ **203/777-7752.** Reservations not accepted. Main courses $7–$17.95. AE, MC, V. Sun–Thurs noon–10:30pm, Fri–Sat noon–11:30pm; brunch Sun noon–3pm. CONTEMPORARY AMERICAN.

This chic brasserie and bar is at the corner of Crown Street, a block west of the green. Black bentwood chairs and tables are the main feature of the simple but elegant decor here. To the left as you enter is the well-stocked bar; to the right, the dining rooms and huge vertical grills with spits loaded with chickens, ducks, and whole roasts of pork and beef. At dinner you can start with something like root vegetable chips, then order the spit-roasted half duckling with a cinnamon-hoisin crust, pizza mistral, or the seared pepper tuna with tomato-caper salsa. There's good luncheon fare as well. Add a glass or two of some premium vintage or brew from the well-selected wine and beer lists. The late hours also make this a good place for an after-theater drink and snack.

Claire's Corner Copia
100 Chapel St. ☎ **203/562-3888.** Menu items $2.75–$7.75. No credit cards. Sun–Thurs 8am–10pm, Fri–Sat 8am–11pm. VEGETARIAN/KOSHER.

Claire's is a great place to stop for breakfast or lunch. It started out as a small, local place, but over the years it has grown into a very popular restaurant. Breakfast here might include frittatas, wonderful homemade muffins, scones, and quiches. Sandwiches on homemade bread are popular at lunch, and there's a wide variety of Mexican specialties (meatless of course) available. At dinner the menu takes an international twist and features main courses influenced by the cuisines of India, Italy, and France. The restaurant keeps kosher (under supervision), and owner, Claire, has just published a cookbook called *Claire's Corner Copia.*

✪ Louis' Lunch

261–263 Crown St. ☎ **203/562-5507.** Reservations not accepted. Hamburgers $2.30–$3.10. No credit cards. Mon–Thurs 11am–4pm, Fri–Sat 11am–1am. AMERICAN.

It may seem an audacious claim to say that Louis' Lunch was the "purveyor of the first hamburger sandwich in the U.S.A.," but so it is. Louis' started in 1895, serving the first thinly sliced steak sandwich in 1900 and then, using the trimmings from the steak sandwiches, developed the vertically grilled ground-beef sandwich (also in 1900). The restaurant has been owned and operated by the same family for over 100 years now, and the beef is still ground fresh daily and grilled in the original antique vertical grills. Served on toast with tomato and onion, the hamburger is also available as a cheeseburger (introduced in 1931) for no extra charge. Threatened by downtown redevelopment some years ago, Louis' was rescued by faithful fans who saw to it that the brick structure was picked up and moved safely to its present location two blocks west of the green. Today Louis' continues to cater faithfully to New Haven's weekday lunch crowd.

Scoozzi Trattoria and Wine Bar

1104 Chapel St. ☎ **203/776-8268.** Reservations required. Main courses $4.95–$19.95. AE, DISC, MC, V. Mon–Sat noon–2:30pm; Sun–Thurs 5–10pm, Fri–Sat 5–11pm. CONTEMPORARY ITALIAN.

Scoozzi Trattoria and Wine Bar is one of New Haven's most popular restaurants. It's absolutely impossible to get a table if you haven't made a reservation, so if you're planning a before-theater dinner, call well in advance for a reservation—perhaps even a night or two ahead.

Very popular items on the menu are the pizzettes—small pizzas for one (aptly named). The Jasper pizette with bitter greens, pignoli nuts, garlic cloves, hot red peppers, and smoked mozzarella is a seasonal favorite. If you'd rather have pasta, linguine alla Maremmana is a good choice—it's linguine tossed with grilled chicken, sun-dried tomatoes, arugula, sweet peppers, toasted fennel seeds, and romano cheese. Of course, there are a few token chicken, veal, lamb, and pork dishes on the menu. There's a good wine list and a full bar. Feel free to go just for appetizers (rather than a full meal) before a show.

RESTAURANTS NEAR WOOSTER SQUARE

About six blocks east of the green along Chapel Street lies Wooster Square, a lovely green park surrounded by some of this city's most interesting old houses. In this area, Chapel Street and Wooster Street (parallel, one block south) hold many restaurant choices, many of them featuring Italian cuisine.

Frank Pepe's

157 Wooster St. ☎ **203/865-5762.** Reservations not accepted. Pizza $5–$18. No credit cards. Mon and Wed–Thurs 4–10:30pm, Fri–Sat 11:30am–midnight, Sun 2:30–10:30pm. PIZZA.

For pizza, this is New Haven's favorite, two storefronts in which you'll find bare wooden booths, brick walls, and little in the way of atmosphere, but fantastic pizza. People line up in front of the restaurant to receive the hot pizzas that issue from the huge ovens in the back. The assortment is bewildering, ranging from a small grated-cheese pizza to large pies; large ones with chicken or fresh clams cost more.

AN EASY EXCURSION SOUTH OF NEW HAVEN

Just 30 minutes south of New Haven, via I-95, is Westport, one of many bedroom communities for wealthy New York City executives. The Saugatuck River winds its way through the center of town; on one side is the stately Inn at National Hall (see below) and on the other a handful of coffeehouses, cafes and fine dining establishments. Visitors also enjoy strolling the bricked sidewalks lined with boutiques with familiar Fifth Avenue names. Westport is a romantic destination for an afternoon or evening even if you can't afford to stay overnight.

WHERE TO STAY

❂ The Inn at National Hall

2 Post Road West, Westport, CT 06880. ☎ **203/221-1351** or 800/NAT-HALL. Fax 203/ 221-0276. 15 rms. A/C TV MINIBAR $195–$450 double. All rates include breakfast. AE, DC, MC, V.

Simply put, the Inn at National Hall has no competition in the state of Connecticut. As a labor of love, deluxe motorcoach tour guru Athur Tauck restored this 1873 Italiante brick building to its original state and then continued his work to make this place exceptional. Each of the 15 rooms is individually decorated—and I mean individually. Every one was hand stenciled in exquisite detail and furnished with the most luxurious appointments (both antiques and more modern pieces). Expect to be overwhelmed and seduced by the decor from the moment you arrive. The four-poster canopied beds are bathed in rich fabrics, drapes puddled as in an elegant manor home, and the baths are faced with marble and stocked with milled toiletries. In the elevator, a tromp l'oeil painting of bookshelves is remarkable. Service is discreet, and the independently operated on-premises restaurant gets kudos from the *New York Times.* Manager Nick Carter is the former keeper of the roal apartments for the British yacht, *Brittania.* This inn is not for children, and smoking is not permitted. Coffee and a newspaper followed by a full breakfast are delivered to your room each morning. If you'd rather, continental breakfast may be taken in the drawing room.

3 Connecticut River Valley

Strictly speaking, the Connecticut River Valley extends all the way from Long Island Sound to northern New Hampshire. It's the lower valley that we're interested in, though. Besides being particularly beautiful, the last 100 or so miles of the river's course has figured prominently in Connecticut history. The small towns retain the charm of a bygone era, and the river's banks are scattered with state parks and forests.

From New Haven, it's about 30 miles along I-95 to the mouth of the river. About midway you pass **Hammonassett Beach State Park,** which has facilities for camping and picnicking, hiking trails, and a fine beach for boating, swimming, and scuba diving.

Before reaching the river's edge, the highway passes Westbrook, where there's a nice inn, and then Old Saybrook, a town with picturesque views. On the east bank of the river is Old Lyme, with several fine inns. Heading northwest up the river on Conn. 9 brings you to Essex, perhaps the busiest and most charming river town, with one of Connecticut's most acclaimed inns. Ivoryton, to the west, also has several fine inns, and an old steam railroad. Due north of Ivoryton lies Chester, a charming village with good possibilities for dining and lodging, and just across the river from it, by an antique car-ferry, is Hadlyme, with its own hilltop castle. North of Hadlyme, on the same (east) bank of the river is East Haddam, home of the famous Goodspeed Opera House and several good inns. All this is yours in a distance of 20 miles, from Westbrook to East Haddam.

The **telephone area code** for the Connecticut River Valley is **860.**

OLD SAYBROOK

Old Saybrook is the gateway to scenic Saybrook Point, with its two lighthouses. If you have time for a pretty drive, come up from Westbrook on U.S. 1 East, then follow Conn. 154 through Knollwood, Fenwick (where Katharine Hepburn once lived), and Saybrook Point to Old Saybrook. To cross the river to Old Lyme, you'll have to leave all this tranquillity and climb back onto I-95 eastbound.

WHERE TO STAY & DINE

In Saybrook

Saybrook Point Inn & Spa

2 Bridge St., Saybrook, CT 06475. ☎ **860/395-2000.** 55 rms, 7 suites. A/C MINIBAR TV TEL. $170 superior double, $195 deluxe double, $235 luxury double; $290–$495 suite. AE, DC, DISC, MC, V.

If you're interested in a luxury hotel right on the water, the Saybrook Point Inn is probably your best choice—there are even slips available if you're coming by boat. The rooms hold reproduction Chippendale and Queen Anne furnishings and king-size beds with floral comforters. Many rooms have balconies, and 42 have fireplaces. The rooms on the third floor have cathedral ceilings and paddle fans. All junior suites boast Jacuzzi tubs, and the one- and two-bedroom suites with separate sitting and dining areas are ideal for families.

Dining/Entertainment: Terra Mar, the hotel's award-winning dining room, overlooking the marina, offers continental cuisine as well as seafood. There's also a more casual patio area available for dining. The 18th-century mahogany bar is open daily and provides live entertainment on weekends.

Facilities: Exercise room, indoor and outdoor pools, hot tub, sauna, spa (massage, facials, aromatherapy, and accupressure available), marina; bikes available.

Near Old Saybrook

Captain Dibbell House

21 Commerce St., Clinton, CT 06413. ☎ **860/669-1646.** 4 rms. A/C. $80–$100 double. MC, V.

The Captain Dibbell house was built in 1866 for Capt. Edwin A. Dibbell and his wife, Mary. Captain Dibbell remained in residence until he died in 1907. His wife continued to occupy the house until her death in 1917, after which the house remained a private residence until it was taken over by the present owners, who have done their best to keep the house the way it was over a hundred years ago.

You'll cross an old footbridge to get to the inn, and once inside, you'll feel at home in the comfortable sitting room with its upright piano and puzzle-in-progress on the table. It will be no surprise that the rooms are equally comfortable.

The Captain's Room, for instance, is Victorian in style and houses a queen-size brass bed, antique furnishings, and a blanket chest. In contrast, Elizabeth's Room is bright and airy with its king-size white iron bed, green-and-white quilts, and sitting area with a wingback chair and oak furnishings.

Breakfast is served buffet style in the dining room. You might have fresh fruit muffins, scrambled eggs or an omelet, and freshly ground coffee. If the weather is nice and you'd prefer to eat outside, you can arrange to have breakfast in the gazebo.

OLD LYME

This village is a painter's paradise—and has been so for quite a while. During the early years of this century, Miss Florence Griswold opened the doors of her mansion on Lyme Street to painters, mostly American impressionists, whom she admired, including Charles Ebert, Childe Hassam, Willard Metcalfe, Henry Ward Ranger, and Guy and Carleston Wiggins. Painters being painters, no matter how talented, they were sometimes unable to scrape together the month's rent for a room in the mansion, so instead they did what they could: They painted the door panels of the house with scenes from around Old Lyme. The house is now a museum and one of your prime reasons for stopping here. The other reason is that Old Lyme has several fine inns, good for lodging and for dining.

WHAT TO SEE & DO

Florence Griswold Museum

96 Lyme St. ☎ **860/434-5542.** Admission $4 adults, $3 seniors and students, free for children under 12. June–Nov, Tues–Sat 10am–5pm, Sun 1–5pm; Dec–May, Wed–Sun 1–5pm.

This late-Georgian mansion, built in 1817, was home to America's best-known impressionist art colony. Visit the first-floor rooms where Miss Florence's artist guests used to paint. Upstairs are galleries concentrating on the works of this "Lyme School" of American impressionism, and on changing exhibits, including New England furnishings and decorative arts.

Lyme Academy of Fine Arts

84 Lyme St. ☎ **860/434-5232.** Free admission. Tues–Sat 10am–4pm, Sun 1–4pm.

Primarily a school in a gracious house dating from 1817, the Lyme Academy of Fine Arts has a gallery of changing exhibits of traditional painters and sculptors.

WHERE TO STAY

✪ Bee and Thistle Inn

100 Lyme St., Old Lyme, CT 06371. ☎ **860/434-1667.** 12 rms (10 with bath). A/C. $78–$195 double. AE, DC, MC, V. Directions: From Exit 70 (off I-95), turn left off the ramp and take the first right onto Halls Road (U.S. 1 East); go to the T in the road and turn left; the inn is the third house on the left.

Bob and Penny Nelson's inn dates from colonial times (1756), with many later additions. Its situation, on its own estate of more than five shady acres bordering the Lieutenant River, is superb. The guest rooms have furnishings reflecting the inn's long history—canopy, four-poster, or spool beds with handmade quilts and afghans, washstands, wing chairs—but also private baths in most cases. One room (the cottage) has a TV. The dining room is open for all meals (closed Tuesday). The Bee and Thistle Inn's dining room is open for lunch, dinner, and brunch (on Sundays), and is one of the top-rated restaurants in the area. Contemporary American fare is the chef's specialty, and you might find such delights as lamb sausage and roasted garlic polenta, goat cheese and apple tart, and peanut trout on the menu when you're in town.

Old Lyme Inn

85 Lyme St. (P.O. Box 787), Old Lyme, CT 06371. ☎ **860/434-2600** or 800/434-5352. Fax 860/434-5352. 13 rms. A/C TV TEL. $99–$158 double. Additional person $30 extra. All rates include continental breakfast. AE, DC, DISC, MC, V. Closed first two weeks in Jan. Directions: Go north on I-95, take Exit 70, and turn left off the ramp; turn right at the second light and follow this until the second light; the inn will be on your left. Going south on I-95, take Exit 70 make a right turn off the ramp; the inn is the first driveway on the right.

This gracious and elegant mansion, dating from the 1850s, is the village's prime hostelry. Innkeeper Diana Field Atwood has found period furnishings from many New England locales for the rooms, so you'll find canopy beds, marble-topped dressers and vanities, and antique mirrors. Eight of the guest rooms are in the new (1985) North Wing, which is designed to harmonize with the original mansion and other structures on historic Lyme Street. North Wing rooms are preferable because they are bigger and quieter, though the five rooms in the original mansion are certainly charming. Each room has a clock radio.

The Old Lyme Inn's dining room is open Monday through Saturday for lunch from noon to 2pm and for dinner from 6 to 9pm; Sunday brunch is from 11am to 3pm, dinner from 4 to 9pm. A recent redecoration of the dining room includes an 8×12-foot copy of Winslow Homer's *Breezing Up* done by bachelor of fine Arts students at the Lyme Academy of Fine Arts. The atmosphere is formal in the high-ceilinged dining room, renowned for its fine cuisine, especially local seafood and veal. There's also a less formal grill room, open daily.

ESSEX

This was a shipbuilding and sea captains' town, founded in 1648. At first life in Essex was centered on farming, but within 100 years the shipbuilding industry grew and brought Essex much greater prosperity. The early name, by the way, was the Native American one of Potapaug, which served to identify the town until well into the 19th century.

Today Essex is one of the most picturesque towns in Connecticut, its old houses well kept, its boatyards and marina bobbing with sleek yachts and powerboats. Walk up Pratt Street for a look at the old houses, and then from Essex Square take a drive out North Main Street to view the fine old mansions. This quick tour leaves out lots of interesting side streets, corners, and crannies of Essex, and if you have the time, you could do worse than to poke around town, turning up quaint vignettes and fine river views.

WHAT TO SEE & DO

Connecticut River Museum

Main St. ☎ **860/767-8269.** Admission $4 adults, $3 seniors, free for children under 9. Tues–Sun 10am–5pm.

From Essex Square (the intersection of Main, North Main, South Main, and Pratt Streets), walk down Main Street past the Griswold Inn to the end, known as the Foot of Main, where you'll come across this warehouse for steamboats built in 1878 and recently restored. Ships' models, paintings, photographs, and other exhibits recall life on the Connecticut River in years gone by. Kids will love the replica of the first submarine, the *Turtle*. The museum is open year-round with permanent and changing exhibitions.

WHERE TO STAY & DINE

Griswold Inn

36 Main St., Essex, CT 06426. ☎ ☎ **860/767-1776.** Fax 860/767-0481. 26 rms. A/C TEL. $90–$175 double. All rates include continental breakfast. AE, MC, V.

This fine old inn in the center of town is famous throughout Connecticut for its location, food, and lodging. The rooms are quaint and old-fashioned, with low ceilings and exposed rough-hewn rafters, hooked rugs on the floors, perhaps a marble-topped vanity or a similar piece in one corner. Both double beds and twin beds are available. Note that in summer it may be necessary to reserve a weekend date two months in advance, so call or write to the inn.

The Griswold's several dining rooms are well done and interesting. At lunch, have the Griswold's own brand of sausages or a sandwich. Dinner specialties are hearty, with seafood and steaks under $20. The wine list is quite good; you can find both domestic and imported beer, and one of the drafts is the English lager named John Courage.

The Griswold is known for its Sunday "Hunt Breakfasts," when for $12.95 (11am to 2:30pm) you can help yourself to unlimited amounts of eggs, bacon, and ham, sausage, grits, fried potatoes, kippers, chicken, lamb kidneys, creamed chipped beef, smelts, or whatever else is offered for the day. For children 6 and under, breakfast is on the house, and sodas come in a "bottomless carafe."

EN ROUTE TO IVORYTON

On the way from Essex to Ivoryton, the road (Railroad Avenue) passes the station of the **Valley Railroad** (☎ 860/767-0103). You can ride the old steam train five miles upriver to Chester and back. At Deep River Station, if you wish, you can get off the train and onto the riverboat *Becky Thatcher* to motor farther upriver past Gillette Castle (see below). Trains leave anywhere from 2 to 6 times daily; they connect with the boat for a 2¹/₂-hour combination trip. The combination trip costs $14 for adults and $7 for children 2 to 11. Call for the latest information on schedules and fares.

IVORYTON

Ivoryton is a part of Essex for municipal government purposes, but it has a character and history of its own. The name came from the ivory industry set up here by the Comstock family, and many of the ivory keys for America's pianos and organs were made here. The ivory industry is gone, but the company that makes witch hazel, that soothing and astringent distillate, is still going strong on the Essex/Ivoryton boundary.

WHERE TO STAY & DINE

✪ Copper Beech Inn

46 Main St., Ivoryton, CT 06442. ☎ **860/767-0330.** Reservations recommended, especially on weekends. Main courses $20.75–$26.25. AE, DC, MC, V. Tues–Thurs 6–8pm, Fri–Sat 6–9pm, Sun 1–7pm. Directions: Take Exit 3 from Conn. 9 North and go 1³/₄ miles west to the inn. COUNTRY FRENCH.

The reason to go to Ivoryton is to eat in the inn, built as the home of a prosperous ivory merchant and now one of New England's most gracious places to dine: Tables have fresh flowers and a full French service in silver. The Comstock Room has fine dark-wood paneling; the garden porch is mostly windows and plants, with a floor of quarry tiles and a unique pineapple chandelier. Beside the front parlor of the inn is the Victorian-style conservatory with elegant cast-iron garden chairs and small tables, and it's here that cocktails are served. The menu for dinner is among the best in New England: filet of salmon, poached and served with a champagne-cream sauce and a julienne of mushrooms, artichoke bottoms, and tomatoes; and roast boned breast of pheasant filled with minced wild mushrooms and leeks, and served with a sauce of pheasant glaze and red wine—it goes on to 14 items, none common, all interesting. Appetizers, such as *salade de homard aux truffes du Périgord* (half a fresh lobster, steamed and chilled, served out of the shell with muchrooms and a julienne of truffles in a truffle-scented vinaigrette) and *escalope de foie gras aux raisins* (fresh duck foie gras, seared and served warm with fresh grapes and a glaze of veal stock and armagnac) are offered. Favorite main courses include *escalope de saumon, sauce champagne* (poached salmon served with a champagne cream sauce, and a julienne of mushrooms, artichoke bottoms, and tomato) and *selle d'agneau rotie au thym* (boneless saddle of lamb roasted and served sliced with a thyme-scented lamb glaze and a garnish of goat cheese wrapped in crisp, thin pastry). Desserts include a *trilogie de sorbets tropicaux* (passionfruit, coconut, and blood-orange sorbets served with fresh mango, berries, and a kiwi sauce), and *gateau au citron* (layers of crisp meringue, lemon mousse, and sponge cake, served with a vanilla custard sauce).

The Copper Beech also has 13 fine guest rooms with air conditioning and private bath for $118 to $190 double, continental breakfast included.

CHESTER

The picture-perfect little Connecticut riverside village of Chester is nestled in the valley of the Pattaconk Brook. Its buildings are of white clapboard, yellow brick, or somber granite, its fences of fieldstone. Little shops line the short main street, along with the general store, the post office, and the library. It's charming, scenic, small, and wealthy.

Native American deeds to the land once known as the district of Pattaconk date from the 1660s. Colonial settlers moved to the district from Saybrook in the early 1700s and by 1836 the town was incorporated as Chester. During the colonial period Chester was an industrial town, with a gristmill, a sawmill, and shipyards. The ferry service across the Connecticut River to Hadlyme was inaugurated in 1769—and continues to this day.

There's little to do in Chester except to enjoy the place itself, to stroll its main street, and to ride or walk through the surrounding countryside.

EN ROUTE TO HADLYME

If you're driving, the most enjoyable way to get from Chester to Hadlyme is to take the old **Chester-Hadlyme ferry** (☎ 860/526-2743). Cars and pedestrians travel at prices more antique than the fairly modern boat that makes the run—$2.25 for car and driver, 75¢ for pedestrians and each passenger in the car other than the driver. The history of the ferry run goes back to 1769, when one Jonathan Warner would drag you across the river for a small fee. Today the ferry is run by the state of Connecticut, and it operates April through December 19, daily from 7am to 6:45pm. The trip across the river is made right in the shadow of Gillette Castle, and takes about five minutes, not counting the short waiting time.

HADLYME

Shortly after the turn of the century, an actor named William Gillette realized a lifelong dream by building himself a castle to live in. His stage career, including a very successful period in the role of Sherlock Holmes, had brought him the wealth he needed, and in 1914 he began. Over five years and a million dollars later, the result was a strange-looking mansion of fieldstone named "The Seventh Sister," complete with a commanding view of the Connecticut River and its own three-mile-long excursion railroad. Inside the castle, on River Road in East Haddam, Gillette gave vent to his passion for detail and exotica, bringing furnishings from around the world and specifying in great detail the form that was to be given to the intricately carved oak trim and the ingenious wooden door latches. Today William Gillette's fantasy house is known as **Gillette Castle** (☎ 860/526-2336), and it's a state park open to all and sundry. The narrow-gauge railroad is gone, but forest paths, picnic tables, and river-vista spots have replaced it. Tours of the house itself are given daily Memorial Day to Columbus Day from 10am to 5pm at a charge of $4 for adults, $2 for children 5 to 11, free for children under 5. Gillette Castle is either Connecticut's most distinguished medieval castle or the largest backyard barbecue ever constructed—you decide.

EAST HADDAM

From Hadlyme, drive northwest a few miles to East Haddam, where you'll find the wonderful old **Goodspeed Opera House** (☎ 860/873-8668). This riverside Victorian gem, built in 1876, has now been carefully restored to serve as a venue for American musical theater. The setting by the river and bridge is so picturesque that it's worth the ride just to see the exterior, but if you have the time, take a tour of the interior. It's on view June through August, on Monday from 1 to 3pm and on Saturday from 11am to 1:30pm; $2 for adults, $1 for children. Best of all, see a play; the specialty is the revival of early musicals and the production of new works. Fourteen Goodspeed shows have moved to Broadway (including *Annie*). Three musicals are offered each season beginning in mid-April and continuing through mid-December with performances Wednesday through Sunday, and matinees on Wednesday, Saturday, and Sunday. Tickets cost $19 to $33. Call for the latest information and ticket reservations. Located four miles from the Opera House in Chester is Goodspeed's second stage, Goodspeed-at-Chester/The Norma Terris Theatre which is used for developing new musicals and nurturing emerging artists. Three new musicals are presented each season and tickets are available through the Goodspeed Box Office (☎ 860/873-8668).

RIVER CRUISES

Across the river from East Haddam in the village of Haddam is the office of **Camelot Cruises, Inc.,** 1 Marine Park, Haddam, CT 06438 (☎ 860/345-8591). March through December, you can board the MV *Camelot* for a lunch, Sunday brunch, or Murder Mystery dinner cruise along the placid river. There's no better way to enjoy the scenery, and you get a meal and live entertainment to boot. This is fairly formal dining, and you are expected to dress "appropriately"— suit or sport jacket for men; a dress, skirt and blouse, or a nice slacks outfit, for women.

Cruises depart rain or shine. The evening Murder Mystery dinner cruises board at 6:30pm and depart on Friday and Saturday at 7pm, returning at 10pm. The price, meal (but not tax and tips) included, is $35 per person for the Murder Mystery luncheon cruise, $29 for the Sunday brunch cruise; The Murder Mystery dinner cruise costs $47.75 per person.

WHERE TO STAY

Bishopsgate Inn

Goodspeed Landing, East Haddam, CT 06423. ☎ **860/873-1677.** 6 rms. $75–$100 double. DISC, MC, V. Directions: Take Exit 69 off I-95 to Conn. 9; from Conn. 9, take Exit 7 to East Haddam; from the Goodspeed Opera House, follow Conn. 82 two-tenths of a mile to Bishopsgate on the left.

This colonial home was built in 1818 by East Haddam merchant/shipbuilder Horace Hayden. Four rooms have fireplaces, and each floor has a comfortable sitting area with inviting couches and chairs, so you'll have somewhere to go to read or socialize with the other guests. The rooms are furnished with period pieces or family antiques. The Jenny Lind Room has a wooden pine canopy bed with netting, an Oriental carpet, a wingback and a Windsor chair, pine side tables, and a fireplace. The ground-floor room (also with a fireplace) has a cannonball bed with a pink quilt, a pine hutch, a wingback chair, and lace-edged curtains. The bathroom for this room is located across the hall, but don't worry about privacy— the walk to the bath is hidden by a well-placed screen.

Breakfast here is served in the country kitchen and might include stuffed French toast, fresh fruits, homemade breads and coffee cake, a breakfast meat, and some kind of eggs.

WHERE TO DINE

The Gelston House

8 Main St., Rte. 82., East Haddam. ☎ **860/873-1411.** Reservations recommended. Main courses $6.75–$9.75 at lunch, $16.95–$23.95 at dinner. Prix fixe $25.50. Mon–Sat 11:30am–2:30pm, Mon–Thurs 5–9:30pm, Fri–Sat 5–10:30pm; Sun brunch 11am–2:30pm. AE, MC, V. AMERICAN/CONTINENTAL/FRENCH.

Built in 1853, The Gelston House restaurant offers diners exceptional views of the Connecticut River. Located next door the the Goodspeed Opera House, it's an excellent choice for lunch or dinner. The lunch menu features a variety of sandwiches (including a grilled tequila lime swordfish sandwich for which the fish is thinly sliced and quickly grilled) as well as a short selection of entrée salads and hot main courses (like chicken pot pie and pasta with spring vegetables). At dinner, feast on The Gelston House country-style terrine served with cornichons and plum chutney to start, and follow it with the grilled leg of lamb (marinated in garlic and herbs and served with braised escarole, sundried tomatoes, roasted garlic, and pine nuts). The chocolate bread pudding is the best dessert (in my opinion) at The Gelston House.

4 New London & Groton

46 miles E of New Haven, 45 miles SE of Hartford, 9 miles W of Mystic

Most visitors to these navy towns are here to see the U.S. Coast Guard Academy or the navy submarine base at Groton. But there are other things to see and do as well. New London has a state park and a beachfront amusement park, as well as car-ferry services to Block Island, R.I., Fishers Island, N.Y., and Orient Point, Long Island, N.Y. Groton has Fort Griswold State Park.

The big draw in this region is, of course, Mystic Seaport (see "Mystic and Stonington," later in this chapter). Many visitors choose to stay near Mystic and tour New London and Groton on a day trip. There are some lodging possibilities, however, in New London, Groton, and the nearby towns of Niantic and East Lyme, to the west. Lodging establishments in this area consist almost exclusively of highway motels. Many are geared to the tourist trade rather than to the business or armed-forces traveler.

GETTING THERE   By Car   Speedy access to New London is provided by I-95 and Conn. 52. A warning is in order: Rush-hour traffic (8 to 9am and 5 to 6pm) in the Groton/New London area is extremely heavy, especially along I-95 and its feeder roads. Make your getaway before 5pm, or stay and have dinner until the roads empty out.

By Train   Amtrak runs trains daily from New York City to Boston along the coastal route via New Haven, Old Saybrook, New London, Mystic, and Providence. The trip from New York City to New London takes about 2³/₄ hours; to Mystic, about 3 hours.

By Bus   Bus transportation in the region is provided by **Southeastern Area Rapid Transit (S.E.A.T.)** (☎ 860/886-2631).

ESSENTIALS   The **telephone area code** is **860.** For information, contact **Connecticut's Mystic & More!,** P.O. Box 89, New London, CT 06320 (☎ **860/444-2206** or 800/TO-ENJOY), for a free vacation kit.

NEW LONDON

The major tourist attraction in New London is the **U.S. Coast Guard Academy,** 15 Mogehan Ave. (☎ 860/444-8270). Start your tour of the grounds at the Visitors Pavilion (open daily from 9am to 5pm), where you can visit the museum and gift shop. A special treat here is a visit to the Coast Guard's training barque *Eagle,* generally in port at the academy in April and May (open to visitors on Friday, Saturday, and Sunday from noon to 5pm when in port). If you miss the *Eagle,* perhaps you can catch the colorful dress review of the Corps of Cadets, usually held (weather permitting) in April, May, September, and October. For times and dates, contact the Public Affairs Office at the above number.

New London's major beach-and-amusement complex is at **Ocean Beach Park,** located at the southern end of Ocean Avenue; take Exit 75-76 from I-95 (☎ 860/447-3031). Besides walking on the white sand beach, you can stroll along the boardwalk, play a game or two of miniature golf, test your reflexes in the arcade, and take a quick trip down the triple water slide. Ocean Beach Park is open Memorial Day to Labor Day and costs $8.50 maximum per carload (you pay 75¢ per half hour up to $8.50); after 6pm the most you'll pay is $1.50.

FERRY TO THE ISLANDS

New London is a major ferryboat port, with frequent summer sailings to Block Island, R.I., and Fishers Island as well as Orient Point, N.Y., on the tip of Long Island.

BLOCK ISLAND   See "Block Island" in Chapter 9 for details. The pier in New London is north of the railroad station (☎ 860/442-7891 or 442-9553). Follow the red-and-white signs to the dock.

FISHERS ISLAND   Daily ferries go to this New York island a few miles off the Connecticut coast, departing from the dock on State Street. For fares and schedules, call ☎ 860/443-6851.

ORIENT POINT, LONG ISLAND   The dock is on Ferry Street; details from the Cross Sound Ferry Service are available by calling ☎ 860/443-5281; for reservations from Orient Point, call ☎ 516/323-2525. Cars are carried ($28, several dollars less Tuesday through Thursday except during the summer), and reservations for the 1½-hour cruise (adults, $9.50 one-way, $15 same-day round-trip; kids, half price) are a must in high summer.

GROTON

Groton, the "Submarine Capital of the World," makes its living from General Dynamics' Electric Boat Division and from Pfizer Pharmaceuticals, besides the naval facilities at the submarine base.

No one comes to Groton to see anything but submarines—and there are plenty to see. Your tour here should be an auto cruise along **Submarine Drive,** the waterfront road along the eastern bank of the Thames River (named Thames Street) south of I-95 and Military Highway to the north. Take Exit 85 from I-95 and follow Bridge Street to Thames Street.

Near the point where Bridge Street runs into Thames, just south of the Gold Star (I-95) Bridge, is the **USS *Flasher* National Submarine Monument.** The conning tower of this World War II Angler-class sub has been established here as a memorial to the American submarine sailors who lost their lives during that war. The *Flasher* sank more than 100,000 tons of enemy shipping during the war, and its crew members were repeatedly cited by the president for their services.

While you're down in Groton, see the **Fort Griswold Battlefield State Park** (☎ 860/445-1729), at Monument Street and Park Avenue (Monument runs parallel to Thames Street). The heroic, tragic story of the American force that defended the fort in 1781 against the British is told in the museum, open from Memorial Day to Columbus Day. The Memorial Tower (view from the top) was erected for the courageous defenders who fought until overpowered and then perished in the massacre by the victorious British. The state park is open all year, and both the park and the museum are free of charge. The Monument House Museum and Groton Monument are open Memorial Day to Labor Day, daily from 10am to 5pm; and Labor Day to Columbus Day, on weekends from 10am to 5pm.

North of the Gold Star (I-95) Bridge, Submarine Drive continues along the Military Highway. Near the entrance to the U.S. Navy's Groton Submarine Base (Exit 86 from I-95) is the **USS *Nautilus* Memorial** (☎ 860/449-3174 or 800/343-0079), and the Submarine Force Library and Museum, featuring the world's first nuclear-powered submarine. Launched in Groton in 1954, the *Nautilus* saw its finest hour when it passed beneath the ice cap at the geographic North Pole in 1958, the first ship ever to reach that geographically significant spot. Decommissioned after 25 years of service in 1980, the sub is now open for free to visitors Monday and Wednesday through Sunday from 9am to 5pm, from 1 to 5pm on Tuesday; to 4pm in winter (mid-October to mid-April). Note that the sub is closed New Year's, Thanksgiving, and Christmas Days. Displays in the library and museum chronicle the history of the U.S. submarine force since the Revolutionary War. You can peer into working periscopes, inspect miniature submarines, wonder at the Revolutionary War–era *Turtle,* all at no charge.

WHERE TO STAY

Radisson Hotel

35 Governor Winthrop Blvd., New London, CT 06320. ☎ **860/443-7000** or 800/
333-3333. Fax 860/443-1239. 116 rms, 4 suites. A/C TV TEL. $119–$159 double. AE, CB,
DC, MC, V. Directions: Take Exit 83 or 84S from I-95 to Governor Winthrop Boulevard and
the hotel.

If you want to stay downtown in New London, this is perhaps the best and most
comfortable place. Well located near the railroad station and just a short distance
off I-95, the Radisson has many services, including an indoor pool, a restaurant,
a lounge, and a whirlpool bath.

Windsor Motel

345 Gold Star Hwy., Groton, CT 06340. ☎ **860/445-7474.** 58 rms. A/C MINIBAR TV.
$48–$70 double. Children stay free in parents' room. Discounts available during off-season
and for stays of a week or more. AE, MC, V. Directions: Take the Conn. 184 exit from I-95.

Thirty-three of the motel rooms here come with complete kitchens. Use only one
double bed and you pay only $48 to $58; use both double beds and the price is
$60 to $70. Since children of any age stay free with their parents, the two-bed price
could cover a family of four.

5 Mystic & Stonington

Mystic: 9 miles E of New London, 5 miles NW of Stonington

GETTING THERE   By Car   Speedy access to Mystic is provided by I-95 and
Conn. 52. Take Exit 90 from I-95 for Mystic Seaport. A warning is in order:
Rush-hour traffic (8 to 9am and 5 to 6pm) in the area is extremely heavy,
especially along I-95 and its feeder roads. Make your getaway before 5pm, or stay
and have dinner until the roads empty out.

By Train   **Amtrak** runs trains daily from New York City to Boston along
the coastal route via New Haven, Old Saybrook, New London, Mystic, and
Providence. The trip from New York City to Mystic takes about 3 hours; from
Boston, about 1¹/₂ hours.

By Bus   Bus transportation in the region is provided by **Southeastern Area
Rapid Transit** (S.E.A.T.) (☎ 860/886-2631).

ESSENTIALS   The **telephone area code** is **860.** Both these towns have their
own information booth and office. For general inquiries, your best bet is the
Mystic and Shoreline Visitors Information Center, Olde Mistick Village,
Mystic, CT 06355 (☎ **860/536-1641**). Olde Mistick Village is the new
colonial-style shopping complex just south of I-95 on Conn. 27, very near
Mystic Seaport. The information center is in Building 1, and is open Monday
through Friday from 9am to 5pm, Saturday from 9am to 6pm, and Sunday from
10am to 5pm.

Connecticut's maritime life, past and present, is all on view in the area
comprising the open-air museum called Mystic Seaport, and the pretty old seaside
town of Stonington. Mystic Seaport is one of the top tourist attractions in New
England, drawing very large crowds every day of the summer. The huge open-air
"museum" is big enough to handle the crowds, but the capacity of nearby motels
is not—the motels are packed in July and August, and guests must prepay their
entire stay.

You can avoid the hotel crush altogether by taking an Amtrak train through this area and getting off for the day at Mystic, where a bus will take you from the station to Mystic Seaport. After your day roaming around the ships, old buildings, and exhibits, board an afternoon train to Providence or Boston (or New Haven or New York). There's no extra charge for the stopover if you buy a through ticket and you obviate the need for a room.

MYSTIC
WHAT TO SEE & DO

✪ Mystic Seaport

Mystic. ☎ **860/572-5315.** Admission $16 adults, $8 children 6–15, free for children under 6. June–Aug, daily 9am–8pm; Apr–May and Sept–Oct, daily 9am–5pm; Nov–Dec, daily 9am–4pm; Jan–Mar, daily 10am–4pm. Closed Christmas Day. Directions: Take Exit 90 from I-95 and follow the signs.

One could return again and again to this impressive museum to see the various indoor exhibits, walk through the preserved 19th-century town, or climb aboard one of the venerable sailing ships moored and preserved here. (Foremost among these is the *Charles W. Morgan,* the last wooden whaling ship in the United States.) Although this is a nonprofit museum, there's much more life to it than just rows of glass cases housing exhibits. You'll see scrimshaw, old tools, watches, clocks, chronometers, navigational instruments, and so on, but most of your time will be taken walking through the village and watching the interpreters (staff) do their jobs and explain what they're doing. You'll see half a dozen crew members high in the rigging of the square-rigged ship *Joseph Conrad,* furling a sail in time to a chantey they sing, with one rope supporting all of them high above the deck— among other demonstrations.

Mystic Seaport began in 1929 as the Marine Historical Association, founded by three citizens of Mystic who were interested in preserving aspects and objects from the town's maritime past. The site of the museum is the former shipyard of George Greenman and Company, which built wooden clipper ships in the 19th century.

To get the feel of the place, stay at least three or four hours; if you've arrived late in the day, you can buy a ticket and have it validated for the next day as well. With your ticket you'll be given a very handsome map of the village and its exhibits, plus a list of the daily events, from special lectures to sea-chantey sings. In winter, interpreted exhibits and craft demonstrations don't begin until 10am. Look at the list to get an idea of what'll be in action for the hours you're in the village. The museum can be divided basically into four areas: the indoor exhibits of small boats, models, figureheads, and the like, mostly near the Seamen's Inne entrance gate; changing exhibits; the restored village and waterfront area; and the shipyard at the southern end of the grounds where the seaport cares for its ships.

The **Coastal Life Area** is the official name of Mystic Seaport's 19th-century village. The village includes the shops of a shipsmith, ship-carver, and printer, a cooperage, bank, shipping office, grocery, chapel, schoolhouse, pharmacy, rope walk, clock and nautical instrument shop, mast-hoop shop, ship's chandlery, and tavern.

Indoor exhibits are housed in several buildings. In the three-story Stillman Building are ship's models, paintings, and scrimshaw. The Mallory Building is devoted to exhibits explaining the Victorian-era shipping business of the Mallory family, and also shipbuilding in Mystic. In the Wendell Building are collections

Mystic Seaport

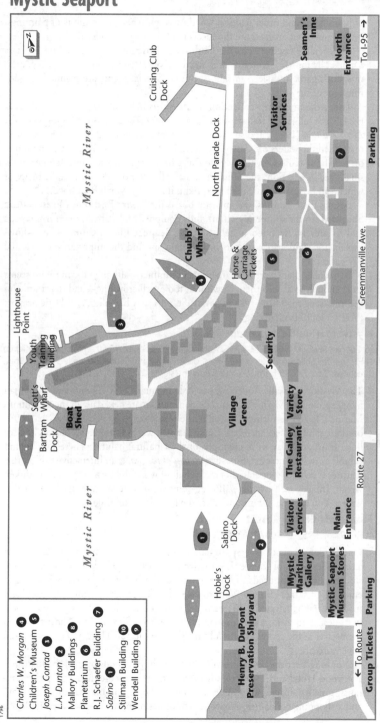

1796

Charles W. Morgan ❹
Children's Museum ❺
Joseph Conrad ❸
L.A. Dunton ❷
Mallory Buildings ❽
Planetarium ❻
R.J. Schaefer Building ❼
Sabino ❶
Stillman Building ❿
Wendell Building ❾

Mystic River

Lighthouse Point

Youth Training Building

Scott's Wharf

Bartram Dock

Boat Shed

Cruising Club Dock

Chubb's Wharf

North Parade Dock

Horse & Carriage Tickets

Security

Village Green

The Galley Restaurant

Variety Store

Visitor Services

Main Entrance

Route 27

Sabino Dock

Hobie's Dock

Mystic Maritime Gallery

Mystic Seaport Museum Stores

Henry B. DuPont Preservation Shipyard

Group Tickets

← To Route 1 Parking

Greenmanville Ave.

Visitor Services

Seamen's Inne

North Entrance

To I-95 →

Parking

N

of figureheads and other nautical wood carvings. Changing exhibits of paintings, prints, and other artifacts are the specialty of the R. J. Schaefer Building.

Children are fascinated by the **Children's Museum,** where the theme is "It's a Sailor's Life for Me." Kids can swab the deck, move cargo, cook in the galley, dress in sailor's garb, and sleep in sailors' bunks. Special events are planned for kids throughout the year.

Today the museum's **collection of old ships** includes the *Charles W. Morgan* (1841), the full-rigged training ship *Joseph Conrad* (1882), and the fishing schooner *L. A. Dunton* (1921). It also owns a steamboat called the *Sabino* (1908), which once plied the waters off Casco Bay in Maine but that now takes museum visitors on half-hour cruises on the Mystic River from mid-May to mid-October, for a small fee. In addition, the museum has a collection of 300 small craft, many of which can be seen in the Small Boat Exhibit and the North Boat Shed.

Besides these exhibits, the museum boasts the **Henry B. duPont Preservation Shipyard** (in the southern section), fully equipped and staffed to perform repairs and to preserve wooden vessels; and the **Seaport Planetarium,** where shows explain the significance of stars in the night sky and the importance of celestial navigation.

Remember that the crowds are heavy in summer—although the museum seems large enough to absorb them all without too much crowding—and that traffic on the mile-long road from I-95 to Mystic Seaport may be pokey. At Mystic Seaport there's a lot of free parking.

Mystic Marinelife Aquarium

55 Coogan Blvd. ☎ **860/572-5955.** Admission $9.50 adults, $8.50 seniors, $6.50 children 3–12, free for children under 3. July–Aug, daily 9am–7pm; Sept–June, daily 9am–4:30pm. Directions: Take Exit 90 from I-95 and follow the signs.

The Mystic Marinelife Aquarium has 40 living marine life exhibits and more than 3,500 specimens. Marine mammal demonstrations are held daily in the aquarium's Marine Theater featuring Atlantic bottle-nosed dolphins and beluga whales. An outdoor exhibit area called Seal Island lets you watch four species of seals and sea lions sport and play in re-creations of their natural habitat. There's a penguin exhibit as well. A new exhibit called *Robots of the Sea,* is an interactive exhibit that features a remotely operated vehicle that allows visitors to "explore" a sunken wreck. Images seen by the exploring mini-submarine are displayed on a video screen. You can stay 90 minutes after the last admission time.

Foxwoods Casino Resort

At Exit 92 off I-95. ☎ **800/PLAY-BIG.**

One of Connecticut's newest attractions is the the Foxwoods Casino Resort, just a few miles north of Mystic. It started with the casino, which features over 3,000 slot machines, hundreds of table games, and a poker room. Gamers can also enjoy "high-stakes" Bingo. Want to take a break from the gaming tables and slot machines? Each week a different celebrity performer arrives at Foxwoods, but guests and visitors can also enjoy giant-screen films at Fox Theatre or find themselves at the center of action in the Cinedrome 360 Theater. There's even an adventure ride.

Not long after the development of the casino, Foxwoods opened the luxurious **Foxwood Hotel** and **Two Trees Inn.** Within the resort are three gourmet restaurants, nine less-formal food outlets, an indoor pool, a health spa, a beauty salon, and a shopping concourse. Foxwoods continues to expand. Most recently there's been talk about creating a museum chronicling the history of the Native American, as well as a monorail to transport visitors quickly from one end of the resort to the other. To get here, take Exit 92 off I-95.

WHERE TO STAY

During much of the year, especially in high summer, Mystic is crowded with visitors who've come to tour famous Mystic Seaport. Though there are lots of lodging places, most will be full in July and August, so advance reservations are good to have.

Lodgings in Mystic proper are mostly hotels and motels, with a few guesthouses. In the nearby quiet village of Noank, a few miles south and east along Conn. 215, there are some quiet inns.

Hotels/Motels

In addition to the hostelries listed below, remember that the cluster of motels at Exit 90, the Conn. 27 interchange on I-95, includes several branches of big chains and several local establishments.

Comfort Inn

132 Greenmanville Ave., Mystic, CT 06355. ☎ **860/572-8531** or 800/228-5150. 120 rms. A/C TV TEL. $118–$139 double. All rates include continental breakfast. AE, DC, MC, V. Directions: Take I-95 to Exit 90.

The Comfort Inn at Mystic is clean, well located, and comfortable. It offers all the amenities you might expect of the major hotel chain, such as an outdoor pool and an exercise facility, direct-dial telephones, and individual climate control; some rooms even have whirlpool baths or Jacuzzis. The continental breakfast is served between 6 and 10am. The Eatery is the hotel's neighboring restaurant, and it serves breakfast, lunch, and dinner.

Inn at Mystic

At the junction of U.S. 1 and Conn. 27 (P.O. Box 216), Mystic, CT 06355. ☎ **860/536-9604** or 800/237-2415. Fax 203/572-1635. 68 rms. A/C TV TEL. $55–$225 double. Children stay free in parents' room. AE, DC, DISC, MC, V. Free parking. Directions: Follow U.S. 1 to the intersection with Conn. 27.

One of Mystic's longtime favorites is this expansive inn. The large complex has several different classes of accommodation in separate buildings, all set atop a hill overlooking the water. As you drive up, you first approach the tidy motel units in several large buildings. The office and the Flood-Tide Restaurant are here. The motel rooms are modern, clean, and attractive, with some colonial reproductions to put you in the proper mood for visiting old Mystic. Above the motel, along a drive shaded by large trees is the inn, a fine old mansion at the summit of the hill. Green lawns complete with miniature waterfall surround the house, which has a number of fine guest rooms decorated with period furniture and replicas. The inn's wide veranda is a favored place to sit and take in the view. Beyond the inn is the Gatehouse, a smaller building, also very pretty. The inn has its own boat dock, tennis court, pool and hot spa, and walking trail. This is a dependable favorite, worthy of your consideration. Rooms in the main mansion are most desirable.

Mystic Hilton

20 Coogan Blvd., Mystic, CT 06355. ☎ **860/572-0731** or 800/445-8667. Fax 860/572-0328. 184 rms. A/C TV TEL. $189 double. Additional person $20 extra. Children stay free in parents' room. AE, DC, DISC, MC, V.

Across from the Mystic Marinelife Aquarium and Olde Mistick Village is the Mystic Hilton. All the modern conveniences, comforts, and luxuries are here, in the guest rooms, in the indoor pool, and in the Mooring (the hotel restaurant) and Soundings (its lounge). It's just off Exit 90 of I-95.

Steamboat Inn

73 Steamboat Wharf, Mystic, CT 06355. ☎ **860/536-8300.** 10 rms. A/C TV TEL. $95–$250 double (depending on the season). All rates include continental breakfast. MC, V.

Located quite literally on the banks of the Mystic River, the Steamboat Inn is a lovely alternative to the areas larger hotels and motels. Antique-appointed rooms all have working fireplaces, and each is named for a famous schooner. Continental breakfast includes homemade baked goods, fresh fruit, coffee, tea and juice.

Taber Inn and Townhouses

29 Williams Ave., Mystic, CT 06355. ☎ **860/536-4904.** 28 rms. A/C MINIBAR TV TEL. May 15–Oct 30, $75–$150 single, $85–$185 double; Oct 31–May 14, $65–$150 single, $75–$185 double. Additional person $10 extra. MC, V. Directions: Go east on U.S. 1 a short distance to the motel, on the right-hand side.

This is more than a motel: Besides its very tidy motel rooms, it can rent you a room in a restored inn (1829), a restored farmhouse, a two-bedroom cottage, or two-bedroom town houses. In high summer, rooms go for $100 a double in the motel, about $15 less in the inn and farmhouse, about double that in the town houses.

Guesthouses

Harbour Inne & Cottage

Edgemont St. (U.S. 1; P.O. Box 398), Mystic, CT 06355. ☎ **860/572-9253.** 4 rms, 1 cottage. A/C TV. $55–$125 double; $150–$250 cottage. Additional person or pet $10 extra. No credit cards. Directions: From the Amtrak station, take the dead-end street to the right of the station, then turn right on to Edgemont Street; the guesthouse is on the left.

The Harbour Inne & Cottage is right next to the water, in a part of town that's part residential and part industrial but clean and quiet. The two small buildings of bright natural cedar, once a fisherman's house, are neat as a pin. In the guesthouse, the rooms are cozy and cheerful with that same honey-colored wood, a private bath with shower stall, a TV, and air conditioning. In the cottage next door are one bedroom (with a fireplace), a kitchen, bath, Jacuzzi, and sofas that convert to beds (the place can sleep up to six people). There's also a waterfront gazebo and boat dock.

✪ Randall's Ordinary

Conn. 2 (P.O. Box 243), North Stonington, CT 06359. ☎ **860/599-4540.** 15 rms. A/C. $75–$195 double. All rates include continental breakfast. AE, MC, V. Directions: Off I-95 drive a third of a mile north of Exit 92 on Conn. 2.

Randall's Ordinary is actually quite extraordinary. Situated on 27 acres, the inn and restaurant include the John Randall House (1685) and the Jacob Terpenning Barn, which was moved from New York and attached to a silo. The three rooms in the John Randall House don't have TVs or telephones, but they do have fireplaces and queen-size canopy or four-poster beds. One of the rooms has teal-green paneling, a large bathroom, a blanket chest, a table, and a Windsor chair. The rest of the rooms, located in the barn, have canopy or four-poster beds (either double or queen-size, some with trundles)—Room 4 has a brass bed—and three of the rooms have sitting-room lofts.

Randall's Ordinary also features hearth cooking (the colonial way) in its huge fireplace for breakfast, lunch, and dinner. Lunch is served daily from noon to 3pm and features a daily special such as roast pork loin or grilled venison sausage, a daily soup, and brick-oven–baked breads. A full meal will cost somewhere around $15 per person. If you'd like to try dinner here instead, arrive at 7pm for the one seating of the evening. Ready yourself to embark on a food odyssey from start to finish. You'll begin with hearth-roasted popcorn and Vermont Cheddar crackers while you decide on your main course and a beverage. Soup is your first course, and it's served at around 7:30pm. The menu changes daily as well as seasonally, and on any evening you'll have your choice of meat or poultry or seafood. Desserts also change daily and are served with fresh whipped cream and coffee or tea. This will all cost around $30 per person (plus tax and tip). A reservation is a must. On Saturday, seatings are at 5 and 7:30pm.

The Whaler's Inn

20 E. Main St., Mystic, CT 06355. ☎ **860/536-1506** or 800/234-2588. Fax 203/ 572-1250. 41 rms. Winter $65–$99; spring $79–$115; summer $89–$130; fall $85–$125. AE, MC, V. Directions: From I-95 North, take Exit 89, turn right onto Allyn Street, go left at the second light onto U.S. 1 and look for the sign just over the drawbridge. From I-95 South, take Exit 90, go left onto Conn. 27 to U.S. 1, go right on U.S. 1 and look for the sign.

In the main building of The Whaler's Inn there are traditionally decorated and furnished rooms with canopy beds, wingback chairs, humpback couches, and rich color schemes, such as Chinese red and forest green. The 1865 House has eight rooms decorated with dusty-rose carpets and floral bed coverings with green accents. Ask about special packages—they offer some good ones.

The hotel's restaurant, Bravo-Bravo, features Italian cuisine at reasonable prices.

WHERE TO DINE

The great number of Mystic's restaurants—and there are many of them—are part of the many hotels and motels. There are exceptions, however. One quite good restaurant is on the grounds of Mystic Seaport, just outside the admission ticket office. Other good places to dine are in the town of Mystic, south of Mystic Seaport; head south on Conn. 27, then right onto Main Street, to reach the center of town. The restaurants are located in the commercial district, on the far side of the quaint old bascule bridge.

At Mystic Seaport

41 North

21 W. Main St. ☎ **860/536-9821.** Reservations not accepted. Main courses $8.95–$22.95. AE, DC, MC, V. Sun–Thurs 11am–10pm, Fri–Sat 11am–11pm. Bar stays open until 1am. AMERICAN/ITALIAN.

In the center of Mystic, 41 North always has an interesting chalkboard menu out on the sidewalk. Last time I was there it listed fresh mako shark, fresh tuna steak, and a shore dinner featuring a one-pound lobster with a pound of steamed clams. Nautical flotsam, jetsam, and memorabilia decorate the dining room, and seafood fills the menu (along with prime rib and Italian specialties).

Seamen's Inne

65 Greenmanville Ave. ☎ **860/536-9649.** Reservations recommended. Main courses $10.95–$19.95. AE, MC, V. Mon–Thurs 11:30am–9pm, Fri–Sat 11am–10pm, Sun 11am–2pm and 3:30–10pm. SOUTHERN AMERICAN/SEAFOOD.

The Seamen's Inne, a beautiful colonial restaurant located at Mystic Seaport, features Yankee fare and seafood. At lunch, try the oyster stew or grilled mussels with garlic butter and lemon-honey-mustard dip to start. There are light lunches, sandwiches, and salads available, as well as more substantial fare, such as the Yankee pot roast, which comes with a vegetable and potato. Fish and chips is on both the lunch and dinner menus, and, of course, dinner also offers fresh fish. You might also consider trying the red beans and rice with smoked ham hocks and corn bread, or the Inne's carpetbagger (butterflied filet mignon with fried oysters and béarnaise sauce). There's a special Dixieland Country breakfast buffet served from 11am to 2pm every Sunday ($10.95 per person), which consists of southern fried chicken, bacon, sausages, scrambled eggs, cheddar-cheese grits, creamed chipped beef, waffles, chicken fried steak, fresh baked muffins, candied sweet potatoes, mashed potatoes, home fries, fried fish, biscuits and honey, plus a lot more (including the grand finale, chocolate bread pudding with whiskey sauce). There's also a children's menu.

⑤ 2 Sisters Deli

4 Pearl St. ☎ **860/536-1244.** Reservations not accepted. Main courses $2.50–$6.50. No credit cards. Daily 8:30am–7pm. AMERICAN.

Looking for just a sandwich, a salad, or dessert? Head here, just off Main Street, where the sandwiches are fresh and the menu is long. There are 42 sandwiches, plus various soups, bagels, salads, salad plates, cakes, pies, brownies, and cookies. Come for breakfast, lunch, a picnic, or an early supper, any day.

In Noank

⑤ Abbott's Lobster in the Rough

117 Pearl St. ☎ **860/536-7719.** Reservations not accepted. Dinner $14–$25. MC, V. First Fri in May–Labor Day, daily noon–9pm. Labor Day to mid-Oct, Fri–Sun noon–7pm. Directions: Follow Conn. 215 South to Noank, go left on Main Street, and then right on Pearl Street. SEAFOOD.

If you love seafood, if you love shore dinners, if you love the real New England, Abbott's is a must. Here you'll find a parking lot, a large restaurant, and numerous seaside picnic tables. Approach the cashier's window and order what you like: clam chowder, steamed clams or mussels, oysters, shrimp in the shell, steamed lobster, a lobster or crab roll, cheesecake, and carrot cake. Pay the tab and then take a table and wait for your number to be called. When your order is ready, you get to enjoy some of the finest seafood in the region. It's not fancy, but it's fantastically delicious. The lobsters at Abbott's are steamed (the way I do them), not boiled, and I can personally attest to the difference; a steamed lobster is sweeter and more tender. Abbott's handy tabloid newspaper-style menu bears full directions on how to eat a lobster. But when lobster is this good, you learn fast anyway.

STONINGTON

As you drive into the delightful village of Stonington, five miles east of Mystic along U.S. 1 and U.S. 1A, you'll cross a bridge over the railroad tracks, turn left, and proceed down Water Street, the town's main street. Water Street holds many boutiques, antiques shops, restaurants, and real estate offices. Beyond this commercial area is a residential one, ending in **Cannon Square.** The square is small, with two 18-pound cannons used in repelling a naval attack mounted by five English ships on August 10, 1814, during the War of 1812. The pretty square is surrounded by a neoclassical bank building, a fine old granite house, and several houses in Federal style.

Beyond Cannon Square, continue south along Water Street to visit the **Old Lighthouse Museum,** at 7 Water St. (☎ 860/535-1440), a fine old granite structure that was the first government lighthouse in Connecticut. Inside are displays of maritime gear from the days of wooden whaling and fishing craft, swords, firearms (some made right here in Stonington), local stoneware, toys, decoys, and 19th-century portraits. There's a special room for children's exhibits. Each season there's a changing feature exhibit. The museum is open May through October, Tuesday through Sunday from 11am to 5pm, daily July and Aug. Adults pay $3 admission; children 6 to 12 are charged $1; children under 6 are free.

WHERE TO STAY

The village of Stonington is a traditional New England seacoast village, just the place to stay if you want to escape the crowded highways and modern motels. Stonington's bed-and-breakfast guesthouse list is beginning to grow. If you can't get a room at the following place, drop by the **State of Connecticut Tourism Division Information Center,** off I-95 southbound at North Stonington, for help.

✪ Antiques & Accommodations

32 Main St., North Stonington, CT 06359. ☎ **860/535-1736.** 6 rms, 1 cottage. $99–$149 double weekdays; $129–$189 weekends; $230–$360 cottage rooms and suites. MC, V. Directions: Take Exit 92 off I-95, head west on Conn. 2 for 2¹/₂ miles, and turn right on Main Street; the inn is located two-tenths of a mile down, on the right.

The furnishings in the sitting room of this Victorian bed-and-breakfast inn change all the time because they're for sale. If you're an antiques lover, you'll like Antiques & Accommodations with its antique four-poster beds, blanket chests, Queen Anne and Empire chairs, Federal mirrors, and Oriental rugs. The cottage has two units and a three-room suite that are perfect for families, with brass beds, wicker pieces, wingback chairs (including a kid-size version), stenciling, and kitchens with electric stoves. The gardens are lovely, and outside on the stone patio you can sit and relax on the wooden garden furniture. The innkeepers use the herbs, berries, and vegetables grown in the garden to make the complimentary English breakfast that's served every morning by candlelight. At the formal dining table you might find walnut and banana waffles and ham steak with pumpkin bread.

WHERE TO DINE

Harbor View Restaurant

66 Water St., Cannon Sq. ☎ **860/535-2720.** Reservations recommended. Main courses $14–$22. AE, DC, MC, V. Daily 11:30am–10pm; brunch Sun 2–6pm. FRENCH.

As you enter from Water Street, the darkish, cozy bar is to your right, and it features a special menu of lighter fare for lunches, snacks, and suppers. In the dining rooms, the atmosphere is nautical, with lots of ocean views, bentwood, and low lamps, but the service is polished and professional as well as friendly. The menu here is fairly classical, with appetizers such as Brie en croûte (baked in puff pastry), French onion soup, and smoked salmon. Your main course might be peppered tenderloin of beef with brandy, mushrooms, and heavy cream; or coquilles St-Jacques, with mushrooms, tiny shrimp, and white-wine sauce. There's a wide variety of seafood featured, of course.

Noah's

113–115 Water St. ☎ **860/535-3925.** Reservations recommended. Main courses $8–$17; breakfast $8; dinner $14–$25.MC, V. Tues–Sat 7–11am, Sun 7am–noon; Tues–Sat 11:15 am–2:30pm, Sun 12:30–2:30pm; Tues–Thurs and Sun 6–9pm, Fri–Sat 6–9:30pm. REGIONAL/INTERNATIONAL.

Right in the center of Stonington's commercial district is this informal restaurant of two rooms with tin ceilings, booths sporting nice etched glass, and wood tables draped with cloths. Prints and paintings ornament the walls, and Noah's has a feeling of the authentically old-fashioned. You can come for breakfast, when a tuck-in of the standard fare of eggs, pancakes, and muffins can be yours; or come for lunch, with a varied menu of light meals; or for dinner, you can order seafood, filet mignon, or pork chops and get vegetable, potato, salad, bread, and butter with your main course.

Skipper's Dock

66 Water St. ☎ **860/535-2000.** Reservations recommended. Dinner $11–$35. AE, CB, DC, MC, V. Daily 11:30am–4pm; 6–10pm. Closed Nov–Mar. SEAFOOD.

Behind the Harbor View is another restaurant under the same management, right by the docks and meant to be convenient to the yacht crews who tie up nearby. The restaurant has nice waterside decks set with dining tables, as well as two indoor dining rooms with bentwood furniture. The air smells of the sea, the landward wall of the restaurant is hung with hundreds of salvaged lobster buoys, and the sound of bell buoys wafts easily on the air. The menu here focuses on seafood. Have a big bowl of steamed clams, linguine with shrimp and clams, Stonington fish chowder, or fisherman's stew Portuguese. If you choose a fresh fish of the day, you can have it prepared four different ways: with herb butter, in a scallion-ginger sauce, with lobster sauce, or topped with honey-mustard sauce. For those who don't like fish, a few selections of steak and chicken are available.

6 Hartford

102 miles SW of Boston, 113 miles NE of New York City, 74 miles W of Providence, 34 miles E of Litchfield

Hartford is Connecticut's capital, a fairly small (pop. 150,000) and manageable city with an admirable range of attractive architectural styles and a business-like spirit. It is and has been a city with a good amount of wealth, much of it generated by the tens of thousands of workers who sit in the thousands of offices of Hartford's great insurance companies and banks. Insurance companies seem to have a penchant for expressing their wealth and prestige through skyscrapers like the Prudential Tower in Chicago, and the John Hancock Tower in Boston, among others. Hartford has four dozen insurance companies and therefore lots of skyscrapers. The downtown area has been given a new attractiveness by redevelopment, which has left most of the buildings of great historical value intact.

The city was founded by the Rev. Thomas Hooker, who left Newtown (Cambridge, Mass.) on foot with a band of followers in 1636 after a dispute with another clergyman over the strict rules that governed the colony of Massachusetts Bay. In 1639 Hooker and others drafted the Fundamental Orders as the legal constitution of their settlement, and it is upon this early document that Connecticut bases its claims as the *first place in the world* to have a written

Hartford

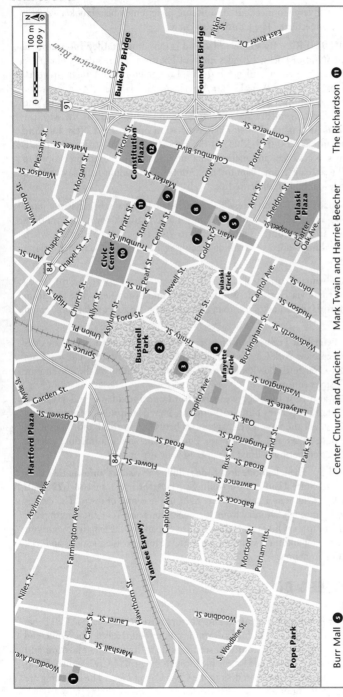

Burr Mall **5**
The Bushnell **4**
Bushnell Park **2**
The Capitol and Lafayette Square **3**

Center Church and Ancient
Burying Ground **7**
Civic Center **10**
Constitution Plaza **12**

Mark Twain and Harriet Beecher
Stowe Houses (Nook Farm) **1**
Old State House **9**

The Richardson **11**
Travelers Tower **8**
Wadsworth Atheneum **6**

1799

constitution. Every Connecticut auto license plate remembers Hooker when it proclaims Connecticut "The Constitution State."

GETTING THERE **By Plane** Hartford is served by **Bradley International Airport** in Windsor Locks, 12 miles north of Hartford. There's direct one-plane service between Bradley and more than 60 other North American airports, operated by United, TWA, Delta, American, and USAir. Buses leave the terminal for downtown Hartford and for Springfield, Mass., periodically, and limousines shuttle from Bradley to most cities in Connecticut. By the way, the Connecticut Aeronautical Historical Association operates the **New England Air Museum** (☎ 860/623-3305) at the airport, with more than 70 aircraft, plus engines, accessories, and memorabilia, on display. The collection is open to visitors all year, daily from 10am to 5pm. Admission for adults is $6.50; children 6 to 11, $3; for children under 6, free.

By Car Hartford is easily accessible by Interstate highways, being at the junction of I-91 and I-84. Hartford is very much a commuters' town, and traffic is very heavy at rush hours. The best day to visit the city is Saturday, when almost everything is open and parking is easily available. On Sunday many places are closed.

By Train **Amtrak** runs trains daily from New York City to Boston along the inland route via Hartford, Windsor Locks, and Springfield. The trip from New York to Hartford takes less than 3 hours; from Boston to Hartford, about $2^{1}/_{2}$ hours.

By Bus **Peter Pan Trailways, Bonanza,** and **Vermont Transit** all operate daily buses between New York City, New Haven, Hartford, and Boston. The trip from New York to Hartford takes about 3 to $4^{3}/_{4}$ hours, depending on the line and the number of stops en route.

Bonanza also runs buses between Hartford and Providence and Hyannis; Vermont Transit operates buses to Vermont, New Hampshire, Montréal, and Québec City. All the large lines have buses between Hartford and Boston. In Hartford, buses arrive at 1 Union Place. For schedules and information, call the branch offices of the above-listed bus lines in your city or town.

ESSENTIALS The **telephone area code** is **860.** The **visitors' information desk** is in the Old State House, 800 Main St., Hartford, CT 06103 (☎ **860/ 522-6766**), in Old State House Square, right in the center of town. The desk is open Monday through Saturday from 10am to 5pm. There is no short-term parking convenient to the Old State House, so plan to park for the length of your visit in a downtown lot and then walk to the Old State House to ask questions and pick up maps and brochures.

WHAT TO SEE & DO
THE WALK

The **Greater Hartford Convention and Visitors Bureau** (☎ 800/446-7811) has organized all the sights in Hartford's downtown into what is called **The Walk,** and has published this walking tour and scenic guide in its annual "Hartford and Southern New England Guide," available through the mail (1 Civic Center Plaza) or from the visitors information desk in the Civic Center Plaza. The following are the highlights of The Walk.

(*Note:* In addition to its other sights, Hartford has a surprising number of palatial houses, most still occupied by wealthy families. Anyone interested in domestic architecture should take a drive through the residential sections northwest of downtown.)

The Old State House Pure Bulfinch, the Old State House served as Connecticut's state capitol from 1796 to 1878. You can see the inside Monday through Saturday from 10am to 5pm and Sunday from noon to 5pm; admission is free. On the Main Street side, have a look at the statue of Hartford's founder, the Rev. Thomas Hooker (1586–1647). Compare this state house with the one in Boston or the Capitol in Washington, both Bulfinch achievements. Outdoor concerts are often held in the precincts of the Old State House, and three galleries inside hold exhibits which change frequently. Warm weather finds farm markets, festivals, and concerts outside on the large lawn. The information center and museum shop are open during regular hours.

The Richardson North on Main Street a block from the Old State House is the mass of Connecticut brownstone built in 1877 by Henry Hobson Richardson for the Cheneys, a Connecticut family of silk manufacturers (for many years it was known as the Cheney Building). It now houses the Brown, Thomson & Company restaurant (see "Where to Dine," below).

Constitution Plaza Just east of the Old State House is Constitution Plaza, Hartford's triumph of urban renewal. The plaza has nice copses of trees (one of willows), a fountain designed not to splash or spray passersby in the wind, and the elliptical Phoenix Mutual Life headquarters, perhaps Hartford's most striking building. Hartford is particularly rich in works by Alexander Calder (who lived and worked in the state), and one of his mobiles is suspended from the ceiling of the commercial banking room in the Connecticut Bank and Trust Company.

Travelers Tower Between Main and Prospect Streets, right next to the Old State House, rises Hartford's tallest observation point, the **Travelers Insurance Company Tower** (☎ 800/842-6568). On weekdays in summer from 10am to 3pm there are tours to the top of the building, leaving every half hour on the hour and half hour. In the 30 minutes spent at the top, you'll get the best possible view of the entire city, the suburbs, and the surrounding tobacco country. You must call and reserve a spot on the tours in advance. Please note that the elevator does not go all the way to the top of the tower, and visitors should be prepared to climb 100 steps. There is no handicapped access. The Travelers Tower stands on a spot where there was once a tavern. In this tavern, during a dispute between colonials and royal officials, Connecticut's royal charter disappeared and was hidden in the cavity of a nearby oak tree. This was the famous "Charter Oak" incident. The king's men ruled Connecticut illegally for a time (they could not find the charter and thus could not destroy the legal instrument of Connecticut's self-rule), but the charter survived and it's now on view at the State Library (see below).

Also note that tours are run off-season, but you must call to make reservations.

Wadsworth Atheneum Hartford's art museum, at 600 Main St. (☎ 860/278-2670), has a fine collection of more than 45,000 items of painting, sculpture, decorative arts, costume, textiles, Pilgrim-century furniture, and contemporary and African American art. Don't miss a visit. As you enter, ask for a guide leaflet to the collections. Major exhibits change seasonally, so there's always something new to see. The museum's pleasant cafe serves soups, salads, sandwiches, pasta, and a few heartier dishes at very reasonable prices ranging from $5 to $9. Admission costs $5 for adults, $4 for seniors, free for children under 13; free for everyone on Saturday before noon and all day on Thursday. The museum is open Tuesday through Sunday from 11am to 5pm.

Burr Mall   Between the Wadsworth Atheneum and the attractive city executive office building, Burr Mall is a shady, fragrant spot with a fountain and a fine—if incongruously placed—stabile of Calder's called *Stegosaurus* (1971).

Across Prospect Street from Burr Mall, take a look at the interesting buildings: the **Masonic Temple** and the **Hartford Times Building.** The facade for the latter was once the front of a church in New York, which explains its architecture, odd for a newspaper building!

Center Church & Ancient Burying Ground   Across Main Street from the Travelers Tower is the site of the first church in Hartford, whose pastor was Thomas Hooker (he's thought to be buried under the church). The present church dates from 1807. The gravestones in the cemetery date as far back as 1640.

Bushnell Park   With 500 trees of 150 varieties, Bushnell Park is an oasis in the middle of the busy city. It was laid out by the famous landscape architect Frederick Law Olmsted, the Hartford resident who also landscaped Central Park in New York, the Fenway parks in Boston, and Montréal's Mount Royal Park. The twin-towered Gothic gateway on Trinity Street is Hartford's memorial to its Civil War dead. Be sure to visit the park's carousel, one of the finest restored merry-go-rounds you'll ever see, complete with calliope and automatic drums and cymbals. Rides cost 10¢, and it is by no means only children who take advantage of this low price. The carousel has three types of seating accommodation: "lovers' chariots" for the unadventurous, stationary wooden horses, and horses that move up and down. Remember to grab at the brass ring. Note that the carousel doesn't operate on Sunday, and you must see it with all the lights on and the music trilling to really get the feeling.

The Capitol & Lafayette Square   Richard M. Upjohn is the architect responsible for the Hartford state capitol, a great potpourri of architectural styles and periods, including Gothic niches housing soldiers in Civil War uniforms. For all its eclecticism, the capitol is fine to look at. At one time it was topped by a statue of *The Genius of Connecticut,* a woman. You can see that statue inside the building, and also the battle flags and memorabilia preserved here. Across Capitol Avenue is the **State Library** and **Supreme Court,** a pretty building housing the paper treasures of Connecticut history, including the famous royal charter once hidden in an oak tree. Besides preserving the documents, the library is now the repository of the Samuel Colt collection of more than 1,000 firearms. All together, the collections here make up the **Museum of Connecticut History,** (231 Capitol Ave., ☎ 860/566-3056) and you can visit it Monday through Friday from 9am to 4:45pm and Saturday from 9am to 12:45pm; no charge for admission.

The Bushnell   Near the capitol and State Library, in Lafayette Square, is the Bushnell, where many of the city's concerts, plays, and recitals are held. The interior is of the purest 1930s art deco, a style that has seen a resurgence in recent years. The Vienna Boys Choir or the Boston Symphony—you may find either on the playbill here depending on current schedules. For current information, call the Bushnell Memorial (☎ 860/246-6807).

The Civic Center   A complex of several city blocks, the Civic Center follows some of the best modernistic architecture, with fine shopping arcades, lots of open spaces, and mezzanines with hanging plants, small potted trees growing up a story or two, and meeting rooms, restaurants, and clubs. The thing to do, especially on a hot summer day, is to enter the air-conditioned spaces and wander around enjoying the sights, perhaps stopping for a snack or a meal.

The Mark Twain House   The famous American author from Hannibal, Mo., settled in Hartford in the early 1870s. One of the wealthiest young men in town, Samuel Clemens (1835–1910) had a house designed by Edward Tuckerman Potter. It was finished in 1874 at a cost of $131,000, and is extremely rich in the sort of detail that makes Victorian architecture so much fun to inspect. Twain lived here for 17 years, moving out only after bad investments forced him to take a lecture tour of Europe for some quick money. He loved this place for the best years of his life, and *Tom Sawyer, Huckleberry Finn, Life on the Mississippi, The Prince and the Pauper,* and *A Connecticut Yankee in King Arthur's Court* were all written while he lived here. To see the Mark Twain House, 351 Farmington Ave. (☎ 860/493-6411), you must take the tour, which is just as well, for the guides have an encyclopedic knowledge of the house and its occupants. The Mark Twain House is open Monday and Wednesday through Saturday from 9:30am to 5pm and Sunday from noon to 5pm; between June 1 and Columbus Day, and in December, the museum is also open Tuesday from 9:30am to 5pm. Admission for the 45-minute guided tour is $7.50 for adults, $7 for seniors, $3.50 for children 6 to 12. See "Harriet Beecher Stowe House," below, for directions.

The Harriet Beecher Stowe House   In the same complex of buildings, known as Nook Farm, is a house once lived in by Harriet Beecher Stowe (☎ 860/525-9317). Although Stowe wrote *Uncle Tom's Cabin* while living in Brunswick, Me., she lived and wrote in Nook Farm from 1873 until she died in 1896. Lots of the original furnishings of the author's remain in this Victorian "cottage." The Stowe House is open Monday through Saturday from 9:30am to 4pm, Sunday noon to 4pm (the gift shop stays open until 4:30pm). Admission is $6.50 for adults, $6 for seniors, and $2.75 for children 6 to 16, under 6 are admitted free.

To get to the Mark Twain and Harriet Beecher Stowe houses, take Exit 46 off I-84, go right onto Sissan Avenue and then right again on Farmington Avenue for about 15 blocks. Look for the art deco steeple of Trinity Church, and four blocks later, turn left. If you want to take the bus, wait at the Old State House or along Asylum Street and take the E1 ("Westgate–Health Center"), E-2 ("Unionville"), E-3 ("Bishops Corner"), or E-4 ("Corbins Corner").

NEARBY ATTRACTIONS

The region around Hartford has numerous other sights to see. In West Hartford is the birthplace of America's first great lexicographer, Noah Webster. And the colonial town of Old Wethersfield, about 10 miles south of Hartford, has a treasure trove of old houses.

WEST HARTFORD

Noah Webster (1758–1843) was born in a farmhouse on the outskirts of Hartford. He lived there with his strict Calvinist parents and four siblings, helping to work the land until he was 16. Webster left home to attend Yale on the eve of the American Revolution, and was caught up in the intellectual ferment of the time. He served with the American forces and later returned to Hartford to practice law. Webster saw it as his purpose in life to give Americans a new "national language" to go along with their new order of government and society. By 1828, working alone with pen and paper, he had completed a 70,000-word dictionary, which included 12,000 words never previously included in a dictionary. The dictionary sold more than 300,000 copies in some years. Along with his *Elementary Spelling Book* and grammar, the dictionary standard-ized Americans' distinctive spelling, pronunciation, and usage. His spelling book alone sold more than one million copies annually after 1850, and that was in a nation of only 23 million people! After Webster, Americans no longer had to use schoolbooks and dictionaries written and published in England; thus, we are indebted to him for such simplified spellings as "honor" instead of the English "honour," and "neighborhood" instead of "neighbourhood."

West of central Hartford is Webster's boyhood home and a modern museum, the **Noah Webster House Museum of West Hartford History,** 227 S. Main St., West Hartford (☎ 860/521-5362). The house, a simple center-chimney colonial dwelling, is furnished authentically in period style, and costumed guides give you a tour and explain what life was like in the America of two centuries ago. A new permanent exhibition focuses on Noah Webster and his role in American history. There's a garden typical of the period with herbs and dye plants. Admission costs $5 for adults, $4 for seniors, and $1 for children 6 to 12; children under 6 are free. The museum is open from mid-July to August on Mondays, Tuesdays, Thursday, and Fridays, from 10am to 4pm; on Saturdays and Sundays from 1 to 4pm; from September to June, on Mondays and Tuesdays and Thursdays through Sundays, from 1 to 4pm. It's best to arrive before 3pm for the last tour. To get there, take I-84 to Exit 41.

Another museum of interest in West Hartford is the **Museum of American Political Life**, located at Hartford University, 200 Bloomfield Avenue (☎ 860/768-4090). It holds an enormous collection (said to be the largest anywhere) of presidential campaign memorabilia. Here you'll find everything from buttons to bumper stickers and posters. It's a great place to poke around for a couple of hours. The museum is open Tuesday through Friday from 11am to 4pm and Saturday and Sunday from noon to 4pm. Donations are appreciated.

If you've got the kids in tow, you might want to take them to the Science Center of Connecticut (950 Trout Brook Dr., ☎ 860/231-2824) where they'll be amused at the mini-zoo, planetarium, and by the many hands-on activities kids love. The center is open Tuesday through Friday from 10am to 4pm, Saturday from 10am to 5pm, and Sunday from noon to 5pm. Admission is $5 for adults and $4 for seniors and children ages 3 to 15. Children under 3 are admitted free of charge.

OLD WETHERSFIELD

Take I-91 south for about 10 miles to Exit 26 and follow the signs to the town.

Buttolph-Williams House

Broad St. ☎ **860/529-0460** or 860/247-8996. Admission $2 adults, $1 children. May–Oct, Wed–Mon 10am–4pm;Nov–Apr, Sat–Sun 10am–4pm.

This mansion from the early 1700s has excellent authentic period furnishings. The kitchen is especially good and may be the most real-to-life of any extant in New England. It has a fine collection of treenware, iron cooking utensils, a rare clock-jack, and settle.

Webb-Deane-Stevens Museum

211 Main St. ☎ **860/529-0612.** Admission $6 adults, $5 seniors, $2.25 students, $1 children 5–11, free for children under 5. May–Oct, Wed–Mon 10am–4pm (last tour at 3pm); Nov–Apr, Sat–Sun 10am–4pm (last tour at 3pm).

This museum is actually three separate houses that are situated on their original properties. The **Webb House,** built in 1752, was the site of a strategy conference between Gen. George Washington and his French ally, the Comte de Rochambeau, in 1781. At the conference, Rochambeau outlined his plan to engage the British at Yorktown. It worked and the battle ended the Revolutionary War. The house now contains period furnishings, fabrics, porcelain, and silver.

The **Isaac Stevens House** was built in 1788 as home to a leatherworker and still contains the family's original furnishings. Of particular note here are the collections of toys and women's bonnets.

Finally, the **Deane House,** built in 1766 by a member of the First Continental Congress (1774–76) and commissioner (ambassador) to France (1776), is an elegant place for an elegant gentleman, with some interesting architectural details. Although he was a patriot, Silas Deane was ill-used by some of his American diplomatic colleagues, and he found himself condemned for profiteering by Congress. He lived the rest of his life in exile, but in 1842 Congress made amends to his family and restored his good name and fortune.

Wethersfield Historical Society

150 Main St. ☎ **860/529-7656.** Old Academy, free; Keeney exhibits, $2 adults, $1 children 6–12, free for children under 6; Dunham House $3 adults, $2 children 6–12, free for children under 6. Old Academy, Tues–Thurs and Sat 1–4pm; Keeney, Tues–Sat 10am–4pm, Sun 1–4pm; Dunham, Tues–Sat 10am–4pm, Sun 1–4pm.

If you've now become intrigued by Wethersfield's deep history, drop in at the Historical Society, located in the Old Academy, a fine Federal-style brick building dating from 1804.

The society is in charge of the nearby Keeney Memorial Cultural Center at 200 Main St., with visitor orientation, a museum shop, and exhibits on Wethersfield, and also the Dunham House, which had just opened when this book was going to press.

WHERE TO STAY

As of this writing, Hartford has no wonderful little hotels and inns made from converted Victorian townhouses or renovated farmhouses on the city's outskirts. The lodging stock here is large business-oriented downtown hotels and highway motels. Generally speaking, the hotels offer more convenient locations. Many of them are within a few minutes' walk of all the downtown sights. The motels, on the other hand, are not really very far out of the city, and they offer clean and comfortable accommodations at moderate, and even budget, prices.

Note: If you're coming to Hartford for a weekend, you'd do well to make arrangements to stay in a downtown hotel. Most of the hotels feature weekend package plans that can save you substantial amounts of money from regular rates. In any case, regular weekend rates are significantly lower than the rates charged on business days. In many cases, this rule holds for the highway motels also.

Finally, if you're willing to stay some distance out of the city and just drive in for the day, the surrounding countryside has some lovely old inns in quiet small towns.

Downtown

Holiday Inn Hartford Downtown–Civic Center

50 Morgan St., Hartford, CT 06120. ☎ **860/549-2400** or 800/HOLIDAY. 343 rms. A/C TV TEL. $99–$125 double. Additional person $10 extra. Children stay free in parents' room. AE, DC, DISC, MC, V. Parking $5 per night in hotel garage.

Conveniently located on the northern side of I-84, with access to Main Street's shopping, the Old State House, and the Civic Center, the Holiday Inn offers comfortable guest rooms, some with views of the river. Services and facilities include an outdoor pool, an exercise room, a guest laundry, a gift shop, a business center, and a full-service restaurant/lounge. There's a complimentary shuttle service to and from Bradley International Airport.

Ramada Inn–Capitol Hill

440 Asylum St., Hartford, CT 06103. ☎ **860/246-6591** or 800/272-6232. 96 rms. A/C TV TEL. $60.95 double. AE, CB, DC, MC, V.

The Ramada, near the Amtrak train station and the Greyhound bus station, has a very convenient location. The hotel has the advantage of being small, which allows for more personal service, and is also quite moderately priced, considering its excellent location.

Sheraton Hartford

315 Trumbull St., Hartford, CT 06103. ☎ **860/728-5151** or 800/325-3535. Fax 860/522-3356. 383 rms. A/C TV TEL. $134–$144 double. AE, CB, DC, DISC, MC, V. Parking $10 per day.

This modern 15-story tower is without a doubt the most convenient hotel to the Hartford Civic Center and is also well located for seeing the sights in the center of the city. Being the city's largest hotel and the favorite with convention and meeting groups, it features a full list of services, including a pool and health club with sauna and conditioning equipment, a cocktail lounge, a parking garage, 55 shops, and bright, modern rooms. If you plan to be in Hartford over a weekend, take advantage of the weekend special rate.

The Stage Café restaurant specializes in New England and continental favorites that range from $15 to $25 at dinner; an extensive breakfast buffet and full lunch are also served.

Nearby

Super 8 Motel

57 W. Service Rd., Hartford, CT 06120. ☎ **860/246-8888** or 800/800-8000. Fax 860/246-8888. 104 rms. A/C TV TEL. $44.88 double. Additional person $4 extra. Children under 12 stay free in parents' room. Rates include continental breakfast. AE, DC, DISC, MC, V. Directions: Take Exit 33 off I-91, north of the intersection with I-84.

The inexpensive Super 8 is within a mile of the center of town. Rooms are simple but adequate, and the price is unbeatable. If you have a car and want to save money, this is the place to go.

WHERE TO DINE

Although it's not a particularly large or cosmopolitan city, Hartford has an interesting selection of restaurants. You should find it easy to please your appetite, your taste buds, and your budget, whatever they may be.

To satisfy a pang of hunger at any time of the day or night, Hartford's citizens head for the Hartford Civic Center, which has its own collection of restaurants and fast-food shops, some operating 24 hours a day. See "Specialty Dining in the Civic Center," below.

Brown, Thomson & Company

942 Main St. ☎ **860/525-1600.** Reservations suggested for parties of five or more. Main courses $7–$15. AE, DISC, MC, V. Mon–Thurs 11:30am–12:30am, Fri 11:30am–1:30am, Sat 5pm–1:30am, Sun 4pm–midnight. AMERICAN.

At least once, drop in here, just a one-block stroll north of the Old State House. The dark stone building (1877)—a wonder of American Romanesque architecture with lots of arched windows, columns, and turrets—was designed by Henry Hobson Richardson. The restaurant preserves the feeling of a century ago: matchboard walls, glass that's beveled or etched or stained, stamped-metal ceilings, ceiling fans, and even a great old elk's head. The menu lists everything from French onion soup and buffalo wings to broiled swordfish and prime rib of beef. You'll find pastas, barbecued ribs, and popcorn shrimp. You might get intellectual indigestion if you read the entire menu, but you're certain to find something you fancy. Dessert and drink offerings are equally profuse, from mud pie to chocolate-chip-cookie pie, and from frozen daiquiris (with or without alcohol) to Dom Perignon (at the retail-store price!). You can suit your budget as well as your appetite, spending anywhere from $12 to $35 for a meal. There's a special coloring-book menu and a strolling magician on the weekends for kids. For adults, there's live comedy on Friday and Saturday evenings. The bar features big-screen TVs and pool tables.

Specialty Dining in the Civic Center

If you enter from Asylum Street near the corner of Ann Street, you'll be on the Market Level. If you enter from Trumbull Street at the corner of Asylum Street, you'll be on Level One. There are a number of fast-food outlets here. Additionally, there are some full-service restaurants as well.

Of the full restaurants in the Civic Center, the best is **Gaetano's** (☎ 860/249-1629), open for lunch (Monday through Saturday from 11:30am to 2pm) and dinner (Monday through Saturday from 5 to 10pm). The setting here is casual but stylish, and the cuisine is continental, inspired by various Italian regions. Start with a hot antipasto and go on to "veal birds" Gaetano or lamb chops Vienna. Of course there's pasta as well, everything from fettuccine de francesca to penne garden bolognese. A full dinner will cost about $30 per person.

7 Litchfield's Lakes & Hills

Northwest of Hartford is tobacco country. The Connecticut River Valley has very good conditions for growing a premium wrapper leaf for cigars, the famous Connecticut Valley shade-grown tobacco. The long barns next to the fields are for drying; and part of the year the crop will be covered with gauze enclosures to protect it from too much direct sun—hence the "shade-grown" name.

A pleasant morning or afternoon can be spent driving through part of the tobacco country on the way to Litchfield, which is certainly among the most beautiful towns in New England. Litchfield County is all forest, rivers, and rolling hills—some of the prettiest country in this exceptionally pretty state.

Deeper into the northwest corner of the state, you'll come upon other charming towns, country inns, and resorts nestled in the Litchfield Hills (Connecticut's "Berkshires") and scattered on the shores of clear lakes. This is vacation country. In the charming old town of Salisbury, you're only 4 miles from the Massachusetts state line, 12 miles from the southern Berkshire town of South Egremont. (For the Berkshires, see Chapter 8.)

As you drive west toward the Litchfield Hills, you might want to make several attractive detours. Head out of Hartford on U.S. 44, and soon you'll be in **Avon,** where there's a nice hotel and restaurant. Farther along U.S. 44, just before Winsted, turn north for **Riverton,** the charming village where Hitchcock chairs are made and Seth Thomas clocks are sold. Back on U.S. 44, just eight miles west of Winsted, is the quiet ambience of **Norfolk,** where you'll find a lovely town green, three state parks, and Yale's Summer School of Music.

From Norfolk, you can continue west on U.S. 44 to Canaan, Salisbury, and Lakeville, or you can take U.S. 44 to Conn. 8 south through Torrington to U.S. 202 west, which will eventually bring you to **Litchfield.**

From Litchfield, drive along U.S. 202 south and west for 12 miles to New Preston. Then head north on Conn. 45, and you'll come to pretty **Lake Waramaug.** Continue north on Conn. 45 to Cornwall Bridge. Then head north on U.S. 7 and cross westward on Conn. 112 to pick up Conn. 41 north to **Salisbury;** or take Conn. 4 west from Cornwall Bridge to Sharon, then Conn. 41 north through Lakeville to Salisbury.

If you want to go on once up in Connecticut's northwest corner, you're very close to one of America's oldest and finest resort areas, the Berkshire Mountains of Massachusetts. The towns of South Egremont, Great Barrington, Lee, and Lenox have great charm, good restaurants, fine old inns and guesthouses, a bewildering array of cultural activities, and more antiques shops than you've ever seen before in one area at one time. For details, see Chapter 8.

AVON

Head out of Hartford on U.S. 44 to reach Avon, nine miles to the west.

WHERE TO STAY & DINE

Avon Old Farms Hotel

U.S. 44 and Conn. 10 (P.O. Box 1295), Avon, CT 06001. ☎ **860/677-1651.** Fax 860/677-0364. 160 rms. A/C TV TEL. Hotel, $109–$129 double; motel, $79 double; mini suites $165. AE, DC, DISC, MC, V.

For decades, residents of Hartford have escaped to the country to find this hotel at the intersection of U.S. 44 and Conn. 10. Escaping to the country doesn't mean giving up the city's comforts, for the spacious rooms at the hotel are furnished with king-size, queen-size, or twin double beds; antique reproduction lamps; mirrors; tables and chairs; clock radios; original paintings; and lots of little extras like shower caps, bath oil, and mending kits. You choose from several types of rooms here. Those in the hotel are larger and more modern and open onto a corridor; the motel-style rooms are a bit smaller and open (as motel rooms do) to the outside. The registration lobby is elegantly done in Georgian style, with comfortable sofas and a fine marble fireplace. Guests have the use of the hotel's restaurant, exercise room and sauna, hairstyling salon, and outdoor pool.

Litchfield Hills

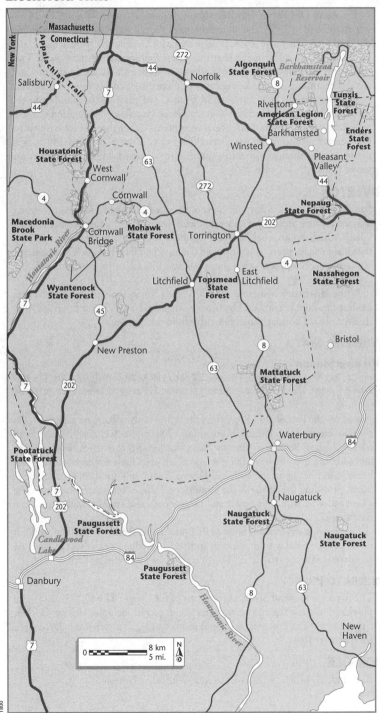

The **Avon Old Farms Inn Restaurant**, across the street (☎ 860/677-2818), was established in 1757, and all the rooms of the old inn now serve as charming dining rooms. The Forge Room is decorated with blacksmith's paraphernalia, and in chilly weather a fire in the hearth casts an appropriately mellow glow. Two other, smaller rooms near the front door are among the oldest in the inn and are also charming. A large dining room of more recent construction is decorated with Early Americana, dark-wood beams, old pine boards, and country curtains. The menu is American with continental touches: New England seafood, roast beef with popovers, and several continental dishes that change frequently. On Sunday, brunch is an eat-all-you-like buffet. Expect to spend $40 to $50 per person for dinner, with wine, tax, and tip included. Lunch and dinner are served daily.

RIVERTON

Farther along U.S. 44, a few miles west of the vast Barkhamsted Reservoir, in lovely wooded country (much of it state forest land) lies Riverton, a fine Connecticut hill village which looks much as it did in the 1800s. Driving or strolling along the village's main street, you'll pass the Grange Hall, the Hitchcock Museum, the Village Sweet Shop, and other shops selling antiques, herbs, and contemporary crafts.

At the **Hitchcock Museum** (☎ 860/738-4950), in Pleasant Valley, look over the fine furniture in Lambert Hitchcock's original factory. Visiting hours are April to December, Thursday through Sunday from noon to 4pm.

WHERE TO STAY

Old Riverton Inn

Conn. 20 (P.O. Box 6), Riverton, CT 06065. ☎ **860/379-8678** or 800/378-1796. Fax 860/379-1006. 12 rms. $75–$175 double. Additional person $15 extra. All rates include full breakfast. MC, V.

Just across the Farmington River from the center of the village, on Conn. 20, lies the Old Riverton Inn. Originally opened in 1796 by Jesse Ives, the inn (now listed on the National Register of Historic Places) has seen many changes, modifications, and additions over the years, but it retains much of its Early American charm, with heavy wood beams in the Colonial Dining Room and grindstones from Nova Scotia providing the paving in the Grindstone Terrace. The guest rooms are done in period style, with four-poster and canopy beds and country wallpaper; some have fireplaces.

Luncheon is served from noon to 2:30pm; dinner from 5 to 8:30pm (to 9pm on Saturday); Sunday from noon to 8pm; open Wednesday through Sunday. At dinnertime expect to pay $17.95 for veal française or broiled scallops.

WHERE TO PICNIC

The **Riverton General Store,** in the center of the village (☎ 860/379-0811), can provide all the raw ingredients for a marvelous picnic, including deli sandwiches, cheese, meat, other groceries, cold beer, and hot coffee. It's open seven days a week from 6am to 8pm.

NORFOLK

Back on U.S. 44, just eight miles west of Winsted, is Norfolk.

WHERE TO STAY

Manor House

69 Maple Ave. (P.O. Box 447), Norfolk, CT 06058. ☎ **860/542-5690.** 8 rms. $95–$190 double. All rates include breakfast. AE, MC, V.

In an area full of graceful homes–turned–bed-and-breakfasts, the Manor House stands with the best. This stucco, timber, and stone inn, on five acres, was built in 1898 by Charles Spofford, the architect of London's underground; that helps explain the English overtones. A massive stone fireplace and authentic Tiffany windows set the tone for the common rooms. The guest rooms have antique beds with down comforters; some rooms boast a fireplace, a private balcony, a two-person soaking tub, or a two-person Jacuzzi. A full breakfast, with homemade harvested honey, is served in one of three places: in bed, in an elegant dining room, or on the sunlit porch.

LITCHFIELD

Connecticut's answer to the pretty Massachusetts towns in the Berkshires is Litchfield, which a National Park Service writer has called "probably New England's finest surviving example of a typical late 18th-century town." The town was incorporated in 1719, and in the next 100 years it grew and prospered as a center for small industry and an important way station on the Hartford–Albany stagecoach route. With this prosperity came the urge, and the wherewithal, to build very fine, graceful houses, which is what the citizens did, making sure that the houses were set well back from the roadway. Progress in the 19th century robbed Litchfield of much of its wealth. Water-powered industry drove Litchfield's small-time craftspeople out of business, and the railroads bypassed the town. But the town's decline may have been a blessing in disguise. Today Litchfield retains its late 18th-century beauty, unsullied by the workers' tenements and textile mills that have changed the face of so many other New England towns.

WHAT TO SEE & DO

At a tiny **information booth** on the green, you can get a free booklet on the town's history, architecture, and activities, complete with a small map. The sightseeing is simple enough: Drive down South Street just to get the feel of the gracious neighborhood.

In addition to the following, other Litchfield curiosities include the **Ethan Allen House,** thought to be the one in which the famous patriot and leader of Vermont's "Green Mountain Boys" was born; it is at the southern end of South Street, in the road's fork. A **milestone** dating from 1787, which informed the traveler that it was 33 MILES TO HARTFORD, 102 MILES TO NEW YORK—J. STRONG AD 1787, stands on West Street, northern side, just at the end of the town green. And the **jail,** right on the green at the beginning of North Street, is connected to the bank next door! Whether it's for the convenience of thieves who wish to escape or for police who may nab burglars in the bank is not clear.

Haight Vineyard

29 Chestnut Hill Rd. ☎ **860/567-4045.** Free admission. Mon–Sat 10:30am–5pm, Sun noon–5pm.

On Chestnut Hill Road off Conn. 118, a mile east of Litchfield, this quaint and inviting place prides itself on being Connecticut's first farm winery (established

1975). Besides guided winery tours and wine tastings, you can take the Vineyard Walk, a self-guided tour of the vineyards during which you can inspect the types of grapes that make Haight wines.

Some of the favorite wines here are Convertside White, Chardonnay, Riesling, and Merlot. There's even a sparkling wine made in the classic *méthode champenoise*. Prices are moderate.

Litchfield Historical Society

7 South St. ☎ **860/567-4501.** Admission (including the Tapping Reeve House, see below) $3 adults, free for children. Mid-Apr to mid-Nov, Tues–Sat 11am–5pm, Sun 1–5pm.

The Litchfield Historical Society was founded in 1856 and is dedicated to preserving the history of Litchfield County. The museum has permanent exhibits in four of its five galleries, as in the Liggett Gallery, which highlights "Litchfield's Golden Age" (1780–1840), and the Nelson Gallery, which focuses on everyday life in the early 1800s. The Cunningham Gallery houses changing exhibits and community events.

Tapping Reeve House (1773)

82 South St. ☎ **860/567-4501.** Admission (including admission to the Historical Society museum, see above) $3 adults, free for children. Mid-May to mid-Oct, Tues–Sat 11am–4pm, Sun 1–5pm.

Stop at this house and take a look at the small, unprepossessing edifice beside it, which was the nation's first school of law, established here by Tapping Reeve in 1775 (the school moved into the one-room building in 1784). North Street is as attractive as South Street, and after a drive has given you the lay of the land, park at the green and stroll along either street to see the houses more closely. The hours and admission information is for both the Tapping Reeve House and Law School.

White Memorial Conservation Center

80 Whitehall Rd. ☎ **860/567-0857.** Trails, free. Museum, $2 adults, $1 children 6–12, children under 6 free. Museum, Mon–Sat 9am–5pm, Sun noon–4pm. Grounds are always open.

South of U.S. 202, just $2^1/2$ miles west of Litchfield, this is the state's largest nature center, with more than 35 miles of trails open year-round for hiking, cross-country skiing, and horseback riding. Some of the trails are interpretive nature trails that allow you to observe the bird life of a marsh pond. The Holbrook Bird Observatory is an area that has been designed specifically to attract birds in all seasons. There are sheltered viewing stations in this area. Also on the property is a museum that includes dioramas, mounted specimens, live animals, a touch center, and a children's room.

LAKE WARAMAUG

From Litchfield, drive along U.S. 202 south and west for 12 miles to New Preston. Then head north on Conn. 45 and you'll come to Lake Waramaug. Attractive inns front Lake Waramaug, as does a state park with picnic and camping facilities. **Lake Waramaug State Park,** New Preston, CT 06777 (☎ 860/868-0220), has 88 campsites open May 15 through Labor Day. You can reserve in advance, but only by mail. Picnic grounds and swimming are here, too.

Next door to the Hopkins Inn is the **Hopkins Vineyard,** on Hopkins Road in Warren (☎ 860/868-7954). The quaint red-barn winery is open for tours and tastings from 10am to 5pm seven days a week from the beginning of May through the end of the year. From January 2 through April, you can visit on Friday,

Saturday, and Sunday only, from 11am to 5pm. The winery is closed New Year's Thanksgiving, and Christmas Days.

Whoever heard of a vineyard in Connecticut? You'll be telling all your friends about Connecticut wines once you taste Hopkins's fine, dry Seyval Blanc, perfect for a seafood meal at the inn across the street. Wine prices are moderate and quality is high. The vineyard is not affiliated with the Hopkins Inn, although the vineyard barn was obviously part of the same estate at one time.

WHERE TO STAY

The Hopkins Inn, listed under "Where to Dine," also has rooms for rent.

The Boulders Inn

Rte. 45, New Preston, CT 06777. ☎ **203/868-0541.** 17 rms. Modified American Plan $250–$300 double; bed and breakfast plan $200–$250 double. Modified American Plan rates include breakfast and dinner. AE, MC, V.

Nestled in the Berkshire Hills, the luxurious Boulders Inn overlooks Lake Waramaug. There's a private beach for swimming, and canoes, sunfish, bicycles, and a tennis court are all available for guest use. The main building was constructed in 1895 of fieldstone and shingles and features six rooms, all of which are decorated with Victorian touches. In addition, there are four cottages (each holds two rooms) and the carriage house (with three rooms). Each cottage room has a fireplace and a porch that faces the lake.

The Boulders also has a fine dining establishment featuring creative Continental cuisine. It's open for breakfast daily and dinner in the spring and summer every day except Tuesday. In winter the restaurant is open for dinner from Thursday to Sunday only.

Inn on Lake Waramaug

North Shore Rd., New Preston, CT 06777. ☎ **860/868-0563** or 800/LAKE-INN. Fax 860/868-9173. 23 rms. A/C TV TEL. $204–$229 double. Children 1–14, $45; under 1, free. All rates include breakfast and dinner. AE, MC, V.

This is actually a mini-resort with all kinds of attractions. An indoor pool, a tennis court, air-conditioned rooms, a restaurant, and water sports (rowing, canoeing, sailing) are among the many offerings. There's even a small launch designed like an old "showboat" for tours of the lake. Even so, the inn retains an antique flavor. Only five guest rooms are in the original inn, while the others are in more modern but attractive guesthouses. Most rooms have working fireplaces. The inn offers many special events, like old-fashioned ice harvesting and "Turkey Olimpiks," which have become traditions over the years.

WHERE TO DINE

Hopkins Inn

Hopkins Rd., New Preston, CT 06777. ☎ **860/868-7295.** Reservations recommended; required on Sat. Main courses $15–$19. No credit cards. May–Oct, Tues–Sat noon–2pm; Apr–Dec Tues–Thurs 6–9pm, Fri–Sat 6–10pm, Sun 12:30–8pm. Directions: From Conn. 45, follow the shore road around Lake Waramaug to the inn. INTERNATIONAL.

Not far from where the shore road rejoins Conn. 45, look for signs that point the way to this graceful old mansion set on a hill above the lake. The menu changes daily, but you can be sure of finding interesting, appetizing dishes. I had a difficult choice between clams casino and smoked salmon to start, and an even harder time choosing among Backhendl (chicken) with lingonberries, steamed lobster, wienerschnitzel, and live trout meunière (you can choose your own trout from the tank!). When it came to those Austrian desserts, the choice was impossible. In warm weather, you can dine on the shady patio outside, with a grand view of the lake.

The Hopkins Inn is most famous for its restaurant, but 11 rooms and 2 apartments are for rent as well, April through December. If you share a bath, a double room will cost $61; with private bath, prices start at $66.

EN ROUTE TO SALISBURY

Continue north on Conn. 45 to **Cornwall Bridge,** famous for its picturesque covered bridge. **Housatonic Meadows State Park** (☎ 860/672-6772) is here with camping and picnic areas, north of town on U.S. 7. Head north on U.S. 7, then cross westward on Conn. 112 to pick up Conn. 41 north to Salisbury; or take Conn. 4 west from Cornwall Bridge to Sharon, then Conn. 41 north through Lakeville to Salisbury.

SALISBURY

Salisbury is an aristocratic, historic town on the edge of the Berkshires. Late in September there's a big flea market here, and at the height of the fall foliage color, the Salisbury Antiques Fair is held in the town hall. Come any time of year, though. The town is pretty, tranquil, surrounded by gorgeous country, and only 20 miles from the heart of the Berkshires' summer and winter activities. Stay in Cornwall Bridge on the way if you like, and consider a short trip to Lakeville for a meal.

WHERE TO STAY AND DINE

Under Mountain Inn

482 Undermountain Rd., Rte. 41, Salisbury, CT 06068. ☎ **860/435-0242.** Fax 860/435-2379. 7 rms. $170–$200 double. Special packages are available. MC, V.

If you're looking for a special place to spend a romantic weekend, the Under Mountain Inn is a perfect choice. Built in the early 1700s, it's situated on three acres of birch-, fir-, and maple-dotted land and is rumored to have the oldest thorned locust tree on its property. Rooms are individually decorated. One has a queen-size four-poster bed, wingback chairs, and a bathroom with a beautiful cedar ceiling. The Covent Garden room has been done in English Country style and features a five-foot tub. A full English breakfast is served on most mornings.

There are several dining rooms in the inn's restaurant, each of which has a working fireplace (great in winter). The pub, with its antique paneling, is quite charming. The evening menu might include Scottish salmon, roast goose, pork Normandie, or everyone's British favorites, bangers and mash, shepherd's pie, and steak-and-kidney pie. Dinner is served to the public on Friday and Saturday nights by reservation only from 6 to 9:30pm. If you're a guest at the inn, you may dine in the restaurant every night during the week at 7pm. Main courses range in price from $11 to $19.

New Hampshire

"**L**IVE FREE OR DIE" says the motto on every auto license plate from New Hampshire, echoing the stirring words of Gen. John Stark, victor at the Battle of Bennington (1777) and a New Hampshire native. New Hampshire folk are still very patriotic in an old-fashioned way, and committed to material progress: Modern facilities abound, and the road system is perhaps the best maintained in New England. On a vacation, "living free" in New Hampshire is a snap—mountains, beaches, lakes, amusements, special activities, and good restaurants are all available to the visitor.

SEEING NEW HAMPSHIRE

On our tour through New Hampshire, we'll look first at the state's seacoast. (Yes, New Hampshire has a seacoast!) Next we'll visit the charming colonial town of Portsmouth on the border with Maine. Then we'll head north into the state's heart, passing through Manchester, the state's largest city, and Concord, its capital, on our way to Lake Winnipesaukee. From this veritable inland sea, we'll head north again into the White Mountains National Forest and the skiing/hiking center of North Conway, then even farther north to Bretton Woods. Moving west, we'll cover Franconia Notch, North Woodstock, and Waterville Valley. Finally, we'll visit Lake Sunapee and then Hanover, the hometown of Dartmouth College.

Throughout New Hampshire, a **rooms-and-meals tax** of 8% will be added to your hotel, motel, or inn bill, and you'll also have to pay it every time you have a meal in a restaurant. Except where noted, tax is not included in the prices listed.

New Hampshire's **telephone area code** is **603**.

GETTING THERE   New Hampshirites are committed to highway travel, so air links and rail lines are played down in favor of bus and car. Amtrak, in fact, has no trains in New Hampshire proper, although it does run along the New Hampshire Vermont border for a bit, stopping in Brattleboro, Bellows Falls, Essex Junction (near Burlington), and White River Junction on the route between New York and Montréal.

By Limousine & Bus   Airport limousines run regularly from Boston's Logan Airport to many points in New Hampshire. First Class Limousine (☎ **800/252-7754** or **603/883-4807**) goes from

What's Special About New Hampshire

Museums
- Strawbery Banke, in Portsmouth, 10 acres of 18th-century buildings brought back to life and filled with working artisans.
- Manchester's Currier Gallery of Art's surprisingly good collection, beautifully displayed.
- A visit to a Shaker village at Canterbury—you can even share in a traditional dinner.

Cool for Kids
- A cruise on the MS *Mount Washington* on Lake Winnipesaukee from Weirs Beach.
- A ride up a mountainside on the historic Mount Washington Cog Railway.
- A nostalgic train ride through the mountains on the Conway Scenic Railroad in North Conway Village.
- A visit to the Old Man of the Mountain at Franconia Notch State Park.
- Gliding through the air in a gondola of the Cannon Mountain Aerial Tramway, near Franconia Notch.

Outdoor Adventures
- Hiking up Mount Washington, the highest peak in New England.
- Swimming, boating, and fishing on Lake Winnipesaukee.
- Cross-country skiing on 90 miles of trails starting from Jackson.
- Hiking and camping along the Appalachian Trail in the White Mountains National Forest.
- Traveling the scenic Kancamagus Highway from Lincoln to Conway.
- Canoeing from Center Conway on the Saco River.
- A hot-air balloon ride along the Connecticut River Valley.

Logan to Manchester, Merrimack, and Nashua and 30 other towns offering a shared limousine or town car. You must reserve in advance.

C&J Trailways runs hourly daily trips from Logan to New Hampshire's seacoast region and Portsmouth; call for schedules and reservations (☎ **603/431-2424** in Portsmouth, or 800/258-7111 in New York and New England).

Concord Trailways, 7 Langdon St., Concord (☎ **603/228-3300,** or toll free 800/639-3317 in New England), has bus service from Boston through Manchester and Concord to Laconia on Lake Winnipesaukee; from there the bus continues to Plymouth and through Franconia. Concord Trailways also has buses from Boston to Conway, North Conway, Glen, Jackson, Pinkham Notch AMC Camp, Gorham, and on to Berlin.

Vermont Transit, operating out of Boston's Greyhound terminal near the Park Plaza Hotel (☎ **617/292-4700** or **800/451-3292, 800/642-3133** in Vermont), has routes from Portland, Me., to St. Johnsbury, Vt., via Boston, besides running from Logan Airport in Boston to the cities of Manchester, Concord, and Hanover. Vermont Transit also runs buses from Montréal south into Vermont and a few points in New Hampshire, but Montréal visitors will have to transfer at least once to reach most of the vacation locations in the state. Vermont Transit buses depart from the Voyageur Terminal in Montréal (☎ **514/287-1590,** or 800/451-3292).

New Hampshire

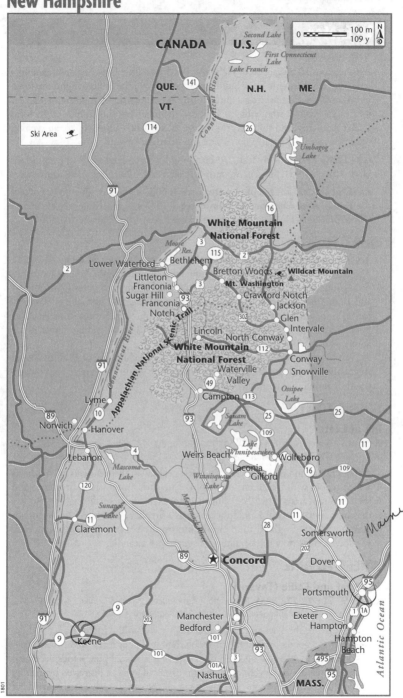

1   Exeter

45 miles N of Boston, 10 miles SW of Portsmouth

Exeter, about 10 miles west of Hampton Beach, is a little New England town dotted with Georgian-style brick buildings. Founded by John Wheelwright, the town served as New Hampshire's capital during the American Revolution. Today, it hosts many visitors who come to walk the quaint streets, the campus of the local **Exeter Academy,** and along the riverbanks. Exeter makes a fine stop for an evening meal or a romantic stroll and as a side trip from Portsmouth.

GETTING THERE   By Car   At Hampton I-95 Exit 2, take N.H. 51 west to the N.H. 101 east/N.H. 108 Portsmouth/Stratham exit; follow N.H. 108 to Exeter.

ESSENTIALS   The **telephone area code** is **603.** If you have questions, contact the **Exeter Area Chamber of Commerce,** 120 Water St., Exeter, N.H. 03833 (☎ 603/772-2411), open Monday through Friday from 8:30am to 4:30pm.

WHAT TO SEE

The **American Independence Museum,** 1 Governor's Lane (☎ 603/772-2622), displays 17th- and 18th-century documents and furnishings. Among its prized possessions are an original seven-page copy of the United States Constitution and an original Order of the Purple Heart Award designed by George Washington. It's open May to mid-October, Wednesday through Sunday from noon to 5pm. Adults pay $4, children 6 to 12 are charged $2, and children under 6 are admitted free.

For more than 200 years, the beautiful Georgian architecture of **Phillips Exeter Academy** has attracted students from around the world. Be sure to stop by and wander around the campus.

WHERE TO STAY

Inn of Exeter

90 Front St. Exeter, N.H. 03833. ☎ 603/772-5901 or 800/782-8444. Fax 603/778-8757. 50 rms, 1 suite. TV TEL. $67–$95 double; $170 suite. AE, DC, DISC, MC, V. Free parking.

This Georgian inn is a wonderful romantic getaway in the trendy town that hosts a prep school with the accent on preppy. The parlor rooms have fireplaces, and the restaurant has a porchlike country atmosphere and a small cozy bar. Rooms may have four-poster beds, and the suite has a fireplace. This is an ideal overnight stop on a New England tour in autumn or any season. At Christmas, each window in this lovely brick building is aglow with a candle.

WHERE TO DINE

The Loaf and Ladle (Tavern)

9 Water St. ☎ 603/778-8955. Reservations not required. Salads $3; main courses $7–$11. AE, DC, DISC, MC, V. Mon–Sat 7:30am–9pm, Sun 9am–9pm. CAFE.

I dropped into the Loaf and Ladle after a rainy visit to the Inn of Exeter and decided it was a good opportunity for a scone and tea. They make all their own bakery products, including cinnamon buns. Inside is seasoned pine woods decorated with trout pictures. The view of the Exeter River will only be distracted by the folk music often played evenings. You might sample the stews, sandwiches, or salad bar and even sit out on the deck in good weather.

Masseno's—The Cook's Choice

33 Water St. ☎ **603/778-7585.** Reservations not required. Soups $2.95–$3.50; salads $2.50; sandwiches $4.50; main courses $9–$13. MC, V. Mon–Wed 10am–5pm, Thurs–Sat 10am–8:30pm. AMERICAN/REGIONAL.

The river running behind the back door adds to the rustic, country appeal of Masseno's. They sell cookware, coffee beans, spices, and food. It's the closest this town gets to having a gourmet shop. You might cozy up to the counter and order curry-broccoli-Cheddar soup, a roast chicken BLT sandwich, or something more original. They've just begun serving dinner. An outdoor cafe operates in summer. It's worth a quick look.

SPECIALTY DINING

Chocolatier

27 Water St. ☎ **603/772-5253.** Reservations not required. From $1.25. MC, V. Mon–Sat 9:30am–5:30pm. DESSERTS/CHOCOLATE.

Everything here is a treat from the white-, milk-, and dark-chocolate items to the truffles, creams, and peppermint patties. You can even buy a chocolate greeting card for chocolate lovers back home. And they'll mail your purchase, if you like.

The Coffee Mill

107 Water St. ☎ **603/778-4801.** Reservations not required. Specialty coffees, bagels, croissants $1–$3. No credit cards. Mon–Thurs 7am–6:30pm, Fri 7am–10pm, Sat 8am–10pm, Sun 9am–4:30pm. COFFEEHOUSE.

The Coffee Mill specializes in—what else?—coffee. Inside are black-and-white floors and a few tables. Stop by for tea, a fresh pastry, or an espresso.

2 Hampton Beach

45 miles N of Boston, 11 miles S of Portsmouth

Many visitors to New England forget that Vermont is the only New England state without a seacoast, and that New Hampshire is in fact a maritime state, even though its coastline is only about 20 miles long. The 20 miles are almost all beach, with some rocky headlands and coves, and four state parks with their own uncommercial stretches of beach.

GETTING THERE   By Bus   See the beginning of this chapter.

By Car   Take I-95 north or south and exit at the Hampton toll plaza. The beach is five minutes east.

ESSENTIALS   The **telephone area code** is **603.** If you have questions, contact the **Hampton Beach Area Chamber of Commerce,** 836 Lafayette Rd. (P.O. Box 790), Hampton Beach, N.H. 03842 (☎ **603/926-8717**).

WHAT TO SEE

Hampton Beach State Park is the most southerly, and the public parking and bathing facilities here are run in the clean, well-ordered way of state park management. But just north of the state park is the town of Hampton Beach, two streets wide (north along the waterfront, south along the inland street, as far as cars are concerned). Hampton Beach is a riot of closely packed motels and cottages, ice-cream and hot-dog stands, penny arcades, and watering places. Lights, glitter, and throbbing crowds of the young, tanned, and adventurous make it a nonstop circus, something out of a "beach party" movie, to revel in or abhor as your taste dictates.

WHERE TO STAY

Lamie's Inn

490 Lafayette Rd., Hampton, N.H. 03842. ☎ **603/926-0330.** Fax 603/929-0017. 32 rooms. TV TEL. Mid-May to mid-Sept, $69–$89 double; mid-Sept to mid-May, $59–$79 double. AE, DC, MC, V. Free parking.

This lively colonial-inspired inn was once affiliated with Omni hotels and today, under independent ownership, still welcomes seacoast guests as it has for decades. Individually decorated rooms feature some canopy beds, stenciled borders, armoires concealing TVs, and papered baths. Friendly folk run the inn, and there's a restaurant and tavern where you can spend your leisure time.

FROM HAMPTON BEACH TO PORTSMOUTH

North of Hampton Beach, the state park beaches at Rye Harbor and Wallis Sands are not as bubbly with activity as Hampton, but to some tastes are all the more pleasant for that. At the state park beaches in New Hampshire, expect to pay a small parking fee, which includes use of all other facilities as well.

The drive along U.S. 1A north to Portsmouth is very pretty, winding along the coast past a succession of ever more sumptuous and meticulously maintained summer mansions, still inhabited by the wealthy and powerful of New Hampshire, Maine, and Boston.

3 Portsmouth

55 miles N of Boston, 54 miles SW of Portland, 51 miles E of Manchester

Of the gracious maritime towns along the New England coast, Portsmouth is one of the prettiest and most interesting. A morning or afternoon spent wandering through the town's restored historic side streets, perhaps with lunch, tea, or dinner in one of its restaurants, is both relaxing and entertaining.

GETTING THERE **By Bus** See the beginning of this chapter.

By Car I-95, running between the Boston area and Portland, passes right by Portsmouth.

ESSENTIALS The **telephone area code** is **603.** The **Greater Portsmouth Chamber of Commerce** maintains a visitors information center at 500 Market St. (Exit 7 off I-95), Portsmouth, N.H. 03801 (☎ **603/436-1118**), and also an **information kiosk** in Market Square.

WHAT TO SEE & DO

Strawbery Banke Outdoor Museum

Marcy St. ☎ **603/433-1100.** Admission $10 adults, $7 children 7–17, free for children 7. Daily 10am–5pm. Closed Nov–Apr. Directions: Follow the directional signs, with arrows, posted throughout the town and on approach roads toward the waterfront, just south of the U.S. 1 bridge.

Portsmouth's jump from wilderness to settlement started in 1630, when a group of settlers sailed into the Piscataqua River's mouth in search of fresh water and good land. As they climbed up the rise from the shore, they found not only the water and land they'd been looking for but also wild strawberries, which delighted them so much that they named the place Strawbery Banke. Today that name serves to identify the center of the city's historic restoration effort, a 10-acre section of buildings dating from 1695 to 1955 brought back to life. For the price of admission you can wander about, looking at the 42 houses and buildings, exhibits, period gardens, workshops, and artisans' galleries on display.

A walk through Strawbery Banke is educational as well as entertaining, for you'll see how chairs, tables, and cabinets were made besides seeing examples of the work itself; boatbuilding, wood carving, and stoneware potting are explained, and early tools and architectural designs are spread out for your examination.

Strawbery Banke is the major part of Portsmouth's Old Harbour area, the cornerstone of which is **Prescott Park,** a waterfront park, dock, and amusement area donated to the city by the Prescott sisters in the 1930s and 1940s.

John Paul Jones House

Middle and State Sts. ☎ **603/436-8420.** Admission $4 adults, $2 children 6–12, free for children under 6. Mon–Sat 10am–4pm, Sun noon–4pm. Closed Mid-Oct to late May.

No place in this pretty city is more notable than the National Historic Landmark house of John Paul Jones (1758), located right downtown. The stately house was actually a rooming house when Jones stayed in it while his frigate, the famous *Ranger,* was being built in a nearby shipyard. It's now the headquarters of the Portsmouth Historical Society, and you can visit the house and museum on a one-hour guided tour.

WHERE TO STAY

Sise Inn

40 Court St., Portsmouth, N.H. 03801. ☎ **603/433-1200** or 800/267-0525. 26 rms, 8 suites. TV TEL. $99–$115 double; $125–$175 suite. Rates include continental breakfast. AE, DC, MC, V. Free parking.

The rooms and suites in this 1881 Queen Anne style inn take you back to late 19th-century Portsmouth, and it's easy to imagine yourself as the guest of a wealthy Portsmouth merchant family. Guest rooms have rich carpeting, fine furniture, and period pieces, but also such modern conveniences as cable TVs and VCRs. The inn caters to businesspeople, but off-the-road travelers won't feel out of place.

WHERE TO DINE

Izzy's Premium Frozen Yogurt

33 Bow St. ☎ **603/431-1053.** Reservations not required. Coffees $1.25–$2.60; dairy items $1.50–$3. No credit cards. Mon–Fri 10am–9pm, Sat–Sun 11am–9pm. COOL LIBATIONS/COFFEES.

In winter, Izzy's is great for a caffè latte, a mochaccino, or an espresso. In summer they're busy dishing out yogurt to kids and grandparents. Stop in to check the changing menu on the chalkboard. The decor is rather mod, with black-and-white-checked tiles. If you come by in summer, you'll likely to find they stay open until 11pm as long as there's business.

Library Restaurant

401 State St. ☎ **603/431-5202.** Reservations recommended. Main courses $11–$19; dinner $30–$35. AE, CB, DC, DISC, MC, V. Daily 11:30am–3pm and 5–11pm, Sept–May; Sun brunch 11:30am–3pm. CONTINENTAL.

Located in the Rockingham House, in the center of town, the Library is a good choice no matter what your culinary preference. The menu lists such varied delights as Long Island duckling, rack of lamb, and veal and fish specials, along with more familiar fare and money-saving daily-special plates. The old hotel was converted to condominiums.

Old Ferry Landing

10 Ceres St. ☎ **603/431-5510.** Reservations not required. Soups $2–$5; main courses $5–$13. AE, DISC, MC, V. Daily 11:30am–9pm. Closed Sept 25 to mid-Apr. SEAFOOD.

You'll know the Old Ferry Landing by the red awnings outside. It's located off Bow Street, on the waterfront, almost on top of the tugboats. Outside dining is on plastic furniture; inside, the decor is a bit nicer, but the food is what people come here for. Steak and chicken specials are on the menu, but the fresh seafood is best. It's casual, fun, and reasonably priced.

Poco Diablo Restaurant & Cantina

37 Bow St. ☎ **603/431-5967.** Reservations not required. Main courses $7.35–$10.95. AE, DISC, MC, V. Sun–Thurs 11:30am–10pm, Fri–Sat 11:30am–11pm. MEXICAN.

This isn't exactly a palace, but the atmosphere is engaging enough with its brick, beams, pine, and views of the tugboats. You can start with a few margaritas and move on to more hearty Mexican dishes. The staff is friendly and casual.

The Stockpot

53 Bow St. ☎ **603/431-1851.** Reservations not required. Sandwiches $2.25–$4.25; main courses $6–$12. MC, V. Daily 11am–11:30pm. AMERICAN.

Situated in an 1800s building, The Stockpot was once the Eldridge Brewery. You can still see the huge wheel on the ceiling that once ran the elevator used to bring goods from the dock below to the upper stories. The decor is a blend of brick and knotty pine, with views of the river. There is outdoor dining and an upstairs lounge. Fish and chips is popular, as is the homemade meatloaf with fries. Or you might order a local catch on special, possibly baked stuffed scrod. The chef's specialty is New England clam chowder.

Szechuan Taste & Thai Café

54 Daniel St. ☎ **603/431-2226.** Reservations recommended. Main courses $7.25–$14; fixed-price lunch $5–$6.50. AE, DISC, MC, V. Sun–Thurs 11:30am–10pm, Fri–Sat 11:30–11pm. SZECHUAN/THAI.

This family-run place offers a refreshing change from Portsmouth's mostly seafood restaurants. The simple, dimly lit restaurant is the kind of place you go with friends, where you might not venture without a recommendation. There are many Szechuan dishes on the menu. In winter, hours might be shorter.

A COFFEEHOUSE

Breaking New Grounds

16 Market St. ☎ **603/436-9555.** Reservations not required. Coffees and teas $1.25–$2.75. No credit cards. Sun–Thurs 7am–11pm, Fri–Sat 7am–midnight. COFFEEHOUSE.

One day about Christmas time I was visiting Portsmouth's little shops with friends when we stumbled into this coffeehouse to be charmed by its hardwood floors, antique lights, exposed brick and wired ice cream parlor chairs. The friendly staff was busy serving up mochas, cappuccino, teas, and espresso. Besides the gourmet coffees are delicious pies and cakes. They also sell retail coffee and coffee-related merchandise.

4 Manchester

51 miles W of Portsmouth, 53 miles NW of Boston, 19 miles S of Concord

Manchester borders the Merrimack River, and the cheap waterpower brought the city wealth in the textile boom of the mid- and late 19th century. The very impressive **Amoskeag Mills** still border the river and the canals in the center of town, the brick facades stretching for almost a mile. The mills are used for various purposes today, including the manufacture of textiles and shoes (plenty of factory-outlet stores in town); continued use preserves these monuments of American architectural and industrial history.

GETTING THERE   By Plane   Manchester's airport is served by Continental, Delta, Northwest, and USAir.

By Bus   See the beginning of this chapter.

By Car   I-93, the main route between Boston and northern New Hampshire, passes through Manchester, as does U.S. 3 (the Everett Turnpike). From the Hampton Toll on I-95, take N.H. 101 34 miles into Manchester.

ESSENTIALS   The **telephone area code** is **603.** Call the **Manchester Chamber of Commerce** (☎ **603/666-6600**) with your questions.

WHAT TO SEE & DO

Currier Gallery of Art

192 Orange St. ☎ **603/669-6144.** Admission Gallery, $4 adults, $3 seniors and students, free for children under 18; free for everyone Thurs 1–9pm. Zimmerman House (including entry to the Currier Gallery), $6 adults, $4 seniors and children 7 or older (children under 7 not permitted). Tues–Wed and Fri–Sat 10am–4pm; Thurs 10am–9pm; Sun 1–5pm. Directions: Cross the Queen City or Amoskeag Bridge to downtown, and drive along Elm Street (U.S. 3) to Orange Street; go east on Orange six blocks and the museum is on your left.

The collection of this fine museum is strong in 19th- and 20th-century European and American glass, English and American silver and pewter, and colonial and Early American furniture. It also has a nice collection of American and European paintings and sculpture. Degas, Monet, Jan Gossaert, and a follower of Meliore are represented, along with other masters. Until March the main gallery is closed for renovation, but tours of the **Zimmerman House,** a Frank Lloyd Wright designed home owned by the museum, are still available.

Anheuser-Busch Brewery

221 Daniel Webster Hwy., Merrimack. ☎ **603/595-1202.** Free admission. May–Oct, daily 9:30am–5pm; Nov–Apr, Wed–Sun 10am–4pm. Directions: Take the Everett Turnpike five miles south of Manchester to Exit 11, in the town of Merrimack.

The company that offers Budweiser and Michelob is the largest brewer of beer in the world, with an annual capacity of about 90 million barrels at 13 breweries across the country. For tours, running continuously throughout the day, assemble in the special alpine-looking tour building.

After the tour there's sampling of the brew, of course, and perhaps a visit to the Clydesdale Hamlet, home for a dozen of the huge, majestic draft horses. You've probably seen them in eight-horse hitches pulling a brewer's wagon in advertisements or local parades.

WHERE TO STAY

Bedford Village Inn

2 Old Bedford Rd., Bedford, N.H. 03110. ☎ **603/472-2001** or 800/852-1166. Fax 603/472-2379. 14 rms. A/C TV TEL. Including continental breakfast: $110–$165 double. AE, DC, MC, V. Free parking.

In a suburb of Manchester lies a wonderful city inn on landscaped grounds so picturesque that TV networks routinely use the inn as a locale for interviews or programming during the presidential primary. This is the preferred address to the Sheraton in Manchester proper because it offers more New England home-spun character. The clapboard, stone and architectural detail will entice the most jagged traveler. Lots of colonial appointments, fireplaces, fresh flowers, and good service make this extra-appealing, especially compared to some of the drab roadside motels nearby. There is a tavern, and they make candy in the sweets shop. There's also a restaurant in a separate building.

Howard Johnson Hotel

298 Queen City Ave., Manchester, N.H. 03102. ☎ **603/668-2600** or 800/654-2000. Fax 603/668-2600, ext. 634. 100 rms. A/C TV TEL. Sept–Oct, $84 double; Nov–Aug, $69–$74 double. Children under 18 stay free in parents' room. AE, DC, DISC, MC, V. Free parking. Directions: Take the Queen City Bridge exit (no. 4) from I-293.

At this convenient motel just off I-293 you'll find king- and queen-size beds, HBO movies, an indoor pool, saunas, a lounge, and a restaurant (open from 7am to 10pm).

Sheraton Tara Wayfarer Inn

121 S. River Rd., Bedford, N.H. 03110. ☎ **603/622-3766** or 800/325-3535. Fax 603/666-4454. 194 rms. A/C TV TEL. $85–$130 double. AE, DC, DISC, MC, V. Free parking.

As chain hotels go, the Sheraton is the best in Manchester. Despite its size, it manages to impart a genuinely warm feeling with woodsy, rustic touches. The outdoors pours in through big windows in the public areas. The restaurant, with an adjoining bar, overlooks a small river. Rooms are just what you'd expect from a first-class hotel with all the amenities. The Sheraton adjoins a shopping mall and offers complimentary shuttle service to the airport four miles away.

WHERE TO DINE

Bedford Village Inn

2 Old Bedford Rd., New Bedford. ☎ **603/472-2001.** Reservations recommended. Main courses $17–$25, dinner for two $60. AE, DC, MC, V. Mon–Fri 7–10:30am, Sat–Sun 8–10:30; Mon–Sat 11:30am–2pm; daily 5:30–9:30pm. AMERICAN/REGIONAL.

Besides having a lovely and romantic inn—one that's more appealing than Manchester's other choices—this country inn has a delightful restaurant where regional fare is presented with care and flair. Some of the items prepared by the chef include veal scampi, Atlantic salmon, duck, and lobster altaire. Come for a visit and dinner if you can't stay here.

Newicks Seafood Restaurant

696 Daniel Webster Hwy., (N.H. 3), Merrimack. ☎ **603/429-0262.** Reservations not accepted. Main courses $9–$22. AE, DISC, MC, V. Sun–Thurs 11:30am–8:30pm, Fri–Sat 11:30am–9pm. SEAFOOD.

About three miles from the Busch Brewery is this fish market and restaurant where fresh fish is served to the masses. Everything from lobster to haddock, clams, and combination plates are popular. The decor is simple and the food hearty.

5 Concord

19 miles N of Manchester, 24 miles S of Laconia, 55 miles SE of Lebanon

The capital of New Hampshire is a pleasant little city with an appropriate frontier-mountain feeling. First settled in 1725, the town was called Rumford for the first 40 years; the name later found its way into the title of Count Rumford, inventor of a certain sort of shallow fireplace. Since 1816 Concord has been the capital of the state. Granite, printing, electrical equipment, and leather goods, as well as a surprisingly small amount of state bureaucracy, keep the town going.

GETTING THERE   **By Bus**   See the beginning of this chapter.

By Car   Concord is near the junction of I-89 and I-93, making it easily accessible from Boston, Manchester, central and northern New Hampshire, and central and northern Vermont.

ESSENTIALS   The **telephone area code** is **603.** If you have a question, call the **Concord Area Chamber of Commerce** (☎ **603/224-2508**) or contact the **New Hampshire Office of Travel and Tourism Development,** P.O. Box 1856, Concord, N.H. 03302 (☎ **603/271-2666**).

WHAT TO SEE & DO

Pierce Manse

14 Penacook St. ☎ **603/224-7668.** Admission $2 adults, 50¢ children and students. Mon–Fri 11am–3pm. Closed Labor Day to mid-June.

Franklin Pierce, 14th president of the United States, was speaker of the New Hampshire General Court (legislature) as well as one of the town's prominent lawyers. His house, now a National Historic Site at the farthest reaches of North Main Street, was saved from demolition by a civic-minded group named the Pierce Brigade. It was his family home from 1842 to 1848. You might want to make an appointment by calling ☎ **603/224-7668** or **603/224-0094.**

The State House & Visitor's Center

107 N. Main St. ☎ **603/271-2154.** Admission free; self-guided tours. Nov–June, Mon–Fri 8am–4:30pm; July–Aug, Mon–Fri 8am–4:30pm, Sat 11am–4pm; Sept–Oct, Mon–Fri 8am–4:30pm, Sat–Sun 11am–4pm.

The state capitol, called the State House, was built in 1819 of—you guessed it—New Hampshire granite. It's the oldest state capitol in which a legislature still occupies its original chambers. Inside, the state's battle flags and portraits of its notable military commanders are proudly displayed. A statue of Daniel Webster, one of several native New Hampshire boys who made good on a national scale, stands before the building. The small size of the State House will surprise you; compared with the mammoth buildings in Providence, Hartford, and Boston, it seems barely big enough to hold just the governor's staff. But many of the tax-burdened citizens of other states are lured to New Hampshire every year by the low tax rate, kept low in part by keeping bureaucracy small. It's in the center of town.

Canterbury Shaker Village

288 Shaker Rd., Canterbury. ☎ **603/783-9511.** Admission $8 adults, $4 children 6–12, free for children under 6. Open (for guided tour): May–Oct, daily 10am–5pm (last tour at 4pm); Apr and Nov–Dec, Fri–Sun 10am–5pm (last tour 4pm). Closed Jan–Mar. Directions: Take Exit 18 off I-93 and follow the signs 6¹/₂ miles to the village.

On the way to Laconia, you can visit a restored village founded by the Shakers in 1792. Members of the United Society of Believers in Christ's Second Appearing were called Shakers because of the religious ecstasies they sometimes experienced. Their community at Hancock, Mass., in the Berkshires (see "Stockbridge," in Chapter 8) is the best known, but there were others, notably at Sabbathday Lake, Me., and here in Canterbury.

Besides producing the much-admired Shaker furniture and craft items, the Canterbury Shaker community specialized in producing herbs and herbal medicines, which were sold throughout the country. You can still visit the herb garden, as well as the original meeting house (1792), an apiary (bee house), the ministry, a Sisters' shop, a laundry, a horse barn, the infirmary, and the schoolhouse (1826).

You can see dovetailed and oval box making in the carpentry shop, and look over reproductions of Shaker designs in furniture and crafts in the carriage-house gift shop and the gallery in the carpentry shop. There are other traditional Shaker crafts demonstrations on site and also a self-guided nature trail to the mill sites and mill ponds.

All year on Friday and Saturday evenings you can also enjoy a traditional candlelight dinner here. There is one seating (family style at long tables) at 7pm sharp. The four-course meal (choose from a poultry, meat, or fish main dish) costs $32 per person. Recipes, ingredients, and cooking methods are all true to Shaker form and philosophy. After dinner has transported you to another era, you'll be guided through the village by candlelight, or if it's off-season and the village is closed, on Saturday you'll be treated to an evening of folk singing. You'll have an enjoyable evening either way. The Creamery restaurant is open for lunch from 11:30am to 2:30pm and for brunch on Sunday from 11am to 2pm.

WHERE TO DINE

The Coffee Mill

124 Main St. ☎ **603/224-8081.** Reservations not required. Coffees and teas 70¢–$1.25. No credit cards. Mon–Fri 7am–5pm, Sat 8am–3pm, Sun 8am–3pm. COFFEEHOUSE.

In the center of town, The Coffee Mill sells New York bagels, iced tea, cappuccino, gourmet coffees, and a delicious assortment of special iced drinks.

Phil A. Busters

1 Eagle Sq. ☎ **603/228-1982.** Reservations not required. Soups $3–$4; main courses $7–$13. AE, DISC, MC, V. Mon–Thurs 11:30am–9pm, Fri–Sat 11:30am–10pm. AMERICAN.

This place opposite the State House is working hard to please and is getting much repeat business. The natural wood, tartan fabrics, and friendly staff are a few of the reasons they seem to be making it. Another is the outdoor dining area, where a summer salad will tempt you—perhaps a Caesar or chicken salad. Desserts are made fresh. There's a happy hour, called Business After Hours, with 50¢ drafts.

6 Lake Winnipesaukee

Laconia: 24 miles N of Concord, 56 miles S of Franconia Notch

The largest of the lakes in New Hampshire's Lakes Region is grand indeed: 28 miles long, close to 300 miles of shoreline, 72 square miles of water to swim in or boat on, and almost 300 islands. The name has been translated as "smile of the Great Spirit," and while the lake's irregular shoreline might suggest a wry grin rather than a sunny smile, the lake's large size would certainly do the Great Spirit justice. Summer is when the lake is busiest with swimmers, boaters, waterskiers, and the like, but winter snows draw crowds to the **Gunstock** ski area near the lake's shore.

GETTING THERE   By Bus   See the beginning of this chapter.

By Car   I-93 is the major road to the lake; from Portsmouth, take the Spaulding Turnpike (N.H. 16) to N.H. 11.

ESSENTIALS   The **telephone area code** is **603**. The **Greater Laconia/Weirs Beach Chamber of Commerce,** 11 Veteran's Sq., Laconia, N.H. 03246 (☎ 603/524-5531 or 800/531-2347), provides information.

LACONIA & GILFORD

Laconia, Lake Winnipesaukee's largest town, is also its business and commercial center. Many of the area companies with large shoe factories have factory-outlet stores here where shoes sell at bargain prices. Downtown next to city hall, the **Belknap** (*Bell*-nap) **Mill** (☎ 603/524-8813), a textile mill built in 1823, has been restored and you can tour it to see the hydroelectric machinery that ran the mill from 1918 to 1969. The mill now serves as the region's center for culture and the arts. It's open Monday through Friday from 9am to 5pm and Saturday from 9am to 1pm, all year. In part of the gallery is a permanent exhibit called *The Mill and the Community,* which represents the 1800s to 1950s, when the area was the knitting capital of the world.

WHAT TO SEE AND DO

BEACHES   Ellacoya State Beach, on N.H. 11 southeast of Glendale, is one of the nicest beaches on the lake. The entrance fee is $3 for adults and children 12 and older, free for children under 12. There's plenty of parking, and if you go early in the day you can get one of the picnic tables. There's a snack bar, and a lifeguard is on duty all the time the beach is open. The slope of the beach is very gradual, making it ideal for small children; for more experienced swimmers, a swimming dock floats in the water farther out.

Weirs Beach, on N.H. 11B near its intersection with U.S. 3, is a town beach with a similar admission charge, free parking at several lots in the town of Weirs Beach (look for the signs to the free lots—everything on the main street is metered). The town is known more for its honky-tonk penny arcades, candlepin bowling alleys, pinball machines, fortune-tellers, and fast-food stands than it is for the beauty of its beach. These amusements are open during the day, and in the evening in summer, and give the town a character that differs greatly from what it once must have been: The grand old turn-of-the-century mansions around the town are some of the finest of their genre, with lots of cupolas, turrets, gables, and all the other paraphernalia that make late-Victorian architecture so intricate.

You can stay overnight at Weirs Beach in one of the hotels, motels, or guesthouses, although the low lakefront situation seems to lend a mustiness to most accommodations.

BOAT RIDES   Many boats make tours of the lake several times daily. Most famous is the 230-foot **MS** *Mount Washington* (☎ **603/366-2628**), which runs cruises from Weirs Beach between late May and late October, with the schedule varying depending on the time of year. The cruise around the lake takes 3 hours and costs $14 for adults, $6 for children 4 to 12, free for children under 4. Breakfast, luncheon buffet, a Sunday champagne brunch, cocktails, snacks, and gifts are available on board. Ports of call are Centre Harbor, Wolfeboro, and Alton Bay. Shorter cruises are offered on smaller vessels operated by the same company.

WHERE TO STAY

When coming to the lake for fun, people stay in the many motels and inns on parts of the lake's shore near Laconia, or in a small, pretty town such as Wolfeboro, due east of Laconia. Skiers stay at the inns located near the slopes or in a lakefront establishment with winterized cabins.

To get away from the hustle and bustle of the highway, drive along N.H. 11 and watch for signs pointing out a scenic shore road off to the left. N.H. 11 has been remade in recent years and is farther away from the lakeshore, while the motels are still along the old road which used to be N.H. 11. Most of the traffic uses the new road, leaving the old one much quieter.

Belknap Point Motel

107 Belknap Point Rd. (R.F.D. 8), Gilford, N.H. 03246. ☎ **603/293-7511.** 16 rms. A/C TV TEL. Mid-June to mid-Oct $88–$108 double; off-season $58–$78 double. Additional person $10 extra. AE, DISC, MC, V. Free parking. Directions: From N.H. 11, turn left on Belknap Point Road, then go half a mile down.

Those looking for quiet accommodations with all the conveniences will enjoy the Belknap Point. It has two sections: Down on the shore of the lake, a number of efficiency units with kitchens and decks reaches out almost over the water; and up the steep slope of the hill between the old road and the new (you can enter from either road) are a number of motel rooms, all with ceramic tile bath, a little balcony, and gorgeous views of the lake. The new owners work hard to make sure each guest is comfortable. The Belknap Point has its own swimming area and a grassy patio.

Estate Motel and Cottages

Scenic Dr. (R.F.D. 4), Gilford, N.H. 03246. ☎ **603/293-7792.** 8 rms, 2 efficiencies, 3 cottages. A/C TV. $70 double; $75 efficiency for two; $350 or $500 per week cottage. Weekly rates available. MC, V. Free parking. Directions: Go to the end of the N.H. 11 bypass, turn left onto N.H. 11 east, go 3½ miles, and take a left on Scenic Drive; the motel is half a mile on the left.

Here, in another establishment along the scenic lakefront road, are eight motel rooms and two efficiencies in white buildings. The rooms look out over a grassy lawn down to the lake; the lake boating and swimming dock are convenient. The Estate is secluded and quiet, and it's best to reserve in advance for one of its rooms. Rooms have two double beds, refrigerators, and cable TV; the efficiencies have the same, plus a sink, and stove, and kitchen utensils. Three cabins are rented by the week for $350 for one bedroom or $500 for two bedrooms.

WOLFEBORO

Wolfeboro is among the prettiest and most interesting towns on the lake. It escaped the blight that hit such textile-producing towns as Laconia because Wolfeboro never industrialized; it has escaped the honky-tonk commercialism that has taken over some other lake towns, perhaps because of its "inconvenient" position at the southeastern tip of the lake. So today Wolfeboro is a fine, almost typical, New England town with the requisite historical society, white-steepled churches, gracious old houses, and some very good views of the lake.

There's less hustle and bustle in Wolfeboro than in some other lake towns, less to "see and do," but that makes it all the better for those who really want to relax. The MS *Mount Washington* stops here to pick up and discharge passengers for its tours of the lake (see "What to See and Do" under "Laconia and Gilford," above, for details); and a good number of the motels and resorts in town have their own stretches of beach. Wolfeboro is proud to call itself "the oldest summer resort in America," because in 1763 Gov. John Wentworth built what is thought to be the first summer house in the United States within the town's boundaries.

WHAT TO SEE AND DO

Libby Museum

N.H. 109. ☎ **603/569-1035.** Admission $1 adults, 50¢ children. Tues–Sun 10am–4pm. Closed Oct–Memorial Day. Directions: Go three miles north of Wolfeboro on N.H. 109.

Dr. Henry F. Libby, a Boston dentist who was born and raised near the shores of Winnipesaukee, devoted the latter part of his life to the study and collection of natural history specimens: fish, animals, and birds. Other interests of his included early Native American lore of the region, and artifacts from the times of early settlers. All these diverse exhibits are brought together in the Libby Museum.

Castle in the Clouds

N.H. 171, Moultonboro. ☎ **603/476-2352.** Admission $10 adults, $7 students, free for children under 10. May to mid-June, Sat–Sun 9am–5pm; mid-June to mid-Oct, daily 9am–5pm. Closed Mid-Oct to Apr. Directions: Take N.H. 109 north from Wolfeboro for 17 miles, turn right (east) onto N.H. 171, and go three miles to the entrance.

Around the turn of the century, Thomas Gustav Plant decided to build himself a retreat in the New Hampshire wilderness. While he was not alone in this—lots of rich men were building lavish estates in the region—his accomplishment is certainly among the grandest. Lucknow, as the estate was named, cost millions to build; the name comes from a castle in Scotland, and originally from a city in India, although the mansion has distinctly central European touches to it. Today, Lucknow is called Castle in the Clouds; its grounds are very beautiful, and the view of the mountains and lakes is nothing short of spectacular. Horseback trail rides are available.

WHERE TO STAY AND DINE

In Wolfeboro

Wolfeboro Inn

44 N. Main St., Wolfeboro, N.H. 03894. ☎ **603/569-3016** or 800/451-2389. Fax 603/569-5375. 43 rms. A/C TV TEL. Summer and fall, $109–$219 double; winter and spring, $79–$179 double. Rates include continental breakfast. AE, DISC, MC, V. Free parking.

Among the most serviceable of the town's hostelries is this venerable inn, where the rooms have some antique pieces. It was built in 1812, but it has been thoroughly modernized and prides itself on giving the "glitter-weary traveler" a comfortable and tasteful place to lodge and dine. As the inn, in the center of town, is often full in high summer, it's best to reserve in advance. In summer, enjoy the sandy beach on Lake Winnipesaukee or take a cruise in the inn's own launch, included in the room price. In winter, outdoor activities are skating, cross-country skiing, and iceboating.

The dining areas have wooden chairs and tables and several fireplaces, including three in Wolfe's Tavern (open from 9am to 11pm) and a large brick one in the Dining Room (dinner is served from 7 to 9pm). The menu offers a fairly standard selection of the popular beef, seafood, and fowl dishes, but the daily specials (available at both lunch and dinner) are always interesting, and often the best values. Sandwiches at lunch are priced at $4.50 to $6. At dinner, main courses with side dishes cost $8 to $18; the daily specials are usually nearer the lower end of that range.

7 North Conway/Mount Washington Valley

73 miles NE of Concord, 49 miles NE of Laconia, 39 miles E of Lincoln

On the edge of the White Mountain National Forest and at the end of Mount Washington Valley, North Conway is the sports capital of the White Mountains. It's not a particularly large town, although the mile or two of motels and eateries along N.H. 16 south of town do seem to extend the boundaries. But basically you can walk to almost anything except this southern extension by parking downtown, somewhere near the antique railroad station.

North Conway has taken well to its role of mountain town, and the people talk hearty and look healthy. Some of the businesses are old-time mom-and-pop affairs, but a lot of shops have been citified to cater to the hiking and ski trades. But still the town has not been "taken over" by city people. Perhaps the character and charm of North Conway are best exhibited by the town library building on Main Street not far from the railroad station: Although small, it's built of massive granite blocks and has a slate roof that will last forever; it's open on weekday afternoons, and Friday to 7pm.

GETTING THERE **By Bus** See the beginning of this chapter.

By Car North Conway is on U.S. 302 (N.H. 16). The most beautiful way to approach is via I-93 to Lincoln, then the scenic Kancamagus Highway east. Coming from Lake Winnipesaukee, N.H. 25 to N.H. 113 to N.H. 16; the more scenic approach is up the eastern shore of the lake from Alton on N.H. 28 to N.H. 109 to N.H. 25, then to N.H. 113 and N.H. 16.

ESSENTIALS The area along N.H. 16 from Madison through North Conway and Gorham, including the town of Bartlett on U.S. 302, is organized for tourist reasons as the Mount Washington Valley. Situated in the shadow of the Northeast's tallest peak, the valley offers camping, rafting, climbing, hiking, and biking, as well as three nordic ski-touring centers. The towns of North Conway and Jackson are centers for these activities and for winter skiing. The nordic ski areas are known as Mount Washington Valley Ski Touring Association, Jackson Ski Touring Foundation and Great Glen Trails. Nearby are the ski areas of Attitash Bear Peak, Black Mountain, King Pine, Mount Cranmore, and Wildcat. Viewing the fall colors is famous in the area in late September, but be prepared to face the traffic.

The **telephone area code** is **603.** The **Mount Washington Valley Chamber of Commerce and Visitors Bureau,** P.O. Box 2300, North Conway, N.H. 03860 (☎ **603/356-3171** or **800/367-3364**), has its main information center on Main Street in North Conway village, open Monday through Friday from 8:30am to 5pm and Saturday and Sunday from 10am to 4pm. The guides are very helpful and can assist you in making room reservations if you're having trouble. You can also book reservations on the toll-free number or order the color guidebook to the valley.

WHAT TO SEE & DO

SHOPPING

North Conway has become synonymous with shopping and outlet stores. A spectrum of stores has opened, beckoning as many bargain hunters here as skiers. On hand you'll find such trendy names as **Ralph Lauren, Anne Klein, Banana Republic, Dansk,** and, of course, **L. L. Bean.** Bean's has a good-sized factory store here that's immensely popular. There's also a shopping center adjacent to the Sheraton hotel, with two dozen stores and a handful of eateries. This is the next best thing to going to Freeport or Kittery, Maine, for outlet shopping.

SKIING

The Mount Washington Valley includes five **alpine ski areas:** Attitash, Black, Cranmore, King Pine, and Wildcat. Altogether there are about 100 downhill trails and two dozen lifts, and the slopes range from those for the beginner to those that present a challenge even to some experienced skiers. Many of the inns recommended below under "Where to Stay" offer special ski packages that include lift fees for all five areas.

Besides the five developed ski areas in the valley, it's possible to ski in the cirque at **Tuckerman's Ravine,** where the shadows protect the snow long past the time when the cover on other slopes has begun to melt. The special excitement at Tuckerman, besides the challenge of the au naturel slopes, comes from climbing the mountain you're going to ski down, for there are no lifts. Follow the line of black dots up the mountain to the top. This is old-time skiing, with only a run or two a day, and only those with real stamina and strong legs should and will accept the challenge. But going back to the basics is exhilarating, everyone you meet here is your friend, and the fling down the mountain after the climb is a fitting way to end the season. Park in the Wildcat lot and recuperate in the cafeteria or lounge.

Every alpine ski area in the valley has some **cross-country trails,** some of which are very easy and some of which are only for experts. The center of the ski-touring activity in the valley is Jackson, where the **Jackson Ski Touring Foundation,** P.O. Box 216, Jackson, N.H. 03846 (☎ **603/383-9355**), maintains and grooms about 100 miles of cross-country trails. The foundation is a nonprofit village organization dedicated to encouraging ski touring in and around Jackson, and it has a small office in the center of the village. Skiing magazines have rated this the number one spot in the East. Check here for passes, information, and maps. There's a nominal fee for the use of the trails; a season membership is available. Clinics, tours, and rentals can all be found both in Jackson and in North

Conway at the several ski shops. At Mount Washington, **Great Glen Trails**, (P.O. Box 300), Gorham, N.H. 03581, ☎ **603/466-2333,** is a new entry in the market with 100 kilometers of back country ski trails. In summer the ski trails are transformed into riding trails for mountain bikers. At the base lodge, food and other refreshments are available.

OTHER WINTER SPORTS

Because of the state parks, national forest, and private reserves in the valley, lots of other winter sports are popular here. **Winter camping** is possible, using a tent or the Appalachian Mountain Club (AMC) huts (see "Where to Stay," below), a few of which are open all winter. Note that many areas in the White Mountains have extremely severe weather—blizzards with temperatures of 14°F and winds gusting to 100 mph on top of Mount Washington are possible in *August*. This does not mean you'll hit impossible weather, but it does mean you should check with rangers and AMC personnel, and have good equipment and knowledge of winter camping before you go in.

    Snowmobiling is also pretty big in the valley, and places in North Conway will rent you a machine by the hour or the day. Ice-skating rinks are maintained by the towns of North Conway, Conway, and Jackson. Various ponds and lakes aren't bad for ice fishing—the locals will be glad to give visitors tips on the most-visited ice-fishing spots.

    Tennis courts are available all year at the indoor courts of the Mount Cranmore Recreation Center (☎ **603/356-6301**). Guest memberships are open to the public on a daily basis.

SUMMER ACTIVITIES

Besides **hiking and camping** in the state parks and national forests, Mount Washington Valley offers many other activities.

    Right in North Conway village center is the romantic old station of the **Conway Scenic Railroad** (☎ **603/356-5251**), built in 1874 and restored to its present condition in 1974. For $7.50 (adults) or $5 (kids 4 to 12; free for children under 4), you can buy a ticket for the scenic ride through the mountain country; choose your seat from among those in the enclosed cars or the open-air "cinder collectors." A steam locomotive and a 45-year-old and a 46-year-old diesel engine are on hand to provide the power, and if you go a little early, you can visit the roundhouse to see where the locomotives are turned around. Trains run daily from mid-June through late October and on weekends only from mid-April to mid-June and late October through December. Departure times are 10am, noon, and 2 and 4pm. The trip takes about an hour. The "Sunset Special" at 6:30pm runs Tuesday through Saturday in July and August. On Friday, Saturday, and Sunday of Thanksgiving weekend and on the first three weekends on December (with Santa aboard), the train makes special trips at noon and 2pm.

    The **Mount Washington Valley Theater Company,** North Conway, N.H. 03860 (☎ **603/356-5776**), currently performs at the playhouse on Main Street in the Eastern Slope Inn complex. The season, from late June through Labor Day, features four lively musicals. Of course, it's most fun to see the entire series, watching the various members of the company take on different roles every other week, but even if you can't afford to stay in North Conway the entire season, you'll enjoy seeing a play here. The box office opens daily at

The White Mountains

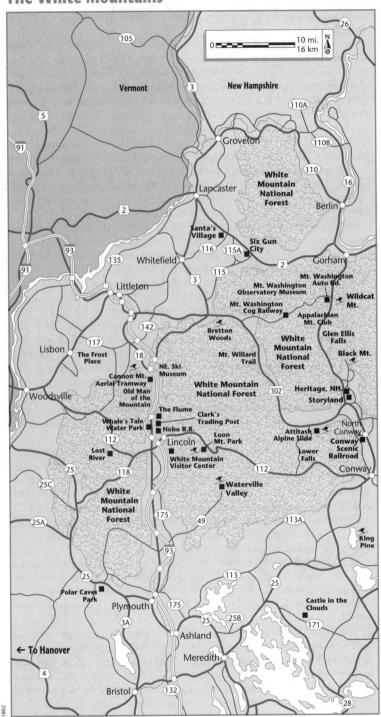

noon, and curtain time is 8pm sharp. Tickets run $13 to $16.50. Group rates are available.

A considerable part of northern New Hampshire is included in the **White Mountain National Forest,** which is not to be confused with a national park. The forest does have a number of developed sites, however. Camping areas ($5 per night, cold running water and pit toilets only) are dotted here and there, as are very pretty picnic areas. A maze of trails, some very easy and some not so easy, covers a lot of the forest's vast expanse. Signs by the roadside mark the trail's beginning, but don't wander in just for a 30-minute walk if you're not familiar with the area. Instead, buy detailed maps of the trails and a trail guide from the **Appalachian Mountain Club,** 5 Joy St., Boston, MA 02108 (☎ **617/523-0636**), or from the club's **Pinkham Notch Visitor Center** (☎ **603/466-2721**) on N.H. 16 north of Jackson. The *AMC White Mountain Guide* ($16.95) will tell you all about the trail: how difficult it is, how long it is, the vertical rise, the average walking time, reference points along the way, and what to see as you walk.

Another option is to **rent a canoe** for the day or the week from **Saco Bound Inc.,** two miles east of Center Conway on U.S. 302 (☎ **603/447-2177**). The Saco River has lots of smooth and easy areas. Overnight trips and canoe pickup service are available, as well as daily canoe rental at a daily rate of $25.50 and pickup charge of $10 a canoe. The season runs April through October.

Heritage New Hampshire, on N.H. 16 in Glen (☎ **603/383-9776**), has a variety of lifelike scenes and dioramas with talking figures which outline New Hampshire's history, from the docks of an English port town through the Industrial Revolution at the Amoskeag Mills in Manchester. You can walk at your own pace through the maze of displays, and costumed guides will answer any questions you may have about New Hampshire's history. The history lesson on New Hampshire passes through three centuries. And there is also a 120-foot historic mural, which is New England's largest. Don't pass on the vintage trolley ride. The price is $7.50 for adults, $4.50 for children 6 to 12, free for children under 6; it's open daily from 9am to 6pm in July and August, and until 5pm in June, September, and October.

Right next to Heritage New Hampshire is **Story Land** (☎ **603/383-4293**), a children's amusement park with rides, clowns, animals, and lots of other treats. Once you've paid the $15 admission fee, all the rides are free; children under 4 are admitted without charge. Open from 9am to 6pm daily from mid-June through early September, and then weekends only until mid-October.

The **ski areas** at Attitash and Wildcat Mountain don't fully close down in summer. They've developed full warm-weather recreation programs to keep the visitors coming and the bills paid.

At **Attitash** (☎ **603/374-2368**), the lifts keep working to take you up to the top of the Alpine Slide, a long track that you schuss down on a little cart—an exhilarating ride, and safe for all ages. You can buy an all-day ticket for $16 or single-ride tickets for $6.50 per adult, $5 per child 6 to 12, free for children under 6.

At **Wildcat Mountain** (☎ **603/466-3326**), the snack shop stays open for those wanting a snack before boarding the gondolas for the 25-minute round-trip ride up the mountainside (in operation from late May to late October daily from 9am to 6pm; from September 12 to October 11, daily from 9am to 5pm). The area around Wildcat Mountain and its base camp are kept immaculate because they're within the national forest and subject to its regulation.

Two Scenic Drives

A private business, the **Mount Washington Auto Road,** Gorham, N.H. 03581
(☎ **603/466-3988**), operates an alpine toll road to the top of the highest peak
in the Northeast, 6,288-foot Mount Washington. Start from N.H. 16 in
Pinkham Notch. You can drive your own car (no trucks or campers) to the
top of the mountain at $15 for car and driver (including an audio tour on
cassette) and $5 for each passenger ($3 for kids 5 to 12, free for children under
5); vans operated by the company will take you on a guided tour to the top
and back down a gain (1¹/₂ hours) for $19 per person (kids, $10) if you'd
rather not drive. Hours are 7:30am to 6pm for the road, 8:30am to 5pm for the
guided van tour. The season is normally from mid-May to mid-October, but
remember that Mount Washington's summit has the most severe weather in
the Northeast, and it's altogether possible for the road to be temporarily
closed because of snow even in June or September. This, by the way, is only
one of three ways to reach the Mount Washington summit, the others being
on foot following the Appalachian Mountain Club trails or by cog
railway, described under "Crawford Notch and Bretton Woods," later in this
chapter.

New Hampshire 112 between Conway and Lincoln is known as the
Kancamagus Highway and has been designated a National Scenic Byway. Its
33-mile length exhibits some of the finest scenery in the White Mountains, including the view from the 2,860-foot Kancamagus Pass. Almost the entire length of
the road is within the boundaries of the national forest and is therefore protected
from any development more civilized than a campground (there are six along the
road) or a picnic area. The drive is a must: This is White Mountains beauty in its
purest form.

WHERE TO STAY AND DINE

North Conway has dozens of places to stay and to dine, including a good number of motels along the southern extension of Main Street (N.H. 16), but I'll
concentrate mainly on the small inns in the town and on those in the neighboring towns of Jackson and Glen, most of which have excellent dining rooms. Many
of the lodging establishments listed here have midweek and ski packages; be sure
to inquire if you're planning an extended or active stay. The best dining in this
area is often found in the restaurants of hotels—those that come to mind include
the **Inn at Thorn Hill, Hale's White Mountain Hotel, The Wentworth,** and
the **Snowvillage Inn.**

IN SNOWVILLE

Snowvillage Inn Restaurant

Two miles off N.H. 153, Snowvillage. ☎ **603/447-2818.** Reservations accepted. Main
courses $13–$22, dinner for two $45. AE, DC, DISC, MC, V. Daily 8–9:30am, 6–9pm.
REGIONAL/FRENCH.

> This off-the-beaten-path inn was put on the map for its attractive guest rooms but
> lately has earned a reputation for its regional and French cuisine that may include
> Hungarian mushroom soup, poached salmon, or beef dishes. Barbara and Kevin
> Flynn are the new owners. Getting here takes about 15 minutes from North
> Conway and even less from Conway. You should call ahead to be sure there's room
> for you.

In North Conway
Inns & Guesthouses
The Center Chimney
River Rd. (P.O. Box 1220), North Conway, N.H. 03860. ☎ 603/356-6788. 4 rms (none with bath). $44–$55 double. Rates include muffins and coffee. Additional bed $10 extra. Midweek stay of three days, $15 off. No credit cards. Free parking. Directions: Turn down River Road at the Texaco Station in North Conway village.

The Center Chimney is just that: a big center-chimney Federal house built in 1787, now accepting guests. Look for the house north of town, just off Main Street near the Saco River. There's a fireplace in the living room and cable TV and phone for guest use. Cathedral Ledge, a popular rock-climbing spot, is just down the road.

Cranmore Inn
Kearsarge St. (P.O. Box 1349), North Conway, N.H. 03860. ☎ 603/356-5502 or 800/526-5502. 18 rms (14 with bath). $56 double without bath, $49–$68 double with bath. Rates include breakfast. Add $10 per room in foliage season. AE, MC, V. Free parking. Closed Christmas. Directions: From Main Street, turn onto Kearsarge Street and follow it one block to the inn.

Perhaps the best for price, convenience, and pleasantness is the Cranmore Inn, just off Main Street on the street leading to the Mount Cranmore ski area, and only a few blocks from the intercity bus stop. The inn is over a century old, with guest rooms in Victorian style. Two-bedroom units (sharing one bath) are available for families and friends traveling together, with a hearty country breakfast included in the rates. There are bonuses: a huge parlor with fireplace, a games room, and a TV room; nice big lawns suitable for games and Frisbee (in summer); and an outdoor pool. From the inn, you can walk to the slopes of Mount Cranmore in 10 minutes and to the center of town in 5 minutes or less. A 5-minute walk will bring you to the Mount Cranmore Health Club, with full privileges included in the rates in season (there's a nominal charge off-season). Note that winter rates are different for weekdays and weekends. Dinner is served only to in-house groups reserving the entire inn.

The 1785 Inn
N.H. 16, North Conway, N.H. 03860. ☎ 603/356-9025 or 800/421-1785. Fax 603/356-6081. 17 rms (12 with bath). $70–$100 double without bath, $90–$130 double with bath. Rates include breakfast. AE, CB, DC, MC, V. Free parking.

The dining room and tavern are homespun with a combination of Victorian accents and a country rustic decor. The dining room is open for all meals in ski season, but not for lunch other times. They do all their own baking, from the dinner rolls to desserts. The TV room has a fireplace and a VCR. The guest rooms are simple and rather dated. Many have hand-made quilts and the odd antique may be found. The views and food are most noteworthy.

Sunny Side Inn
Seavey St., North Conway, N.H. 03860. ☎ 603/356-6239. 9 rms. A/C. $53–$107 double. Rates include breakfast. AE, MC, V. Free parking. Directions: Turn onto Kearsarge Street at the traffic light, go right again at the top of the hill, and it's on the left.

On a quiet back street stands the two-story dormered Sunny Side Inn, an affordable and cozy bed-and-breakfast place. There's a living room with fireplace and a reading nook you can relax in or walk to the village for shopping and dining. You won't need an early start since rates include breakfast with home-baked goods.

Hotels & Motels

Best Western Red Jacket Mountain View

On a slope above South Main St., North Conway, N.H. 03860. ☎ **603/356-5411** or 800/752-2538. Fax 603/356-3842. 164 rms. A/C MINIBAR TV TEL. $79–$173 double. Package rates available. AE, DC, MC, V. Free parking.

This is one of North Conway's better choices, ranking behind the Sheraton, but always in demand. At the height of the season (summer or winter), rooms go quickly because of the inn's central location and many accoutrements: an indoor pool covered by a dramatic wood roof, and an outdoor pool as well; saunas; a heated whirlpool and Jacuzzis; a games room with table tennis and electronic games; a bocce court; shuffleboard courts; tennis courts; and a dining room and cocktail lounge. A children's program is offered in summer. Many rooms have views and balconies, and some offer lofts so that a family can sleep more comfortably. Ceramic tile baths, two double beds to a room, air conditioning and heat, and other luxury touches add to the draw, but it's the view and the convenience that convince many people to stay here. Package plans are always available. At dinner, main courses are in the $12-to-$16 range. Lunch and a Sunday buffet breakfast are served in the Birchmont Tavern in the summer.

Hale's White Mountain Hotel and Resort

West Side Rd., North Conway, N.H. 03860. ☎ **603/356-7100** or 800/533-6301. 80 rms. A/C TV TEL. $59–$139 single or double. AE, DISC, MC, V. Free parking.

In the guest rooms, you'll sink into the plush carpets and enjoy the comfortable decor of fine woods and four-poster beds. Room service is provided. The fieldstone fireplace is the focal point in the lobby. The panorama from the dining room and lounge is unmatched in North Conway. Besides the nine-hole golf course, there's an outdoor pool and a year-round outdoor whirlpool, along with a fitness center and saunas.

Sheraton Inn North Conway Inn

N.H. 16 at Settler's Green, North Conway, N.H. 03860. ☎ **603/356-9300** or 800/648-4397. 200 rms. A/C TV TEL. $79–$165 double. AE, DC, DISC, MC, V. Free parking.

The pedestrian mall that adjoins the hotel keeps everything busy around here. Peaked roof lines accent the gray clapboard structure. The Sheraton has many amenities to offer, including its full-service restaurant and lounge, indoor pool, whirlpool, fitness room, tennis courts, and skating rink on the pond in winter. The rooms are first class, just as you'd expect from a well-known upscale competitor.

IN INTERVALE

A mile or two north of North Conway along scenic N.H. 16 are several inns and motels also worth considering. Although you won't be able to walk easily to town from here, these establishments have their own restaurants and you're only a short drive from most of the hiking and ski points.

Inns

The Forest, a Country Inn

N.H. 16A, Intervale (P.O. Box 1736, North Conway, N.H. 03845). ☎ **603/356-9772** or 800/448-3534. 11 rms. $60–$159 double. Additional person $25 extra. Rates include breakfast. AE, MC, V. Free parking. Directions: Follow N.H. 16 north through North Conway; in Intervale, take N.H. 16A to the inn.

This large 1890 Victorian house, converted to take guests, has nine rooms (three with fireplaces) in the inn itself; there are also two rooms with fireplaces in a nearby cottage. You'll get a nice living room (with fireplace) in which to meet new friends, a heated pool in summer, and 39 miles of cross-country skiing in winter on groomed trails, as well as summer hiking trails.

Old Field House

N.H. 16A, Intervale, N.H. 03845. ☎ **603/356-5478** or 800/444-9245. 18 rms, 2 suites. A/C TV TEL. $59–$109 double; $110–$175 suite. Rates include continental breakfast. Stays of three to six nights discounted 15%. AE, MC, V. Free parking. Directions: From North Conway on N.H. 16, bear right on N.H. 16A.

The Old Field House is in a field, yes, but it's not old. It's hard to tell at first whether this hostelry is an old building redone from top to bottom or a new building made to look good and last long. Despite its sturdy granite facade and gambrel-roofed wings meant to conjure up the romantic New Hampshire past, it's quite modern. The rooms are clean and shiny, with beamed ceilings and colonial-style furniture; beds range from one or two doubles to a queen-size or a tremendous king-size. All rooms are non-smoking and have cable TV, and a refrigerator. Both suites boast a fireplace and a private Jacuzzi. You get lots of extras at the Old Field House, such as a heated outdoor pool, a whirlpool, tennis, laundry facilities, background music, a games room, and shuffleboard.

Ⓢ Wildflowers Inn

N.H. 16, North Conway, (P.O. Box 597, North Conway, N.H. 03860). ☎ **603/356-2224.** 6 rms (2 with bath). $50–$80 double without bath, $60–$92 double with bath. Rates include continental breakfast. MC, V. Free parking. Closed Nov–Apr. Directions: Go 1¹/₂ miles north of the center of North Conway on N.H. 16; you'll see the sign on the left as you head north.

Wildflowers is another charming guesthouse—homey, simple, convenient, and friendly. With the colorful array of flowers, it's aptly named. The guesthouse is Victorian, from marble-topped bureaus to spindle beds. And Mount Washington serves as a delightful backdrop.

JACKSON

About seven miles above North Conway on N.H. 16 is Jackson, right at the geographical center of the Mount Washington Valley and the central point for cross-country skiing in the region. Besides being right in the middle of the downhill ski areas, Jackson has its own ski-touring organization. It also has a collection of delightful inns open winter and summer. The **Jackson Chamber of Commerce,** P.O. Box 304, Jackson, N.H. 03846, will send you information, or you can phone the **Jackson Chamber of Commerce Information and Reservation Center** (☎ **603/383-9356,** or toll free 800/866-3334).

Inns

Christmas Farm Inn

N.H. 16B (P.O. Box CC), Jackson, N.H. 03846. ☎ **603/383-4313.** 30 rms, 5 cottages. $136–$190 double; $95 per person cottage. Rates include breakfast, dinner, and service. Children under 12 stay in parents' room for $25 (which is for meals). AE, MC, V. Free parking. Directions: Follow the road from the village toward the Black Mountain Ski Area.

Just outside the center of Jackson village proper, on the road up the hill to the Black Mountain Ski Area, is the Christmas Farm Inn. Here the proprietors hold that "hospitality makes the difference," but one must admit that the resort-style facilities help: The inn has its own pool and putting green (there are two professional golf courses near Jackson), a games room, a sauna, a lounge, a living room, shuffleboard, and a dining room done in Early American. The Christmas Inn has five separate places of accommodation, from the original inn (built in 1786) to a maple-sugaring house. Five two-bedroom cottages with fireplaces are also on hand for two couples or families, with prices based on four adults sharing each unit. The barn has four family rooms, and there's even a log cabin.

Dana Place Inn

N.H. 16, Pinkham Notch, N.H. 03846. ☎ **603/383-6822** or 800/537-9276. 35 rms. $125–$185 double. Rates include breakfast and dinner. AE, CB, DC, DISC, MC, V.

Dating to 1860, this farmhouse has had a few additions and today boasts many fine country-inn rooms, a good restaurant, an indoor pool and whirlpool, and four tennis courts. A TV is situated in a parlor for communal viewing or videos. The dining room has a fireplace, and there's a separate breakfast room. Deluxe rooms have views of the Ellis River. Children may be accommodated in many rooms at an extra charge for meals only. The former shared baths rooms have been combined to form family suites. Some rooms have exposed brick, and one has an ornamental fireplace. The inn is located seven minutes north of Jackson and five minutes south of Tuckerman's Ravine on N.H. 16.

Ellis River House

N.H. 16 (P.O. Box 656), Jackson, N.H. 03846. ☎ **603/383-9339** or 800/233-8309. Fax 603/383-4142. 18 rms (15 with bath). A/C TV TEL. $69–$99 single or double without bath, $79–$229 single or double with bath. Rates include breakfast. AE, DC, DISC, MC, V. Free parking.

In addition to the original four guest rooms in the lovely clapboard inn, the Ellis River House has less charming (more contemporary) rooms done with whirlpools for two, central air conditioning, fireplaces, and balconies or patios. In all, there are 11 rooms with fireplaces and three with whirlpools. There's also a whirlpool for those without private ones in their rooms. You'll have a hearty breakfast in the morning to get you ready for hiking in summer or skiing in winter.

✪ Inn at Thorn Hill

Thorn Hill Rd., Jackson, N.H. 03846. ☎ **603/383-4242** or 800/289-8990. 19 rms. A/C. $140–$275 double. Rates include breakfast and dinner. AE, DC, MC, V. Free parking, across the street. Closed Weekdays in Apr. Directions: From Jackson Village, take N.H. 16A through the covered bridge to Thorn Hill Road, turn right, and go up the hill to the inn.

The Inn at Thorn Hill is quite wonderful. The hospitality is genuine, the surroundings gracious, and the mood romantic and appealing. Designed by Stanford White, this 1895 yellow clapboard inn is just the ticket for unwinding or rewinding after a day on the slopes or bargain-hunting in North Conway's factory outlets. The living rooms are worldly and designed with detail. The bar is just big enough for a few close friends yet small enough to feel as though it's open just for you. The dining room is a treat; dinner may be romantic by candlelight and breakfast sumptuous as you look out at the glistening snow (usually not in summer!). Charming country rooms are in several buildings and cottages, including the roomy main inn. Among the changes going on is the addition of fireplaces and whirlpools in three cottages, which feature lovely sitting rooms and decks or a porch. The two-story cottage has a half bath upstairs along with a king-sized bed and a first-floor level with a sitting area, full bath with a whirlpool, and fireplace. You can open the shutters from the tub and see the fireplace—how romantic. Come here to eat even if you can't stay. The whole inn is nonsmoking.

Village House

N.H. 16A, Jackson, N.H. 03846. ☎ **603/383-6666** or 800/972-8343. Fax 603/383-6464. 15 rms (13 with bath). $55–$120 standard double without or with bath. Rates include breakfast. DISC, MC, V. Free parking. Directions: From N.H. 16 north, take N.H. 16A into Jackson.

In the center of Jackson, very near the covered bridge leading into the town from N.H. 16, is the Village House. The rooms here have an antique flavor. There's cable TV in the living room. Five rooms include kitchenettes, TVs, and balconies. Two units are for families, and one has its own whirlpool tub. They offer a swimming pool, a clay tennis court, and an outdoor spa. Rates include full breakfast in winter and continental breakfast in summer. The 50 percent repeat guest ratio attests to the inn's success.

Whitneys' Inn

N.H. 16B, Jackson, N.H. 03846. ☎ **603/383-8916** or 800/677-5737. 30 rms. $64–$126 double. Rates include breakfast. AE, DISC, MC, V. Free parking.

Just up the hill from the cross-country ski-touring center is Whitney's Inn. I've been visiting this inn for more than a decade, and its always a lovely and quiet respite. It offers a dining room with Hitchcock-style appointments, and there's a tavern in the barn. Rooms are graded standard or deluxe and impart a country flavor. An inddoor pool is planned, but if you can't wait, there's always the brook-fed pond for cooling off! The inn's own cross-country trails connect with the trails of the Jackson Ski Touring Foundation nearby.

Old-Fashioned Resorts

Eagle Mountain House

Carter Notch Rd., Jackson, N.H. 03846. ☎ **603/383-9111** or 800/966-5779. Fax 603/383-0854. 94 rms. TV TEL. $105–$210 double. AE, DC, DISC, ER, MC, V. Free parking. Directions: Drive out of Jackson Village a mile or so, past a series of cascading waterfalls, to find the Eagle Mountain House.

This is one of the remaining premier grand old resorts in New England. Originally built in 1879 and completely rebuilt in 1986, the five-story white clapboard hotel commands a magnificent view of the surrounding mountains. New management is breathing new life into this landmark property and some investment in the "back of the house" will bring added convenience with such modernization as a computer system. Facilities include a heated outdoor pool, whirlpool, tennis courts, a health club, a nine-hole golf course, a playground, and well-marked walking trails. The lobby is filled with rich leather sofas and the guest rooms with specially made furniture. The dining room serves traditional New England fare while the tavern serves more casual meals. You'll enjoy staying here.

Wentworth Resort Hotel

Jackson, N.H. 03846. ☎ **603/383-9700** or 800/637-0013. Fax 603/383-4265. 62 rms. TV TEL. $69–$159 double; $195–$350 condominium. AE, MC, V. Free parking. Directions: From N.H. 16 north, take N.H. 16A into the center of Jackson.

The Wentworth is a turn-of-the-century hotel, complete with a rambling frame main building, a lounge, elegant dining rooms, various cottages and overnight rooms, an 18-hole PGA golf course, a pool, and clay tennis courts. It was redone a couple years ago from top to bottom and all is shiny and bright. Lately, new central air conditioning and heating have been installed. The hotel is definitely of a graceful, older time. Condominium units (rentable by the day, week, or month) have been added in clusters. the restaurant takes great pride in its menu, featuring such choices as citrus-marinated boneless duck breast, honey-roasted rack of lamb, and certified Angus beef. End with a berry tart or lemon sponge pie.

A Motel

The village of Jackson is known for its country inns, and staying in one of these excellent places is a real treat. But—as you'll see—it's not inexpensive, especially when you add the 8% state room tax and the 15% "service charge," which are often found only in the fine print. For more reasonable prices in Jackson, try the motel listed below.

Covered Bridge Motor Lodge

N.H. 16 (P.O. Box V), Jackson, N.H. 03846. ☎ **603/383-6630** or 800/634-9151. 32 rms, 4 efficiencies. A/C TV TEL. $44–$84 double; $95 efficiency for two (two-night minimum). Rates include continental breakfast. AE MC, V. Free parking.

For reasonable prices in this high-priced village, try this attractive hostelry on the far side of the red covered bridge from the village. It has a tennis court, an indoor spa, and an outdoor pool. The modern units here are designed not to clash with Jackson's forest mood, and prices are reasonable. Four additional efficiency apartments rent by the week.

Mountain Hikers' Huts

The **Appalachian Mountain Club,** the organization that has done so much to preserve and maintain wilderness trails in New England, operates several lodging facilities in the White Mountain National Forest. At the **AMC's Pinkham Notch Visitor Center** in Gorham, N.H. 03581 (☎ **603/466-2721**), 11 miles north of Jackson on N.H. 16, people of all ages, whether AMC members or not, can find inexpensive bunkroom-type accommodations (106 bunks in all) and simple but hearty meals. A bunk and breakfast costs $35 per adult; bed and supper is $40; bed, breakfast, and supper is $45. Children 12 and under receive a discount for the beds and meals, and as a convenience the kitchen will make up trail lunches for $5 per person. Discounts are also available for AMC members. Note that you must have reservations, and they must be secured by a nonrefundable per-person per-night deposit. If you'd like a room alone, you'll have to pay $20 extra for each unused bunk in the room, if others are turned away as a result. All these rules seem quite sensible. Note that *the 8% tax is already included* in these prices. MasterCard and Visa are accepted. Every Saturday and daily during July and August a free lecture program is given in the evening and may include topics on natural history, cultural history, or adventure travel.

Besides the Pinkham Notch Visitor Center the AMC maintains a laudable system of **mountain huts** along its hiking trails in the mountains. Similar accommodations and meals are provided at similar prices, and with similar reservation arrangements. The huts are attended and trail meals prepared by "hutmen" and "hutwomen," a hearty breed of New England youth who pride themselves on being able to pack on their backs all the supplies needed in the huts—to a weight that would make a normal person stagger—and almost run up the mountains with the load several times a week. Guided hikes are featured throughout the summer. Write or call for details.

8 Crawford Notch & Bretton Woods

About 20 miles NE of North Conway

North and east on U.S. 302 from Glen will take you through scenic **Crawford Notch** to **Crawford Notch State Park.** The park is a fine place for hiking and fishing, and you can see two impressive waterfalls—the Flume and the Silver Cascades—from the highway. Facilities include a 24-site campground, a picnic area, an information booth, and a shop featuring the products of New Hampshire artisans. The ruins of the **Willey House** hold a mystery and a story from the 1820s, when the road was being cut and the Willey family set up house in Crawford Notch to provide for the teams that would pass through the valley. In August 1826, one of the worst storms ever to hit the White Mountains wreaked havoc in the valley, with floods, landslides, wind, and rain that left the Willey House unharmed but resulted in the death of every member of the household.

GETTING THERE   By Bus   See the beginning of this chapter.

By Car   Crawford Notch and Bretton Woods are on U.S. 302.

ESSENTIALS   The **telephone area code** is **603.** If you have questions, contact the **Mount Washington Valley Visitors Center,** at the information booth on Main Street in North Conway (☎ **603/356-3171**). Or contact P.O. Box 2300, North Conway, N.H. 03860 (☎ 800/367-3364); they'll send you a free 68-page guide to the area.

WHAT TO SEE AND DO

Certainly the quaintest way to get to the top of Mount Washington is by the **Mount Washington Cog Railway** (☎ **603/846-5404** or **800/922-8825**). It's a 3¹/₂-mile track along a steep trestle up the mountainside. The locomotive (powered by steam) drives a cog wheel on its undercarriage which engages with pins between the rails to pull the locomotive and train up the slope. In operation since 1869, the three-hour round-trip scenic excursion is a lot of fun. At the portion of the run known as Jacob's Ladder the grade is a surprising 37°, but the little engine pulls along trustworthily despite the steepness. At the top, the average summer temperature is 40°F and there may be a stiff wind. Stroll to the new visitors center for a snack, drink, or souvenir, and then tour the mountaintop: See the displays highlighting the worst of Mount Washington's weather. If you pick a clear day to ascend the 6,288-foot summit, it will seem as though you can see all the way to Europe!

The base station, where you board the train, is six miles off U.S. 302 east of Twin Mountain, N.H. The season is May 1 through Columbus Day (Canadian Thanksgiving), with weekends-only runs until Memorial Day, then daily runs sometimes starting at 8am, and continuing hourly after June 26, with the last train leaving at 4pm. Have reservations, or try to take an early train—perhaps the 8am—to avoid having to wait in line. Round-trip fares are $35 for adults, $24 for children 6 to 12, and free for children under 6 who sit on a parent's lap. Remember to wear a sweater or jacket, or both, for the cool weather at the top, no matter how warm it is at the bottom.

WHERE TO STAY

Mount Washington Hotel & Resort

U.S. 302, Bretton Woods, N.H. 03575. ☎ **603/278-1000** or 800/258-0330. 230 units. $185–$625 double in hotel (with breakfast and dinner); $90–$189 double in the Bretton Arms; $70–$129 double in the lodge. AE, DC, DISC, MC, V. Free parking. Hotel closed mid-Oct to mid-May. Directions: From North Conway, follow U.S. 302 28 miles north to Bretton Woods.

The Mount Washington Hotel and Resort, a National Historic Landmark, is synonymous with the White Mountains region. Ever since this once-grand hotel hosted the famous 1944 Bretton Woods Conference, which established the world monetary system for the postwar period, it has warmed the hearts of many guests. The grounds are lovely, actually spectacular, with a golf course (29 holes), and the hotel's white frame building has a red roof that makes a grand impression. This year the hotel reopens for its 94th season, one the collection of owners hopes will be a banner year since the renovation program begun four years ago has come to a close. The wonderful lobby has a working fireplace, and the observation lounge overlooks the links. Other facilities include tennis courts, an outdoor pool, and stables.

The casual and fine dining room continue to improve and there are also lounges for revitalizing after a round golf. Guest rooms are attractive and get spruced more and more each year.

The Bretton Arms, a Victorian inn on the grounds, has more intimacy for some folks, and the Bretton Woods Motor Inn, at the entry, is likely to please those with less lofty expectations.

Notchland Inn

Harts Location, N.H. 03812. ☎ **603/374-6131** or 800/866-6131. 11 rms. $110–$160 double with breakfast, $146–$200 double with breakfast and dinner. Rates depend on season; a minimum stay may be required. AE, DISC, MC, V. Free parking. Directions: From North Conway, follow U.S. 302 north 19 miles to Harts Location.

At Crawford Notch, one of the most spectacular sites on the East Coast, stands the Notchland Inn. Also quite magnificent in its own right, the granite mansion set on 400 acres has rooms with working fireplaces and antiques. When I last visited the inn, I was given the grand tour by the new owners—and it was a grand tour. Les Schoof and Ed Butler have put their own brand of hospitality into the place, and old-timers and new guests will be equally pleased with the result. The architecture is stately, the grounds pruned to perfection and the furnishings quite commendable—including the dining room where five-course dinners are served nightly. The owners love to explain the lore of the land. I like the ground-floor room just past the stairs in the corner. It has the most country ambience, but the others offer their own charm. The hot tub sits in a gazebo by the pond. Activities include wagon and sleigh rides, cross-country skiing, hiking, canoeing, and cycling from the inn.

NEARBY

Venture about 15 minutes farther north on U.S. 302 from Bretton Woods and you'll come upon the little town of Bethlehem (no pun intended), with a fine inn of its own that makes a nice alternative to Bretton Woods's selections.

Adair—a Country Inn

U.S. 302 (P.O. Box 850), Bethlehem, N.H. 03574. ☎ **603/444-2600** or 800/441-2606. Fax 603/444-4823. 7 rms, 1 suite. $105–$175 double; $145–$175 suite. Rates include breakfast. AE, MC, V.

This three-story white clapboard home is as pretty in summer as it is bathed in snow each winter. With 200 acres of pastoral grounds, the inn offers you an opportunity to go exploring at your own pace. The attention to detail is commendable: note the square nails in the maple floor in the entry, the granite foundation in the downstairs tavern replete with a billiards table and fireplace, a parlor for reading, an attractive dining room, and a sun porch. If you've been shopping in North Conway, about an hour away, you'll return here to fresh cookies and cakes served with tea at 4pm. Coffee and tea are brewing at 8am each day too, followed by a full breakfast served between 8 and 9:30am once you've jump-started your day. Accommodations contain a quaint mix of period appointments, both reproductions and antiques. One suite is available with a fireplace, and there are also fireplaces in some bedrooms. The Lincoln and Cabor rooms are good choices.

9 Waterville Valley

10 miles NE of I-93 at Campton Upper Village

GETTING THERE By Car   Take I-93 to Campton Upper Village, then follow N.H. 49 for 10 miles to Waterville Valley.

ESSENTIALS   The **telephone area code** is 603. The **Waterville Valley Lodging Bureau,** Waterville Valley, N.H. 03215 (☎ **603/236-8371** or **800/ 468-2553**), provides a free reservations service.In 1829 a small settlement in a remote New Hampshire valley was incorporated as a town. A few farms, perhaps a small store, and a tiny public library—that was all there was to Waterville Valley. Today the little settlement is still there, in a beautiful spot deep within the White Mountains National Forest. A tasteful, tactful developer owns the valley and has dictated the shape of the new resort community. The results so far are very encouraging, almost a marvel: hotels and condominium developments under different ownership, all of striking and interesting design, furnished in good taste and staffed with competent, concerned personnel. Two ski areas are handy, a golf course and lots of tennis courts await players, and hiking, bicycling, fishing, and snowshoeing are right at a visitor's doorstep. This is a very fine resort.

WHAT TO SEE & DO

IN SUMMER   It seems as if they've thought of everything here. First and foremost, the valley is deep within the national forest, so hiking and fishing are easy to find. For tennis, there are 18 clay courts and lessons by a professional staff. The golf course in the valley is 9 holes, and not too far away at White Mountains Country Club is an 18-hole course. Guests at the Valley Inn can use its paddle-tennis courts for free; the general public can use them, day and night, for a fee. Bikes can be rented in the town square. And then, of course, there's shopping in the town square or a ride to the top of Mt. Tecumseh on the "High Country Express," the fastest gondola in the east.

IN WINTER   Although snowshoeing, hiking, skating, and general taking of country-mountain air are all possible and enjoyable in Waterville Valley, most people come to ski the trails and slopes of Mt. Tecumseh and Snow's Mountain. **Mount Tecumseh** is the larger and more elaborate of the two, with two triple-chair lifts, five double-chair lifts, a T-bar, a J-bar, and a platter-pull lift. The vertical drop is more than 2,000 feet, and there are 48 trails and slopes. Rentals and lessons are easily available, as is a quick meal at the base cafeteria. A schuss bus takes guests from Waterville Valley hotels to Tecumseh and back. The other area, **Snow's Mountain,** is right in the valley near the hotels of the village, and has three intermediate and beginners' slopes. It's for first-timers and learners, with one double-chair lift and a vertical drop of less than 600 feet. To keep the crowds down, Mt. Tecumseh and Snow's Mountain operate on a limited-ticket basis (no more than a 15-minute wait for the lift on average). For information about snow at both areas, call ☎ **603/236-4144.**

Ski packages for two, three, five, or seven nights are offered, and all facilities in the valley participate. Depending on what you want, you can get a package that includes lodging, meals, lifts, and/or lessons. Prices depend on which hotel you choose and what options you need to do the sort of skiing you're after. Options are also offered for ski touring (trail fees, lessons, equipment, and lodging) in the packages.

WHERE TO STAY

Golden Eagle Lodge

Snowsbrook Rd., Waterville Valley, N.H. 03215. ☎ **603/236-4600** or 800/910-4499. Fax 603/236-4947. 139 condominium units. TV TEL. $89–$319 per unit. Children stay free in parents' room. AE, DC, DISC, MC, V. Free parking.

Fashioned in the style of 19th-century grand New England resorts, the Golden Eagle rises proudly to the occasion. It was designed by Graham Gund Architects, one of the most distinguished firms in the United States. The crescent-shaped six-story building with green shutters and turrets is a mass of oversize windows, more than half of which look out onto Corcoran Pond, named after the man who so carefully developed much of this valley. The 139 condominium units vary in size from 650 to 1,050 square feet, sleeping two to eight people, and are fully furnished with understated accoutrements. Rates include use of the pool, sports center, and many other facilities in the valley.

Snowy Owl Inn

Village Rd., Waterville Valley, N.H. 03215. ☎ **603/236-8383** or 800/766-9969. 82 rms. TV TEL. $60–$150 double. Rates include continental breakfast and wine and cheese in the afternoon. AE, DC, DISC, MC, V. Free parking.

This four-story inn is situated close to the slopes and spotlights a fieldstone fireplace in the knotty-pine lobby, a lounge with another fireplace for aprés-ski, an indoor pool, an outdoor pool, a whirlpool, and a sauna. Sturdy rooms are built to take skiers' abuse, and half of them have whirlpools and wet bars.

Valley Inn

Tecumseh Rd., Waterville Valley, N.H. 03215. ☎ **603/236-8336** or 800/343-0969. Fax 603/236-4294. 52 rms. TV TEL. Summer/foliage season, and late fall to late spring, $55–$185 double; late spring and late fall, $55–$165 double. Children 12 and under stay free in parents' room. AE, DISC, MC, V. Free parking.

The attractive design of the Valley Inn adds to the area scenery and provides some unexpected bonuses to guests. Many rooms overlook the valley and mountains; others, the forest and settlement. Most guest rooms have a king-size bed, whirlpool bath, pull-out sofa bed, and air conditioning. The inn's heated indoor/ outdoor pool is open all year: Part is enclosed by the building, but a huge window comes down just to water level and you can swim underneath it to the outdoor portion of the pool, winter or summer. The Valley Inn has other athletic goodies: two platform (or paddle) tennis courts, saunas, a Jacuzzi, and a games room. The inn's dining room has a treetop-level view, and the lounge has live entertainment on weekends and holidays.

LONG-TERM STAYS

Several of the condominium developments in the valley have long-term (by the month or the season) rental rates for those who want an apartment rather than a hotel room. Accommodations range from one-bedroom apartments for one or two people to three-bedroom apartments that can take 8 to 10 people. Each apartment is completely furnished, including kitchen utensils and dinner service, all linens, and cable color TV. There are various package and weekly plans, both for normal and holiday periods, and low-season specials are available.

For information, contact **Windsor Hill Condominiums,** Jennings Peak Road, Waterville Valley, N.H. 03215 (☎ **603/236-8321** or **800/343-1286**). Their apartments also rent by the day (two-day minimum) for $278 to $590 for a weekend, or $340 to $660 for a five-night ski week. In summer you'll pay $364 to $665 per week. MasterCard and Visa are accepted.

Another firm to contact is **Condominium Vacations,** P.O. Box 389, Waterville Valley, N.H. 03215 (☎ **603/236-4101** or **800/468-2553**). Their 40 privately owned condos have from one to four bedrooms, and may be rented by the night. Rates range from $89 for a one-bedroom condo sleeping up to four people on a midweek night in summer, to $179 per night for a four-bedroom condo sleeping 8 to 10 people on a weekend night in high summer. Call for full information.

AN EXCURSION TO SQUAM LAKE

If you want to take a delightful detour for a couple of hours or, better yet, take an overnight trip, take the Holderness/U.S. 3 exit off I-93 and make your way a short distance to Squam Lake.

The movie *On Golden Pond* was filmed here and highlighted the beautiful shoreline and famous loons. My favorite spot in New England is here at the Manor on Golden Pond. You might elect to take one of the day tours of the lake from the dock of the Manor on Golden Pond.

Continue to Center Sandwich for a glimpse of an old New Hampshire town. It's a charmer. If you happen to be here when the "over the mountain road" is open, you can cut across the 10 or so miles and get into Waterville Valley. Keep in mind that the potholes may sometimes seem like sink holes. On my last trek across this road, I thought I might blow a tire, but my compact disc player never skipped a beat!

WHERE TO STAY & DINE

✪ Manor on Golden Pond

U.S. 3, Holderness, N.H. 03245. ☎ **603/968-3348** or 800/545-2141. 24 rms, 4 cottages. A/C TV TEL. $180–$325 double with breakfast and dinner; $825–$1,500 per week cottage without meals. AE, MC, V. Free parking. Directions: Take I-93 to Exit 24, Ashland/Holderness; take a right on U.S. 3 south and travel for 4.7 miles.

Bambi and David Arnold had something superlative in mind when they purchased the Manor and transplanted themselves from Orange County, California, to Squam Lake, the site of the movie *On Golden Pond.* On 13 acres and overlooking the lake famous for its loons, the marvelous retreat will seduce even the most hard-to-please guest. It ranks with Cape Cod's Whalewalk Inn as my two favorite's in all New England. Dating back to 1907, this rich French vanilla colored establishment is enchanting with its columned entry, a gravel drive (to preserve the integrity of the inn), tennis courts tucked to one side, an outdoor pool, and two shoreline acres where you can take out a paddleboat or occupy a private lakeside cottage (the water laps at your porch). Inside, the main inn is a delightfully designed English manor estate with several burning fireplaces, a beamed-ceiling dining room, a reading nook outside the pub with a baby grand piano, and a separate breakfast room with its own fireplace and adjoining deck overlooking the lake. At breakfast, a gourmet feast, soft music and the sound of loons can be heard. Guest rooms are like the pages of *House Beautiful* brought to life. Seven have working fireplaces; some have four-poster rice beds, others have canopy beds, and all are wonderfully decorated. Treat yourself and someone special by booking the Windsor, or another room with a view of the water. A few cottages, more modestly decorated, are also available— they're perfect for families. Children under 12 are only permitted in the cottages. At the edge of the lake is one of the cottages and there are a handful of small boats there too. Few places anywhere will provide the romance in store for guests here.

10   The Franconia Notch Area

14 miles SE of Littleton, 11 miles N of Lincoln

GETTING THERE   By Bus   See the beginning of this chapter.

By Car   Follow I-93 to U.S. 3 to Franconia Notch.

ESSENTIALS   The **telephone area code** is **603.** The local **visitors center** is at the intersection of I-93 and the Kancamagus Highway (☎ **603/745-8720**). It's run both by the White Mountains Association personnel and also by national forest rangers; it's open daily from 8:30am to 5pm (to 6pm in July and August). Interstate 93 comes up from Manchester and Concord to pass through the White Mountains National Forest. The towns of North Woodstock and Lincoln form the center of the developed area within the forest, and it's here that most people come to look for a room, a meal, or any of the other services of civilization. At this point the Kancamagus Highway heads east through the most scenic 33-mile drive in the mountains; north of Lincoln and North Woodstock are several natural curiosities, including the famous Old Man of the Mountain at the narrow pass called Franconia Notch.

The area centered on North Woodstock and Lincoln is very rich in possibilities for outdoor activities, especially hiking, camping, picnicking, and skiing at Cannon Mountain and Mittersill in Franconia Notch itself, and at Loon Mountain near Lincoln on the Kancamagus Highway.

WHAT TO SEE & DO
SIGHTS

Franconia Notch State Park is surrounded by the **White Mountains National Forest.** The natural wonders of the park are impressive indeed, including the

Notch (pass, or gap) itself, the Flume, the Basin, several lakes, and the rock out-crop in the shape of a man's profile that has all but become the state symbol of New Hampshire, the famous Old Man of the Mountain. The state park offers a wealth of outdoor activities: Lafayette Campground, the Appalachian Mountain Club's system of trails and huts, a nine-mile paved bike path, trout fishing, swim-ming in the mountain lakes, a number of beautiful picnic sites, and a ski area, Cannon Mountain with an aerial tramway that operates winter and summer.

THE OLD MAN   The Old Man of the Mountain, also called the Great Stone Face, is one of New Hampshire's most famous features. After thousands of years in the making, it was "discovered" by white settlers at the beginning of the 19th century. The profile is formed by several ledges of granite, and in a cubist sort of way the representation is quite striking. But don't expect a mammoth image: The face is only about 40 feet high, and it's set on a cliff 1,000 feet above the valley floor. Its grandeur comes not from its size, but rather from its fidelity (it really does look like a human face in profile) and its impressive perch high in the sky, gazing out over the mountains. In recent years the state has spent a good deal of money preserving the face from the ravages of nature, for even granite formations crumble given enough wind, rain, and ice. From the highway parking lot, a path leads down to the shores of Profile Lake, and descriptive plaques tell you all about the Old Man.

South of the Old Man along U.S. 3 and to the east lies the undulant crest of Mt. Liberty, which to some people resembles George Washington lying in state. Take a look and feel free to concur or disagree!

THE BASIN & THE FLUME   Also south of the Old Man along U.S. 3, signs will point to a side road and the Basin, a huge glacial pothole in the native gran-ite, 20 feet in diameter. The hole is at the foot of a waterfall and was presumably made by the action of small rocks and stones whirled around by the force of the water. It's a cool spot, good for contemplation.

Four miles north of North Woodstock, but still south of the Basin, is the Flume, a natural gorge or cleft in the granite. A boardwalk has been erected along the 800-foot length of the Flume, and for $6 ($3 for children) you can walk through its cool depths, the granite walls rising to 60 or 70 feet above you, mosses and plants growing precariously in niches here and there. Signs explain how nature formed the Flume and point out interesting sights along the way. Near the Flume is a covered bridge thought to be one of the oldest in the state, perhaps erected as early as the 1820s. There's a seasonal information office (☎ 603/745-8391) here, which, like the Flume, is open from mid-May to mid-October.

CANNON MOUNTAIN AERIAL TRAMWAY   An impressive view of Franconia Notch and the mountains is yours if you take the Cannon Mountain Aerial Tramway (☎ 603/823-5563) to the top of the line. The tramway operates from the end of May to October, daily from 9am to 4:30pm, at a round-trip cost of $8 for adults, $4 for children 6 to 12, free for children under 6. The tramway station is just off I-93 Exit 2 and U.S. 3 north of the Old Man, and has its own parking lot. In the weathered-shingle building at the base and the summit station are cafeterias, should you be in need of a light meal, and the New England Ski Museum.

ROBERT FROST'S FARM   Only a mile or two from the town of Franconia is the Frost Place, Ridge Road (☎ 603/823-5510), the farm that the great poet bought in the early part of this century. He lived here with his wife and children during some of the most productive and inspired years of his life and wrote many of his best and most famous poems to describe life on this farm and the scenery surrounding it. Among these are "The Road Not Taken" and "Stopping by Woods on a Snowy Evening."

The price of admission includes a 20-minute video shown in the barn behind the house. The show explains much about Frost's early life and work and about the countryside here. The farmhouse has been kept as faithful to the period as possible, and there are numerous interesting exhibits of Frost memorabilia, though much of the furniture is from other places. It's spare and simple, as was the rural lifestyle at the time. Behind the house in the forest is a half-mile-long poetry-nature trail. Frost's poems are mounted on plaques in sites appropriate to the things they describe. In several places the plaques have been erected at the exact spots where Frost composed the poems. The various trees, shrubs, and flowers along the path are marked, though only some will be in bloom when you visit.

Admission to the site costs $3 for adults, half price for children 6 to 15, free for children under 6, $2 for seniors. It's open late May through June, Saturday and Sunday from 1 to 5pm; and July through the Columbus Day weekend, Wednesday through Monday from 1 to 5pm.

To get to the Frost Place, leave Franconia on N.H. 116 south, and after exactly a mile look for a sign on the right indicating Bickford Hill Road. Then turn left onto Ridge Road, a dirt road, and the Frost Place will be up a way on your right. You come to the parking lot before the house; obey the sign and park in the lot, and walk up the road to the house.

THE LOST RIVER   As you travel through New Hampshire, you'll see many bumper stickers proclaiming "I FOUND THE LOST RIVER." You can find it, too—six miles west of North Woodstock on N.H. 112 in Kinsman Notch. Explore the narrow gorge and caverns with the help of walkways, ladders, and bridges. Like most of the attractions in this neck of the woods, it's open from mid-May to mid-October. Admission is $7 for adults, $4 for children 6 to 12, free for children under 6.

CLARK'S TRADING POST   Clark's on U.S. 3 just north of Lincoln has been a traditional shop for families traveling in the White Mountains since 1928. In addition to an old-fashioned photo parlor, water-bumper boats, a magic house, a narrow-gauge steam locomotive, and a gift shop selling moccasins, a family of native black bears performs daily. It's a bit on the campy side, but it's also part of many people's childhood.

SKIING

There are two notable ski resorts in the Franconia Notch area: Cannon Mountain near the Notch itself and Loon Mountain in Lincoln, at the western end of the Kancamagus Highway.

CANNON MOUNTAIN   Besides the 70-passenger aerial tramway, Cannon Mountain (☎ 603/823-5563) has one triple-chair and two double-chair lifts, one quad-chair, and a pony lift, all with an hourly capacity of close to 7,000 skiers. There are 29 trails, about a quarter of them novice, another quarter expert, and the remaining half intermediate. The vertical drop is 2,145 feet, and besides having snowmaking equipment for the snowless days, the slopes are positioned so that they naturally receive and retain more than the average amount of white stuff. Cannon Mountain is operated by the state, as it's in a state park. Besides the three cafeterias and the base station and lounges nearby, you'll find a ski school, a nursery, and a ski shop where you can rent equipment. This operation had been attempting to acquire parts of the former Mittersill ski area to expand but has yet to be successful.

LOON MOUNTAIN   A drive two miles east of Lincoln along the Kancamagus Highway brings you to Loon Mountain (☎ 603/745-8111, or 603/745-8100 for snow information), a modern ski area with a gondola (four-passenger cars), two triple-chair lifts, and five double-chair lifts to take 12,150 skiers an hour up the mountain. The vertical drop is 2,100 feet, and the longest run is 2^1/$_2$ miles. Loon has a limited-lift-lines policy and top-to-bottom snowmaking capacity. The Mountain Club on Loon, managed by Marriott, has 240 rooms and a restaurant; other services at the base lodge include a cafeteria, lounge, nursery, ski shop, and rental shop. Lift fees are $43 on weekends, slightly less on weekdays.

In summer and fall, Loon Mountain's gondolas operate from 9am to 7pm daily to take visitors on the 7,100-foot trip (1,850-foot rise) to the summit, at $8.50 per adult, $4.50 per child, free for kids 6 and under. You can also rent in-line skates and mountain bikes. There are cafeterias at both the base and summit stations.

Several ski areas offer package arrangements through the **Ski 93 Association,** named because the areas involved are all accessible by Interstate 93. Bretton Woods, Cannon Mountain, Loon Mountain, and Waterville Valley are among the members, and you can get three- or five-day cut-price lift tickets. Midweek passes good at all five areas are a real bargain. The association will be glad to help with reservations at area hotels, lodges, and inns. Write or call P.O. Box 517, Lincoln, N.H. 03251 (☎ 603/745-8101).

WHERE TO STAY

You can make your base at any of several places in the area. At the southern end of Franconia Notch State Park lies **North Woodstock,** at the junction of U.S. 3 and N.H. 112, a small and fairly attractive commercial center with a few inns. Just across the Pemigewasset River, where I-93 Exit 32 meets the Kancamagus Highway, is the town of **Lincoln,** basically a commercial strip with some motels and residences.

At the northern end of the state park, near I-93 Exit 38, are the towns of **Franconia** and **Sugar Hill,** with a good number of nice inns. Finally, at I-93 Exit 42, only a few miles from the Vermont state line, is the town of **Littleton,** the largest settlement in these parts. It has two nice old inns for you to consider.

IN NORTH WOODSTOCK

Woodstock Inn

80 Main St. (U.S. 3; P.O. Box 118), North Woodstock, N.H. 03262. ☎ **603/745-3951** or 800/321-3985. Fax 603/745-3701. 19 rms (11 with bath). TEL. $39–$75 double without bath, $59–$140 double with bath. Rates include full breakfast. Packages available. AE, DISC, MC, V. Free parking.

This century-old Victorian house has six guest rooms that share three baths. Decor is Victorian, of course, except for the color TVs and air conditioners in some rooms. Downstairs in the inn is a full restaurant and lounge (see "Where to Dine," below). Behind the inn is the Victorian Deachman House, which contains two more guest rooms, and across the street in the 100-year-old Riverside Building are 11 rooms with private baths. Attached to the rear of the main inn is the area's original train depot, which today offers pub-style lunches and dinners with entertainment in the lounge.

IN LINCOLN

Kancamagus Motor Lodge

N.H. 112 (Kancamagus Hwy.), Lincoln, N.H. 03251. ☎ **603/745-3365** or 800/346-4205 outside New Hampshire. 34 rms. A/C TV TEL. Summer, $64–$74 double; winter, $42–$74 double. DISC, MC, V. Free parking. Directions: Take I-93 to Exit 32, then drive east on N.H. 112 just over one mile.

On the Kancamagus Highway a mile west of the Loon Mountain ski area is this modern motel. It has a heated outdoor pool and rooms in a modern style furnished with private steambath, one queen-size or two double beds, and wall-to-wall carpeting. Its main draw is its location, very close to Loon Mountain and not far at all from the attractions of Franconia Notch. The Kancamagus has a dining room, which serves a filling and well-priced breakfast ($1.90 for bacon, egg, home-fries, and toast). An adjacent restaurant has a lounge.

Lincoln Motel

5 Church St., Lincoln, N.H. 03251. ☎ **603/745-2780**. 7 rms. A/C TV. High season, $52–$63 double; low season, $35 double. Kitchenette unit $5 per day extra. DISC, MC, V. Free parking.

Right in town on N.H. 112 is an unprepossessing two-story structure with rooms that constitute one of the best bargains in the area, especially for skiers. You'll see the Lincoln Motel from the Kancamagus Highway, set back from the road half a block on the left-hand side as you go from North Woodstock east toward Loon Mountain. Advantages here include good, if basic, rooms, low prices, and Loon Mountain less than two miles away.

IN FRANCONIA & SUGAR HILL

In the small town of Franconia, a reference point is the confluence of N.H. 18 and N.H. 116. After coming from the south and meeting, the two routes head north to Littleton.

Franconia Inn

Easton Rd., Franconia, N.H. 03580. ☎ **603/823-5542** or 800/473-5299. 34 rms, 3 suites. $65–$97 double; from $108 suite. AE, MC, V. Free parking. Closed Apr. Directions: In Franconia, turn onto N.H. 116 at the Mobil station; the inn is two miles down the road on the right.

Just over two miles south of Franconia along N.H. 116 (Easton Road) is the Franconia Inn, a nice old white clapboard place built in 1868. It still provides many of the services that once brought wealthy Bostonians here: riding horses, outdoor pool, four clay tennis courts, a family-size hot tub, bicycle tours, and hiking trails. Several golf courses are nearby. Right across the road from the inn is **Foxfire Aviation, Inc.** (☎ **603/823-8881**), which will take you up for sailplane (glider) rides. Besides so many things to do, there is the tranquillity and beauty of the verdant Easton Valley, with fine views of Cannon Mountain, Mt. Lafayette, and the Franconia and Kinsman mountain ranges.

The guest rooms at the inn are well maintained and somewhat old-fashioned, but all have newly renovated baths. Prices depend on view and room size. An adult can have breakfast and dinner daily for $32.50; meal plans for children depend on their ages. Add taxes and tips. When you call, ask for a corner room, and also about package plans, which may save you some money.

For rainy days and evenings, there are movies, a games room with coin-operated games for the kids, a billiards room, an oak-paneled library with fireplace, and a screened porch set with wicker furniture. Downstairs, the Rathskeller Lounge has quiet entertainment many nights. The nice candlelit dining room adds considerably to the feeling that you've settled yourself into a huge old summer estate owned by one of your rich uncles in the heart of Robert Frost country. The "uncles" in this case are innkeepers Richard and Alec Morris. It's comfy here. Ski season, by the way, is one of the inn's best times, with trails radiating from the inn throughout the valley.

Horse & Hound Inn

205 Wells Rd., Franconia, N.H. 03580. ☎ **603/823-5501** or 800/450-5501. 10 rms (8 with bath). TEL. $100–$120 double with bath. Rates include breakfast and dinner but not tax, tip, and drinks. AE, CB, DC, DISC, MC, V. Free parking. Directions: Go south out of Franconia on N.H. 18; after 2$^1/_2$ miles, look for Wells Road on the right, and it's half a mile to the inn.

This is a real true-to-life country inn according to the old style. It's not plush and fancy with priceless antiques everywhere, but rather simple, well kept, and attractive. It's well off the main roads and, blissfully, perfectly quiet except for the crackle of a fire in the fireplace on a cool day or the murmur of conversation in the lounge. Rooms come with phones for outgoing calls (free local calls) and a double, a queen-size, or two double beds. Two units for families or couples traveling together offer two bedrooms sharing a single bath (when only one bedroom is needed, the other is locked off). The inn's dining room serves good, hearty, honest food, such as sirloin steaks and surf-and-turf; a full dinner might cost $25 to $30 per person, drinks, tax, and tip included if you're not on a meal plan.

Sugar Hill Inn

N.H. 117, Sugar Hill, Franconia, N.H. 03580. ☎ **603/823-5621** or 800/54-VISIT. 10 rms, 6 cottages. $169–$209 double or cottage. Rates include breakfast and dinner. MC, V. Free parking. Directions: Take N.H. 18 out of Franconia and turn left onto N.H. 117 for about a mile.

In the village of Sugar Hill, a few miles west of Franconia along N.H. 117, is the Sugar Hill Inn, perched up on a hill and surrounded by grassy lawns. The original farmhouse was built in 1789, but I doubt that it then had such a commodious and welcoming front porch. In any case, the house became an inn in 1929, still with its original fireplaces (some now fitted with Franklin stoves), old board floors, and wood beams. Now the rooms have very pretty country furnishings, quilts, old paintings, rocking chairs, and hand-stenciled designs on the walls. Each of the rooms has twin beds, a double bed, or a queen-size bed. Beside the inn are six small guest cottages with similar decor, private bath, carpeting, and TV; they're open all year since gas fireplaces were added. The higher rates for the cottages are for the foliage season and include dinner. An adjoining roadside pub now has a player piano. Small, quiet, congenial, authentic—that's the Sugar Hill Inn. Jim and Barbara Quinn are your hosts.

IN LITTLETON

White clapboard churches with graceful steeples and the solid four-square brick facades of Main Street's commercial district: This is Littleton, N.H., a fine New England town. It's neither a quaint village nor an industrial town, but something in between; Littleton may be to New Hampshire what Lake Wobegon is to Minnesota.

The local chamber of commerce and historical society have put together a pamphlet that will take you on a guided tour of the town's landmarks, including the post office and courthouse, Masonic Temple, public library, and Tilton's Opera building.

Rabbit Hill Inn

N.H. 18, Lower Waterford, VT 05848. ☎ **802/748-5168** or 800/76-BUNNY. 20 rms. A/C. $179–$259 double. Rates 15% less in winter midweek. Rates include breakfast and dinner. MC, V. Free parking. Directions: From I-93 North, take Exit 44 onto N.H. 18 North and go about two miles to the inn. From I-91 North or South, take Exit 19 to I-93 South briefly, then take Exit 1 onto Vt. 18 for about seven miles.

Though it's actually in Vermont, the Rabbit Hill Inn is connected to Littleton, N.H., by cultural and commercial ties. Established in 1795, the inn was bought by John and Maureen Magee in 1987. Most rooms have views of the mountains; these views are significant, as the inn is set into the side of a hill with a magnificent panorama of the mountains and the Connecticut River Valley. The plan to have breakfast and dinner here makes sense, as Lower Waterford is a tiny hamlet with few other dining opportunities.

The elegant Rabbit Hill Inn is homey in its welcome. Beautiful antique furnishings are in the dining room, Irish pub, parlor with Federal period furnishings and guest rooms, 12 of which have fireplaces, some with a Jacuzzi for two. Across the road from the inn is the village church, built in 1859, and next to that the small library. Besides these public-service buildings, the village of Lower Waterford has fewer than a dozen houses. The Rabbit Hill Inn sometimes accounts for fully half the village's active population! It's idyllic and special here—"like Brigadoon," as John Magee says—and you'll love it.

WHERE TO DINE

Woodstock Inn

80 Main St., North Woodstock. ☎ **603/745-3951.** Reservations recommended. Main courses $10–$19. AE, DISC, MC, V. Daily 7am–10pm, Directions: From Exit 32 off I-93, turn right on N.H. 112, then right on N.H. 3; the inn is on the left. AMERICAN.

The Woodstock has perhaps the best full menu in the area. For a light lunch or a drink before or after dinner there's the Woodstock Station (the dining room) or the more formal Clement Room. The favored place to sit for dinner in the inn is on the enclosed porch next to one of the large windows looking out onto Main Street. The menu includes such selections as duck with peach sauce flamed with amaretto; sautéed chicken with pesto, artichokes, and sun-dried tomatoes; roast rack of lamb; beef Wellington; and salmon baked in parchment paper with fresh vegetables, capers, and Pernod. The Woodstock Station & Stock Room (the pub) has a wonderful selection of soups, salads, main dishes, desserts, and more, contained in a 16-page menu. You can dine sumptuously here for a mere $20, but your dinner bill will more likely be higher when drinks, dessert, tax, and tip are included. The Woodstock Inn provides some of the best dining in the area.

11 Lake Sunapee

Sunapee Harbor: 40 miles NW of Concord, 25 miles SE of Lebanon

GETTING THERE   By Plane   Northwest Airlines serves the airport at West Lebanon, 29 miles northwest of Sunapee Harbor.

By Bus   See the beginning of this chapter.

By Car   Follow I-89 to N.H. 11 South.

ESSENTIALS   The **telephone area code** is **603**. For information, contact the **Lake Sunapee Lodging Bureau,** P.O. Box 400, Sunapee, N.H. 03782 (☎ **603/ 763-2495** or **800/258-3530**). Lake Sunapee is a pleasant regional vacation spot in southwestern New Hampshire, not very far from the town of Hanover, which is home to Dartmouth College. Besides summer sports such as swimming, boating, and canoeing, the area around Lake Sunapee has its own small ski area in Mount Sunapee State Park. On a trip to Vermont or north to Hanover for a visit to Dartmouth, the shores of Lake Sunapee are a fine place to stop for a night or even a week.

Of the towns around the lake, Sunapee (sometimes called Sunapee Harbor), on the western shore, is the nicest, with a good collection of inns, motels, and resorts. Although in its early days Sunapee held a tannery, a gristmill, and several shops for woodworking industries, it now makes its living from summer visitors; in recent years, skiers have brought business to the town in winter as well.

The town of Mount Sunapee, on the southwestern shore, is not really a town at all, regardless of what it may say on your road map. The intersection of N.H. 103 and N.H. 103B, with a motel and the state park and state beach entrance, is the "town."

WHAT TO SEE & DO

To see Lake Sunapee, there's no better way than to catch the **MV *Mount Sunapee II*** (☎ 603/763-4030), which leaves Sunapee Harbor marina at 2:30pm on Saturday and Sunday from mid-May to mid-June for tours of the beautiful, very pure lake. From mid-June to Labor Day there are daily sailings at 10am and 2:30pm. And until mid-October the ship sails on weekends at 2:30pm. The tour lasts 1¹/₂ hours and costs $9 for adults. Kids under 12 pay $5; kids under 5 ride free. The *Mount Sunapee II* holds 150 people and the tour is narrated by the amiable captain.

In the summer, Sunapee hosts very well attended **flea markets** out on N.H. 103B at the blinking light (between Sunapee Harbor and Sunapee Lower Village). Both buyers and sellers flock to the intersection's roadsides, and everything from craftwork through antiques to junk is available.

The best **beach** in the area is the state park beach, near the state park entrance. The entrance fee covers use of changing rooms. Lake Sunapee is a Class A reservoir—the water is about as pure and unpolluted as you'll find anywhere.

Across the large traffic circle from the entrance road to the beach is the entrance to the state park and its chair lift to the summit of **Mount Sunapee** (☎ 603/ 763-2356). In summer the round-trip price in three-person chair lifts is $5.50 for adults, $2.50 for children 6 to 12, free for children under 6. The trip takes you over 1¹/₂ miles (1,510 feet straight up) to the summit at 2,743 feet. At the top there are walking trails (not difficult) to an overlook and to a glacial tarn named Lake Solitude. At the base of the mountain is a cafeteria; spacious lawns, hiking trails, and picnic areas are all open to the public at no charge.

For **skiing,** the Mount Sunapee area has three double-chair lifts, three triple-chair lifts, and a pony lift. The vertical drop is 1,500 feet on 36 slopes and trails (☎ 603/763-2356 for information). A ski school, a ski shop with rental equipment, a cafeteria, and a nursery are all available.

WHERE TO STAY

Though the Lake Sunapee region is perfect for vacationers, there is some spirit among the local people to limit touristic growth. Thus many of the long-standing inns here are more like self-contained mini-resorts. There are a few motels for those on a vagabond tour.

Dexter's Inn and Tennis Club

Stagecoach Rd. (P.O. Box 703F), Sunapee, N.H. 03782. ☎ **603/763-5571** or 800/232-5571. 19 rms. A/C. $135–$175 double. Rates include breakfast and dinner. Off-season package rates available. DISC, MC, V. Free parking. Closed Nov–Apr. Directions: From I-89, take Exit 12 and N.H. 11 west for 5¹/₂ miles to a left turn on Winn Hill Road for 1¹/₂ miles.

Dexter's is hidden away on a back road, but it has a fine view of Lake Sunapee and its surrounding mountains. Built in 1801, the yellow clapboard house was renovated in the 1930s and converted to an inn in 1948. It has been owned and run by the Simpson-Durfor family for well over two decades and has that family feel about it that makes even first-time visitors comfortable. Some of the rooms have antique pieces, including the beds; other rooms have more modern furnishings. Annex rooms have air conditioning. A cottage is available weekly. Breakfast will be delivered to your room if you like, and dinner is taken in the dining room.

Amusements include a well-equipped library and a piano in the living room, a pretty outdoor swimming pool, and three professional-grade tennis courts (complete with pro and pro shop). Tournaments include matches sanctioned by the USTA/NE. Other games include shuffleboard, croquet, and horseshoes.

Mount Sunapee Motel

N.H. 103, Mount Sunapee, N.H. 03255. ☎ **603/763-5592**. 22 rms. TV. $56–$63 double; $60–$78 two-room unit for two. Credit card payments cost 5% extra. AE, DC, MC, V. Free parking. Directions: From I-89, take Exit 9 and follow N.H. 103 west to the motel.

This very popular motel is right near the entrance to Mount Sunapee State Park. It's modern, with tile bathrooms, tub-shower combinations, and at least two beds in each room. Half the motel consists of 11 two-room units, each with a kitchenette; the outdoor pool is shared by all.

12 Hanover

5 miles N of Lebanon, 64 miles NW of Concord, 20 miles E of Woodstock, Vt.

GETTING THERE **By Plane** **USAir System** and **United Express** serve the airport at West Lebanon, six miles south of Hanover.

By Train **Amtrak** serves White River Junction, Vt., five miles south of Hanover.

By Bus See the beginning of this chapter. Short-run intercity bus service is operated by **Advance Transit** (☎ 603/448-2815).

By Car Follow I-89 to Exit 18 at Lebanon, then N.H. 120 north to Hanover; or follow I-91 in Vermont to Exit 13 in Norwich, then go east across the Connecticut River to Hanover.

ESSENTIALS The **telephone area code** is **603.** For visitor information, contact the **Hanover Area Chamber of Commerce,** P.O. Box 5105, Hanover, N.H. 03755 (☎ 603/643-3115).

The small town of Hanover is the home of one of the country's oldest and most prestigious colleges. **Dartmouth College** (named for the earl who was colonial secretary to King George III) was founded in 1769, and its charter gives a hint of why it was located in such a remote place: It was meant primarily "for the education and instruction of Youth of the Indian Tribes," and only secondarily for the education of "English Youth and others." Today, Dartmouth is more than a small undergraduate college; its graduate schools of medicine, engineering, and business administration are well respected, and the Hopkins Center for the Arts is the cultural focus of the entire region.

In many ways the college is the town and vice versa. College buildings of exceptional beauty and grace are scattered or clustered throughout Hanover, and most are shaded by trees of a prodigious height and girth. Anyone out for a drive would enjoy a walk through the campus, perhaps on one of the guided college tours (free) that leave from the college information booth during the summer; in winter, tours depart from McNutt Hall. To order tickets to performances, or to find out what's showing at the **Hopkins Center,** call **603/646-2422.**

In winter, Dartmouth's **Winter Carnival** is the major fun and social event, with special art shows, drama and concerts, and ice-sculpture contest, and other amusements.

WHAT TO SEE & DO

Everyone takes a tour of Dartmouth College, but for a more offbeat view of the campus and surrounding area, take a **hot-air balloon ride.** At the Post Mills Airport (P.O. Box 51, Post Mills, VT 05058; ☎ **802/333-9254**), you can take a sunrise or sunset balloon ride with trained professional balloonists who will float you up or down the Connecticut River Valley, depending on the whim of the wind. After you've helped with the set-up process, you'll be airborne for 1 to 1 1/2 hours, and finish with a champagne reception at the touchdown site. Oh, and don't worry, they'll take you back to the airport to pick up your car if you want. Balloons fly daily, weather and wind permitting. The cost for all this fun is $150 per person. To reach the airport from Hanover, cross the bridge to Vermont, take I-91 to Exit 14, turn left on Vt. 113, go six miles, and turn east onto Vt. 244. The airport is a quarter mile down the road on the right at the fork.

WHERE TO STAY & DINE
In Hanover

Hanover Inn

At the corner of Main and Wheelock Sts., Hanover, N.H. 03755. ☎ **603/643-4300** or 800/443-7024. Fax 603/646-3744. 70 rms, 22 suites. A/C TV TEL. $186 single or double; from $239 suite. AE, DC, DISC, MC, V. Parking $5 per night in underground garage, free in outdoor lot.

Hanover's prime hostelry is right in the center of town. Some rooms have views of the lawns and buildings of the college. It fills up quickly at major college events, such as orientation, graduation, and the big football games played at home. Decor is colonial, to fit in with the rest of Hanover, but modern comfort has been given great consideration. There are larger and slightly newer rooms in the east wing. Room service is available from 7am to 10pm.

The Hanover Inn's formal dining room and restaurant are supplemented by a lovely outdoor patio, under an awning, in summer. The feeling is very much that of an exclusive country club. At lunch, sandwiches are only about $5 and full luncheon meals (the daily specials) can be had for $8 to $10. The dinner menu offers a good and balanced selection of well-known meat, fish, and fowl dishes: Start with coconut-fried shrimp with apple-and-pear chutney, and then have anything from pan-fried brook trout to native spring lamb, and the total bill will be about $35 per person. The waitresses in black uniforms with white trim are silent, efficient, and friendly, waiting attentively at their stations when all the diners have been served. Room service is available for all three meals. You might elect to come for one of the wine-tasting dinners that so many rave about.

IN LYME

Alden Country Inn

On the Common, Lyme, N.H. 03768. ☎ **603/795-2222** or 800/794-2296. Fax 603/795-9436. 14 rms. $65–$105 double. Rates include breakfast. AE, MC, V. Free parking. Directions: From Lebanon, take N.H. 120 to N.H. 10 to Lyme Center.

If Hanover is the busy college town, Lyme, N.H., 10 miles north on N.H. 10, is the peaceful New England village. At the center of Lyme you'll see the high-pillared facade of the inn, built in 1809. Until 1995, it was known as the Lyme Inn and although the name has changed—along with the decor—the owners remain the same. The rooms here have an eclectic array of furnishings including many of the Federal period—both antiques and reproductions. You should know that the inn has its own tavern, replete with fireplace, a new chef, and now features dining on the porch.

IN NORWICH, VT

Norwich Inn

Main St., Norwich, VT 05055. ☎ **802/649-1143**. 22 rms. A/C TV TEL. $55–$109 double. AE, MC, V. Free parking, next to the inn.

Just across the Connecticut River from Hanover, in Vermont, you'll find the Norwich Inn, a nice hostelry known for its charm, dignity, and warm welcome as well as for the excellence of its dining room. The inn has been here since 1797 and its furnishings reflect its heritage, with brass and canopy beds in many rooms. The Victorian pub is called the Jasper Murdoch Alehouse, after the man who opened the inn almost 200 years ago. The current innkeepers are Sally and Tim Wilson. The cuisine in the pretty, formal dining room, or on the porch, is of a high order. The restaurant and some other areas have just been redone and look terrific. The alehouse brews 15 kinds of beer, so you'll never be without a cool libation. Take a look in the new micro-brewery housed in its own building.

12 Maine

There's something quintessentially American about this rugged and sparsely populated state, the largest in New England. It's as though the vast forests of the north and the jagged coastline of "downeast" Maine are the last American frontier, rich in natural resources yet waiting for people equally rugged to tame them.

Imagine the exhilarating feel of a cool breeze on your face while watching a tomato-orange sun rise over Acadia National Park as it kisses America with the first warmth of a new day. You might try camping and cooking on an open fire—the smell of maple-smoked bacon will rouse even the sleepiest of travelers. Little wonder the sun shines first here in Maine; it's a grand preview of what this state has to offer.

Although there are still areas of wilderness in Maine, some of the state's potential was exploited long ago, soon after its discovery by Europeans. When the French and English came to these shores, they found miles and miles of virgin forest. The tremendous white pines have been replaced by other varieties, and lumber products again comprise a good deal of the state's economy.

Besides its forests, Maine has great stores of granite for building, but most are untapped as yet. Although agriculture is difficult because of the rocky soil and short growing season, Maine potatoes are known and used throughout the eastern United States. Maine's fishers yearly pull great quantities of fish, scallops, shrimp, and the famous lobsters from freezing Atlantic waters. But the largest industry in Maine these days is the vacation trade: campers, hikers, and fishers in the mountains and lakes, yachting and summer residents in the beautiful old coastal towns. Good food—especially fresh seafood—and clean air draw the crowds from Boston, Montréal, and New York, and life in the southern coastal towns is lively and interesting from mid-June through Labor Day, after which the visitors become those looking for the quiet of Indian summer and the autumn foliage season. Most resorts close up by the last week in October.

SEEING MAINE

Of the vacation areas in Maine, certainly the most popular is the southern coast, where such pretty towns as Ogunquit, Kennebunkport, Boothbay Harbor, and Camden provide an atmosphere either

What's Special About Maine

Seacoast
- The famous "rockbound coast of Maine," more than 1,000 miles long, offering an endless array of beautiful vistas and charming villages and towns.
- Acadia National Park, one of the few national parks east of the Mississippi.
- Beach resort towns of Ogunquit and Kennebunkport.
- A cruise aboard a swift schooner in Camden, center of the sail-charter business.

Shopping
- Antiques shops and flea markets on both sides of U.S. 1 between Kittery and Ogunquit on Saturday in summer.
- Maine's most famous store, L. L. Bean, in Freeport, open 24 hours a day, 365 days a year.
- Factory-outlet stores in Freeport and many other coastal towns.

Dining
- Memorable dining in Portland and along the coast.

restful or lively, cultural or natural, as you like it. Next in popularity comes the famous old resort of Bar Harbor, which is a good ways "downeast." The crowds these days come to commune there with the rugged beauty of Acadia National Park. Finally, a smaller number of hardy souls head into the hinterland among the mountains, forests, and glacial lakes for a share of the outdoor life.

GETTING THERE   By Plane   Maine's major airport is the Portland International Jetport, served by many major American air carriers. Bar Harbor Airport is served by Colgan Airlines (☎ 800-272-5488).

By Train   Amtrak does not operate in Maine, but its trains do connect with buses at Boston's South Station that will take you north into Maine. Plans to initiate rail service in Maine are stalled, but the state is still hopeful; call 800/USA-RAIL for an update.

By Bus   Greyhound Lines in conjunction with Vermont Transit operates buses from Boston to Bangor with stops in Newburyport, Mass., Portsmouth, N.H., and Portland, Brunswick, and Bangor, Me. The schedule has been cut back considerably for midway points and for connections from or to Canada.

Vermont Transit (☎ 800/451-3292, 800/642-3133 in Vermont) and Greyhound travel to Bangor from Montréal with stops in Burlington, Vt., Boston, and Portland. In summer there are usually buses from Bangor to Ellsworth and Bar Harbor, but you should check in advance to see whether they're running.

Concord Trailways (☎ 207/828-1151 or 800/639-5505) operates six daily round-trips between the Amtrak station in Boston or Logan International Airport and Portland. This is the only nonstop service available between the cities.

By Car   The Maine Turnpike (I-95) is a toll road. U.S. 1 or its scenic alternate route, U.S. 1A, parallels the Maine Turnpike all the way to Brunswick, and while it's a bit slower, it costs nothing. Besides, it's more scenic, and in my opinion no other highway in the entire country could possibly have as many flea markets, antiques shops, and white-elephant sales as does U.S. 1 in Maine, all the way from Kittery to Ellsworth. Weekends are the best times to catch them, but in July and August any day will do.

Note: If you're heading for Ogunquit, take the exit from I-95 soon after you cross the state line at Kittery—follow the signs for U.S. 1 and the "shore" or "scenic" route through York, and this will save you a toll.

ESSENTIALS For travel information and answers to your questions, contact the **Maine Publicity Bureau,** P.O. Box 2300, Hallowell, ME 04347 (☎ **207/ 623-0363,** or 800/533-9595).

The state of Maine also operates **information centers** at several points of entry to the state such as at Kittery, between I-95 and U.S. 1 (☎ 207/439-1319); at Houlton, at the junction of I-95 and U.S. 1 (☎ 207/532-6346); at Calais, 7 Union St. (☎ 207/454-2211); at Hampden, on I-95 northbound, Mile 169 (☎ 207/862-6628) and southbound at Mile 172 (☎ 207/862-6638); in Fryeburg (gateway to the White Mountains), in the center of town (☎ 207/935-3639); and at Yarmouth, between I-95 (Exit 17) and U.S. 1 (☎ 207/846-0833).

Maine's **telephone area code** is **207.** Meals and rooms in Maine are taxed at a rate of 7%, so look for this tax to be added to your bill each night, and at mealtimes.

1 Ogunquit

73 miles NE of Boston, Mass.; 18 miles NE of Portsmouth, N.H.; 35 miles SW of Portland

The Native American name means "beautiful place by the sea," and it holds true even today, because Ogunquit's town government has ensured that the town remains tidy and picturesque despite its tourism development. Visitors feel welcome in the town, whether they're strolling along Ogunquit's picturesque "Marginal Way," a path along the rocky coast; relaxing at the Ogunquit Beach; or dining in one of the many excellent restaurants. At Perkins Cove, a tiny peninsula is festooned with the quaint low waterfront shops and shacks from Ogunquit's fishing-village heyday. Right along U.S. 1 is the Ogunquit Playhouse, which presents Broadway plays and musicals from late June through Labor Day. Ogunquit has been a summer resort for over a century, and it's no wonder that people come back year after year. Ogunquit is popular with and embraces the gay community in summer, much like Provincetown on Cape Cod. A handful of guesthouses (the Yellow Monkey), restaurants (Valerie's), and bars (Le Club and the Front Porch) cater to a gay clientele.

GETTING THERE By Bus See the beginning of this chapter.

By Car See the beginning of this chapter.

ESSENTIALS The **telephone area code** is **207.** The **Ogunquit Chamber of Commerce** maintains an information office on U.S. 1 (P.O. Box 2289), Ogunquit, ME 03907 (☎ **207/646-2939**), south of the center of town, and as Main Street is U.S. 1, you'll come to the office just south of the downtown area. It's open daily in season and Monday through Friday from 10am to 4pm off-season. Free year-round directories are available on request.

WHAT TO SEE & DO

To walk Marginal Way, start at the town's information office, pick up a map, and you'll come out right at **Barnacle Billy's** in Perkins Cove, a mile or so away. The

Maine

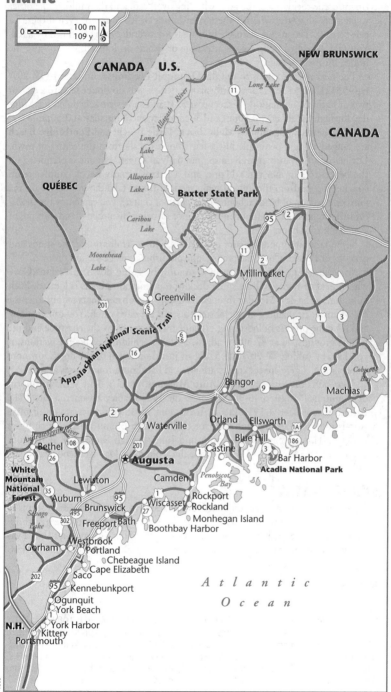

Atlantic, the rocky coast, the gulls wheeling overhead, and the smiles of the other walkers are all a treat whether the sun is shining or it's misty, or even if there's a gale coming. The inlet at Barnacle Billy's has a drawbridge that's operated by hand. You may be called upon by yachtspeople or fishers on lobsterboats to raise the bridge for their passage!

The next thing to do is to call the **Ogunquit Playhouse,** on U.S. 1 (☎ 207/ 646-5511), to get seats for a performance, which will no doubt feature a star or two of national reputation. Tickets cost $21, and shows are scheduled for Monday through Saturday at 8:30pm and Wednesday and Thursday at 2:30pm.

As for beaches, Ogunquit's **Main Beach, Little Beach,** and **Footbridge Beach** are ranged along a peninsula just a few minutes' walk from the center of town. Lifeguards are on duty from 8am to 5pm daily in season. No one is permitted on the beach in summer after 11pm, and a patrol usually keeps couples from straying too far from the lighted main section. If you take the footbridge on the northerly section of beach (about a mile north of center), you can enjoy the peaceful surf late at night, without much chance of being disturbed—and you might snatch a kiss to boot.

Some lazy afternoon, be sure to leave time for a stroll around the shops and galleries of Perkins Cove, the picturesque old fishing-village section of town.

You can get to know the sea in Ogunquit by going down to Perkins Cove where, next to Barnacle Billy's, the dock of the Finestkind boats is located. Each hour during the day, Monday through Saturday, the **lobster boats** set out to cruise the Maine coast, hauling in the lobster pots and the day's catch. You can go along and have the process of lobstering explained while you view the coastline and the fishing grounds, all at $7.50 for adults, $5.50 for children. Make reservations, if you like, by calling ☎ 207/646-5227, or just drop down to the docks for more information. There are cocktail, starlight, and lighthouse-tour cruises as well.

Auto buffs can visit the **Wells Auto Museum,** on U.S. 1 in Wells just north of Ogunquit (☎ 207/646-9064), where the 1907 Stanley Steamer, a rare 1912 Pathfinder roadster, a 1918 Pierce Arrow, and 75 other classics are on display. Admission costs $4 for adults, $2 for children over 6, and is free for children under 6. The museum is open from mid-June through September, daily from 10am to 5pm; Memorial Day through the Columbus Day weekend, weekends only, from 10am to 5pm.

WHERE TO STAY

Ogunquit has a good selection of accommodations in all price ranges. It seems as though every place in town rents rooms, from the gas station to the gift shop. Many are on U.S. 1, however, which is busy with traffic. If you don't find a vacancy among the following selections, search along Shore Road toward Perkins Cove, where it's quieter.

MODERATE

Cliff House
Bald Head Cliff (P.O. Box 2274), Ogunquit, ME 03907. ☎ **207/361-1000.** Fax 207/ 361-2122. 162 rms. A/C TV TEL. July–Aug, $165–$195 double; Apr–June and Sept to mid-Dec, $105–$120 double. Rates include breakfast. AE, MC, V. Free parking. Closed mid-Dec to Mar. Directions: Heading north, take the York/Ogunquit exit off I-95, then take U.S. 1 north 3¹⁄₃ miles to River Road; take a right and follow River Road to the end; turn left onto Shore Road and the Cliff House will be 3¹⁄₂ miles ahead.

Originally, guests stayed in the large old house perched on the cliff 90 feet above the surf, but now the house is overshadowed by several large and very modern motel units, all with a view of the sea. Seventy pine-covered acres, heated indoor and outdoor pools, fitness center, sauna, and tennis courts add to the lure of the Cliff House's remote location and its view. The rooms are very handsome, with picture windows for the sea view, and balconies. Off-season, prices are somewhat lower, and special money-saving packages are offered. There's free transportation in season into town, to the beach, and to other points of interest in and around Ogunquit.

Country Squire Motel

On U.S. 1 at Bourne's Lane, Ogunquit, ME 03907. ☎ **207/646-3162.** 35 rms. TV. High season, $75–$89 double; off-season, $52–$85 double. MC, V. Free parking. Closed late Oct to late Apr.

The inspiration for this modern, attractive hotel is colonial, with an arched portico along the front of the motel, bay windows in each room, pots of plants, and colonial-style furniture. The facilities are an uncolonial matter, however, for there's a swimming pool, and each room has wall-to-wall carpeting. Fifteen rooms have cathedral ceilings and skylights; half have telephones. Coffee and doughnuts are served each morning. The Country Squire is located just four blocks or so from the center of town.

Nellie Littlefield House

9 Shore Rd., Ogunquit, Me 03907. ☎ **207/646-1692.** 8 rooms (including two suites). TV A/C. $140–$195 double. Rates include continental breakfast. MC, V. Free parking. Closed Dec 11 to mid-Apr.

The new owners of the Nellie Littlefield House are transplanted here from Lake Forest, Illinois—well, sort of. They've also had a home nearby for many years and another in Vero Beach, Florida, where they smartly spend the winter. Inside are eight lovely country-inn-inspired rooms and suites. Three have water views. Besides the neatly trimmed and landscaped grounds to enjoy, guests may spend their leisure moments in the dining room, on the shaded veranda, or in the living room. This new offering has been artfully restored and decorated, and will earn a preeminent position among the bed and breakfast choices. It's just a few steps from the movie house and Einstein's Deli in the center of town.

INEXPENSIVE

The Colonial

61 Shore Rd. (P.O. Box 895), Ogunquit, ME 03907. ☎ **207/646-5191** or 800/233-5191. Fax 207/646-3993. 58 rms, 22 suites. A/C TV TEL. July–Aug, $78–$95 single or double; $120–$140 room with kitchenette; $110–$190 apts. May–June and Sept to mid-Oct, rates are 50% lower. AE, DISC, MC, V. Free parking. Closed mid-Oct to Apr. Directions: Follow U.S. 1 to Shore Road toward the sea.

Of Ogunquit's cozy Victorian seaside hotels, The Colonial is brimming with life, having been renovated by Chet and Sheila Sawtelle. Besides the rooms in the inn, the motel section has suites with kitchens, plus some units with kitchenettes. The Colonial has a heated pool, a whirlpool spa, a breakfast coffee shop, an elevator, and more important, a spacious veranda in the turn-of-the-century fashion, the perfect place for sitting, viewing, reading, and napping. A higher price is charged for the rooms with the best ocean views.

Hayes Guest House

133 Shore Rd. (R.R. 1, Box 12), Ogunquit, ME 03907. ☎ **207/646-2277.** 5 rms, 2 apartments. $80–$85 twin or double; $85–$135 apartment. Additional person $15 extra. No credit cards. Free parking. Closed Oct–May. Directions: Follow U.S. 1 to Shore Road toward the sea.

Elinor Hayes is very kind and friendly and has decorated her rooms and apartments with interesting old pieces, such as a rope-frame bed made in Maine, old sea chests, and patchwork quilts. Guests have use of a refrigerator and the swimming pool. It's a charming place, and Mrs. Hayes a charming lady, and you're within walking distance of Perkins Cove with its restaurants, shops, and galleries.

Seafair Inn

14 Shore Rd. (P.O. Box 1221), Ogunquit, ME 03907. ☎ **207/646-2181.** 13 rms (9 with bath), 5 efficiencies. A/C TV. $40–$65 double without bath, $60–$95 double with bath; $99 efficiency. Rates include continental breakfast. MC, V. Free parking.

As you head down Shore Road from the main crossroads, you'll come to the Seafair Inn, on the right-hand side. Pass the two millstones at the beginning of the path, walk up through the garden, go through the sunny front porch with wicker furniture, and enter the formal parlor of this one-time Victorian summer house. A tribute to the owners, the rates have not changed since 1993.

WHERE TO DINE

Perkins Cove, at the seaside end of Shore Road, has several good restaurants. In July and August, it can be very difficult and expensive to park your car here, and you'd be well advised to take one of the "trolleys" (open buses) that run along Shore Road to the cove.

Barnacle Billy's

Shore Rd., Perkins Cove. ☎ **207/646-5575.** Reservations not accepted. Main courses $8–$21. AE, MC, V. Daily 11am–10pm. Closed mid-Oct to mid-Apr. Directions: Follow Shore Road to Perkins Cove. LOBSTER POUND.

At Barnacle Billy's, you'll find good prices, good food, and good service as only you yourself could provide. The routine here is to enter, choose what you want from the chalkboard menu, pay the cashier and get a slip, and submit it to the counterperson; then wander off into Barnacle Billy's waterfront dining room, done all in pine with tables and chairs to match, and a hardwood fire going in two big stone fireplaces. The view of the marina and the cove is as good as the food: Lobster, steamed clams, corn on the cob, salad, and garlic bread are all available. When the weather's fine, you can even order at a window on the brick terrace and have your meal while sitting in the sunshine, either on the terrace or on a deck a flight up; both terraces are right next to the Finestkind Boat Dock.

Now you can enjoy more of Billy's at "Barnacle Billy's etc.," which was for almost 50 years the Whistling Oyster Restaurant. It's located just across the garden and, like the original Billy's, offers free parking across the road with valet service.

Cafe Amore

37 Shore Rd., Ogunquit. ☎ **207/646-6661.** Fax 207/646-0938. Reservations not accepted. Sandwiches $3–$4.75, salads $3–$3.75, coffees $1–$2.70. No credit cards. Daily 7:30am–10pm. Closed mid-Mar to mid-Dec. COFFEEHOUSE.

Cafe Amore is a charmer. It's just what Ogunquit needed. Stop in for a sandwich and pastry after the beach, coffee before going to the Ogunquit Playhouse, or for your morning coffee and bagel. The look is very artistic and you'll love the interior with its old display cooler filled with wonderful desserts. Or take your

Southern Maine Coast

Bethel
Bryant Pond
219
Livermore
17
Winthrop
5
North Waterford
26
117
Turner
4
202
11
South Paris
Norway
118
Mechanic Falls
495
201
Richmond
Lovell
117
Auburn
Lewiston
95
302
Bridgton
Long Lake
11
196
Lisbon Falls
Bath
Casco
136
Brunswick
Saco R.
Naples
5
117
11
Gray
Freeport
209
Hiram
N. Windham
Yarmouth
Cornish
Sebago Lake
35
202
302
Casco Bay
5
25
Westbrook
Portland
Limerick
4
South Portland
Hollis Center
Cape Elizabeth
11
Shapleigh
5
Old Orchard Beach
Saco Bay
Alfred
111
Saco
Biddeford
109
Sanford
1
TNPK.
4
109
Kennebunk
202
North Berwick
Kennebunkport
Rochester
Berwick
95
ATLANTIC OCEAN
Somersworth
Wells
Dover
Ogunquit
MAINE
New Hampshire
Maine
York
Durham
Kittery
108
Portsmouth
1A
Exeter

0   16 km / 10 mi.   N

1804

coffee to one of the patio tables and watch the street scene. It's a prime people-watching spot.

Clay Hill Farm

Agamenticus Rd. ☎ **207/361-2272.** Reservations recommended. Main courses $13–$23; dinner $35–$40. AE, DISC, MC, V. May–Oct, dinner only, daily 5:30–9pm; Nov–Mar, dinner only, Thurs–Sun 5:30–9pm. Directions: Go south on Main Street (U.S. 1) from the center of Ogunquit for a third of a mile, to a blinker at a crossroads next to the Admiral's Inn; turn right onto Agamenticus Road and go 1³/₄ miles to the tavern, which will be on your right. AMERICAN.

The farmhouse has been converted into a tavern with several large dining rooms with lots of windows. Start with clam chowder or Maine crab cakes, and go on to haddock stuffed with lobster. Before and after dinner, you can relax in the lounge and enjoy the piano entertainment provided.

Einstein's Deli

At the corner of Shore Rd. and U.S. 1. ☎ **207/646-5262.** Reservations not accepted. Main courses $5.25–$9. DISC, MC, V. Summer, daily 6am–midnight. Off-season, hours vary. DELI.

Ogunquit is prepared for New Yorkers who come north for the summer or others in search of good corned beef, pastrami, bagels, and the like. Einstein's has all these delights and lots more—homemade soup and turkey club sandwiches—besides several dining areas and a take-out service. The clam chowder is true New England style.

Hurricanes

Orweed Dr., Perkings Cove, Ogunquit. ☎ **207/646-6348.** Reservations recommended. Main courses $14–$20; dinner for two, $50 with wine. AE, DC, DISC, MC, V. Daily 11:30am–4pm; Sun–Thurs 5:50–9:30pm, Fri–Sat 5:30–10pm.

Hurricanes is a long-established restaurant in Perkins Cove. I had an outstanding dinner there when I came through town unexpectedly in the fall. The views of the surf are wonderful, the fireplace glows, and you can even order a full meal at the cozy bar if it's too busy for a reservation or table waiting. Among the specialties are baked salmon and brie baklava, rack of lamb, and the plank-roasted fresh haddock. Dining here is superlative.

Old Village Inn

30 Main St. ☎ **207/646-7088.** Reservations recommended. Main courses $8–$10 at breakfast, $13–$20 at dinner; dinner $30. AE, MC, V. Breakfast Sat–Sun 7:30–11:30am; dinner daily 5:30–10pm. AMERICAN/SEAFOOD.

The Old Village Inn is popular because of its location and because of its several low-ceilinged dining rooms with their heavy beams barely six feet from the floor, all decorated with old crockery; if the weather's fine, you'll want to dine in the inn's glassed-in conservatory amid the flowers and plants. At dinner, have the delicious lobster bisque to start, then a dish such as seafood imperial or perhaps roast duckling; the fish-of-the-day is always a good choice. A small bar provides for the thirsty. You might even decide to stay here as the inn offers a handful of rooms.

EASY EXCURSIONS
"THE YORKS"

Just south of Ogunquit is York, or "The Yorks," as the town actually consists of Old York, York Harbor, and York Beach. York Harbor, at the mouth of the York River, is a summer resort much like Ogunquit. York Beach tends to be more honky-tonk, with amusements and snack shops. Another attraction is Nubble Light, a picturesque 1879 lighthouse.

WHAT TO SEE & DO

What you come to see is **Old York Village,** a "living history museum" operated by the Old York Historical Society (☎ 207/363-4974). Settled by Europeans in 1624, Old York received a royal charter in 1639, the first English town in the country to have this privilege. The historical society has preserved six historic buildings. Guides explain the details of daily community, commercial, and family life in Old York from 1740 to 1940. The tours are run mid-June through September, Tuesday through Saturday from 10am to 4pm and Sunday 1 to 5pm. Tickets cost $6 for adults, $2.50 for children 6 to 16, and are free for children under 6.

Take a look at the **Old Gaol,** built as a jail in the 1700s, now a museum of colonial artifacts administered by the Old York Historical Society (☎ 207/ 363-4974). It's open mid-June through September, Tuesday through Saturday from 10am to 5pm and Sunday from 1 to 5pm.

Jefferds Tavern (1750) and the **Old School House** (1745) are next door to one another, providing an authentic glimpse of two aspects of life over two centuries ago. The **Emerson-Wilcox House** (1740) is now a museum.

Down at the water's edge is the **John Hancock Warehouse and Wharf,** once owned by the great patriot who signed the Declaration of Independence with a signature so large that the king could read it without his glasses. It now holds exhibits on the maritime industry.

Near Sewall's Bridge on the York River is the **Elizabeth Perkins House,** built in 1730 but preserved with Colonial Revival furnishings.

Finally, you may want to visit the **Old York Cemetery.** It has a fascinating collection of old New England tombstones.

WHERE TO STAY

Edwards' Harborside Inn

Stage Neck Rd., York Harbor, ME 03911. ☎ **207/363-3037** or 800/273-2686. 8 rms (6 with bath), 2 suites. A/C TV. $50–$170 double without bath; $75–$170 double with bath; $140–$220 suite. Rates include continental breakfast. MC, V. Directions: From U.S. 1, take U.S. 1A about two miles through York Village into York Harbor and go right on Stage Neck Road.

This quaint three-story gray clapboard Victorian home sits on the harbor right at the ocean. The little town is a breeze to walk through, and you can stroll along the shoreline. The inside is pleasant with views all around. One suite has a spa, and several have fireplaces.

KITTERY ✓

South of York is Kittery, which is best known as the **outlet center** of Maine with hundreds of shops on both sides of U.S. 1. Kittery is more popular than Freeport for its shopping because of the abundance of stores with designer labels.

If you drive along U.S. 1, you might get bogged down in traffic during the summer season, but you'll also be rewarded with fine shoreline restaurants and lobster pounds.

WHERE TO DINE

Cape Neddick Lobster Pound

60 Shore Rd. (U.S. 1A), Cape Neddick. ☎ **207/363-5471.** Reservations accepted for parties of five or more. Main courses $9–$16. AE, MC, V. Summer, daily noon–4pm; 5–9pm. Off-season, call for hours. SEAFOOD.

This waterside lobster pound and restaurant is just across the street from the Cape Neddick Campground and has views of the harbor. The restaurant has decks outside where you can enjoy the view and weather. The menu lists baked stuffed lobster, broiled scallops, reef and beef kebabs, and some teriyaki dishes.

2 Kennebunkport

30 miles NE of Portsmouth, 29 miles SW of Portland

The several communities with similar names—Kennebunk, Kennebunkport, and Kennebunk Beach—are clustered together on the Maine coast and constitute one of the state's most popular vacation areas, particularly since they were put on the map by former President Bush and his family. Other areas worth exploring are Goose Rocks Beach and Cape Porpoise.

Of the towns, Kennebunkport is perhaps the most interesting. As its name implies, Kennebunkport was the waterfront part of the Kennebunk area. It has been a resort for years, drawing both the well-to-do and the student crowd living on summer earnings. Prices for rooms and meals tend to be a bit high, but for most people the price is not so important as long as they can just find a room open in this delightful Maine town.

GETTING THERE **By Bus** See the beginning of this chapter.

By Car Coming from the south, follow I-95 (the Maine Turnpike) to Exit 2 (Wells), then U.S. 1/Me. 9 north to Kennebunkport. Coming from the north, take I-95 to Exit 3 (Kennebunk), then Me. 9A east to Kennebunkport. Note that there are other settlements with similar names, including Kennebunk and Kennebunk Beach.

ESSENTIALS The **telephone area code** is **207.** The **Kennebunk Kennebunkport Chamber of Commerce**, P.O. Box 740, Kennebunk, ME 04043 (☎ **207/ 967-0857** or 800/982-4421), maintains an information center on Me. 35 in Lower Village, Kennebunk. Ask for a copy of their "Experience Kennebunk Kennebunkport."

WHAT TO SEE & DO

Shops and galleries around **Dock Square** draw lots of shoppers who enjoy spending their time browsing.

Gooch's Beach is right at the southern end of Beach Street, on the western shore of the Kennebunk River; **Kennebunk Beach** is west of Gooch's, along the coast. These beaches are good for swimming, especially on very hot days (the water tends to the chilly), and for walking, thinking, or jogging on almost any day.

Be sure to take a drive or a walk along **Maine Street** for a look at Kennebunkport's fine old mansions. For a look at the rocky coast, go south on Ocean Avenue to **Spouting Rock**.

The **Kennebunk Historical Society,** (☎ 207/967-2751), offers tours of the fine old homes and buildings. The **Intown Trolley** offers a 45-minute narrated tour featuring such points of interest as the Spouting Rock/Blowing Cave, Franciscan Monastery, and the estate of former President George Bush. The **Nott House** (☎ 207/967-2513) is a Greek Revival home with Victorian furnishings and is open mid-June to early October, Wednesday to Saturday from 1 to 4pm. Adults are $3 and children between 6 and 12 pay $2.

SPECIAL TIMES IN KENNEBUNKPORT

Of course summer is the most popular time in this area but late autumn is a wonderful time to take advantage of off-peak rates at the romantic inns of this area and special weekends are set aside to celebrate each season.

Each December the Kennebunk Business Association presents the **Christmas Prelude,** celebrating 15 years during this yuletide season. The festival and events include an art show, children's Christmas stories, a bonfire with caroling at the Village Marketplace, church recitals, a holiday fair, blueberry pancake breakfast, tours of historic homes, hayrides, a parade with Santa arriving by boat and many other activities.

In February the country inns offer several **weekends of romance** with the chamber of commerce sponsoring a winter carnival, carriage rides, hayrides, and an ice-skating party.

WHERE TO STAY
EXPENSIVE

Austin's Inn—Town Hotel
Dock Sq. (P.O. Box 609), Kennebunkport, ME 04046. ☎ **207/967-4241** or 800/227-3809. 14 rms. TV. High season, $99 double; off-season, $69 double. DISC, MC, V. Free parking.

Austin's is for those who want to be smack in the middle of town, right next to Dock Square, the Kennebunk River, and the dock. It's a new and modern hostelry in an older-style building where it's possible to fit three, four, or even five people in several of the rooms, which is good for traveling families to note. Ten rooms have air conditioning.

Breakwater
Ocean Ave., Kennebunkport, ME 04046. ☎ **207/967-3118.** 20 rms. TV. $75–$140 double. Rates include full breakfast. AE, MC, V. Free parking. Closed mid-Oct to Mar. Directions: In Kennebunkport, turn left at the traffic light, then go over the drawbridge; turn right at the monument onto Ocean Avenue and follow Ocean to the hotel, on the right side.

The situation at the Breakwater is excellent—the open sea is right next door. Prices vary, the cheaper rooms being in the Breakwater building, and the more expensive ones in the Riverside building, which is more modern and preferable. You can watch the boat come up the mouth of the river from some rooms and hear the waves break from others. For dinner, the Breakwater has one of the best restaurants around (see "Where to Dine," below).

The Captain Jefferds Inn
Pearl St. (P.O. Box 691), Kennebunkport, ME 04046. ☎ **207/967-2311.** 12 rms, 4 suites. $85–$135 double; $145–$165 suite for two. Minimum stay two nights July–Oct. Rates include full breakfast. MC, V. Free parking. Closed Jan–Mar. Directions: In Kennebunkport, turn left at the traffic light, then go over the drawbridge; turn right at the monument onto Ocean Avenue and go five short blocks; turn left onto the one-way street, then another left onto the corner, and look for the white fence.

This inn is one of those old sea captains' houses so immaculately restored that it made the cover of *House Beautiful;* the owners have added unusual antiques, lots of them, and comfortable furnishings. There's an antiques shop on the premises and another nearby under the same ownership. Children are welcome with prior notice, as are pets. Besides being everything a quaint inn should be, the Captain Jefferds is just off Ocean Avenue—walking distance to everything in town.

Captain Lord Mansion

Pleasant and Green Sts. (P.O. Box 800), Kennebunkport, ME 04046. ☎ **207/967-3141** or 800/522-3141. Fax 207/967-3172. 16 rms. $79–$225 double. Rates include breakfast. DISC, MC, V. Free parking. Directions: In Kennebunkport, turn left at the traffic light, then go over the drawbridge; turn right at the monument onto Ocean Avenue and look for the mansion on the left-hand side after several blocks.

In 1812 a naval captain and his sailors were blockaded in Kennebunk Harbor by the British, so Captain Lord put his men to work on building the mansion, and they did an impressive job. Today in this guesthouse there are antiques everywhere, and gas fireplaces in all but one of the rooms. Air conditioning is one new feature not often found in historic buildings that's a welcome change for August days. Driving from Dock Square down Ocean Avenue, keep glancing to your left and soon you'll see the stately yellow mansion topped by its cupola/ observatory at the back of a rich greensward a block long: Captain Lord meant this first sight of the mansion to be impressive, and it certainly is. Children over 6 are welcome.

Maine Stay Inn and Cottages

34 Maine St. (P.O. Box 500AF), Kennebunkport, ME 04046. ☎ **207/967-2117** or 800/ 950-2117. Fax 207/967-8757. 13 rms, 4 suites. TV. Late June to mid-Oct, $95–$185 single or double; mid-Oct to late June, $75–$165 single or double; year-round, $100–$200 suite. Rates include full breakfast. AE, DISC, MC, V. Free parking.

Only a short walk from town, this charming place is surrounded by gardens and lofty trees. Though the rooms, including two suites, are equipped with all the modern conveniences, the spirit—and the welcome (tea is served to guests at 4pm)—befits a cozy inn. The cottages are clean, bright, and a good value; five have a working fireplace. Upon request, breakfast is served in your cottage.

MODERATE

Chetwynd House

Chestnut St., Kennebunkport, ME 04046. ☎ **207/967-2235.** 4 rms. $75–$160 double. Rates include breakfast. MC, V. Free parking. Directions: Take the second left off Ocean Avenue; the street is not marked, but Chetwynd House is a short distance up on the left, and is marked clearly by a sign.

Chetwynd is immaculately clean, with fine wide-board floors of a rich honey color and very decent furnishings, including many four-poster beds. Extra pleasures at the Chetwynd House include tea and cakes, and here you're only two blocks from Dock Square and the center of town.

Green Heron

Ocean Ave. (P.O. Box 2578), Kennebunkport, ME 04046. ☎ **207/967-3315.** 10 rms, 1 cottage. A/C TV. $65–$128 double. Rates include breakfast. No credit cards. Free parking. Closed Jan. Directions: In Kennebunkport, turn left onto Me. 9 at the traffic light, then go over the drawbridge; turn right at the monument onto Ocean Avenue and drive until you see the house on the left-hand side.

The Green Heron has been a dependable Kennebunkport hostelry for years and years. This nice old house and cottage are owned by Charles and Elizabeth Reid, who converted them into guest rooms with simple and comfortable furnishings.

The beaches are within walking distance and there's a cheery breakfast room with lots of big windows overlooking the water.

Welby Inn

Ocean Ave. (P.O. Box 774), Kennebunkport, ME 04046. ☎ **207/967-4655**. 7 rms. $60–$95 double. Rates include breakfast. AE, MC, V. Free parking. Directions: In Kennebunkport, turn left at the traffic light, then go over the drawbridge; turn right at the monument onto Ocean Avenue and continue to the inn.

Located on Ocean Avenue, this inn can be recognized by its handsome hand-painted tile signboard out front. One of the owners, Betsy Rogers-Knox, is the faïence artist who did the tiles for the sign, as well as those for all the private bathrooms, and many of the paintings in this graceful old converted summer cottage. The covered patio in front is new. Children over 10 are welcome.

WHERE TO DINE

The cheapest way to have a lobster dinner is to wander down to the lobster pound. Although many restaurants have appropriated the name "Lobster Pound," a real pound is simply the place where the live lobsters are kept in saltwater vats until a customer comes and buys them. Most lobster pounds these days have a few simple cooking facilities, and will boil up the lobsters, provide salad and french fries, butter and salt and a paper plate, and charge just a little above the price of a live lobster. There are several such lobster pounds in Kennebunkport, where a cooked lobster will cost between $10 and $14, depending on size and season.

Arundel Wharf

43 Ocean Ave. ☎ **207/967-3444**. Reservations recommended. Main courses $9–$19; lunch $3–$9. AE, DC, DISC, MC, V. Daily 11:30am–9:30pm. Closed Jan–Mar. SEAFOOD/STEAK.

As you walk across the parking lot to the restaurant, the gulls will be squealing overhead; as you enter, you'll see a modern back deck, a beamed ceiling, and several windows with water views, for the Arundel is indeed on a wharf by the Kennebunk River. The staff here is young and friendly, and for lunch they mostly serve sandwiches with a few platters offered, but for dinner you can have a choice of five lobster entrees, prime rib, or swordfish steak.

The restaurant's name comes from the fact that Kennebunkport was once named Arundel, after England's Earl of Arundel; in fact, it bore that name all through the better part of its maritime prominence, changing only in 1821.

Breakwater

Ocean Ave. ☎ **207/967-3118**. Reservations suggested. Main courses $13–$20; meals $25–$40. AE, MC, V. May–June and Sept–Oct, breakfast daily 8–10am; dinner daily 6–9pm. July–Aug, breakfast daily 8–10am; dinner daily 5:30–10pm. Closed Nov–Apr. Directions: In Kennebunkport, turn left at the traffic light, then go over the drawbridge; turn right at the monument onto Ocean Avenue and follow Ocean to the hotel, on the right-hand side. SEAFOOD/BEEF.

A local favorite, the dining rooms are elegant without being overly formal and the sun porch—which is a dining room—affords a beautiful view of the sea. You can order a beef kebab or baked haddock; the broiled scallops are popular. The delicacies proceed to swordfish and roast prime rib, with the lobster clambake priced according to the day's market. Have reservations, but be sympathetic when you're told that specific tables can't be reserved (the ones with the sea view are the hot ones).

White Barn Inn

Beach St. ☎ **207/967-2321.** Reservations recommended. Four-course fixed-price dinner $49 Sun–Fri, $52 Sat. AE, MC, V. Jan–Mar, dinner only, Wed–Sun 6–9:30pm. Apr–Dec, dinner only, daily 6–9:30pm. MODERN AMERICAN/REGIONAL.

This is one of Maine's most noted restaurants, highly respected and highly priced. The reputation is well deserved. The chef prepares an array of modern American regional dishes. For starters, you might have the cream of red pepper soup with diced fennel and lemon-scented crème fraîche, or marinated tenderloin of lamb with garlic confit, a salad of assorted endives, and a roasted-tomato oil. Main courses include lightly grilled native salmon with sliced spring leeks, grilled onion, and an orange-basil oil; or steamed Maine lobster nestled on fresh fettuccine with carrots and ginger in a Thai-inspired honey-and-sherry vinegar sauce. When you dine here during foliage season, the view through the tall window in the rear is nothing short of spectacular with its extravagant spray of fall flowers and vegetables arranged like a work of art. Beach Street is parallel to Ocean Avenue but across the inlet from it, to the south. If in doubt, ask for the Franciscan Monastery; the White Barn's very near, on the other side of the street. The accommodations here are equally lovely and expensive. You won't be disappointed.

AN EXCURSION TO CAPE PORPOISE

Three miles northeast of Kennebunkport along Me. 9, on the shore, is the village of Cape Porpoise. This charming little bit of Maine coastal life is a vacation haven for a small, knowledgeable few. Not fancy, not crowded, it has only a few crafts shops, a few eateries, a few guesthouses, and a lot of Maine atmosphere. For pretty views of the sea, drive out and head for the pier. A brass plaque on a rock atop the sand hill there bears this legend: "August 8, 1782, a British ship of 18 guns attacked a small force of inhabitants gathered on Goat Island and was driven away by severe musket fire, losing 17 men. James Burnham of this town was killed. This tablet erected by the Maine State Council, Daughters of the American Revolution, August 8, 1921."

Well, not an awful lot that's exciting has happened in Cape Porpoise since this signal victory, and it's just as well, for the quiet is what makes it nice.

WHERE TO DINE

Nunan's Lobster Hut

50 Mills Rd. (Me. 9 East), Cape Porpoise. ☎ **207/967-4362.** Reservations not accepted. Dinner $12–$20. No credit cards. Dinner only, daily 5–9pm (sometimes closes a bit later). Closed mid-Oct to mid-Apr. Directions: Follow Me. 9 east to the restaurant, on the right-hand side. SEAFOOD.

Nunan's is an unprepossessing low-roofed shack where you can order fish chowder, boiled lobster, steamed clams, salads, homemade pies, beer, and wine. Some patrons return night after night. Authentic Maine coastal dining—that's Nunan's.

3 Portland

108 miles NE of Boston, 161 miles SW of Bar Harbor

Cities in Maine have never had a reputation for chic or avant-garde ambience because Maine is a rural state, and it's the farmlands, woodlands, and coastal industries, such as lobstering, that count. But Portland, the state's largest city and its transportation hub and business center, may be changing all that. The Civic

Center draws sports events, conventions, and big-name entertainers, and its revitalized waterfront area, known as the Old Port Exchange, is now even more attractive than it was in its Victorian heyday when the railroads, the huge sailing fleet, and the trade in lumber and fish made Portland what it is.

In Portland, you can visit the city's colonial, Early American, and Victorian landmarks, browse through the Portland Museum of Art, designed by I.M. Pei, or take a cruise in Portland Harbor or Casco Bay. Portland is also the American end of the Prince of Fundy Cruises, which will take you and your car to Yarmouth, Nova Scotia, on an 11-hour overnight cruise.

GETTING THERE   By Plane   Portland International Jetport is served by numerous national airlines.

By Bus   See the beginning of this chapter.

By Car   Follow I-95 to I-295, which makes a loop through downtown Portland.

ESSENTIALS   The **telephone area code** is **207**. The **Convention & Visitors Bureau of Greater Portland Information Center,** 305 Commercial St., Portland, ME 04101 (☎ **207/772-5800**; fax 207/874-9043), on the waterfront, can fill you in on Portland life.

WHAT TO SEE & DO
BOATS & CRUISES
Portland is the prime dock for Casco Bay and indeed northern New England, and you can climb aboard a boat with your car or without, for a few hours or overnight. Here are the major lines:

Casco Bay Lines, Commercial and Franklin Streets (☎ 207/774-7871), will take you (but not your car) over to Bailey's Island in summer. While on the 5¹/₂-hour cruise, you'll be told all about the island's history and its geologic features, plus lots of Portland and Casco Bay lore. On a sunny day, this is a very fine way to "take the air." The price for this cruise is $13.50 for adults, $6 for children. Other cruises are a bit shorter and a bit cheaper: There's a year-round sunset cruise to the islands (2¹/₂ hours), a seasonal music cruise every Sunday around Casco Bay (3 hours), plus other seasonal runs, and the year-round cruise on the United States Mail boat, which goes to six of the Calendar Islands (3 hours).

May through October on most days, the **MS *Scotia Prince*** leaves Portland in the evening for Yarmouth, Nova Scotia, on an 11-hour overnight cruise. Return sailings from Yarmouth are in mid-morning. If you had to drive, you'd go 858 miles! The ship provides satisfactory cabin accommodations, buffet and à la carte dining, live entertainment, a casino, and duty-free shopping. The ship was designed for interior use and is not built for much outdoor use. The wind on the crossing is brisk and cool, even in August, and there are benches on each deck but limited lounge chairs. The overnight crossing is a pleasant experience for those with cabins, which are at a premium in summer, so plan ahead. Day cabins (for the Yarmouth Portland segment) are inexpensive and worth the extra tab. There has been a concerted effort to upgrade the cabins and redesign the public areas. A scaled-down version of a traditional cruise line variety show is presented free of charge in each direction. Current high-season (late June to mid-September) prices for the cruise are from $77 per adult, half price for children 5 to 14 accompanied by an adult, and free for children under 5. The fare for a car is normally $98. A cabin for two costs in the range of $32 to $95. A family of four can easily spend

$350 one-way. But there are several special fares that might suit your needs and will save you money. Be sure to call **Prince of Fundy Cruises** for the latest fares, schedules, and other particulars; credit and charge cards are accepted for passage. In Portland, call ☎ 207/775-5616; elsewhere in Maine, call 800/482-0955; ☎ 800/341-7540 in other states and Canada. In Yarmouth, Nova Scotia, call ☎ 902/742-3411.

SIGHTS

Wadsworth-Longfellow House

485 Congress St. ☎ **207/879-0427.** Admission $4 adults, $1 children under 12. June–Oct, Tues–Sun 10am–4pm. Closed Nov–May. Directions: Follow Me. 22, which leads to Congress Street, to the house.

This boyhood home of poet Henry Wadsworth Longfellow was built in 1785–86 by the poet's maternal grandfather, Gen. Peleg Wadsworth. The house holds furnishings that once belonged to the famous Wadsworths and Longfellows. If you happen to be in town in mid-December, "Holidays at Henry's" is a warm and wonderful visit celebrating Christmas from a bygone era. There's a beautiful garden, and the Maine Historical Society, which received the bequest of the house in 1901, is located right next door.

Tate House

1270 Westbrook St. ☎ **207/774-9781.** Admission $4 adults, $1 children under 12. July to mid-Sept, Tues–Sat 10am–4pm, Sun 1–4pm; May–June and mid-Sept to Oct, by appointment. Closed Nov–Apr. Directions: Go southwest on Congress Street for 3¼ miles, cross the stream, and turn left on Westbrook Street, very near Portland Jetport.

The Maine forest was for a long time the prime source of masts for the British navy, and the man who managed the whole trade was George Tate, who had this house built in 1755.

Victoria Mansion (Morse-Libby House)

109 Danforth St. ☎ **207/772-4841.** Admission $4 adults, $1.50 children 6–18, free for children under 6. June–Labor Day, Tues–Sat 10am–4pm, Sun 1–5pm. Labor Day–Columbus Day, Fri–Sat 10am–4pm, Sun 1–5pm. Closed Columbus Day–May.

Built between 1858 and 1860, the Victoria Mansion has fascinating Victorian decorations and many original furnishings. It's the headquarters of the Victoria Society of Maine. If you're a Victoriana fan, this is a stop not to be missed.

Portland Museum of Art

7 Congress Sq. ☎ **207/775-6148.** Admission $6 adults, $5 students and seniors, $1 children 6–12, free for children under 6; free for everyone every Thurs evening and the first Sat of the month. Tues–Wed and Fri–Sat 10am–5pm, Thurs 10am–9pm, Sun noon–5pm.

Particularly strong are the collections of 18th- through 20th-century American art relating to Portland and to Maine, with paintings by Andrew Wyeth, Winslow Homer, and Edward Hopper. Highlights include the Joan Whitney Payson Collection featuring Renoir, Degas, Monet, Picasso, and other masters. The building was designed by I. M. Pei in 1983.

Back Cove

Baxter Blvd.

Here's a treat that won't cost you a cent. "The Boulevard," as it's known locally, is a popular rendezvous with its 3½-mile jogging track around Back Cove. Since the city extended the walkway over Tukey's Bridge and adjoining the Interstate,

Portland

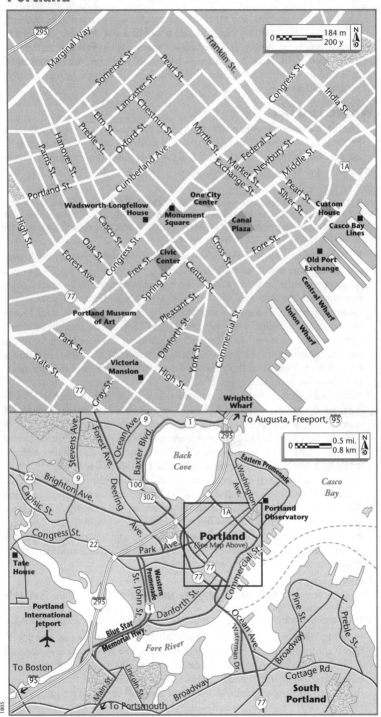

walkers, joggers, cyclists, and other outdoors enthusiasts can make the circle trip as fast or as leisurely as they like. The area is well lit and scenic with the shoreline all the way around. Parking is located on one side at Payson Park and on the other by the rugby field. From April through November you'll find windsurfers in the cove and in winter cross-country skiers on the walking path. There are even exercise stations along the way.

WHERE TO STAY

The city has a few lodging places downtown, but many visitors, especially those here on business, stay in motels near Exit 8 or Exit 7 at the Maine Mall; both exits are off the Maine Turnpike. You'll find a Holiday Inn, Howard Johnson, Super 8, and Fairfield Inn, to name a few.

✪ The Danforth

163 Danforth St., Portland, ME 04102. ☎ **800/991-6557.** Fax 207/879-8754. 9 rms. A/C TV TEL. $95–$155 double. Rates include breakfast. AE, MC, V. Directions: From Longfellow Square, take State Street (one-way) south to Danforth Street and turn right; the inn is on the right at the corner of Winter Street.

I took particular interest in the makeover of this wonderful three-story brick mansion on the edge of Portland's West End as it got on its feet last year. That was a good call since the innkeeper and the inn itself is wowing visitors—many already repeat guests. Dating back to 1823, just after Maine became a state, it was constructed for a silver merchant and later sold to the owner of Canal Bank (which later became Key Bank). In the early 1900s John Calvin Stevens took the building's best assets and improved on them with an addition. It was even a girls' school for a short time before going into service as the rectory of St. Dominic's Catholic Church next door. Then the present owner came to town to restore this once-grand mansion to its former glory.

Up for a nightly adoption now are fewer than a dozen rooms—seven with working fireplaces and most with sitting areas. These are classic and rather stately rooms blended to appeal to both the carriage trade and business executives who tire of blueprint hotel rooms. Here, the rooms are individually decorated. Expect to find luxurious guest rooms with antiques, designer fabrics, two-line phones with fax machines brought in for your convenience, and more. This is a choice that now makes others play catch-up to compete. In all, there are 12 fireplaces, an artfully restored billiards room, a majestic parlor, a library, and a breakfast or morning room to enjoy a full breakfast. Outside the gardens are still maturing, but the landscaping is neat and trim. Access to a full health club is available. The Danforth provides just what Portland needs: a little class, a sophisticated innkeeper the big-city guest will be comfortable with and exhibiting the warmth Mainers are known for, and, for couples, a little romance.

Pomegranate Inn

49 Neal St., Portland, ME 04102. ☎ **207/772-1006** or 800/356-0408. 8 rms. $95–$155 double. Rates include full breakfast. AE, DISC, MC, V. Free parking on the street. Directions: From Longfellow Square, go up Pine Street to Neal Street and turn left; the inn is on the left.

In an ideal West End setting, this inn is a wonderful find for couples who appreciate warm surroundings and enjoy exploring. The fine detail work is exceptional as displayed in the faux-marbre woodwork and painted hardwood floor. Rooms feature four-poster beds, period furniture, designer fabrics, and Oriental carpets. Rooms may be hand-painted with many fine details. A favorite is the garden suite.

Portland Regency

20 Milk St., Portland, ME 04101. ☎ **207/774-4200** or 800/727-3436. Fax 207/775-2150. 95 rms. A/C MINIBAR TV TEL. $115–$195 single or double. AE, DC, DISC, MC, V. Valet parking, $5 per day.

A few steps from the port district and the commercial center of town is the Portland Regency, a new hotel located in a fine old waterfront building that was constructed in 1895 as an armory. The guest rooms are decorated in Early American reproductions, not exactly accurate to the hotel's age, but very nice nonetheless. This is Portland's most luxurious downtown hostelry. Services include an appealing restaurant, bar, excellent health club with aerobics, and room service.

Radisson Plaza Hotel

157 High St., Portland, ME 04101. ☎ **207/775-5411** or 800/333-3333. Fax 207/775-2872. 202 rms. A/C TV TEL. $99–$155 single or double. AE, CB, DC, DISC, MC, V. Parking $5.

In the city center, within walking distance to the museum, civic center, and Old Port district, is the renovated Sonesta Hotel Portland—trying again to lure guests with a new name and some renovations that make it at least as inviting as the Holiday Inn, but still lagging behind the cozier Portland Regency. Guests have use of two restaurants, two bars, and a limited fitness room. A free shuttle is provided to the jetport. Ask the hotel about weekend packages when you call for reservations.

West End Inn

146 Pine St., Portland, ME 04102. ☎ **207/772-1377** or 800/338-1377. 5 rms. TV. With breakfast. $75–$139 double. AE, MC, V. Directions: From Longfellow Square, take Pine Street toward the West End.

The West End's owner is trying to give his three-story brick inn the look of an old-style country inn. With a few more old-world appointments and a little seasoning, the place will be on its way. In the meantime, this mansard-roofed corner inn has a handful of quaint rooms with pretty fabrics and wall coverings. One room has a skylight and a cathedral ceiling. The West End is within walking distance of the West Side Restaurant (see below), one of my favorite places for breakfast or a dessert and tea at night. Parking is free on the street.

WHERE TO DINE AND BE ENTERTAINED

The renaissance of Portland's waterfront district has given rise to numerous restaurants in recent years, and a short walk through the tidy and picturesque restored blocks of Fore, Exchange, Middle, and Moulton Streets will reveal interesting and moderately priced places for snacks, meals, or relaxing drinks. Fore Street and the cobblestoned Wharf Street run side by side between Moulton Street and Union Street. In this short stretch are a number of excellent spots to enjoy a drink or meal. Among the notable drinking establishments are Three Dollar Deweys (at Union and Comercial), Taps, Cadillac Jacks, Gritty's, the Old Port Tavern, The Big Easy, and the Moon. Sunday River was poised to open a micro-brewery here also—supplementing the microbrew of Gritty's. The Pavillion opened in late summer in the former Canal National Bank building on Middle Street and was bringing in crowds of dancers who pay a small cover charge to dance. Another dance club is Zootz at the top of Forest Avenue (behind the Radisson) for a taste of industrial strength house music. Portland's gay populace gravitates to the Underground (for the youth market) and Blackstones (for the post-graduates). And in addition to the following restaurants, try Street & Company, Gilbert's Chowder House,

Squire Morgan's, Erik's, Della's Catessen, Dock Fore or any of a number of neat dining and drinking spots operating in the Old Port District.

Baker's Table

434 Fore St. ☎ **207/775-0303.** Reservations recommended on weekends. Main courses $8–$13; meals $18–$22; special lunch $5–$9. AE, DC, MC, V. Lunch Mon–Fri 11am–5pm, Sat–Sun 10am–5pm; dinner daily 6–10:30pm. AMERICAN.

Salad here is almost a meal in itself, and with a big bowl of fish chowder it'll fill you for sure. The heartier and more expensive dinner menu (bouillabaisse, tournedos, or perhaps chicken provençal) is served amid linen-clad tables and sparkling stemware. There's soft background music, paintings by local artists, an interesting crowd, a well-stocked bar, and an espresso machine. You might even eat outside in good weather.

Bella Bella

606 Congress St., at High St. ☎ **207/780-1260.** Reservations not accepted. Main courses $7–$10; desserts $2.95; dinner for two $25. No credit cards. Dinner only, daily 5–10pm. ITALIAN.

The funky interior is a pleasant introduction to this youthful addition to Portland's dining scene. Every day there are specials, usually one with fish and some type of filled ravioli served with a green salad. If you see a few things on the menu you'd like to try, the chef will even make up a special combo plate as a sampler. Add a little Italian, Chilean, German, or domestic wine or a cold beer to complete your dinner. There's often a wait of 10 minutes or so, and if it's a bit longer the hosts will page you at the nearby Coffee By Design a couple of doors away. After you eat dinner, a 10-minute walk down to the Old Port Exchange will revive you for an evening of merriment, or you might saunter into Portland's West End for a look at the neighborhood and lovely old homes.

Café Always

47 Middle St. ☎ **207/774-9399.** Reservations recommended. Main courses $10–$19. AE, MC, V. Dinner only, Tues–Sat 5–10pm. NEW AMERICAN.

A colorful and stylish refuge of the designer set, Café Always has a menu as interesting as the clientele and the decor. Victorian wallpaper murals catch your eye; the white linen tablecloths are topped with butcher's paper. Chef/owner Cheryl Lewis might start you off with a grilled duck and wild-rice nori roll, then move on to a lobster-and-goat-cheese burrito, followed by a salad of sun-dried tomatoes, garlic croutons, toasted pine nuts, fresh greens, and parmesan cheese. For dessert, there's mocha-pecan pie. All breads, desserts, ice creams, and sorbets are made right in the restaurant. The wine list, with more than 100 items, is heavy with California vintages. You'll love the four-course tasting menu from around the globe.

Fresh Market Pasta

43 Exchange St. ☎ **207/773-7146.** Reservations not accepted. Main courses $4.50–$8. AE, MC, V. Mon–Thurs 9am–10pm, Fri–Sat 9am–11pm, Sun noon–8pm. ITALIAN.

Located in the Old Port Exchange, this pasta market offers delicious dishes in a simple though upbeat environment. If you're looking for fancy pasta, go down Exchange Street another block to Walter's, but come here if you want a good (and not expensive) pasta spread to eat in or take out. The decor is little more than ice-cream-parlor chairs, posters of Italy, and a few pasta items for sale in a display cupboard. You can see the folks prepare your food right in front of you. You can have the daily pasta topped with marinara, pesto, Alfredo, bolognese, or another sauce. For dessert try Izzy's cheesecake or the five-layer chocolate-mousse cake.

Pepper Club

78 Middle St. ☎ **207/772-0531.** Reservations not accepted. Main courses $5.50–$10.95. No credit cards. Dinner only, Sun–Wed 5–9pm, Thurs–Sat 5–10pm. AMERICAN/VEGETARIAN.

Imagine the look of a colorful Caribbean restaurant with the atmosphere of a San Francisco coffeehouse. That's the Pepper Club. The menu at this casual, fun restaurant is written on the chalkboard and the daily specials might include vegetarian lasagne, fresh salmon, and homemade pies or cake. You can enjoy wine or beer with your meal.

The Seamen's Club

1 Exchange St. ☎ **207/772-7311.** Reservations required on weekends. Main courses $7–$11; sandwiches $5–$6. AE, CB, DC, MC, V. Sun–Thurs 11am–9:30pm, Fri–Sat 11am–11pm. AMERICAN.

This is a good place to meet Portlanders who work in or near the waterfront, particularly at lunchtime, when sandwiches and the table d'hôte draw a crowd. Sunday brunch is good, too. At dinner, the menu is filled with the popular classics: baked stuffed shrimp, fresh fish catch, filet mignon, and lobster. Don't miss the fish or lobster chowder and roast turkey served on honey-wheat bread at lunch. Everything is fresh—the freezer is used only for ice cream!

Walter's Café

15 Exchange St. ☎ **207/871-9258.** Reservations not accepted. Salads $5–$7; main courses $11–$16; desserts $2.95. AE, MC, V. Lunch Mon–Sat 11am–3pm; dinner daily 5–10pm. ECLECTIC.

Walter's Café is one of the best places for a meal in Portland. The eclectic menu ranges from three wok specials to angel-hair pasta with lobster to Java shrimp. Upstairs is a bar serving beer and wine where you might elect to dine if there's a long wait. Downstairs you'll find a wonderfully preserved tin ceiling, exposed-brick walls, and a display kitchen. You might savor your dinner, go for a walk around the Old Port, and then stop almost next door at Java Joe's for a "cup o' Joe" and a great dessert.

West Side Restaurant

58 Pine St. ☎ **207/773-8223.** Reservations not accepted. Main courses $9–$14. AE, CB, DC, MC, V. Breakfast Mon–Fri 7–11am, Sat 8am–2pm, Sun 9am–2pm; dinner Sun–Thurs 5:30–9pm, Fri–Sat 5:30–10pm. Directions: From Longfellow Square, go up Pine Street, through the stop sign, and the restaurant is on the left. AMERICAN.

What I enjoy most about the West Side are the breakfasts. You can choose from a host of items to make an omelet that's served with hearty whole-wheat or white toast (the bread is made fresh daily right out back) and garnished with fresh fruit. You might also try the waffles or the Mexican or Oriental eggs. In summer the backyard dining area is open. The serving staff is energetic and fun.

FOR SNACKS & DESSERTS

Portland has a number of casual haunts for something as simple as coffee and dessert. In addition to the two choices below you might try the Victory Deli, Java Joe's, Vermont Coffee Roasters, and Raffles Cafe.

Big Sky Bread Company

536 Deering Ave. ☎ **207/761-5623.** Reservations not accepted. Breads $2.85–$3.50; cookies $1; cinnamon rolls $1.50. No credit cards. Tues–Sat 7am–6:30pm, Sun 8am–2pm. BAKERY.

Martha Elkus and her husband, Bill Harris, have managed to bring new life into the old Engine Eight firehouse at Woodfords Corner, near Forest Avenue and Woodfords Street. Their Big Sky flag hangs over the firehouse doors in front where the engines once roared. Inside are a handful of tables and chairs big enough to sit and enjoy the Sunday newspaper while having a freshly brewed coffee or tea you pour yourself. Not to be missed are the cinnamon rolls with raisins and walnuts, raisin or chocolate-chip cookies, or fat-free muffins (if you're trying to be good). All the grains are organically grown in Montana. Each loaf of bread weighs two pounds and three ounces.

Coffee by Design

620 Congress St. ☎ **207/772-5533.** Reservations not accepted. Desserts $1–$2.25. MC, V. Mon–Wed 7am–8pm, Thurs–Sat 7am–10pm, Sun 9am–8pm. COFFEEHOUSE.

Portland needed another coffeehouse, and Coffee by Design hits the spot for many java lovers. The funky interior is long and narrow, with local artwork on display throughout; every month or so the art changes, so you'll never know quite what surroundings you'll be enjoying your specialty coffee or tea in. Overhead is a tin ceiling with whirling fans. On the menu board are wonderful desserts: plain or marble cheesecake ($2.25), carrot cake ($2.25), oversize cookies (95¢), muffins ($1), and cinnamon rolls ($1.60). You might even elect the chocolate-pecan-pie bar. This place makes a great stop before or after visiting the nearby Portland Museum of Art.

EASY EXCURSIONS SOUTH OF PORTLAND
CRESCENT BEACH

Just south of Portland lies the charming town of **Cape Elizabeth.** About three miles from downtown Portland, pick up Me. 77 for the speedy drive to the cape.

Or you might elect to go along the Shore Road and stop at **Portland Headlight,** the first lighthouse in the United States, commissioned by George Washington and completed in 1791. The grand headlight and park area is widely photographed, and the lawns of the old fort are a wonderful spot to have a picnic. There's also a small rocky beach for wading. On July 4th weekend, you can find the Portland Symphony Orchestra performing here with the magnificent headlight and beautiful Casco Bay Islands as a backdrop.

If you take Me. 77, look for the Old Ocean House Road. Just down on the left is a **fine old New England home** with a long tree-lined drive where Bette Davis lived during her marriage to actor Gary Merrill.

About seven miles from Portland, off Me. 77, is Two Lights Road. Drive a mile for the turnoff to Two Lights State Park. Another half mile down are the **two lighthouses** from which this area takes its name. Today, one working light is operated by the Coast Guard. The second, once owned by Gary Merrill, is a home. Don't miss the spectacular views from here; you might even go climbing on the rocks—but be careful of the high waves.

The **Lobster Shack Restaurant** is open between April and Columbus Day and provides local seafood in a rustic atmosphere. There are plenty of picnic tables outside too. Expect a long line in summer—but it moves quickly.

Keep driving along the shore for a quick stop at **Kettle Cove,** a mile from Two Lights State Park. You can park for free here and walk along the beach into Crescent Beach State Park. Crescent Beach is popular with locals for romancing and is also the best nearby beach to Portland.

OLD ORCHARD BEACH

Go to Pine Point Road, 15 minutes south of Portland, at U.S. 1. Less than a mile from the turnoff is the **Scarborough Marsh Nature Center,** operated by the Maine Inland Fisheries and Wildlife in conjunction with the Maine Audubon Society. Daily programs are offered on the marshes by nature interpreters. You can even experience the marsh by canoe at night. Other programs include activities for children, wildflower lectures and tours, and canoe rentals. Call 207/883-5100 for more information.

Beyond the nature center is a little restaurant with fine take-out food. The **Portside Seafood Restaurant** offers clam cakes, fried clams, haddock, and fried Maine shrimp at reasonable prices.

At the bottom of Pine Point Road (three miles from the U.S. 1 turnoff) is the more pricey and commercial **Lobster Bake.** Here the road (also known as Me. 9 West) turns south toward Old Orchard Beach. Pine Point Beach and Old Orchard melt together forming almost seven miles of beachfront. Mid-rise condominiums are popping up these days.

You can still get a feel of decades gone by at **Bailey's Lobster Pound** (☎ 207/883-4571). Instead of turning right to Old Orchard, make a sharp left to Bailey's. The pound is open daily from 9am to about 6 or 7pm.

Old Orchard Beach is largely forgettable according to local folks. In the 1940s and 1950s, big bands came to play in the huge dance hall at the end of the pier. Over the years, fire claimed the pier piece by piece until it was little more than a stub. It was rebuilt but never regained its appeal.

The amusement section with rides and carnival atmosphere is popular with French Canadians who come by the thousands from Québec to soak up the sun. The beach is still in excellent condition and a popular rendezvous with teenagers from Portland to Portsmouth. Each summer fireworks are set off Thursday evenings during July and August.

EASY EXCURSIONS NORTH OF PORTLAND

Most people head east from Portland, aiming at Camden, Boothbay, Bar Harbor, or the Canadian border. But an excursion up U.S. 302 and Me. 26, deep into Maine's forested hinterland, will bring you right up against North Woods life.

SEBAGO LAKE

Of Maine's hundreds of beautiful clear lakes, Sebago Lake is one of the largest and most accessible. The eastern shore is somewhat developed with small villages, highway establishments, and the like; at the southern tip, the town of Sebago Lake is hardly more than a few dozen houses, two stores, and a gas station. But along the western shore, in the area of the settlement called East Sebago, are a number of places that rent rooms and cabins, mingled among the larger private summer cabins and houses.

Although the roads that skirt the lake do have collections of cabins and houses here and there, it's hardly what you'd call thickly settled. You'll come across Sebago Lake State Park at the northern tip of the lake, where there's also a fine beach, picnic facilities, and a camping area. Although very busy in summer, the park is yours to enjoy with only a handful of others in early June or after Labor Day.

SABBATHDAY LAKE

Thirty miles north of Portland along Me. 26 is the settlement of Sabbathday Lake, the last living Shaker community in the country. Founded in the 1700s, the Sabbathday Lake community still has a handful of active members who continue to work and live in the Shaker tradition. A shop selling community products, a museum, and a welcome center are open to visitors, though most of the other buildings are not. While other Shaker villages remain, one in Massachusetts and another in Kentucky for instance, this is the only remaining village still operated by the Shakers. For more on Shaker history and beliefs, see "Stockbridge," in Chapter 8.

The spare white buildings of the village are plain but extremely well kept. Most notable is the Brick Dwelling House. In the fields near the village are several small, simple cemeteries, each with only one monument, bearing the legend SHAKERS and the dates of interment.

Up the road a few miles is the village of Poland Spring, which gained fame in the 1800s when a man was miraculously cured by its waters. The water from the spring has been bottled and shipped throughout the country since that time.

Continue north on Me. 26 and you'll soon come to one of the prettiest towns in Maine, right at the edge of the White Mountains and a vast national forest.

BETHEL

Tucked away in the mountains on the western edge of Maine is the village of Bethel, on U.S. 2, the highway that heads west along the border of the White Mountains National Forest. There are two attractions: a well-known preparatory school called **Gould Academy** (founded 1836) and **an excellent inn.**

Should you have an extra hour to spend in Bethel, drop in at **Dr. Moses Mason House,** 14 Broad St. (☎ 207/824-2908), on the common, open in July and August, Tuesday through Friday from 10am to 4pm and Saturday and Sunday from 1 to 4pm; the rest of the year, Monday through Friday from 10am to 4pm. Moses Mason was a congressman during the Jackson administration and had this Federal house built in 1813. Today it's furnished in antiques of the period and also holds several murals attributed to Rufus Porter. There are research facilities, special exhibits, pictures, films, and a gift shop. Admission costs $2 for adults, $1 for children.

North on Me. 26 is **Grafton Notch State Park,** which has a pretty waterfall named Screw Auger. West on U.S. 2 is the **White Mountains National Forest.** Between Gilead, Me., and Shelburne, N.H., the highway is lined with the **famous Shelburne birches.** It's rare to see so many of these unusual, lovely trees in one spot.

For more on the national forest in New Hampshire, see Chapter 11.

WHERE TO STAY

Chapman Inn
Broad and Church Sts. (P.O. Box 206), Bethel, ME 04217. ☎ **207/824-2657.** 9 rms (5 with bath). winter, $75 double without bath, $85 double with bath, $25 bed in dormitory; summer, $55 double without bath, $65 double with bath, $25 bed in dormitory. Rates include full breakfast. AE, MC, V. Free parking.

This has been a bed-and-breakfast full of cheery, homey rooms since 1865. The white clapboard inn offers use of a games room, a living room with a fireplace, a nearby pond with canoes, and private saunas. There's also a 24-bed dormitory for groups and others. You can walk to golf, shops, and restaurants.

EASY EXCURSIONS AROUND PORTLAND
CHEBEAGUE ISLAND

This little island, actually part of the town of Cumberland, measures about 1¹/₂ miles wide and less than 5 miles long. It sits in the waters of Casco Bay, 45 minutes from Portland via boat. Take a picnic or mountain bikes for a fun day outing.

To get here, you can take the **Casco Bay Islands Transit boat** (☎ 207/ 774-7871), which costs $7.85 round-trip, departs from a Commercial Street wharf in Portland, and arrives at the west end of Chebeague Island about 45 minutes later; you then need to take a $3 taxi ride for about four miles to get to the Chebeague Island Inn.

Or you can take the **Chebeague Transportation Company boat** from Cousins Island in Yarmouth, a 10-minute drive north of Portland. There's plenty of parking (for about $8) near the Cousins Island dock, and the 15-minute boat trip costs $9 round-trip for adults and children over 12, and 75¢ each way for children 1 to 12. The boats make at least eight round-trips each day and they arrive 100 yards from the Chebeague Island Inn. Call 207/846-3700 for the schedule.

Where to Stay & Dine

Chebeague Island Inn

South Rd. (P.O. Box 492), Chebeague Island, ME 04017. ☎ **207/846-5155.** 21 rms (16 with bath). $75–$100 double without bath, $100–$125 double with bath. Rates include breakfast. DISC, MC, V. Free parking. Closed Oct–Apr.

It's hard to decide what I like best about the Chebeague Island Inn—the simple island rooms or the romantic atmosphere for dinner. This white clapboard inn with dormers on the third floor has an expansive lawn out front and a porch that goes on and on. It's up the hill from the boat landing on the east end. The sunset from the Great Room, where a huge fieldstone fireplace commands attention, will send chills up your spine. The old woods and the homey appointments create a romantic ambience. The rooms are simple, with a great water view in front or island view in back, fresh linens on the beds, light curtains, a dresser, and, in a few cases, some four-poster beds.

The dining room is well respected for its menu. Owners Jan and Dick Bowden sometimes wander from table to table and chat with the customers. The menu changes daily but is likely to include clam chowder or grilled shrimp with roasted-garlic mayonaise as appetizers, or such main dishes as charcoal-broiled filet mignon with bleu cheese, island crab, and, of course, lobster. Desserts are terrific too—try the three-berry pie or hazelnut-mocha torte.

Chebeague Orchard Inn

Chebeague Island, Maine 04017. ☎ **207/846-9488.** 5 rooms (all with shared baths). $75–$95 double. Winter, 15% less. Rates include breakfast. MC, V.

Vickie and Neil Taliento have been living on the island for more than a dozen years, and this is the fourth year they've been welcoming guests to this small Greek Revival home on two acres. Each room is country-simple, with some island views, and two of the rooms have private half baths (a toilet and sink), but they share a shower. Full breakfast is served in the sunny dining room. Guests may choose to bring their bicycles and roam the island. No lunch or dinner is served at the inn, but an island market and the Nellie G. Cafe do provide sustenance. You can always visit the dining room at the Chebeague Island Inn during the summer.

HALLOWELL

Fifty-five miles north of Portland (and 3¹/₂ miles south of Augusta on Me. 20/27) is the charming old town of Hallowell. It's filled with antiques shops and a couple of wonderful little artsy restaurants.

Where to Dine

Slates

167 Water St. ☎ **207/622-9575.** Reservations not required. Soups and salads $3.95–$5.95; main courses $8.95–$16.95. MC, V. Mon 7:30am–2:30pm, Tues–Sat 7:30am–9 or 9:30pm, Sun 9am–2:30pm. ECLECTIC.

Slates is a funky kind of place with a slate floor, a counter with polished wood, a tin ceiling, and ice-cream-parlor chairs. Ceiling fans whirl above your head. The menu is eclectic with gypsy stew, Brazilian black-bean soup, steak-and-sausage pie, country chicken pie, and a variety of salads. In the morning you can order crepes, quiches, and sandwiches. Dinner is by candlelight.

A FALL FOLIAGE DRIVING TOUR

If you happen to be in Portland during New England's wonderful foliage season, then you'll want to drive through the area to see the color. But don't get here too early—the foliage comes into full color in early October, and you can usually count on peak time in southern Maine to be around October 10.

From Portland, drive along U.S. 302 past Sebago Lake State Park. Continue north to Naples, past Long Lake on Me. 35 to Lynchville, where Maine's famous international signpost points the way to China, Denmark, Mexico, Naples, Norway, Paris, and Poland. Take Me. 5 along the edge of the White Mountains National Forest. On the way is the Sunday River ski area, with its panoramic views.

Go east on U.S. 2 to the covered bridge built in 1872, one of the most photographed bridges in New England. Soon you'll arrive in Rumford on the Androscoggin River.

Maine 108 from Rumford will take you past apple orchards with fine views of many lakes and ponds. Drive past Auburn Lake on Me. 4 through the hardwood forest. Follow U.S. 202 into Gray and take Me. 26 into Portland. The entire route is about 175 miles—unless you've made some detours of your own.

AN EXCURSION NORTHWEST OF PORTLAND

Perhaps the most common way into New Hampshire from Portland is south on the Maine Turnpike towards Portsmouth or north and west toward North Conway via US 302. But consider this westerly route out of Portland via Me. 25 through several quaint towns. Westbrook is a suburb best-known as being home to a mill owned by Scott Paper Company. Shortly you wind your way to Gorham, home of the University of Southern Maine and a rural town with stately homes. Continue through Standish (there's a regular Saturday night antique auction in town where deals are often had because of the remote location). At the 32-mile mark from Portland is Cornish where the homes are mostly clapboard frame structures. A handful of local shops and antique halls dot the main street, replete with a general store and a two-story yellow clapboard town hall.

In the center is the **Cornish Inn** (☎ 207/625-8501 or 800/352-7235), which makes a nice stop for a refreshment and dinner. Prime rib is a specialty ($13.95). The decor is traditional country, and there's even a tiny tavern for a cold brew.

Continue on Me. 25 four miles west through Porter, where the pretty three-story white clapboard Riverside United Methodist Church is in the center square. You'll also find a couple more antique shops here. Continue across the New Hampshire border (now 43 miles from Portland) into Freedom, N.H. (remember this state's motto on its license plates is "LIVE FREE OR DIE"). Continue three miles to N.H. 153 in Effingham. If you were to continue west on Me./N.H. 25 the road would bring you into Center Ossipee 10 miles further on. We'll continue on N.H. 153 north (in Effingham it's only 15 miles south of Conway). At the turn onto N.H. 153 you'll notice King Pine Ski Area where night skiing is offered. Continuing to the town of Eaton you'll see another general store called—what else?—the Eaton Village Store. At this point you've driven only 57 miles from Portland but it's taken 2$^{1}/_{2}$ hours with stops. On the right is Crystal Lake and you'll shortly see signs for the Snowvillage Inn. Now if you planned ahead or are arriving close to supper time, then call the inn for dinner reservations. If not, the short drive from here on N.H. 153 will direct you into Center Conway and North Conway via N.H. 16 and U.S. 302. For dining information in Snowville, see North Conway in Chapter 11.

EN ROUTE TO BOOTHBAY HARBOR

North of Portland, the next major tourist destination is Boothbay Harbor. However, you'll pass several interesting towns along the way, each with an attraction peculiar to Maine.

FREEPORT

This small Maine town is known all over the country and throughout the world as the headquarters of **L. L. Bean** (☎ 207/865-3111 or 800/221-4221), the company that sells equipment, clothing, and supplies for outdoor activities. L. L. Bean has been in Freeport for decades, but in recent years the store's popularity has burgeoned to epic proportions. Half a dozen parking lots, administered by Bean employees, fill up quickly every day with cars bearing license plates from all over America and Canada. The large, attractive store, open 24 hours, is always mobbed during the day and busy at night. The same shopping policy applies to the catalog—you can order 24 hours a day, seven days a week.

You're likely to find the rich and famous shopping here. Rock bands or other celebrities playing in Portland can usually be found here late at night following their performance. Don't forget to stop by Bean's trout pond in the men's department.

Bean's reputation was built by selling sturdy, good-quality items at reasonable prices. The returns policy is absolute: If you find a Bean item unsatisfactory at any time, return it for a refund. Should you stop at Bean's, remember that the store carries hundreds of items for which there is no room in the catalog, and that there's also a "factory store" for end-of-season and distressed merchandise. It's located across Main Street in its own building. You should also know that Bean's will mail your packages home for you from the store—now with a charge. Keep it in mind if your trunk's too full; take the item you've just bought to the customer service counter and they'll take care of the rest. The store will charge $4.50 per address to ship orders both via catalog and retail store.

The boom at Bean's has brought prosperity to Freeport, and a dozen other shops—Banana Republic, The Gap, Dansk, Anne Klein, Ralph Lauren, Reebok, you name it—have opened in order to profit from the press of Bean buyers. The old Mobil gas station was razed to make way for a new Levi's store and thankfully the building designers managed to impart some style to make it blend with the rest of Freeport. Additionally, the Ralph Lauren Polo store has added a second floor and new merchants. Bookland has moved above Dansk too. Freeport still lacks the quintessential coffee house but a couple of street vendors try to fill the gap.

Where to Stay

Harraseeket Inn

162 Main St., Freeport, ME 04032. ☎ **207/865-9377** or 800/342-6423. 54 rms. $150–$225 single or double. AE, DC, DISC, MC, V. Free parking.

This is a favorite, a cheerful upscale country inn with all the modern conveniences of a hotel. Green shutters accent this white clapboard inn, well respected for its restaurant and downstairs tavern. You'll find cozy fireplaces burning, afternoon tea, lovely rooms, and good Maine regional cooking. The inn's tavern—the Broad Arrow Tavern—got its name from the broad arrow symbolizing naval property of the king of England. The king sent his navy to claim the best trees for masts that would be used for gun ships to protect his royal property and lands. Much of Freeport was forest, and its white pine trees (standing 200 feet) were cut and transported to England. The tavern and the main dining room are a treat for lunch or brunch even if you don't stay here. And it's a pine cone's throw from L. L. Bean.

Isaac Randall House

Independent Dr., Freeport, ME 04032. ☎ **207/865-9295** or 800/865-9295. Fax 207/865-9003. 9 rms (all with bath). A/C TEL. $70–$115 double, $125 in caboose. MC, V. Free parking. Directions: Drive half a mile south of L. L. Bean on U.S. 1 (Main Street).

The Isaac Randall House, Freeport's first bed-and-breakfast, has been hosting guests for more than a decade. This isn't the only B&B in town anymore, but it's still the best. The old clapboard farmhouse dates from 1823, just after Maine became a state. You'll love the old Glenwood stove in the country kitchen, where a full breakfast is served; upstairs is a sitting room with pumpkin-pine floors. Beyond that is a little area with a refrigerator for guests to keep picnic fare or drinks cold. All the rooms are delightfully done; some have brass fixtures in the bath that ordinarily would be found in very fine old homes. A caboose out back has been converted to an unusual room accommodating up to four persons. You'll want to slip down the drive to the Country Café and Bakery for other delights or walk into the center of Freeport for shopping.

Where to Dine

One of this town's most appealing aspects is the fact that there are almost as many restaurants as there are factory stores. They dot Main Street like umbrellas in the sand.

You'll find everything from Ben and Jerry's famous ice cream in the shadow of L. L. Bean's front door to the greasy spoon across the street. McDonald's serves up its hamburgers from inside the historic Gore House, a white clapboard house where you'll find carpeting in the dining room. Now that's progress! You might enjoy a hot pretzel from a street vendor or opt to sit on a bricked patio of a seafood take-out. This is prime real estate for people-watching.

Jameson Tavern

115 Main St. ☎ **207/865-4196.** Reservations recommended. Main courses $10–$19; sandwiches $4.50–$5.95. AE, DC, DISC, MC, V. Lunch daily 11:30am–2:30pm; dinner daily 5–10pm in the dining room, 11:30am–11pm in the tavern. SEAFOOD/STEAKS.

Here is a colonial choice you won't want to pass up. Dating back to 1779, the inn takes pride in being the site where papers were signed separating Maine from Massachusetts. It has a colonial dining room in front and an equally inviting tavern/restaurant in back. You'll find tombstone rubbings framed in the hallway. The locals love the tavern, and you'll want to sample the mud pie or chalkboard specials. It has local charm and is easy to find—next door to Bean's.

Ocean Farms Restaurant

23 Main St. ☎ **207/865-3101.** Reservations not required. Main courses $4–$10 at lunch, $10–$20 at dinner. AE, MC, V. Daily 7am–10:30pm. SEAFOOD/STEAKS.

The decor has been updated for the coming years but still is done to reflect its native roots. The service is casual at breakfast and lunch, but more formal at dinner. The menu is mostly seafood, though other items are always offered as well.

BRUNSWICK

Surrounded by coastal resort towns, Brunswick is the cultural center of this part of Maine: Both **Bowdoin College** and Maine's only professional music theater are here. The **Maine State Music Theater** (☎ 207/725-8769), on the Bowdoin campus, presents musical productions from mid-June through Labor Day each summer.

Much of Bowdoin's fame comes from the distinguished alumni who have spent their time in Brunswick and then moved on to fame and glory: Longfellow, Hawthorne, and President Franklin Pierce were all Bowdoin graduates. The college is at Pine and College Streets, and free tours are available year-round. While you're here, visit Bowdoin's art museum to see its collection of colonial works.

Where to Dine

Stowe House

63 Federal St. ☎ **207/725-5543.** Reservations recommended. Main courses $10–$16. AE, DC, MC, V. Lunch daily 11:30am–2pm; dinner daily 5:30–8:30pm. STEAKS/SEAFOOD.

Near Bowdoin College, this famous inn, where Harriet Beecher Stowe wrote *Uncle Tom's Cabin,* serves up regional cuisine in lovely, warm surroundings. Specialties include the broiled seafood sampler and veal médaillons sautéed with Maine crabmeat and white asparagus.

BATH

A 10-mile drive along U.S. 1 north from Brunswick brings you to Bath, a fine town of colonial and Federal houses built when the town was a wealthy seaport and shipbuilding center.

To see these houses, take a drive down Washington Street and stop at no. 243, the headquarters of Bath's famous **Maine Maritime Museum** (☎ 207/443-1316). One admission ticket ($6 for adults, $2.50 for children 6 to 16, free for children under 6; $20 for a family) admits you to the exhibit on the maritime history of Maine, the restored Percy & Small Shipyard and its buildings, the Apprentice Shop boatbuilding school, a lobstering exhibit (seasonal), and, when in port, a 142-foot fishing schooner. Just about everything you'd associate with the sea is represented in these exhibits: early fishing methods, shipbuilding, small boats, engines and steam yachts, lobstering, navigation, ships' models and paintings, sailors' memorabilia, and all sorts of coastal lore. There's even a play boat for children complete with crow's nest and a "cargo" of sand.

The 10-acre museum complex is along the river, with plenty of space for picnickers. Wear outdoor clothing and good shoes. You'll need several hours to see everything; or you can have your ticket validated for the next day also, at no extra charge. The museum is open daily from 9:30am to 5pm.

WISCASSET

Wiscasset bills itself "the prettiest village in Maine," and as you pass through the center of town on U.S. 1, you can confirm this. As you cross the Sheepscot River bridge to Damariscotta, look south and note the two enormous hulks standing in the water. The four-masted schooners *Hesperus* and *Luther Little* once carried cargoes along the Atlantic coast. But the many-masted schooners (a few were even built with six masts!) were the last of a proud breed, replaced by the more reliable steamboats. These two relics of a romantic age sit forlorn in the mud, awaiting restoration or final destruction.

The best spot to eat here is probably **Le Garage** on Water Street (☎ 207/882-5409). With views of the old ships below, it sits on the Sheepscot River in a yellow clapboard building that was once a garage and a blacksmith's shop. Chef Alan Dodge's eatery is open for lunch and dinner, with meals costing $6 to $20. It's closed in January.

Directly across the street is the **Old Customs House,** dating back to 1870. It houses a gift shop today containing many fine items with a country flavor.

Three miles south of U.S. 1 on Me. 27, north of Wiscasset, is **Edgecomb Pottery;** it's just down the Boothbay Harbor turnoff. The best pottery along the coast may be found here. Some of the work is rather pricey ($20 coffee mugs), but the workmanship is exceptional. A big deck and terrace area loaded with everything from bowls and vases to soap dispensers will immediately catch your eye. There are some seconds and discontinued items on sale at one-third off, but the selection can be slim in summer. (They also have shops in Freeport, downtown Wiscasset, and Boothbay Harbor.)

4 Boothbay Harbor

11 miles S of U.S. 1, 59 miles NE of Portland, 52 miles SW of Camden

North and east of Portland, the Maine coastline is a choppy succession of peninsulas, sea inlets, islands, and river outlets. The country here is beautiful, and vacation communities abound. Reaching many of these communities means driving down a peninsular road for quite a number of miles to the tip and, upon departure, driving back up to U.S. 1—few bridges or causeways span the inlets or rivers.

Boothbay Harbor is the principal town in a region of vacation settlements that include Boothbay, Boothbay Harbor, East Boothbay, Southport, and Ocean Point. A whole guide could be written on this region alone, and so recommendations have been limited to Boothbay Harbor itself, which is the center of the action.

GETTING THERE   By Bus   See the beginning of this chapter.

By Car   Follow I-95 or U.S. 1 to Brunswick, then U.S. 1 to Bath and Wiscasset. East of Wiscasset, take Me. 27 south to Boothbay Harbor.

ESSENTIALS   The **telephone area code** is **207.** Contact the **Boothbay Harbor Region Chamber of Commerce,** P.O. Box 356, Boothbay Harbor, ME 04538 (☎ **207/633-2353**), for information.

As you drive down Me. 27 from U.S. 1, several miles from town you'll come to a seasonal information bureau, on the right. If it's closed, don't worry, for there's another one a bit farther along, right at the edge of town, that's open year-round.

WHAT TO SEE & DO

Wander down to the shore in town and you'll see lots of signboards and ticket stands for the boats that operate on **cruises** out of Boothbay Harbor. Ticket prices range from about $10 to $15 and may include a search for seals, water birds, whales, and other marine life, or perhaps a clambake or a chicken bake afloat. When the moon is nearly full, special moonlight cruises are arranged. Cruises can be anywhere from one to three hours in length. Ask around to find a style, length, and price that's right for you.

The Boothbay Harbor region celebrates several **festivals** each year. Among them are the Fisherman's Festival, Windjammer Days, Antique Auto Days, Friendship Sloop Days, and a fall foliage festival.

A CLAMBAKE ON CABBAGE ISLAND

Go down to Fisherman's Wharf on Main Street, look for Pier 6, and climb aboard the **MV** *Argo* for a cruise out to Cabbage Island in Linekin Bay and a real downeast-style clambake. Clams and lobsters are steamed amid seaweed the old-fashioned way and served up twice a day from Memorial Day through Labor Day. The *Argo* sails to the clambake Monday through Friday at 12:30pm (returning by 4:15pm) and Saturday at 12:30pm and 5pm (returning before dark); on Sunday departures are at 11:30am (returning by 2:45pm) and 1:30pm (returning by 4:45pm). The total cost for the clambake is $34.95 per person, and that includes the delightful round-trip boat cruise, a cup of fish chowder, two lobsters, steamed clams, corn on the cob, new Maine potatoes, and blueberry cake and coffee for dessert. The scenic island has games, paths, and sitting areas for you to enjoy as well. Call ☎ 207/633-7200 for clambake reservations at least half an hour before sailing time.

A BOOTHBAY MUSEUM

Boothbay Region Art Foundation

7 Townsend Ave. ☎ **207/633-2703.** Admission free. Mon–Sat 10am–5pm, Sun noon–5pm.

The work of local artists and others is displayed in this gallery and arts center on a year-round basis. It premiered to replace the former Brick House Art Gallery.

WHERE TO STAY

I've chosen mostly establishments in town or in special locations outside. The Boothbay region does have a number of bed-and-breakfast houses, most off the beaten track. For information, check (or call) the information booth.

IN TOWN

Admiral's Quarters Inn

105 Commercial St., Boothbay Harbor, ME 04538. ☎ **207/633-2474.** 7 rms. TV. $75–$95 single or double. Rates include morning coffee and light breakfast. MC, V. Free parking. Closed Nov–Apr.

Monhegan: The Picture-Perfect Isle

The *Balmy Days* is a motor craft that makes the daily 16-mile run out from Boothbay Harbor to Monhegan Island, Maine's famous, windswept resort-at-sea. You cannot stay overnight on the island without previous hotel reservations, but the *Balmy Days's* schedule allows you to have between three and four hours on the island if you return on the same day. Monhegan is noted for its captivating paths and hiking trails through Cathedral Woods and to the sea. A round-trip ticket to Monhegan Island costs $28 for adults; children under 10 are charged $15. While at Monhegan, the *Balmy Days* makes one run around the island so you can see the rugged cliffs, and this costs $1 extra. By the way, if you're energetic, you can easily hike all over the island in one four-hour stay on Monhegan. There's also a supper cruise ($21.50 to $26 for adults, half price for children), including a chicken or lobster dinner. For detailed information, call 207/633-2284 or 800/298-2284.

Visitors arrive on the island from Boothbay Harbor or Port Clyde at the boat dock near the Island Inn. Most visitors come for the day, but overnight accommodations are available and often last-minute reservations can be found. So remember to call the hotels before you take the boat over. Bicycles are not permitted on the island; there's only a handful of cars and pick up trucks which take luggage to the few inns here. There is no bank on the island, and the few existing public phones don't accept coins. You must use a phone credit card— even for a local call. Also, whatever comes with you to the island goes back with you on the boat. There simply are no trash receptacles.

About 60 families live all year on Monhegan. In summer the population swells markedly here since this is also a long-time art colony. Painter Jamie Wyeth still has a home here (it's a 10-minute walk from the dock to Lobster Cove) although he spends more time at his Port Clyde home on the mainland.

Several trails, 17 miles of them, zig-zag over the island. One to Lobster Cove takes you to Wyeth's home romantically facing the open sea. Another goes to the cliffs which are the tallest in Maine and usually are a surprise to visitors both for their height and ruggedness. Swim Beach is the only place for a cool—make that cold—dip in the water. In summer, the lobster traps and other gear sit idle because the season is closed from June 25th until January 1.

The Monhegam Museum is located in the former keeper's residence at the lighthouse. Open daily (11:30am to 3:30pm) from July 1 to mid-September, it offers an intriguing glimpse of island life with special exhibits including photos of local birds and flora. The museum is also stocked with many antiques such as fishing gear. The galleries are free, although a $2 donation is welcome. The lighthouse next door was built in 1824 and manned until 1959. The view is wonderful from this lonely spot. You can see the village, much of the island, neighboring Manana Island, the Camden Hills on the mainland, and from the southerly side—around 7 and 10pm—the *Scotia Prince* heading toward or away from Portland.

Two places to stay on the island are the superior **Island Inn** (☎ 207/596-0371 or 800/722-1269), with 33 rooms and its own dining room (open for all meals during set hours), and the **Monhegan House** (☎ 207/594-7983 or 800/599-7983), with its 32 rooms and breakfast cafe (dinner is served only twice a week). Both hotels take credit cards, and both close from October to May. Rates for the Island Inn are $73 to $78 for a single, and $116 to $140 for a double. Prices for the Monhegan House are $40 to $44 for a single and $70 for a double.

This large, old, white clapboard sea captain's house built around 1820 commands marvelous views of the harbor. Upper and lower sun decks allow you to take in the view from each room. The inn was poised to be sold as I came through Boothbay and reportedly will have some renovations done but will retain much of its ambiance.

Anchor Watch Bed and Breakfast

3 Eames Rd., Boothbay Harbor, ME 04538. ☎ **207/633-7565.** 4 rms. $70–$105 double. Rates include breakfast. MC, V. Free parking.

Here is a charmer, small and intimate and run by friendly folks who also run the *Balmy Days* cruises over to Monhegan Island. When I last visited the inn on a sunny summer day, the dining room was brimming with guests having quiche and coffee, toast and pastries, and more. You could see the haze over the water on this hot day and the enthusiasm in everyone who was finishing up in time for the 9:30am boat to Monhegan. Country-flavored rooms have views of the water and lawn sloping down to the shore. The coffee pot is always on, and you're just a short walk to the local shops for exploring.

Captain Sawyer's Place

87 Commercial St., Boothbay Harbor, ME 04538. ☎ **207/633-2290.** 10 rms. TV. $45–$95 double. MC, V. Rates include continental breakfast. Free parking. Closed Mid-Oct to mid-May.

Run by Kim Reed-Upham and sons Nick and Aaron, this guesthouse is a classic yellow-and-white Boothbay Harbor residence—complete with rooftop "observatory." A small patio overlooks the pedestrians on Main Street, and the house's long wraparound veranda overlooks everything. The bright and tidy rooms have some period furnishings and Martha Washington bedspreads. The location couldn't be any better, nor the welcome warmer.

Topside

McKown Hill, Boothbay Harbor, ME 04538. ☎ **207/633-5404.** 23 rms, 1 cottage, 1 house. TEL. $50–$95 single or double; $95–175 cottage; $1,000–$1,350 per week house. Rates include morning coffee. MC, V. Free parking. Closed Oct to mid-May.

Topside says it all about this charming hilltop house just two blocks from the center of town atop McKown Hill. Several fine old houses have been meticulously restored down to the marble fireplaces (in the living rooms) and stocked with antiques for the pleasure of Topside's guests. Nine rooms have refrigerators, microwave ovens, and coffee percolators; nine others have coffee makers and refrigerators. And what a view—from many of the rooms or simply from a lawn chair in the midst of Topside's lush green grass, where you can take it all in as the cool breezes waft up from the harbor. Although there are other places on McKown Hill, Topside is smack at the top. A full house is now available for rental, too.

NEARBY

Five Gables Inn

Murray Hill Rd., East Boothbay, ME 04544. ☎ **207/633-4551** or 800/451-5048. 16 rms. $80–$130 double. Rates include breakfast. MC, V. Free parking. Closed Dec–Apr. Directions: Follow Me. 96 east to Murray Hill Road and the inn.

I missed Ellen and Paul Morissette, owners of this 150-year-old inn when I came through Boothbay, but the hospitality hasn't changed, and the response from readers about their home is very encouraging. All the rooms in this superbly restored old Maine coastal inn have a great view of Linekin Bay; five have a working fireplace. After your wonderful buffet breakfast here, enjoy the view from the large veranda, take the sun on the lawn, or cross the road for a swim. Bustling Boothbay Harbor is three miles away; here in East Boothbay, it's much calmer and quieter.

Lawnmeer Inn and Restaurant

Me. 27, Southport, ME 04576. ☎ **207/633-2544** or 800/633-7645. 32 rms. TV. $45–$120 double. MC, V. Free parking. Closed Mid-Oct to mid-May. Directions: From U.S. 1, take Me. 27 south to West Boothbay, across the bridge to Southport Island.

A short drive from Boothbay Harbor, across the drawbridge in Southport, the Lawnmeer offers motel-style rooms with modern conveniences. Most rooms have water views, decks, or both. Breakfast and dinner are served during set hours. The menu includes steamed clams and pasta dishes. In a quiet country setting, this is the place to go if you need to get away from it all.

Ocean Point Inn

Shore Rd. (P.O. Box 409), East Boothbay, ME 04544. ☎ **207/633-4200**. 61 rms. TV. $85–$122 double. DISC, MC, V. Free parking. Closed Mid-Oct to mid-May. Directions: Follow Me. 96 east through East Boothbay to the end of the road at Ocean Point.

Way down at Ocean Point by the lighthouse, on the southern tip of a peninsula overlooking the harbor mouth, is a collection of about 100 cottages, all in a serene location. Ocean Point Inn is the only commercial establishment here, and it offers a wide choice of accommodations. All rooms are decorated in colonial/ modern resort style, with small refrigerators and electric heat, and each guest has access to the outdoor heated pool. The Ocean Point has its own restaurant open for breakfast and dinner. Meal service may vary from continental breakfast to full breakfast and from six days a week to daily service, depending on the season, so check ahead. It's just $6^{1}/_{2}$ miles to town, where many restaurants are situated.

WHERE TO DINE

Andrews' Harborside Restaurant

At the footbridge. ☎ **207/633-4074**. Reservations recommended for large parties. Main courses $9–$15. MC, V. Daily 7:30am–9pm. Closed Mid-Oct to Apr. AMERICAN/SEAFOOD.

Andrews' offers mako-shark burgers, chowders, and a lobster roll that's not gigantic but is positively stuffed with succulent lobster meat—no filler. Tables are covered in nautical blue-and-white cloths, and you have your choice of an indoor dining room with lots of windows or a screened-in porch, both with fine views of the harbor. A full bar and wine list are offered. For dessert, go downstairs to the Round Top Ice Cream booth beneath the terrace. At breakfast, Andrews' is known for its homemade fresh cinnamon rolls.

Chowder House

In the Granary, 49 Townsend Ave. ☎ **207/633-5761**. Reservations not accepted. Main courses $10–$18; dinner $20–$30. AE, DISC, MC, V. Daily 11am–9pm. Closed Early Sept to mid-June. SEAFOOD.

A few steps from the center of Boothbay Harbor, down near the footbridge, is the Chowder House, where you can have a drink in the Loading Dock Lounge, a woody place filled with nautical paraphernalia, then eat in the dining room with its inside water-view room and outside terrace. The clam chowder and lobster stew are made fresh daily and are served with freshly baked bread. You might choose the lobster sandwich or seafood salad, but there's meat and fowl as well. Popular choices are the native scallops sautéed in wine and butter with shallots and pars-ley and surf-and-turf kebabs. The Chowder House has been family owned and run for 16 years. The big bar has as many as 40 stools—often busy with patrons enjoying the food and views. Regulars here (those who make several visits during a week's vacation) rave about this outdoor bar under a yellow awning; it was a former wooden sailboat.

Lobster Dock

Eastside, Boothbay Harbor. ☎ **207/633-7120.** Reservations not accepted. Main courses $8–$16; dinner for two $25. MC, V. Summer, daily 11:30am–8:30pm. Off-season, hours vary. SEAFOOD.

Enjoy lunch or dinner in a casual atmosphere where you can watch your lobster prepared before your eyes. There's no table service here, but the "downeast" hospitality still shows through. Fried seafood is on the menu, along with several lobster items. Beer and wine are served.

Lobsterman's Wharf

On the waterfront, off Me. 96, E. Boothbay. ☎ **207/633-3443.** Reservations not accepted. Soups and salads $2.75–$8.50; main courses $12–$17; desserts $4; dinner for two $35. AE, MC, V. Summer, daily 11:30am–midnight. Off-season, hours vary. SEAFOOD/AMERICAN.

This restaurant overlooks Linekin Bay, within an easy walk to the East Boothbay General Store. Lobster, grilled seafood, and barbecued shrimp are specialties; the seafood combos are popular. The decor has nautical overtones, and the service is friendly. Full liquor service is provided.

Rocktide

45 Atlantic Ave. ☎ **207/633-4455** or 800/762-8433. Reservations: See below. Main courses $11–$18; dinner $25–$35. MC, V. Dinner only, daily 5:30–9pm. AMERICAN/SEAFOOD.

Located across the bay from downtown Boothbay Harbor (use the footbridge), Rocktide is a big place with four dining areas. On the Seadeck, in the Chart Room and Buoy Room, you can dress as you like and no reservations are taken; in the Dockside and Harborside Rooms, diners should observe "jacket" formality and reservations are taken. The menu is old New England: fried Maine shrimp, ocean scallops, seafood casserole, finnan haddie, New England lobster pie, or a fisherman's platter. But there are unexpected items as well, such as a kebab of shrimp, scallops, lobster, and swordfish and sole Duxelleois and roast duck. Every main course comes with rights to the salad bar, a popover, and rice or potato.

5 Camden

85 miles NE of Portland, 77 miles W of Bar Harbor

A small coastal town wedged between the salt waters of Penobscot Bay and a range of rocky hills, Camden has a population of barely 4,000—it's small, picturesque, and manageable. Poet Edna St. Vincent Millay came from this region, but today Camden's chief claim to fame is that it's the home port for several two-masted schooners taking eager landlubbers for cruises along the Maine coast. The hills behind the town are included in the Camden Hills State Park.

GETTING THERE   By Bus   See the beginning of this chapter.

By Car   Follow U.S. 1 to Camden.

ESSENTIALS   The **telephone area code** is **207.** The **Rockport-Camden-Lincolnville Chamber of Commerce,** P.O. Box 919, Camden, ME 04843 (☎ **207/236-4404;** fax 207/236-6252), maintains an information booth on the public landing in Camden where you can get a directory of the area and also a brochure describing the walking and bike tours of Camden and Rockport outlined by the Camden Historical Society.

WHAT TO SEE & DO

If you have a car, drive north from town along U.S. 1 and follow the signs to the entrance to **Camden Hills State Park** and the auto road to the top of **Mt. Battie,** the highest hill of the range. Besides the town itself, the drive up will afford you a view of the rocky hills, the countryside beyond, and Penobscot Bay—as described by Millay in her "Renascence."

Camden's **Windjammer fleet of schooners** provides the adventurous with a very different vacation: dipping in and out of the myriad of small harbors and inlets along the Maine coast. Cruises usually leave on Monday and last a week; they cost about $450 per person and space must be reserved in advance. Half-day and one- to three-day cruises range in price from $35 to $300. Contact the chamber of commerce (see above) for current information.

Go southeast along Bay View Street and you'll come to **Laite Memorial Park and Beach**, with picnic areas and restrooms, as well as a nice, chilly Maine beach. For the rest of your time in Camden, latch onto a copy of the walking tour brochure (mentioned above) put out by the Camden Historical Society and stroll through the town to get the flavor of it.

From the **Rockland Ferry Terminal** (☎ 207/596-2202), you can take a car-ferry to **Vinalhaven Island**, in Penobscot Bay, for a taste of island vacation life. The *Governor Curtis* (State Ferry Service, P.O. Box 645, Rockland, ME 04841) makes the 1¹/₂-hour run to and from Vinalhaven six times a day. You can also take a car-ferry to North Haven Island from here. The *Neal Burgess* makes the 1¹/₄-hour round-trip three times a day.

WHERE TO STAY

Camden is not packed with places to stay, and that's part of its charm. Many people stay at the motels scattered along both sides of U.S. 1 north and south of town. Here, I'll mention the best inns and guesthouses right in town, within walking distance of everything.

EXPENSIVE

Camden Harbour Inn
83 Bay View St., Camden, ME 04843. ☎ **207/236-4200** or 800/236-4266. 22 rms. $175–$225 Mid-June to mid-Oct; $95–$175 double mid-Oct to mid-June. Two-night minimum stay in summer. Rates include breakfast. AE, DISC, MC, V. Free parking. Directions: When U.S. 1 turns left in the center of town, turn right to reach the inn.

A nice old inn (1874) with white clapboards and beautiful views of Penobscot Bay, the Camden Harbour could be a model for the typical coastal Maine inn. Break-fast is served to guests (full breakfast in summer and continental breakfast offpeak) and the public, and dinner is served to both during the summer. The tavern is a gathering spot as well. Almost all the rooms have water views, eight have fireplaces, and eight have private patios. You can have cocktails or dinner on the nice Victorian veranda, which also has a fabulous view. Children over 12 are welcome.

Norumbega
61 High St., Camden, ME 04843. ☎ **207/236-4646.** 9 rms, 3 suites. $135–$290 double; $195–$450 suite. Rates include breakfast. AE, MC, V. Free parking. Directions: From the center of town, go north along U.S. 1.

This vast stone Victorian summer "cottage" (really a mini-castle) dates from 1886, when it was built by inventor Joseph Stearns. Having improved telegraphy, Stearns grew rich on the proceeds and built himself a veritable castle-mansion with rich woods, worked stone, and sumptuous furnishings, many of which survive. The games room is furnished with a pool table and TV. Many of the guest rooms have fine views of Penobscot Bay, some have working fireplaces, and all have king-size beds. Children over 7 are welcome.

Whitehall Inn

52 High St. (P.O. Box 558), Camden, ME 04843. ☎ **207/236-3391** or 800/789-6565. Fax 207/236-4427. 50 rms. TEL. $150–$170 double. Rates include breakfast and dinner. AE, MC, V. Free parking in a private lot. Closed Mid-Oct to late May. Directions: On U.S. 1, go just north of the town center.

The graceful old inn, under the same ownership for 25 years, has been Camden's prime place to stay for almost a century, and is easily recognizable by its pillared porches. Camden's most famous daughter, Edna St. Vincent Millay, gave a reading here when she was just a girl. The decor is refined in both the public rooms and the guest rooms. The mood in the dining room is casual nowadays. The hotel offers a tennis court and shuffleboard.

MODERATE

Blue Harbor House

67 Elm St., Camden, ME 04843. ☎ **207/236-3196** or 800/248-3196. Fax 207/236-6523. 8 rms, 2 suites. $85–$110 double; $135 suite. Rates include full breakfast. AE, DISC, MC, V. Free parking.

This friendly inn, just a few blocks south of downtown on U.S. 1, serves a full breakfast on the sun porch. Dinner is available by reservation only for $30 per person. The menu may include lobster stew, stuffed rack of lamb, roasted red potatoes, seasonal vegetables, and chocolate brownie soufflé. In the separate carriage house (built 1806) are two suites with king-size beds, whirlpools, and TV/VCRs. Bicycles are provided free, and beer and wine are available for purchase. This inn may be situated on a quiet street, but it's also on the super-highway and can be reached via E-mail addressed to MKKE83A@prodigy.com.

Edgecombe-Coles House

64 High St., Camden, ME 04843. ☎ **207/236-2336.** 6 rms. $120–$180 double. Rates include breakfast. AE, DISC, MC, V. Free parking.

This huge turn-of-the-century summer cottage retains its earlier glory, with period furnishings filling the rooms and lovely views of the garden. Three rooms have king-size beds and fireplaces, three rooms have ocean views, and three have TVs. Smoking is not permitted.

Goodspeed's Guest House

60 Mountain St., Camden, ME 04843. ☎ **207/236-8077.** 8 rms (6 with bath), 1 suite. $65 double without bath, $95 double with bath; $135 suite. Rates include breakfast. No credit cards. Free parking.

This house, half a mile up the hill on Me. 52, has been beautifully redone and furnished with antiques by its owners, who provide a warm welcome. A tiny deck, set with umbrella-shaded tables and chairs, allows you to enjoy the quiet of this location.

Hawthorn Inn

9 High St., Camden, ME 04843. ☎ **207/236-8842.** 7 rms, 3 suites. $75–$175 double. Rates include breakfast. AE, MC, V. Free parking.

This big Victorian house with a view of Camden Harbor is just a few minutes' walk north of the commercial district on U.S. 1, and has been carefully and lovingly restored—the large, airy rooms are furnished with antiques and there are Jacuzzis and fireplaces in the carriage-house rooms. You might enjoy breakfast on the outdoor deck with distant harbor views. Afternoon tea is served at 4pm by the new owners.

Maine Stay

22 High St., Camden, ME 04843. ☎ **207/236-9636.** 8 rms (6 with bath). $75 double without bath, $80–$120 double with bath. Rates include full breakfast and afternoon tea. MC, V. Free parking next to inn.

This big white house built in 1802 has very charming rooms with antiques and Oriental rugs, some of which share baths, and two pretty living rooms and a deck that overlooks the backyard. Located in the center of the historic district, the inn is about a five-minute walk to the town center. I love this place—the rooms are great and the hospitality genuine. And too, while the highest priced room is $115, half the others are only $75. A small brook runs behind the barn, and there's a narrow path back there and a new rose arbor with a bench so that you can linger to read or chat.

The Owl and the Turtle Harbor View Guest Rooms

8 Bay View St., Camden, ME 04843. ☎ **207/236-9014.** 3 rms. A/C TV TEL. $75–$85 double; $50–$55 double mid-Oct to May. Rates include continental breakfast. MC, V. Free parking. Directions: Entering the commercial center northbound on U.S. 1, turn right onto Bay View Street when U.S. 1 turns left.

This is perhaps the strangest name for a guesthouse, but it's explained when one realizes that the building that houses the Owl and the Turtle Bookshop also houses a few very nice motel-type rooms, each with a marvelous view of Mt. Battie and the inner harbor. The Owl's rooms are nicely decorated, but there are so few of them that you must reserve in advance by phone or mail. Nonsmoking.

Swan House

49 Mountain St., Camden, ME 04843. ☎ **207/236-8275** or 800/207-8275. 6 rms. June to mid-Oct, $85–$120 double. Rates include full breakfast. Mid-Oct to mid-June, rates are lower. MC, V.

This fine Victorian house dates from 1870 and has six guest rooms in the house and the Cygnet Annex. It specializes in generous breakfasts. Nestled at the foot of Mt. Battie, the inn is next to a state park trail that leads to the summit.

Windward House Bed and Breakfast

6 High St., Camden, ME 04843. ☎ **207/236-9656.** 7 rms, 1 suite. $65–$125 double; $85–$135 suite. Rates include breakfast. AE, MC, V. Free parking.

Personal service and beautiful accommodations are a hallmark here. It's a delightful atmosphere with flowers and shrubs all around. Inside, fireplaces, Oriental rugs on hardwood floors, and antiques combine to make a stay here everything a Maine B&B experience should be. The room overlooking the garden in the back has a four-poster bed and skylights, and is particularly fine. Lots of attention is also paid to landscaping. Children over 12 are welcome.

WHERE TO DINE

Cappy's Chowder House

1 Main St. ☎ **207/236-2254.** Reservations not accepted. Main courses $10–$18 at lunch, $18–$26 at dinner. MC, V. Daily 7:30am–midnight; hours vary off-season. AMERICAN/ SEAFOOD.

The two dining levels (the upstairs one with a water view and raw bar) have rich nautical decor and an eclectic menu. The seafood—clam, fish, and lobster chowders, salads—is excellent, plus there are burgers, daily fish specials, stir-fries, and steaks. You can get breakfast here as well. Downstairs is the bakery with fresh breads, doughnuts, and sandwiches. Management prides itself on the desserts, especially the crunch-a-nutter pie. Liquor is served at the bar, which provides a social center and quick-lunch place for many of the local yacht crews; tables and booths are for serious diners.

AN EASY EXCURSION TO ROCKPORT

A few minutes south of Camden is Rockport, a charming seaside town with a lovely harbor and the **Sail Loft Restaurant** (☎ 207/236-2330). Lunch and dinner are offered daily, and its reputation of more than 30 years stems in part from its blueberry muffins and clam chowder. The Sail Loft has a small bar tucked into one corner and views of the harbor from many tables in the restaurant. The restaurant is entirely nonsmoking.

6 Castine & Blue Hill

These little villages, set apart on a peninsula in Penobscot Bay, are gems. With only a few places to stay and to dine, these towns draw a steady crowd of summer regulars who come for the beauty, the seclusion, the quiet, the easy summer life. At the end of the section, I've also included Deer Isle, which is south of Blue Hill.

CASTINE

20 miles S of Bucksport, 20 miles W of Blue Hill

In the winter of 1613, Sieur Claude de Turgis de la Tour founded a small trading post here among the Tarrantine people. The struggle for North America's forest, natural, and maritime wealth was already beginning, and the French Fort Pentagoet founded by Turgis de la Tour would be conquered by the English in 1628. A treaty returned Pentagoet to France in 1635, and during the tumultuous period until 1676 the place changed hands many times. The British took it and called it Penobscot Fort; the French retook it and built the formidable Fort Saint Peter. At one time the village was the capital of all French Acadia (the lands in what is now Atlantic Canada). Even the Dutch coveted the fort, and ruled here from 1674 to 1676. In the latter year, Baron de Saint Castin recaptured the town for France and opened a trading station. Fortifications were strengthened and, despite raids by the British, the family of Baron de Saint Castin ruled over the town (then called Bagaduce) even after the wealthy baron himself returned to France in 1703. By 1760, however, the fate of French North America was sealed, and Castin's Fort, or Bagaduce, was to be held by the British after that year.

English settlers brought new life to Bagaduce during the 1760s, and dissatisfaction boiled in the English colonies at this period. Some of the townspeople were loyal to the king, others sympathized—actively and passively—with the American revolutionaries. But in 1779 a British naval force came from Nova Scotia, intent on making the town safe for British Loyalists (and thereby influencing the negotiations that would determine the fledgling United States' northern border). The British built Fort George to defend the town.

The challenge to American sovereignty was taken up by the General Court (legislature) of Massachusetts, which governed the territory at the time, and the ill-fated Penobscot Expedition was outfitted and launched at an ultimate cost of $8 million. Bad luck and bad commanding resulted in the destruction of most of the American force, almost bankrupting the Commonwealth of Massachusetts. Fort George was enlarged and strengthened over the years, and the town thrived until the border between the United States and Canada was determined. Unhappily for residents of Bagaduce, the boundary was to be the St. Stephen River (the present boundary) and not the Penobscot. Those loyal to the British Crown put their houses on boats and sailed them to sites along the coast of what is today New Brunswick at St. Andrews. Some of the houses moved still stand in St. Andrews.

In 1796 the name of Bagaduce was changed to Castine, and although it was occupied by British forces during the War of 1812, there was never again to be much military action. But in the 350 years of Castine's history, its forts—Fort Pentagoet, Fort George, and the American Fort Madison—saw a surprising number of attacks.

GETTING THERE **By Bus** See the beginning of this chapter.

By Car Turn right onto Me. 175 at Orland, east of Bucksport, and continue on Me. 166 and 166A to Castine.

ESSENTIALS The **telephone area code** is **207.** The **Castine Town Office** (☎ 207/326-4502) may be able to answer your questions.

WHAT TO SEE & DO

Visit the sites of the forts: **Fort Pentagoet,** near the Wilson Museum on Perkins Road; **Fort George,** near the entrance to town; and **Fort Madison.** Fort George is now a state memorial, kept up by the Bureau of Parks and Recreation.

Historical signboards placed around the village outline Castine's fascinating history. For a closer look, visit the **Wilson Museum,** on Perkins Street (☎ 207/326-8753), three blocks from Main Street to the southwest. Open late May through September, Tuesday through Sunday from 2 to 5pm, the admission-free museum has exhibits explaining the rich local history and prehistoric artifacts from the Americas, concentrating on the growth of the human ability to fashion tools. On Sunday and Wednesday afternoons in July and August, you can also visit the museum's authentic working-blacksmith shop, see Castine's century-old hearses, and take a guided tour (for a nominal fee) of the John Perkins House (1763–83).

WHERE TO STAY & DINE

Castine Inn
Main St. (P.O. Box 41), Castine, ME 04421. ☎ **207/326-4365.** 20 rms. $75–$125 double. Additional person $20 extra. Rates include breakfast. MC, V. Free parking. Closed Nov-Apr.

The Castine Inn is a three-story 1898 clapboard summer hotel, long a landmark in this town. Many rooms and the broad porch offer views of the deep harbor and the inn's gardens. Dinner is served nightly between 5:30 and 8:30pm, and features innovative regional cuisine. A mural of Castine is painted on all four walls of the dining room.

Pentagoet Inn

Main St. (P.O. Box 4), Castine, ME 04421. ☎ **207/326-8616** or 800/845-1701. 16 rms. $160–$180 double. Rates include breakfast and dinner. MC, V. Closed Nov–Apr.

This beautiful gabled-and-turreted pale-yellow house with dark-green trim is right in the center of the village. The inn building dates from Victoria's time, 1894, and several rooms next door date back 200 years. The comforts are modern and drinks are served on the porch daily in the summer. The common rooms are lovely, and chamber music is often presented. The multicourse evening meal offers several choices, usually including Maine lobster. Lindsey and Virginia Miller have a charming place, and I recommend it for those who want a quiet getaway to a beautiful town. Parking is available on the street.

BLUE HILL

20 miles E of Castine, 14 miles SE of Ellsworth

Blue Hill is a town of majestic elm trees, with prim white clapboard homes and churches. It attracts visitors because its most outstanding "attractions" are peace, quiet, and an easy pace.

Blue Hill was settled in 1762 by colonists from Andover, Mass., and by 1792 it was turning Maine's forests into ships, and was sending these ships around the world. In 1816 granite quarries were opened and stonecutting complemented shipping, and from 1879 to 1881 there was also a copper mine.

GETTING THERE **By Bus** See the beginning of this chapter.

By Car Coming from the west and south, take U.S. 1 to Orland, then Me. 175 south to South Penobscot, then follow the signs eastward to Blue Hill. Coming from the east and north, take U.S. 1 to Ellsworth, then Me. 172 south and west to Blue Hill.

ESSENTIALS The **telephone area code** is **207.** The **Blue Hill Chamber of Commerce,** P.O. Box 520, Blue Hill, ME 04614 (**no phone**), is helpful. **Liros Gallery** on Main Street is acting as the chamber for now and can be reached at ☎ **207/374-5370.**

WHAT TO SEE AND DO

Today, if you're not coming to Blue Hill on vacation, you're probably coming to enroll your child in the **George Stevens Academy** (1803), a preparatory school. Or perhaps you've arrived to attend a chamber music concert in **Kneisel Hall,** performed by students and faculty of the summer music school twice weekly in July and August at 8pm.

You may want to visit the **Holt House** (1815), home of the Blue Hill Historical Society, open in July and August, Tuesday through Friday from 1 to 4pm. The stocky but dignified four-chimney home remains much as it did during Federal days. Take a look also at the pretty stained-glass windows in the **First Congregational Church.** Also worth visiting is the 1814 **Parson Fisher House.**

WHERE TO STAY

Arcady Down East

South St., Blue Hill, ME 04614. ☎ **207/374-5576.** 7 rms (5 with bath). $75–$85 double without bath, $95–110 double with bath. Rates include breakfast. AE, MC, V. Free parking. Directions: Go one mile south along Me. 172 and Me. 175.

As you drive up, you'll see a fantastic shingled castle of a place, looking as though it really belongs in Bar Harbor. If a summer cottage could be called "baronial," it would be this one run by Bertha and Gene Wiseman, with lots of public rooms, views of Cadillac Mountain in the distance, and a great variety of guest rooms, one with a fireplace. And if you're here in winter and venture out, they have an ice-skating rink.

Blue Hill Farm

Me. 15 (P.O. Box 437), Blue Hill, ME 04614. ☎ **207/374-5126.** 14 rms (7 with bath). $70 single or double without bath, $85 single or double with bath. Rates include breakfast. MC, V. Free parking. Directions: Go two miles from the center of the village on Me. 15 (turn at the Exxon station).

It's quiet here, with ducks cruising serenely on the pond, and you'll think you're visiting some comfortably established country cousins. This is an authentic Maine farm now run as a bed-and-breakfast place by Jim and Marcia Schatz. Rooms in the converted farmhouse and barn have private or shared bath (two rooms to a bath). Some of the farm's 48 acres are laced with nature paths.

Blue Hill Inn

Union St. (P.O. Box 403), Blue Hill, ME 04614. ☎ **207/374-2844.** 11 rms. High season, $100–$130 double with breakfast, $130–$170 double with breakfast and dinner. Off-season, rates are about 25% lower. MC, V. Free parking.

This has served as the town's prime hostelry since about 1840, and is an even better place to stay and dine since innkeepers Mary and Don Hartley took over in 1987. Four of the inn's rooms have working fireplaces and furnishings authentic to the period. Dinner is served by candlelight each evening in summer and on weekends and holidays in the off-season. The food gets very high marks locally. You might enjoy hors d'oeuvres before dinner in the garden or by the fire in the living room.

WHERE TO DINE

Jonathan's

Main St. ☎ **207/374-5226.** Reservations recommended. Main courses $12–$17; dinner $20–$25. MC, V. June–Oct, dinner only, daily 5–9:30pm. Nov–Feb, Apr–May, dinner only, Tues–Sun 5–8pm (but call first to double-check). Closed March. NEW ENGLAND.

The fare here is moderately priced and varied, and includes everything from New American cuisine to Szechuan stir-fried beef to braised rabbit dijonnaise. Diners have more than 200 wines to choose from.

AN EXCURSION TO DEER ISLE

You can continue southward, taking Me. 15 to Deer Isle and Stonington, its southernmost town. Just after you cross the humpback bridge onto Deer Isle proper, you'll see a little chamber of commerce information booth, open in summer. Shortly after passing the booth you'll enter the village of Deer Isle.

Stonington is a fishing village, summer resort, and former granite-quarrying town. Beyond Stonington is Isle au Haut, part of Acadia National Park. A **mail boat** (☎ 207/367-2468) will take you over to the island in less than an hour, and you can hike along the park trails. Call ahead to be sure it's running.

WHERE TO STAY

Pilgrim's Inn

Deer Isle, ME 04627. ☎ **207/348-6615.** Fax 207/348-7769. 13 rms (8 with bath). $140–$150 double without bath, $165–$175 double with bath. Rates include breakfast and dinner. No credit cards. Free parking. Closed Mid-Oct to mid-May.

The inn, dating from 1793, is furnished with many antiques, Laura Ashley fabrics, and nice country touches. Each evening, hors d'oeuvres are served in the common room, with its eight-foot-wide fireplace, and dinner follows in the dining room, a converted barn. Innkeepers Jean and Dud Hendrick will lend you a bicycle so you can explore on your own, or will give you advice about local excursions, including those to Isle au Haut and the Haystack School of arts and crafts.

Note that no smoking is allowed in guest rooms or in the dining room. Should you want to stay for a full week, you can take advantage of special rates. The Pilgrim's Inn has been placed on the National Register of Historic Places.

7 Bar Harbor & Acadia National Park

161 miles NE of Portland, 20 miles SE of Ellsworth

When a Yankee talks about a "downeaster," he's talking about somebody from Maine, but when somebody from Maine talks about a downeaster, he means somebody from the region of Bar Harbor or even farther east. Most of us think of the Maine coastline as running its ragged way north, yet a quick look at the map will show that Bar Harbor is at about the same longitude as San Juan, Puerto Rico, and that indeed the Maine coastline heads more directly east than it does north at this point. These are the wilder shores of Maine and the settlements are fewer, the vegetation is not so lush, and the climate is a bit harsher than in other parts of the state, but at the same time the scenery is more dramatic, the air is charged with life, and there's a sense of wild nature.

The French influence was for a long time paramount in these parts, and many downeasters today speak French as a second language. In fact, it was Samuel de Champlain who gave Mount Desert Island its name, in the form of "L'Ile des Monts-Deserts," and even today the local pronunciation is "dez-*zert*," following the French style.

When steamships and railroads were opening up America in the 1800s, they also opened up downeast Maine, and by the end of the century, Bar Harbor, a small town on rocky Mount Desert Island, boasted almost as many palatial summer homes as Newport, although the ones here were perhaps not quite so lavish. In any case, only a small number of the original dozens of mansions are still standing, for a great number were wiped out in the Great Fire of 1947.

Today, Bar Harbor has a wonderful collection of little inns and lots of motels, most lining the roads into town from Ellsworth. The big attractions in the area, for which so much housing must be provided, are the town itself, the cruise boats to Yarmouth, Nova Scotia, and, of course, Acadia National Park. The park takes up something like half the land area of Mount Desert Island and much of that on the smaller surrounding islands, and is one of the few national parks in the eastern United States and the only national park in New England.

GETTING THERE   **By Plane**   Colgan Air serves Bar Harbor Airport, eight miles northeast of the town.

By Bus   See the beginning of this chapter.

By Car   Follow U.S. 1 to Ellsworth, then Me. 3 south to Bar Harbor.

ESSENTIALS   The **telephone area code** is **207.** The **Bar Harbor Chamber of Commerce,** 93 Cottage St. (P.O. Box 158), Bar Harbor, ME 04609

(☎ **207/288-5103**), maintains information booths at their Cottage Street office and at the *Bluenose* **Ferry Terminal** on Me. 3 (☎ **207/288-2402**).

WHAT TO SEE & DO

BICYCLING   Should you want to rent a bike for trips around town or into Acadia National Park, check with **Bar Harbor Bicycle Shop** at 141 Cottage St. (☎ 207/288-3886), at the corner of Eden Street, Me. 3 (Cottage Street is parallel to West Street but one block south of it, away from the water). Rates are $9 for up to 4 hours, $14 for up to 12 hours. Fees include maps, locks, and helmets.

CRUISES   The **Frenchman Bay Boating Company** (☎ 207/288-3322) organizes all sorts of boat trips: sightseeing, sailing, whale-watching, lobstering, and nature cruises. The *Whale Watcher* motors out to the Gulf of Maine twice daily in search of the leviathans of the deep; the four-hour whale watch costs $28 per adult, $18 for kids 6 to 15, free for the little ones. If sail power is your preference, hop aboard the schooner *Bay Lady* for one of its four daily two-hour cruises in Frenchman Bay, the saltwater shushing along its hull, the wind singing in the rigging, and nary a motor's chug or growl.

For sightseeing cruises, the diesel-powered *Acadian* is the boat to take. Cruise the shores of Bar Harbor and Acadia National Park to a detailed narration of the sights. Cruises last one or two hours and cost $15.00 for adults, $10.50 for kids 6 to 15, and are free for kids under 6. Perhaps the most thoroughly authentic cruise offered is aboard the 40-passenger *Katherine,* which the captain takes out as a lobster boat to check his traps. Along the way, he'll introduce you to the local seals as well. Fares are $16.75 for adults, $10.75 for kids 6 to 12, and free for those under 6.

You can sail aboard a traditional three-masted schooner, the *Natalie Todd.* This 101-foot historic wooden vessel offers two-hour sails from the Bar Harbor Inn Pier for $17.50 per adult, $10 for children under 12. The *Natalie Todd* sails three times a day, at 10am, 2pm, and 6:30pm. Tickets are available at the pier or at the *Natalie Todd* ticket office at 27 Main St. (☎ 207/288-4585). For information in the off-season, call 207/546-2927 or write Capt. Steven F. Pagels, P.O. Box 8, Cherryfield, ME 04622.

A HARBOR-VIEW WALK   If you're willing to walk for 30 to 45 minutes, you can enjoy one of Bar Harbor's nicest little hikes. Follow Main Street (Me. 3) south out of town, past the park on the right, and about a mile down the road (15 to 25 minutes' walk) is a pull-off spot for cars (capacity: four vehicles). If you reach the Ocean Drive Motor Inn, you've gone too far. Walk down the dirt road, closed by a chain, near the little metal sign marking the boundary of U.S. government land, posted on a tree. It's less than a 10-minute walk to Rocky Harbor along the dirt road through the fragrant forests. When you come to a fork, bear left with the road (a path goes off straight). When you reach the viewing point, you'll find a grassy clearing furnished with litter barrels for picnickers (no tables). If you've brought a picnic, you can share it with the gulls and ducks. It's secluded, beautiful, quiet, and within walking distance from town—a fine place.

ACADIA NATIONAL PARK   The rugged terrain of **Mount Desert Island,** sculpted by a mammoth glacier, has attracted lovers of natural beauty for over a century, and soon after summer visitors arrived in significant numbers,

Acadia National Park

preservation efforts began. By the end of World War II, Acadia National Park was well along to its present size of more than 30,000 acres, or something like half the land on the island (the other half is still in private hands). This park is unusual because it was not created on public land or acquired by public funding. The focal point of activities here is **Cadillac Mountain,** at 1,530 feet the highest point on America's Atlantic coast. The thing to do at Cadillac is to hike (or drive) to its summit for the majestic views. In fact, local people have recognized that those who see the sun break forth on the horizon from the mountain are the first people in the United States to greet the new day, so there's a "Sunrise from Mount Cadillac Club." You can join by picking up a blank from the Bar Harbor information bureau and filling it out with the help of your hotel manager the night *before* you plan to see the sunrise. Then, if you follow through, you get to be a member of this most exclusive club.

Besides visiting Cadillac Mountain, the first agenda is to drive the **Loop Road,** a one-way scenic ocean drive that takes you past many of the most fascinating scenic, topographic, and geologic features of the island. Admission to the park is $5 per car, and a pass is good for seven days (you can visit the area free up to the toll Loop Road; an annual pass costs $15. Stop at **Thunder Hole** below Otter Cliffs when the surf's up to witness the drama of the waves, or at **Sand Beach** for a chilly yet invigorating ocean swim. There's National Park camping at Black Woods (follow the signs)—the only campground where you can reserve ahead. Call **the Mistix Outlet** (☎ 800-365-2267) as early as spring for reservations.

On Mount Desert's western peninsula, **Echo Lake** is the Park's freshwater swimming area; there's a lookout tower atop **Beech Mountain,** and a park campground is located near the peninsula's southern tip at **Seawall**—$12 per night for those lucky enough to arrive early in the morning. And throughout the park are 120 miles of hiking trails from short and level to precipitous (maps sold at park headquarters), and 45 miles of turn-of-the-century, stone "carriage roads" good for bike trips, horseback riding, and even cross-country skiing and snowmobiling. A good place to rent a bicycle or canoe is, not surprisingly, **Acadia Bike and Canoe** on Cottage St. in Bar Harbor, ☎ 207/288-5483. For kayak tours, contact **Coastal Kayaking** at the same phone number.

Not far from the town of Bar Harbor, in the park at Sieur de Monts Spring, is the **Robert Abbe Museum of Stone Age Antiquities** (☎ 207/288-3519), a wildflower garden, and a nature center. Admission is $2 for adults, $.50 for children.

The beach at **Seal Harbor,** southeast of Blackwoods, is very fine and open to the public for free. It's one of Mount Desert Island's poshest summer resorts, with all sorts of famous and wealthy people inhabiting the big houses tucked away on the forested streets of the village. Park in the lot across the street.

A visit to Acadia National Park wouldn't be complete without tea and popovers ($5.50) at **Jordan Pond** (☎ 207/276-3610). A tradition for almost 100 years, the restaurant serves lunch on the porch from 11:30am to 5pm, afternoon tea on the lawn from 1 to 6pm, and dinner by the fireside from 5 to 9pm. You can get snacks and beverages on the overlook throughout the day from 9am to 6pm. Whether you dine or not, you're invited to stroll around the gardens and spacious grounds; the panoramic view of the lake and mountains from the lawn is stunning. It's open from late May to late October.

TOURS   National Park Tours (☎ 207/288-3327) runs two tours daily from Bar Harbor, beginning from Testa's Restaurant, at 53 Main St. The cost is $15 per adult, $5 per child under 12. The tour takes you past Bar Harbor's mansions left from its heyday, and stops at Cadillac Mountain, Sieur de Monts Spring, and Thunder Hole. Traditionally the tours have left at 10am and 2pm, but call in advance to check the times and to make a reservation.

If you have a car, you can rent a cassette tape recorder with a prerecorded tour narration from Sightseeing Tapes, Inc. You pay the $11 rental fee for the tape and player ($8 if you rent only the tape), and start out to follow the description of many interesting points in the national park. The advantage here is that this tour is cheaper overall if you have several people in your car, and you can turn off the tape at any time should you want to spend a while at some point. Tapes and machines are for rent at the National Park Visitor Center at Hulls Cove, the first park entrance you come to when approaching Bar Harbor from the north on Me. 3.

A FERRY TO NOVA SCOTIA   The Marine Atlantic ship **MV** *Bluenose* sails from Bar Harbor to Yarmouth, Nova Scotia, and back again daily in summer between late June and late September. It's a car-ferry with room for 1,000 passengers and 250 cars, a sun deck, buffet, dining room, cafeteria, bar, casino, and duty-free shop. The *Bluenose* leaves Bar Harbor every morning in summer and returns from Yarmouth in late afternoon, arriving back in Bar Harbor at night. The trip takes about six hours each way, and costs $41 per adult, $22.50 per child 5 to 13 (under 5 free); cars cost $50; trailers and campers cost $110 for up to 30 feet long, with a summertime minimum charge of the normal car's fare. You can rent a day-use cabin for an extra $36 to $40. Off-season schedules are such that the ferry leaves Bar Harbor one day and returns the next; fares are about 25% lower. The vehicle fees don't include the driver's ticket, so a car-and-driver crossing in summer would pay about $100, and a family of four with a car would pay over $350 for the journey round-trip. Note that you must make reservations in advance: **Marine Atlantic Reservations Bureau,** P.O. Box 250, North Sydney, NS B2A 3M3, Canada (☎ 207/288-3395 in Bar Harbor, 902/742-6800 in Yarmouth, or 800/341-7981 in the continental United States).

WHERE TO STAY

While there are plenty of rooms to handle the thousands of visitors each year, the problem is to get the room you want rather than one you're forced to take. Reservations are advisable in all recommended places, and as these are some of the choicer spots, I'd suggest that you reserve early.

If you arrive without a reservation, make your way to Mount Desert Street, which was a favorite locale of those who built palatial "summer cottages" and which today has an abundance of wonderful old inns.

EXPENSIVE

Bar Harbor Inn

Newport Dr. (P.O. Box 7), Bar Harbor, ME 04609. ☎ **207/288-3351** or 800/ 248-3351. 153 rms. A/C TV TEL. $69– $235 double. AE, DISC, MC, V. Free parking.

Set amid its own lush grounds on a point overlooking Frenchman Bay, this was once a private club that has been converted, expanded, and renovated to take in visitors year-round, and the feeling is that of a posh resort in the 1920s. White pillars frame the front porch; attendants pad quietly here and there. The inn's hot tub and large heated pool are next to a little copse of trees only a few yards from the waters of the Atlantic, and here, as everywhere else at the inn, the views are magnificent. The rooms are not old-fashioned, however, with lots of windows looking onto either the bay or the inn's lush grounds; in 1994, 23 new rooms were added. Oceanfront rooms feature private balconies and oversize beds. The atmosphere is formal but friendly. One can dress for dinner, served in the semicircular dining room that overlooks the bay.

Cleftstone Manor

Me. 3 (Eden St.), Bar Harbor, ME 04609. ☎ **207/288-4951** or 800/962-9762. 16 rms. A/C. $95–$198 double. Rates include breakfast and evening refreshments. DISC, MC, V. Free parking. Closed Nov–Apr.

Farther from the center of town, 500 yards from the *Bluenose* dock, up on a hillside, is the Cleftstone Manor, one of Bar Harbor's finest inns. A Victorian summer house in the grand manner, the inn has spacious public rooms, good views from many of the guest rooms, and many elegant touches. No smoking is allowed in the manor. Breakfasts are of home-baked breads and pastries. Afternoon tea and evening refreshments are served. Repeat guests will likely notice all the changes taking place here such as repapered guest rooms, some with fireplaces, and other nice touches, not to mention the restored exterior.

Holbrook House

74 Mount Desert St., Bar Harbor, ME 04609. ☎ **207/288-4970.** 10 rms, 2 cottages. High season, from $115 single or double. Off-season, $65–$85 single or double. Year-round, $115–$145 cottage for two. Rates include breakfast and afternoon refreshments. MC, V. Free parking. Closed mid-Oct to Apr.

Built in 1880, the Holbrook House, in the center of town, has rooms that pro-vide enough space for even the most enormous Victorian family. Also on hand are two cottage suites decorated in chintz and with period furnishings. The breakfast served here is wonderful. The owners have done so well that they purchased another inn called The Inn at Bay Ledge (see below).

The Inn at Bay Ledge

1385 Sand Point Rd, Bar Harbor, ME 04609. ☎ **207/288-4204.** 7 rooms, 3 cottages rooms. $145–$250 double; $85–$150 off-season. Rates include breakfast. MC, V. Free parking. Closed Dec–Mar.

The folks at the Holbrook House decided to open this early 1900s residence that sits atop an 80-foot cliff. What's ideal here is that every room in the main inn has a view of the ocean. The rooms are country-inn-simple but pleasing enough, with an assortment of furnishings ranging from modern to more cherished pieces. The cottage rooms do not have ocean views and are situated across the street; one has a fireplace, a big stone one at that. For recreation, there's the private rocky beach, the hot tub, a pool, and sauna. It's a short drive into downtown. The owners are friendly and exacting—after all, one is a retired executive from McDonald's Corporation, so everything's neat as a pin. Breakfast includes a hot entre and is usually served outdoors, weather permitting.

Ledgelawn Inn

66 Mount Desert St., Bar Harbor, ME 04609. ☎ **207/288-4596** or 800/274-5334. Fax 207/288-9968. 33 rms. TV TEL. $95–$250 double. Rates include continental breakfast. AE, DISC, MC, V. Free parking. Closed Jan–Apr.

Having escaped destruction in the Great Fire of 1947, the "cottage" built for Boston shoe magnate John Brigham has been fully converted to a bed and breakfast. The public rooms are attractive, the lawns and trees nicely kept, the guest rooms commendable. Many rooms have working fireplaces and private sauna-and-whirlpool baths. The Ledgelawn has a widow's walk on top, open for the view or the warm rays of the sun until 6pm. The inn has a hot tub. It seems the continental breakfast is sometimes rather sparce according to some readers, and cereal bowls scarce. A little more attention to details is probably in order.

Manor House Inn

106 West St., Bar Harbor, ME 04609. ☎ **207/288-3759** or 800/437-0088. 14 rms. Late June to mid-Oct, $85–$165 single or double. Off-season, $55–$125 single or double. Rates include breakfast. MC, V. Free parking. Closed mid-Nov to mid-Apr.

Period furnishings fill all the guest rooms of this huge Victorian home. The chauffeur's cottage, two guest cottages, and five gardens also occupy the acre of grounds, which is listed in the National Register of Historic Places. Guests can eat breakfast in a lovely garden.

Mira Monte Inn

69 Mount Desert St., Bar Harbor, ME 04609. ☎ **207/288-4263** or 800/553-5109. Fax 207/288-3115. 12 rms, 3 suites. A/C TV TEL. $90–$145 single or double; $140–$180 suite. Rates include breakfast. AE, MC, V. Free parking. Closed late Oct to early May.

The Mira Monte Inn is a fine old Victorian house (1864) lovingly restored and maintained by Bar Harbor native Marian Burns, who will happily give you advice on nature trails and local activities. All rooms come with period furnishings, and each room has something different: a canopy bed, brass bed, fireplace, porch, or bay window. Several fireplaces are on hand, and there are some baths with two-person whirlpool tubs. The inn is wheelchair accessible.

MODERATE

Anchorage Motel

51 Mount Desert St., Bar Harbor, ME 04609. ☎ **207/288-3959** or 800/336-3959. 48 rms. TV TEL. High season, $69–89 single or double; off-season, from $49 single or double. AE, CB, DC, MC, V. Free parking.

This is a tidy two-story motel set back from Mount Desert Street, the street with all the inns. The standard modern motel comforts cost a bit more here because this is Bar Harbor, and the location is good.

Hearthside B&B

7 High St., Bar Harbor, ME 04609. ☎ **207/288-4533.** 9 rms. $85–$125 single or double. Rates include full breakfast. DISC, MC, V. Free parking. Directions: Stay on Me. 3 as it becomes Mount Desert Street and take the third left (High Street), a one-way street, before the Episcopal church.

This inn is run by Susan and Barry Schwartz on a quiet street close to town. Its living room has a fireplace and other touches of past Bar Harbor elegance. Afternoon tea is served. Three rooms have a fireplace, two have a whirlpool tub, a few have air conditioners, and all have ceiling fans. The inn has a no-smoking policy. Unlike most inns that close in winter, the Hearthside is open all year.

Stratford House Inn

45 Mount Desert St., Bar Harbor, ME 04609. ☎ **207/288-5189** or 800/550-5189. 10 rms (8 with bath). TV. $75–$85 double without bath, $90–$150 double with bath. Rates include continental breakfast. AE, MC, V. Free parking. Closed Mid-Oct to mid-May.

Stratford House looks like Elizabeth I's own summer cottage, for it has everything you could imagine in the way of Tudor domestic architecture—it's gabled and half-timbered. Though built by a publishing magnate, this inn was the summer home of musical greats Fritz Kreisler and Jan Paderewski. The music room is appointed with a grand piano and an organ. Some guest rooms have a fireplace, and each is furnished with a four-poster mahogany or brass bowbottom bed.

Thornhedge Inn

47 Mount Desert St., Bar Harbor, ME 04609. ☎ **207/288-5398.** 13 rms. TV. $80–$140 single or double. Rates include breakfast. AE, MC, V. Free parking. Closed Mid-Oct to mid-May.

In 1900 a retired Boston publisher named Lewis Roberts built himself a "cottage" in Bar Harbor. It has gone through several hands since then, lately having been owned by a former dean of Harvard Medical School, and today it's among Bar Harbor's most desirable places to stay. The aim of its owners is to "recapture the spirit of Bar Harbor at the turn of the century," and they have done so by arranging to purchase many of the house's original furnishings. Today the large, sunny, gracious master bedroom on the second floor is done in turn-of-the-century style; adjoining is the original bathroom, which is a good deal larger than the standard motel room today. Many rooms have working fireplaces, in which fire laws allow artificial logs to be burned. You can tell that I like the Thornhedge, and when you stay there you'll know why. As you're driving or walking along Mount Desert Street, you can't miss the Thornhedge, for it's painted a bright, cheery yellow.

Villager Motel

207 Main St., Bar Harbor, ME 04609. ☎ **207/288-3211,** 207/288-3011 or 800/ 988-8212. 63 rms. A/C TV TEL. Apr–June, $45–$69 single or double; July–Aug, $70–$92 single or double; Sept–Oct, $49–$72 single or double. AE, MC, V. Free parking. Closed Nov–Mar. Directions: Take Me. 3 heading south out of town.

The Villager is a very neat two-story motel of moderate size and the usual comforts: a heated outdoor pool, modern rooms, and a convenient location that still leaves you within walking distance of the sights, shops, and restaurants in town. All these advantages, plus the moderate rates, ensure that the Villager is often full, so it's good to make reservations in advance.

BUDGET

Acadia Hotel

20 Mount Desert St., Bar Harbor, ME 04609. ☎ **207/288-5721.** 10 rms. TV. $55–$79 single or double. Children are charged $5 extra. Rates include continental breakfast in summer. AE, DISC, MC, V. Free parking.

Rooms here are in the budget class, tidy but simple. Some rooms have air conditioners and private entrances (the "motel" rooms), while others are entered through the hall ("hotel"). Continental breakfast is served on the wraparound porch in good weather.

Bass Cottage in the Field

"The Field," Main St., Bar Harbor, ME 04609. ☎ **207/288-3705.** 10 rms (6 with bath). $45–$65 double without bath, $65–$85 double with bath. No credit cards. Free parking. Closed Mid-Oct to mid-May.

One of the most centrally located and inexpensive authentic cottages in Bar Harbor, Bass Cottage has been operated and run by sisters in the Maddocks family since it was purchased in 1928. Most rooms in this inn, built in 1885, have private baths, and some have an ocean view. Walk to one of the many restaurants less than a block away, then relax on the wicker-furnished, glass-enclosed porch. This is a real find!

McKay Lodging

243 Main St., Bar Harbor, ME 04609. ☎ **207/288-3531** or 800/86-MCKAY. 23 rms (17 with bath). TV TEL. $55–$85 double without bath, $75–$95 double with bath. Rates include continental breakfast. MC, V. Free parking.

The McKay cottages are a mere 1^1/2 blocks from the park and the center of town. They offer simple but comfortable and fairly homey accommodations at an unbeatable price. Rooms in the main house are air-conditioned, and all rooms with private bath have a refrigerator. The folks operating the cottages under a lease arrangement have been doing so for more than three years.

Mount Desert Island YWCA

36 Mount Desert St., Bar Harbor, ME 04609. ☎ **207/288-5008.** 35 rms (none with bath). $85 per week single; $70 per person per week double. No credit cards. Free parking.

Individual women travelers can stay at the YWCA, where rooms rent by the night and by the week and include clean bed linens, use of the laundry room, and kitchen privileges. Weekly rates are available only if paid in full at the beginning of your stay. Upon arrival, you will be charged a membership fee of $10 (for stays of a week or more) and a $25 returnable security deposit. Rooms are hard to come by in the summer, so write ahead for reservations. Open year-round.

WHERE TO DINE

As you drive toward Bar Harbor from Ellsworth, the road is lined with little shacks and stores bearing the magic word LOBSTERS. Outside each is a strange arrangement of backyard barbecues in a row, with large pots or drums on them and stovepipes (in some cases very rickety ones) shooting up. These contraptions are used to prepare a traditional lobster clambake. The drums or kettles are filled with lobsters, clams, corn on the cob, and seaweed, and then saltwater is poured in, the fire is started, and the whole business is cooked up and served to the droves of motorists. Some places have tables where you can sit to consume your feast, at others you take the goodies home with you, but in any case this is the way to get the most seafood for your dollar, and the eating couldn't be better! This is the real Maine experience, and shouldn't be missed.

How do you pick the right place to stop? Every single place seems to have a signboard out front giving the price per pound of lobster, and you can go by this to some degree. But the price and poundage depend on how the lobster is stored: Some places store the live lobsters on ice and not in seawater, as the seawater can add weight to the lobster when it's put on the scale. In any case, make sure the lobster is alive, not dead and limp.

MODERATE

Freddie's Route 66 Restaurant

21 Cottage St. ☎ **207/288-3708.** Reservations recommended. Main courses $8–$13; dinner $18. AE, MC, V. Dinner only, daily 5–10pm. Closed Late Oct to mid-May. SEAFOOD/STEAKS.

It seems appropriate that the "66" is almost as proud of its decor as it is of its cuisine. Owner Freddie Pooler has re-created the 1950s and '60s here, with an astounding variety of memorabilia collected from gas stations, diners, and a soda fountain. Liquor is served and wine is available by the glass or bottle.

Opera House

27 Cottage St. ☎ **207/288-3509.** Reservations not accepted. Dinner $15–$27. AE, DISC, MC, V. Dinner only, Tues–Sun 5:30–9pm or later. ECLECTIC.

Opera aficionados and lovers of fine food will be delighted by this unique restaurant. Although the restaurant is open only at night, the "Listening Room" is open throughout the day and everyone is invited to wander through the gallery and listen to a portion of the 90-minute taped program of the day while paying homage to the opera greats whose pictures grace the walls. A placard at the entrance advises DINING FOR ADULTS and YOU ARE WELCOMED DRESSED AS YOU ARE. The à la carte menu includes crayfish étouffée ($19.95). The menu features roast duck in cognac or Cajun blackened halibut. If you've dined elsewhere, at least have dessert and a cordial or coffee; the rich crème brûlée is a wonderful way to end an evening.

INEXPENSIVE

Island Chowder House

38 Cottage St. ☎ **207/288-4905.** Reservations recommended. Main courses $7–$17; dinner $8–$17. AE, DISC, MC, V. Daily 11am–10pm or later. Closed Nov–Apr. SEAFOOD.

Have a table in the attractive, woody dining room and order the shore dinner of clam chowder, steamed clams, lobster, french fries, and coleslaw, and the bill will be a reasonable $18, tax and tip included. Fish and chips is a third of that price. Chicken and steak are available for those who don't want seafood.

Miguel's

51 Rodick St. ☎ **207/288-5117.** Reservations not accepted. Main courses $7–$14; dinner $12–$20. MC, V. Dinner only, daily 5–10pm. Closed Mid-Nov to Mar and Mon off-season. MEXICAN.

Located behind the firehouse, this quaint, attractive storefront eatery offers delicious quesadillas, burritos, tacos, chiles rellenos, even shrimp fajitas and carne asada. For an appetizer, try the chimitas for $4.50. Huge frozen margaritas (and other liquor) are served, and on summer evenings you can dine on the patio.

BUDGET

Bubba's

30 Cottage St. ☎ **207/288-5871.** Reservations not accepted. Sandwiches and full meals $4–$11. No credit cards. Daily 11:30am–1am. AMERICAN.

This is a favorite sandwich-and-drinks place for many of the more interesting people in Bar Harbor on vacation. Soups, salads, and sandwiches make up the bill of fare all day, but sipping and socializing are what it's all about. The choice of 10 kinds of burgers is noteworthy. The big bar and the bentwood make it all upbeat and enjoyable.

EVENING ENTERTAINMENT

At **Geddy's,** on Main Street near the corner of West Street (☎ **207/288-5077**), every night in summer is witness to some sort of live performance. Jazz, pop, and rock all issue forth from its sidewalk windows. Check the playbill out front and then walk in. There's no cover or minimum, and beer is $1.50 to $3 or a bit more (for Heineken and the like).

AN EASY EXCURSION FROM BAR HARBOR

Besides Bar Harbor, Mount Desert Island is home to **Seal Harbor, Southwest Harbor,** and **Northeast Harbor.** Take Me. 3 around the island for a look at each of these harbors, all distinctive areas. **Mount Desert Island** hosts many summer homes of old-money families, such as the Rockefellers.

Just outside Northeast Harbor is Somes Sound and **Abel's Lobster Pound** (☎ 207/276-5827). Open between May 25 and October 15, Abel's is well known for its shore dinners. The lobster pound is an open-air hut arrangement down the hill from the restaurant. The rustic-inspired dining room is on a split level and provides views of the sound. The staff takes your lobster order and runs it down to the pound, where it's cooked. The food isn't fancy, but the atmosphere is real New England.

WHERE TO STAY

Grey Rock Inn

Northeast Harbor, ME 04662. ☎ **207/276-9360.** 7 rms, 1 suite, 1 cottage. $105–$155 double; $265 suite; $175 cottage. Rates include breakfast. No credit cards. Free parking. Closed Mid-Oct to mid-May.

This small and lovely inn is run by a mother and son who take pride in their vintage 1911 clapboard-and-fieldstone house. Afternoon tea is served in the cozy living room warmed by a fireplace. Three guest rooms also have fireplaces.

Breakfast might be served on the porch or in the dining room. The cottage offers two bedrooms and two baths, plus a full kitchen.

8   From Bar Harbor to Canada

The coastal highway, U.S. 1, winds east and north from Ellsworth. You might want to wander south along Me. 186 for views of the scenic **Schoodic Peninsula**. If not, head ever northeastward, toward the Canadian frontier.

When you get to Cobscook Bay, you will have reached the easternmost limits of the United States. **Cobscook Bay** can boast two state parks, **Cobscook Bay State Park** and **Quoddy Head State Park.** But the following park is even more interesting.

ROOSEVELT CAMPOBELLO INTERNATIONAL PARK   A Canadian island with an Italian-sounding name on which an American president spent his summers? These little mysteries are not at all as difficult to solve as one might suppose. Campobello Island is officially part of Canada, even though the major access road comes from Lubec, Me. (You must pass through Customs.) And the "Italian" name is nothing more than the name of a former Nova Scotian governor, William Campbell, with two "o's" added for exotic flavor. When the island was granted to Capt. William Owen by Governor Campbell in 1767, it was still part of the Canadian province of Nova Scotia. (The province of New Brunswick was not formed until 1784, when large numbers of United Empire Loyalists fled New England to live in George III's still-loyal dominions to the north.)

Franklin Delano Roosevelt's father, James, bought some land on the island in 1883, at a time when lots of important city people were building vast "summer cottages" at Bar Harbor, Passamaquoddy Bay, and other northern coastal locations. Young Franklin—to solve that last little mystery—came here long before he was president of the United States, and spent many a summer as a teenager rowing, paddling, and sailing on the waters, and hiking through the woods.

In 1920 FDR ran for the vice presidency—and lost. Taking on a banking job instead, he looked forward to a relaxing summer at Campobello in 1921. On August 10 of that year, the first signs of illness showed, and two weeks later the doctors diagnosed the crippling disease as polio. When he left the island in September, he had no way of knowing that the few more times he would see the summer cottage and his Campobello friends would be brief weekend visits—as president of the United States. The day-to-day lives of the great and powerful are fascinating to explore in detail, and a visit to the Roosevelt house on Campobello Island gives one a peek at the early years of this incredibly courageous man who went on to become governor of New York and president of the United States. It is no less intriguing to see how a well-to-do family spent its summers at the turn of the century, with long and leisurely days filled by sports, games, and family fun. Servants saw to the chores, and even they must have enjoyed getting away from the city to such a beautiful spot.

The Roosevelt Cottage is now part of Roosevelt Campobello International Park, a joint American-Canadian effort open from the Saturday prior to Memorial Day through Columbus Day from 9am to 5pm eastern standard time. Guides at the reception center will point out the path to the Roosevelt Cottage, show you movies about the island, and map out the various walks and drives in the 2,600-acre nature preserve. There's no charge for admission. For park information, call the **Campobello Island Chamber of Commerce** (☎ 506/752-2233).

CALAIS AND ST. STEPHEN   Residents of Maine and New Brunswick, while the best of friends, cling to memories of their ancestors' fervent support for, respectively, George Washington and George III. With the success of the American Revolution, United Empire Loyalists flocked across the frontier into Canada so as not to be disloyal to the monarch. The "Loyalist" and "Revolutionary" towns preserve this good-natured rivalry.

But things are different in Calais, Me. (pronounced "callous"), and its neighboring city, St. Stephen, N.B. Folks in these two towns, cheek-by-jowl on the St. Croix River, make a point of telling visitors how they ignored the affinities of *both* sides during the War of 1812, and St. Stephen even supplied powder-poor Calais with gunpowder for its Fourth of July celebrations! In fact, by the time the war came, families in the twin towns were so closely intermarried that no one wanted to take the time to sort out who should be loyal to whom.

These days, residents celebrate this unique plague-on-both-their-houses philosophy with an **International Festival** in the first week of August. The two bridges over the river between the towns are thronged with merrymakers moving back and forth—under the watchful but benevolent eye of Customs, of course—and Canadian and American flags fly everywhere.

You can get more information from the **Greater Calais Area Chamber of Commerce** (☎ 207/454-2308).

Despite its interesting history, there's little to detain you in Calais, and soon you'll be heading onward, into Canada (see *Frommer's Canada*), or back down U.S. 1 to points south and west. When you return home, however, you'll know what the maritime forecasters mean when they predict weather for the coastline "from Eastport (on Cobscook Bay) to Block Island (Rhode Island)." And you'll be able to say that you've been at the easternmost point in the United States.

9 The Moosehead Lake Region

165 miles NE of Portland, 45 miles SE of Jackman, 75 miles NW of Bangor

Think of Maine and you'll immediately envision the state's rockbound coast. However, many visitors come to experience inland Maine—in particular, the Moosehead Lake Region. Moosehead represents the way Maine used to be, in its natural state. For many Mainers, that's a bit too remote; after all, it's a production just to go to a movie theater.

The region has much to offer outdoors types: white-water rafting, cross-country skiing, ice fishing, snowmobiling, and, of course, hunting and fishing in season. There's little doubt you'll see a moose or two during your stay as well.

Some of the camps and lodges still require you to arrive by float plane and bring your groceries and essentials with you. Those places are for the real Daniel Boones. The rest of us can take great comfort in a good brisk sit on the lakeshore, casting a line into the cold water, or drinking in the sun on a boat in summer.

If you plan on going to Moosehead Lake, remember: Don't fool with the moose! They are big and command attention and respect. Besides, if you happen to run into one doing even 10 miles per hour, your car will most likely crumple like aluminum foil as if you had hit a brick wall.

GETTING THERE   By Bus   There is no bus service into Greenville.

By Car   From the south, take I-95 to Exit 36 (north of Waterville) at U.S. 201, go north on U.S. 201 about 38 miles to Me. 16 east to Abbot Village, and then north on Me. 15/6 to Greenville. Or you can take I-95 north to Exit 39 at

Newport (105 miles north of Portland) and then Me. 11 to Me. 7 to Me. 23 until you reach Me. 16/6, where you go west through Guilford to Abbot Village; then turn north to Greenville on Me. 15/6. Both routes are about 160 to 170 miles total and take less than three hours.

ESSENTIALS   The telephone area code is **207**. The **Moosehead Lake Region Chamber of Commerce,** P.O. Box 581, Greenville, Me. 04441 (☎ **207/ 695-2702**), maintains an information office on Me. 15/6 before you come into town; it's open Memorial Day through October 15, daily from 9am to 5pm; off-season, weekdays from 10am to 4pm.

WHAT TO SEE & DO

Everything revolves around Moosehead Lake. At 40 miles outstretched, this is the largest lake in the Northeast, with 400 miles of shoreline, some of it accessible only by canoe. For most arrivals, Greenville is the beginning (and possibly the destination) of their introduction to Moosehead. There's one blinking traffic light in town, and directions are usually centered around "go left at the blinker," "go through the blinker," or "at the blinker." To get to Greenville, see "Getting There," above.

The adventuresome or those on a tight schedule will want to see all of Moosehead from aloft. **Folsom's Air Service, Inc.** (☎ 207/695-2821), can take you on a float-plane ride. Flights are offered daily, weather permitting. For $20 you can sample the lake for 15 minutes; for $50 the trip lasts 75 minutes and covers Wilson Pond, Horseshoe Pond, White Cap Mountain, Elephant Mountain, the Penobscot River, and the top of Mount Katahdin. In all, nine flights are on the menu.

There are many surrounding ponds and streams where a good deal of trout bite. On the Moose and Kennebec Rivers, fly fishing is popular in midsummer and fall. Hunting is another favorite pastime. October is deer archery season, while November is for firearms. September through November is black bear season. The month of October is also the time for partridge.

Wilderness Expeditions (☎ 207/534-7305 or 800/825-WILD) offers a wide array of programs—from canoe trips, rafting the Maine waters, and outfitting trips to mountain biking and pack-and-paddle trips for those who want to combine horseback riding and rafting.

The Moosehead Marine Museum, through the blinker on North Main Street (☎ 207/695-2716), is a little bit of a place with steamboat history dating back to 1836. The last remaining lake steamer (now it's operated by diesel), the *Katahdin,* is still operating for lake trips as it did in the 1930s, when logs were moved over the water before roads laced the Moosehead Lake shoreline. From Memorial Day through early October, you can board the vessel for a daily three-hour cruise, although early and late in the season, it operates weekends only. The staff requests no smoking and no high-heeled shoes (in the Great Maine Woods without pumps?). At this point, you should have already shopped your way through **L. L. Bean.**

WHERE TO STAY

Foster's Maine Bush Sporting Camps
P.O. Box 1230, Greenville, ME 04441. ☎ **207/695-2845.** 8 cabins. Summer, $65–$100 cabin; off-season and winter, $45–$100 cabin. No credit cards. Directions: Drive four miles north of the center from blinking light; it's on the eastern side of the lake.

Katahdin: Mountain of the People

Baxter State Park lies 45 miles north of Greenville and 18 miles north of the town of Millinocket. Even for some Mainers, Baxter State Park is a long trek into the wilderness. But for those adventurers who love the outdoors and the sporting life, this parcel of land provides the ultimate recreational holiday.

Percival P. Baxter, a former governor of Maine, began acquiring undeveloped regional tracts here back in 1930. His first purchase was slightly less than 6,000 acres, but it included Maine's highest peak—mile-high Mount Katahdin. A year later, Baxter donated the land to his state with the proviso that it be kept wild forever. Over the years Governor Baxter purchased additional property, now totalling more than 200,000 acres. In 1933 the Maine Legislature named the park after Baxter, and its tallest peak Baxter Peak.

As part of his legacy, Baxter left the following verse to inspire us with the spirit of the park:

> Man is born to die, His Works are Short-lived
> Buildings crumble, Monuments decay, Wealth Vanishes
> But Katahdin in All Its Glory
> Forever shall remain the Mountain of the
> People of Maine.

In all, one finds 46 ridges and peaks here. Eighteen are higher than 3,000 feet, but Baxter Peak itself stands alone at 5,267 feet. The park is laced with some 175 miles of trails popular with hikers, mountain climbers, and naturalists. Bring your camera to capture the wildlife and to record the ever-shifting colors of this noble mountain. A plethora of plants grow along the way, from alpine ferns to orchids.

Camping at Baxter is very popular in summer and fall for an average of 115,000 annual visitors, and space in the cabins or in any of the eight campgrounds should be reserved far in advance. These 1,200 sites operate between May 15 and October 15. There are some winter facilities available, too (cabins for $30 per person, for instance). But you should note that the park closes from mid-October to December 1, and from April 1 to mid-May, due to hazardous conditions. Facilities may range from tenting space and leantos to bunkhouses. Fireplaces and picnic tables also dot each campground. Day passes cost $8 per car. Bunkhouses cost $7 per person, tenting space $6 per person, cabins $17 per person. Reservations are made through **Baxter State Park, Reservations Clerk,** 64 Balsom Dr., Millinocket, Me. 04462, ☎ 207/723-5140.

For canoe trips or rentals, write or phone **Allagash Wilderness Outfitters,** 30 Minuteman Dr., Millinocket, Me. 04462, ☎ 207/723-6622. For river rafting expeditions, you should contact: **Magic Falls Rafting Company,** 2820 Banton Ave., Winslow, Me. 04901, ☎ 207/873-0938; or **Unicorn Rafting Expeditions,** P.O. Box T, Brunswick, Me. 04011, ☎ 207/725-2255. And for lists of nearby lodgings, reach the **Katahdin Area Chamber of Commerce,** 1029 Central St., Millinocket, Me. 04462, ☎ 207/723-4443.

The new owners here are working hard to get everything ready for new arrivals. Since some of the cabins are no more than 10 feet from the shore, you can swim

Baxter State Park

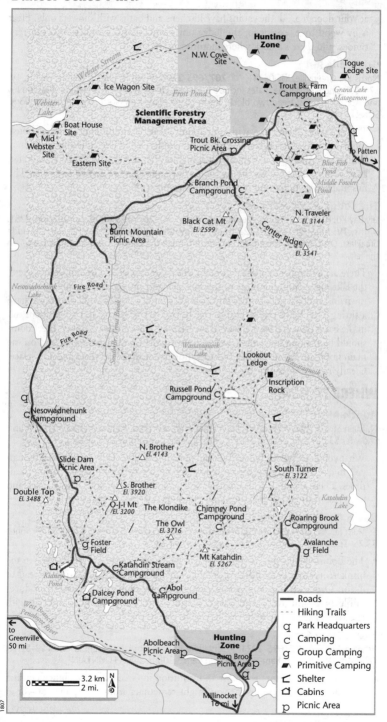

Hunting Zone

N.W. Cove Site

Togue Ledge Site

Webster Stream

Ice Wagon Site

Webster Lake

Trout Bk. Farm Campground

q

Grand Lake Matagamon

Scientific Forestry Management Area

Frost Pond

Boat House Site

Mid Webster Site

Eastern Site

Trout Bk. Crossing Picnic Area
p

To Patten
27 m

Blue Fish Pond

Middle Fowler Pond

S. Branch Pond Campground
C

Burnt Mountain Picnic Area
p

Black Cat Mt
El. 2599

N. Traveler
△ *El. 3144*

Center Ridge

△ *El. 3541*

Nesowadnehunk Lake

Fire Road

Sandy Str. Trout Brook

Fire Road

Wassataquoik Lake

Lookout Ledge

Inscription Rock

Wassataquoik Stream

Russell Pond Campground
C

Nesowadnehunk Campground
q
C

N. Brother
△ *El. 4143*

South Turner
△ *El. 3122*

Slide Dam Picnic Area
p

S. Brother
△ *El. 3920*

Katahdin Lake

Double Top
△ *El. 3488*

O-J-I Mt
△ *El. 3200*

The Klondike

Chimney Pond Campground
C

Roaring Brook Campground
C

Nesowadnehunk Stream

The Owl
△ *El. 3716*

Avalanche Field
g

Foster Field
g

Kidney Pond

Katahdin Stream Campground
C

Mt Katahdin
△ *El. 5267*

Daicey Pond Campground

Abol Campground

West Branch Penobscot River

to Greenville 50 mi

Abolbeach Picnic Area
p

Hunting Zone

Rum Brook Picnic Area
p

q

Millinocket 18 mi

▬	Roads
- - -	Hiking Trails
q	Park Headquarters
c	Camping
g	Group Camping
◣	Primitive Camping
⌐	Shelter
⌂	Cabins
p	Picnic Area

0   3.2 km
    2 mi.

N

1807

at your doorstep. All the cabins have kitchens and baths with showers only. Heat is by woodstove, except for the lodge unit, which has a fireplace. You can rent canoes, and there's a dock where motorboats are rented.

Greenville Inn

Norris St., Greenville, ME 04441. ☎ **207/695-2206.** 9 rms, 1 suite, 6 cottage rooms. TV. $75–$95 single or double. Rates include breakfast. DISC, MC, V. Free parking. Closed Nov and Apr. Directions: Head two blocks north of the blinker on North Main Street to Norris Street.

This is a sweet little place, with nine rooms in the main inn plus a carriage house room and two cottages containing the remainder. The Greenville Inn is run by a family, with the son and daughter helping out. Besides the individually decorated guest rooms, there's a fine dining room where outsiders are invited to dinner. The hospitality is genuine and the location convenient.

The Lodge at Moosehead

Lily Bay Rd. (P.O. Box 1167), Greenville, ME 04441. ☎ **207/695-4400.** Fax 207/695-2281. 8 rms. TV. June–Oct $140–$225 double; Nov–May $125–$175 double. Rates include breakfast. DISC, MC, V. Directions: Go north through the blinker 2^1/$_2$ miles to the lodge, on the left.

There are a number of assets that make this lodge special: the friendly atmosphere, the lake views (nothing short of spectacular), and the rooms (handily the best in town and good enough to rival any New England country inn). All the rooms have a sitting area, hand-carved four-poster beds, a gas fireplace, and a whirlpool tub in the bath; only one has no view of the lake. By this summer, another three rooms should be making their introduction. Downstairs is a billiards room, and on the main floor you'll find a lovely and romantic parlor with lake views and a fireplace. Clearly no one does it better at Moosehead.

WHERE TO DINE

Auntie M's

N. Main St. ☎ **207/695-2238.** Reservations not accepted. Sandwiches $3.50–$5; soups/ chowder $3.95; main courses $6–$10. MC, V. Daily 5am–8pm. AMERICAN.

What you'll get here is home-cooking, pure and simple. This isn't Kansas, though you might imagine a twister came through after a rush with locals during meal-times. There are sandwiches such as the tuna roll or Dagwood; a daily special; and baskets with fried haddock, scallops, chicken, and liver and onions.

Boom Chain Restaurant

S. Main St. ☎ **207/695-2602.** Reservations not accepted. Breakfast $2.50–$4.50; lunch $3.75–$6.50. No credit cards. Daily 6am–2pm. DINER.

The Boom Chain runs akin to the Road Kill Café (see below) and is close to the blinker; its owners spend most of their energy on food preparation instead of decor. Order up blueberry pancakes (you know, Maine is the largest producer of blueberries in the United States), a daily special, or possibly a sandwich with chowder or chili. The homemade pies are good, too.

Harris Drug Store

Pritham Ave. ☎ **207/695-2921.** Reservations not accepted. Ice-cream favorites $2–$2.10. DISC, MC, V. Mon–Sat 8am–5:30pm, Sun 9am 5:30pm. SODA FOUNTAIN.

The Harris Drug Store is almost an institution in Greenville. The lunch counter and soda fountain are just as you might remember from a by-gone era—or at least imagine it to have been. There are nine stools where you can sit up and order a root-beer float, sundae, milkshake, or cherry Coke. The present owners' grandfather started the business in 1896, and the spirit of that generation lives on today as you look back at a slice of real Americana.

Lakeview Restaurant

At the Lodge at Moosehead Lake, Lily Bay Rd. ☎ **207/695-4400.** Reservations required. $25 per person. DISC, MC, V. Dinner only, Nov–May 5:30–8:30pm. REGIONAL AMERICAN.

Roger and Jennifer once served dinner here all year but they decided the summer season was too hectic and they wanted to concentrate their efforts on their inn so dinner only is served in the off-peak season. The view from this dining room is award-winning: Big windows frame the wonderful lake and partial sunsets. Attentive service makes this the top choice in town, with a menu that's adventurous and not too serious (where else can you order moose-shaped pasta?). Come a little early and have a drink on the deck overlooking the lake. You might even catch a glimpse of a moose in the gravel driveway out front. And, by the way, if you need a place to stay, this is numero uno (see "Where to Stay," above).

Road Kill Café

Me. 15 at Greenville Junction. ☎ **207/695-2230.** Reservations not accepted. Main courses $9–$14; dinner for two $22. MC, V. Daily 11am–10pm. Closed Apr to mid-May and Dec–Jan. CAFE.

Ask locals in the Moosehead region the name of a place to eat that's a staple in this part of Maine and they'll say the Road Kill Café. However, they'll say this not because the food is memorable—as the name implies, this place has a sense of humor and the cooking is good if basic. License plates and roadsigns make up the decor. There's a yellow line on the floor just like on the road outside, but thankfully the deer and ribs served aren't road kill. The place is popular enough for a second one to have opened on U.S. 302 in Bartlett, N.H. Try it if you get up that way.

13 Vermont

The Green Mountain state is one of the nation's most rurual, with lots of trees and very few people—only about half a million in total. But the greenery is Vermont's glory—green is even the color of the state's auto license plates. To protect the sylvan beauty of the state and to keep the roads from becoming cluttered with "off-site advertising," the state government has devised a plan whereby participating stores, restaurants, lodging places, and attractions put information on their establishments in a little book called the *Vermont Visitors' Handbook,* yours free by writing to the Vermont Development Agency, Montpelier, VT 05602. The establishments in the handbook have numbers, and an attractive green sign out on the highway nearby will direct you to the store, restaurant, or motel and will also bear its number.

Only in Vermont would some enterprising citizens come up with a promotion to support the dairy industry and its hard-working farmers in an effort to preserve the small dairy farms of the state. Nowhere but in Vermont can you adopt a cow. With one cow for every two residents, Vermont has almost 2,400 dairy farms. The "Adopt a Cow" program lets you support a cow and its farmer while receiving an "Info-Pak" and T-shirt. This enlightened policy is just one of the glories of visiting the Green Mountain State.

Skiing is another of Vermont's glories, and resorts in this state are usually more winter- than summer-oriented. Heavy precipitation gives many ski areas a good, long season, and the mountain scenery and imported "alpine" architecture help get one into the spirit of winter fun. No Vermont lodge would think of opening without its fireplace stocked with logs to give the glow to an après-ski cocktail and conversation.

Don't be too surprised by Yankee humor, especially during mud season, as some of the locals may refer to Vermont as the state with four seasons: early winter, mid-winter, late winter, and next winter. They'll be pleased to show you around and show off all the wonderful features that beckon visitors any time of year.

Although winter is its prime season, Vermont is also beautiful in summer. Room rates are lower, many ski resorts run their chair and gondola lifts for sightseers, and the state parks do a booming business with campers, hikers, and picnickers. And, winter or summer, most places in Vermont have the distinct advantage of being quite accessible, whether you plan to come by car, bus, train, or air.

What's Special About Vermont

Museums
- The Bennington Museum, with its excellent Revolutionary and Early American collection, as well as a superb exhibit of paintings by Grandma Moses.
- Shelburne Museum, south of Burlington, a huge complex of more than 37 historic buildings, a steamboat, and art galleries, holding the fullest collection of Americana ever assembled.
- Hildene, in Manchester, the former gracious country mansion of Robert Todd Lincoln, Abraham's son.

Shopping
- The Vermont State Craft Center at Frog Hollow in Middlebury, a gallery of Vermont artisans' achievements.
- Small factories in Grafton and Plymouth selling delicious locally made Vermont Cheddar.

Especially for Kids
- Alpine slides at Manchester and Stowe, adding an outdoor thrill to a summer vacation.
- The elevator ride to the top of the Bennington Battle Monument and the panoramic view.
- The magnificent steeds at the Morgan Horse Farm in Middlebury.
- Billings Farm & Museum in Woodstock, where kids can get close to farm animals and even milk a cow or two.

Beautiful Towns & Villages
- Grafton, Dorset, Woodstock, Manchester, Newfane, and many other small Vermont settlements—all picture-perfect New England towns.

Resorts
- Vermont's ski resorts in summer—vacation resorts featuring play houses, hiking, mountain biking, and many other indoor and outdoor pursuits.

SEEING VERMONT

GETTING THERE **By Plane** Burlington is served by several major air carriers and their regional commuter subsidiaries, such as Business Express (Delta Connection), United Express, USAir Express, and Continental Express. In addition, USAir and United Airlines have direct flights to Burlington in large aircraft. Direct flights go to Burlington from many cities.

By Train Two Amtrak trains serve Vermont, and both run between New York City and Montréal. The *Vermonter* runs daily between Washington, D.C., via New York City to Montréal, stopping in Brattleboro (for Mount Snow), Bellows Falls, White River Junction (for Woodstock and Killington), Montpelier, Waterbury (for Stowe), Essex Junction (for Burlington), and St. Albans. The *Vermonter* is a night train, and passengers must transfer to a bus in St. Albans before continuing to Montréal.

The *Adirondack* runs daily between New York City and Montréal, skirting Vermont as it runs up the Hudson. Stops at Whitehall (for Rutland), Port Henry, and Port Kent (for Burlington) are the most convenient for reaching points in Vermont, although there are lots of other stops. The *Adirondack* is a day train.

By Bus   Vermont has its own large bus line, **Vermont Transit Lines** (☎ 802/864-6811 or 800/451-3292, 800/642-3133 in Vermont), which operates from New York (in conjunction with Greyhound), Montréal (in conjunction with Voyageur), and Boston to virtually all points of interest in Vermont. Other services run from Portsmouth, N.H., Portland, Me., and Concord, N.H., to points in Vermont.

By Car   Take the Interstates: I-95 to I-91 from New York City and Connecticut, I-93 to I-89 from Boston, and Canada 10 to 133 to I-89 if you're driving from Montréal. Vermont's Route 100, which winds through the center of the state from north to south, links most of the resort areas.

ESSENTIALS   State information booths are maintained on the major access roads to the state; stop at one for a map and for the *Vermont Visitors' Handbook* mentioned above.

Vermont has a law that prohibits skis from sticking out beyond the normal width of the car. Roads are very well maintained in Vermont in winter, but remember that the roads into the mountains are gradients, so it's best to have snow tires. Dry gas, to prevent your fuel lines from freezing, isn't a bad idea either.

The Vermont tax on rooms and meals is 8%, and the **telephone area code** for the entire state is **802.**

1 Brattleboro

8 miles W of Marlboro

The first town you're likely to encounter if you come from New York or Boston is Brattleboro, and in a way this is as it should be, for Brattleboro was the site of Vermont's first colonial settlement. In 1724 a small fortress was built at the spot now marked by a granite commemoration stone and named Fort Dummer. There had been white settlers in the area before that, but the fort became the focal point of a community as well as its principal defense against the Native Americans.

Today Brattleboro is one of the state's larger towns, with a population around 13,000 and industries that range from printing and book manufacture to furniture making and the manufacture of optical products. As for famous sons, the great Mormon leader Brigham Young was born (1801) nearby in Windham County, and Rudyard Kipling married a Brattleboro woman in 1892 and they lived near the town for some time.

GETTING THERE   By Train   There's one train nightly between New York and St. Albans (see the beginning of this chapter).

By Bus   Vermont Transit Lines (☎ 802/864-6811 or 800/451-3292, 800/642-3133 in Vermont) serves Brattleboro.

By Car   Follow I-91, the major north-south route along the Connecticut River Valley, or Vt. 9 (east-west) in Vermont and New Hampshire.

ESSENTIALS   The **telephone area code** is **802.** The **Brattleboro Chamber of Commerce** information office is at 180 Main St., right in the center of town (☎ 802/254-4565), and is open during business hours.

WHAT TO SEE AND DO

If you have an hour to spend in town before you rush off to the music festival at Marlboro or the hiking and skiing at surrounding resorts, check out the

Vermont

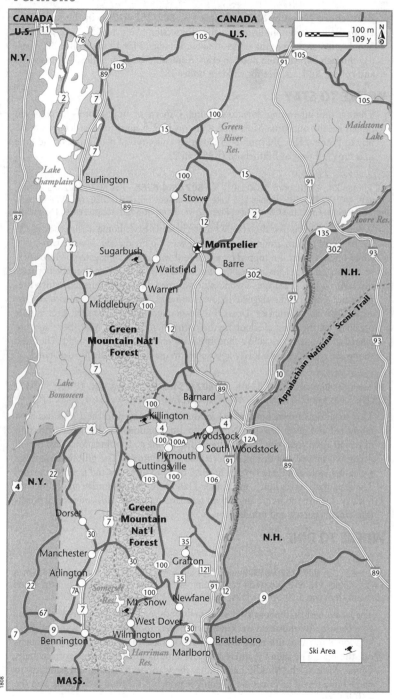

Brattleboro Museum & Art Center (☎ **802/257-0124**), in the town's old Union Railroad Station down near the intersection of Vt. 119, Vt. 142, and U.S. 5, only a few steps from the center of town. It's open May 15 to October 30, Tuesday through Sunday from noon to 6pm. Admission is $2 for adults, $1 for seniors and college students; free for children under 18.

WHERE TO STAY

There is one interesting downtown hotel. Otherwise, Brattleboro's lodgings are motels on the outskirts. Most motels are on U.S. 5 north of Brattleboro on the way to Putney (Exit 3N from I-95); another collection of places to stay and dine in is on Vt. 9 west of Brattleboro (I-95 Exit 2).

40 Putney Road

40 Putney Rd., Brattleboro, VT 05301. ☎ **802/254-6268.** Fax 802/258-2673. 4 rms, 1 suite. A/C TV. $80–$85 double; $95 suite. Rates include breakfast. DISC, MC, V. Free parking. Directions: Cross the Connecticut River on Vt. 9 and go south to the center 1¹/₂ miles.

When I first drove past this stately French baronial-style home dating back to the 1930s, I had to turn around to see what it was. To my delight, it was a two-story, white-brick country inn topped by a slate roof with a matching garage. The owners have changed since I first visited the inn, and now Joan and Pete Broderick operate this lavish home. It features a wonderful two-tone dining room replete with a fireplace and draped and swagged window treatments, and a living room with an Oriental carpet and a fireplace. Upstairs is a fancy sun room. You might elect to take breakfast on the patio overlooking the fountain and lawn in back. Beverages are offered in the afternoons, and a chocolate is left on your pillow each night. The guest rooms are sprinkled with lovely appointments and are individually decorated.

Latchis Hotel

50 Main St., Brattleboro, VT 05301. ☎ **802/254-6300.** 30 rms. A/C TV TEL. $49–$72 double. Rates higher in foliage season. AE, MC, V. Free parking.

This small downtown hotel where lumber traders stayed in the 1930s has been renovated and given new life. Now a pleasant monument to the local expression of the art deco style, the Latchis offers comfortable accommodations with period decor, within walking distance of everything downtown. The grill restaurant has a pleasing look, and there's even a brewery that produces ales and lager for the inn. The restaurant serves lunch and dinner Tuesday through Saturday and brunch on Sunday. Deluxe rooms are larger than standard and come with continental breakfast, cinema passes, and minibars.

WHERE TO DINE

Common Ground

25 Elliot St. ☎ **802/257-0855.** Reservations recommended. Main courses $3–$11; lunch $3–$5; dinner $16–$18. No credit cards. Summer, Mon and Wed–Sat 11:30am–9pm, Sun 10:30am–2pm and 5:30–9pm; winter, Wed–Mon 11:30am–8pm. INTERNATIONAL.

The location of Brattleboro's oldest natural-foods restaurant also serves as a popular coffeehouse (live music on weekends) and gallery for local artists. Its second-floor location allows it to utilize a glassed-in patio terrace where diners may sit throughout the year. The menu is interesting and international, with dishes from Italy, China, Mexico, the Middle East, India, the Caribbean, Japan, and America, to name but a few. The prices are certainly reasonable, the food is delicious, and the staff is friendly.

2 Marlboro & Wilmington

West of Brattleboro are some of Vermont's loveliest unspoiled villages, worthy of a few days' stay, or at least a meal or a rest stop. Marlboro and Wilmington are on Vt. 9, west of Brattleboro, in the direction of Bennington.

MARLBORO

8 miles W of Brattleboro, 10 miles E of Wilmington

GETTING THERE   By Car   Follow Vt. 9 west from Brattleboro.

ESSENTIALS   The **telephone area code** is **802.** The nearest **visitors center** is on Interstate 91 in Guilford (☎ **802/254-4593**), about eight miles away.

WHAT TO SEE & DO

The town's name brings to mind immediately the summertime **Marlboro Music School and Festival,** directed by Rudolf Serkin for many years. The festival brings together dozens of the most talented musicians in the country, some famous and some soon to be famous, for two months of practice, consultation, and tutorial. On weekends from mid-July to mid-August, the school is opened to concert audiences, most of whom have ordered their tickets weeks or months in advance and have also made early lodging reservations. The auditorium at Marlboro College seats fewer than 700 people, and to keep the spirit of the chamber music, directors and performers resist demands for a larger hall.

If you're interested in attending weekend festival concerts, write early to Marlboro Music, Marlboro, VT 05344 (☎ 802/254-2394); this is the address to use from late June through mid-August. From September through mid-June, write to Marlboro Music, 135 S. 18th St., Philadelphia, PA 19103 (☎ 215/569-4690). Or you can phone the box office (☎ 802/254-2394) and ask for schedules, prices, and ticket-purchase forms. Then, when you've got your tickets, make a reservation in Marlboro or nearby Brattleboro or Wilmington, or even in Bennington—that city is only a 45-minute drive away through the forests of southern Vermont.

WHERE TO STAY

Marlboro is a location more than a bustling town, and when you drive to the dot on the map, you'll find a church, a small town office building, and several houses. But that's about all, and so for many products and services you must drive to Brattleboro. Several inns and restaurants in the area, however, provide well for travelers year-round, as well as for festival visitors. The inn recommended below has excellent dining rooms.

Whetstone Inn

South St., Marlboro, VT 05344. ☎ **802/254-2500.** 12 rms (8 with bath). $60–$70 double without bath; $60–$80 double with bath. Three-night minimum stay required in summer. No credit cards. Free parking.

The Whetstone has been an inn for close to two centuries: The upstairs was once a "ballroom" where the local gentry could stage their get-togethers; the downstairs was a tavern along the stagecoach route between Boston and Albany. In winter, cross-country ski trails start at the inn's back door. The inn's pond (the reservoir in case of fire) is right out back. As there's no great activity in the town, nothing will disturb you unless you take to your feet or your bicycle to go to the music festival, two miles away. Higher rates are for rooms with a private bath or a kitchenette; meals are not included, but you can get breakfast each morning (waffles, pancakes, popovers, and home-baked muffins and biscuits) and dinners on concert nights during the summer and on weekends and certain weekdays at other times in the year.

WILMINGTON

10 miles W of Marlboro, 21 miles E of Bennington

Almost equidistant between Brattleboro and Bennington is Wilmington, a crossroads town where Vt. 9 meets Vt. 100. Many people pass through Wilmington as they begin their journey northward along Vermont's central scenic artery, Vt. 100. There are many good inns here, partly because it's a crossroads and partly because it's close to the ski slopes of Mount Snow.

GETTING THERE   By Car   Vermont 9 meets Vt. 100 in Wilmington.

ESSENTIALS   The **telephone area code** is **802.** The **Mount Snow/Haystack Region Chamber of Commerce,** P.O. Box 3, Wilmington, VT 05363 (☎ **802/ 464-8092**), can answer your questions.

WHERE TO STAY

Hermitage Inn

Coldbrook Rd. (P.O. Box 457), Wilmington, VT 05363. ☎ **802/464-3511.** Fax 802/ 464-2688. 15 rms. $200–$225 double. Rates include breakfast and dinner. AE, DC, MC, V. Free parking. Directions: Follow Vt. 100 north about 2 1/2 miles and turn left onto Coldbrook Road; the inn is about three miles down.

When you see the inn, you'll understand why it's named Hermitage: Jim McGovern raises his own game birds, makes his own maple syrup and jam, and has a vast and well-selected wine cellar. If he ever wanted to be a hermit, he'd be set for life. You can become a hermit in this plentiful hideaway, which was once the home of the editor of the *Social Register.* The main house is over a century old and has some of the original furnishings and many others from the same period, and all the guest rooms have working fireplaces. The inn's other attractions include fine views of Haystack Mountain and a shop. For recreation there's the course of 15 field sporting clays (targets thrown from various positions), and they even have release pheasant hunts. It's a real country experience, not a citified country inn.

As you might expect from the bounty described above, the dining here is superb and exceptional, with lots of game fowl, home-raised venison, trout, and fresh vegetables, plus wines from that venerable cellar, which has been abuilding for almost three decades. Lunch is sometimes served during the busy winter season, at an extra charge. The inn's other attractions include 34 miles of cross-country ski trails, ski rentals, a tennis court, and a trout pond. Golf and ski packages are offered.

✪ Trail's End

Smith Rd., Wilmington, VT 05363. ☎ **802/464-2727** or 800/859-2585. 13 rms, 2 suites. $90–$150 single or double; $140–$180 suite. Rates include breakfast. AE, MC, V. Free parking.

Despite its woodland location (about five miles from Mount Snow, four miles north of the traffic light in Wilmington, and half a mile east of Vt. 100), Trail's End is no backwoods establishment, for it has a heated outdoor pool, clay tennis court, and trout pond, and a dining room in which remarkably delicious meals are the rule. Six rooms have TV sets. Four rooms have fireplaces in addition to the two fireplace suites. Trail's End is certainly one of Mount Snow's most attractive, architecturally interesting, congenial places to stay.

The White House of Wilmington

Vt. 9, Wilmington, VT 05363. ☎ **802/464-2135** or 800/541-2135. Fax 802/ 464-5222. 23 rms. $170–$240 double. Rates include breakfast and dinner. AE, DC, MC, V. Free parking.

This could well be this area's most elegant and gracious inn. Housed in an imposing turn-of-the-century (1914) mansion with lofty porticoes and high-ceilinged public rooms with elegant furniture, it has charming, spacious guest rooms, nine of which have a fireplace. The White House is a complete resort, with a lovely rose garden replete with fountain. The dining room, which is very well regarded, serves breakfast and dinner daily. On Sunday, there's brunch and, in winter, a special skiers' lunch. Facilities include a 60-foot outdoor pool, an indoor pool, a sauna, a whirlpool, and 45 kilometers of hiking and cross-country ski trails. Children over 10 are welcome.

3   Bennington

21 miles W of Wilmington; 14 miles N of Williamstown, Mass.; 140 miles NW of Boston, Mass.

"Vermont's most historic area" is how the citizens of Bennington tout their town. The reason for this civic pride is that the Revolutionary War's Battle of Bennington was fought near here (the actual site is now in neighboring Walloomsac, N.Y.) in 1777. The battle is looked upon as a turning point in the war, since the British troops expected to encounter little resistance at Bennington and instead were forced to retreat after having lost a good number of casualties and prisoners to the Revolutionaries. Soon afterward, at the Battle of Saratoga, the British soldiers thus weakened were forced to surrender, giving the Americans their first great victory of the war.

Although the Battle of Bennington was certainly influential in the winning of the war, it is doubtless remembered so well today because of a 306-foot-high obelisk that was built in 1891 to commemorate it. Both the monument (which has an observation platform) and the well-known Bennington Museum's collection of Americana are open to visitors.

GETTING THERE   By Car   U.S. 7 is the main north-south route and Vt. 9 the main east-west one.

ESSENTIALS   The **telephone area code** is **802.** The **Bennington Area Chamber of Commerce** (☎ 802/447-3311) is at Veteran's Memorial Drive (U.S. 7 North), about a mile from the intersection of Main and North/South Streets. Open during business hours, the chamber can give you a good, detailed map of the town and lots of information on both the town and the surrounding region.

WHAT TO SEE & DO

The historic sights of the town are mostly grouped along West Main Street, in the section called Old Bennington. You can buy a single ticket that admits you to the town's three most important sights—**the Bennington Museum,** the **Bennington Battle Monument,** and the **Park-McCullough House**—for $10 for adults, $9 for seniors, $8 for students, or 50¢ for children 6 to 11 (those under 6 get in free).

The ticket represents a small savings over the price of three individual admission tickets. Pick yours up at the Bennington Area Chamber of Commerce, the Bennington Museum, or the Park-McCullough House.

While you're at the Park-McCullough House in North Bennington, drive or walk through the campus of **Bennington College,** a unique loosely structured four-year college that stresses artistic creation and an acquaintance with nature. The situation of the college is particularly beautiful and is particularly well adapted to the creative efforts of the students. It's located on 550 acres dotted with biking trails, playing fields, tennis courts, and a spring-fed lake. The college is respected for its summer programs, including its summer writing workshops. Call 802/442-5401 for more information.

THE BENNINGTON MUSEUM   The Bennington Museum, West Main Street (Vt. 9) (☎ 802/447-1571), has a collection dominated by Revolutionary and Early American history. Paintings, glass items (molded, blown, and pressed), American-made furniture and carvings, arms, toys, and costumes are all included, and there are considerable numbers of very attractive treasures. The Bennington pottery, for instance, is more like china with its gold or colored trim; it was made here for wealthy customers for over 100 years. Of the paintings, the most fascinating are the ones in the Grandma Moses collection. Anna Mary Moses (1860–1961) was a farm girl in nearby New York State, and later as a farmer's wife she did all the heavy, hard work that life on a farm demands, yet still found time to paint. After she was 70 years old and could no longer keep up with the heavy farm work, her paintings took on such a charming and primitive character and such spirit that one of her paintings now hangs in the Metropolitan in New York and many others are here in the Bennington Museum. At the age of 100 she was still at work, and she died at 101. You can look back into what life was like for her in the exhibit called *And Life Is What You Make It* in the Grandma Moses Schoolhouse Museum, also in the Bennington Museum.

The museum is open daily from 9am to 5pm. Admission is $5 for adults, $4.50 for young people 12 to 17 and seniors, free for children under 12; or $12 per family. The museum is closed Thanksgiving Day and Christmas week.

THE BENNINGTON BATTLE MONUMENT   This impressive obelisk is more than 306 feet tall, which makes it the tallest structure in Vermont. It took four years (1887–91) to build, and when it was finished one could walk to the top by means of an interior staircase. Today, the staircase is closed and an elevator hums up and down. A small admission fee is charged, and tickets are available in the souvenir shop to the west of the monument entrance. Pick up a copy of the free leaflet describing the battle and the monument. The monument is open April 1 to November 1, daily from 9am to 5pm.

This was not the site of the battle but of the colonists' arsenal, which was the object of the British advance. His supplies depleted by the action at Fort Ticonderoga, "Gentleman Johnny" Burgoyne sent two of his units toward Bennington to capture the Revolutionaries' arms stores. But Gen. Burgoyne misjudged the size of the rebel force and was unaware that Gen. John Stark, who had fought at Bunker Hill and under Washington at Trenton and Princeton, commanded the Americans. Stark cleverly headed off the British advance at Walloomsac (N.Y.), six miles west of the arsenal. Stark is said to have exclaimed, "There are the Redcoats! They will be ours tonight or Molly Stark sleeps a widow."

The pitched battle on August 16, 1777, lasted two hours, and when the smoke cleared the American forces were victorious. On the way back to Bennington, Stark's troops were surprised by British reinforcements, but Col. Seth Warner and his Green Mountain Boys arrived in time to save the day for the Americans. The losses at Bennington and lack of supplies weakened the British force, and Burgoyne surrendered his entire command in October following the Battle of Saratoga.

The view from the monument is very fine. Though you wouldn't recognize it, you can look west to where the battle actually took place, less than six miles away. For a closer view, follow "Bennington Battlefield" signs from the monument through a covered bridge to North Bennington, then west on Vt. 67 to the Bennington Battlefield Historic site near Walloomsac, N.Y. Plaques describe the battle, and shaded picnic tables provide a good place for a rest and a snack.

PARK-MCCULLOUGH HISTORIC HOUSE MUSEUM Of Bennington's outstanding Victorian mansions, one is exceptionally well kept. The Park-McCullough House, just off Vt. 67A at the corner of West and Park Streets in North Bennington (☎ 802/442-5441), is open for guided tours through the house from early May through October, daily from 10am to 4pm (last tour leaves at 3pm). Adults pay $5, seniors and students pay $4, children 12 to 17 are charged $3, and children 11 and under accompanied by an adult enter free. Besides the house, still stuffed with period furnishings and personal effects, there's a pint-size "manor" for a children's playhouse and a cupola-topped carriage house complete with century-old carriages.

WHERE TO STAY

Bennington has dozens of motels on the highways that approach it, but as is my custom I will concentrate most heavily on the establishments right in town. However, one of the following inns, the Hill Farm Inn, is in the village of Arlington, about 15 miles north of Bennington, which has a number of its own hostelries, in the town proper and on Vt. 7A between Bennington and Arlington.

Moderate

Four Chimneys Restaurant & Inn

21 West Rd. (Vt. 9 West), Old Bennington, VT 05201. ☎ **802/447-3500.** 7 rms. A/C TV TEL. $100–$125 double. Rates include continental breakfast. AE, CB, DC, MC, V. Free parking. Directions: Follow Vt. 9 west to the inn, on the right-hand side.

Noted mostly for its restaurant (see "Where to Dine," below), Four Chimneys does have several pleasant, comfortable guest rooms. The inn is set on spacious grounds good for walks, reading, and just sitting. If you decide to dine here as well, you'll feel right at home.

Hill Farm Inn

R.R. 2, Box 2015, Arlington, VT 05250. ☎ **802/375-2269** or 800/882-2545. 11 rms (8 with bath), 2 suites. $75 double without bath; $90 double with bath; $110 suite. Rates include breakfast and dinner. AE, DISC, MC, V. Free parking. Directions: Go north of Bennington, and four miles north of Arlington, just off Vt. 7A.

This inn has been receiving guests since 1905 but was actually built as two farmhouses in the early 1800s. For a handful of years, George and Joanne Hardy leased the inn to a couple who operated it. They have now come back into the picture and have aggressively updated the rooms, service, and dining. Of the 11 guest rooms and two suites, seven are in the inn proper, and six in the 1790 guesthouse next door.

Budget

Bennington Motor Inn

143 W. Main St., Bennington, VT 05201. ☎ **802/442-5479** or 800/359-9900. 16 rms. A/C MINIBAR TV TEL. $52–$56 double with one queen-size bed, $58–$62 double with two beds. Additional person $5 extra; additional bed $5 extra. Rates higher during foliage season. AE, DC, DISC, MC, V. Free parking.

The little extras at this motor inn, located 3 1/2 blocks west of the U.S. 7 intersection, include coffeemakers in the rooms, color TV (with cable and in-room movies), and individual thermostats. Some of the larger rooms, designated as family units, can sleep up to six people, and these rooms also have little refrigerators.

Best Western New Englander Motor Inn

220 Northside Dr., Bennington, VT 05201. ☎ **802/442-6311** or 800/528-1234. Fax 802/442-6311. 58 rms. A/C TV TEL. $55–$95 double. Additional person $7 extra. AE, CB, DC, DISC, MC, V. Free parking.

Between Bennington and North Bennington is the New Englander, a fairly large motel arranged around a central court with a swimming pool and the motel's restaurant, which helps block noise from the busy street. As this is Bennington, the rooms have been done with Early American inspiration, although all furnishings are modern. In the clutter and strip development of Northside Drive, the New Englander is a very pleasant oasis, complete unto itself, and rooms are moderately priced. The New Englander's rooms are comfortable and contain coffeemakers and cable TVs with remote control. The suites have whirlpool tubs.

Kirkside Motor Lodge

250 W. Main St., Bennington, VT 05201. ☎ **802/447-7596.** 23 rms. A/C TV TEL. $50 double with a double bed, $58 with a queen-size bed, $68 with a king-size bed. Off-season, about 15% less; during foliage season, rates are $78–$98 double. AE, DC, DISC, MC, V. Free parking.

The pleasant rooms here may have antiques, and some are more individualized than others; they don't all come from a cookie-cutter motel blueprint. There's little problem with street noise because of the motel's position and location on Vt. 9 West, just 1 1/2 blocks from U.S. 7. If you stay here, you'll be right beside the handsome Gothic-style church and about equidistant from the center of town and the museum and monument.

WHERE TO DINE

Alldays & Onions

519 Main St. ☎ **802/447-0043.** Reservations recommended. Main courses $7–$20; lunch $5–$8. AE, DISC, MC, V. Breakfast and lunch, Mon–Sat 8:30am–5:30pm; dinner, Thurs–Sat 6–8pm. AMERICAN.

Bennington's purveyor of the daily fresh and delicious is a combination country store, delicatessen, gourmet food shop, restaurant, and bistro. Drop by and join the assortment of locals and travelers, Bennington College students and professors, for freshly baked morning muffins and Colombian coffee, a wonderful create-your-own sandwich, or a cool pasta salad. From 4 to 6pm the lunch menu changes to a bar menu with lighter fare. Evening suppers often feature enticing pasta dishes or fish. They have a small but good eclectic wine selection.

Bennington Station Restaurant

150 Depot St. ☎ **802/447-1080.** Reservations not required. Main courses $11–$18.50. AE, CB, DC, DISC, MC, V. Mon–Thurs 11:30am–9pm, Fri–Sat 11:30am–10pm, Sun 11am–8pm. AMERICAN.

Back at the turn of the century Bennington was a busy town, so busy that a train depot was constructed to accommodate the flow of passengers who boarded the 18 daily trains during its heyday in 1915. Constructed in 1897, this old depot saw its last train pull out in 1933. The exterior's blue marble was quarried in West Rutland. Today the depot is a popular dining spot, serving such specialties as Vermont Tom Turkey, a seafood sampler, and a salad bar. There's an early-bird special offered between 4:30 and 6pm. The specialty of the house is prime rib. This is a fine choice for local dining.

Brasserie

324 County St. ☎ **802/447-7922.** Reservations not accepted. Main courses $6–$14. AE, MC, V. Daily 11:30am–8pm. Directions: Turn off Main Street by the Dunkin' Donuts (460 Main) and go straight; the street ends at County Street at Potter's Yard, a complex that includes the restaurant. NEW AMERICAN.

In Bennington there's a place called the Potter's Yard, a complex of shops and galleries in which local works of art and crafts are displayed and sold, and in this same complex at School and County Streets is the Brasserie. As the name might suggest, the Brasserie is fashioned on a French tavern restaurant, with beer and wine and delicious dishes, such as the pâté maison with French bread or chicken curry. A chef's salad or Greek salad and a variety of sandwiches or omelets are similarly good choices. The patio is the choice place to dine in good weather.

Four Chimneys Restaurant & Inn

21 West Rd. (Vt. 9 West), Old Bennington. ☎ **802/447-3500.** Reservations recommended. Main courses $12–$22; lunch $5.50–$11; dinner $25–$35. AE, CB, DC, MC, V. Lunch, Tues–Sun 11:30am–2pm; dinner, Mon–Sat 5–10pm, Sun 2–9pm. Directions: Follow Vt. 9 West to the inn, on the right-hand side. FRENCH.

Only half a mile west of the Bennington Museum, this imposing and many-chimneyed white mansion shaded by huge old trees set in spacious, well-tended grounds was once the home of a prominent Bennington businessman. Now its formal salons, informal solarium, patio, and terraces are set up for elegant dining. Chef Alex Koks's English-language menu is admirably straightforward: What would be "*maigret de canard, sauce framboise*" in a more pretentious place is "broiled breast of duck with raspberry-vinegar sauce" at the Four Chimneys—and it's just as delicious. Classics, such as beef Wellington, rack of lamb, and roast Cornish game hen, come in preparations that are interesting and original without being hyperexotic. The food is excellent, the service the same, and luncheon, on a pleasant summer's day, is a special treat. House wines are under $15 per bottle, several good selections cost $20 or less, and most bottles are under $35.

4 West Dover & Mount Snow

6 miles N of Wilmington; 3 miles SE of Mount Snow ski area

Because of its southern Vermont location within driving distance of the metropolitan centers of Boston, Hartford, Providence, and New York, Mount Snow is one of Vermont's most popular ski resorts. The ski resort encouraged the inn trade, and the inns began playing host to summer travelers, and now this area is as popular in the warm months as in the cold.

The ski area is immense, with three different faces of the mountain covered with trails and lifts—13 lifts in all, including two enclosed skis-on gondolas. The highest vertical drop is almost 2,000 feet, and you could take the same lift a dozen times and never come down the same trail or slope. It's crowded, yes, because it's close to the cities, and is a good mountain for beginners and intermediate skiers, but it also has a lot of variety, and certainly a lot of activity. A resort this big has all the facilities: a "Pumpkin Patch" nursery for small children, a bar, a cafeteria, equipment rentals, a ski school, and 40 miles of cross-country trails.

GETTING THERE   By Car   Follow Vt. 100.

ESSENTIALS   The **telephone area code** is **802**. The **Mount Snow/Haystack Region Chamber of Commerce,** P.O. Box 3, Wilmington, VT 05363 (☎ **802/ 464-8092**), can answer your questions. Or you can stop by the information booth at the intersection of Vt. 9 and Vt. 100 in Wilmington, open May to September, daily from 9am to 5pm.

WHERE TO STAY

About 100 inns, lodges, hotels, and motels are clustered near the ski area, on the approach roads, or in the villages near Mount Snow. From this bewildering assortment of choices, several stand out:

✪ The Inn at Sawmill Farm

Vt. 100 (P.O. Box 367) at Crosstown Rd., West Dover, VT 05356. ☎ **802/464-8131.** Fax 802/464-1130. 20 rms. $350–$400 double. Rates include breakfast and dinner. AE, MC, V. Free parking at main entrance.

Here's a deluxe country inn that began as an inn with an attitude, then later developed into a warm venue set amid romantic surroundings. It appears regularly in designer magazines with lavish spreads showing the guest rooms—Victorian, Federal, turn-of-the-century—in the inn's various buildings. The dining rooms are particularly wonderful, providing the perfect ambience for romantic dinners of elegant, carefully prepared dishes from a positively sumptuous menu. In the evening, even in summer, the public rooms are all aglow with a multitude of candles—trays of them set on antiques here and there—adding a soft, warm mood everywhere. Be sure to note the temperature-controlled wine cellar with more than 36,000 bottles and over 870 labels.

On the inn's carefully tended grounds are a pool, two trout ponds, and a tennis court. The inn proper, an old farmhouse and barn, houses 10 guest rooms, and in other buildings there are 10 rooms, each with a fireplace; all rooms have air-conditioning. Prices are a bit higher in foliage season and holidays. Children under 10 cannot be lodged at the inn.

Kitzhof

Vt. 100, West Dover, VT 05356. ☎ **802/464-8310** or 800/388-8310. 25 rms. TV. Mid-May to mid-Sept (including breakfast), $58 double; mid-Sept to Mar (including breakfast and dinner), $92–$128 double. DISC, MC, V. Free parking. Closed Apr to mid-May. Directions: Go about 10 miles north of Wilmington on Vt. 100; the inn is on the right just beyond West Dover.

Kitzhof is a particularly nice alpine-style lodge set back from the highway, charging moderate prices. No two rooms are alike except in their comfort and sparkling cleanliness. An outdoor pool is heated for summer use, and an eight-foot hot tub is new. There's a BYOB bar with setups. Reductions are in order for lots of things, such as five-day economy ski weeks and arrivals early or late in the ski season. The

Kitzhof takes bus tours in summer and can provide lodging for hikers and bikers when there's room.

WHERE TO DINE

Brush Hill Restaurant

Vt. 100. ☎ **802/896-6100.** Reservations required. Main courses $17–$25; dinner $45–$50. MC, V. Dinner only, Wed–Sun 6–10pm. CONTEMPORARY.

North of West Dover is Brush Hill, a late 18th-century post-and-beam barn that has been restored and turned into a romantic dining spot. A 12-foot-long brick fireplace takes the chill off in foliage season; all diners enjoy it, as there are fewer than a dozen tables. The menu changes monthly, but recently dinner started with an unusual antipasto of grilled artichokes, shallots, red pepper, and smoked scamonza and was followed by a rack of lamb with mint essence, grilled leeks, and garlic. Dessert may be the dieter's to-order-or-not dilemma, but who can resist pastry puffs filled with French vanilla ice cream and topped by chocolate-rum sauce?

5 Newfane & Grafton

NEWFANE

14 miles NW of Brattleboro, 16 miles NE of West Dover, 15 miles S of Grafton

Newfane and Grafton are two of Vermont's most picture-perfect towns, with tall old trees, white churches with high steeples, and gracious old houses designed with classical touches. Come early in spring when they're "sugaring off" and see town children tap the maple trees along village streets. Come in summer and explore for yard and antiques sales. Come in autumn for the blazing color. Or come in winter to hide away in a comfy inn and dine each night from a superb menu.

GETTING THERE By Car   Follow Vt. 30 north from Brattleboro; from West Dover, follow unnumbered roads via East Dover, Brookside, South Newfane and Williamsville to Vt. 30, then north.

ESSENTIALS   The **telephone area code** is **802.** The nearest **visitors center** is on Interstate 91 in Guilford (☎ **802/254-4593**).

WHERE TO STAY & DINE

Four Columns Inn

West St. (P.O. Box 278), Newfane, VT 05345. ☎ **802/365-7713.** 15 rms. A/C TEL. $100–$175 double. Rates include breakfast. AE, MC, V. Free parking.

The Four Columns Inn is perfect for a delectable meal or an overnight stay. You can come here for dinner Wednesday through Monday from 6 to 9pm. Find a table in the cozy dining room, and settle back for a delightful evening of regional fare prepared with the freshest ingredients and great care. The atmosphere is romantic and the service friendly and fine-tuned. The wine list has vintages priced from $19 to $50, and a full dinner for two here might cost $80 to $125.

As for the guest rooms, they're as charming as the inn and the town, with private bath, air conditioning, and breakfast included. The inn also has a pool, and hiking trails pass near the back door. Note that there's no smoking in either the dining room or the guest rooms.

GRAFTON

15 miles N of Newfane, 7 miles S of Chester

GETTING THERE   By Car   Follow Vt. 35 north from Newfane, or south from Chester; from I-91 northbound, take Exit 5, then Vt. 121 west to Grafton; from I-91 southbound, take Exit 6, then U.S. 5 south to Bellows Falls and North Westminster, then Vt. 121 west to Grafton.

Like Newfane, Grafton is a part of old New England, but there's a nobility about this town—something like Woodstock—that makes it special. Carefully preserved houses and public buildings from a century or two ago are joined unobtrusively by more modern structures on the outskirts. Summer or winter, Grafton is a place bewitching in its beauty. Stop for a cup of coffee, a drink, or a meal, or even for overnight. Be careful, though—one overnight easily leads to week-long stays here.

ESSENTIALS   The **telephone area code** is **802.** The nearest visitors center is on Interstate 91 in Guilford (☎ **802/254-4593**).

WHAT TO SEE & DO

Grafton is perfect just for relaxing walks and sitting by the fireplace, but there are lots of other things to do as well. Start with **a horse-and-carriage ride** (in summer) around town. You'll see the driver, the steed, and the buggy at the stand in front of the Old Tavern Monday through Saturday between mid-June and the end of October. The ride is not just for fun—you'll get a complete narrative tour of Grafton as the horse trots along.

Grafton harbors a number of antiques shops, artists' galleries, a village store, and the **Grafton Village Cheese Company** (☎ 802/843-2221). The Cheese Company makes Cheddar, and you can see it being made and try samples or buy Vermont products by following the Townshend Road about half a mile south of the village. Hours are 8:30am to 4pm Monday through Friday and 10am to 4pm Saturday; closed in April.

By now, no doubt, you are completely enchanted with the town. To delve into its history, pay a visit to the **Grafton Historical Society Museum,** on Main Street just down from the post office (☎ 802/843-2584). The exhibits of Grafton memorabilia, old photographs, history, and genealogical files are open from 1:30 to 4:30pm Saturday and Sunday from June through mid-October, and on holiday weekends and holiday Mondays; it's open daily during foliage season.

WHERE TO STAY & DINE

The Old Tavern at Grafton
Vt. 35, Grafton, VT 05146. ☎ **802/843-2231** or 800/843-1801. 66 rms. TV TEL. $115–$165 single or double; $460–$550 Guest House. MC, V. Free parking.

The center of Grafton's social life since it was built in 1801 as a way station on the stagecoach road, The Old Tavern is also a town landmark. In its long history as a place to stay the night, The Old Tavern has played host to General Grant, Woodrow Wilson, Rudyard Kipling, and even woodsman-philosopher Henry David Thoreau. With its annexes, the inn can lodge about 130 people. Its rooms have private baths and modern conveniences, but the ambience is still old New England. The Old Tavern is not what one would call "quaint," but it's an authentic landmark, charming, hospitable, and very comfortable. Facilities include a pond for swimming, two tennis courts, a paddle-tennis court, mountain-bike rentals, and a games room. There are also 18 miles of cross-country ski trails.

You have a choice of dining rooms. For a drink before dinner, make your way to the Phelpsbarn Pub, with its own separate bar, several fireplaces, live music, and a TV room. Lunch is served at The Old Tavern from noon to 2pm, and dinner from 6:30 to 8:30pm, by reservation. At dinner, main courses range from $13 to $25.

6 Manchester

24 miles N of Bennington, 7 miles S of Dorset

GETTING THERE   **By Bus**   See the beginning of this chapter.

By Car   Follow U.S. 7 north from Bennington or south from Rutland.

The town of Manchester was once a summer resort on the order of the Berkshire towns. Settled before the Revolution, the town has a wide main street and handsome houses that retain the charm of the early Federal period.

As the county seat of Bennington County, Manchester was an important place long before Mt. Equinox (3,800 feet), to the west, drew crowds of hikers and skiers.

In the modern town of Manchester Center, just a few miles north along U.S. 7, all is bustle and activity, with traffic lights, filling stations, shopping centers, supermarkets, restaurants, and motels.

As the story is told, in the early days the village of Manchester wanted to attract business and visitors but decided that folks would not come to a town without sidewalks. The local quarry of the only stone available was enlisted to provide the necessary materials for sidewalks. As a result, today Manchester enjoys the distinction of having 17 miles of *marble* sidewalks.

ESSENTIALS   The **telephone area code** is **802.** The **Manchester and the Mountains Chamber of Commerce** (☎ **802/362-2100**) maintains an information office on Vt. 7A in Manchester Center for your convenience.

WHAT TO SEE & DO

What do you do in winter? That's easy: You go **skiing.** Big Bromley, Snow Valley, Magic Mountain, Stratton Mountain, and numerous ski-touring centers are located within a few miles of Manchester Center. Right in Manchester is the ski-touring center at Hildene.

As for summer activities, you can play golf, swim, hike, or ride a bike. Rent a bike from **Battenkill Sports,** in the stone house 1¼ miles east of U.S. 7A along Vt. 11/30, Manchester Center (☎ 802/362-2734). They offer mountain bikes, road bikes and helmets are included. Men's, women's, and children's bikes are available.

At the Bromley ski area on Vt. 11, six miles east of Manchester, an **Alpine Slide** (☎ 802/824-5522) draws downhill racers in summer. You take the ski lift to the top and then choose among the three alpine slide tracks, two-thirds of a mile long, controlling the speed of your little cart as you travel to the bottom. The slide is open late May to mid-October daily from 9:30am to 6pm, if the weather's good. The slide is fun, and the chair-lift ride that takes you up over the verdant hills is equally enjoyable.

What about famous residents? Abraham Lincoln had four sons, but only one of them lived to adulthood. When President Lincoln was assassinated in 1865,

Robert Todd Lincoln was an officer serving under General Grant in the Union Army. Later a successful lawyer and businessman, Lincoln came to Manchester in 1902, bought 412 acres of land, and began construction of **Hildene.** The mansion was completed in 1904, and Lincoln spent the summers there until his death in 1926. The estate was inherited by his wife and then his granddaughter, who left it to the Church of Christ, Scientist, in 1975. It's now owned and maintained by a nonprofit group, the Friends of Hildene (☎ 802/362-1788).

Robert Todd Lincoln built more than a house here. Hildene's 22 buildings include a dairy barn, a horse barn, a sugar house, a greenhouse, even a small observatory. You can roam the grounds, tour the 22-room **Georgian Revival mansion**, and inspect Lincoln family heirlooms mid-May through October, daily from 9:30am to 4pm (last tour). Admission costs $6 for adults, $2 for children. In winter, Hildene is the site of a ski-touring center. To find it, go two miles south along Vt. 7A from the intersection with Vt. 11/30—the intersection is the main crossroads in Manchester Center.

WHERE TO STAY

Christmas tours and a June food-and-wine fest are featured at some of the historic inns of Manchester. The first two weekends of December are very special.

✪ 1811 House

Manchester Village, VT 05254. ☎ **802/362-1811** or 800/432-1811. 14 rms. A/C. $110–$200 double. Rates include full breakfast. AE, MC, V. Free parking.

Think of someone special you'd like to spend a romantic, fun time with and picture yourselves here at the 1811 House. This historic 1770s house (the name came from when the inn first started taking guests) sits on seven acres of lawns and gardens, and you can take a stroll around the pond. If you sit in the tartan-clad pub (usually on the honor system), you can see out the back door across the gardens right up to the Equinox's new golf course. Bravo on the food. And the inn has so many single-malt liquors that the folks at the liquor store usually direct inquiries and samplers here for a taste test. The rooms are exquisite. Six have fireplaces, and three are contained in a separate carriage house. Children 16 and older are welcome. This is my favorite historic inn in Vermont.

✪ Equinox Hotel, Resort & Spa

Vt. 7A, Manchester, VT 05254. ☎ **802/362-4700** or 800/362-4747. Fax 802/362-1595. 144 rms, 19 suites. A/C TV TEL. $159–$289 single or double; $349–$549 suite. AE, DC, DISC, MC, V. Free parking behind the hotel.

The sprawling Equinox Hotel right in the center of town has undergone another face-lift. The Equinox saw its heyday in Victorian times, with four presidents as guests over the years. (It was almost five: Lincoln had reservations for 1865 but was assassinated.) As the inn's fame and clientele grew, wings and additions were added to the original building, making at last a vast, rambling wonder of a place. The extensive renovations a couple years back have set the hotel up for welcoming the 21st century. The Equinox has all the facilities of a luxury hotel and then some: an 18-hole golf course, a heated pool, three tennis courts, a health fitness center, a lounge, and a restaurant. You have a choice of the fine dining room or the inviting smart-casual dining room with its burning fireplace and adjoining lounge where entertainment is featured.

With the extensive renovations complete, guests find themselves in Vermont's best hotel, as it exhibits more style, class, and poshness than any other found in

Burlington or the major ski areas. The rooms are plush and comfortable, with fine furnishings, warm colors, and a tasteful and expensive look. For a real treat, book yourself into one of the cupola rooms, such as the Grant Suite.

Inn at Manchester

Vt. 7A (P.O. Box 41), Manchester, VT 05254. ☎ **802/362-1793** or 800/273-1793. Fax 802/362-3218. 14 rms, 4 suites. A/C. $95–$110 double; $130 suite. Rates include breakfast. AE, DISC, MC, V. Free parking.

This restored Vermont Victorian inn between Manchester Village and Manchester Center is surrounded by four acres on the outside and has plenty of room for guests in 14 rooms and suites in the inn, plus 4 more in the restored carriage house, where there's a separate lounge. The rooms bear the names of delightful mountain and meadow flowers, such as primrose, black-eyed Susan, and blue phlox. Antiques are placed carefully in all the rooms, and each bedroom has a different style of coordinated linens and comforters. Old prints, paintings, and posters, picked up by innkeepers Stan and Harriet Rosenberg during their travels, are found on walls throughout the inn. The inn has a pool and offers afternoon tea with wine and a cheese party on weekends.

Reluctant Panther Inn and Restaurant

West Rd., Manchester Village, VT 05254. ☎ **802/362-2568** or 800/822-2331. Fax 802/362-2586. 12 rms, 4 suites. A/C TV TEL. $165–$275 double; $275–$325 suite. Rates include full breakfast and à la carte dinner. AE, MC, V.

This lavender clapboard inn sitting on a marble foundation and surrounded by marble sidewalks and a marble terrace has a longstanding reputation in the village. The restaurant is wonderful and a good reason to stay put for dinner. The bar area is quaint and inviting, and the parlor room at the entry has real ash and maple leaves woven into the wallcovering. Rooms are equally as original and may feature a fireplace in the superior category or suites with whirlpool baths and fireplaces.

Village Country Inn

Vt. 7A, Manchester Village, VT 05254. ☎ **802/362-1792** or 800/370-0300. 16 rms, 18 suites. TV TEL. $140–$215 double; $210– suite. Rates include full breakfast and dinner. AE, DISC, MC, V. Free parking.

This historic 1889 inn has a big front porch that beckons you to come and linger. Inside is a stone fireplace, a tavern, and a garden-style dining room. The rooms are country-inspired with French overtones, with all the frilly details such as lace and down pillows. Rooms include all bed arrangements, even twins, to accommodate most needs. You can request an air-conditioned room. In 1995 the owners converted their former living quarters into three additional suites, so there's even more choice now.

Wilburton Inn

River Rd., Manchester Village, VT 05254. ☎ **802/362-2500** or 800/648-4944. 35 rms. A/C TEL. $150–$230 single or double. Rates include breakfast and dinner. AE, MC, V. Free parking. Directions: Go past the Equinox Hotel on Vt. 7A, turn right on River Road, and follow River Road a mile or so to the entrance on the left.

What a view. I mean, what a view! The stone wall winds up to the circular entry to this former retreat owned by RKO and now a no-smoking country inn with a handful of individual brick cottage buildings on 20 acres. To keep you busy (as if strolling the grounds with the valley below isn't enough), there's an outdoor pool and three tennis courts. This big old brick structure was built in 1902 and features a fine dining room with a view and some big public rooms with fireplaces. The furnishings are rather dowdy in the public areas, but the smiles and hospitality are genuine. Three of the guest rooms have fireplaces, and all have queen-size or king-size beds.

AN EASY EXCURSION

About eight miles south of Manchester is a lovely old village called **Arlington.** Forefathers of Arlington offered a princely sum of 50 acres to the first person to build a gristmill in the village—back in 1764. Through the years Arlington came into its own as the site of the state's first furnace foundry and then of the state's first chair factory; the furniture-building industry expanded, and the manufacture of railroad-car wheels soon followed.

Many of the original one-room schoolhouses that accent the pastoral countryside have been made into quaint (and sometimes stately) private residences. One famous resident, Ira Allen—brother of Ethan Allen (who is probably better known for upscale furniture than for his days as leader of the Green Mountain Boys)—created the University of Vermont with a sizable endowment in 1791, the same year Vermont became a state.

Norman Rockwell spent 1939 to 1953 in Arlington, using some of its residents as inspiration for his *Saturday Evening Post* covers. He lived in two homes on the shore of the Battenkill River, which weaves itself through the town. You can fly fish or canoe in the river or just sit on its shoreline and read a tome.

Special events include **Ethan Allen Days,** held during the third weekend in June; an **arts-and-crafts show** during the second weekend of August; **foliage season,** at its height in very late September to about October 10; and a Christmas event called the **St. Lucia Festival of Lights,** held on the second weekend in December.

WHERE TO STAY

Arlington Inn

Vt. 7A, Arlington, VT 05250. ☎ **802/375-6532,** or 800/443-9442. 13 rms. A/C. $65–$175 single or double. Rates include breakfast. AE, CB, DC, DISC, MC, V. Directions: Head eight miles south of Manchester Village on Vt. 7A.

Step back to the mid-1800s when Vermont politico Martin Chester Deming built this Greek Revival mansion. All the rooms, fitted with antiques, are named after family members and others who have owned this home (most of whom are buried in the cemetery across the street). You might walk around the lovely landscaped grounds or grab a match of tennis on the inn's own court. Besides the guest rooms, three with working fireplaces, there's a tavern/pub and a full dining room with attentive dinner service. Dining may consist of blackened breast of chicken on caramelized onions with wild blueberries and thyme, medallions of Vermont-raised beefalo crusted with peppercorn and herbs, or merlot demi-glace.

7 Dorset

7 miles N of Manchester

Settled in 1768, Dorset is one of the many villages in New England that are older than the American republic. It's a gem of a village, having kept its rural spirit and fine buildings intact over the centuries, and any new structures are required to add to the harmony of the village and its setting.

For a number of years, Dorset was an artists' and writers' summer resort, but these days it's usually only the successful in those fields who can afford to stay in one of Dorset's few charming old inns; rather, the village now caters to those who have become successful in the city and who need to get away to the peace of the countryside for a few days or weeks.

In Dorset the sidewalks are marble, and so is a nice church with Gothic touches not far from the town green. There's a marble quarry about a mile south of town, and besides supplying the soft, easily cut stone for a myriad of uses in Dorset, the quarry supplied most of the marble for the New York Public Library building.

GETTING THERE   By Car   Follow Vt. 30 north from Manchester.

ESSENTIALS   See "Manchester," above.

WHAT TO SEE AND DO

For recreation, Dorset has the **Dorset Playhouse** (☎ 802/867-5777), down past the church just near the end of the town green on Cheney Road. Plays are performed by professional actors June through August and community players September through May.

The **J. K. Adams Company Factory Store,** on Vt. 30 a mile south of town, makes fine wood products—carving boards, butcher blocks, kitchen worktables, even kitchen organizers like a spice block that holds 16 glass jars and revolves on a lazy Susan. All the items are available at a reduced price, and the "seconds" are sold at prices up to 40% off the norm, but compared to other outlet prices in New England, these are not too special.

WHERE TO STAY & DINE

Barrows House

Dorset, VT 05251. ☎ **802/867-4455** or 800/639-1620. 28 rms. A/C TV. $180–$230 double. Rates include breakfast and dinner. AE, DISC, DC, MC, V.

Besides loving the town of Dorset, you'll love the Barrows House with its main inn dating back to 1784 and the seven other white clapboard buildings on the property. There's a heated outdoor pool and two tennis courts, not to mention the fancy gardens to walk through. I even found fiddleheads growing in one patch outside the front door. Guest rooms are a mix of country inn and modern appointments. There are a handful of rooms upstairs in the main inn, but the ground floor is used mostly for dining. Small groups enjoy this place to hold their powwows and executive think-tank sessions. It's located six miles north of Manchester in the center of town.

Dorset Inn

Church St., Dorset, VT 05251. ☎ **802/867-5500.** Fax 802/867-5542. 31 rms. $150–$195 double. Rates include breakfast and dinner. AE, MC, V. Free parking.

The Dorset, which claims to be Vermont's oldest continuously operated inn, has several older rooms in the original building and a larger number of rooms in an artfully disguised modern addition that blends in well with the older part; 29 rooms are air-conditioned. The inn has a dining room, where lunch ranges from $7 to $12.50 and dinner courses go for $10 to $20.

8   Woodstock

16 miles W of White River Junction, 20 miles E of Sherburne Center (Killington), 14 miles NE of Plymouth

Woodstock was chartered in 1761, and within five years it had been designated the shire town (county seat) of Windsor County. The particular significance of these little facts is that they explain why the town is so beautiful today, why so many lovely buildings survive, and why the town escaped the ravages (and riches) brought by 19th-century industry. The industry here was government, the only pollutant from which is hot air, and this rises out of sight at once.

Besides its fine buildings, Woodstock boasts no fewer than four church bells made by Paul Revere. Three are still in service, but one cracked after two centuries of use and is now on display on the south porch of the Congregational church.

Woodstock is particularly well situated in a beautiful valley of the Ottaquechee River, with mountains all around. In winter, skiers can be put up in the town while they spend the day on the slopes of Mount Tom or Suicide Six.

GETTING THERE   By Car   From I-89 or I-91, follow U.S. 4 west.

ESSENTIALS   The **telephone area code** is **802.** From late June through the foliage season, there's a **town information booth** (☎ 802/457-1042) in service on the village green, where you can get a free village map and list of town businesses. Otherwise, contact the **Woodstock Area Chamber of Commerce,** 18 Central St. (P.O. Box 486), Woodstock, VT 05091 (☎ **802/457-3555**).

WHAT TO SEE & DO

SIGHTS   The Woodstock Historical Society's **Dana House Museum,** on Elm Street (☎ 802/457-1822), just around the corner from the green, is open for visits from early May through late October, Monday through Saturday from 10am to 5pm and Sunday from 2 to 5pm. They once charged admission but lately have changed that policy, so everyone visits for free now. The collections include furniture, decorative arts, antique toys, paintings, textiles, historic clothing, and local artifacts. There's a research library and museum gift shop on the premises.

In your walks around town, you might want to look for the **three covered bridges** across the Ottaquechee, including one built in 1969 and rebuilt five years later—Middle Bridge, just off the green in the middle of town.

On the far side of the Ottaquechee from the town green is a cemetery, and at the east edge of the cemetery is the beginning of a walking trail. The **Billings Park Trails** are maintained by the town and are yours to enjoy for free.

SKIING   Woodstock was the site of the first ski tow in the United States—a rope on a pulley that pulled skiers up the slopes in a farmer's field. Today a well-known ski area called Suicide Six is close by. In addition, the **Woodstock Ski Touring Center,** at the Woodstock Country Club, Vt. 106, Woodstock, VT 05091 (☎ 802/457-6674 or 800/448-7900), has nearly 50 miles of marked trails for skating and classic technique, plus equipment rental, a cross-country ski shop, a restaurant and lounge, lessons, ski tours, a wood-fired trailside log cabin, and midweek ski-free plans with the Woodstock Inn (☎ 800/448-7900). An indoor sports center is located a mile away and connects to cross-country trails (discounted combination cross-country-ski/sports-center passes are available).

Suicide Six (despite the terrifying name) is a fine midsize family ski area with two double-chair lifts and a J-bar on the beginners' slope. Located three miles north of Woodstock on Vt. 12, it also offers midweek ski-free plans with the Woodstock Inn. Package plans are available through the inn; there is 50% snowmaking capability, and lessons and equipment can be had on the spot in a new base lodge that also houses a ski-rental shop, a restaurant, and a lounge (☎ 802/457-1666). This number does not operate in summer.

You can stay in Woodstock and ski elsewhere, of course; the **Killington and Pico ski areas,** just a short drive away, present all the challenge and facilities a skier could want.

ESPECIALLY FOR KIDS   Less than half a mile north of the village center is **Billings Farm & Museum,** Vt. 12 and River Road (☎ 802/457-2355). This working farm dates back to 1871, when owner Frederick Billings, a railroad entrepreneur, began importing purebred cows from the Isle of Jersey. His farm prospered, and today it is operated as an agricultural museum. Children have the opportunity to milk a cow, see basket weavers at work, watch an oxen pull, learn about chickens, walk through historical gardens, and view an 1890 farmhouse where butter is churned and ice-cream treats are served on the adjoining patio. Admission, which allows you to leave and return the same day, is $6 for adults, $5 for seniors, $3 for children 6 to 17, and free for those under 6. The farm and museum are open May to October 31, daily from 10am to 5pm; on November weekends and the last two weekends in December, 10am to 4pm.

A NEARBY ATTRACTION   While in Woodstock, take a spin over to the **Quechee Gorge,** eight miles to the east. The highway bridge carries U.S. 4 right across the picturesque gorge; below, the Ottauquechee River slips swiftly between boulders and jagged rock walls. The Grand Canyon it's not, but pretty? Definitely.

For the best view, follow the signs to the viewpoint north of the highway. Or enter Quechee State Park, on the east side of the gorge, and take the short hiking trail down to the edge of the gorge. The walk will take 15 minutes, one-way. By the way, there's camping and picnicking at Quechee State Park.

WHERE TO STAY

✪ Jackson House Inn
37 U.S. 4 West, Woodstock, VT 05091. ☎ **802/457-2065.** 9 rms, 3 suites. $135–$165 double; $195–$250 suite. Rates include full breakfast. No credit cards. Free parking.

The Jackson House vies for the top spot in my heart as Vermont's best inn (and best-kept secret) along with the 1811 House of Manchester Village and the Inn at the Round Barn Farm in Waitsfield. Come here if you want to be enveloped by country warmth. The inn was the home of a lumber baron who artfully decorated each room in different woods, from maple to cherry. The room Gloria Swanson used to stay in is popular today and is furnished with old photos; other rooms may have New England country, Victorian, or French Empire antiques. Breakfasts are an event and feature such items as a Santa Fe omelet or baked apples stuffed with mincemeat. Hors d'oeuvres and wine and champagne are offered in the evenings. New to the inn is a spa and an exercise room and steam room. You'll find Jackson House 1 1/2 miles west of the oval in the center of Woodstock. Children under 14 are not recommended—and no pets.

Kedron Valley Inn

Vt. 106, South Woodstock, VT 05071. ☎ **802/457-1473.** 27 rms, 2 suites. TV. $97–$195 double; $195–$215 suite. Rates include breakfast. AE, DISC, MC, V.

Innkeepers Max and Merrily Comins offer warm hospitality, gourmet cuisine, and some of Woodstock's most charming accommodations at the Kedron Valley Inn, located just five miles south of town. The inn has been lovingly decorated by Merrily, who displays treasured family heirlooms throughout, from her grandmother's wedding dress to a wonderful collection of antique quilts. Each room has unique features; most have queen canopy beds, while others offer the cozy warmth of Franklin stoves or fireplaces. A few have private decks. One deluxe suite even boasts a Jacuzzi.

Each morning there's a different kind of homemade muffin at breakfast, which you can enjoy along with an omelet or blueberry pancakes. The dinner menu features dishes ranging from rack of lamb or grilled pork to veal and salmon, along with an impressive selection of wines. And you'll certainly want to curl up by the fire to enjoy a nightcap in the bar, which is graced with a grand piano.

Sports lovers will find no shortage of activities at the Kedron, no matter what the season. In winter, there's downhill or cross-country skiing, and sleigh rides at the Kedron Valley Stables; the summer months bring fishing and swimming in the inn's private pond, as well as horseback riding, tennis, and golf. And pet owners, take heart: Your dog will receive an enthusiastic welcome at the Kedron.

Shire Motel

46 Pleasant St., Woodstock, VT 05091. ☎ **802/457-2211.** 33 rms. A/C MINIBAR TV TEL. $48–$95 double. AE, DISC, MC, V. Free parking.

If you want a fancy place to stay, try the Woodstock Inn. But if you want comfortable and convenient lodgings at a good price, head straight for the Shire Motel, just east of the center. I've found the proprietors to be particularly helpful and friendly. It's well kept and has the advantage of being within walking distance of the village green. Their latest amendment is to update the existing rooms and to add seven new ones.

Twin Farms

Barnard, VT 05031. ☎ **802/234-9999** or 800/894-6327. Fax 802/234-9990. 4 rms, 2 suites, 7 cottages. MINIBAR TV TEL. $700–$850 double; $850 suite for two; $1,050–$1,500 cottage for two. 15% gratuity extra. Rates include all meals and liquor. AE, DISC, MC, V. Closed Apr. Directions: From the village of Woodstock, take Vt. 12 north to Barnard and the General Store, turn right, and proceed about half a mile to the gate on the right.

Simply put, Twin Farms is the most luxurious and expensive lodging establishment in New England as well as one of the finest operations in the United States. Staying here is like having a few days at your very own estate. Twin Farms—once the home of Nobel Prize winner Sinclair Lewis and his wife, writer Dorothy Thompson—captures the romance and splendor of a bygone era. The 1795 farmhouse is nothing short of sumptuous. The entry hall boasts a wonderful hand-painted pastoral scene that leads up the stairs to the two second-floor guest rooms, a parlor with game boards where afternoon tea is served, a living room with another blazing fireplace overlooking the small terrace and the valley, the Great Room with its loft library, a colonial dining room once used by the writing team to entertain, and the inn's formal dining room with two fireplaces.

All the guest rooms offer finely crafted fireplaces, luxury baths with tubs designed for relaxing, billowy beds with Egyptian cottons and down comforters in designer fabrics, and ample details to keep you poking around for hours. The main house contains four rooms, while the lodge offers two spacious suites (one with a private entrance and terrace overlooking a slope of wildflowers and ski runs) sharing an extra common living room with impressive artwork and its own fireplace. Also on the nearly 240 acres are seven separate cottages with museum-quality artwork and magnificent designs inside and secluded surroundings outside.

Four of the cottages were new in 1995. The Orchard Cottage is set under a spruce tree surounded by an apple orchard and features two hand-carved granite fireplaces. Heavenward is a herringbone woven split-ash ceiling, and underfoot are white-ash floors whereupon designers have set cranberry chenile club chairs and hand-woven rugs. The Barn Cottage is designed in Scandinavian Grambrel architecture, with local stone and cedar shingles. The fireplace rises from the floor to the top of the post-and-beam ceiling. A split-log staircase rises up to a loft with a day bed and tall windows.

For lingering, there's the pub with a full help-yourself bar, a pool table at one end, and a commanding fireplace framed by sofas and other lodge-type appointments at the other. A remote-control jukebox plays everything from country to Gershwin. Below is a full-size fitness center with a complete line of workout stations. As a special treat, a Japanese soaking tub contained in its own building nearby is open 24 hours for a relaxing time amid the towering trees you can almost reach out and touch. Two unlit tennis courts, hiking and cross-country ski trails, downhill ski trails with a lift, and mountain bikes and canoes are all provided for your exclusive diversion. After lunch in winter, you might enjoy mulled wine in the pub, followed by a sleigh ride through the woods. The pond is groomed for skating in winter and stocked for fishing in summer.

Meals and cocktails are taken in a variety of locales—from along the stream, to the terrace, to a picnic at the pond (replete with canoes). All meals are an event, but dressing up for dinner isn't required; after all, you're on vacation. A maximum of 26 adults are accommodated on the premises.

Woodstock Inn and Resort

14 The Green, Woodstock, VT 05091. ☎ **802/457-1100** or 800/448-7900. Fax 802/457-3824. 143 rms. A/C TV TEL. $145–$299 double. AE, MC, V. Free parking.

This deluxe inn was the pet project of Laurance Rockefeller. The inn, a stately white clapboard mansion with a bricked townhouse addition, faces South Street on one side and the village's oval green in front. The service is attentive; the food very well prepared, with the accent on regional fare; and the accommodations first rate. The premier rooms are in the townhouse section artfully adjoining the original inn, where rooms have colonial-inspired appointments, luxury baths, VCRs, cable TVs, alcoves with book shelves, and fine linens and window treatments. The courtyard features a Paul Revere bell as its focal point. There's an extensive health facility owned by the inn down the road about two miles, with everything from swimming to aerobics and a Robert Trent Jones, Sr., championship golf course. Suicide Six ski area and the Woodstock Ski Touring Center are both owned and operated by the inn.

WHERE TO DINE

Bentleys of Woodstock

3 Elm St. ☎ **802/457-3232.** Reservations recommended in peak season. Main courses $12–$19; lunch $10–$14; dinner $25–$35. AE, DC, MC, V. Sun–Fri 11:30am–2am, Sat 11:30am–1:30am. Closed Thanksgiving. CONTINENTAL.

In its various dining rooms, Bentleys, in the center of town, has captured the spirit of a Victorian tavern but without the heaviness: a pillared bar with potted palms, bentwood chairs, and Victorian sofas. The crowd is eclectic, the prices are moderate, and the food is good and simple or good and fancy. Lunch is burgers, sandwiches, light-lunch plates, and salads; for dinner, these same dishes are on order, or you can indulge in a maple-mustard chicken, trout, duckling, or creative pasta dishes. There's live entertainment some evenings. The chef is earning rave reviews, and if you're here on Friday or Saturday at 10pm, you'll see the ceiling roll back to transform the dining room into a dance club replete with a sophisticated light show. Bentley's is just a few steps across the village green.

Mountain Creamery

33 Central St. ☎ **802/457-1715.** Reservations not accepted. Ice cream $1.25; pie $3.25; sandwiches $4.25–$5.50. No credit cards. Daily 7am–5pm. ICE CREAM/COFFEE SHOP.

Right in the center of town, this unpretentious coffee shop does a brisk local and tourist business. Many people stop by for an ice cream from the lower-level fountain, while others drop in for something more substantial such as the mountainhigh apple pie ($3.50) made on the premises. If you stop in for breakfast, there are plenty of egg dishes and muffins to jump-start your morning. Grab something quick and head for the slopes in Killington or Pico 25 minutes away!

The Prince and the Pauper

24 Elm St. ☎ **802/457-1818.** Reservations recommended. Fixed-price dinner $30. DISC, MC, V. Dinner only, Sun–Thurs 6–9pm, Fri–Sat 6–9:30pm. CONTINENTAL.

The Prince and the Pauper is down an alley named Dana Lane, which runs alongside the Woodstock Historical Society's building in the center of town. Lowbeamed ceilings, candle lanterns casting a golden aura onto the small tables, a worldly clientele, and good conversation are what make the mood here, but the exotic array of dishes and delicacies adds to it: Where else would you find boneless rack of lamb baked in a puff pastry? Roast duckling is on the menu, too, which changes frequently, of course, but the intimate atmosphere and the international flair remain. A lighter tavern or bistro menu is offered for $9.95 to $14.95, and you can order à la carte from the main menu, too. The lounge opens at 5pm. There's outdoor seating in summer.

9 Plymouth

14 miles SW of Woodstock, 36 miles N of Grafton, 10 miles S of Sherburne Center (Killington)

GETTING THERE   By Car   Follow U.S. 4 west from Woodstock, then Vt. 100A; Vt. 100, the main north-south road through central Vermont, passes one mile west of Plymouth.

ESSENTIALS   See "Woodstock," above.

WHAT TO SEE AND DO

Calvin Coolidge was born in this tiny Vermont hamlet not far from the intersection of Vt. 100 and Vt. 100A, and you can visit the **Coolidge Homestead** and the **Calvin Coolidge Birthplace** (☎ 802/672-3773). The former president's early history is interesting, but the story of his "inauguration" is full of fascination. While he was vice president, Mr. Coolidge came to Plymouth for a vacation in August 1923. Before he could even unwind, news came that President Harding was dead and that he, Calvin Coolidge, was the 30th president of the United States. But he had to take the oath of office! The local notary public in the tiny town was none other than the new president's own father, Col. John Coolidge, and it was Colonel John who—as the only judicial official handy—administered the oath to his son by the light of a kerosene lamp at 2:47am, August 3, 1923.

You can visit the Homestead, the Birthplace, the **Wilder Barn** (a farmer's museum), the village church, the cemetery where President Coolidge is buried, and **Wilder House,** once the home of Coolidge's mother. Wilder House today holds a small restaurant and lunch counter. Coolidge Hall served as the summer White House in 1924.

The historic site is open from late May through mid-October, daily from 9:30am to 5:30pm. Admission for adults costs $4.50, children under 14 years of age enter for free, and a family ticket costs $16.

Don't miss Plymouth's outstanding attraction, the **Plymouth Cheese Company** (☎ 802/672-3650). The company's president, John Coolidge, is a scion of the famous village clan. Come to see the delicious Vermont granular-curd cheese being made on Monday through Wednesday from 11am to 1pm, or come to sample and purchase the cheese Monday through Saturday from 8am to 5:30pm and Sunday from 9am to 5:30pm. The cheese comes cut to order by the ounce or the pound, or in three- and five-pound wheels, and it's aged 3, 6, or 12 months to produce mild, medium, or sharp Cheddar. Cheeses are also available flavored with sage, caraway, garlic, or dill. By the way, watching the cheese-making costs nothing; a five-pound wheel costs $32.

10 Killington

10 miles N of Plymouth, 20 miles W of Woodstock, 12 miles E of Rutland

For many skiers, Killington is the only word they have to hear before they begin thinking snow. The resort is one of Vermont's prime ski areas and is especially noted for its progressive approach to development of its facilities (for instance, the addition of "gladed" ski trails, which give one the feeling of skiing right in the forest) and its snow-making and grooming capabilities. But in recent years Killington has expanded its breadth of activities so that now you can go there for skiing in winter, organized backpacking and camping trips in the summer, tennis practice and lessons, a golf course, or the summer playhouse and the Hartford Ballet. The resort is booming, but it's laid out so well on the side of the mountain that there's plenty of room for all the activities and the visitors.

GETTING THERE   By Car   Follow U.S. 4 or Vt. 100 to Killington Road.

ESSENTIALS   The **telephone area code** is **802.** The whole Killington area, which is part of the town of Sherburne, is organized with the **Killington Lodging Bureau** (☎ **802/773-1330,** or **800/621-6867**) in charge of making room reservations for you. You can call or write to a lodge or motel directly, or you can call the lodging bureau to see what's available. The **Killington and Pico Areas Association,** P.O. Box 114, Killington, VT 05751 (☎ **802/773-4181**), also maintains an **information booth** (☎ **802/775-7070**) at the junction of U.S. 4 and Vt. 100 in Sherburne, at Southworth's Ski Shop; the booth is open in summer and fall, daily from 10am to 6pm.

WHAT TO SEE & DO

SKIING AT KILLINGTON & PICO   Well, here you have it: one of the best-managed ski areas in the United States, with good snow-making capability, a variety of trails, a well-organized ski school, a very accessible location, lots of parking, three lounges, quick food service or a nice restaurant, several bars, and a long skiing season—what more can I say? The vertical drop is more than 3,000 feet; there are six chair lifts, a gondola said to be the longest in the world, and four Poma lifts, all with a total capacity of 10,000 skiers per hour. If that sounds like a mob scene, I must admit that it does get crowded but also that it's a big mountain and there seems to be room for everyone.

If you don't choose a package plan that includes room, meals, and lift tickets, Killington Resort has various packages just for the slopes, including special rates on lifts for two to seven days, or plans with which you get lifts and lessons for two to seven days at reduced rates, or all three—lifts, lessons, and equipment rentals—for one price.

At Pico (*pie*-ko) Peak near Killington, there are five chair lifts, two T-bars, a vertical drop of 2,000 feet, and plenty of easy parking. It's a good, challenging area. With the resort's powerful snow-making capabilities, the Killington area traditionally has the longest ski season in the East, from October to mid-June.

SUMMER AT KILLINGTON   Everyone coming to the Killington area will want to take the **Killington Chairlift** (☎ 802/422-3333 or 800/372-2007) to reach the 4,241-foot summit of Mount Killington. They say that this was the point from which the territory of "Verdmont" (green mountain) was christened in 1763. At the top you'll find a cafeteria, cocktail lounge, observation deck, and a self-guided nature trail. The chair lift operates all summer.

The base station for the chair lift is at the top of Killington Road; it runs from early June through Labor Day, and mid-September to early October, daily from 10am to 4pm. Round-trip tickets are $10 for adults, $5 for children 6 to 12, free for kids under 6.

A SHOPPING EXCURSION   One of Vermont's widely acclaimed crafts is hand-forged wrought iron. Companies like L. L. Bean, Eddie Bauer, and Pottery Barn sell items forged in Vermont. A main supplier of these beautiful lamps, candleholders, cabinetry hardware, fireplace utensils, and other wrought-iron furniture is **Hubbardton Forge.** An afternoon excursion there from Killington or via Rutland (depending on where in the Killington area you're staying) makes for an interesting and productive trip.

The foundry, located on Vt. 30 in Castleton (just west of Rutland), no longer offers tours of Hubbardton Forge, but its products can be purchased, often at 30% savings or more, in nearby Cuttingsville. **Vermont Industries,** Vt. 103 in Cuttingsville (☎ 800/639-1715), was once the factory store (until October 1993) of Hubbardton Forge when private ownership took over the retail portion. Hubbardton still supplies all its factory store quality items to Vermont Industries, which will ship your item home if you don't want to take it with you. The red barn with seven rooms of furniture and other tin, pewter, and wrought-iron items is located about 10 miles south of Rutland and is open daily from 10am to 5pm; call ahead for holidays hours, as they may decide to close.

From Vt. 4, go south four miles on U.S. 7 to Vt. 103 south toward Ludlow. The store is five miles ahead on the left. From Killington, take Vt. 100 south to Vt. 103 north to the store on the right. For a catalog, send $2 to Vermont Industries, Vt. 103 (Box 301D), Cuttingsville, VT 05738. Your $2 will be refunded with your first order.

WHERE TO STAY

Killington is a well-organized resort community, and so virtually all activities here are organized around various package plans designed to save visitors money over the normal daily rates. A package usually includes lodging, meals, and the price of the activity: lift tickets, tennis lessons, horseback riding, backpacking trips. In ski season, most inns operate on the Modified American Plan (MAP), in which you are required to take breakfast and dinner with your room. Call the lodging bureau (☎ 802/773-1330 or 800/621-6867) to ask about the package plans, or to make reservations; or send a card to Killington Ski Area, Killington, VT 05751, asking for information on ski, hiking, or tennis package plans.

Trailside Lodge at Killington

Coffee House Rd., Killington, VT 05751. ☎ **802/422-3532** or 800/447-2209. 28 rms. Fall foliage season (Sept 15–Oct 15; including breakfast), $65 double. The rest of the year (including breakfast and dinner), $45–122 double. MC, V. Free parking.

This former farmhouse, near Vt. 100 about 2 ¹/₂ miles off U.S. 4, is youthful and energetic and the best of its type in Killington. You won't find friendlier folks than Fred and Susan Field anywhere. Imagine Club Med on the cheap sans the beach atmosphere, and you'll understand the feeling here. Bike tours make this popular in summer, and skiers love it in winter, especially the family table servings in the dining room, where you'll always have plenty to eat. There's a full-service bar and a whirlpool for socializing or maybe even late-in-the-evening romancing. Accommodations are dormitorylike—some come with several twin beds and a double arrangement, but most with bunk styling. Don't be dismayed: If you book a double, there will be only two of you, no matter how many beds the room takes! And there's cross-country skiing at your doorstep to boot. As an added attraction, the new Green Mountain National Golf Course is almost in the front yard. Packages with meals might be as low as $35 per person.

WHERE TO DINE

Hemingway's Restaurant

U.S. 4. ☎ **802/422-3886.** Reservations recommended. Fixed-price four-course dinner $36–$48. AE, CB, DC, MC, V. Dinner only, Wed–Sun 6– 10pm. Closed mid-Apr to mid-May. AMERICAN.

Established in a restored Vermont farmhouse, the restaurant has won several awards for its dishes. You might start dinner (the only meal served) by ordering hand-rolled fettuccine with smoked trout and scallions or consommé of rabbit; then go on to shrimp with dark rum and currants or grilled pheasant with beaujolais. There's also a tasting menu that includes wine. The wine list is full and well balanced, everything from Château Lafite-Rothschild to Sutter Home white zinfandel.

11 Middlebury

32 miles N of Rutland, 34 miles S of Burlington

Like its more famous counterpart of Hanover, N.H., the town of Middlebury is replete with beautiful old Georgian and 19th-century buildings, a small college of a high quality, and a pretty town green. Hanover has Dartmouth, and Middlebury has Middlebury College, but only Middlebury has the Vermont State Craft Center at Frog Hollow and the University of Vermont's Morgan Horse Farm—but more of that later.

GETTING THERE   By Car   Several highways converge at Middlebury, including U.S. 7, Vt. 23, Vt. 30, and Vt. 125.

ESSENTIALS   The **telephone area code** is **802.** The **Addison County Chamber of Commerce,** 2 Court St., Middlebury, VT 05753 (☎ **802/388-7951**), has an information office in the center of town, on the left-hand side as you come into Middlebury from the south (on U.S. 7) or the east (Vt. 125). The office is open during normal business hours.

WHAT TO SEE & DO

Once you've settled in and taken a stroll around this charming town, wander over to **Middlebury College** for a look at its exceptionally pretty campus and old granite buildings. Those in need of information about the college can get it by dropping in at the admissions office in Emma Willard House on Main Street (Vt. 30). Middlebury was founded by local people in the 19th century and went on to become a high-quality school. Robert Frost's participation in the Breadloaf Writers' Conference (held on Middlebury's mountain campus, close to nearby Ripton) spread the college's reputation even further.

Robert Frost wasn't the only person of renown to tramp the streets of Middlebury. A man named John Deere was an apprentice here from 1821 to 1825, after which he moved to Illinois and invented the world's first steel moldboard plow, making his name a household word in farms across the nation.

Deere's apprenticeship took place at Frog Hollow, which is down the hill from Court House Square. Today the **Vermont State Craft Center** at Frog Hollow, on Mill Street (☎ 802/388-3177), features traditional and modern crafts in various media by more than 300 juried Vermont craftspeople. It's open all year, Monday through Saturday from 9:30am to 5pm and Sunday from noon to 5pm. They also have a center in Burlington, at 85 Church St. (☎ 802/863-6458), and in Manchester, across from the Equinox Hotel (☎ 802/362-3321).

To see the magnificent steeds at the **University of Vermont's Morgan Horse Farm** (☎ 802/388-2011), head west on Vt. 125 from Middlebury, turn right onto Vt. 23 (Weybridge Street), and follow the signs to the farm for about 2 ¹/₂ miles. Admission to the farm is $3.50 per adult, $2 for teens (kids under 12 get in for free); it's open from May through October, daily from 9am to 4pm. Once on this working farm, you'll get a guided tour of the stables, an audiovisual presentation about the farm and the Morgan horse, and the chance to roam the farm's spacious grounds to see the Morgans in training or playing, and perhaps have a picnic at the picnic area.

WHERE TO STAY & DINE

The Addison County Chamber of Commerce, 2 Court St., Middlebury, Vt. 05753 (☎ 802/388-7951; fax 802/388-8066), maintains a list of homeowners who rent rooms to visitors. When crowds of parents swell the town for graduation or alumni return for homecoming, the town's lodging places are always filled. The "Homeowners Listing" is a very useful service. Drop by or call the chamber's information office.

Middlebury Inn and Motel

20 Court House Sq., Middlebury, VT 05753. ☎ **802/388-4961** or 800/842-4666. 75 rms. A/C TV TEL. $86–$170 double. Children under 18 stay free in parents' room. Pets $6 per day extra. AE, DC, DISC, MC, V. Free parking.

This historic 1827 inn dominates the square even more than the red-brick courthouse just up the hill from it. Guest rooms are in several locations: in the inn itself, in the Hubbard House attached to the inn, in the Victorian-style Porter Mansion, and in a modern motel annex. Price is determined by room size and location (and thus the views). The inn has its own dining room, which serves breakfast, brunch, lunch, and dinner.

Waybury Inn

Vt. 125, East Middlebury, VT 05740. ☎ **802/388-4015** or 800/348-1810. 14 rms. summer, $85–$115 double; off-season, $75–$115 double. Rates include breakfast. Children get their own room at half the room price. DISC, MC, V. Free parking.

As soon as you come up the front walk, you'll recognize the Stratford Inn, or rather, the Waybury Inn. You see, the Waybury Inn is the real-life inspiration for the hit television comedy "Newhart," set in a Vermont country inn. You won't find Bob Newhart or Mary Frann tending the front desk, but you'll find lots of other familiar connections with the show. Rooms in the cozy, quaint (1810) inn have been refurbished in period style; five rooms are air-conditioned. The inn provides guests with bikes and croquet equipment. The Waybury's dining room serves dinner and Sunday brunch at moderate prices. At dinnertime, a full-course meal of garden salad, main course, vegetables, potato, and bread made right in the inn will cost between $13 and $17. There's also a fully licensed tavern.

12 Sugarbush, Warren & Waitsfield

WAITSFIELD

20 miles SW of Montpelier, 22 miles S of Stowe, 6 miles N of Warren

GETTING THERE By Car Both Warren and Waitsfield are on Vt. 100. The area centered on Warren, along Vt. 100, can boast three well-known ski resorts: Sugarbush Valley, Mad River Glen, and Sugarbush North. Although much of the crowd here comes to stay in its own condominiums, a number of inns, motels, and guesthouses amply provide for the rest.

ESSENTIALS The **telephone area code** is **802.** The **Sugarbush Chamber of Commerce,** Vt. 100 (P.O. Box 173), Waitsfield, VT 05673 (☎ **802/496-3409** or **800/828-4748**), will help you out with information regarding lodging, dining, events, and activities, and will also reserve accommodations for you, if you wish. The chamber of commerce is open daily during the summer and winter seasons, weekdays at other times of the year.

WHAT TO SEE & DO

Sugarbush has lots of opportunities for good skiing, and although the resort is not so highly ramified as those at Mount Snow, Killington, or Stowe, well, perhaps that's part of the charm here—an absence of big-time crowds. That doesn't mean you'll have no wait for the lift lines, though. Short lift lines these days are only at places with reserved-seat lift tickets or at places not worth skiing—and Sugarbush, Sugarbush North, and Mad River Glen are not among them.

SUGARBUSH VALLEY At Sugarbush proper, the slopes and trails come down almost 2,500 feet from top to bottom, and they're laid out so that close to half of them are rated as suitable for expert skiers. Lifts include a gondola almost two miles long, four chair lifts, and a Poma. Rentals, instruction, and cross-country ski trails are all part of the establishment. The ski school offers a ski-week "saturation skiing workshop," which claims to instruct students in centeredness and energy awareness as well as techniques on the slopes. Lots of package plans are up for grabs—call the information numbers given at the beginning of this section.

MAD RIVER GLEN   Mad River Glen is an easy drive from Waitsfield center on Vt. 17. This is a smaller area than Sugarbush, but still a good size, with four chair lifts all radiating out from one base area. The vertical drop is 2,000 feet, and the preponderance of trails (three-quarters of them) are for moderately well-trained or expert skiers. Mad River Glen has a ski shop, a rental shop, a ski school, and a nursery. For information, contact Mad River Glen, Waitsfield, VT 05673 (☎ 802/496-3551). Or call the ski and snow line (☎ 802/496-2001, or 800/ 696-2001 outside Vermont).

SUGARBUSH NORTH & SOUTH   Sugarbush consists of two mountains: Sugarbush South and Sugarbush North. Together they provide 80 trails and 16 lifts, the majority rated intermediate and expert. Equipment and lessons are yours at the base stations for the appropriate fees.

Sugarbush South rises to two peaks nearly 4,000 feet high. Below, nine lifts whisk you around the rolling ridges. The trails and slopes at Sugarbush North descend 2,600 feet from top to bottom, and about half the runs are classed as good for the median-level skier. But a look at the mountain trail plan will show you that taking the four-person chair lift to the top of Mt. Ellen will start you on some very long and pretty tricky runs. Sugarbush North has 36 trails and slopes in all— and usually a good amount of cover for a long season. For lodging information, call ☎ 802/583-2381 or 800/53-SUGAR.

The air currents around Sugarbush make it good for soaring or gliding, and the Sugarbush Soaring Association, P.O. Box 123, Warren, VT 05674 (☎ 802/ 496-2290), can fill you in on getting airborne. Glider rides and lessons are offered from May through November, daily from 9am to 5pm; call or write for details. Just so you'll know: You can qualify for solo glider flights in less than two weeks of full daily lessons and flights.

WHERE TO STAY & DINE

✪ Inn at the Round Barn Farm

East Warren Rd., Waitsfield, VT 05673. ☎ **802/496-2276.** 7 rms, 4 suites. A/C TV TEL. $100–$185 double; $155–$185 suite. Rates include breakfast. AE, MC, V. Free parking.

This is one of my favorite places to be. From the outside it looks typical of the rural Vermont countryside; inside has a delightful, cheerful, and designer atmosphere. Five ponds dot the landscaped backyard on this 85-acre former dairy farm. The library has wide pine floors, a fireplace, and classical music. The breakfast room is French-inspired and overlooks the ponds and gardens in the rear. A games room offers billiards and board games. The round barn has been restored and has an indoor pool; it's used mostly for functions. The rooms and suites are luxurious, especially the latter, and may be the best inn rooms in the state. Five rooms have four-poster beds, three have private whirlpools. You'll be hard-pressed to find better anywhere in New England. It's about 1 1/2 miles off Vt. 100 at Bridge Street.

Sugarbush Inn

Sugarbush Access Rd., Warren, VT 05674. ☎ **802/583-2301** or 800/53-SUGAR. 46 rms. A/C TV TEL. $96–$150 double (including breakfast). AE, DC, DISC, MC, V. Free parking.

With its own pools (indoor and outdoor), batteries of tennis courts, golf course, and nature paths through the woods, the Sugarbush Inn, two miles north of Warren, is the area's poshest resort inn. Rooms are tasteful and very comfy. The inn is part of the Sugarbush ski resort but doesn't enjoy the reputation it once had.

EASY EXCURSIONS

MONTPELIER   The reason to take a detour and visit Montpelier, the state capital of Vermont, is to take a look at the **capitol building,** a comely classical structure modeled on the Grecian Temple of Theseus. It's made of granite from nearby Barre, of course, but the dome is of wood covered in copper and then gilded. The State House will surprise you—it's so small—but then you'll notice that the capital city, Montpelier, is pretty small, too; and thus you realize that you're in the midst of the most rural state in the Union, 48th in population (only about half a million Vermonters in all, spread through almost 10,000 square miles). In fact, a Vermont schoolchild once wrote that in Vermont "the trees are close together and the people are far apart."

BARRE   The first thing you must know about Barre is that its name is pronounced like the name "Barry," and not like a drinking place. The next thing to know is that Barre is the **granite capital of the world,** having the world's largest quarry for the stone, and also a good number of the world's finest craftspeople to work it. Guided tours of the quarries and the workshops are offered daily and prove a fascinating way to spend a few hours, but even more fascinating is a visit to the **Hope Cemetery** on Vt. 14, eight-tenths of a mile north of the U.S. 302/Vt. 14 intersection. The cemetery has two gates and is open until sunset. We speak of making "monuments to survive ourselves," and in Barre the phrase is literal! Stonecutters here create the monument of their dreams for their own resting places. You'll see a balanced granite cube resting precariously on one corner, self-portraits and statues, a ponderous granite armchair, even a relief of a husband and wife sitting up in bed, hands joined in eternal friendship. Hope Cemetery is more like a sculpture garden, a touching memorial to artisans and artists who came here from many parts of the world.

The **Rock of Ages quarry** (☎ 802/476-3119) is open from the beginning of May through October, with tours every day from 8:30am to 5pm, free. A shuttle-bus tour costs $3.50 for adults, $1 for children.

13 Stowe

22 miles N of Waitsfield, 36 miles E of Burlington

GETTING THERE   **By Bus**   See the beginning of this chapter.

By Car   Stowe is on Vt. 100, 10 miles north of I-89 Exit 10.

ESSENTIALS   The **telephone area code** is **802.** Businesses in the area are organized into the **Stowe Area Association,** P.O. Box 1320, Stowe, VT 05672 (☎ **802/253-6617** or **800/24-STOWE**). The information office there, in the center of Stowe very near the intersection of Vt. 100 and Vt. 108 (the Mountain Road), is open daily in ski season from 9am to 9pm, to 6pm the rest of the year. If you don't have a reservation when you arrive in Stowe, drop in here for help.

For **information on snow conditions** in the area, call **802/253-3600** in the winter. The lodges and inns around Stowe adopt alpine or central European names, and although the terrain here is hardly "alpine," somehow the names make sense. The village is dominated by Vermont's highest mountain, Mount Mansfield (4,393 feet), certainly no Matterhorn; but there's definitely a European feeling in Stowe, the feeling one has in some tiny Austrian village amid emerald-green rolling hills, winding roads, and steep slopes. Perhaps it's the lushness (in summer) of the lawns, forests, and wildflowers, or perhaps it's the rain and mists—Lamoille County is said to have the greatest amount of precipitation in the state—which make everything so lush. Whatever, there is certainly an especially attractive air about Stowe.

The frequent rain is not a liability either, for local people learn to plan on it, and the earth scents after the rain are part of the pleasure of Stowe. And besides, it's all this precipitation that makes Stowe one of the best skiing areas in the East, with plenty of deep cover and a long season.

Winter or summer, the narrow rocky mountain defile known as Smuggler's Notch is a dramatic place for a hike or a drive, and is just another one of those things that make Stowe special.

WHAT TO SEE & DO

Much of the territory around Stowe is part of Vermont's **Mount Mansfield State Forest and Park,** and for summer visitors that means hiking trails (especially the Long Trail from Massachusetts to Canada), camping areas, and picnicking. Winter visitors will want to note the state ski area, and Spruce Peak ski area.

SKIING STOWE   The trails are down both Mount Mansfield and Spruce Peak, the mountains on either side of the Smuggler's Notch defile, and the variety of trails is such that there's plenty of adventure for everyone, no matter what your ability. In fact, the mountains, the staff in charge of trail maintenance, and especially the Sepp Ruschp Ski School have all worked hard over many years to earn for Stowe the high regard it has among skiers. The vertical drop is more than 2,000 feet, and the lifts include five chairs, three T-bars, and a gondola with four-passenger cars. Beginners will want to start off at the Toll House Slopes, near the base of the toll road up Mount Mansfield; the next logical step is to Spruce Peak; and after you've mastered that, go on to the more difficult among the Mount Mansfield trails and slopes. Lessons and rentals are available, and there are restaurants at Cliff House (top of the Mansfield gondola) and Octagon (top of the toll road), as well as at the base camps.

A big event of the winter season at Stowe is the annual **Winter Carnival,** held during the second week in January, when special races, church suppers, square dances, hockey and skating matches, a snow-sculpture contest, and even a queen's ball are held. Hotel rates are not raised for this event. Check with the Stowe Area Association for a carnival schedule.

SUMMER AT STOWE   Some of Stowe's pleasures are best appreciated during warm weather. The breathtaking ride to the top of Vermont's highest mountain in a **gondola** (☎ 802/253-7311) costs $9 round-trip for adults, $4 for children (and one child rides free for each paying adult). Or you can drive to the top of Mount Mansfield on the toll road, climbing even higher into the mist, past bunches of exotic wildflowers, feeling the air get cooler. The toll-road base station is near the ski areas just south of Smuggler's Notch; you pay for your car ($12) and then proceed up the road, which is paved only for a quarter of a mile; the rest is stabilized dirt. (But the quarter mile at the bottom is so perfect for skateboarding that the management has had to erect a sign prohibiting the fast and fancy rollers from monopolizing this stretch of its land!) Both the gondola and the toll road are open daily from mid-June through mid-October, weather permitting. The gondola is the fastest in the world.

It's hardly less exciting just to make the drive through **Smuggler's Notch.** You approach the mountains and the defile, and start turning the sharp bends in the road as you meet a sign saying "SHIFT TO LOW GEAR NOW"—and it means it. The road begins to twist among tremendous boulders fallen from the steep sides of the defile over the eons; the foliage gets very thick, the trees block much of the sun's light, and as you grind along up the switchback slope, a sense of wildness and excitement takes over. Just over the pass is a stopping place (you dare not stop unless you can pull off the road) with benches, toilets, a snack stand, and several impromptu trails that invite one to clamber—at least for a few hundred feet—into the rocks.

It's no exaggeration to say that something's always happening in Stowe in June, July, and August: **Antique-car rallies, horse and dog shows, a craft fair,** even **a fiddlers' meeting,** and a surprisingly authentic **Oktoberfest** (in October, natch) crowd into the schedule. **Topnotch,** that posh resort on Mountain Road near Mount Mansfield, is the place to rent horses by the hour or for a trail ride: Call 802/253-8585 and ask for the stables; the going rate is $22 per hour.

Stowe has an **alpine slide,** operated by the Mount Mansfield Company (☎ 802/253-7311). You start by taking a cool and scenic ride up a chair lift. At the top, you mount a small sled and begin your descent along a concrete runway that weaves and turns like a bobsled run all the way to the bottom of the mountain slope. The idea (and the alpine slide design) came from Germany. The slide is open daily 10am to 5pm from mid-June to September, and on weekends and holidays only from Memorial Day through mid-October; on rainy days, the slide closes down. Rides cost $6.50 per adult, $5.50 per child; five-ride ticket books are available. Take your slide-ride between 10am and 5pm, weather permitting. The alpine slide is six miles north of Stowe village on Vt. 108 at Spruce Peak.

The more familiar summer pastimes are well covered, too. The Stowe Country Club has an 18-hole golf course; tennis courts abound (many hotels and lodges have their own); hiking, bicycling, fishing, and photographing can fill whole weeks.

Last, the Stowe Theater Guild offers **summer theater** during July and August, every weekday. Performances are at their new stage at the Town Hall Theater, next door to the Stowe Area Association.

A CINEMA Stowe now has a movie house, called **Stowe Cinema,** which is exactly a mile north of Stowe village, along Mountain Road. Call 802/253-4678 to see what's playing. When you get there, you can choose a regular theater seat or a comfy corner of the Projection Room—a cocktail lounge—from which to see the film.

WHERE TO STAY

Stowe has a good variety of lodging places, posh or modest, dauntingly expensive or surprisingly cheap. In summer there's no problem finding exactly the room you want at the price you want to pay. But on busy winter weekends you'd be well advised to reserve in advance. Just give the Stowe Area Association a ring (see above), and reservations will be made for you. In winter the toll-free number is in operation; in summer call on the regular line.

Most hostelries in Stowe require winter visitors to have breakfast and dinner; in the jargon, this is called the Modified American Plan. Smaller places generally have BYOB bars or lounges, which helps greatly in reducing the expense of an after-ski glow. For supplies, trundle down to the Vermont State Liquor Store on Vt. 108, open Monday through Saturday from 9am to 9pm and Sunday from 11am to 6pm.

What follows is a selection of my favorite places to stay in Stowe, summer or winter. Bus service along Vt. 108 (the Mountain Road) connects the ski slopes to Stowe Village during the busy winter season.

EXPENSIVE

Stowehof Inn
Edson Hill Rd. (P.O. Box 1108), Stowe, VT 05672. ☎ **802/253-9722** or 800/932-7136. Fax 802/253-7513. 46 rms. A/C MINIBAR TV TEL. $110–$190 double. Rates include breakfast and dinner. Weekly rates and special package deals available. AE, DISC, MC, V. Free parking.

This is my first choice in Stowe. The inspiration of the bold, unusual, and exciting place is definitely alpine, and the public rooms give a sense of coziness and charm such as one might get in a small European schloss. Architect Larry Hess's masterful planning of spaces—split levels, strange angles, nooks, crannies, high ceilings and low ceilings—has resulted in a truly delightful place to spend time. There's a sunken fireplace pit, a cardplayers' nook decorated with giant playing cards (a royal flush, no less), a library seating area, and a living room with a panoramic view of the valley. One motif used throughout the inn, from the main entrance to the dining and living rooms, is that of support "columns" of massive tree trunks stripped of bark and dried to a silvery, ringing hardness. Additionally, the grounds are lovely to enjoy.

Each of the guest rooms is decorated differently, and each has a private balcony or patio. Some "demi-suites" have extra Murphy beds, or fireplaces or kitchenettes. There are several dining rooms, but one in particular is among the area's best. On the menu will be Vermont venison medallions, Atlantic salmon, rainbow trout, fresh duck, and pork chops. Guests can imbibe in the downstairs pub.

Additional attractions at the Stowehof Inn include a heated pool, tennis courts, shuffleboard, a pitch-and-putt green, a sauna, a library, a games room, and horseback riding. The inn is about 3 ¹/₂ miles northeast of Stowe Village, just off the Mountain Road (Vt. 108).

Trapp Family Lodge
Luce Hill Rd., Stowe, VT 05672. ☎ **802/253-8511** or 800/826-7000. 93 rms. TV TEL. $222–$242 double. Rates include breakfast and dinner. AE, CB, DC, DISC, MC, V. Free parking. Directions: Take Vt. 108 (Mountain Road) from the center of Stowe two miles to a fork by a white church; Vt. 108 bears right, but you bear left and follow this side road up the mountain slope, following the signs to the lodge.

The singing Trapp family of *Sound of Music* fame left the mountains of their native Austria before World War II and settled here in Stowe, later using this as home base for their worldwide concert tours. Members of the family are still involved in operating the resort. The main lodge, destroyed by fire in 1980, has been rebuilt; there's also a lower lodge. Many of the rooms have balconies. Other facilities include indoor and outdoor pools, 36 miles of cross-country ski trails, a sauna, and a fitness room. Maria von Trapp is buried here.

MODERATE

Andersen Lodge

3430 Mountain Rd., Stowe, VT 05672. ☎ **802/253-7336** or 800/336-7336. 17 rms. A/C TV. $68–$120 double. Rates include breakfast. AE, MC, V. Free parking.

This small, friendly Tyrolean inn between Mount Mansfield and Stowe has an authentic European ambience lent by its Austrian proprietors, Trude and Dietmar Heiss. Mr. Heiss is an Austrian-trained chef as well, and so the meals (which come with your room in ski season) are particularly hearty and "alpine." You can play tennis, the piano, or bumper pool; swim in the pool; use the sauna and Jacuzzi; or just sit in front of the fire. Some rooms have telephones and refrigerators.

Gables Inn

1457 Mountain Rd., Stowe, VT 05672. ☎ **802/253-7730** or 800/GABLES-1. 19 rms. Summer, $60–$150 double; winter (including breakfast, après-ski snacks, and dinner), $120–$240 double. AE, MC, V. Free parking.

This homey, congenial inn a few miles northwest of Stowe has mostly large rooms with a queen-size bed, and some have a fireplace and hot tub; most rooms have air conditioning and TV. The Gables also has a pool, a picnic area, a common hot tub, and a front porch where you can have breakfast (to noon) while gazing at Mount Mansfield.

Golden Eagle Resort Motor Inn

Mountain Rd., Stowe, VT 05672. ☎ **802/253-4811** or 800/626-1010. 59 units. A/C TV TEL. $89–$149 room, suite, or efficiency for two; $111–$199 apartment. AE, DC, DISC, MC, V. Free parking.

You can bed down in a comfortable room, suite, efficiency unit, or vacation apartment; such amenities as fireplaces, balconies, refrigerators, and private whirlpool baths are available in some accommodations. The Golden Eagle, half a mile north of Stowe Village, has many facilities, including a hot tub, indoor and outdoor pools, a fitness room, a sauna, a whirlpool bath, a tennis court, nature trails, and even two stocked trout ponds for fishing buffs. There are three restaurants. Service here is friendly, experienced, and dependable. Weekly and monthly rates can bring the apartment prices down somewhat.

Green Mountain Inn

Main St., Stowe, VT 05672. ☎ **802/253-7301** or 800/Stowe-Inn (800/786-9346). Fax 802/253-5096. 64 rms. A/C TV TEL. $89–$160 double. AE, MC, V. Free parking.

I've been coming to Stowe for years, and I've seen the Green Mountain Inn in all seasons. I particularly like fall and winter. Around Christmas it's wonderfully romantic in Stowe, and when the soft snow falls around this red-brick hostelry and the fresh powder collects in the windows, it's quite pretty. I also enjoy the classic colonial look of the restaurant, which has fiddleback chairs and small-paned windows. A second restaurant faces the outdoor pool. The health club has everything from a sauna, steam room, and whirlpool to cardiovascular exercise equipment and a full Nautilus circuit. With colonial colors, some Victorian styling, canopy beds, and other antiques, the guest rooms have a romantic ambience.

Scandinavia Inn

Mountain Rd., Stowe, VT 05672. ☎ **802/253-8555** or 800/544-4229. 18 rms. TV TEL. $55–$95 double. Rates include breakfast. AE, DISC, MC, V. Free parking. Closed Apr–May and Nov.

Keeping close to the spirit of its name, this inn, two miles northwest of Stowe village, is a dark-wood building with peaked gables and white trim, decked with Scandinavian flags. In summer there are lounge chairs on the front porch, flower boxes that provide splashes of color, and picnic tables. This inn has a surprising range of services, including a sauna, a hot tub, a pool, a whirlpool bath, a fitness room, a games room, barbecue grills, and bicycles.

Stoweflake Inn and Resorts

Mountain Rd., Stowe, VT 05672. ☎ **802/253-7355** or 800/253-2232. 71 rms, 25 townhouses. A/C TV TEL. $74–$148 double; $130–$325 townhouse for two. DC, DISC, MC, V. Free parking.

The Stoweflake is a long-standing favorite in Stowe, a family-run operation that has grown steadily over the years and today provides some of the best accommodations and service around. There are two tennis courts, an outdoor pool, an indoor pool, a PGA-approved putting green, a 370-yard driving range, nearby golf, and a health club with saunas, Jacuzzi, and fitness equipment. The restaurant is well regarded locally. Come in the summer and you might just see the Stoweflake's hot-air balloon. Rooms have all the comforts of a first-class hotel, and the town houses are even bigger.

WHERE TO DINE

During ski season, of course, most people will want to eat at their inns, or will be obliged to do so. Stowehof, the Golden Eagle, and the Green Mountain Inn are some of the preferred dining places in the valley. Almost every other inn serves meals as well.

14   Burlington

225 miles NW of Boston, Mass.; 98 miles S of Montréal, P.Q.; 36 miles W of Stowe

GETTING THERE   By Plane   Burlington is served by several major air carriers and their regional commuter subsidiaries, including Business Express (Delta Connection), USAir Express, United Express, and Continental Express. In addition, USAir, United Airlines, and Continental Airlines have direct flights to Burlington in large aircraft.

By Train   Amtrak's day train *Adirondack* runs daily between New York City and Montréal, skirting Vermont as it runs up the Hudson. It stops at Port Kent, N.Y., from which you can take a cross-lake ferryboat to Burlington. The train runs from mid-May to mid-October.

By Bus   Vermont has its own large bus line, Vermont Transit Lines, 135 St. Paul St., Burlington, VT 05401 (☎ 802/864-6811, or 212/971-6300 in New York City; or 800/451-3292, 800/642-3133 in Vermont), which operates from New York City (in conjunction with Greyhound), Montréal (in conjunction with Voyageur), and Boston to virtually all points of interest in Vermont, including its home base at Burlington. Burlington's Vermont Transit bus station (☎ 802/864-6811) is at the southeastern end of the Church Street Marketplace across from City Hall Park.

By Car   Follow I-89, which runs between Boston and the U.S.–Canadian border north of Burlington.

ESSENTIALS   The **telephone area code** is **802.** In the midst of the Church Street Marketplace, near the corner with Bank Street, is an **information gallery** (no phone) with brochures and maps. For more elaborate or detailed information, contact the **Lake Champlain Regional Chamber of Commerce,** 60 Main St. (P.O. Box 453), Burlington, VT 05402 (☎ **802/863-3489**).

The largest city in Vermont is a town of only about 55,000 people, but in this state, small is beautiful. Burlington's situation on the shores of Lake Champlain brings it extra attractiveness and aquatic-sports opportunities as well. The town is the seat of the University of Vermont, and student activities and cultural events add an extra dimension to Burlington's daily life. Of the city's native sons, the educator and philosopher John Dewey is the most famous, and Ethan Allen, while not born here, chose Burlington as his home in his later years. Today part of his farm is encompassed by Ethan Allen Park.

Besides being a college town, Burlington is industrial: Weapons, data-processing equipment, textiles, and consumer products are all made here, and Burlington's medical facilities serve the northern part of the state. Burlington is one of two termini for Lake Champlain ferryboat crossings (the other is Port Kent, N.Y.).

Downtown Burlington is a fairly compact area easily negotiated on foot. The heart of town for visitors and locals alike is the Church Street Marketplace, a four-block stretch of Church Street from Pearl Street to College Street closed to vehicular traffic, beautified with trees, benches, and sidewalk cafes, and busy with strollers, street vendors, shoppers, lovers, performers, and sidewalk-bench conversationalists. At the northwestern end of Church Street stands the pretty Unitarian church, built in 1816.

WHAT TO SEE & DO

Much of Burlington's cultural life centers on the **University of Vermont** campus, and on the campuses of the other three colleges in the area: **St. Michael's, Trinity,** and **Champlain.**

The University of Vermont stages an annual summer **Champlain Shakespeare Festival,** held at the Royall Tyler Theatre (☎ 802/656-2094), on the Main Street side of the campus. A **Mozart Festival** is held in summer as well. See below for information on the university's museum.

Much of the lakefront land in Burlington is encompassed by **parks,** including Oak Ledge Park and Red Rocks Park in South Burlington, Battery Park near Burlington's center and only five blocks from the ferries, and Burlington Municipal Beach on Institute Road north of the ferry dock along the lake shore. Ethan Allen Park is north of the center of town; take North Avenue (Vt. 127) starting at Battery Park.

MUSEUMS

Robert Hull Fleming Museum
Colchester Ave. ☎ **802/656-0750.** Free admission; $2 donation suggested. Tues–Fri 9am–4pm, Sat–Sun 1–5pm. Closed Labor Day–Apr. Directions: From the center of town, go east on Pearl Street, which merges with Colchester Avenue; look for the museum on the right-hand side.

The University of Vermont's museum, on its campus not far from downtown Burlington, has a good collection of fine arts and anthropological holdings (including some good pre-Columbian objects), changing exhibitions of contemporary art, works by Vermont artists, historic art from around the world, and a bona-fide Egyptian mummy.

Shelburne Museum

U.S. 7, Shelburne. ☎ **802/985-3346.** Ticket good for two consecutive days, $17.50 adults, $6 children 6–14, free for kids under 6. Late May to late Oct, daily 10am–5pm; late Oct to late May, guided tour of selected buildings and collections daily at 1pm. Directions: Take Exit 13 off I-89 and head south on U.S. 7, seven miles south of Burlington.

Visitors to Burlington must make a detour to the town of Shelburne to see the Shelburne Museum, a gala festival of Americana collected into 37 historic buildings arranged on 45 acres, including an authentic one-room schoolhouse, six fully furnished early New England homes, a jail complete with stocks, an Adirondack hunting lodge, a print shop, and a lighthouse that once guided ships on Lake Champlain. The buildings you see date from the 17th, 18th, and early 19th centuries; each was moved here from its original location in Vermont, New Hampshire, New York, or Massachusetts, and all are now filled with the artifacts of earlier American life. The museum is said to have about the best and fullest collection of Americana ever assembled. Among the artifacts are a 1920s carousel, a round dairy barn (1901), and even the huge 220-foot side-wheel steamship SS *Ticonderoga*, docked here after its last run on the lake. Four art galleries feature paintings and sculpture by European and American artists (Andrew Wyeth, Grandma Moses, Ogden Pleissner, Rembrandt, Monet, Manet, Degas), and other buildings hold displays of folk art both charming and authentic: quilts, decoys, glassware, and furniture, plus the tools used to make these items. The museum has a cafe and snack bar, picnic tables, stores, and free parking.

LAKE CHAMPLAIN FERRIES

One of the favorite things to do in Burlington is to take the **ferry** (☎ **802/864-9804**) over to Port Kent, N.Y., whether you're actually interested in getting to Port Kent or not. Ferries, leaving from the King Street Dock in Burlington, operate in spring, summer, and fall, leaving each terminus at about one-hour intervals from 7:15am to 5:30 or 6:30pm, a bit more frequently in summer, with 14 trips a day in each direction. You can take your car across if you're going somewhere: Price for car and driver, one-way, is $12.50; each additional adult pays $3.50 one-way; children 6 to 12 are charged $1. The trip, a marvelous way to get to know Lake Champlain, takes about an hour each way. This ferry doesn't run in winter, but ferries between Grand Isle, Vt., and Plattsburgh, N.Y., operate year-round. You'll also find a ferry chugging between Charlotte, Vt., and Essex, N.Y., from early April through early January.

WHERE TO STAY
EXPENSIVE

Radisson Burlington Hotel

60 Battery St., Burlington, VT 05401. ☎ **802/658-6500** or 800/333-3333. Fax 802/658-4659. 255 rms. A/C TV TEL. $89–$149 double. Additional person or bed $10 extra. Children under 18 stay free in parents' room. AE, CB, DC, DISC, ER, MC, V. Free parking.

The Radisson bills itself as "Vermont's most luxurious hotel," and although many other hotels may dispute the claim, there's no disputing the Radisson's quality. Tropical plants bring freshness to an enclosed garden court next to the pool and whirlpool bath. Many rooms have gorgeous views of Lake Champlain, while others

The Northeast Kingdom

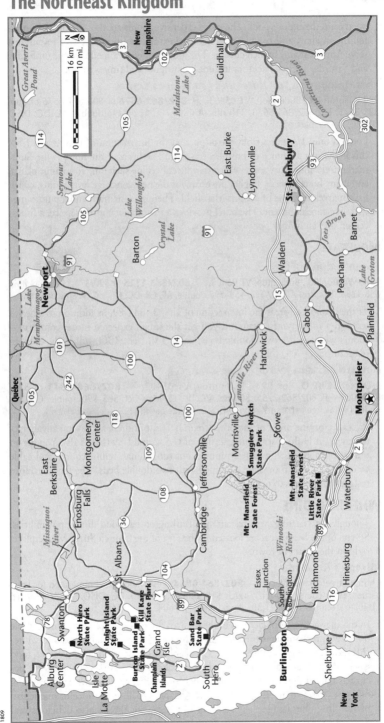

1809

open onto the indoor pool. The more expensive rooms are those with a lake-and-mountain view, and the plaza rooms have extra amenities. The two restaurants serve American and French cuisine. The lounge offers a comedy troupe on Friday and Saturday nights. Facilities include a whirlpool and fitness room.

Sheraton-Burlington Hotel and Conference Center

870 Williston Rd., Burlington, VT 05403. ☎ **802/862-6576** or 800/677-6576 or 800/ 325-3535. Fax 802/865-6670. 310 rms. A/C TV TEL. $82–$146 double. AE, DC, DISC, ER, MC, V. Free parking.

Located only $1^1/_2$ miles from the airport, at the intersection of U.S. 2 and I-89, this is the prime choice of business travelers. The heart of the hotel is the Summerhouse, a four-story space with a translucent ceiling sheltering fountains, plants, and many hotel services. Higher prices are for the new concierge level rooms, which have marvelous views of Mount Mansfield. There's a restaurant and a pub/lounge with live entertainment. The hotel provides a free airport shuttle service, a fitness center, and an indoor pool.

MODERATE

Econo Lodge

1076 Williston Rd., Burlington, VT 05403. ☎ **802/863-1125** or 800/371-1125. Fax 802/ 658-1296. 177 rms. A/C TV TEL. $59–$92 double. AE, CB, DC, ER, MC, V. Free parking.

At the Econo Lodge, at the intersection of U.S. 2 and I-89, in addition to a health spa and a full-service restaurant, you get the usual, expected motel comforts—rooms with one or two double beds, color TV, free HBO, full bath, even an outdoor pool.

Howard Johnson Motor Lodge

1 Dorset St. (P.O. Box 993), Burlington, VT 05402. ☎ **802/863-5541** or 800/ 654-2000. Fax 802/862-2755. 89 rms. A/C TV TEL. May–Oct, $85–$90 double. Children under 18 stay free in parents' room. AE, MC, V. Free parking.

Prices are on the order of the other chain hotels, but there are several advantages to staying at HoJo's, at the intersection of U.S. 2 and I-89 (Exit 14E). You get an indoor-outdoor pool, a fitness room, a hot tub, saunas, tennis courts, and cable color TV. Lots of rooms are equipped with two double beds. The familiar HoJo restaurant operates to midnight.

WHERE TO DINE

Though not bursting with restaurants, Burlington has good dining possibilities. Several of the best places are located in the area of the Church Street Marketplace, right in the center of town.

Alfredo's Restaurant

Church Street Marketplace. ☎ **802/864-0854.** Reservations recommended for large parties. Main courses $6–$13; lunch $10; dinner $15–$20. DC, DISC, MC, V. Mon–Fri 11:30am–10pm, Sat–Sun 11:30am–midnight. ITALIAN.

In the alley across from city hall in the Church Street Marketplace are three simple but cozy and charming storefront dining rooms with lace curtains, red-and-white-checked tablecloths, and live lobsters in a tank by the door. In good weather, food is served under an open-air awning in the back. With its latest expansion, the decor has moved toward cafe styling, with a row of French windows running along one side. Pasta in all its variations—fettuccine, capellini, vermicelli, manicotti, ravioli, linguine, lasagne—is a strong suit here, but there's also delicious veal sorrentino (veal with eggplant and mozzarella in a marsala sauce), chicken in garlic with peppers and mushrooms, and many other Italian delights.

Bourbon Street Grill

213 College St. ☎ **802/865-2800.** Reservations recommended. Main courses $5—$17; full lunch $10; full dinner $20. AE, DC, MC, V. Mon–Wed 11:30am–10pm, Thurs–Sat 11:30am–midnight; Sun brunch 10:30am–3pm, dinner 3–10pm. Directions: Follow College Street to the corner of South Winooski. AMERICAN/CAJUN.

At South Winooski, this is a tidy little storefront bistro with whirling ceiling fans and a menu for any time of day. Soups, salads, burgers, and sandwiches share space on the menu with jambalaya, Cajun flank steak, and shrimp étouffée. For a little Louisiana thrill, preface your meal by ingesting an authentic Louisiana Hurricane, a powerful rum-based concoction that calms you down if you're in the midst of a storm, or starts a storm if you aren't. For something a little tamer, try the Southwest dishes.

Carbur's

115 St. Paul St. ☎ **802/862-4106.** Reservations accepted only for preferred seatings. Main courses $7–$13. AE, DC, DISC, MC, V. Sun–Thurs 11:30am–midnight, Fri–Sat 11:30am–1am. ECLECTIC.

Carbur's is done in heavy mod-Victoriana and tends to the quietly outrageous: A sign in the window says "FAMOUS SINCE 1974." The dining room has a tremendously high ceiling equipped with ceiling fans that spin slowly even on cool days, just for atmosphere. The menu is a book, 16 pages long, filled with sandwiches, soups, salad plates, almost all—with a few exceptions like the monster five-decker sandwich—for around $8. The menu, by the way, is laden with enough drawings and amusing patter to keep you entertained all through your meal. Come for lunch or dinner any day. It faces City Hall Park at the southeastern end of the Church Street Marketplace. There's another Carbur's restaurant in Portland, Me., too, but it's under different ownership.

Index

The following Frommer's guides are available from your favorite bookstore, or you can use the order form on the preceding page to request them as part of your membership in Frommer's Travel Book Club.

FROMMER'S COMPLETE TRAVEL GUIDES

(Comprehensive guides to sightseeing, dining and accommodations, with selections in all price ranges—from deluxe to budget)

Acapulco/Ixtapa/Taxco, 2nd Ed.	C157	Jamaica/Barbados, 2nd Ed.	C149
Alaska '94-'95	C131	Japan '94-'95	C144
Arizona '95	C166	Maui, 1st Ed.	C153
Australia '94-'95	C147	Nepal, 3rd Ed. (avail. 11/95)	C184
Austria, 6th Ed.	C162	New England '95	C165
Bahamas '96 (avail. 8/95)	C172	New Mexico, 3rd Ed.	C167
Belgium/Holland/Luxembourg,		New York State, 4th Ed.	C133
4th Ed.	C170	Northwest, 5th Ed.	C140
Bermuda '96 (avail. 8/95)	C174	Portugal '94-'95	C141
California '95	C164	Puerto Rico '95-'96	C151
Canada '94-'95	C145	Puerto Vallarta/Manzanillo/	
Caribbean '96 (avail. 9/95)	C173	Guadalajara, 2nd Ed.	C135
Carolinas/Georgia, 2nd Ed.	C128	Scandinavia, 16th Ed.	C169
Colorado '96 (avail. 11/95)	C179	Scotland '94-'95	C146
Costa Rica, 1st Ed.	C161	South Pacific '94-'95	C138
Cruises '95-'96	C150	Spain, 16th Ed.	C163
Delaware/Maryland '94-'95	C136	Switzerland, 7th Ed.	
England '96 (avail. 10/95)	C180	(avail. 9/95)	C177
Florida '96 (avail. 9/95)	C181	Thailand, 2nd Ed.	C154
France '96 (avail. 11/95)	C182	U.S.A., 4th Ed.	C156
Germany '96 (avail. 9/95)	C176	Virgin Islands, 3rd Ed.	
Honolulu/Waikiki/Oahu, 4th Ed.		(avail. 8/95)	C175
(avail. 10/95)	C178	Virginia '94-'95	C142
Ireland, 1st Ed.	C168	Yucatán '95-'96	C155
Italy '96 (avail. 11/95)	C183		

FROMMER'S $-A-DAY GUIDES

(Dream Vacations at Down-to-Earth Prices)

Australia on $45 '95-'96	D122	Ireland on $45 '94-'95	D118
Berlin from $50, 3rd Ed.		Israel on $45, 15th Ed.	D130
(avail. 10/95)	D137	London from $55 '96	
Caribbean from $60, 1st Ed.		(avail. 11/95)	D136
(avail. 9/95)	D133	Madrid on $50 '94-'95	D119
Costa Rica/Guatemala/Belize		Mexico from $35 '96	
on $35, 3rd Ed.	D126	(avail. 10/95)	D135
Eastern Europe on $30, 5th Ed.	D129	New York on $70 '94-'95	D121
England from $50 '96		New Zealand from $45, 6th Ed.	D132
(avail. 11/95)	D138	Paris on $45 '94-'95	D117
Europe from $50 '96		South America on $40, 16th Ed.	D123
(avail. 10/95)	D139	Washington, D.C. on $50	
Greece from $45, 6th Ed.	D131	'94-'95	D120
Hawaii from $60 '96 (avail. 9/95)	D134		

FROMMER'S COMPLETE CITY GUIDES

(Comprehensive guides to sightseeing, dining, and accommodations in all price ranges)

FROMMER'S FAMILY GUIDES

(Guides to family-friendly hotels, restaurants, activities, and attractions)

FROMMER'S WALKING TOURS

*(Memorable strolls through colorful and historic neighborhoods,
accompanied by detailed directions and maps)*

FROMMER'S AMERICA ON WHEELS

*(Guides for travelers who are exploring the U.S.A. by car, featuring a brand-new
rating system for accommodations and full-color road maps)*

FROMMER'S SPECIAL-INTEREST TITLES

Arthur Frommer's Branson!	P107	Frommer's Where to Stay U.S.A.,	
Arthur Frommer's New World		11th Ed.	P102
of Travel (avail. 11/95)	P112	National Park Guide, 29th Ed.	P106
Frommer's Caribbean Hideaways		USA Today Golf Tournament Guide	P113
(avail. 9/95)	P110	USA Today Minor League	
Frommer's America's 100 Best-Loved		Baseball Book	P111
State Parks	P109		

FROMMER'S BEST BEACH VACATIONS
(The top places to sun, stroll, shop, stay, play, party, and swim—with each beach rated for beauty, swimming, sand, and amenities)

California (avail. 10/95)	G100	Hawaii (avail. 10/95)	G102
Florida (avail. 10/95)	G101		

FROMMER'S BED & BREAKFAST GUIDES
(Selective guides with four-color photos and full descriptions of the best inns in each region)

California	B100	Hawaii	B105
Caribbean	B101	Pacific Northwest	B106
East Coast	B102	Rockies	B107
Eastern United States	B103	Southwest	B108
Great American Cities	B104		

FROMMER'S IRREVERENT GUIDES
(Wickedly honest guides for sophisticated travelers and those who want to be)

Chicago (avail. 11/95)	I100	New Orleans (avail. 11/95)	I103
London (avail. 11/95)	I101	San Francisco (avail. 11/95)	I104
Manhattan (avail. 11/95)	I102	Virgin Islands (avail. 11/95)	I105

FROMMER'S DRIVING TOURS
(Four-color photos and detailed maps outlining spectacular scenic driving routes)

Australia	Y100	Italy	Y108
Austria	Y101	Mexico	Y109
Britain	Y102	Scandinavia	Y110
Canada	Y103	Scotland	Y111
Florida	Y104	Spain	Y112
France	Y105	Switzerland	Y113
Germany	Y106	U.S.A.	Y114
Ireland	Y107		

FROMMER'S BORN TO SHOP
(The ultimate travel guides for discriminating shoppers—from cut-rate to couture)

Hong Kong (avail. 11/95)	Z100	London (avail. 11/95)	Z101